Data-Centric .NET Programming with C#

Fabio Claudio Ferracchiati

Jay Glynn

Zach Greenvoss

Jerry Hoff

P. G. Muraleedharan

Christian Nagel

Jacob Hammer Pedersen

Rob Schieber

Kent Tegels

Neil Whitlow

Donald Xie

Wrox Press Ltd. ®

Data-Centric .NET Programming with C#

First Printed December 2001

Published by Wrox Press Ltd,
Arden House, 1102 Warwick Road, Acocks Green,
Birmingham, B27 6BH, UK
Printed in Canada
ISBN 1-861005-92-X

Trademark Acknowledgements

Wrox has endeavored to provide trademark information about all the companies and products mentioned in this book by the appropriate use of capitals. However, Wrox cannot guarantee the accuracy of this information.

Credits

Authors
Fabio Claudio Ferracchiati
Jay Glynn
Zach Greenvoss
Jerry Hoff
P. G. Muraleedharan
Christian Nagel
Jacob Hammer Pedersen
Rob Schieber
Kent Tegels
Neil Whitlow
Donald Xie

Additional Material
Niranjan Kumar
Brian Reisman
Saurabh Nandu

Technical Architect
Ian Blackham

Technical Editors
David Barnes
Victoria Blackburn
Claire Brittle
Gary Evans
Martin Lau
Douglas Paterson

Author Agent
Chris Matterface

Project Administrators
Rob Hesketh

Category Manager
Sonia Mullineux

Illustrations
Natalie O'Donnell

Cover
Chris Morris

Technical Reviewers
Imtiaz Alam
Uriah Blatherwick
Richard Bonneau
Andreas Christiansen
Cristian Darie
Slavomir Furman
Radha Ganesan
Costas Hadjisotiriou
Hope Hatfield
Brian Hickey
Ben Hickman
Mark Horner
Amit Kalani
Dianna Leech
Jason Montgomery
Johan Normen
Aruna Panangipally
Venkataramanan Poornachandran
Phil Powers-De-George
Juan Ramon Rovirosa

Technical Reviewers
Scott Roberston
Kristy Saunders
Trevor Scott
Keyur Shah
David Shultz
Gavin Smyth
Kent Tegels
Adwait Ullal
Helmut Watson

Production Coordinator
Emma Eato

Proof Reader
Chris Smith

Index
John Collin

About the Authors

Fabio Claudio Ferracchiati

Fabio Claudio Ferracchiati is a software developer and technical writer. In the early years of his ten-year career he worked with classical languages and old Microsoft tools like Visual Basic and Visual C++. After five years he decided to dedicate his attention to the Internet and all related technologies. In 1998 he started a parallel career writing technical articles for Italian and international magazines. He works in Rome for CPI Progetti Spa (http://www.cpiprogetti.it) where he develops Internet/intranet solutions using Microsoft technologies. Fabio would like to thank all his Wrox contacts and CPI colleagues. In particular he would thank Angelo for his kindness.

A great embrace goes to "Nonny" who has been ill recently. We need you, so don't make "tricks". Finally, I would scream to the world that I love Danila. She gives me the force and the inspiration when I write books for you. She is my muse. If you want discover her intelligence and start to appreciate her ideas, visit her site at http://www.danilabarbara.com.

Jay Glynn

Jay started developing software in the late 1980's, writing applications for the Pick operating system in Pick BASIC. Since then he has created applications using Paradox PAL and Object PAL, Delphi, Pascal, C/C++, Java, VBA, and Visual Basic. Currently, Jay is a Project Coordinator and Architect for a large insurance company based in Nashville TN. For the past five years he has been developing software for pen-based computers and, more recently, for ASP and server-based systems. When not sitting in front of a keyboard, Jay is busy restoring a house in Franklin TN, playing a round of golf whenever possible, and watching Disney movies with his wife and three year old son. Jay can be reached at jlsglynn@hotmail.com.

I would like to thank my wife Lydia and my son Samuel for being patient and understanding for all of the late nights. They are my motivation and inspiration.

Zach Greenvoss

Zach Greenvoss, MCSD, is a Senior Consultant with Magenic Technologies, a Microsoft Gold Certified consulting firm in Northern California. He specializes in middle-tier architecture and implementation, utilizing various technologies including COM+, MSMQ, BizTalk, XML, and the .NET Framework. Before Magenic, Zach worked at the Defense Manpower Data Center in Monterey California, where he developed client-server applications for the Department of Defense. Zach and his wife, Amanda enjoy globetrotting, caving, gaming, and playing with their two cats. He can be reached at zachg@magenic.com.

I would like to thank my wife Amanda for all her patience, love, and understanding of the time required to both work and write. A special thanks to Chris Madsen and Magenic for providing me the time and environment in which to work on this book. Finally, I am proud to say that I am a CSU Monterey Bay graduate – Go Otters!

Jerry Hoff

Jerry Hoff lives in Saint Louis, Missouri where he delivers computer-programming seminars at Washington University's CAIT program. Among the classes he teaches are Java, JavaScript, Visual Basic, PL-SQL, Transact-SQL, PERL, VB.NET, C#, and ASP.NET. Previously, he taught for several years at the Microcomputer Program at University of Missouri, where he taught classes in C, Unix, ASP and Java.

When not teaching, Jerry does private consulting via his company, Mind Technologies. His hobbies include scuba diving, and finding victims upon whom he can practice his shaky Japanese and Italian language skills. He can be reached at Jerry@mindtechnologies.com.

I would like to deeply express my gratitude to those who supported me while I was contributing to this book, including Geri Hoff, Jenny Hoff, and Atsuko Hashimoto. I would also like to thank my grandfather, Salvatore Guercio, and uncle, Carlo Guercio. Finally, I cannot forget my other uncle Roy Guercio, who first taught me DOS years ago, setting my life's path.

Other people I would like to thank are Cheryl Roth and everyone in Microdata, Bob Thomas, Allan Crean, Andrew Arett, Keith Sproull, and Wrox's Chris Matterface, a great author agent.

Lastly, I would like to take a moment to remember Justin Bhansali who was tragically killed while volunteering in Africa through the Peace Corps January 7, 2000. Justin was an exceptionally talented and intelligent programmer, and a good friend.

P. G. Muraleedharan

Muraleedharan lives in Trivandrum in India, where he works for XStream Software India (P) Ltd, a subsidiary of XStream Software Inc. Ottawa. He graduated in Electronics and Communication Engineering and worked for two decades in electronics manufacturing industry. Subsequently he did his Masters in Computer Science and Engineering and has 14 years of programming experience. He has written many papers in technical journals of professional societies. He is also a regular contributor to many international conferences. He is a member of several professional organizations. His areas of interest include Image Processing, Artificial Intelligence, Internet and web-based applications, and Multimedia applications. He can be reached by e-mail at: pgmurali@vsnl.com.

My thanks go to the Wrox team for helping with this book. In particular, I want to thank the reviewers for making innumerable corrections in the structure and style.

To my wife, Valsalakumari, and our children Abhijith, Abhinand, and Aiswarya for the support and love they have given me.

Christian Nagel

Christian Nagel is working as a trainer and consultant for Global Knowledge, the largest independent information technology training provider. Having worked with PDP 11, VMS, and Unix platforms, he looks back to more than 15 years of experience in the field of software development. With his profound knowledge of Microsoft technologies – he's a certified as Microsoft Certified Trainer (MCT), Solution Developer (MCSD), and Systems Engineer (MCSE) – he enjoys teaching others programming and architecting distributed solutions. As founder of what is now called .NET User Group Austria, and as MSDN Regional Director, he is a frequent speaker at European Developer conferences. You can contact Christian via his web site at http://christian.nagel.net.

I would like to thank the editors at Wrox Press who made my text readable. My thanks also go to many people at Microsoft, in particular Alex Holy, Sabine Fleischmann, and the developers of the .NET platform. Finally, and most importantly, I would like to thank my wife Elisabeth for her patience when I was working day and night.

Jacob Hammer Pedersen

Jacob Hammer Pedersen is a systems developer at ICL Invia – a member of the Fujitsu Group.

He pretty much started programming when he was able to spell the word 'basic', which, incidentally is the language he's primarily using today. He started programming the PC in the early 90s, using Pascal, but soon changed his focus to C++, which still holds his interest. In the mid 90s his focus changed again, this time to Visual Basic . In the summer of 2000 he discovered C# and has been happily exploring it ever since.

Primarily working on the Microsoft platforms, other expertise includes MS Office development, COM, COM+, and Visual Basic.Net.

A Danish citizen, he works and lives in Aarhus, Denmark.

Rob Schieber

Rob Schieber is a consultant in Columbus, Ohio, where he has developed in the manufacturing, telecom, resale, insurance, and information sectors. Rob's primary areas of expertise include enterprise systems, cryptography, and system security. Rob has a Bachelors Degree in Management Information Systems from the University of Dayton where he also played collegiate football for four years. Rob is a Microsoft Certified Professional, and has written multiple articles for *ASPToday* and *CSharpToday*.

When Rob isn't around a computer, he will probably be near his wife Kristy or his 2 dogs: Keo and Chloe.

To my wife Kristy, and Keo and Chloe.

Kent Tegels

Kent is a system developer and engineer living in Omaha, Nebraska. He works for HDR, Inc., a leading Engineering, Architecture, and Consulting Firm. He is a Microsoft Certified Professional plus Site Builder, System Engineer (plus Internet), and Database Administrator. He has contributed to other Wrox Press titles and web sites. In his spare time, Kent enjoys cooking, American football, and spending time with his friends.

Deepest thanks for Janell for putting up with yet another "project", and to "the Mom squad" for being there for us, over all the years. Also thanks to the staff of Wrox for being so easy to work with. Finally, thanks to my fellow authors and reviewers for doing the hard work that makes technology fun.

My efforts for this title are dedicated to the brave members of the all of the national Armed Forces that make up North American Treaty Organization. Standing tall for freedom, your bravery, commitment, and sacrifices are never forgotten.

Neil Whitlow

My first experience with recreational programming was with Basic on a Commodore Vic 20, and as the years went by it became an addiction that grew into QuickBasic 4.5 and Visual Basic 1.0 in DOS and Windows. Meanwhile, another sick obsession called Accounting was consuming my formal education. It was only after completing all my BBA requirements for Accounting that I began to realize there were now professional options for PC programmers, not just mainframe, AS/400, and Unix. I delayed graduation and slaved for two more years at school to get a double major with Management Information Systems. Ironically, it was COBOL (albiet MicroFocus PC-based COBOL for OS/2 and DOS) that landed me my first paying programming job out of college. From there it was on to QuickBasic 4.5 and Visual Basic versions 3-6. I've also had my fingers into goodies such as Java, Perl, ASP, and SQL Server, to name a few. Currently, I'm a Senior Systems Analyst developing software for pen-based computers with a large insurance company in Nashville, TN. When not programming or doing yardwork, I enjoy woodworking, watching football and hockey, and re-reading fiction from H. Beam Piper, J.R.R. Tolkien, Robert A. Heinlein and the like. Neil can be contacted at authorwhitlow@home.com.

I thank Jesus Christ for his unconditional love. I thank my wife, Lillian, for loving me despite my inner geek and for her patience with my profession. Thanks to my parents for buying their son a Commodore Vic 20 on that Christmas long ago. Thanks to all the Wrox folks for their patience and guidance. Finally, thanks to some friends at previous jobs who have been influential and inspirational in my professional programming career: Mac Gardner, Curt Nazor, Analiese Merrill, Becky Moore, and most of all Shane Russell.

Donald Xie

Donald Xie has 14 years experience in enterprise application development for various types of businesses. He is a co-author of "*Professional CDO Programming*" and a contributing author for a number of books including "*C++ Unleashed*" and "*VB MTS*". Donald currently works as a consulting system architect for the Department of Training in Western Australia, Australia. You can contact Donald at donald@iinet.net.au.

Niranjan Kumar

Niranjan lives in Chennai, South India. You can reach him at KNiranja@chn.cognizant.com. He's been working in the IT industry for the past four years and enjoys working in C-based languages. He initially started with C on Unix platforms, then migrated to C++ and Visual C++. Apart from official work, Niranjan is exploring C# and .NET technologies and is currently employed by Cognizant Technology Solutions, India. He likes diving, swimming, playing guitar, and solving 2D picture puzzles.

I would like to thank my parents and close friends for their consistent support and encouragement at every stage my life, particularly during this write-up. I am extremely delighted to be part of this Wrox team.

Brian Reisman

Brian started writing programs in BASIC, Pascal and C for his Tandy 1000. He has worked as developer and consultant for many companies in both Florida and Delaware. Now his main focus is as a trainer and consultant for Online Consulting (http://www.onlc.com) in Wilmington, Delaware. As a trainer, Brian keeps up on the certifications, holding MCDBA, MCSD, MCSE, MCT, CNA, and OCP titles. Brian has skills in a myriad of technologies including: C#, VB, ASP, COM, SQL, HTML, DHTML, ASP.NET, XML, and of course .NET.

Brian is in the process of building a site for new developers to help one another. You can check it out at www.joltcoder.com. He can be reached at either brian@joltcoder.com or brianr@onlc.com.

Dedication: First I'd like to thank my wife, Tami, and son, Thatcher, whose patience and love made this possible. I'd also like to thank my parents Joel and Alice for all of the support they have given to me.

I would also like to extend my sympathy for all of the families affected by the attacks against the United States on September 11, 2001. In addition, I would like to thank all of the heroes: the firemen, policemen, and volunteers whose unity is showing that something wonderful can come from even the most terrible of tragedies. God Bless America!

Saurabh Nandu

Saurabh Nandu is the webmaster of the site http://www.MasterCSharp.com, which concentrates on teaching C# and .NET. He worked on HTML, JavaScript, and Flash 5.0 before he started learning Java. He got introduced to .NET by his friend and after being influenced by the power and flexibility of .NET he sticks to working as a freelance writer/reviewer on .NET and related technologies in his free time. He is currently working as Technical Evangelist at YesSoftware.

I would like to thank my friend Nanu Jogi without whose direction I would have never got into working on the .NET Platform. I would also like to thank my family especially my brother Pritesh for their support (in every way), without which I would not have been here.

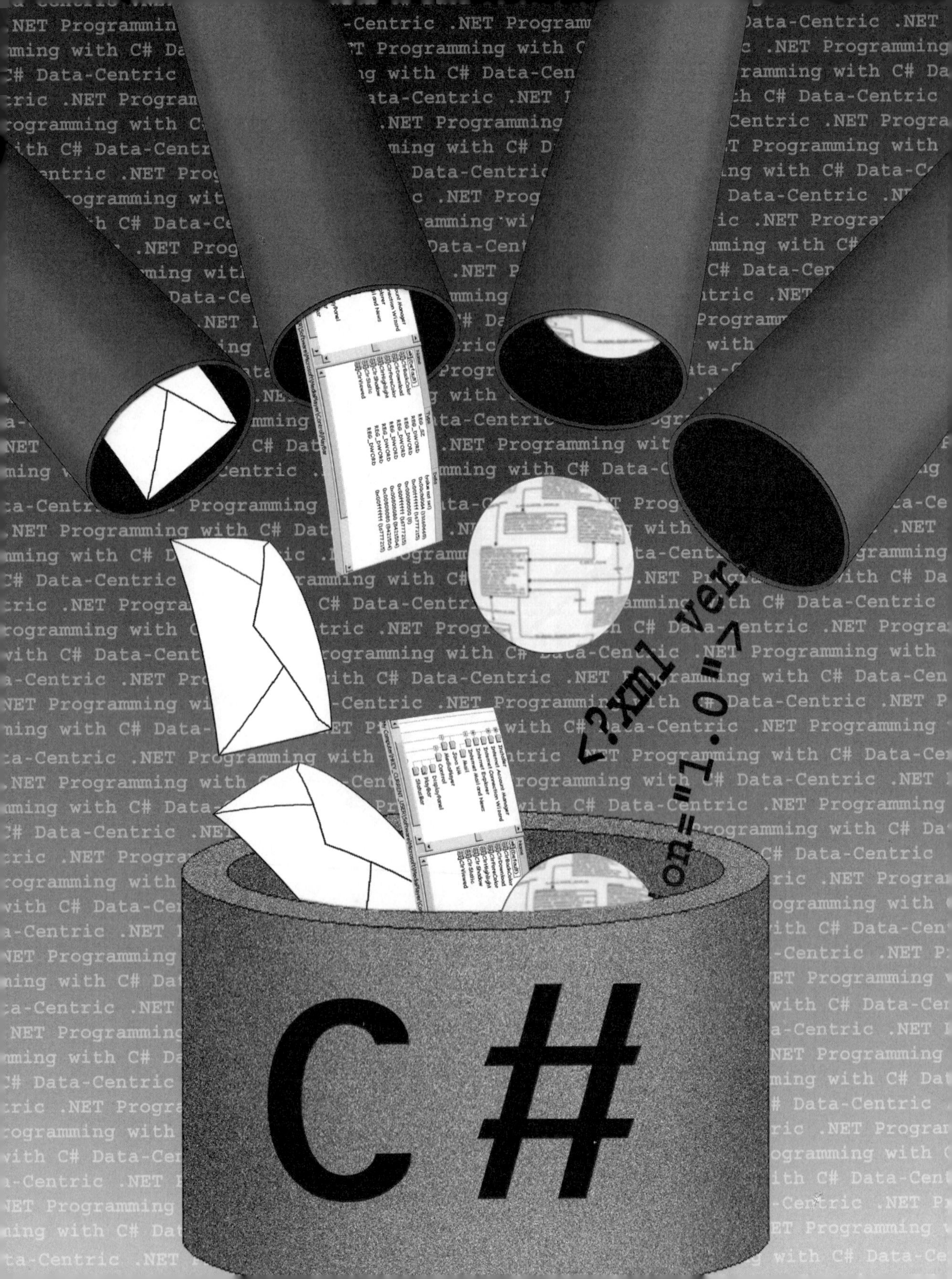
Data-Centric .NET Programming with C#
<?xml ver
on="1.0"?>
C#

Table of Contents

Table of Contents

Table of Contents

Table of Contents

Table of Contents

Introduction

The .NET Framework offers developers working in a Microsoft environment a major change in the way they design, code, and deploy new applications. From the language being worked in, to the architecture being employed, through to the functionality available, the release of .NET will present a wide vista of opportunities and new information to be assimilated.

This book is aimed at tackling just one small part of this revolution – here we're going to concentrate on the parts of the .NET Framework concerned with data. Even more specifically, we're just going to discuss how these parts can be made to work using the C# language.

Our focus within the book has been to highlight the data-centric aspects of .NET, and attempt to show how to consume and use data, at a number of points in the application – whether it be data from relational databases, non-relational data sources such as directories, or even incoming data from messages.

Who is this Book For?

This book is aimed at providing solution developers with the information they need to be able to interact with, and effectively utilize, a variety of data sources in the development of sophisticated applications. This involves consideration of obvious topics such as ADO.NET and XML, alongside less familiar data inputs such as messages, Active Directories, and the Registry. Given the current status of the .NET Framework (at the time of writing the final release of the framework was still being anticipated) issues such as COM Interop, integration with DNA based applications, and use of 'legacy' approaches such as ADO are also tackled.

This book is aimed at intermediate to advanced level programmers who are already familiar with the syntax of the C# language, have an appreciation of RDBMS and SQL, and understand the fundamentals of the .NET Framework.

What Does This Book Cover?

This book can be basically sub-divided into three main sections after Jacob Hammer Pedersen's introduction (**Chapter 1**).

First, we consider the technology basics for those aiming to build data-centric applications. Jerry Hoff and Kent Tegels take us through working with ADO (**Chapter 2**) and ADO.NET (**Chapters 3 – 5**), before Donald Xie discusses how more advanced application development features, such as connection pooling and transactions, can be used inside the .NET Framework (**Chapter 6**). Following that, Jay Glynn runs through aspects of utilizing and working with XML (**Chapters 7 and 8**).

Our second major area concerns some of the other non-relational data sources and inputs we may need to deal with. Christian Nagel describes using the Active Directory and messaging in **Chapters 9** and **10** respectively, while in **Chapter 11**, Zach Greenvoss provides information on using files and dealing with the Registry. To round off this block, P. G. Muraleedharan gives a brief taster of Web Services (**Chapter 12**) and Rob Schieber discusses the .NET Enterprise Server range of products (**Chapter 13**).

Our third section pulls the topics covered in the previous two sections together in a set of case studies to illustrate various aspects of .NET data-centric application development. In **Chapter 14** Neil Whitlow describes how to construct a .NET application that works with an open source (MySQL) database. Donald Xie picks up the baton in **Chapter 15** with a study describing how to extend and migrate a Visual Basic 6 application using .NET. Lastly, Fabio Claudio Ferracchiati looks at a legacy scenario where Messaging Services and Host Integration Server are used to develop an application (**Chapter 16**).

Finally, our coverage is supplemented with three appendices. In **Appendix A**, Saurabh Nandu details some differences between the Beta 1 and Beta 2 releases of the .NET Framework, in **Appendix B**, Brian Reisman provides a reference of the ADO.NET object model, while in **Appendix C** Niranjan Kumar shows how to connect to, and work with, some non-SQL Server databases – namely Access, Oracle 8i, and DB2.

What You Need to Use this Book

The .NET Framework will run on Windows 2000 or XP and we suggest rather than using the framework alone, obtaining either the Beta 2 or RC1 release of Visual Studio .NET. There are issues associated with using these different versions and Chapter 1 contains comments about this subject.

Over the course of the book we'll discuss a number of different technology areas involving many different pieces of software. We make considerable use of a RDBMS (primarily in this book SQL Server 2000, although connecting to databases such as Access, Oracle 8i, MySQL, and DB2 is discussed), and the chapters using the Active Directory and Messaging Services require use of a Windows 2000 Server installation.

Conventions

We've used a number of different styles of text and layout in this book to help differentiate between the different kinds of information. Here are examples of the styles we used and an explanation of what they mean.

Code has several fonts. If it's a word that we're talking about in the text – for example, when discussing a `for (...)` loop, it's in this font. If it's a block of code that can be typed as a program and run, then it's also in a gray box:

```
for (int i = 0; i < 10; i++)
{
    Console.WriteLine(i);
}
```

Sometimes we'll see code in a mixture of styles, like this:

```
for (int i = 0; i < 10; i++)
{
    Console.Write("The next number is: ");
    Console.WriteLine(i);
}
```

In cases like this, the code with a white background is code we are already familiar with; the line highlighted in gray is a new addition to the code since we last looked at it.

Advice, hints, and background information comes in this type of font.

> **Important pieces of information come in boxes like this.**

Bullets appear indented, with each new bullet marked as follows:

❑ **Important Words** are in a bold type font

❑ Words that appear on the screen, or in menus like File or Window, are in a similar font to the one you would see on a Windows desktop

❑ Keys that you press on the keyboard like *Ctrl* and *Enter*, are in italics

Customer Support

We always value hearing from our readers, and we want to know what you think about this book: what you liked, what you didn't like, and what you think we can do better next time. You can send us your comments, either by returning the reply card in the back of the book, or by e-mail to feedback@wrox.com. Please be sure to mention the book title in your message.

How to Download the Sample Code for the Book

When you visit the Wrox site, http://www.wrox.com/, simply locate the title through our Search facility or by using one of the title lists. Click on Download in the Code column, or on Download Code on the book's detail page.

The files that are available for download from our site have been archived using WinZip. When you have saved the attachments to a folder on your hard-drive, you need to extract the files using a de-compression program such as WinZip or PKUnzip. When you extract the files, the code is usually extracted into chapter folders. When you start the extraction process, ensure your software (WinZip, PKUnzip, etc.) is set to Use Folder Names.

Errata

We've made every effort to make sure that there are no errors in the text or in the code. However, no one is perfect and mistakes do occur. If you find an error in one of our books, like a spelling mistake or a faulty piece of code, we would be very grateful for feedback. By sending in errata you may save another reader hours of frustration, and of course, you will be helping us provide even higher quality information. Simply e-mail the information to support@wrox.com; your information will be checked and if correct, posted to the errata page for that title, or used in subsequent editions of the book.

To find errata on the web site, go to http://www.wrox.com/, and simply locate the title through our Advanced Search or title list. Click on the Book Errata link, which is below the cover graphic on the book's detail page.

E-mail Support

If you wish to directly query a problem in the book with an expert who knows the book in detail then e-mail support@wrox.com, with the title of the book and the last four numbers of the ISBN in the subject field of the e-mail. A typical e-mail should include the following things:

❑ The **title of the book**, the **last four digits of the ISBN**, and the **page number** of the problem in the Subject field.

❑ Your **name**, **contact information**, and the **problem** in the body of the message.

We **won't** send you junk mail. We need the details to save your time and ours. When you send an e-mail message, it will go through the following chain of support:

❑ Customer Support – Your message is delivered to our customer support staff, who are the first people to read it. They have files on most frequently asked questions and will answer anything general about the book or the web site immediately.

❑ Editorial – Deeper queries are forwarded to the technical editor responsible for that book. They have experience with the programming language or particular product, and are able to answer detailed technical questions on the subject. Once an issue has been resolved, the editor can post the errata to the web site.

❑ The Authors – Finally, in the unlikely event that the editor cannot answer your problem, they will forward the request to the author. We do try to protect the author from any distractions to their writing; however, we are quite happy to forward specific requests to them. All Wrox authors help with the support on their books. They will e-mail the customer and the editor with their response, and again all readers should benefit.

The Wrox Support process can only offer support to issues that are directly pertinent to the content of our published title. Support for questions that fall outside the scope of normal book support, is provided via the community lists of our http://p2p.wrox.com/ forum.

p2p.wrox.com

For author and peer discussion join the P2P mailing lists. Our unique system provides **programmer to programmer™** contact on mailing lists, forums, and newsgroups, all in addition to our one-to-one e-mail support system. If you post a query to P2P, you can be confident that it is being examined by the many Wrox authors and other industry experts who are present on our mailing lists. At p2p.wrox.com you will find a number of different lists that will help you, not only while you read this book, but also as you develop your own applications.

Particularly appropriate to this book are the ado_dotnet, c_sharp, and dotnet_framework lists.

To subscribe to a mailing list just follow these steps:

1. Go to http://p2p.wrox.com/

2. Choose the appropriate category from the left menu bar

3. Click on the mailing list you wish to join

4. Follow the instructions to subscribe and fill in your e-mail address and password

5. Reply to the confirmation e-mail you receive

6. Use the subscription manager to join more lists and set your e-mail preferences

1

Connecting with .NET

The release of the Microsoft .NET Framework is one of the most significant events for developers on Microsoft platforms in years. It will provide a feature-rich development platform for the construction, deployment, and execution of Internet-enabled distributed applications. The .NET Framework offers the attractions of simplified application development (with programmers able to choose from a number of languages), easier application deployment, an emphasis on XML usage, and the tools and technology for creating and consuming Web services.

This book is aimed at just exploring a part (but a highly important one at that), of this revolution in application development – data-centric application programming. As we've already mentioned, with the .NET Framework, the language used in application programming may become a matter of personal preference but here we're going to concentrate on C#. C# is being touted as the language of the .NET platform and Microsoft is planning to rely on this language for future development. Additionally, C# is being submitted for standardization, which means that others can have a go at creating C# compilers and variants for platforms other than Windows (and for Windows if they so desire). Hopefully this means that we'll soon see C# compilers appearing on other platforms, so increasing its user base.

In this introductory chapter, we'll attempt to highlight some of the most prominent features of the .NET environment and provide some lead into the rest of the book. Many of these features are not specifically data-centric, but describe many of the building blocks that you will be using when programming .NET and that provide the foundation on which our data programming is based.

Our brief introduction consists of four main sections:

- ❑ A quick recap of the .NET Framework
- ❑ A discussion of the relationship between Windows DNA and .NET application architectures
- ❑ An overview of .NET applications
- ❑ Information about .NET releases and aspects of this book

The .NET Framework

As mentioned above, the .NET framework provides a model for programming desktop and distributed applications that is full of elegance and thrives on powerful simplicity. Over the next few pages, we'll touch on some of the more prominent features that are likely to make your life as a developer easier in the future, namely:

❑ The Common Language Runtime

❑ Assemblies

❑ The .NET class framework and namespaces

Common Language Runtime

The **Common Language Runtime** (**CLR**) provides a run-time execution environment for .NET applications with code running under its control being termed **managed code**. The CLR allows access to the Windows API (in a simplified and object-oriented manner) as well as **unmanaged code** (code running on Windows outside the CLR) like COM components.

The managed code that runs in the CLR is virtually identical no matter which programming language it was written in. This is achieved by each of the programming languages that work with .NET (C#, Visual Basic .NET, Visual C++ .NET and many others) being compiled to **Microsoft Intermediate Language** (**IL**) rather than platform-dependent code. It is this IL that is run inside the .NET runtime and the CLR actually compiles the IL to platform-specific code just before the code executes.

Thus managed code has a number of attractive features including:

❑ It can, potentially, be run on any platform that provides a means of interpreting it (when appropriate CLRs are produced)

❑ It provides the basis for language-independence (see below)

On the downside, managed code is slower than unmanaged code because it needs to be compiled to platform-specific code at run-time. Also intermediate language is rather a lot easier to read than the platform-specific code, thus it may invite people to attempt to reverse engineer your applications

Just-In-Time Compilation

As mentioned above, managed code needs to be compiled to platform-specific code at run-time, to which end a number of **Just-In-Time** compilers are provided (JIT'ers). These compilers are designed to target the specific needs of the environment and, as such, one JIT'er can generate code that is optimized for fast execution at the cost of space in memory – a type of code that is highly appreciated on workstations with plenty of RAM, while another can provide code that is optimized for minimum memory requirements, at the cost of speed – something that might be preferable on hand-held devices.

IL and Language-Independence

The fact that the IL is the same no matter what the original language is a great advantage – with a minimum of care, we'll be able to share code and data types seamlessly between different programming languages in .NET. Moreover, we'll be able to write classes in language X that derive from classes written in language Y – something that has been impossible before. While it is true that COM in theory provides that very same possibility, anybody who has attempted to pass complex data types (or just a string for that matter) between Visual Basic and Visual C++ will know that it often requires quite a bit of effort.

Within the CLR the **Common Type System** (**CTS**) defines the basic data types that are supported in the .NET Framework and also the rules for defining custom classes. Furthermore the **Common Language Specification** (**CLS**) provides a minimum set of standards that guarantees that code can be accessed from any language. For example, among the nearly forty conventions to which a CLS-compliant language must conform there are issues such as public identifiers being case-sensitive, and properties and events needing to follow naming rules.

Garbage Collection

Garbage collection, or automatic memory management, is probably one of the most important features of the runtime. No program that must run over long periods of time can afford to leak memory, since it will (regardless of the amount of storage on that machine) eventually run out of resources and crash. The garbage-collection utility in the .NET Framework ensures that objects allocated memory space, and no longer referenced by the application, are collected – thus freeing memory. Interestingly, there will be some unpredictability as to when the garbage will be collected because the timing of the garbage collection is influenced by the level of available memory. When available memory is low, the garbage is collected more frequently; however, this unpredictability means there is still no excuse for not programming wisely.

Another thing to remember about automatic memory management is that it only works with managed code. Unmanaged C# or C++ code will not be garbage-collected – you will have to remember to free the memory you allocate if you are using this.

It should also be stressed that it is not just memory that is being managed and cleaned out from time to time. The same holds true for database connections, printer resources, and so forth.

Assemblies

With the introduction of .NET we will celebrate the end of "DLL Hell", or so we hope. Prior to .NET, registering and updating DLLs could be a nightmare – many people have experienced huge amounts of frustration when installing a new piece of software only to find a shared DLL is overwritten with the latest version, which is unfortunately not fully backward compatible. At this point the poor user finds other software residing on the machine fails to operate. The problem is compounded by the inability to have more than one version of the DLL registered at any time on the OS.

.NET introduces **assemblies** to replace traditional DLLs and COM components hosted in DLLs or EXEs. An assembly can consist of one or more files; however, no matter the number of files, it is considered to be atomic. Assemblies are self-describing and contain **metadata**, which gives details such as the types and methods contained in them. Additionally, assemblies contain metadata that describes the assembly itself – a data structure known as a **manifest**.

Among the things found within this manifest is information about the version of the assembly. A normal Windows DLL or COM component would write this information in the Registry, overwriting any information previously there. With the assembly it is possible for several versions of an assembly to be running at the same time, or side by side. On top of that, it is possible for a given application to instruct the CLR that it wants to run with a given version of an assembly. Thus multiple versions of the same assembly can co-exist peacefully enabling the applications accessing them to run smoothly without compatibility problems.

The Registry thus becomes slightly less significant in .NET programming – while you may still want to use the registry for storing information of various kinds, the Registry no longer holds the central role in a component's life that it used to. With the information that COM components previously stored in the Registry safely stored away in the manifests of the individual assemblies, it becomes much easier to find the settings an application is using, and when an assembly is deleted, the manifest is automatically removed as well.

Deployment

This brings us neatly to another benefit of the assembly concept – **Zero Impact Installation**. If an assembly is private (that is only intended to work with one application), since it is self-contained and self-describing (unlike COM components, which have separate type library files and GUID entries in the Registry), to be installed it merely needs placing in the appropriate folder in the file system. Such an approach will greatly simplify the deployment of large applications.

Shared assemblies (those intended to be common libraries) require a little more thought and have to be installed in an appropriate special directory – the **assembly cache** – and given a cryptographically derived name – a **strong name**.

Class Framework and Namespaces

From a developer's point of view, the .NET Framework may by described glibly as the vast framework of classes that we are gifted with. These classes allow us to write simple code that targets the Windows environment more easily than before, and which does so in a completely object-oriented way.

The **base class library** is the set of fundamental classes that can be inherited and extended by other (framework or custom) classes or used directly. The **extended class libraries** found in the .NET Framework are class libraries focused on a particular aspect of application development – for example ASP.NET includes classes specifically aimed at supporting the development of Web Services.

The framework classes are divided into a number of **namespaces**, which organize the classes into a hierarchical structure of related groups. The base (or root) namespace for the .NET Framework is `System`, and all of the other base classes in .NET (such as `System.Drawing` and `System.IO`) derive much of their functionality from the classes in this namespace – indeed every .NET class is ultimately derived from the `System.Object` class.

Let's just get a taste of what lies ahead by running through some of the data-related namespaces we'll be using over the course of the book:

❑   `System.Data` – The `System.Data` namespace contains the classes you will be using when working with ADO.NET. The namespace also functions as the base of other namespaces, most important of which are the `Common`, `SqlClient`, and `OleDb` namespaces (see below). We'll be discussing many aspects of using these namespaces as we discuss various aspects of ADO.NET in Chapters 3 – 6.

❑   `System.Data.Common` – This namespace contains classes that are shared between .NET data providers. A data provider in .NET consists of a number of classes that describe how to get at data sources such as databases.

❑   `System.Data.SqlClient` – This is the namespace that provides the .NET data provider that targets SQL Server, more specifically SQL Server 7 and 2000. While it is possible to access SQL Server from the OLE DB data provider mentioned shortly, it is recommended to use this provider since the implementations of the classes found in this namespace are optimized for use with SQL Server.

❑   `System.Data.OleDb` – This is the general .NET data provider. Use this provider when you are working with data sources other than SQL Server. The classes found in this namespace are similar to those found in the `SqlClient` namespace, making switching back and forth between providers trivial.

- ❏ `System.Xml` – XML is used virtually everywhere in the .NET framework and unsurprisingly it has a dedicated namespace – `System.Xml`. It contains several classes and namespaces for accessing and manipulating XML, including the `Schemas`, `Xsl`, `Xpath`, and `Serialization` namespaces. We'll be considering XML specifically in Chapters 7 and 8.

- ❏ `System.DirectoryServices` – The `System.DirectoryServices` namespace provides access to two classes that use the ADSI interface to access the Active Directory from managed code, as we'll discuss in Chapter 9.

- ❏ `System.Messaging` – This namespace includes classes for accessing, administering, and monitoring message queues as we'll cover in Chapter 10.

- ❏ `System.IO` – This namespace provides a wide range of classes and namespaces that concern themselves with input and output, primarily to and from disk, but also in other ways as we'll see in Chapter 11.

After this brief introduction to some of the new features included in .NET, let's step back from it all and look at development using Microsoft technologies from an architectural viewpoint.

DNA and .NET

A number of years ago, Microsoft announced an initiative called **Windows Distributed interNet Architecture** (**Windows DNA**), a term referring to an n-tier logical application model, coupled with a framework designed to support and enable the development of distributed applications.

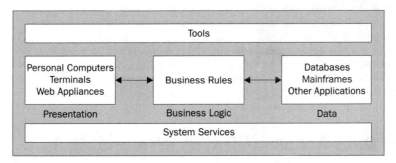

Windows DNA subsequently evolved into **Windows DNA 2000**. This latter term was both a marketing term that was used to help promote the Windows 2000 family of operating systems, and a reference to the development of the original tools and services into a complete development platform.

The n-tier model provides a number of clear benefits to the developer – it enables tiers to be worked on in parallel, since the tiered separation of functionality provides encapsulation of features. It gives flexibility in software distribution, facilitates scalability, and allows for easier maintenance and support.

In the old Windows DNA platform we made use of products and technologies including:

- ❏ Active Server Pages (ASP) for building dynamic, interactive Web pages

- ❏ Microsoft Component Object Model (COM) for creating component-based distributed applications

11

❑   Microsoft Transaction Server (MTS) to provide services to support and perform transactions

❑   Universal Data Access (UDA) to access and work with data

❑   Microsoft SQL Server 7.0 to provide a data store

In Windows 2000, COM and MTS evolved and consolidated into COM+ and became an integrated part of the operating system (unlike MTS).

So how much of this has survived into the .NET era? Actually, most of it, albeit with some rebranding and evolution of features. Thus, SQL Server 2000 is now designated as a member of the .NET Enterprise Server family (which we'll discuss in Chapter 13). Development of .NET applications is still component-based (although using a .NET-compliant language), although, as we've discussed above, the assembly approach makes deployment a lot easier. Indeed, as we'll see in Chapter 6 and in the DNA application migration case study in Chapter 15, .NET assemblies and COM+ can be used together relatively easily and features such as connection pooling, object pooling, transactions, and just-in-time activation are all still crucial parts of application development.

.NET does offer new ways to program the tiers themselves as reviewed below, but one conceptually important new development is that of Web Services (detailed in Chapter 12).

.NET Web Services

Web Services are distributed business components that may standalone or act in conjunction with other such services. Crucially, these components are able to receive and respond to requests using open standard protocols. Thus, in the heterogeneous computing world such services offer access to functionality and data from applications running on incompatible operating systems and in different languages.

Architecturally this will have an impact on the precise design of the business-logic tier, since no longer does the application itself have to contain all the functionality it needs itself; it can leverage resources made available by external parties over the Internet (or other such network). Of course, at the time of writing, with the RTM of the .NET Framework still just around the corner, large-scale deployments of .NET-based applications making use of sophisticated Web Services have yet to be widely realized.

Universal Data Access (UDA) in DNA and .NET

Time for a little more history, but some which will help us when we move on to discussing data access via ADO (in Chapter 2) and ADO.NET in subsequent chapters.

Under Windows 2000 DNA, UDA referred to the part of the architecture designed to provide access to information across the enterprise and it streamlined the Microsoft data access strategy by combining ODBC, OLE DB, and ADO. It did so by providing a simple programming interface that can be used with multiple programming languages and database platforms.

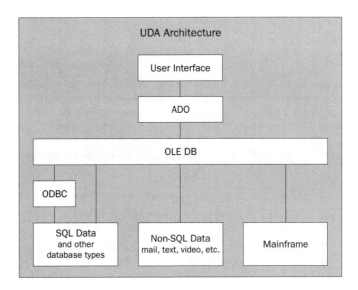

In .NET, the term universal data access has changed and now means the device-independent ability to access data anytime from anywhere. Thus the term UDA has evolved to mean that an appropriately equipped PDA can access the same data with the same ease as a desktop user or roaming laptop client.

Let's return to our diagram for a moment – the layering of data access technologies such as ADO and OLE DB and ODBC were all designed to make accessing data easier; however, as we'll find in Chapter 2, it has it's limitations. ADO.NET addresses these by giving us a radically improved new approach, which as discussed in Chapters 2 and 3, is:

❑ Data-centric – far easier to deal with both structured and semi-structured data

❑ More closely aligned with n-tier development methodology – it's emphasis on using disconnected data and basis on XML allows loosely coupled, distributed systems to be supported

XML

XML is an essential building block in so many technologies under .NET that it is certainly worth drawing specific attention to it. As an open standard text-based, extensible system of organizing information, XML has huge power in being used as a basis for information transfer between different applications.

Additionally, since it is entirely text based (which means it can be passed along with HTML through firewalls) it is an excellent medium to call methods that reside behind firewalls (hence XML being very good news for n-tier enterprise applications and as a technology to enable Web Services). The downside is that there can be rather a lot of text involved, which increases the data transmitted, but the benefits are great enough to make this a minor issue in most cases.

In a data-centric application, XML is interesting because it can be used to describe complex structures or objects, and thus can be used as the bearer of all the data that was previously contained in objects such as an ADO `Recordset`. As you will see later in this book, ADO.NET includes excellent features to support the use of XML, both to define the schema of a database, and as a data bearer.

In the .NET framework, you will encounter XML time and time again even when not dealing with data explicitly, for example:

❑   Assembly manifests can be dumped as XML files for browsing and editing.

❑   In the development environment of Visual Studio .NET, C# supports documentation of the code by using XML tags directly in the code and an XML file can be constructed whenever components are built. The resulting file can be used for documentation of the code, and IntelliSense can use this to present hints when you use the methods and classes in other projects.

Finally for this whistle-stop tour let's quickly identify the different types of applications that you can build in .NET.

Programming .NET Applications

We can sub-divide .NET applications into the following areas (excluding text-only applications running in a DOS window – simple Console applications):

❑   Windows Forms applications

❑   Windows Service applications

❑   ASP.NET Web applications

❑   Web Services

❑   Windows Forms controls

While the bulk of the book deals with the interaction with data, the case studies at the end of the book provide a more rounded view – the Scientific Data Center application in Chapter 14 uses both Windows Forms and a Windows Service; the DNA application migration study in Chapter 15 involves coding a Windows Form application, and the legacy project of Chapter 16 is based around an ASP.NET application and Windows Services.

As we've already mentioned Web Services, let's have a quick look at the others.

Windows Forms Applications

Windows Forms is the .NET equivalent of the traditional Windows-based application that provides a form based UI. Windows Forms provide a rich set of components that can be used in essentially the same manner as you would use ActiveX controls in Visual Studio 6. Most of the functionality that is used in Windows Forms is found in the namespace `System.Windows.Forms`.

Creating a Windows Application project in Visual Studio .NET creates a project that is targeted at the Windows environment, but it is important to understand that this cuts you off from very little of the functionality found throughout .NET. If you are familiar with the Visual Basic 6 development environment you are likely to feel right at home in the environment presented to you by Visual Studio .NET. Windows Forms is the perfect choice for you if you are developing either a standalone or distributed application, to be run on the Windows 98, 2000, or XP platforms.

Windows Service Applications

These applications are executables running in independent NET Windows sessions with no user interaction (the evolution from NT Services). Such applications have certain special requirements – for example they need to be compiled with a set of resources that allow, say, the Services Control Manager to recognize and administer the service, and they don't have user interfaces. They do however, like standard applications, respond to events.

Most Windows 2000 machines have a large number of such services present such as the Distributed Transaction Coordinator and IIS Admin service.

ASP.NET Web Applications

The .NET framework provides the `System.Web.UI` namespace that includes many of the objects you will need to create impressive web applications.

When you create an ASP.NET Web Application project in Visual Studio .NET you are presented with a form designer that looks very much like the one used to create Windows Forms, and you are given the choice of using controls as well. These controls include what are seemingly the same controls as mentioned above, but on closer inspection you will find that the `DataGrid` is not the same. The reason being that this control will exist in a browser, rather than on a Windows Form, which adds some limitations and changes some behaviors. However, working with the controls has a very familiar feel to it, making it much easier to delve into programming for the Web.

One of the new things in ASP.NET is the ability to use the C# language, or any other language that is supported by the CLR, as the scripting language. This means that when you are writing the application code, there is no difference in the code used in the presentation layer and the code in the business layer.

ASP.NET will probably become the technology of choice for a large part of the web development community, and must now be considered whenever you need to write an application that must reside in a browser of some sort.

Windows Forms Controls

These are the successors to ActiveX controls – they are reusable components that provide a user interface and are responsive to user events. The `System.Windows.Forms.Control` class provides the basis for such controls.

Versions of .NET

As we detail in Appendix A, different versions of the .NET Framework have been released to the public over the course of its development cycle. Significant changes were made between the Beta 1 and the Beta 2 releases (some of which are documented in Appendix A). The Beta 2 version of the code is almost feature-complete and stable enough for developers to begin some early deployments of live code.

At the time of writing this book the .NET Release Candidate 1 had just been made available, although according to Microsoft, this release is only recommended for users who have not installed Beta 2. It appears that certain areas of operation, particularly related to COM+ interoperability and COM+ services (such as serviced components in Chapter 6 and queued components in Chapters 10 and 16) contain some interesting under-the-hood differences between Beta 2 and RC1. Additionally the ODBC .NET Data Provider Beta 1 add-on for the .NET Framework SDK Beta 2 (which we use in Chapter 14) fails with RC1.

Following the Microsoft comments, this book is written with the Beta 2 version of the Framework in mind, and, where possible, we have flagged differences that are noted (or needed) when the code is executed on RC1. When the final release becomes available any changes having impact on this book will be identified on www.wrox.com, and an updated code download will be made available.

Software Requirements

The .NET Framework will run on Windows 98/NT 4, 2000, or XP and we suggest, rather than using the framework alone, obtaining either the Beta 2 or RC1 release of Visual Studio .NET (bearing in mind the above comments about different versions), and running Windows 2000 or XP.

Over the course of the book we'll discuss a number of different technology areas involving many different pieces of software. We make considerable use of an RDBMS (primarily in this book SQL Server 2000, although Appendix C discusses how to connect to databases such as Access, Oracle 8i, and DB2, and Chapters 2 and 14 discuss MySQL), and the chapters using the Active Directory and Messaging Services (Chapters 9, 10, and 16) require a Windows 2000 Server installation. Chapter 15 considers migrating an application from the DNA model to .NET, and as such makes use of Visual Studio 6 (although the code built using Visual Basic 6 is downloadable).

Summary

In this opening chapter we've just attempted a rapid overview of some of the .NET Framework's major points and provided a brief introduction to some of the namespaces we'll be encountering within this book. In so doing, we've touched on the variety of data sources that are involved in data-centric applications – relational databases, non-relational data such as directories, and isolated data inputs such as messaging.

The relationship between DNA and .NET has been commented on – more specific comparisons are best treated as the appropriate technologies are described. Furthermore, we've identified the different types of .NET applications we may be encountering.

We rounded off our discussion by identifying the different versions of the .NET Framework available at the time of writing, and some issues related to using them.

As we mentioned above .NET is a substantial advance on the DNA methodologies and technologies being pushed a couple of years ago, however it *is* related and, for many, inter-operation of .NET and DNA will be crucial both for advancing their existing application functionality and interacting with existing data stores. It is with this diversity of development in mind that the book closes with cases studies that look at:

❑   Development of a .NET application accessing a non- .NET data store

❑   The migration of a DNA application to a .NET enabled application

❑   The development of .NET applications dealing with legacy data

In fact, our first task in this book is to look at the role old technology – ADO – may play in our new .NET world.

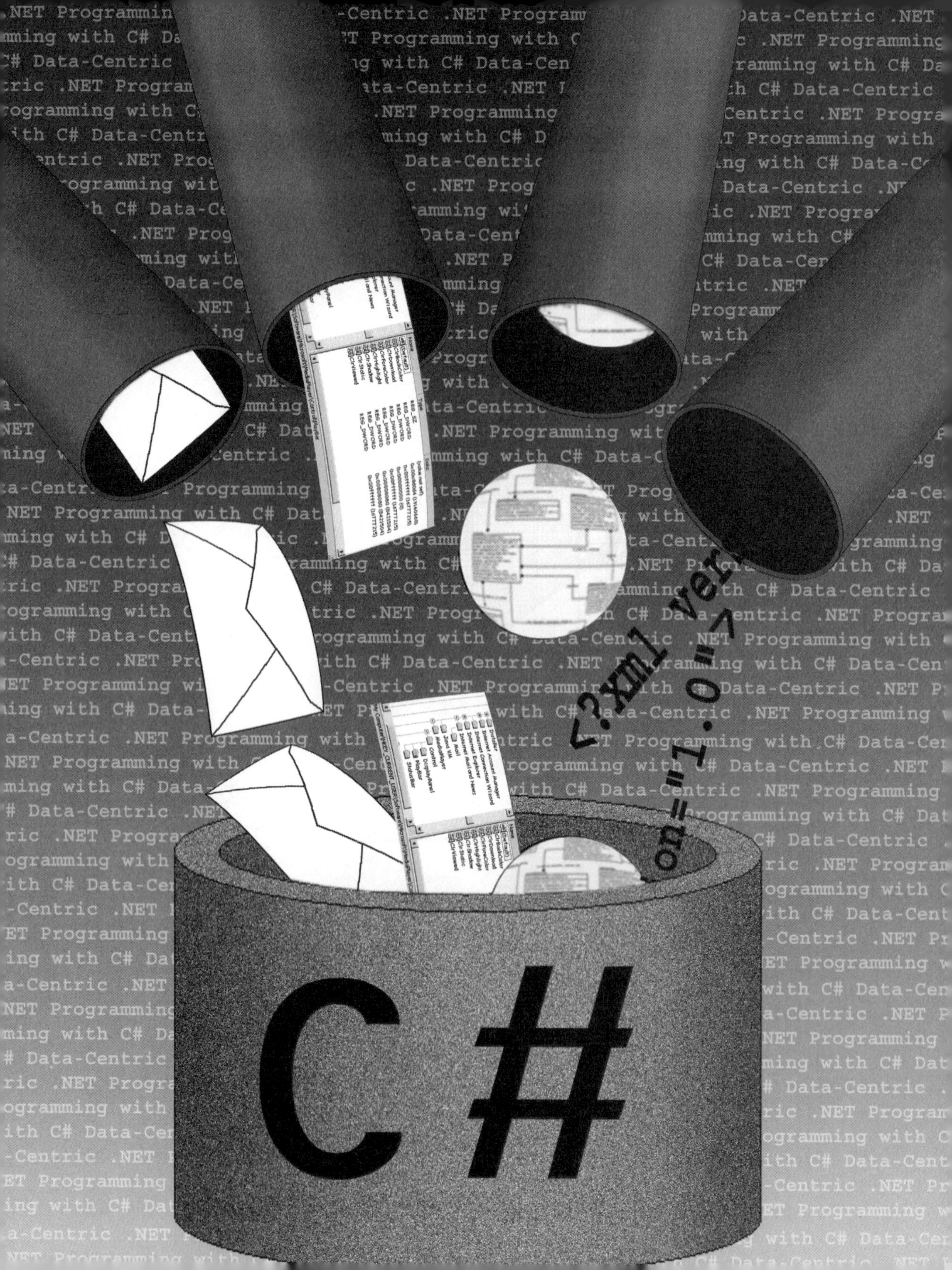
Data-Centric .NET Programming with C#
<?xml ver
on="1.0"?>
C#

2

ADO and C#

Contrary to popular belief, ActiveX Data Objects (ADO) is far from dead in the .NET era. In fact, it may be the only way you will get your job done. Since you are reading this book, it's quite likely that you have an appreciation of the benefits of the .NET Framework for writing data-centric applications. In the following chapters, you will read much about how to use .NET classes and managed providers to get your work done. All of that is fine, but what if your data source is a MySQL database, an Exchange Server or even DB2 running on an AS/400? Can you still get the benefits of .NET, and "eat your cake" using an ODBC data source?

If you couldn't, this would be a very short chapter indeed. In this chapter, we are going to look at what are, at least for some of us, old friends: **ActiveX Data Objects** (**ADO**) and **Open Database Connectivity** (**ODBC**) data source providers and investigate how they can be used in the .NET environment by:

❑ Looking at the background to ADO and then drilling through the ADO object model to gain a better understanding of it

❑ Comparing and contrasting classic ADO with ADO.NET and seeing how ADO fits in the distributed application model commonly used with .NET

❑ Looking forward to the graying of ADO, and a time when ADO may be retired

To understand the present and future, sometimes it is helpful to reflect on the past, and that will be our first task as we look at ADO itself.

What is ADO?

Just over a decade ago, Bill Gates introduced the world to the concept of "information at your fingertips". The idea is that data, in whatever form, should be accessible from virtually any device – regardless of its form, at virtually any time. Of course, we know that no single data storage system will fit every need. We also know that it is expensive (in terms of time and personal effort, if not cash as well) to master every data access method we are likely to need to know.

An early attempt to create uniform way to access data in relational databases was the Open Database Connection standard. While powerful, the Applications Programming Interface for this tended to be cumbersome for Visual Basic programmers to use. Microsoft then layered different data access technologies on top of ODBC to make life easier. To this end, DAO (for the JET engine used by Microsoft Office products) and RDO (used for accessing relational database management systems) were initially introduced. However, these technologies were geared specifically toward product families and offered almost no support for semi-structured data sources like Exchange.

OLE DB was later introduced as "the way" to access any form of data – relational, hierarchical, or semi-structured – through a COM-based interface. OLE DB is much less dependent on the actual physical structure of the data than ODBC. OLE DB layered the solution to data access models into providers (which hold and serve data) and consumers (which use providers and present data to the application). Both consumers and providers are materialized as COM objects. They interact with each other through a set of COM interfaces. Once again, however, Microsoft traded easy programmability for higher performance and designed OLE DB to work best with C++ in high-performance middle-tier objects.

However, Visual Basic proved to be a much more popular way to accomplish these goals, so Microsoft introduced the ActiveX Data Objects (ADO) library as a preferred technology for data access. ADO is a high-level library built on top of OLE DB. Through ADO we can work with non-relational data such as directory data, data in mail stores, or data in Excel files. Access to such a broad range of data sources was impossible with DAO or RDO before.

ADO, built on COM, provided a key solution to the problem of having to master the "Data Access Technology Du Jour".

The components involved in making the COM, OLE DB, and ADO plumbing work can get very complicated. They must translate between their native environment and the standardized interfaces demanded by the ODBC environment. They must be able to express data in the format, and within the data types, used by the environment, and they must behave (at least somewhat) consistently with any other data source. This obviously requires a significant amount of programming to accomplish and even more to produce a well-tuned, performance-geared provider. This, in turn, explains why it will take time for native providers for these data sources to appear – cost, time, and expertise.

As well thought and intentioned as ODBC is, it has an inherent limitation. The abstraction of data access methods at the provider level takes a "least common dominator" approach. Even if a data store *could* do more, the rules about being a compliant provider mean that it cannot. In order to overcome this, another solution was needed, and put forth in OLE DB. OLE DB changes the expectation of a provider. In effect, it allows a greater amount of the data source's native functionality to be exposed to ADO, and thus to your application.

For a long time ADO, ODBC, and OLE DB got us a lot closer to the ideal of information at your fingertips. Then along came XML. By its very nature, XML can bypass the whole need for the plumbing, giving us direct access to data. Only a very small portion of the data we need to access today actual presents and persists itself as XML. So while the future for that technology appears glowing, we still need to make do with what we have.

Of course, SQL Server 2000 has excellent facilities for generating and consuming XML. For a comprehensive look at this technology, consider Professional SQL Server 2000 XML, *Wrox Press (1-861005-46-6).*

Exploring ADO

ADO as we know it today (ADO 2.6 being the current production version at the time of writing) consists of five major classes: `Connection`, `Command`, `Record`, `Recordset` and `Stream`. In turn, each of these classes except for `Stream`, has one or more associated collections. We will look at the object model graphically later in the chapter.

❑ `Connection`: Used to define, establish and control a connection between your application and the database. The `Connection` object has two collections: `Properties` and `Errors`. The `Properties` collection contains key-value pairs describing the attributes of the connection, while the `Errors` collection holds a list of errors occurring in the connection. The `Connection` class has a number of methods and events for controlling connections and transactions.

❑ `Command`: Used to define, execute, and hold partial results from queries. The `Command` object is commonly used to execute stored procedures requiring one or more parameters. Like `Connection`, `Command` also has a `Properties` collection. It has an aptly named collection representing the `Parameters` associated with the command. These can be input, output or bi-directional. The `Command` object throws no events, but does have methods for executing and controlling the stream of execution that it is part of.

❑ `Record`, `Stream`: `Records` are used as data structures in `Streams`, whereas `Streams` result from queries to hierarchical data sources. From early on, ADO was geared to work with data from relational database systems. As different hierarchal data based provider technologies evolved, it became essential to develop ADO objects that adhered more closely to the data model of these systems. Each `Record` has a collection of `Properties` representing attribute values of that record. One can consider a `Stream` to be a collection of collections, with a `Record` being an individual collection of attributes. `Records` have no events, but do have a limit set of methods to traverse, for cloning and pruning them and their children. `Streams` also have no events, but a rich set of methods for loading and persisting data.

❑ `Recordset`: Used to present and store the results of a query where those results can be expressed in rows and columns. Each `Recordset` has a `Fields` collection and a `Properties` collection. Like other objects in this set, the `Properties` of a `Recordset` represent certain attributes of the query result. The `Fields` collection effectively contains key (column name)-value (row data) pairs. `Recordsets` have a full set of methods and events.

This terse listing of the ADO object model really does two things. It demonstrates the elegant simplicity – from a programmer's point of view – that makes ADO a great tool to work with. However, it leaves out big chunks of the total ADO picture such as:

❑ ADO MD for working with multidimensional data cubes

❑ ADOX for working with data schemas and metadata

ADO is all this and more, of course. If you really need or want to get into the deep, dark recesses of ADO, then ADO 2.6 Programmers Reference, *Wrox Press (1-1861004-63-x) is just what you are looking for.*

ADO Programming in C#

The typical ADO program – at least in part and mostly from the higher-level language developer's perspective – tends to do the following (hardcore C++ programmers are probably left rolling their eyes at how simplified this is, compared to their reality):

- ❏ Add a reference to ADO to current project.

- ❏ Create a `Connection` object and open it. In order to open successfully, a Data Source Name (DSN) or connection string needs to be specified. Either one will specify a provider, a set of authentication credentials, and information on how and what to connect to.

- ❏ Create one or more `Command` objects, populate the command text, then create, load up, and attach some `Parameter` objects to the `Command`.

- ❏ Create one or more `Recordset` objects, setting them to receive the results of an executed command.

- ❏ Iterate through the `Recordsets` and their rows, extracting the data into some working storage.

- ❏ Once the data processing is completed, post the data back into the data store using new or recycled `Command` objects, probably as sets of transactions.

- ❏ Clean up any references to the created objects.

Of course, hardened Visual Basic programmers can also be seen rolling their eyes when they consider how fast and lightweight COM components can really be if they are built from the ground up using the Active Template library.

Errors can occur at any point along the way, bubbling up from the data source (at least usually). Errors are caught in the `Errors` collection of the `Connection` object. Well-written code should check to see if this collection is populated after each major action.

As you will learn in the following chapters, there are many similarities between writing ADO.NET and ADO, but some of your methods and thinking will change.

.NET to COM Interoperations

A design goal for the .NET runtime was to avoid recreating the problems introduced by COM in terms of recycling of components (the infamous "DLL Hell") and hairy data type translations. This has been accomplished neatly with the Common Type System and the Common Language Runtime. It also replaces the different "p-Code" approaches taken by different languages, with a common approach to just-in-time compilation and Microsoft Intermediate Language.

These fundamental changes mean that COM and .NET cannot natively share resources with each other. Microsoft realized early on, however, that everybody using its tools probably has substantial investment in existing COM-based solutions. Therefore, some method of sharing will be required for the foreseeable future. This is achieved using a solution known as "COM Interoperability". This solution bridges the gap between .NET and COM so that either can use the resources of the other.

While a comprehensive drill-down on using COM Interoperability via C#, lies outside the scope of this book, we do consider the topic from a practical perspective in Chapter 15.

COM Interoperability services are exactly how we access classic ADO in our C# examples. Doing so is a fairly simple process. Since we anticipate most developers will be using Visual Studio .NET, we will demonstrate how to use that tool in the rest of this chapter. Most of our examples will be based on a simple C# console application. This simplifies development, and allows us to focus on core techniques.

Referencing ADO

So to demonstrate ADO, after creating the shell of a C# console application project, right-click on **References** and select **Add Reference....** On the **Add Reference** screen, click the **COM** tab. When you have the desired version of ADO highlighted, click on the **Select** button. Visual Studio .NET then queries the binary bits of the Dynamic Link Library selected to enumerate the accessible components.

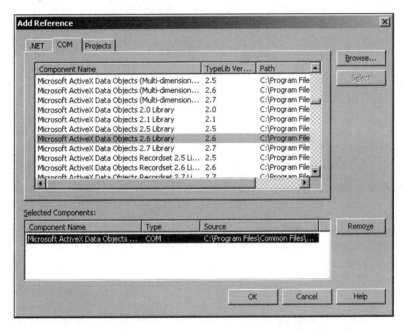

Once you are satisfied with your selections, click **OK** to finish adding the reference.

> *Here we use version 2.6 of the ADO libraries in our example. Although ADO 2.7 is available with the various .NET SDKs, at the time of writing version 2.6 was the current production version.*

If you are not using Visual Studio .NET, you need to manually import the referenced namespaces. This can easily be done with the following steps:

❑ Start a command-line session, and issue the command

```
tlbimp "c:\program files\common files\system\ado\msado15.dll"
```

❑ Add using adodb.dll to your .cs files

Now you can start writing code. Here's a little class that creates and opens a connection to nowhere in particular, or more precisely, to no provider.

```
using System;
namespace Wrox.ProCSharpData.Chapter2.Sample1
{
    /// <summary>
    /// Demonstrates how to access classic ADO in C#
    /// </summary>
    class Class1
    {
        /// <summary>
        /// The main entry point for the application.
        /// </summary>
        [STAThread]
        static void Main(string[] args)
        {
            // Let the compiler know what objects we plan to work with
            ADODB.Connection objConn;
            // Create a connection object to work with
            objConn = new ADODB.Connection();

            // Open the connection for use
            try
            {
                objConn.Open("","","",-1);
            }
            catch (Exception e)
            {
                // What? Something went wrong? Tell me what...
                Console.WriteLine("Error:\n" + e.Message);
                // Wait for the user to hit Enter...
                Console.ReadLine();
            }
            finally
            {
                // Do nothing for now
            }
        }
    }
}
```

This probably looks a bit different from the ADO code that we are used to seeing (unless you use C++). Notice that we use the new operator to create an instance of ADO's Connection class. Running in this in debug mode gives us a chance to see, however, that we can use C#'s try ... catch ... finally blocks.

What we can gain from this failed code is hope that our previously presented seven-step model for programming with ADO will not change greatly.

Using ADO with Relational Databases

Let us start our drill down into ADO programming in .NET using a slightly more interesting example. We will follow the theme of Chapter 14 of this book, which presents a case study about data, collected from oceanographic buoys, that is stored in a MySQL database.

The case study in Chapter 14 covers the steps you will need to go through to get MySQL running. This includes creating the "Buoy Database" DSN we will use in the following example. Although this step may seem arcane, it will help to demonstrate that you can still use DSNs with .NET.

The following slightly modified version of our first sample class connects to the database and returns a simple count of the number of buoys. As you will find out as you use Visual Studio .NET to write C# that calls classic ADO, you might be able to get away with some of the lazy habits that Visual Basic or ASP let you get by with. These include:

❑   The C# compiler will have issues with the optional nature of some method parameters. In C#, all function parameters for at least one method signature must be provided. To work around this, you can use an essentially empty instance of the Object class.

❑   Directly accessing the values of property collection elements may not be possible. You may find it easier to iterate through these collections, and extract the desired value from the enumerated instance. It seems to be best practice to precisely match data types where possible.

❑   The set of constants you may be used to working with will not be available here. For example, when calling the Open method of the Connection object, there is an optional parameter that defines if the connection is treated as synchronous or asynchronous. The constants adAsyncConnect and adConnectUnspecified are made available in the classic COM type library. However, these are not known in the .NET environment directly. You have some choices about this, of course. You can just hardcode the numeric values (which somewhat defeats the value of having the constants). You can work your way around this and define your own constants.

You could also be a bit masochistic, for example, and try Convert.ToInt16 (ADODB.ConnectOptionEnum.adConnectUnspecified) as the value for the final parameter in the Open method call. It is an option...

Here's the new code:

```
class Class1
{
    /// <summary>
    /// The main entry point for the application.
    /// </summary>
    [STAThread]
    static void Main(string[] args)
    {
```

The first difference we will see is that we're going to add instances of ADO's Recordset and Command objects to work with. First, we add the Command object instance:

```
ADODB.Connection objConn;
ADODB.Command objCmd;
```

Next we create an ADO Recordset object instance:

```
ADODB.Recordset objRS;
```

BETA 2 NOTE: If you are using Beta 2 of Visual Studio .NET, then you will find that when creating the Recordset instance, instead of the above line, you will need to enter the following line in order to successfully execute the code.

```
ADODB._Recordset objRS;
```

We continue by creating an object instance called objOptParm. We will use this as a placeholder value for the situation where the compiler complains that a method call does not have the correct number or type of parameters, even though those parameters are optional as far as the COM signature for the method defines. We can "nullify" this object by setting it a zero-length string.

```
object objOptParm;
// Create our parameter placeholder
objOptParm = "";
```

The next section of code opens a connection to the database. In the previous examples, we just used zero-length strings for the UserID and Password parameters of the Open method. Here, we are using the objOptParm object as a placeholder for the UserID and the Password. We are also calling a new function in this class, Pause(). We will look at the code for that shortly.

```
// Create a connection, then try to connect...
objConn = new ADODB.Connection();
try
{
    objConn.Open("DSN=Buoy Database",objOptParm.ToString(),
        objOptParm.ToString(),-1);
}
catch(SystemException e)
{
    Console.WriteLine("Error:\n" + e.Message);
    Pause();
}
finally
{
    // do nothing yet
}
```

Our next chunk of code creates Recordset and Command instances. We populate the CommandText property of the Command object instance and tie the Connection instance to it:

```
// Make ready a Recordset to receive the query results
objRS = new ADODB.Recordset();
// Setup up the command we want to execute...
objCmd = new ADODB.Command();
objCmd.CommandText = "SELECT Count(BuoyId) AS BuoyCount FROM buoys";
objCmd.ActiveConnection = objConn;
```

We can now try to execute it. Notice the use of the placeholder objects again, and the use of a hard-coded value for the options parameter of the Execute method:

```
// Execute the command
try
{
    //...then execute it
    objRS = objCmd.Execute (out objOptParm,ref objOptParm,1);
}
catch(SystemException e)
{
```

```
        Console.WriteLine("Error:\n" + e.Message);
        Pause();
    }
    finally
    {
        // do nothing yet
    }
```

Finally, we can start looping through the result set to get at the rows returned. Notice the use of a `foreach` loop. We use this to expose the columns in the row as instances of the `Field` object. From there, it is fairly simple (and a compiler-acceptable way) to get at the values returned.

```
    // Dump the result set out
    try {
        while(!objRS.EOF) {
            foreach(ADODB.Field fld in objRS.Fields) {
                Console.WriteLine("There are {0} buoys deployed.",
                    fld.Value.ToString());
            }
            objRS.MoveNext();
        }
    }
    catch(SystemException e) {
        Console.WriteLine("Error:\n" + e.Message);
    }
    finally {
        Pause();
    }
}
```

Finally, we move some of our interactive bits into a function. This helps to keep code more modular:

```
    static private void Pause()
    {
        Console.Write("Press [Enter] to continue...");
        Console.ReadLine();
    }
}
```

Pulling it Together

To wrap up our discussion of using relational databases, ODBC, and ADO in C#, here are the key points to keep in mind:

❑ ADO came forth to provide a seamless way to use different data sources within a common programming model.

❑ ADO is based on using OLE DB providers and object models that manage the plumbing needed to connect an application to a data source.

❑ The key elements in the object model include `Connection`, `Command`, `Record`, `Recordset`, and `Stream`.

❑ Most ADO-based programs follow a seven-part model of referencing the ADODB library, establishing a connection, preparing commands for execution, preparing a `Recordset` to receive results, executing the command, processing the data, updating the data store and then cleaning up.

❑   ADO is based on COM, which is not natively available in .NET. However, .NET does offer an interoperability service that allows you access.

❑   You need to work around some of the requirements of the C# compiler not understanding COM's optional parameters, and the possibility that certain properties may not be directly available. You may need to work around getting constant values defined for your program to use.

It is probably not too hard from here to understand how you could write C# code that inserts, updates, and deletes data in a database. Given some of the limitations of current versions of MySQL, we will not be showing any examples of using stored procedures with parameters. You will find that in most cases, if such features are available to you, you may be able to use the ADO.NET and the OLE DB managed providers instead. There are times, however, where a true OLE DB provider is available, but using ADO may be preferable to using ADO.NET. We will look at that in the next section with the **Internet Publishing Provider**.

Using ADO with Semi-Structured Data Sources

Are there times where *not* using ADO.NET in a .NET application makes sense? We have already covered one instance, when only an ODBC provider is available. There some cases where you may find it easier to use ADO instead of ADO.NET when an OLE DB provider is available. One such case is when using the Internet Publishing Provider. In this section, we will look at the techniques involved in using ADO's Record object as an interface to a **semi-structured** data source provider. Before doing that, however, let's clarify what we mean by a semi-structured provider and the roles they fill.

Traditional database management systems such as Access, MySQL, Oracle, and SQL Server are designed to store, manage, and query "structured" data and its inter-relationships. By organizing data into rows, columns, and tables, the data assumes a regular and somewhat rectangular shape. This high degree of structure and predictability means that high performance query and management systems can be created. Indeed, if we stop to think about it, there is a lot of useful, high-value (in terms of investment of financial and human resources) data that can be normalized to fit within such systems.

However, there is probably a lot more data than cannot be so neatly squared away. Consider the value tucked away in the tons of documents, presentations, and e-mails quietly sitting on the corporate network. It would be unreasonably hard to normalize these objects for use in a database. Granted, each of these items could conform to some object model, and they are all obviously storable in an electronic format. Beyond this, attempting to accommodate such irregular data within the regularity of a relational database simply does not make sense. So, if ADO is ever to accomplish it mission of being a single interface to any data source, it needs to work with data that is "semi-structured".

This was exactly the goal of Microsoft's strategy for **shaped-data** in ADO version 2.5. By being able to **nest** rows of different sizes within a table structure, it became possible to represent semi-structured data with ADO's object model. There was also a need to develop providers that exposed ADO, ODBC, and OLE DB interfaces to these data stores. Microsoft developed a few semi-structured providers to work with. One of the most potent of these providers is the Exchange OLE DB provider that allows developers to interact at the ADO level with the Web Storage System in Exchange 2000.

> *Is Microsoft saying that Exchange is a second-class citizen compared to SQL Server 2000 by not having a .NET managed provider for Exchange 2000? Not really. As we will see later in this chapter when we compare and contrast ADO to ADO.NET, the semi-structured nature of the Web Storage System (the core of Exchange 2000) is easier to work with in ADO, hence Microsoft has not made developing a managed provider a high priority... just yet.*

Another commonly available provider is the Provider for Internet Publishing. This allows you to query HTTP services for information. In turn, the provider presents that information back to ADO as `Recordsets`.

> *For a drill down on using the Internet Publishing Provider, see* Professional ADO 2.5 Programming, *Wrox Press (1-861002-75-0). Do keep in mind that this provider works best with sites that have the FrontPage Server Extensions installed or that support the WebDAV protocols.*

Using the Internet Publishing Provider

Formally known as the Microsoft OLE DB Provider for Internet Publishing Provider, IPP for short, this is your gateway to accessing a web space via ADO. IPP is a very handy way to interact with WebDAV-enabled sites. This includes reading, writing, moving, removing, and renaming files within such spaces. The most straightforward way to use this provider involves the following steps:

- Create an ADO `Connection` object, set it to refer to the target web site, and then open it. Think of the web site as being a container of documents (and, of course, there can be containers within that container with documents in them, and so on, and so on...).

- Create an ADO `Record` object. This will act as the conduit of results from the provider back to our application.

- Call the `GetChildren` method of the `Record` object to fetch the matching documents within a container, depositing the results into an ADO `Recordset`.

- Iterate through the resulting ADO `Recordset` and act on the returned results.

Let's turn our attention to a somewhat more practical discussion. Suppose you have been asked to develop a program that crawls an Intranet site looking for documents that have not been updated for thirty days. You want to use the Internet Publishing Provider to accomplish this, so you are somewhat stuck with ADO for now. For our purposes, we will once again use a fresh C# console application to this end.

> *The complete code is available for download from www.wrox.com. The application we present here is the* WebDB *project.*

Our solution is structured like this:

- The `Main()` function will create any values that need to be shared between functions. It will then proceed to query a URL for files and sub-directories. Finally, it will examine a list of the files to see which of them have become stale.

- We will create a function to open a given URL and collect the list of files and subdirectories. Each of the files will be added to a queue of files for processing. When a subdirectory is discovered, this function will call itself to get the files and subdirectories in that subdirectory.

- We also need a class to act as a property bag for the file attributes we are interested in, such as the filename, its URL, the date it was last updated, and its size.

- A utility function for displaying any errors caught.

This is the beginning of the code for our `Main()` function:

```
static void Main(string[] args)
{
    System.Collections.Queue FileList;
```

29

```
     FileEntry objFE;
     DateTime CutoffIs;
```

We will use a `Queue` data structure for this example. We could have used another collection type, but the queue is first-in, first-out. Thus, the use of a `Queue` data structure allows us to retrieve the files in the order in which they were discovered.

```
     FileList = new System.Collections.Queue();
```

Next, we can call our function that examines a web site, passing it our starting URL and a reference to the just created `Queue` for the discovered files:

```
     CollectFilesOnPath("http://localhost/",ref FileList);
```

When the first call to our discovery function returns, we should have a complete list of the available files to work with. With those in hand, we will compute a "cutoff" date. We will use this value to determine if a file is stale or not:

```
     CutoffIs = System.DateTime.Now.ToLocalTime() - TimeSpan.FromDays(30);
```

Then it is a simple matter to take items out of the queue and compare their last updated date and time to our cutoff. If the comparison result is greater than zero, meaning that the file is stale, we will display the name and timestamp for the file. Once we have emptied the queue, we will pause for a keystroke.

```
     while(FileList.Count > 0)
     {
        objFE = (FileEntry)(FileList.Dequeue());
        if(DateTime.Compare(CutoffIs,objFE.LastUpdated) > 0)
        {
           Console.WriteLine("{0} last update written to{1}"
                                    ,objFE.LocalName,objFE.LastUpdated);
        }
     }
     Console.WriteLine("\nPress [Enter] to continue.");
     Console.ReadLine();
}
```

Our function that opens and scans a given URL for files follows:

```
     static private void CollectFilesOnPath(string URLPath,
                                  ref System.Collections.Queue FileList)
     {
```

We know we need to create ADO `Connection` and `Record` object instances, so we will define them at the top of the function.

```
     ADODB.Connection objConn;
     ADODB.Record objRec;
```

Next we create an ADO `Recordset` object instance:

```
ADODB.Recordset objRS;
```

> *BETA 2 NOTE: As before if you're using Beta 2 of Visual Studio .NET, then instead of the above line, you'll need to use:*

```
ADODB._Recordset objRS;
```

With this out of the way, we can continue. At a later point in this example, we will find that we need an "optional parameter" object as we did in our previous example programs. We will also need a string to hold our ADO `Connection` (which will be based on the `URLPath` parameter passed in). We will also need an instance of the file property-bag container (to be detailed later) to add to the queue. We add all of these now:

```
object objOptParm;
string strConnStr;
FileEntry objFE;
```

One somewhat annoying feature of Visual Studio .NET and the .NET Framework we will have to deal with again is "optional" parameters. IPP uses a set of enumerations to control how the connection to the web site will behave. Unlike our previous experience with optional parameters, we cannot just cheat and use an empty object. Instead, we'll need to create instances of the enumerations and set their values to what we want.

```
ADODB.ConnectModeEnum Mode;
ADODB.RecordOpenOptionsEnum OpenOptions;
ADODB.RecordCreateOptionsEnum CreateOptions;
```

We've seen this before – just creating an empty optional parameter object:

```
objOptParm = new Object();
objOptParm = "";
```

The connection string needs to specify a provider name, a data source, and any credentials we want to use. IPP's provider name is `MSAIPP.DSO`. When we attempt to open that connection, we should test for any exceptions being raised:

```
strConnStr = "Provider=MSDAIPP.DSO;Data Source=" + URLPath + ";" +
                                    "User ID=;Password=;";
objConn = new ADODB.Connection();
try
{
   objConn.Open(strConnStr,objOptParm.ToString(),
                                    objOptParm.ToString(),-1);
}
catch(Exception e)
{
   ReportError(e);
}
```

> **Here is an annoyance to keep in mind: when the provider cannot open the desired web site using the provided credentials, it does throw an exception, but the message property of that exception will be empty.**

Now we can create and set the values of our enumeration objects. For the most part, these can be the default values expected by the `Open` method of our `Record` object. These values are documented in depth in the MSDN library.

```
Mode = new ADODB.ConnectModeEnum();
CreateOptions = new ADODB.RecordCreateOptionsEnum();
OpenOptions = new ADODB.RecordOpenOptionsEnum();

Mode = ADODB.ConnectModeEnum.adModeUnknown;
CreateOptions = ADODB.RecordCreateOptionsEnum.adOpenIfExists ^
            ADODB.RecordCreateOptionsEnum.adCreateCollection;
OpenOptions = ADODB.RecordOpenOptionsEnum.adOpenRecordUnspecified;
```

Note that the ^ operator is C#'s bitwise XOR operator.

Next, we can create instances of the `Record` and `Recordset` objects to work with, and then open the record as our interface with the IPP using the freshly created enumerations. As usual, it is a good idea to catch any errors that may be thrown:

```
objRec = new ADODB.Record();
objRS = new ADODB.Recordset();
try
{
    objRec.Open(objOptParm.ToString(), objConn,Mode,CreateOptions,
            OpenOptions, objOptParm.ToString(), objOptParm.ToString());
}
catch(System.Exception e)
{
    ReportError(e);
}
```

To populate the `Recordset`, we call the `GetChildren` method of the `Record` object. This effectively issues an HTTP GET command for the `_vti_inf.html` in the root of the web site being queried. This in turn tells IPP where to find the `author.dll` file. IPP and FrontPage work together through `author.dll` to get the actual list of resources and return them as a `Recordset`. You can think of the `author.dll` as being the actual data provider; it knows how to map the files and folders into objects that can be used with OLE DB.

```
objRS = objRec.GetChildren();
```

As we have seen before, the next step is to iterate through the `Recordset`. When starting a new record, we need to create a new property bag to hold the information we've found about the file or subdirectory in question. With that ready, we can then iterate through each of the fields (columns, if you will) for certain attributes.

```
while(!objRS.EOF)
{
    objFE = new FileEntry();
    foreach(ADODB.Field fld in objRS.Fields)
    {
```

Instead of returning a rectangular set of columns and rows when the `GetChildren` method is called, IPP returns a `Recordset` of what amounts to property names (as columns) and values (as rows). Of the twenty IPP properties normally found, we are only interested in five for our problem.

Property Name	Property Value Explained
RESOURCE_PARSENAME	Indicates the relative URL of the resource.
RESOURCE_ABSOLUTEPARSENAME	Indicates the absolute URL of the resource.
RESOURCE_LASTWRITETIME	Indicates a FILETIME structure containing the time that the resource was last written. The time is in UTC format.
RESOURCE_STREAMSIZE	Indicates the size of the resource's default stream, in bytes.
RESOURCE_ISCOLLECTION	True if the resource is a collection, such as a directory. False if the resource is a simple file.

The next section of the function determines if the current property is one of the ones we are interested in, and if so, either stores it in our property bag or, if it is a subdirectory, calls itself with the newly found path. If we find the `ISCOLLECTION` attribute is set to `False`, we know we have a regular file, so we can add it to the queue.

```
switch(fld.Name.ToString())
{
   case "RESOURCE_PARSENAME":
   {
      objFE.LocalName = fld.Value.ToString();
      break;
   }
   case "RESOURCE_ABSOLUTEPARSENAME": {
      objFE.FullURL = fld.Value.ToString();
      break;
   }
   case "RESOURCE_LASTWRITETIME":
   {
      objFE.LastUpdated = Convert.ToDateTime(fld.Value);
      break;
   }
   case "RESOURCE_STREAMSIZE":
   {
      if(fld.Value != null)
      {
         objFE.Size = Convert.ToUInt64(fld.Value.ToString());
      }
      break;
   }
   case "RESOURCE_ISCOLLECTION":
   {
      if(Convert.ToBoolean(fld.Value))
      {
         CollectFilesOnPath(objFE.FullURL,ref FileList);
      }
```

```
                else
                {
                    FileList.Enqueue(objFE);
                }
                break;
            }
        }
    }
    // Move on to the found item.
    objRS.MoveNext();
    }
}
```

We have mentioned a property-bag class and have seen it typed as `FileEntry`. This is actually just a very simple class:

```csharp
class FileEntry
{
    private string strLocalName;
    private string strFullURL;
    private System.DateTime dtLastUpdated;
    private System.UInt64 uintSize;

    public string LocalName
    {
        get { return strLocalName; }
        set { strLocalName = value; }
    }
    public string FullURL
    {
        get { return strFullURL; }
        set { strFullURL = value; }
    }
    public System.DateTime LastUpdated
    {
        get { return dtLastUpdated; }
        set { dtLastUpdated = value; }
    }
    public System.UInt64 Size
    {
        get { return uintSize; }
        set { uintSize = value; }
    }
}
```

Finally, our function to report exceptions should look familiar.

```csharp
static private void ReportError(System.Exception err)
{
    Console.WriteLine("Error:\n" + err.Message);
    Console.WriteLine("Press [Enter] to continue");
    Console.ReadLine();
}
```

To wrap up our discussion of ADO programming in C#, there are a few lessons learned worth sharing.

Some Lessons Learned

The points summarized below are not only based on this example, but take into account wider inter-operability issues as well.

❑ First and foremost, if you can avoid using ADO, do so, particularly if you are building a new .NET-based solution. The primary reason for this is that from a performance perspective, the cost of marshaling and inter-process operations for bridging COM to .NET is fairly high. Another reason is that ADO, unfortunately, is fraught with ways to let "lazy" programming practices work and work well. This is inconsistent with the strongly typed and well-structured approach that programming in .NET favors. While finding "workarounds" is certainly possible, doing so may effectively decrease the efficiency of your total development effort. Expect this to be a major issue when porting existing Visual Basic code up to .NET, if you decide to follow that route.

❑ Do not expect that "reuse by cut and paste" or automated transformation will result in a lot of time saving. Early on, I wrote a little script that would "redecorate" a Visual Basic function into C# so that I could then paste it into a class. Although the program worked reasonably well, the output did not because I had taken full advantage of ADO and COM, letting me be "lazy". The result? I probably spent just as much time "fixing the bad" as I would spend "writing the good". Your experience may, of course, be different.

❑ Look for ways to present and access the data needed as an XML stream instead. The .NET Framework has plenty of ways to use that natively.

❑ Consider writing your own custom OLE DB Provider or even .NET Managed Provider. This may sound like daunting task, but if you are working with proprietary data it may be the best overall solution.

❑ Obviously, it will not always be possible to avoid writing ADO code, so consider ways to isolate it. For example, consider our Internet Publishing Provider example. We put considerable effort into working around the eccentricities of .NET relative to ADO in the function that gathered files on a URL path. This code would have been much simpler to write in classic Visual Basic with COM interfaces, and we could then use interoperability to access that. The downside is that we still have a "classic DLL" to cope with, and thus potential "DLL Hell" issues. Consider the trade offs carefully.

We have seen that ADO can be a useful means to an end for the professional C# programmer. This commonly occurs when ADO.NET either cannot work with a given provider or when ADO.NET architecture is less well suited than that of ADO. Experience shows us that working with ADO in a .NET-based application presents a few challenges, but they are addressable. By comparing ADO to ADO.NET, we should get a clear understanding how ADO fits into the .NET environment.

ADO Meets ADO.NET

Although ADO.NET and ADO have similar names, and a common role in providing data access for applications and ease of use, they are completely different things. In many ways, ADO is to ADO.NET what COM is to the .NET Framework. Neither is particularly revolutionary; rather, each represents an evolution of what came before into what will be. ADO was a great stride forward for many of us, as it dramatically simplified the programming needed to access data. In one neat package, we could interact with a wide range of databases, and our programs would have a consistent, well-understood design pattern. And since ADO is built on COM, we certainly could use it in any COM-friendly programming language. It gave us one thing to learn, to use, and to master.

ADO.NET is not so much about learning and mastering one thing, but about being an effective set of tools to use. ADO defined a fairly rich model that OLE DB providers had to adhere to, and providing anything further required working around or changing the ADO model. Conversely, the ADO.NET Data Provider model defines only a minimum set of functionality that a provider must offer, but it is free to do more. The trade off here is that each provider may introduce its own namespace and its own eccentricities to work with, meaning more for us to learn. Similarly, the workhorse object in ADO is the `Recordset`. The manifestation of ADO's heritage as a database access technology is found in the structure of the `Recordset`. When designing ADO.NET, Microsoft decided to act on two important facts.

❑   Not all data is, or can be, effectively or efficiently stored in a database

❑   XML is rapidly become the method of choice for encoding and transmitting data

To this end, `Recordsets` have undergone a metamorphosis into the data source-neutral, XML-based `DataSet` in ADO.NET.

Understanding the Differences

Keeping all of this in mind, we will now compare ADO.NET with ADO so as to complete our understanding of each and how they fit into the .NET programming environment. We will start by looking the design goals of ADO.NET, then at some of its important features.

The design goals of ADO.NET set out to address some of the issues in using ADO in distributed applications. Those goals include:

❑   Leverage developers' knowledge of ADO – Microsoft understands that the last thing we want as professional developers is the need to learn another data access technology. ADO.NET coexists with ADO because each one fills specific roles.

❑   ADO.NET is data-centric, not database-centric – The distinction is important because it opens far more of the valuable information we have to work with. With ADO, we were somewhat limited to working with databases and data that conformed itself nicely to normalization. With ADO.NET, we will find that as long as the data is available in XML, we will probably be able to work normally with it, regardless of its source.

❑   Support the n-tier programming model – ADO.NET's `DataSet` is a disconnected object, using XML as both a data source and as a vessel for the transmission of data between layers.

❑   XML Support – Nowadays it seems pretty hard not to support XML at some level, but ADO.NET goes one step beyond XML support and is actually built squarely on top of the Microsoft XML technology suite. ADO.NET allows us to read XML, from almost any source, as easily as we can fetch data from a database. It also allows us to work with XML using the familiar column and row concepts we have become familiar with as ADO developers.

.NET Data Providers versus COM-Driven Providers

The first major difference that you are likely to find lies in the in the providers. As previously mentioned, .NET's native providers and COM's providers are radically different.

The simplest form of a .NET data provider will only support a `DataSet` object through the `IDataAdapter` interface. The object may add parameterized queries through the `IDataParameter` interface. A complete data provider will support transactions, connected data access, and commands. Complete providers will support the full range of `IData...` and `IDb...` interfaces.

On the other hand, OLE DB providers come in three flavors:

❑ Service

❑ Data

❑ Document Source

Service providers are essentially proxies between services using an OLE DB interface. Service providers rarely control their own data. Data providers on the other hand, control their own data and expose it in tabular form. Document Source providers, like the IPP, manage folders and documents. OLE DB providers can also be classified as simple or complex. A set of mandatory interfaces must be exposed, but these do not need to support the full range of functionality. However, the minimum requirements are far greater for these providers than for the .NET data providers. At a minimum, the provider must support a number of interfaces for each member of the ADO object model.

In theory, a .NET provider will be better than an OLE DB provider for a number of reasons, including:

❑ .NET Managed Providers use XML for transferring data and not a binary format as does OLE DB. This eliminates some potential COM inter-operability delays.

❑ Performance – Because a .NET Data Provider is expected to be written on top of the Common Language Runtime and Common Type system, there should be far less conversion between native types and COM types. There is also direct access to the native wire format of the underlying data source. This is exactly why SqlClient has excellent performance. This .NET Data Provider uses the Tabular Data Stream format and thus effectively "drinks from the firehose".

The Information Technology community is good at creating interesting phrases like "drinking from the firehose. When used in the database sense, it means that the data is flowing from its source at great volume and maximum rate, and the consumer is taking as much of the data as quickly as possible. However, if you imagine yourself trying to drink water from a firefighter's hose turned fully open, you have the right mental image for "drinking from the firehose".

❑ Flexibility – A provider must support a small set of functionality, but is free to define its own additions to that. This contradicts the ADO mindset of forcing functionality to fit one model. This could lead to the problem of one provider becoming a de facto standard, and other providers having to play catch-up with it.

❑ Reuse – Since these providers are based on .NET, it should be easier to inherit and reuse providers to provide new functionality as that develops.

XML/HTTP versus COM/Marshaling

A serious limitation for distributed applications, particularly distributed over the Internet, is that COM relies on Remote Procedure Protocols to marshal Recordsets between COM-based processes. This process is often contrary to the security standards of a well-secured web server (RPC endpoints are well-known holes for exploitation). Along the way, additional functionality to load and save XML was bolted on to ADO. However, it relied on persistence to files, making it cumbersome to work with over a network.

An absolutely key concept in distributed .NET application design is to use XML as the encoding medium for data and transport with the HTTP protocol. The Simple Object Access Protocol (SOAP) became the de facto standard for realizing this in the pre-.NET era. In .NET, the approach is known as Web Services. ADO.NET is build from the start to support this, neatly, cleanly, and directly.

Distributed Application versus Client-Server

ADO rose to power following the rise of the client/server approach to computing. ADO's view of the world works well with this model: continuously connected, state aware, and somewhat limited to databases; and the components of our solutions are distributed to two or maybe three layers: a client (a desktop application or set of web pages); a server (where the data management occurs) and perhaps a business logic layer that mediates actions between the two others. Everything works quietly under the covers, buttressing the simple object model. All of the plumbing is abstracted to the point that as developers, we are seldom aware of what is really going on under those covers. Try to make this approach work over a disconnected, stateless environment, such as the Internet, and it quickly becomes obvious that we do need to be aware of what is going on under the covers. Even if the objective is to create a purely internal multi-tier solution architecture, ADO's roots in COM seep through.

ADO.NET mitigates this in two ways. Firstly, data can always be treated as disconnected, so no connection to its source need be maintained. Secondly, ADO.NET does not particularly care about where or how it got the data. What it does care about is how that data interrelates and keeps track of itself. It also tracks changes to the data so that when the data needs to be posted back, it knows exactly what changes to make. As the developer, it will be up to you to know where those transactions should occur. It should also help us scale upwards because available connections will be turned over faster.

Data Specificity

We have discussed before that despite Microsoft's best efforts, ADO is largely seen as a database access technology. In some ways, ADO's dependence on COM further restricts its adaptation beyond this context. ADO.NET moves away from this by explicitly supporting XML as the first choice data source. In effect, this means that ADO.NET has greater *data* specificity than ADO does (it can handle any data actually as it is, rather than fixing it to some limited schema), but ADO will have greater *database* specificity.

Cursors

This comparison is easy to explain: classic ADO supports server-side cursors, ADO.NET does not.

That probably leads to asking why. The answer goes back to data specificity against database specificity. In classic ADO, there was always some connection back to the data source. This connection was, in part, defined by the type of cursor used when creating the Recordset.

However, ADO.NET wants as little do with a continuous database connection as possible. It wants to store, manipulate and understand the data it has on its own terms. So the idea of a cursor back to the data source just does not make sense in the ADO.NET context.

Transactions

You may be thinking that ADO and ADO.NET agree on very little. One thing both approaches agree on is the need to support transactions when creating, updating, or deleting data. In fact, transactions are more important in the disconnected approach used by ADO.NET.

Transaction support in classic ADO operates on both the database and, where used and support, the COM+ environment. In ADO.NET, and in .NET in general, classes can participate directly in transactions. ADO.NET can also "manually" participate in database transactions in a similar way to ADO.

Object Model Differences

A good way to understand how ADO and ADO.NET relate to each other is compare their object models. We will do this by examining the ADO object model that you may already be familiar with, then attempting to match the ADO.NET objects with those. To start with, the figures below show the relationships within the two object models.

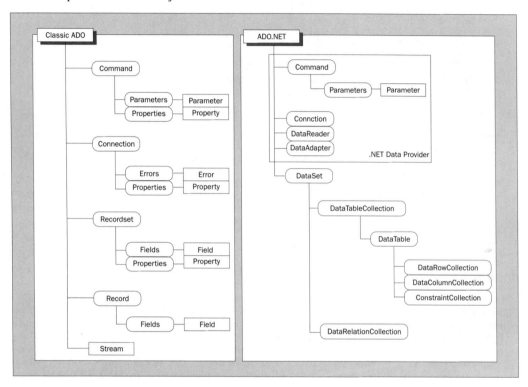

Command

In both classic ADO and ADO.NET, `Command` objects are used to define and execute commands against a data source. Both objects support appending parameters to the command. Commands are typically used to execute stored procedures within a relational database management system.

Using a classic ADO `Command` object in Visual Basic 6 would look like this:

```
Set objCmd = New ADODB.Command
Set objConn = New ADODB.Connection
objConn.Open ("Provider=SQLOLEDB.1;Integrated Security=SSPI;Initial " & _
              "Catalog=northwind;Data Source=localhost;")
Set objCmd.ActiveConnection = objConn
objCmd.CommandText = "[Sales By Year]"
objCmd.CommandType = adCmdStoredProc
objCmd.Parameters.Append objCmd.CreateParameter("@Beginning_Date", _
                              adDate, adParamInput, 16, "12/1/1997")
objCmd.Parameters.Append objCmd.CreateParameter("@Ending_Date", _
```

```
                                        adDate, adParamInput, 16, "12/31/1997")
    Set objRS = objCmd.Execute
```

Using an ADO.NET `Command` object in C# with SQL Server, the code would look like this:

```
objConn.ConnectionString = "Integrated Security=SSPI;Initial " +
                           "Catalog=northwind;Data Source=localhost;";
objConn.Open();
objCmd.Connection = objConn;
objCmd.CommandText = "[Sales By Year]";
objCmd.CommandType = CommandType.StoredProcedure;
objCmd.Parameters.Add("@Beginning_Date",new SqlDateTime(1997,12,1));
objCmd.Parameters.Add("@Ending_Date",new SqlDateTime(1997,12,31));
objDR = objCmd.ExecuteReader();
```

Notice that the differences amount to the following:

❑ There is no need to specify a provider in the connection string.

❑ With ADO.NET you do not need to create and then append parameters, you can simply add them.

❑ Instead of calling an execute method on the `Command` object instance to get a `Recordset`, you call the `ExecuteReader` method to get a `DataReader`. There is more on these objects in the following chapters.

If we were going to use an OLE DB source instead, the `ConnectionString` property and `SqlDateTime` instances would need to be adapted to work with that provider.

Connection

In both ADO and ADO.NET, `Connection` objects are used to define what data source to connect to, how to connect to it, and who to connect as. Both ADO and ADO.NET use connections to establish if a query should be treated as part of a transaction. When comparing these objects between ADO and ADO.NET, there are three major differences to keep in mind:

❑ In classic ADO, all errors occurring between the data source and the application are typically expressed in the `Errors` collection of the `Connection` instance. In ADO.NET, such errors are treated just like any other instance of an exception.

❑ In classic ADO, the connection string syntax is uniform for all providers. In ADO.NET, the syntax of the connection string may vary by provider.

❑ In classic ADO, the connection is conceptually thought of as being at the same hierarchal level as another other ADO object. In ADO.NET, a `Connection` is an object at a Data Provider-specific level.

The actions needed to open a connection to the `Northwind` database, using Windows Authentication, in Visual Basic 6 would look like this:

```
Dim objConn As New ADODB.Connection
objConn.Open "Provider=SQLOLEDB.1;Integrated Security=SSPI;" & _
             "Initial Catalog=northwind;Data Source=localhost;"
If objConn.Errors.Count > 0 Then
   For Each objErr In objConn.Errors
      Debug.Print objErr.Number & ": " & objErr.Description
   Next
End If
```

In C#, the code might look like this:

```csharp
SqlConnection objConn = new SqlConnection();
try
{
    objConn.ConnectionString = "Integrated Security=SSPI;" +
                        "Initial Catalog=northwind;Data Source=localhost;";
    objConn.Open();
}
catch(Exception e)
{
    do
    {
        Console.WriteLine(e.Message);
        e = e.InnerException;
    }
    while(e != null);
    Console.WriteLine("Press [ENTER] to continue...");
    Console.ReadLine();
}
```

If you are using C# to connect to an instance of that same database "downsized" to Access, it would look like this:

```csharp
OleDbConnection objConn = new OleDbConnection();
try
{
    objConn.ConnectionString = "Provider=Microsoft.Jet.OLEDB.4.0;" +
                            "Data Source=c:\northwind.mdb;";
    objConn.Open();
}
catch(Exception e)
{
    do
    {
        Console.WriteLine(e.Message);
        e = e.InnerException;
    }
    while(e != null);
    Console.WriteLine("Press [ENTER] to continue...");
    Console.ReadLine();
}
```

Note how differently we work with the errors between ADO and ADO.NET. Being able to treat database errors like any other exception should be a great time saver!

Errors and Error

In classic ADO, `Errors` collects individual instances of `Error` objects and resides in the `Connection` object. There really is no similar concept in ADO.NET as every data provider is expected to throw instances of an `Exception`. Each provider may derive subclasses of `Exception` to provide additional details about the error encountered. For the `SqlClient` namespace, use the `SqlException` class, and use the `OleDbException` if you are working with that the OLE DB.

Exceptions in ADO.NET are not queued into a specific collection as `Error` instances are placed into the `Errors` collection of ADO's `Connection` object. Instead, exceptions present themselves as a linked list. If more than one exception occurs concurrently, they will all be present. The previous examples for the `Connection` object show how to step through such lists.

Record and Stream

As we have seen earlier in this chapter, the classic ADO `Record` object is used to interface with a semi-structured data provider. One area where ADO.NET has some shortcomings deals with semi-structured data providers like EXOLEDB and the IPP. To a certain extent, this makes sense in the .NET philosophy where semi-structured data is best represented as XML.

> *So what is the best way to work around this? For Exchange 2000, at the time of press, the method Microsoft recommends using to access Exchange is to HTTP-POST a DAV request and get an* `XmlReader` *on the results, and call* `DataSet.ReadXml()` *on that* `XmlReader`. *For the IPP, it would probably be best to wrap that functionality up inside a COM component exposing the result set as an XML document. You could then "feed" that to an* `XmlReader`.

The story for `Stream` is essentially the same. In classic ADO terms, a `Stream` represents a series of binary data flowing from a `Record`. In .NET, `Stream` provides a generic view of a sequence of bytes.

Recordset

The bad news is that there is no direct equivalent for the classic ADO `Recordset` in ADO.NET. The good news is that the bad news is actually good news! In classic ADO, `Recordset`s really grew out of the need to express the results of a query against a data source in a rectangular form, as this was typically what databases worked with. Since tables and the results of most SQL queries expressed themselves as sets of rows and columns, it made sense to represent the data in a similar format for our applications to work with. Along the way, the `Recordset` grew in terms of functionality and features, but the philosophy of ADO – essentially "any data you want, so long as you express it in the ADO objects" – remained largely unchanged. A few key points to keep in mind about the classic ADO `Recordset` include:

- ❑ Given its roots as a database access technology, ADO tends to be highly bound to database functionality. For example, if you wanted to express data from a table of sales and a table of customers, you had to ask the data source to join these two different sources together and express the result as a virtual table. Or worse yet, you had to write the methods for gluing the data together. And many of you have probably had to do exactly that because you had one `Recordset` of data from one provider "A" that you needed to merge with data from another provider "B".

- ❑ The "behind the scenes" behavior of a `Recordset` was largely a function of the cursor type of the connection used during its assembly. For example, if you wanted to work the data in a manner that was "disconnected" from its native data source, you would use either a `Keyset` or `Dynamic` cursor.

- ❑ Sharing a `Recordset` between tiers of distributed applications involved extra resources and developer attention due to marshaling issues. Attempting to ship a `Recordset` through a firewall in a web application scenario opened up a very large set of security issues. Also, since some measure of locks were held on the data at the database level, scalability became significantly limited.

- ❑ Finally, the process of using a `Recordset` to deliver data involves the overhead of the amount of metadata, and the COM and ADO infrastructure.

In practical terms, ADO.NET's `DataSet` object cooperates with the `DataAdapter` object to fulfill the mission of classic ADO's `Recordset`. A `DataSet` is an in-memory representation of the data from one or more `DataAdapters`, which, in turn consist of connections and commands back to the provider. You will primarily use a `DataSet` when you need to read, update, and post back data, or when you need to tie together data from multiple data sources. The really neat thing about the `DataSet` is that you can do all the query, update, and transformation work locally against it, then allow it to figure out how to update its sources. Finally, the `DataReader` acts as a fast-forward, read-only `Recordset`. It is an ideal tool to use if you are just fetching data for the sake of displaying it elsewhere.

From this section, you should now see that growing from ADO to ADO.NET is really much more of an evolution than a revolution. Starting from the ground up, ADO.NET sets aside classic ADO's "your size fits one" approach to providers. This means we can expect a much richer and faster platform to build on. By switching from COM to XML as the message, and from RPC to HTTP as the medium, we should gain a much greater degree of interoperability and reach for our applications. By abstracting data from its source – typically via XML – we gain a more data-centric and less database-centric model to work with. By eliminating cursors, we reduce constraints on scalability. Finally, by providing one container that accepts data for what it is rather than from whence it came, we have a greater degree of flexibility as developers.

The Graying of ADO

It is clearly reasonable to expect that classic ADO will continue to be an important tool even with the introduction of ADO.NET. That should not be taken to say that ADO will continue on forever. Perhaps, it is best to say that ADO is starting to show more than just a few gray hairs. Consider the reasons that classic ADO persists:

❑ No native provider for Data Source X – We spent a good portion of this chapter using ADO to work with a MySQL database precisely because you may find yourself in such a situation. We have also seen that developing a .NET Data Provider is a less daunting task than trying to write one for OLE DB. So it reasonable to assume that database providers will eventually start providing their own native providers. Until then, you have to use ADO.

❑ Semi-structured data sources – The future for Microsoft's willingness to create and support semi-structured data providers is uncertain. We have seen a significant push on the Exchange front to expose its services using XML, which is a perfectly valid source for ADO.NET to consume. Technologies like the Internet Publishing Provider are also likely to be susceptible to similar treatment. In the mean time, it may be best to wrap the functionality for such providers into COM objects with interfaces exposing the result set as XML.

❑ Time and effort to convert – Although there will be some tools that will convert legacy code into a .NET-usable format, to truly realize the fully benefit of .NET it may be more effective and efficient to rethink, restructure, and recode legacy applications.

At some point, we may assume that ADO will retire and enjoy a well-deserved rest. As you have read this chapter, hopefully you have come understand why classic ADO will continue for now, what role it plays in the .NET era, and how it compares with ADO.NET.

Summary

We began this chapter by stating that the rumors regarding the demise of ADO were greatly exaggerated. Along the way we have:

❑ Seen what ADO is, how it is structured, and how it works

❑ Illustrated how to use ADO in C# with both relational and semi-structured data providers

❑ Discussed some lessons learned

❑ Compared and contrasted ADO to ADO.NET

❑ Previewed where ADO may be heading in the future

With this understanding in hand, let us now turn our attention to actually using ADO.NET for all that it's worth.

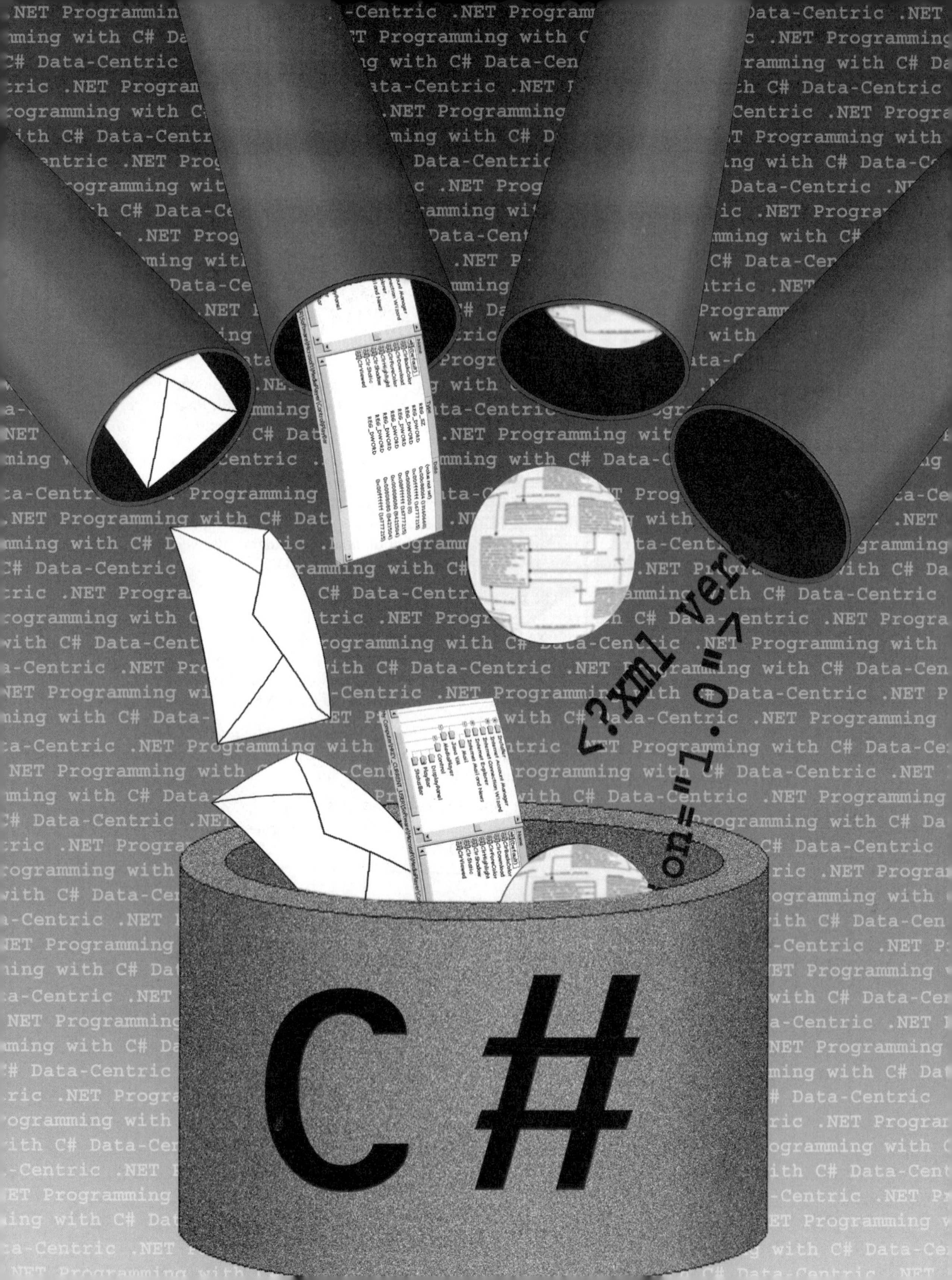
Data-Centric .NET Programming with C#
<?xml ver
on="1.0"?>
C#

3

ADO.NET and C# I: Data Access

To paraphrase Mark Twain, it could be said that ADO.NET is to ADO as "Lightning is to a Lightning Bug". In the previous chapter, we saw how you can leverage your knowledge of classic ADO (that is, ADO running on top of COM) in the .NET environment. We also compared ADO.NET with classic ADO as a way of understanding each of them. In this chapter, we will start our drill-down on ADO.NET. In this chapter, you will be presented with the fundamentals of ADO.NET and how to write simple console C# programs to access data. If you have already done some simple database access programs in C#, this chapter may be a review of the basics. If you have not done any C# database programming at all, this chapter will give you the basics of what you need to know to proceed further in the book. In this chapter we will:

❑ Examine ADO.NET and the ADO.NET namespaces

❑ Look at the .NET data providers, explore the common ADO.NET objects, their methods and properties, and demonstrate how to connect to data sources

❑ Illustrate how to work with databases – in particular how to call and use stored procedures, and use the disconnected `DataSet` to manipulate and persist data

Hopefully, you will see that ADO.NET is a big improvement over Microsoft's many earlier data access technologies, along with being very easy to use.

A key strength of ADO.NET is that it is built totally upon the .NET framework. This means that it is seamlessly accessible from any .NET-based programming language. Although this title is focused on C#, you can use same methods and techniques with Visual Basic .NET, JScript .NET, Managed C++, and even Visual J#. No more dealing with callbacks in one language, automation interfaces in another, and event sinks in yet a third. Now we have just one straightforward, well-behaved class model to deal with! However, ADO.NET is not something special to .NET – as ADO is to COM development – rather is a fully-fledged, first-class member of the technology family.

Microsoft is also setting the expectation that ADO.NET will be the standard for data access technology in its Web Services model. This is because it:

❑ Has out-of-the-box compatibility with all existing OLE DB providers

❑ Provides native usage of the Tabular Data Stream used in SQL 7.0 Server (and higher)

❑ Optimizes data transfer through the use of XML

❑ Has disconnected `DataSets` as standard, rather than as a bolted-on afterthought

The code for the chapter can be downloaded from www.wrox.com.

Overview of ADO.NET

The architecture of .NET applications is based on a set of federated, distributed, and loosely-coupled objects interacting via standardized, inter-networking technologies. Classic ADO has several shortcomings in such architectures. For example, `Recordsets` are transferred using COM marshaling. This, in turn, uses Remote Procedure Calls (RPC) as the transfer agent. However, RPC over TCP/IP is problematic from a security standpoint. Out-of-the-box, classic ADO left workarounds to solve that up to the developer. Another shortcoming is the classic ADO approach to materialization. By this we mean that each `Recordset` was designed to hold only one set of data at a time. Finally, `Recordsets` were originally designed with the assumption that they would be tethered to an active connection at most times. This again proved problematic as that tether commonly used RPC.

On the other hand, ADO.NET has built-in facilities for using XML as the messaging medium, and HTTP as the transport medium. Both of these are much easier to plumb through a firewall-secured network. ADO.NET defines a new data storage class known as the `DataSet`. Instances of `DataSets` provide containers for one or more `DataTables`, constraints, and relationships. For practical purposes, a `DataTable` is just like a table in a database. The `DataSet` has the same structure as a database. `DataSets` are creatable, and act independently of any other data source. This allows programmers to utilize and manipulate several tables at once, before propagating the changes back to the original data source. `DataSets` can be populated from query results as well. But once populated, the connection between the two is purely optional. The process of reconnecting and updating existing data from a `DataSet` also uses the built-in XML and HTTP plumbing.

This structure lends itself well to the distributed architecture .NET is expected to address. In ADO.NET, the entire `DataSet` can be serialized into XML, including its schema. Allowing data to be transferred in this way, regardless of the original data source, easily accommodates the movement between different servers for access, business logic, and presentation.

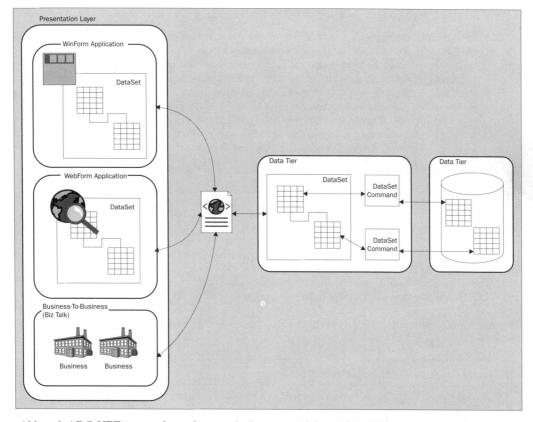

Although ADO.NET is geared mainly towards disconnected data, ADO.NET also accommodates connected, real-time access to data. Disconnected data sources are particularly appropriate in a few cases. The first case is when the data is large enough to justify paging (for example, when you want to read in partial chunks of data in a series), but can be treated as read-only. This is commonly the case for anonymous use of the Internet and intranets. Another case is where data from many sources needs to be brought together for presentation and editing, and the underlying data is relatively free from concurrent change.

Connected recordsets, on the other hand, are best suited when a relatively small portion of the data needs to be locked from changes, and the data changes need to be posted quickly (such as financial transactions).

In this chapter we will demonstrate both. You will notice that some classes are used regardless of the type of connection you wish to make. These classes are also shared between the different ADO.NET providers. You will read more about ADO.NET providers in this chapter.

Namespaces in Detail

Like everything else in .NET, Microsoft has compartmentalized the data classes into a number of namespaces. Out of the box, the .NET Framework supports two .NET data providers. As we saw in Chapter 2, these providers are different from the ODBC and OLE DB providers that are used with classic ADO. These are also known as managed providers. Support for these providers is found within unique namespaces. Here are the namespaces for the two providers you will be using in the next few chapters:

- ❏ `System.Data` – Contains classes used by both managed providers.

- ❏ `System.Data.Common` – Contains base classes used by, and to create, managed providers. This class includes the essential `DataAdapter` class that acts as the intermediary between `DataSets` and the actual database by managing collections of `DataCommands` and `DataConnections`. The `DataColumnMapping` class and its `DataColumnMappingCollection`, as well as the `DataTableMapping` and its `DataTableMappingCollection` are both used to map database objects to `DataSet` members. Another class member, `DbDataAdapter`, is essential for writing your own provider. Finally, the class members `DBDataPermission`, `DBDataPermissionAttribute`, `RowUpdatedEventArgs`, and `RowUpdatingEventArgs` are used to secure and provide events from the `DataAdapter` class.

- ❏ `System.Data.SqlClient` – Contains classes used to connect to SQL Server.

- ❏ `System.Data.OleDb` – Contains classes used to connect to any OLE DB data source.

- ❏ `System.Data.SqlTypes` – Contains information on the different data types used in SQL Server 7.0 and above.

Let's start by taking a closer look at each of the classes involved in some simple examples. We are using mostly the members of the `SqlClient` namespace here. However, as these same classes also exist in the `OleDb` namespace, we could use either with the same functionality preserved. This twin nature of the SQL and OLE DB providers makes it simple to learn an interface that works with multiple managed providers.

There are many important members of the `System.Data` namespace. Here are a few you will need to know for this chapter.

Members	Description
Constraint	A class that represents a constraint against a `DataColumn`.
DataColumn	Represents the makeup of a column in a `DataTable`.
DataException	Represents the error that is thrown by ADO.NET objects.
DataRow	Represents a row of data.
DataSet	Main class in ADO.NET. Stores an in-memory cache of data, which can consist of one or more tables, constraints, and relationships.
DataTable	Represents a database table.
DataView	A data-bindable, customized view of a `DataTable`.

ADO.NET Basics

It would be fair to say that ADO.NET is essentially divided into two halves. The first half, .NET data providers, is where the plumbing of getting data to and from a source occurs. The second half is the `DataSet` class.

In this section, we will look at the .NET Framework classes that collectively make up the data provider half of ADO.NET. The core of this is the `System.Data` namespace. The next chapter addresses `DataSets` at length.

System.Data Namespace

Usually, one of the first things that a programmer would want to know at this point is "What classes do I have to use to connect to data?" If you are familiar with relational database management systems (RDBMS), you will see a great deal of similarity between these classes and the functional objects you would find in a RDBMS. There are several different classes that you will use in almost every data-connecting program. They all reside in the `System.Data` namespace.

Below are descriptions of some of the classes in `System.Data`. At the time of writing, there were 45 different classes within the namespace, not all of which you will need to use immediately. The most important classes are described below:

❏   `DataException` – A `DataException` object will represent the exception thrown when errors occur involving ADO.NET objects.

❏   `DataTable` – An in-memory representation of an actual database table. However, it is not limited to simply this. A `DataTable` will usually house several `DataRow` objects.

❏   `DataRelation` – Allows you to define a parent-child relationship between two `DataTable` objects.

❏   `DataView` – As you would expect, a `DataView` object allows you to create a custom view of a `DataTable`. This is useful for displaying parts of a `DataTable` bound to a control.

❏   `DataSet` – Acts as a container for instances of `DataTables`. We will see much more about this class in the next chapter.

❏   `DataRow` – An object that represents a single record.

❏   `DataRowView` – Allows you to set the "view" of a `DataRow` that will be displayed. It is useful for toggling between the various state-set (new, changed, sorted, filtered) groups of `DataRows`.

❏   `DataColumn` – Like the `DataRow`, the `DataColumn` represents a single `DataColumn` within a `DataTable`.

❏   `Constraint` – A constraint enforces a constraint against one or more `DataColumn` instances.

❏   `ConstraintException` – The exception that is thrown when a constraint is violated.

As mentioned before, the majority of these classes listed above are used when dealing with disconnected data. Classes that provide access to connected data are found within their specific provider namespace. These provider namespaces are discussed in the next section.

.NET Data Providers

At this point, the previous paragraphs have made several references to ".NET data providers". The question remains, "Exactly what are .NET data providers?"

In this section, we'll address that question in detail by looking at:

❏   An overview of .NET data providers including classes like `Connection`, `Command`, and `DataTable`

❏   Connecting to data sources such as SQL Server using the `DataReader`

❏   Storing data in a `DataSet`

Data Providers

If you come to this topic with experience of programming with classic ADO, it would fair to say that a .NET data provider essentially covers the scope of work that the `Connection` and `Command` objects did in classic ADO. If you are new to data access programming, you can think of a data provider as the way to interface with your data source. In either case, the concise description is that the .NET data providers are specialized sets of classes optimized for connecting to particular data sources.

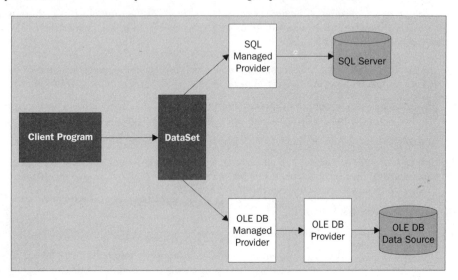

.NET data providers are built by inheriting from the `IDbAdapter` interface found in `System.Data`. Microsoft did exactly this when it created the `SqlClient` namespace and `OleDB` namespace as providers. Each of those namespaces contains the classes required to connect to, and perform operations on, data sources via the `DataCommand` classes.

In its current release of the .NET SDK, Microsoft has included two data providers. The first is specialized for connecting to Microsoft SQL Server 7.0 and above. The classes for this are found in the namespaces `System.Data.SqlClient` and `System.Data.SqlTypes`. This provider knows how to "speak" the native language of SQL Server 7.0 and higher – the Tabular Data Stream protocol. Given this ability, blisteringly fast performance can be achieved.

The second data provider that Microsoft provides is a general data provider for connecting to any other data source that can be reached via a "classic" OLE DB provider. This is an important feature, since not everybody is exclusively using SQL Server. OLE DB remains a widely supported standard for accessing data. Thus, it becomes essential for .NET to have support for it. The OLE DB classes are found in the namespace `System.Data.OleDb`. This is actually meant only as a placeholder until more providers optimized for particular databases are developed. For example, some .NET developers are anxiously waiting for a provider that is optimized for Oracle databases. Until then, they will have to settle for using the OLE DB set of classes.

There are three important concepts to take from this.

❑ Because all .NET data providers are based on `IDbDataAdapter`, they all support the same minimal level of functionality. This means you do not have to learn how to program in each vendor's native format, rather you can just learn ADO.NET. What you use for `SqlClient` will almost always be reusable if you need to use Access instead.

❑ Although all providers must implement the `IDbDataAdapter` interface, the details of how they do this are allowed to be implementation-specific, rather than forced to conform to a standard. This is a big change in direction for Microsoft. In the past, it has "standardized" the implementation in much greater detail and depth.

❑ Most importantly, providers are not materialized as instances of one class, but are instances of classes in different namespaces. In the past, you may have been able to change just a connection string or two if you wanted to switch from Access to SQL Server as the back-end database for your application. With ADO.NET, you will need to create instances of different classes in different namespaces. However, because both `SqlClient` and `OleDb` are rooted in `System.Data`, your changes can mostly be done via search and replace.

The naming schemes for these two providers are nearly identical, usually differing only in their prefixes. Of course, because the `SqlServer` provider is specialized for SQL Server, there are a few objects and methods that have no OLE DB.NET (see below) counterpart.

The `OleDb` data provider enables data access by using OLE DB through COM interoperability. This is accomplished via an element within the framework known as OLE DB.NET. Think of OLE DB.NET as a wrapper for classic OLE DB – when a COM-based OLE DB driver must be used, OLE DB.NET will handle the communications with it.

Some of the drivers include MSDAORA, which is the OLE DB provider for Oracle databases. To connect to an MS Access database, use the Microsoft.Jet.OLEDB.4.0 provider for Microsoft Jet. There is also a provider for SQL Server (SQLOLEDB), which would usually only be used when connecting to older versions of SQL Server. For SQL Server 7.0 or above, you would use the native SQL Server .NET data provider.

> *Note that the OLE DB providers, such as MSDAORA and Microsoft.Jet.OLEDB.4.0, are separate from the OLE DB.NET providers. You still make use of these providers, as the OLE DB.NET provider wraps the OLE DB providers.*

ODBC .NET

As popular as OLE DB and SQL Server are, they are not the only databases and access paths Microsoft has supported. As discussed in the previous chapter, OLE DB is next step forward from the Open Database Connectivity standard (ODBC). However, many product vendors are still "stuck in the 20th century" by supporting only COM-based ODBC providers.

As .NET developers, we have two ways of dealing with that. Chapter 2 went into detail about how to use classic ADO to just that end. Microsoft realizes that ODBC is still important. Given this, it has been quietly working on ODBC .NET. This .NET Data Provider behaves like the `OleDB` provider in terms of bridging COM functionality in the .NET environment. However, ODBC .NET is not currently expected to be an out-of-the-box part of the .NET Framework release. You will need to download and install it if you need to use it.

You can find the ODBC .NET data provider, Beta 1 release, at the time of going to press, at:

http://www.microsoft.com/downloads/release.asp?ReleaseID=31125

Please note that at the time of going to press it did not appear that this driver was fully supported in RC1 – check the Microsoft site for more details and later releases.

Connections

Let us start our drilldown into ADO.NET by looking at connections. We will see how to construct them, what properties they have, and what methods they make available.

Unless specifically noted otherwise, you can assume that the SqlClient and the OleDb data providers will have the same methods and properties with slightly different specific names.

An instance of the Connection class actually makes the connection to the data source. This class is used in connected and disconnected database operations.

Note: When we talk about the connection object we are actually talking about an instance of either of the SqlConnection or OleDbConnection class.

Constructors

The SqlConnection class has two constructors:

❑ SqlConnection()

❑ SqlConnection(connectstring)

If the connection string is omitted, it can be defined with the instance property ConnectionString.

A typical way to create a connection object (instance of the connection class) would look like this:

```
string connectstring = @"uid=sa;pwd=;server=(local)\NetSDK;database=Northwind";
SqlConnection connection = new SqlConnection(connectstring);
```

Properties

Here is a quick code snippet showing some of the useful public properties of the connection object:

```
connection.Open();
    string dbname = connection.Database;
    string dbsource = connection.DataSource;
    string state = connection.State.ToString();

    Console.WriteLine("dbname is " + dbname);
    Console.WriteLine("dbsource is " + dbsource);
    Console.WriteLine("state is " + state);

connection.Close();
```

Some of the properties of the Connection object for SqlClient are:

Property	Behavior	Description
ConnectionString	Writable until opened, read-only thereafter	Gets or sets the string used to open a SQL Server database
ConnectionTimeout	Read/write anytime	Gets the time to wait while trying to establish a connection before terminating the attempt and generating an error
Database	Writable until opened, read-only thereafter	Gets the name of the current database or the database to be used once a connection is open
DataSource	Read-only	Gets the name of the instance of SQL Server to connect to
PacketSize	Read/write anytime	Gets the size (in bytes) of network packets used to communicate with an instance of SQL Server
ServerVersion	Read-only after opening	Gets a string containing the version of the instance of SQL Server to which the client is connected
State	Read-only	Gets the current state of the connection
WorkstationId	Writable until opened, read-only thereafter	Gets a string that identifies the database client

Methods

Two methods of the connection object have been shown in the code above:

- ❑ Open() – Opens the connection using the settings specified in the connection string
- ❑ Close() – Closes the connection

Commands

The Command class is designed to be simply a holder for a SQL statement or a stored procedure, which will execute at a data source. It too is used in both connected and disconnected database operations. The SqlCommand has several constructors, described here:

Constructors

Constructor	Description
`SqlCommand()`	Empty constructor
`SqlCommand(string)`	Constructor with a string (for example, `"SELECT * FROM Customers"`)
`SqlCommand(string, SqlConnection)`	Same as above, except with a connection, not necessarily open
`SqlCommand(string, SqlConnection, SqlTransaction)`	The `SqlTransaction` class, which obviously pertains to transactions will be discussed later.

Properties

The most important public property to know at this point is the `CommandType` property. Its value can be set to one of the three values listed in the `CommandType` enumeration.

`StoredProcedure` – When set, the command object accepts stored procedure names.

```
SqlCommand command = new SqlCommand("@TenMostExpensiveProducts",
                                                connection);
command.CommandType = CommandType.StoredProcedure;
```

`TableDirect` – (this value only applies to `OleDbCommand`). When set to `TableDirect`, the `Command` object accepts a table name, and returns all columns.

```
OleDbConnection connection = new
        OleDbConnection(@"uid=sa;pwd=;server=localhost;database=pubs");
connection.Open();
OleDbCommand command = new OleDbCommand(sql, connection);
command.CommandType = CommandType.TableDirect;
```

`Text` – This is the default of the three. When you set the `Command` object to text, it holds a SQL command.

```
SqlCommand command = new SqlCommand(sql, connection);
//this is not necessary since text is the default
command.CommandType = CommandType.Text;
```

Methods

The following methods of the `Command` object are particularly important. The type of SQL statement you use to construct your `Command` object will dictate which of the following methods you will use.

Note that the `ExecuteXmlReader()` is not available to `OleDbCommand` objects.

`ExecuteNonQuery()` – This method will execute a SQL statement and return the number of rows affected. This method does *not* return any kind of result set, thus is good if executing statements with no results returned (for example, `INSERT`, `UPDATE`, and `DELETE`).

```
SqlCommand command3 = new SqlCommand(nonquerysql, connection);
    int rowsaffected = command3.ExecuteNonQuery();
    Console.WriteLine("Number of rows affected: " + rowsaffected);
```

`ExecuteReader()` – This method also executes a SQL statement, but returns back an instance of the `DataReader` class, which holds the result set while staying connected to the data.

```
SqlCommand command2 = new SqlCommand(sql, connection);
SqlDataReader datareader = command2.ExecuteReader();
while( datareader.Read() )
{
    Console.WriteLine("{0, -20}{1, -20}", datareader[2], datareader[1]);
}
command2.Dispose();
datareader.Close();
```

`ExecuteScalar()` – As its name implies, this method executes a SQL statement but only returns a single value. Good when using aggregate SQL functions, such as SUM, AVG, MIN, MAX, and COUNT.

```
SqlCommand command1 = new SqlCommand(scalarsql, connection);
decimal value = (decimal) command1.ExecuteScalar();
Console.WriteLine("Average freight weight is " + value);
```

`ExecuteXmlReader()` – This method is only available with the `SqlCommand` object. Like the other methods, it takes a SQL statement, but returns the result set as an `XmlReader` object. `ExecuteXMLReader` is an easy way to quickly load an XML document into a `DataSet` for use. Because the `XmlReader` is an abstract class, we need to cast it to an instance of `XmlTextReader`.

```
SqlCommand command4 = new SqlCommand(xmlsql, connection);
XmlTextReader xmltextreader =
    (XmlTextReader) command4.ExecuteXmlReader();

while(xmltextreader.Read())
{
    Console.WriteLine(xmltextreader.ReadOuterXml());
}
```

If you memorize nothing else about the `Command` object, knowing at least the first three methods will allow you to interact with your connected data source for most basic situations.

Just to reiterate, those methods are:

- ❑ `ExecuteScalar` for aggregate SQL functions
- ❑ `ExecuteReader` to populate the `DataReader`
- ❑ `ExecuteNonQuery` for a query with no return value
- ❑ `ExecuteXmlReader` to convert data to XML

DataTable

As mentioned earlier, one of the most important features of ADO.NET is the fact that data can be retrieved, stored and manipulated on the client side, then sent back to the server to propagate the changes. When the data reaches the client application, it is usually stored in a `DataTable`. It is not unusual to find multiple `DataTables` within a `DataSet`. `DataViews` also use `DataTables`.

Here we will examine the structure of the DataTable, and related classes such as DataRow and DataColumn. As you will see, these classes are really nothing more than object-oriented wrappers for familiar table rows and table columns. The following table of properties indicates this – note the Row and Column properties, which represent the table's rows and columns.

Properties

Property	Description
CaseSensitive	Indicates whether string comparisons within the table are case-sensitive.
ChildRelations	Gets the collection of child relations for this DataTable.
Columns	Gets the collection of columns that belong to this table.
Constraints	Gets the collection of constraints maintained by this table.
DataSet	Gets the DataSet that this table belongs to.
DefaultView	Gets a customized view of the table, which may include a filtered view, or a cursor position.
DesignMode	Gets a value indicating whether the component is currently in design mode.
DisplayExpression	Gets or sets the expression that will return a value used to represent this table in UI.
ExtendedProperties	Gets the collection of customized user information.
HasErrors	Gets a value indicating whether there are errors in any of the rows in any of the tables of the DataSet to which the table belongs.
Locale	Gets or sets the locale information used to compare strings within the table.
MinimumCapacity	Gets or sets the initial starting size for this table.
Namespace	Gets or sets the namespace for the XML representation of the data stored in the DataTable.
ParentRelations	Gets the collection of parent relations for this DataTable.
Prefix	Gets or sets the namespace for the XML representation of the data stored in the DataTable.
PrimaryKey	Gets or sets an array of columns that function as primary keys for the DataTable.
Rows	Gets the collection of rows that belong to this table.
TableName	Gets or sets the name of the DataTable.

Constructing a DataRow

If you have ever worked with any type of database program before, you will be familiar with the procedure. In order to hold data in a table you set up the structure of the table. This is usually done by defining the columns – giving them names, data types, and constraints.

Once the structure of the database is determined, you can start to insert data. Row by row, the data is entered until you have a complete table. This is exactly how it is done in ADO.NET as well.

Because the `DataTable`, `DataRow`, and `DataColumn` classes are all found in the `System.Data` namespace, these objects work exactly the same regardless of which managed provider you are working with.

Let's illustrate this theory with an example.

Working with a DataTable

In our example, we are going to create a `DataTable` and then fill it with data that is hard-coded into the program. In other words, we are not going to fill the `DataTable` with data obtained from a database. This is just to let us see the workings of the `DataTable` without that extra complication. This code sample is the `createtable.cs` file found in the `BuildingDataTable` folder of the example code.

```
namespace Wrox.ProCSharpData.Chapter3.BuildingDataTable
{

using System;
using System.Data;

    class CreateTable
    {
        static DataTable datatable;

        public static void Main()
        {
            Console.WriteLine("Creating Table...");
            InitalizeTable();
            Console.WriteLine("Inserting Data...");
            InsertData();
            Console.WriteLine("Displaying Data...");
            DisplayData();

        }
```

First of all, we need to create an instance of the `DataTable`. There are several different constructors for `DataTable`. The constructor we use below simply takes a string that defines the table name.

```
DataTable datatable = new DataTable("CrewTable");
```

Once the table has been created, we must instantiate `DataColumns`, define them by setting various properties, then add them to the table.

Here is a brief list of some properties of the `DataColumn`:

Property	Description
AllowDBNull	Indicates if `null` values are allowed in the column.
AutoIncrement	Indicates if a column automatically increments when new rows are added
AutoIncrementSeed	If `AutoIncrement` is `true`, this determines the starting number. If this value is not set, the default value is 1.

Table continued on following page

Property	Description
ColumnName	Sets the name of the column.
DataType	Sets the data type of the column by setting it equal to a Type object. DataType supports: Boolean, Byte, Char, DateTime, Decimal, Double, Int32, Int64, String, and several other types.
DefaultValue	Designates a default value for the column.
MaxLength	The maximum length of a text column.
ReadOnly	Indicates if a column is read-only or not.
Unique	Determines if a column's values must be unique, for example a primary key.

The first column we will create will serve as the primary key, so we will make it unique. Plus, it will auto-increment and be read-only.

```
public static void InitalizeTable()
{
    datatable = new DataTable("CrewTable");
    DataColumn column1 = new DataColumn();
    DataColumn column2 = new DataColumn();
    DataColumn column3 = new DataColumn();

    column1.DataType = System.Type.GetType("System.Int32");
    column1.ReadOnly = true;
    column1.AllowDBNull = false;
    column1.Unique = true;
    column1.ReadOnly = true;
    column1.ColumnName = "CrewID";
    column1.AutoIncrement = true;
    column1.AutoIncrementSeed = 100;
```

Having done this, we will now make a few more columns, and add them to the table, into the Column collection property, by using the collection's Add() method.

```
    column2.DataType = System.Type.GetType("System.String");
    column2.ColumnName = "Name";

    column3.DataType = System.Type.GetType("System.String");
    column3.ColumnName = "Position";

    datatable.Columns.Add(column1);
    datatable.Columns.Add(column2);
    datatable.Columns.Add(column3);

    datatable.Columns.Add(column1);
    datatable.Columns.Add(column2);
    datatable.Columns.Add(column3);
```

Now comes the matter of defining the primary key. Because the primary key can be composed of one or more columns, the PrimaryKey property of the DataTable expects an array, even if your primary key is composed of only one column. Here is the code.

```
            DataColumn[] primarykey = new DataColumn[1];
            primarykey[0] = datatable.Columns[0];
            datatable.PrimaryKey = primarykey;
        }
```

Finally, we will add rows of data to the empty table. Adding the data is a simple matter of setting a new DataRow using the DataTable's NewRow() method. Then we add the data in the appropriate column.

```
        public static void InsertData()
        {
            DataRow datarow1 = datatable.NewRow();
            datarow1[1] = "Kirk";
            datarow1[2] = "Captain";
            datatable.Rows.Add(datarow1);

            DataRow datarow2 = datatable.NewRow();
            datarow2[1] = "McCoy";
            datarow2[2] = "Doctor";
            datatable.Rows.Add(datarow2);

            DataRow datarow3 = datatable.NewRow();
            datarow3[1] = "Spock";
            datarow3[2] = "Science Officer";
            datatable.Rows.Add(datarow3);
        }
```

Having now completed the table, the columns, and the rows, let's display the data. First we will use a foreach loop to display the column names, putting a tab between each one.

```
        public static void DisplayData()
        {
            Console.Write("\n");
            foreach(DataColumn header in datatable.Columns)
            {
                Console.Write("{0, -10}\t", header.ColumnName);
            }

            Console.Write("\n\n");
```

Then we will use nested foreach loops to actually loop through and display all the data in the table. Using the datacolumn.ColumnName property, we are providing a specific name for the rowdata to display. Although the code makes it clear what we are doing, it does have a slight performance hit (resolving the ColumnName property, then resolving the name to a member of the datarow collection).

```
            foreach(DataRow datarow in datatable.Rows)
            {
                foreach(DataColumn datacolumn in datatable.Columns)
                {
                    Console.Write("{0, -10}\t", datarow[datacolumn.ColumnName]);
                }
                Console.Write("\n");
            }
        }
    }
```

Here is the resulting output:

That's it! The point of this example was to familiarize you with the basic structure of a `DataTable`, and its components. However, up to this point we have not yet seen how to connect to a data source. Let's first connect to a SQL Server data source, then to an OLE DB data source.

Connecting to SQL Server with the DataReader

At this point, you're probably ready to see how to actually connect to a data source. Like classic ADO, to connect requires the objects we just saw in detail, the `Connection` object and the `Command` object.

Before you can run the examples in this section, you will need the to run the SQL Script that is included in the code download. You will need to create the tables that are defined in `ProData.SQL`. Also provided is an MS Access version of the same database.

If you want to use the SQL Server version of this, extract the `ProData.SQL` file to either a machine with SQL Server 7.0 (or higher) installed and running, or any host where you have installed Enterprise Manager for SQL Server. You should run this script from the Query Analyser.

The script will need modifying if you have installed SQL Server to a location other than the default, and if you do not have an instance of SQL Server running named NetSDK.

Here is a sample snippet of code that connects to a SQL Server. Note that you will need to change the connection string to work with how you have set up the `ProTest` database:

```
namespace Wrox.ProCSharpData.Chapter3.SimpleSqlServerDataReader
{

    using System;
    using System.Data;
    using System.Data.SqlClient;

    class sql_datareader
    {
        public static void Main()
        {
            string connectstring =
                    @"uid=sa;pwd=;server=(local)\NetSDK;database=ProTest";

            SqlConnection connection = new SqlConnection(connectstring);
```

The connection string specifies the user name, password, server, and database. Note the @ symbol, which we use to ignore the backslash.

Then we instantiate a `SqlConnection` (for connecting to SQL Server 7.0 or above, otherwise you would use `OleDbConnection`) and give the connection string to its constructor.

Once the connection has been instantiated, we use the `Open()` method and, provided there are no connection errors, we are connected.

Usually, putting the line:

```
Connection.Open();
```

within a `try...catch` block is a good idea since any number of errors can occur when you are connecting.

Once the connection has been established, let's see how to actually read the data. Using the `DataReader`, we can quickly loop over each record, read it in, and print it to the screen. Remember, the `DataReader` allows us to read records in a forward-only fashion, unlike its cousin the `DataSet`. We will see another example using the `DataSet` shortly.

Here is the connection using the `DataReader`:

```
string sql = "SELECT EmpID, Last, Dept, Salary FROM EmpList";
try
{
    connection.Open();
    SqlCommand command = new SqlCommand(sql, connection);
    SqlDataReader datareader = command.ExecuteReader();

    Console.WriteLine("\n\n");

    while(datareader.Read())
    {
        Console.Write("{0, -10}\t{1, -10}", datareader[0],
                                                datareader[1]);
        Console.Write("\t{0, -10}\t{1, -10}\n", datareader[2],
                                                datareader[3]);
    }
    datareader.Close();
    connection.Close();
}
catch(SqlException e)
{
    Console.WriteLine("An error occurred!");
    Console.WriteLine("Check your connect string");
    Console.WriteLine("Your error message is " + e.Message);
}
catch(Exception e)
{
    Console.WriteLine("General Error: " + e.Message);
}
}
}
```

In this block of code, you can see we connect to the data source, then create a Command object, which will hold the SQL statement.

One thing to take note of is that the DataReader is not instantiated using the new keyword, but rather is created by using the Command.ExecuteReader() method. This is a feature, not a bug, as it allows the reader to be tightly integrated with the connection. At this point, the DataReader is like a pointer that is actually positioned *before* the first record. Therefore, you must use the Read() method before you can access any data. Once the loop is started, each time the Read() method is called, it reads a row and advances the DataReader to the next record until every record has been read.

Within the loop, the data is read out by a numeric index indicating the field position.
Notice that the connection and the DataReader are both explicitly closed. Even though the .NET runtime will eventually "garbage-collect" these objects if they go out of scope, while they are in scope, they are consuming resources. So it is considered best practice to close them as soon as possible.

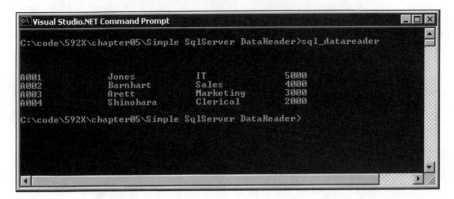

Connecting to an OLE DB Data Source with the DataReader

Now that you have seen the connection to SQL Server, let's examine a connection to an OLE DB data source. This would include any data source that has an OLE DB driver, including Access (which this example connects to), Oracle, or even SQL Server (if needed).

```
namespace Wrox.ProCSharpData.Chapter3.SimpleOLEDBDataReader
{
    using System;
    using System.Data;
    using System.Data.OleDb;

    class oledb_datareader
    {
        public static void Main()
        {
            string connectstring = @"Data Source=c:\protest.mdb;" +
                                     "Provider=Microsoft.Jet.OLEDB.4.0;";

            string sql = "SELECT EmpID, Last, Dept, Salary FROM EmpList";

            OleDbConnection connection = new OleDbConnection(connectstring);
            try
            {
```

```
        connection.Open();
        OleDbCommand command = new OleDbCommand(sql, connection);
        OleDbDataReader datareader = command.ExecuteReader();

        Console.WriteLine("\n\n");

        while(datareader.Read())
        {
            Console.Write("{0, -10}\t{1, -10}", datareader[0],
                                                datareader[1]);
            Console.Write("\t{0, -10}\t{1, -10}\n", datareader[2],
                                                datareader[3]);
        }
        connection.Close();
    }
    catch(OleDbException e)
    {
        Console.WriteLine("An error occurred!");
        Console.WriteLine("Is the database where you said it was?");
        Console.WriteLine("Your error message is " + e.Message);
    }
    catch(SystemException e)
    {
        Console.WriteLine("An error occurred!");
        Console.WriteLine("Maybe the driver is misspelled");
        Console.WriteLine("Your error message is " + e.Message);
    }
    catch(Exception e)
    {
        Console.WriteLine("General Error: " + e.Message);
    }
    }
  }
}
```

This should yield:

Oracle Connection

Accessing an Oracle database would be almost exactly the same as the example shown above. The main difference being of course the connection string. When accessing an Oracle database, you would use the Oracle OLE DB provider. Here is an example:

```
string connection =
            "Provider=MSDAORA;UID=scott;PWD=tiger;Server=yourserver";
```

Storing Data in DataSets

In the previous examples, we saw how you could use a `DataReader` to quickly loop over each record and display the data. Although the `DataReader` is very fast, it is also very limited in what it can do. As mentioned earlier, the `DataSet` is a main class in ADO.NET, because it allows you represent multiple tables, relationships, and constraints on the client side, in fact, you could store an entire database on the client side, modify it, then push the changes back to the data store.

Like any other tool, both the `DataReader` and the `DataSet` have appropriate uses based on their design. For example, `DataReaders` are great for getting a lot of data bound to a read-only control in a hurry. `DataSets`, on the other hand, are better suited when you need to edit data or merge data from many different sources. In other words, there's little point to pushing a few dozen rows into a `DataSet` if your goal is to simply to display them in a Web Form. Equally, it's counter productive to use a `DataReader` to populate a collection that holds the data during editing, then write your own methods for populating the changed data back to its data source.

Other way to think about it is "Do you want to drink water from the firehose or tea from a glass?" `DataReaders` are essentially built on what is known as a "firehose" cursor (fast-forward, read-only blasts of data). `DataSets` are more like the spot of tea – you need to get the water into the teacup first then introduce the tea and let it infuse before drinking.

DataAdapters

Before we dig into `DataSets`, we need to introduce `DataAdapters`. `DataAdapters` are essentially containers for `Command` and `Connection` objects. They bridge the functionality gap between the data source and `DataSets`. The major jobs of `DataAdapters` are to populate `DataSets` with information, and return changed items back to their source. Although you can use `DataSets` without `DataAdapters` (as we did in our earlier examples), they are the most efficient way to get data in from and back to data sources without writing much of your own code.

Both `SqlDataAdapters` and `OleDbDataAdapters` have a number of overloaded constructor methods. The most commonly used one involves passing an instance of `DataCommand` as the parameter. When this is done, the adapter readies itself for that specific use. We will see more about how to use `DataAdapter` later in this chapter.

Using DataSets with SQL Server

In this example, we will query a SQL Server database, store the data in a `DataSet`, then display the data. Notice that the `DataSet` is instantiated with an empty constructor, then given data by using the `DataAdapter`'s `Fill()` method. In this example, we will fill the `DataSet` with all of the rows and columns of the `EmpList` table.

```
SqlDataAdapter dataadapter = new SqlDataAdapter(command);

DataSet dataset = new DataSet();
dataadapter.Fill(dataset, "EmpList");
```

Here is the total code for this simple program. Again, you may need to change the connection string to work with your configuration.

```
namespace Wrox.ProCSharpData.Chapter3.SimpleSqlServerDataSet
{

    using System;
    using System.Data;
    using System.Data.SqlClient;

    class sql_dataset
    {
        public static void Main()
        {
            string connectstring =
                    @"uid=sa;pwd=;server=(local)\NetSDK;database=ProTest";

            // This string defines the data we want use in our DataSet
            string sql = "SELECT EmpID, Last, Dept, Salary FROM EmpList";

            // Create a connection to the database based on our settings
            SqlConnection connection = new SqlConnection(connectstring);

            try{
                // Open the connection, then create a new command to get our
                // data
                connection.Open();
                SqlCommand command = new SqlCommand(sql, connection);

                // Create a DataAdapter and DataSet to work with
                SqlDataAdapter dataadapter = new SqlDataAdapter(command);
                DataSet dataset = new DataSet();

                // Now we can use the fill method to create a virtual table
                // in our DataSet with the name EmpList. It will use the query
                // we defined and associated with the DataSet, via the
                // DataAdapter.
                dataadapter.Fill(dataset, "EmpList");

                // Close the connection as we're done with it.
                connection.Close();

                // Get a reference on the virtual table we've just loaded.
                DataTable datatable = dataset.Tables["EmpList"];
                Console.Write("\n\n");

                // Display a column header based on the column name…
                foreach(DataColumn header in datatable.Columns)
                {
                    Console.Write("{0,-10}\t", header.ColumnName);
                }

                // Now write out the filled-in data.
                Console.Write("\n\n");
```

```
          foreach( DataRow datarow in datatable.Rows )
          {
              foreach( DataColumn datacolumn in datatable.Columns)
              {
                  Console.Write("{0,-10}",
                          datarow[datacolumn.ColumnName].ToString().Trim());
                  Console.Write("\t");
              }
              Console.Write("\n");
          }
      }
      catch(SqlException e)
      {
          Console.WriteLine("An error occurred!");
          Console.WriteLine("Check your connect string");
          Console.WriteLine("Your error message is " + e.Message);
      }
      catch(Exception e)
      {
          Console.WriteLine("General Error: " + e.Message);
      }
    }
  }
}
```

Here is the output of the program:

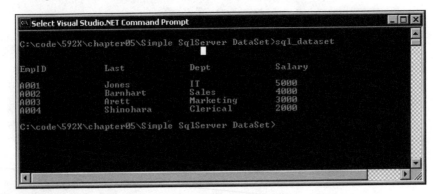

You may note that we broke one our recommended best practices by using a DataSet just to display data. We just did that here to show how simple the DataSet is to use.

Working with Databases

Now that you have seen basic connections to data sources, let's examine how to actually work with the data. The rest of the chapter is dedicated to:

❑ Using stored procedures (blocks of Transact-SQL stored on the server that offer performance benefits, in addition to encapsulation, and abstraction much like class member functions do)

❑ Demonstrating how to save data back to the data source using both the DataReader and DataSet

Stored Procedures

In this example we will call a stored procedure called `GetDept`. This procedure is defined in the `ProTest` database that is provided for you in the sourcecode download.

Here is the code that creates the stored procedure, shown here so that we know what parameters it takes:

```
CREATE PROCEDURE GetDept @EmpID char(5), @Dept varchar(20) output AS
        SELECT @Dept = Dept from EmpList where EmpID = @EmpID
```

As you can see, there is one incoming parameter and one return value. Simply put, you provide the `EmpID` and the stored procedure will return to you the department where that employee works.

The `Connection` and `Command` objects are used here like any other connection, the difference here being that the `Command` object will hold the name of the stored procedure, instead of a SQL statement.

The `CommandType` property is then set to `StoredProcedure`, of course indicating we are going to call a stored procedure.

```
SqlCommand command = new SqlCommand("GetDept", connection);
command.CommandType = CommandType.StoredProcedure;
```

Once that is done, we must now define the input and output parameters. If we think of stored procedures as being like member class functions, the reason becomes clear. For each formal parameter of a function, we need to provide some actual parameter to provide that value. Without these parameters, the server is left to guess what the value should be. If the parameters are inbound only, this only becomes a problem if the developer of that stored procedure left a default value out. Most RDBMS will treat missing outbound parameters as fatal errors – there is no place to report the result to.

The input parameter is the parameter being received by the stored procedure. We will set the name, the type, the size, the direction (input) and, of course, the value. Finally, once those properties have been set, we will add the parameter to the `Command` object.

```
// defines that we creating a new parameter...
SqlParameter inputparameter = new SqlParameter();

// ... and its name in the signature of the procedure, ...
inputparameter.ParameterName = "@EmpID";

// ... and that its data type is character, ...
inputparameter.SqlDbType = SqlDbType.Char;

// ... and that it is ten characters wide, ...
inputparameter.Size = 10;

// ... and that it is an inbound parameter, ...
inputparameter.Direction = ParameterDirection.Input;

// ... and, finally, that it has a value of 'idnum'
inputparameter.Value = idnum;

// now tie the new parameter to our command.
command.Parameters.Add(inputparameter);
```

Setting the output parameter, which is the return value, is just as easy. This is essentially the same process as creating our input parameter.

```
SqlParameter outputparameter = new SqlParameter();
outputparameter.ParameterName = "@Dept";
outputparameter.SqlDbType = SqlDbType.Char;
outputparameter.Size = 20;
outputparameter.Direction = ParameterDirection.Output;
command.Parameters.Add(outputparameter);
```

Remember that the Command object has several methods depending on the type of statement you wish to execute against the database. Since this is a stored procedure, and not a query that will return a result set, we will use the ExecuteNonQuery() method.

```
command.ExecuteNonQuery();
```

Since we obviously have now not received any return result by calling that method, how do we find the department name? The answer is in the parameters. We defined the parameters earlier, giving no value to the "@Dept" parameter. Provided that the stored procedure found the ID we had sent it, the @Dept parameter should now have a value.

```
Console.WriteLine({0}, command.Parameters["@Dept"].Value)
```

Here is the code in its entirety. When printing out the parameters, some cleaning up is achieved by calling the Trim() method to trim away any blank spaces that would normally be there.

```
namespace Wrox.ProCSharpData.Chapter3.StoredProcedure
{

    using System;
    using System.Data;
    using System.Data.SqlClient;
    using System.Data.SqlTypes;

    class StoredProcedure
    {
        public static void Main()
        {
            string idnum;
            Console.Write("Enter a valid ID number: ");
            idnum = Console.ReadLine();

            string connectstring =
                    @"uid=sa;pwd=;server=(local)\NetSDK;database=ProTest";
            SqlConnection connection = new SqlConnection(connectstring);

            connection.Open();

            SqlCommand command = new SqlCommand("GetDept", connection);
            command.CommandType = CommandType.StoredProcedure;

            SqlParameter inputparameter = new SqlParameter();
            inputparameter.ParameterName = "@EmpID";
            inputparameter.SqlDbType = SqlDbType.Char;
            inputparameter.Size = 10;
```

```
inputparameter.Direction = ParameterDirection.Input;
inputparameter.Value = idnum;
command.Parameters.Add(inputparameter);

SqlParameter outputparameter = new SqlParameter();
outputparameter.ParameterName = "@Dept";
outputparameter.SqlDbType = SqlDbType.Char;
outputparameter.Size = 20;
outputparameter.Direction = ParameterDirection.Output;
command.Parameters.Add(outputparameter);

Console.WriteLine("Calling Stored Procedure\n");

command.ExecuteNonQuery();

if(command.Parameters["@Dept"].Value.ToString().
                                    Equals(string.Empty))
{
    Console.WriteLine("Sorry...no department found");
}
else
{
    Console.WriteLine("\nThe person with the ID Number " +
    command.Parameters["@EmpID"].Value.ToString().Trim() +
                                " works in the " +
        command.Parameters["@Dept"].Value.ToString().Trim()
                                + " department\n");
}
connection.Close();
    }
  }
}
```

Here is the resulting output:

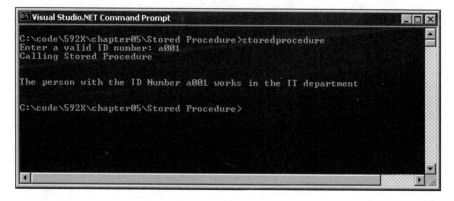

So how do you call a stored procedure that has no parameters? Easy – it's the same process that we have just seen, but you do not define or append any parameters.

Adding and Updating Records

Now it is possible to add and update records using only stored procedures. However, often this is neither convenient nor practical. The following example demonstrates exactly how to do client-side updating and adding first using the DataReader, then the DataSet. We can use DataReaders to simply execute commands, which in turn use stored procedures. However, using DataSets provides a more elegant solution. Keep in mind that DataReaders are read-only, which might be OK so long as you do not expect to edit the results returned. Finally, we have intentionally left the error checking bits out of this example to keep focus on the task at hand.

Using the Command object to Add and Update

This example demonstrates adding, changing, and deleting data using DataReaders. The program itself is not meaningful – it just serves to show examples of how you can do things. It adds, changes, and removes a simple record from a table in the ProTest database. For illustrative purposes the example has been broken up into several different methods. First let's take a look at Main() and see what will be happening here.

```csharp
namespace Wrox.ProCSharp.Chapter03.SqlServerAddAndUpdateDataReader
{

    using System;
    using System.Data;
    using System.Data.SqlClient;

    class sql_datareader_modify
    {
        static SqlConnection connection;

        public static void Main()
        {
            string empid = "B001", last = "Gates", dept = "Management";
            int salary = 10000;

            // set the connection string up and open the connection.
            Initalize();
            Console.WriteLine("Query results");

            // show the current data
            DisplayData();

            // Add a fresh record and display that.
            Console.WriteLine("Adding Data");
            AddingRecord(empid, last, dept, salary);
            DisplayData();

            last = "Smith";
            dept = "Custodial";
            salary = 5000;

            // Update the data with new value.
            Console.WriteLine("Modifying Data");
            ModifyRecord(empid, last, dept, salary);
            DisplayData();

            // Now delete that data and disconnect.
            Console.WriteLine("Deleting Data");
```

```
            DeleteRecord(empid);
            DisplayData();
            DisconnectFromData();
    }
```

As you can see, this program calls `Initialize()` to connect to the data source, displays all records, then adds a record. Again it will display all records, then modify the record that was inserted earlier. Finally, it will delete the record, display them one last time, and then disconnect.

There's nothing major to explain in `Initalize()`, it simply connects to the data source:

```
    public static void Initalize()
    {
        string connectstring =
                    @"uid=sa;pwd=;server=(local)\NetSDK;database=ProTest";
        connection = new SqlConnection(connectstring);
        connection.Open();
    }
```

The `AddingRecord()` method creates a command object. It then inserts the data passed to the method into the data source by executing the command using the `ExecuteNonQuery()` method. In best practice, this function either returns a value indicating in the success or failure of the function, or throws an exception if it, in fact, failed.

```
    public static void AddingRecord(string empid, string last, string dept,
                                                            int salary)
    {
        // Define the query we want to execute.
        string addsql = "INSERT INTO EmpList (EmpID, Last, Dept, Salary)"
                    + " VALUES ('" + empid + "', '" + last + "', '"
                                    + dept + "', " + salary + ")";

        // Create a command based on that query and our existing connection
        SqlCommand addcommand = new SqlCommand(addsql, connection);

        // Execute the query and save the number of rows added
        int rows = addcommand.ExecuteNonQuery();
        Console.WriteLine("Number of rows added " + rows);
    }
```

Updating is very similar as well. Here is the code. Again, if we were writing production code, this function would return some value, or perhaps throw an exception.

```
    public static void ModifyRecord(string empid, string last, string dept,
                                                            int salary)
    {
        // Define the query we want to execute
        string updatesql = "UPDATE EmpList SET Last = '" + last + "', "
                        + "Dept = '" + dept + "', Salary = " + salary
                                    + " WHERE EmpID = '" + empid + "'";

        // Create a command to execute
        SqlCommand updatecommand = new SqlCommand(updatesql, connection);
```

```
        // Execute the query, capturing the number of row changed.
        int rows = updatecommand.ExecuteNonQuery();

        // Display the number of updated records.
        Console.WriteLine("Number of rows updated " + rows);
    }
```

Notice, as before, the return value for `ExecuteNonQuery()` is the number of rows affected. In this example, that value was caught and displayed, but this is not necessary.

The code for deleting a row is similar to adding and updating:

```
public static void DeleteRecord(string empid)
{
    string deletesql = "DELETE FROM EmpList WHERE EmpID = '" +
                                                    empid + "'";
    SqlCommand deletecommand = new SqlCommand(deletesql, connection);
    int rows = deletecommand.ExecuteNonQuery();
    Console.WriteLine("Number of rows deleted " + rows);
}
```

Finally, we have a short function that displays the current state of the database.

```
public static void DisplayData()
{
    // Define our refresh query
    string sql = "SELECT EmpID, Last, Dept, Salary FROM EmpList";

    // define a Command and DataReader to work with.
    SqlCommand command;
    SqlDataReader datareader;

    // Create a command based our query and active connection
    command = new SqlCommand(sql, connection);

    // Execute the command return a datareader with the results
    datareader = command.ExecuteReader();

    // Loop through the results and display the data
    Console.Write("\n");
    while( datareader.Read() )
    {
        Console.WriteLine("{0, -10}\t{1, -10}\t{2, -10}",
        datareader[0].ToString().Trim(),
        datareader[1].ToString().Trim(),
        datareader[2].ToString().Trim());
    }
    Console.Write("\n");

    // Close the reader to free up resources.
    datareader.Close();
}
```

Then the code finishes with a method to close our database connection:

```
    public static void DisconnectFromData()
    {
        connection.Close();
    }
}
}
```

Here is the resulting output:

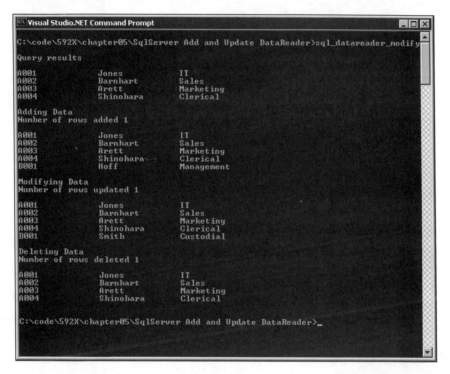

As you can see, adding and updating records using the Command object is very simple and straightforward. But it also exposes some weaknesses:

❑ An active connection has to be kept open during the whole transaction.

❑ We are using what amounts to a read-only connection to make changes in the database.

❑ We have had to create our functions for adding, updating, and removing records.

❑ As simple as our program was, we knew we had total control over the data at times. No one else was likely to add, update, or change our "B0001" key recorded while our program was running. But if they had, our program had no way of coping with it.

These are the issues that DataSets, working through the DataAdapter, address.

Add and Update using a DataSet

In the last example, we saw how to add and update records immediately using the Command object. And we reviewed a few of the reasons why you may not want to use that technique. Using a DataSet instead may work better. By using the DataSet you can:

- ❑ Load the data once from the database, using a just-in-time connection, potentially limiting the amount of bandwidth used

- ❑ Use the DataAdapter bound commands to manage the effort of adding, updating, and deleting data

- ❑ Minimize issues with locked or missing data at final update.

DataSets work very differently from recordsets in many ways, but a key difference of DataSets is that the RowData instances within the DataSet have multiple versions. That is, the DataSet knows which rows have been added, changed, or marked for removal. It also has the ability to extract these rows by versions into sets of data so that they can be processed in batches. It relies on the DataAdapter to make this process work.

The DataAdapter relies on you to define how it should do inserts, updates, and deletes as instances of the Command class. These Commands are then "collected" into the DataAdapter. When the Update() method of the DataAdapter is called, it resolves the changes and processes them through these Commands. The following diagram may help make all of this a bit clearer:

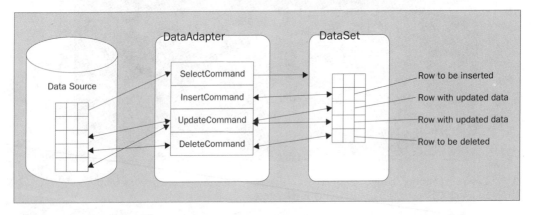

Using a DataSet to do this is only a little more work, the bulk of which stems from the fact that you must let the DataSet know exactly all the information pertaining to the fields you wish to update, by assigning parameter values.

The following is part of the AddAndUpdateDataSetWithParameters sample in the download code. The first snippet is an example of parameter values for persisting new records' data back to a data source:

```
public static void SetInsertParameters(){

    // Define the query used to insert new records
    string insertsql;
    insertsql = "INSERT INTO EmpList (EmpID, Last, Dept, Salary)"
```

```
          + " VALUES (@EmpID, @Last, @Dept, @Salary)";

        // So that the DataAdapter knows how to do inserts, you
        // need to bind a command to the DataAdapter's InsertCommand property
        dataadapter.InsertCommand = new SqlCommand(insertsql, connection);

        // Each of the parameters in the query (or stored procedure)
        // needs to have a command parameter associated with it.
        SqlParameter parameter;
        parameter = dataadapter.InsertCommand.Parameters.Add (
            new SqlParameter("@EmpID", SqlDbType.VarChar));

        // Map this parameter to the column EmpID
        parameter.SourceColumn = "EmpID";

        // Since we are only inserting new records, those rows will be in
        // "current" version of the row.
        parameter.SourceVersion = DataRowVersion.Current;

        // Add a column mapping for the last name
        parameter = dataadapter.InsertCommand.Parameters.Add (
            new SqlParameter("@Last", SqlDbType.VarChar));
        parameter.SourceColumn = "Last";
        parameter.SourceVersion = DataRowVersion.Current;

        // Add a column mapping for the department
        parameter = dataadapter.InsertCommand.Parameters.Add (
            new SqlParameter("@Dept", SqlDbType.VarChar));
        parameter.SourceColumn = "Dept";
        parameter.SourceVersion = DataRowVersion.Current;

        // Add a column mapping for the salary amount
        parameter = dataadapter.InsertCommand.Parameters.Add (
            new SqlParameter("@Salary", SqlDbType.Int));
        parameter.SourceColumn = "Salary";
        parameter.SourceVersion = DataRowVersion.Current;
    }
```

Here is the method, that updates the record, then saves it back to the database:

```
public static void AddingRecord(string empid, string last, string dept, int
salary)
{
    // Add a new row to the first table
    try {
        // Create a new row instance
        DataRow newrow = dataset.Tables[0].NewRow();

        // Populate the row
        newrow[0] = empid;
        newrow[1] = last;
        newrow[2] = dept;
        newrow[3] = salary;

        // Append the new row to the table
        datatable.Rows.Add(newrow);
    }

    // See if any errors occurred
```

```
   catch(SqlException sqlexception)
   {
      Console.WriteLine("You threw a sql exception!");
      Console.WriteLine("error #" + sqlexception.Number);
      Console.WriteLine("Your message is " + sqlexception.Message);
      Console.WriteLine(sqlexception.StackTrace);
   }
   // Update the data source, then refresh it to make sure we have current
   //data
   try
   {

      dataadapter.Update(dataset, "EmpList");
      dataadapter.Fill(dataset);
      datatable = dataset.Tables[0];
   }
   catch(SqlException sqlexception)
   {
      Console.WriteLine("You threw a sql exception!");
      Console.WriteLine("error #" + sqlexception.Number);
      Console.WriteLine("Did you duplicate a primary key value?");
   }
}
```

Here are the update parameters:

```
public static void SetUpdateParameters(){

      string updatesql;
      updatesql = "UPDATE EmpList SET Last = @Last, Dept = @Dept, " +
         "Salary = @Salary WHERE EmpID = @EmpID";
      dataadapter.UpdateCommand = new SqlCommand(updatesql, connection);

      SqlParameter parameter;
      parameter = dataadapter.UpdateCommand.Parameters.Add (
         new SqlParameter("@EmpID", SqlDbType.VarChar));
      parameter.SourceColumn = "EmpID";
      parameter.SourceVersion = DataRowVersion.Current;

      parameter = dataadapter.UpdateCommand.Parameters.Add (
         new SqlParameter("@Last", SqlDbType.VarChar));
      parameter.SourceColumn = "Last";
      parameter.SourceVersion = DataRowVersion.Current;

      parameter = dataadapter.UpdateCommand.Parameters.Add (
         new SqlParameter("@Dept", SqlDbType.VarChar));
      parameter.SourceColumn = "Dept";
      parameter.SourceVersion = DataRowVersion.Current;

      parameter = dataadapter.UpdateCommand.Parameters.Add (
         new SqlParameter("@Salary", SqlDbType.Int));
      parameter.SourceColumn = "Salary";
      parameter.SourceVersion = DataRowVersion.Current;
   }
```

The functions needed to handle updates and deletions are essentially the same as that for inserting a new record, so we will highlight only the significantly different bits.

```
public static void ModifyRecord(string empid, string last, string dept,
                                                    int salary)
{
    // This example updates the last row in table.
    int rownum = datatable.Rows.Count - 1;

    // Select the row to update
    DataRow updaterow = datatable.Rows[rownum];
    updaterow[0] = empid;
    updaterow[1] = last;
    updaterow[2] = dept;
    updaterow[3] = salary;

    // Check for any errors
    try
    {
        dataadapter.Update(dataset, "EmpList");
        dataset = new DataSet();
        dataadapter.Fill(dataset);
        datatable = dataset.Tables[0];
    }
    catch(SqlException sqlexception)
    {
        Console.WriteLine("You threw a sql exception!");
        Console.WriteLine("error #" + sqlexception.Number);
    }
}
```

Not surprisingly, the output of the completed program looks identical to previous code examples. See the code download for the complete program.

Add and Update using a Command Builder

The CommandBuilder automates the tedious work we have just seen, provided that your data is coming from a single table in a single source. It must also have a defined primary key. Both the SqlClient and OleDb namespaces have subclasses for this shortcut. You'll need to use the previously illustrated method if you have data in the DataSet from different tables. In short, the SQLCommandBuilder will retrieve all the information it needs about the fields when it retrieves the data with a simple SELECT statement, relieving you of the burden of specifying each field individually.

The CommandBuilder examines the output of a SELECT statement associated with a SelectCommand in the DataAdapter. From this it quietly creates InsertCommand, UpdateCommand, and DeleteCommand objects, and associates them with the parent DataAdapter. The InsertCommand generated will update most fields, but it will not update an IDENTITY column, or columns with expressions or a timestamp. The UpdateCommand works similarly, and has the same restrictions on what it will update. DeleteCommand obliterates the target row completely.

There are a few side-effects with the CommandBuilder to keep in mind:

❑   By default, the UpdateCommand does not lock records for edit while it's working. Given this, it will only update a matching record if it still exists, and if all of the data in the original version of the row is still in the database with no changes. If the underlying data has changed, a DBConcurrencyException will be thrown.

❏ If you initially use a command builder, then change the CommandText of the SelectCommand, you will probably start experiencing exceptions. This is because the DataAdapter knew one schema when it created the Command sets. Now it has a new, and probably different, schema, which leads to problems when trying to understand the underlying data.

❏ Table and column names containing special characters, even if delimited in brackets, will cause the CommandBuilder problems.

❏ The source DataTable may have no relationships defined within the DataSet.

Now, examine the following program, AddAndUpdateDataSetWithoutParameters in the code download. It is nearly identical to the program we saw before that used parameters; however, because we have used the SqlCommandBuilder we can omit that work. We have eliminated the repeated code as much as possible. What is more important to note, however, is that SetUpdateParameters and its ilk are completely gone from the program.

```
//an example of simple insert, update and delete
//using SqlDataAdapter and a disconnected DataSet
//autogenerated parameters

namespace Wrox.ProCSharpData.Chapter3.AddAndUpdateDataSetWithoutParameters
{
    using System;
    using System.Data;
    using System.Data.SqlClient;

    class sql_modify_noparameters
    {
        // Initialise variables
        ...

        public static void Main()
        {
            // same as for previous example
            ...
        }

        public static void Initalize()
        {
            ...
            dataadapter = new SqlDataAdapter();
            SqlCommandBuilder commandbuilder = new
                                    SqlCommandBuilder(dataadapter);
            ...
        }

        public static void DisplayData()
        {
            ...
        }

        public static void AddingRecord(string empid, string last,
                                            string dept, int salary)
        {
            ...
        }

        public static void ModifyRecord(string empid, string last,
```

```
                                                    string dept, int salary)
        {
            ...
        }

        public static void DeleteRecord(string empid)
        {
            ...
        }
    }
}
```

Summary

This chapter has really covered a lot of material at a lightning-like pace. We have examined the ADO.NET namespaces in some depth, and have demonstrated connecting to data sources. We have also looked at the important ADO.NET classes, their methods, and their properties at length. We have seen how to call stored procedures, and how to use the DataSet and DataAdapter to work with data in a disconnected manner.

The key points to take away from this chapter are:

❑   ADO.NET is not just one set of classes and objects. Rather, it's the framework for data access that is materialized in .NET data providers and the DataSet. Out of the box, there are two managed providers, each with its own unique namespace – OleDb and SqlClient.

❑   Since ADO.NET is built on the .NET Framework, all programming languages based on the .NET framework can use all of the classes with equal agility and with the same technique.

❑   DataSets work well in distributed applications, because they're transportable over HTTP using XML. No active connections to the data source need to be maintained. DataSets rely on DataAdapters to manage the process of synchronizing data on update.

❑   DataReaders are excellent ways to dump data out quickly so long as it does not need to be updated.

❑   The CommandBuilder class of a DataAdapter can be used to quickly generate reasonable Commands for updating DataSets.

In the next chapter, we will see more about how to use DataSets and how to actually do some meaningful work using server controls, data binding, and exceptions.

4

ADO.NET and C# II: Working with Data in .NET

In the previous chapter, we looked at the basic techniques used to hold data retrieved from a database. We covered .NET Data Providers and how to use a `DataSet`. This chapter focuses on using data interactively in our applications.

In particular, we will cover:

❏   Comparing connected and disconnected data

❏   Key object model elements

❏   Exploring the relationships between ADO.NET and XML

❏   Dealing with Exceptions

❏   Data binding to controls

❏   Displaying data

If you are going to get the most from ADO.NET, you will need to know how and when to use disconnected or connected data containers. In order to exploit the offerings of the .NET Framework, you will benefit from understanding data binding. Rather than talk specifically about data binding, we will mostly show examples doing it. Knowing what is offered by different classes will give you better understanding of how you can achieve your goals.

Since the appropriate use of disconnected and connected data is essential to top performing .NET applications, we will start with this topic.

Connected and Disconnected Recordsets

In Chapter 3, we introduced two different classes for working with data once it has been presented to your application from the .NET Data Provider. These two classes are DataReader and DataSet.

The DataReader is the way to retrieve data in a read-only, forward-only manner. A DataReader loads a single row of data at a time. This tends to increase overall application performance and reduce system overhead. Using a DataReader is the way to work with data on a connected basis. You must explicitly close the DataReader to free the connection and memory resources it uses; it will not be subject to complete garbage collection until you do.

> There isn't really a true **DataReader** class as such, .NET Data Providers implement an **IDataReader** interface. Conceptually, and for the purposes of discussion, this interface can be treated like an instance of a class.

The DataSet effectively provides an in-memory cache of the data pulled-up from the data source. Unlike the DataReader, a DataSet reads and holds the entire data in memory at once. Once populated, the DataSet may be disconnected from its original data source completely. Of course, it can subsequently be reconnected to that data source. A DataSet has methods for updating its original data source. Instances of the DataSet class will have several other objects within, particularly DataTable and DataRelation objects. A DataSet also has a handy "dehydration" feature: you can save the data and schema to XML files on disk. Later, or even elsewhere, you can reconstruct the DataSet from these files. This is powerful stuff, as these XML files are easily transportable over HTTP.

A DataReader is most appropriate to use when you need to quickly load data for display. These pump-and-dump situations are common to the Web, where you just need to display data on a page. Another valid use of a DataReader is to load up a custom data container for future processing. For example, you may want to use a SortedList collection to present data in an order different from that made available by the data source. We will look at such an example in the next section. The steps involved in coding DataReader-based solutions are typically:

❑ Create a connection to a data source, and then open that connection.

❑ Create and populate a Command instance with the command statement and the connection.

❑ Call the Execute method on the Command object. The value returned by this method is typically assigned to a DataReader.

❑ Call the Read method of the DataReader to pull out the information desired.

❑ Close the DataReader (to ensure that it gets cleaned up) and close the connection (so that it gets returned to the connection pool and gets cleaned up as well).

On the other hand, if we need to write an application that allows users to add, remove, or edit data, it would probably be best to use the DataSet. The typical DataSet-based solution follows this pattern:

❑ Connect a DataAdapter to a data source

❑ Create one or more DataTable objects (either manually or from DataAdapter)

❑ Disconnect from the data source

❑ Add, edit, or change elements within `DataRows` within the `DataTables`

❑ Call `GetChanges()` to create a "difference" set; a `DataSet` containing only the changed data elements

❑ Loop through this difference set, checking the `HasErrors` property, to see if there are any errors

❑ Extract the errant rows from the `DataTable` using the `GetErrors` method

❑ Loop through difference set and call `AcceptChanges()` or `RejectChanges()` as appropriate

❑ Call the `Merge` method to reconcile the valid changes between the difference `DataSet` and the original `DataSet`

❑ Use the `Merge()` method to update the original `DataSet` with the difference set

❑ Reconnect to the data source

❑ Use the `Update()` method of the `DataAdapter`, passing it the original `DataSet`

❑ Define a series of `DataCommands` so that the `DataAdapters` know how to update the data source with the changed data

❑ Call the `AcceptChanges()` or `RejectChanges()` methods to post the final data back to the source as appropriate

Because they are so vital to this chapter, let's do a quick review of the `DataReader` and `DataSet` classes.

DataReader

A `DataReader` is a manifestation of the `IDataReader` interface. Each .NET Data Provider is obliged to support this interface. A `DataReader` provides a way of reading forward-only streams of result sets generated by executing commands at a data source. It's important to understand that there is not just one `DataReader` class that you use all of the time, but rather, each .NET Data Provider offers its own implementation of the `IDataReader` interface. Out of the box, the .NET Framework offers a `DataReader` specifically for Microsoft SQL Server 7.0 (and higher) and for OLE-DB. Although each `DataReader` looks identical to us as developers, their internal workings are rather different.

For performance reasons, you cannot directly instantiate an instance of the `DataReader` class; it is manufactured for you by the `ExecuteReader` method of a `Command` object. Also keep in mind that if you tinker with the `Connection` instance while a `DataReader` is open, you can seriously disrupt the behavior of the `DataReader`. There is one noteworthy exception to this rule; you can call the `close` method of the `Connection`, but this action will invalidate the `DataReader` for future operations (a `System.InvalidOperationException` will be thrown.) Effectively, this means that a constantly open connection to the data source must be kept going.

Let us take a quick look at a simple program that uses a `DataReader` to populate a `SortedList` collection. Granted, this is a fairly contrived example, but it demonstrates how to implement the steps we discussed earlier. We will only look at the most germane sections of this program. If you want to see the whole thing, the sourcecode can be found in the download code available from www.wrox.com.

Sometimes you might find yourself left in a bind. You need to write a function or program that reads data from some source and display that information in a different sort order elsewhere. That is pretty easy if you can define your own queries for generating the data you need. But as sometimes happens, you just cannot do that. Instead, you have to take what data you can get, load it into some internal data structure, sort it, and then use it in the way that you want. In this chapter, we will be using the ProTest database, created in the previous chapter.

For this example, we will be using a data container class called EmpListItem. This class will store an employee's ID, their last name, their department, and their salary. We have also defined the constructor for this class to accept string and integer values for these attributes:

```
class EmpListItem
{
    string _EmpID;
    string _Last;
    string _Dept;
    int _Salary;

    public string EmpID
    {
        get { return _EmpID; }
        set { _EmpID = EmpID; }
    }
    public string Last
    {
        get { return _Last; }
        set { _Last = Last; }
    }
    public string Dept
    {
        get { return _Dept; }
        set { _Dept = Dept; }
    }
    public int Salary
    {
        get { return _Salary; }
        set { _Salary = Salary; }
    }
    public EmpListItem(string ID, string Last, string Dept, int Salary)
    {
        _EmpID = ID;
        _Last = Last;
        _Dept = Dept;
        _Salary = Salary;
    }
}
```

First, we should identify the variables used. EmpListItem is a class defined in this same namespace.

```
class EmpMain
{
    [STAThread]
    static void Main(string[] args)
```

```
        {
            SqlConnection Conn;
            SqlCommand Cmd;
            SqlDataReader DR;
            EmpListItem NewEmp;
```

Next, we define the data structure we are going to use for storing and sorting the loaded data. One of the really wonderful things about the .NET framework, compared to previous Microsoft offerings, is that many useful data structure designs are ready made for us. In this case, the SortedList class of System.Collections is ideal for the problem at hand. Creating an instance of that is easy, too:

```
            SortedList EmpList = new SortedList();
```

Our next step is to connect to the database:

```
        try {
            // Connect to the database
            Conn = new SqlConnection("Initial Catalog=ProTest;" +
                        "Data Source=localhost;Integrated Security=SSPI;");
            Conn.Open();
```

Now this is where our example gets a bit contrived. We are going to write a direct query that gives us all of the key data elements ordered by the employee's ID. In the real world, we might be stuck calling a stored procedure that does the same thing – and cranky database administrators that will not write a new one for us! Remember, it's just an example...

```
            // Get a list of the employees, their IDs, names,
            // departments and salaries
            Cmd = new SqlCommand("SELECT EmpID,Last,Dept,Salary " +
                                    "FROM EmpList ORDER BY EmpID", Conn);
```

We can now execute this command using the ExecuteReader method. We assign the results of that to a DataReader.

```
            DR = Cmd.ExecuteReader();
```

What happens next tends largely to be a function of how the DataReader is actually implemented. For example, a SqlClient-derived DataReader opens and works with a Tabular Data Stream (TDS) to the SQL Server. Such a reader would step through elements in the stream each time the Read method is called. The DataReader can then access data elements in that stream either by name or position. This method allows a SqlClient-derived DataReader to guzzle data at an amazing rate. We pass these data elements into the constructor.

For what its worth, an OleDb-derived **DataReader** must work through OLE DB to gain access to the data elements. This is a bit slower than working directly with a data medium like TDS, because of the pushing of data between interfaces.

```
            while(DR.Read())
            {
                // Construct a new item to store the employee's data
```

```
            NewEmp = new EmpListItem(DR.GetString(0),DR.GetString(1),
                                  DR.GetString(2),DR.GetInt32(3));
```

It is a fairly simple matter then to enter the freshly created data container into the `SortedList`. Because we wish to access this list sorted by the employee's last name, we specify that as the key value for the sorted list.

```
            // Add that new item to our sorted list
            EmpList.Add(NewEmp.Last,NewEmp);
        }
```

With all of the data read in, we can close down the connection to the database so that it becomes available for other processes to use, and the the garbage collection process cleans up the instance.

```
            // close the connection to return the connection to the pool
            // and so that it can be garbage collected.
            DR.Close();
            Conn.Close();
        }
```

Assuming we did not have any problems working the data source and the query returned some results, we can easily display an alphabetical list of the employees.

```
        // Did records load successfully?
        if(EmpList.Count > 0)
        {
            // Display the sorted list of names and IDs.
            foreach(EmpListItem Emp in EmpList.Values)
            {
                Console.WriteLine("{0} is EmployeeID {1}",Emp.Last,Emp.EmpID);
            }
            Console.WriteLine("Press [Enter] to continue");
            Console.ReadLine();
        }
    }
}
```

One limitation of a `DataReader` is that it works with a single set of results at a time. If you need to work with more than one set of results concurrently, you need to have multiple, active `DataReaders`.

Instances of the `DataReader` class otherwise lack much of an immediate interest to us as developers, with two notable exceptions – the `GetSchemaTable()` and the `NextResult()` methods. The `GetSchemaTable` method returns a `DataTable` populated with schema information about a query just executed. This is a very handy way of exploring the metadata that a query or command returns, particularly if you have no other way of gathering that information. The `NextResult` method advances a result stream to the next result set. For example, the following query will return two result sets in a single result stream:

```
SELECT BonusID,EmpID,BonusMoney,StartDate,EndDate FROM Bonus ORDER BY EmpID
SELECT EmpID,Last,Dept,Salary FROM EmpList ORDER BY EmpID
```

In order to use the data from both of these result sets, you would need to loop through the result set from the query on the `Bonus` table, then use the `NextResult` method to read the results of the `EmpList` table query.

DataSet

We have just seen that a `DataReader` is the lowest-level – and fastest – way to stream data into our applications. A `DataReader`, however, is strictly read-only and forward-only. In most cases, this would be fine. We have just seen a way to work around this behavior to change the order in which the results are presented. However, the nature of the `DataReader` presents four problems:

- ❑ **Read-only:** Although the `DataCommand` may actually execute an INSERT or UPDATE statement, there are no methods provided for changing the data presented by the `DataReader`

- ❑ **Forward-only:** There are no methods on the normal implementation of a `DataReader` that allow you refer to a previously presented data element

- ❑ **Connection-dependent:** A persistent, active connection to the database must be constantly maintained in order for the `DataReader` to function as expected

- ❑ **Serial Data:** In order to work with multiple result sets, you must have them presented by the .NET Data Provider as a series of result sets

In the past, if our applications needed to work with data, it was up to us to define and program the data structures and methods for populating any changes in that data back to their source. Frequently, that amounted to a lot of hand-written code. Thankfully, the .NET Framework offers a great, out-of-the-box way to accomplish this type of functionality – the `DataSet`.

The `DataSet` class actually amounts to an in-memory database with an indefinite lifetime. Unlike the `DataReader`, it can hold several tables. These tables can be programmatically created or filled – via a `DataAdapter` – from a `DataSource`. It also has structures for relating the data in one internal table with other internal tables. It can also manage constraints on the data, as well as persist the data. One of the most potent features of the `DataSet` is its internal ability to know what data has been changed so that when the `DataSet` is reconnected to a data source, only the changed data needs to be updated.

Once the `DataSet` is populated, it loses any need to know anything about its original data source. It holds its data in XML format, and can actually write out its data as an XML file, read data in from an XML file, and store its structure in a schema (XSD) file. We will see examples of this shortly.

There are several object collections within the `DataSet` that are worth discussing. The `DataTable` collection contains references to each data table, which can be referenced numerically or by using the table's name.

```
DataSet dataset = new System.Data.DataSet();
DataTable mytable = dataset.Tables[0];
```

Two other important collections are the `DataRelationCollection` and `ConstraintCollection`. The `DataRelationCollection` holds `DataRelation` objects, while the `ConstraintCollection` holds instances of the `Constraint` class. `DataRelation` objects represent relationships between columns in separate `DataTables`. These objects enable linking between tables, similar to the primary key to foreign key relationships of databases. These relationships can work hand-in-hand with elements in the internal `Constraint` to ensure data consistency. These relationships and constraints can be created programmatically, or created as the `DataSet` is populated from the `DataSource`.

Data Binding to Controls

Controls are an easy, convenient way to accomplish complex tasks. You can think of them as being pre-packaged yet easily customized packages of code. Two types of controls – Web Server Controls and Windows Forms (WinForms) – are commonly used. This section looks at data binding to a commonly used control, the `DataGrid`. There are a number of controls offered in the framework – everything from Ad Rotators to one-step XML rendering. Let us start with the Web Server `DataGrid` control.

We have seen the `ExecuteReader()` method used to fill a `DataSet` in the examples in the previous chapter. We have also seen it used to load data into an in-memory structure. But neither of these are the typical, expected uses of the `DataReader`. Binding a `DataReader` to a control for display is much more the expectation of how a `DataReader` should be used. In the next example, we will see the `DataReader` used to populate a `DataGrid`, and then display the `DataGrid` in HTML format within a web browser.

Binding to ASP: DataGrid

In this example ASP.NET page, a `Command` object is used to populate a `DataReader`. The `DataReader` can then be bound to the `DataGrid`.

The first step is to define what programming language the scripts within the page will use, and to tell the runtime to automatically use our event handlers. Note that we're creating this example in a text editor – for simple demonstrations they are easier than VS .NET.

```
<%@ Page language="c#" AutoEventWireup="True" %>
```

Next, we need to import the namespaces for the .NET framework classes we want to use. Again, we will use instances of the `SqlClient`.

```
<%@ import namespace="System.Data.SqlClient" %>
<%@ import namespace="System.Data" %>
```

Now we can start our actual function. In this case, we want to populate a `DataGrid` (creatively named `DataGrid1`) with the results of our query. We want do to this while the server is building the HTML response, so we need to do our work in the `Page_Load` event.

```
<SCRIPT runat="server">
private void Page_Load(object sender, System.EventArgs e)
{
```

Here is some familiar-looking code to open and connect to a data source, followed by defining and executing a command.

```
// Create and open a connection to the local ProTest Database
SqlConnection Conn = new SqlConnection("Initial Catalog=ProTest;" +
                     "Data Source=localhost;Integrated Security=SSPI;");
Conn.Open();
// Create and define a command to execute
SqlCommand Cmd = new SqlCommand("SELECT Last,Dept " +
                               "FROM EmpList ORDER by Last",Conn );
```

Now this is where the code becomes interesting. In order to display the data in the DataGrid, we execute the command. We know the ExecuteReader method returns an interface to a DataReader, which is conveniently bindable to the DataSource property of a DataGrid. Once the DataReader is bound to data source of the grid, it is simply a matter of calling the DataBind method to finish populating the DataGrid with our result set.

```
    // Use the executeReader method to execute the query and
    // use the IDataReader interface for SqlClient to access the results.
    // Point the data source of the data grid to the DataReader
    DataGrid1.DataSource = Cmd.ExecuteReader(
                                    CommandBehavior.CloseConnection);
    // Populate the grid with the results
    DataGrid1.DataBind();
}
</SCRIPT>
```

Believe it or not, that is about all there is to this effort. If you are familiar with classic ASP programming, this hopefully seems a bit simpler. The next chunk of our ASP.NET page is the familiar HTML page elements:

```
<!DOCTYPE HTML PUBLIC "-//W3C//DTD HTML 4.0 Transitional//EN" >
<html>
    <head>
        <title>Staff Listing</title>
    </head>
    <body>
```

It is common in an ASP.NET page to enclose all of the active page elements (inputs and programmatically controlled items like DataGrids) in a <form> tag set so that they are presented back to the server. This allows our server-side scripts (like ASP.NET pages) to interact with these objects. In this context, these page elements are commonly referred to as *controls*. This next section of the script inserts the DataGrid control into our page after creating a heading. We use one particular optional element of the DataGrid, the HeaderStyle, to have our column headings appear in a bold font.

```
    <form id="form1" method="post" runat="server">
        <h1>DataReader Example</h1>
        <asp:DataGrid ID="DataGrid1" BorderWidth="1"
                    CellPadding="3" runat="server">
          <HeaderStyle Font-Bold="True" />
        </asp:DataGrid>
```

Finally, we have the HTML end-tag elements.

```
        </form>
    </body>
</HTML>
```

This program outputs an HTML table in a web browser:

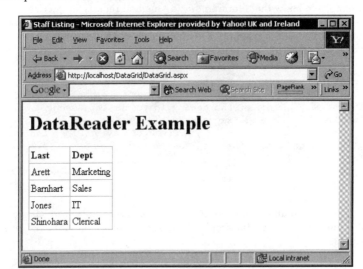

All of you veteran Visual InterDev users may now be rolling your eyes and lamenting that Microsoft is, once again, bringing Design Time Controls (DTCs) to the forefront. Don't panic, Web Server controls in the .NET Framework era are far different from the "poetry" than DTCs inflicted on us. Web Server Controls are much easier to work with and have much more customization potential.

Obviously this is just one use of data binding. Many of the controls made available in the .NET Framework support using essentially this same technique for binding either a `DataReader` or a `DataTable` (from a `DataSet`) to a control. For the sake of completeness, let us take a look at binding a `DataTable` from a `DataSet` to a control.

DataGrids in Windows Forms

For this example, we will look at how to use Visual Studio .NET to create a Windows Form-based application that uses a `DataSet` and a `DataGrid` to display information. Start a new **C# Windows Application** in Visual Studio .NET. Open the toolbox, select the **Data** object pane, then double-click on:

❑ **A DataSet:** Specify that it should be based an **Untyped Dataset**. Access the property sheet for this object and change its name to **EmpInfo**.

❑ **A SqlDataAdapter:** This starts the Data Adapter Configuration Wizard. For the data connection to be used, create a new connection using to the `ProTest` database. Choose **Use SQL Statements** for the query type. For the query, enter:

```
SELECT EmpID, Last , Dept FROM EmpList ORDER BY Last
```

Before clicking **Next**, click on **Advanced Options**. In the Advanced Options dialog, uncheck **Generate Update, Insert and Delete statements**. Click **OK** to accept the Advanced Options and **Finish** to complete defining the `DataAdapters`. Access the properties of this `DataAdapter` and change its name to **daEmpList**.

❑ A second **SqlDataAdapter**: Repeat the same procedure as in the previous, except use the existing connection, and change the query to:

```
SELECT EmpID, Vacation, StartDate, EndDate, BonusID FROM Bonus
                                                  ORDER BY EmpID
```

Change the name of this to **daBonus**.

Now slide open the Windows Forms choice on the toolbox, select **DataGrid** and draw this control on the form.

Once you have the `DataGrid` drawn, double-click on any usused area of the form. This should take you to the `Load` event handler. Add in the following code:

```
// Load up the data from the EmpList table
daEmpList.Fill(EmpInfo);
// Load up the data from the Bonus table
daBonus.Fill(EmpInfo);
// Add a primary key/foregin key relationship
// between the two freshly loaded tables.
EmpInfo.Relations.Add( "Vacation Information",
                        EmpInfo.Tables["EmpList"].Columns["EmpID"],
                        EmpInfo.Tables["Bonus"].Columns["EmpID"]);
dataGrid1.DataSource = EmpInfo.Tables["EmpList"];
```

When you run this application, you should see something like this:

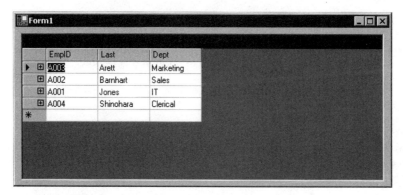

If you click on the first expand button (the + in a square) you get to pick a relationship to explore. Since we have only defined one such relationship, if you follow that, you get:

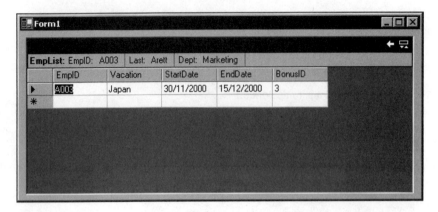

And that's all there is to it!

So far we have examined the differences between disconnected and connected data, and the different roles that `DataReaders` and `DataSets` play in each approach. We've also explored how to use data binding with both of these techniques using a `DataGrid`. Numerous other controls in both Windows Forms and Web Forms also accept data binding. The techniques for using these controls, however, are essentially the same as we have seen here.

Object Models

Back in Chapter 2, we compared ADO.NET's object model to classic ADO. Since then we have learned that ADO.NET is more than an object library. Rather, it is both a class library from which .NET Data Providers are derived and a rich library of ready-to-use functionality. As such, describing the ADO.NET object model is bit more complex. We will attempt to do so in this section.

ADO.NET is rooted in various places in the `System` namespace. This namespace has three physical classes that are fundamental to all of ADO.NET:

- ❑ `Attribute`, and its child class `DescriptionAttribute`. The `DataSysDescriptionAttribute` provides much of the basic functionality that all of the individual objects in ADO.NET use, such as `Equals()` and `ToString()`.

- ❑ `Hashtable`, which has a `PropertyCollection` member. `PropertyCollection` is the basis of the classes that store individual elements. As the parent class name implies, access to elements is accomplished by hashing names into an indexer.

- ❑ `MarshalByValueComponent`, contains the major classes we frequently use in data access programming.

Logically, many of the classes we make the most use of are found in the `System.Data` namespace, although many of them are physically derived from `MarshalByValueComponent`. Here is a list of the key classes we tend to use the most:

Class	Description
Constraint	Defines a constraint for a data column
DataColumn	Column elements in a DataTable
DataException	Base class for exceptions thrown by ADO.NET
DataRelation	Allows for an association between DataColumns
DataRow	Row elements in a DataTable
DataSet	Defines collections of DataTables, Constraints, and DataRelations in memory
DataTable	A collection of rows and columns
DataView	A data bindable view of a DataTable for sorting, filtering, searching, and editing

Let us take a deeper look at these classes. As we discussed in the previous chapter, the classes of a .NET Data Provider will be unique to their base namespace. These classes, however, are generic and can be used with any .NET Data Provider. Put another way, both a SqlDataAdapter and an OleDbDataAdapter can be used to populate a DataTable within any DataSet.

DataSet

As previously noted, a DataSet is an in-memory cache of data. A DataSet holds collections of DataTables. The integrity of a DataSet can be maintained by constraints. A DataSet can both read and write its contained data and metadata via XML. This makes it easy to transport a DataSet over HTTP through a firewall. We will look at an example of this in a following section.

DataSet instances can be constructed in one of three ways: with no name, with a specific name specified in string, or with serialization information. By providing serialization information, you can specify a custom method for persisting information to a given stream.

A DataSet has a number of properties and methods worth discussing:

Property	Description
EnforceConstraints	If set to true, constraints defined for the DataSet are checked and enforced when an updated is attempted. If you want to perform an operation that would violate an otherwise valid constraint, toggle this property to false, and then perform your action. If you do not fix this invalid change before attempting to update the DataSet back to its data source, you will probably encounter an integrity error.
HasErrors	This will be true if any of the rows in any of the tables has an error.
Relations	This is the anchor for the DataRelation collection.
Tables	This is the anchor for the DataTables collection.

Method	Description
AcceptChanges	Posts the DataSet back to the data source
Clear	Empties all of the rows from tables within the DataSet
Clone	Creates an exact replica of the DataSet with no rows in any tables
Copy	Creates an exact replica of the DataSet with rows in the tables
GetChanges	Creates an exact replica of the DataSet containing only the rows with changed data
GetXml	Generates an XML version of the DataSet
GetXmlSchema	Generates an XML schema for the DataSet
HasChanges	Indicates if the any of the data values in the rows have changed
Merge	Merges one DataSet with another
ReadXml	Loads an XML document and its schema into a DataSet, creating instances of classes as needed
ReadXmlSchema	Loads an XML schema into a DataSet, creating instances of classes as needed
RejectChanges	Clears all current changes made to the rows within the DataSet
WriteXml	Persists a DataSet and its schema to a designated destination
WriteXmlSchema	Persists a DataSet schema to a designated destination

We will pay particular attention to the XML persistence methods of the DataSet in a following example.

DataTable

A DataTable is an in-memory container of data represented in DataRow and DataColumn objects. The columns of a DataTable must be defined before the DataTable itself can be created. A DataTable can contain a maximum of a little over sixteen million rows. An instance of a DataTable will have a few interesting properties, methods, and events. Like a DataSet, a DataTable can be constructed with no parameters, with a name, or with serialization information.

Properties	Description
ChildRelations	Anchor for relations of this table
Columns	Anchor for the columns of this table
Constraints	Anchor for the constraints on this table
DefaultView	Holds a DataView of columns and rows in the table
DisplayExpression	Allows for computations or formatting of the data into a value

Properties	Description
HasErrors	Same as `DataSet.HasErrors`
ParentRelations	Reference to collections of `Relations` which involve this table
PrimaryKey	Defines which column or set of columns is the primary key of this table
Rows	Anchors for rows in this table

Methods	Description
AcceptChanges	Posts the changed data in the table back to a data source
Clear	Removes all of the data from the table
Clone	Creates a replica of the structure of the `DataTable`, including constraints, relations, and schemas
Compute	Determines the value of an expression for the rows in the current view
Copy	Replicates the data and structure of the table
GetChanges	Replicates the `DataTable` structure and the current rows with changes
GetErrors	Extracts a `DataRow` array with errors
ImportRow	Copies a `DataRow` from one `DataTable` to another
LoadDataRow	Updates or inserts a row in or into the table
NewRow	Creates a new `DataRow` using the same schema as the table
RejectChanges	Resets any changed rows to the original values

Events	Description
ColumnChanged	Fires *after* a value in a specified row and column changes
ColumnChanging	Fires *when* a value in a specified row and column changes
RowChanged	Fires after a data row has changed
RowChanging	Fires when a data row is changing
RowDeleted	Fires after a data row is deleted
RowDeleting	Fires as a data row is deleted

Two of the more interesting sets of these are the `ParentRelations` and the `ChildRelations` properties. Iterating through these proprieties allows you to access the information in a parent or child table. Each of these properties contains a collection of `DataRelation` objects. By sequentially accessing each of these items, you can access the rows and columns of tables related to the current table.

DataRow

The DataRow and DataColumn work together to provide the actual store for data in a DataTable. The DataRow constructor takes no parameters. Some of the key properties and methods of a DataRow include:

Properties	Description
HasErrors	Gets a value indicating whether there are errors in a columns collection
Item	An indexer that allows you get or set the value of a row data element
ItemArray	Provides access to all of the row elements in an array
RowError	Allows you to set or get a custom error message for the row
RowState	One of added, deleted, detached, modified, or unchanged, reflecting the current state of the data in the row
Table	Provides the DataTable of which this row is a member

Methods	Description
AcceptChanges	Posts the current values in the row to the designated data source
ClearErrors	Empties the current collection of errors associated with this row
Delete	Expunges the row from the table
GetChildRows	Provides access to the child rows of the current row
GetColumnError	Returns the error description for a column
GetColumnsInError	Returns an array of columns that have errors
GetParentRows	Returns a collection of parent rows; there is also a GetParentRow that returns just the first parent row
HasVersion	Allows you to query a row to determine if it has its default values, its original values, proposed values, or current values
IsNull	If the column specified is null, this value will be true
RejectChanges	Undoes all of the uncommitted changes to a row
SetColumnError	Allows you to provide a custom error message for the row
SetParentRow	Allows you to change the parent row for the current row

One aspect of column and row behavior worth discussing more at this point is row versioning. It works like this:

❑ Each DataRow can have different physical sets of data associated with it: Default, Original, Current, and Proposed

- ❏ Once you have called the `BeginEdit` method and you then change the value held by the row, the `Current` and `Proposed` values become available

- ❏ When you call the `CancelEdit` method, any `Proposed` value is expunged

- ❏ The `Proposed` value becomes the `Current` value when the `EndEdit` method is called

- ❏ Calling the method `AcceptChanges` on a row or table sets the `Current` value to the `Proposed` value

- ❏ Calling the method `RejectChanges` on a row, the `Proposed` value is removed and the version becomes `Current`

DataColumn

Whereas rows store data, columns store the schema. They have a number of interesting properties but no special methods other than their constructor. The constructors for a `DataColumn` are a bit different from the other classes we have looked at thus far, so let's pay some extra attention to them.

Constructor	Description
`DataColumn()`	Creates an empty column.
`DataColumn(string)`	Creates a column with the name specified in `string`.
`DataColumn(string, Type)`	Creates a column with the name given in `string` and the data type specified by `Type`.
`DataColumn(string1, Type, string2)`	Creates a column using `string1` as the name, the given data type from `Type` and an expression (for calculated value columns mostly) in `string2`.
`DataColumn(string, Type, string, MappingType)`	Creates a column using the specified name in `string1`, the given data type in `Type`, an expression in `string2`, and value that determines whether the column is an attribute, element or simple text. A `MappingType` is frequently used when mapping to an XML document.

Data types, in this context, are those provided for the .NET Framework or implemented in user classes. Its common to see a data type defined in a .NET Data Provider used in these constructors.

Property	Description
`AllowDBNull`	Controls if `null` values are allowed for this column.
`AutoIncrement`	`true` if the value in this column is automatically incremented as a new row is added.
`AutoIncrementSeed`	The initial value of an auto-increment column.
`AutoIncrementStep`	The difference between a newly auto-incremented value and the previous auto-incremented value.

Table continued on following page

Property	Description
Caption	Controls the caption for the column. Frequently used by data binding controls as the heading for a column and is set to the name of the column (dervied from the data source) by default.
ColumnMapping	Ties a column to an element, or attribute within its data source.
ColumnName	Holds the name of the column relative to the table structure.
DataType	Holds the data type for this column.
DefaultValue	Defines the default used for unspecified elements as added to the table.
Expression	Hold calculatations, the values in a column, or an expression used to filter rows.
MaxLength	Controls the maximum length of a text column.
Ordinal	Defines where this column resides in the sequence of the DataColumn collection of the parent DataTable.
ReadOnly	If set to true, any attempt to change a value in this column causes an exception to be thrown.
Table	Refers to the parent table for this column.
Unique	Requires that all data in this column be unique.

Constraint

Generally, constraints are rules imposed on a column to help ensure the integrity of data in the table. In the ADO.NET context, an instance of the Constraint class achieves this. Three constraints are supported out of the box: a Primary Key, a ForeignKeyConstraint (FKCs) and a UnqiueConstraint. FKCs control what happens to data in related tables when a value is is removed. A UniqueConstraint just helps to make sure that values in a column are unique. Primary Key constraints designate the column as a primary key for the table. Constraints are, by default, unique constraints. That is, a constraint when created will be treated as a unique constraint. However, an overload on the constructor allows you to pass a Boolean flag indicating if the constraint you are creating is actually supposed to be a Primary Key.

The constructor signatures for `Constraints` include:

Constructor	Description
UniqueConstraint(DataColumn)	Creates a new unique constraint on the given column.
UniqueConstraint(DataColumn[])	Creates new unique constraints on an array of columns.
UniqueConstraint(string, DataColumn)	Creates a new unique constraint on the given column with the name given in string.
UniqueConstraint(string, DataColumn[])	Creates new unique constraints on an array of columns with the name given in string.
UniqueConstraint(string, string[], bool)	Creates new unique constraints on an array of columns and with the name given in string. If the Boolean value is true, then it adds the constraint as a primary key as well.

You do not actually have to use the constructor method if you just want to mark a column as uniquely constrained (although we will, so that we can have a unique primary key). Instead, you can just set the `Unique` property of the target column to `true`:

```
ds.Tables[table_name].Columns[column_name].Unique = true;
```

> Keep in mind that Primary Key constraints and Unique constraints are different concepts. You can have any number of columns (or arrays of columns) constrained to uniqueness. However, you can have only one column (or array of columns) acting as the primary key for the table.

As we have previously discussed, if the `EnforceConstraints` on the parent `DataSet` is turned off, these constraints will not be enforced. We will demonstrate how to create a primary key `UniqueConstraint` in the next example.

ForeignKeyConstraint

A `ForeignKeyConstraint` provides a way for defining an action in a table containing a foreign key when the table containing the primary key changes. The principal use for this `Constraint` class is defining what should happen when a delete occurs. There are four constructors for this class:

Constructor	Description
`ForeignKeyConstraint(PrimaryKeyDataColumn, ForeignKeyDataColumn)`	Ties a single column in table holding primary key with a single column in the table holding foreign key
`ForeignKeyConstraint(PrimaryKeyDataColumns[], ForeignKeyDataColumns[])`	Ties an array of columns in table holding primary key with an array of columns in the table holding foreign key
`ForeignKeyConstraint(Name, PrimaryKeyDataColumn, ForeignKeyDataColumn)`	Creates a named constraint then ties a single column in table holding primary key with a single column in the table holding foreign key
`ForeignKeyConstraint(ConstraintName, PrimaryKeyDataColumns[], ForeignKeyDataColumns[])`	Creates a named constraint then ties an array of columns in table holding primary key with an array of columns in the table holding foreign key

Aside from being quite a bit to type, the last constructor offers the most power. In order to get the most out of this constructor, you need to understand the `Rule` enumeration. This enumeration contains the types of actions that can be taken when a constraint is applied. A `Rule` comes in one of two flavors: an `AcceptRejectRule` and a more generic `Rule`. An `AcceptRejectRule` can either cascade or take no action. A `Rule` can cascade the changes, take no action, set all values to a default, or set all values to `null`.

This is one case where an immediate example might help make sense of all of this. Looking again at our `ProTest` database, we know that `EmpList` has an explicit primary key-foreign key relationship shown visually as:

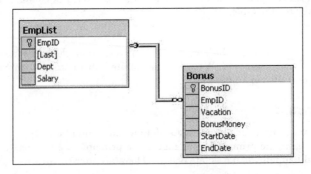

The nature of this relationship probably implies the following business rules:

❏ When a employee is added to the `EmpList` table, there is no need to create a new record in `Bonus` as the new employee probably has not earned a vacation and bonus yet

❏ When a record is updated in `EmpList` is updated, there are no changes required in `Bonus`

❑ When a record is deleted in EmpList, we need to delete the matching record in Bonus

We will see more about relations in the next section.

The following code example shows how to load these tables into a DataSet, create a relationship between them, and then apply a constraint to them. Again, we are using a Command-Line-application to keep the code simple. This application simulates how the ProTest database may actually be used. We have been asked to develop a report showing all of the employees and the total bonus money that they have been paid.

First, we will load the data from the SQL Server data source into a DataSet. Second, we will construct the relationships between the tables in the DataSet as dictated by the business rules. Finally, we will demonstrate how adding, updating, and removing rows in the DataSet affects it. We will do this by adding an employee, then giving her a trip to the Microsoft Professional Developers Conference 2001 in Los Angeles, and a bonus to cover her expenses.

We will use three methods to do our work:

❑ LoadDataSet – loads the tables from our SQL Server into a DataSet with the use of a DataAdapter

❑ ShowStatus – displays some headings, then walks through the data to produce the report desired

❑ Main – simulates the business-type transactions we want to take

The LoadDataFunction is set up to accept a previously created DataSet object passed to the function. It does some very simple exception management, and is quite straightforward.

```
static void LoadDataSet(DataSet ds)
{
    try
    {
        // Create a new DataAdapter for loading the EmpList table
        // then load it into a table with in the given dataset
        // call the new table EmpList.
        SqlDataAdapter daEmpList = new SqlDataAdapter
                    ("SELECT * FROM emplist", "Integrated Security=SSPI;" +
                    "Initial Catalog=ProTest; Data Source=localhost;");
        DataTable empList = new DataTable("EmpList");
        daEmpList.Fill(empList);

        // Create a new DataAdapter for loading the Bonus table
        // then load it into a table with in the given dataset
        // call the new table Bonus.
        SqlDataAdapter daBonus = new SqlDataAdapter(
                                        "SELECT * FROM Bonus",
                    "Integrated Security=SSPI;Initial Catalog=ProTest;" +
                                        "Data Source=localhost;");
        DataTable bonus = new DataTable("Bonus");
        daBonus.Fill(bonus);

        // Add the new tables to the DataSet
```

```
        ds.Tables.Add(empList);
        ds.Tables.Add(bonus);
    }
    catch(Exception e)
    {
        Console.WriteLine(e.Message.ToString());
        Console.ReadLine();
    }
}
```

The ShowStatus function takes a DataSet and a string as parameters. The string passed is displayed in the report headings. The ShowStatus function also sums up the paid bonus before displaying the employee names and total bonus paid.

```
static void ShowStatus(DataSet ds,string header)
{
    // Write some table headers
    Console.WriteLine("\n{0}",header);
    Console.WriteLine("{0} rows in EmpList and {1} rows in Bonus",
                   ds.Tables["empList"].Rows.Count,
                   ds.Tables["bonus"].Rows.Count);
    Console.WriteLine("Last Name\tTotal Bonus Earned");
    Console.WriteLine("---------\t---------");

    // Loop through each of the rows in the EmpList Table
    // so we can display the name and calculate the total bonuses paid.
    foreach(DataRow pdr in ds.Tables["empList"].Rows)
    {
        // Used for summing up the bonuses
        int bonus = 0;

        // Loop through rows of the bonus table looking
        // for any records where the key is found. When found,
        // add the bonus amount to the accumulator
        foreach(DataRow cdr in ds.Tables["bonus"].Rows)
        {
            if(cdr["EmpID"].Equals(pdr["EmpID"].ToString()))
            {
                bonus += Convert.ToInt16(cdr["BonusMoney"].ToString());
            }
        }

        // Display the results
        Console.WriteLine("{0}\t{1:C}",
            pdr["Last"].ToString().PadRight(10,' '),bonus);
    }
}
```

Finally, on to our Main function. A substantial amount of work goes on here, so let's go through it a chunk at a time. To start with, we declare a variable to use as a working DataRow, and create an empty DataSet named EmpInfo. Then we call LoadDataSet to get the data from the SQL Server loaded into the DataSet that we have just created.

```
[STAThread]
static void Main(string[] args)
{
    // temporary working row
    DataRow dr;
    // Create a new DataSet called EmpInfo
    DataSet ds = new DataSet("EmpInfo");
    // Call our loading function
    LoadDataSet(ds);
```

Now we can add our desired primary keys to each table. To accomplish this, we will first type our working Constraint object as an instance of UniqueConstraint. We will then create a new instance of that class using an appropriate name, tie it to the virtual EmpList table and set the primary key parameter flag to true so that our constraint is created as a primary key. Then we just add the Constraint to the collection of Constraints on that table.

```
// Define a UniqueConstraint object called pkey
UniqueConstraint pkey;

//    Add a primary key constraint for the EmpID Table
pkey = new UniqueConstraint("PK_EmpList",
        ds.Tables["empList"].Columns["EmpID"],true);
ds.Tables["empList"].Constraints.Add(pkey);
```

We can just repeat that logic for the bonus table.

```
// And one for the bonus table
pkey = new UniqueConstraint("PK_bonus",
    ds.Tables["bonus"].Columns["BonusID"],true);
ds.Tables["bonus"].Constraints.Add(pkey);
```

We follow virtually the same design pattern to create a ForeignKeyConstraint:

```
// Define a ForeignKeyConstraint object called cnstr
ForeignKeyConstraint cnstr;

// Create the constraint, calling it FKC_EmpList_Bonus,
// setting the primary key table to EmpList and the
// foreign key to Bonus. Note that you have to use the
// actual primary key / foreign key columns
cnstr = new ForeignKeyConstraint("FKC_EmpList_Bonus",
                    ds.Tables["empList"].Columns["EmpID"],
                    ds.Tables["bonus"].Columns["EmpID"]);
```

With the Constraint made ready, we can tweak its proprieties to reflect our business rules, and then add it to the collections of Constraints on the foreign key table.

```
// Implement the first and second business rule -- adding or changing
// a value in the primary key table (EmpID) doesn't affect the
// foreign key table (Bonus)
cnstr.AcceptRejectRule = AcceptRejectRule.None;
cnstr.UpdateRule = Rule.None;
```

```
// Now take care of the third business rule, delete records in bonus
// when the parent record in EmpList is delete
cnstr.DeleteRule = Rule.Cascade;

// Add the constraint to the foreign key table
ds.Tables["bonus"].Constraints.Add(cnstr);
```

> **ForeginKeyConstraints** need to be added to the table holding the foreign key, not the table holding the primary key. Try it the other way to see an interesting run-time exception.

To be certain that we have loaded the data correctly, let's display the report:

```
// Show the status after loading the data
ShowStatus(ds,"After load");
```

```
After load
4 rows in EmpList and 5 rows in Bonus
Last Name          Total Bonus Earned
---------          ------------------
Jones              $2,000.00
Barnhart           $8,000.00
Arett              $4,000.00
Shinohara          $0.00
```

Now let us add an `EmpList` record for Ms. Smyth and see what happens.

```
// Add a new record for Smyth, then reshow the data
// Note that the row count in bonus is uneffected...
dr = ds.Tables["empList"].NewRow();
dr["EmpID"] = "A5000";
dr["Last"] = "Smyth";
dr["Dept"] = "Security";
dr["Salary"] = 5000;
ds.Tables["empList"].Rows.Add(dr);
ShowStatus(ds,"Added Smyth");
```

```
Added Smyth
5 rows in EmpList and 5 rows in Bonus
Last Name          Total Bonus Earned
---------          ------------------
Jones              $2,000.00
Barnhart           $8,000.00
Arett              $4,000.00
Shinohara          $0.00
Smyth              $0.00
```

Let us give Ms. Smyth a bonus for her PDC trip and see what happens.

```
// Give Smyth a bonus, and reshow the data
// Note the new row in the bonus row count...
dr = ds.Tables["Bonus"].NewRow();
dr["BonusID"] = 1000;
dr["EmpID"] = "A5000";
```

```
dr["Vacation"] = "Los Angeles";
dr["BonusMoney"] = 3000;
dr["StartDate"] = new DateTime(2001,10,21);
dr["EndDate"] = new DateTime(2001,10,24);
ds.Tables["bonus"].Rows.Add(dr);
ShowStatus(ds,"Gave Smyth Bonus");
```

```
Gave Smyth Bonus
5 rows in EmpList and 6 rows in Bonus
Last Name         Total Bonus Earned
─────────         ──────────────────
Jones             $2,000.00
Barnhart          $8,000.00
Arett             $4,000.00
Shinohara         $0.00
Smyth             $3,000.00
```

Having seen the .NET and C# exhibitions at PDC, Ms. Smyth decides to quit the firm and become a programmer, giving us a convenient opporunity to demonstrate removing her record from the table. Note that since we set:

```
// Now take care of the third business rule, delete records in bonus
// when the parent record in EmpList is delete
cnstr.DeleteRule = Rule.Cascade;
```

her entry in the bonus table is removed automatically.

```
// Now find the row for Smyth in the EmpList table
// and remove it. Show the results again and notice
// that the row counts in each table is decremented by one.
dr = ds.Tables["empList"].Rows.Find("A5000");
ds.Tables["empList"].Rows.Remove(dr);
ShowStatus(ds,"Removed Smyth");

Console.WriteLine("Press [Enter] to continue.");
Console.ReadLine();
}
```

```
Removed Smyth
4 rows in EmpList and 5 rows in Bonus
Last Name         Total Bonus Earned
─────────         ──────────────────
Jones             $2,000.00
Barnhart          $8,000.00
Arett             $4,000.00
Shinohara         $0.00
```

Clearly, being able to define a `ForeignKeyContraint` greatly simplifies our programming efforts!

DataRelation

We have already seen `DataRelation` objects in action in the previous examples, but we should look at them on their own. `DataRelation` objects are the way to bind the columns of tables together. Keep in mind that when relating columns using a `DataRelation`, these columns must have the same data type. `DataRelation` constructors can get a bit complicated:

Constructor	Description
`DataRelation (RelationName, PrimaryKeyTableColumn, ForeignKeyTableColumn)`	Creates a new `DataRelation` object with the given name relating a primary key table column to a foreign key table column
`DataRelation (RelationName, PrimaryKeyTablesColumns[], ForeignKeyTablesColumns[])`	Creates a new `DataRelation` object with the given name relating an array of primary key table columns to an array of foreign key table columns
`DataRelation (RelationName, PrimaryKeyTableColumn, ForeignKeyTableColumn, CreateConstraints)`	Creates a new `DataRelation` object with the given name relating the primary key table column to the foreign key table column, and a set of existing constraints if `CreateConstraints` is true
`DataRelation (RelationName, PrimaryKeyTablesColumns[], ForeignKeyTablesColumns[], CreateConstraints)`	Creates a new `DataRelation` object with the given name relating an array of primary key table columns to an array of foreign key table columns, and a set of constraints if `CreateConstraints` is true
`DataRelation (RelationName, name1, name2, name3[], name4[], CreateConstraints)`	Creates a `Constraint` with name `RelationName`, using the primary key table named in `name1` and the foreign key table named in `name2`, with the an array of primary key table columns in `name3`, with the an array of foreign key table columns in `name3`, and a set of constraints if `CreateConstraints` is true

A `DataRelation` does not have any special methods that merit attention, but has several properties that do.

Property	Description
`ChildColumns`	Anchors the columns of the foreign key table
`ChildKeyConstraint`	Returns the foreign key constraint, if any, for the relation
`ChildTable`	Provides the name of the foreign key table

Property	Description
DataSet	Provides the name of the DataSet which owns this relationship
Nested	true if the parent object of this relationship has one or more parent relationships
ParentColumns	Anchors the columns of the primary key table
ParentKeyConstraint	Gets any unique constraints for the primary key table
ParentTable	Provides the name of the primary key table
RelationName	Provides the name of relationship

DataExceptions

The DataException class is derived from the SystemException class, and deals with specialized exceptions thrown within ADO.NET. These are normally sub-classed by each of the ADO.NET Data Providers, so you will likely being working with SqlException and OleDbException as instances of the DataException class.

Exception Class	Description
ConstraintException	An action taken has violated a constraint.
DeletedRowInaccessible Exception	An action was attempted on a deleted row.
DuplicateNameException	An attempt to use a name already in use.
EvaluationException	Thrown when an expression cannot be evaluated.
InRowChangingEventException	The row data elements are being changed as an action is affected.
InvalidConstraintException	The request constraint could not be created or has become invalid.
InvalidExpressionException	Thrown when the expression in effect has an error. Parent class of EvaluationException and SyntaxErrorException.
MissingPrimaryKeyException	Occurs if you attempt to use Contains() or Finds() on a column in a DataTable and there is no primary key on that DataTable.

Table continued on following page

Exception class	Description
NoNullAllowedException	An attempt to add a null value where one is not allowed was made.
ReadOnlyException	Occurs when an attempt is made to modify a read-only value.
RowNotInTableException	Thrown if an attempt is made to access a row not in the table.
StrongTypingException	When a null value is requested from a strongly typed table, this exception is thrown.
SyntaxErrorException	Thrown when the expression evaluated has a syntax error.
TypedDataSetGenerator Exception	Thrown when name conflict occurs when attempting to create a strongly-typed DataSet.
VersionNot FoundException	Thrown when an attempt is made to access a version of a row that no longer exists.

The base DataException class has a number of interesting constructors and properties.

Constructor	Description
DataException()	Creates a new instance of the class
DataException(string)	Creates a new instance of the class with the message set to the string provided
DataException (SerializationInfo, StreamingContext)	Creates a new instance of the class with serialization information and information about how to persist the information
DataException(string, Exception)	Creates an instance of the exception with the message set to the string provided, then appends the provided exception as its child.

Property	Description
HelpLink	Anchors a link to the help file for this exception
InnerException	Returns the first child exception
Message	Provides the error message text
Source	Returns the name of the application or the object that caused the error
StackTrace	Anchors the stack trace, helpful for locating the source of an error
TargetSite	Returns the method that threw the exception

As previously mentioned, data providers may implement their own sub-classes of the `DataException` class; the data providers `SqlClient` and `OleDb` both do so.

SqlExceptions

A `SqlException` is generated in response to situations that the data provider cannot handle. SQL Error messages are classified by a severity level, as follows:

Severity Level	Description
10 or less	Informational and tends to indicate a user error
11 through 16	Indicates user correctable errors
17, 18, 19	Software or hardware error, but processing can continue
20 through 25	Software or hardware error, cannot continue and the connection is normally closed

`SqlException` objects do not have a direct constructor, but they do have many interesting properties not found in the base `DataException` class.

Property	Description
Class	Holds the severity level of the error returned
Errors	Anchors a collection of `SqlError` objects
LineNumber	Line number in the batch or stored procedure that generated the error
Number	The SQL error number generated
Procedure	Holds the name of the stored procedure in which the error occured
Server	The SQL Server where the error occured
Source	Provides the name of the provider that generated the error
StackTrace	Anchors the stack trace, helpful for locating the source of an error
State	Provides additional information about the error
TargetSite	Returns the method that threw the exception

The `SqlClient` provider gives you two ways of accessing information about errors that have occurred: through the properties of the `SqlException` (and the nested exceptions within) or within the `Errors` collection. The `SqlError` class itself is nearly identical to the `SqlException` class. We have demonstrated how to display information from `SqlException` in previous examples. Use whichever set of information works best for you.

OleDbException

The major differences between the `OleDbException` class and the `SqlException` class are:

❑ `OleDbException` is derived from `ExternalException`, which derives from `SystemException`, whereas `SqlClient` is derived directly from `SystemException`.

❑ The level of error severity that must be exceeded before a connection shuts down varies more than it does for `SqlClient` due to behavior of the underlying provider.

❑ The items in the `Errors` collection are of the `OleDbError` class.

❑ There is no `Class`, `LineNumber`, `Number`, `Procedure`, `Server`, or `State` property. Instead, an instance of `NativeError` is available. This integer provides database-specific error information.

DataView

A `DataView` object serves a similar purpose to views in the SQL Server context. Both are ways to select a subset of the columns and rows in a table. In SQL Server, it is possible to create a view based on the result of almost any query, but a `DataView` in ADO.NET is limited to operations on one table only. However, unlike views in some versions of SQL Server, a `DataView` can be sorted into a given order. The `DataViewManager` and the `DataViewSetting` classes do allow multiple table views. The `DataView` essentially exists to slim-down a large `DataSet` or `DataTable` for use with data-bound controls. We take a look at these classes in some detail, and then show a short example of how to use them. Let's start with `DataView`.

DataViews

The `DataView` class is fairly straight forward, having just two constructors. It has a rich set of properties that you use to shape the data as you see fit.

Constructor	Description
`DataView()`	Creates an empty `DataView`
`DataView(Data Table)`	Creates a `DataView` using the specified `DataTable`

Property	Description
`AllowDelete`	If set to `true`, you can delete rows in the view once the are created.
`AllowEdit`	If set to `true`, you can edit rows in the view once the are created.
`AllowNew`	If set to `true`, then new rows can be added using the `AddNew` method.
`ApplyDefaultSort`	If `true`, the default sort order is used. See the following discussion.
`DataViewManager`	Anchor for the `DataView` Manager associated with this view.

Property	Description
Item	Indexer for the `DataView` class.
RowFilter	Defines the expression used to filter which rows are seen in the `DataView`. See the following discussion.
RowStateFilter	Defines the row state filter. See the following discussion.
Sort	Defines the sort column(s) and sort order for the view.
Table	Anchor to the source table.

❑   `ApplyDefaultSort` controls if the default sort will be used when presenting this table. The behavior of sorting depends on whether a primary key has been defined for the table and whether the `Sort` property is defined. Essentially, if one or more columns are set to sort on, the rows will be sorted in the order specified. Otherwise, they will be sorted in order by the primary key column value.

❑   `RowsFilter` takes an expression. Rows for which this expression would be `true` are included in the view. The list of supported expressions is similar to that of a SQL WHERE clause.

❑   `RowStateFilter` takes a `DataRowState` enumeration member and includes in the view only those rows whose state matches the enumeration value provided. This is handy way to extract views of tables that the user can view before committing the `DataSet` back to data source.

Method	Description
AddNew	Adds an additional row to the `DataView`
Delete	Removes a row from the view
Find	Locates a row in the `DataView` using a specified primary key value

DataViewSetting

The `DataViewSetting` is the working element of a `DataViewManager` object. Each `DataRowManager` collects `DataViewSettings` to compose a bindable view. From a class model point-of-view, they are essentially the same as a `DataView` with an additional property – `DataViewManager` – which is the parent object of the object.

DataViewManager

The king of the hill, so to speak, of the various classes related to `DataView` is the `DataViewManager`. It holds a collection of `DataViewSettings` for each table in a `DataSet`. The class model of the `DataViewManager` is fairly sparse, so we will touch on it only briefly here before getting to the example.

Constructor	Description
DataViewManager()	Creates a new instance of the DataManager class associated with no DataSet
DataViewManager(DataSet)	Creates a new instance of the DataManager class and associates it with the given DataSet

Property	Description
DataSet	Holds the name of the DataSet associated with the DataViewManager
DataViewSetting CollectionString	Provides the DataViewSettings in a single-string format. Used in persistence.
DataViewSettings	Anchors the collection of DataViewSettings associated with this DataViewManager

Method	Description
CreateDataView(DataTable)	Creates a DataView for the specified DataTable

Although our previous examples using the ProTest have been efficient, they have not made good use of the rich functionality offered by the .NET Framework. To demonstrate using Windows Forms and Data Bound controls, as well as the DataView object, let us look at a slightly different example. In this example, we want to present the employee ID, the last name, and the total amount of the bonuses paid. We also want to show the list sorted by the employee's last name. Finally, we do not want to show any records for employees who have not been given any bonuses.

This time we will have a simple Windows Form, named frmMain, with a DataGrid and an exit button drawn on it. The code behind this form does not do much more than create an instance of a data access class that we will find later. It then calls a method on that instance to load the data, then it binds the DataGrid to a DataView created in the class.

We have organized this application in a namespace called Wrox.ProCSharpData.Chapter4, we need to add this at the top of the section of the form's code-behind file (frmMain.cs):

```
using Wrox.ProCSharpData.Chapter4.DataViewExample;
```

The Form_Load event handler for frmMain starts by creating an instance of the DataAccessClass.

```
private void Form1_Load(object sender, System.EventArgs e)
{
    // Create an instance of the DataAccessClass
    DataAccessClass dac = new DataAccessClass();
```

We can call the LoadDataSet on that instance to load up the DataSet and ready the view for use.

```
// Load the data up for use.
// If that process returns false, we know it failed
// so we need to abort. Otherwise, we can move on.
if(!dac.LoadDataSet())
{
    MessageBox.Show("Failed to load data as expected, " +
                                "check your database connection.",
                "Fatal Error",
                MessageBoxButtons.OK,
                MessageBoxIcon.Stop);
    Application.Exit();
}
```

Once the data and view is ready, we call the `DataForBinding` property to get an object to bind to.

```
// Ask the Data Access for the DataView to display
dataGrid1.DataSource = dac.DataForBinding;
```

Now let us review the `DataAccessClass.cs` file. It starts with the following namespace references:

```
using System;
using System.Data;
using System.Data.SqlClient;
using System.Data.SqlTypes;


namespace Wrox.ProCSharpData.Chapter4.DataViewExample
```

Next, we need to define a few class-level variables to use.

```
public class DataAccessClass
{
    // Working data set
    private DataSet m_ds;
    // Working data view
    private DataView m_dv;
    // Working data table
    private DataTable m_dt;
```

We use the `DataForBinding` property to return a reference to the `DataView` showing the data we want. We offer this up as a property to demonstrate data hiding in the class file.

```
// Property of this class we want to bind the
// Data grid on the form to
public DataView DataForBinding
{
    get { return m_dv; }
}
```

The constructor for the base class is very straightforward: it just creates the `DataSet` used to hold the `DataTable` objects used in the class.

```
// Constructor : just make the data set and return
public DataAccessClass()
{
    m_ds = new DataSet("EmpInfo");
}
```

The `LoadDataSetMethod` actually calls a private version of `_LoadDataSet`, then it calls `_ViewDataSet` to generate the `DataView`. We do this "blind call" to a private function so we can add extra functionality to it without changing the function signature.

```
// This function calls an internal version of LoadDataSet
// which actually loads the data set then calls this function
// calls ViewDataSet to create the DataView
public bool LoadDataSet()
{
    bool rc = true;
    rc = _LoadDataSet();
    if(rc) {
        rc = _ViewDataSet();
    }
    return(rc);
}
```

The `_LoadDataSet` function actually does the work of loading data from the SQL Server into a `DataTable`. Once the `DataTable` is populated, it is given a primary key and is added to the `DataSet`. If an error occurs in this process, the function is set up to return a value indicating failure.

```
// Load the dataset from the server
private bool _LoadDataSet()
{
    // assume that load will succeed
    bool rc = true;
    try
    {
```

Load up all the data from the `EmpList` table:

```
// Create a new DataAdapter for loading the EmpList table
// then load it into a table with in the given dataset
// call the new table EmpList.
SqlDataAdapter daEmpList = new SqlDataAdapter("SELECT * FROM emplist",
            "Integrated Security=SSPI;Initial Catalog=ProTest;" +
                                    "Data Source=localhost;");
DataTable empList = new DataTable("EmpList");
daEmpList.Fill(empList);
```

Load up all the data from the `Bonus` table:

```
// Create a new DataAdapter for loading the Bonus table information
// then load it into a table with in the given dataset
// call the new table Bonus.
SqlDataAdapter daBonus = new SqlDataAdapter("SELECT * FROM Bonus",
```

```
                    "Integrated Security=SSPI;Initial Catalog=ProTest;" +
                                        "Data Source=localhost;");
    DataTable bonus = new DataTable("Bonus");
    daBonus.Fill(bonus);
```

Add the primary keys for these tables, and then add them to the `DataSet`:

```
    // Add primary keys to the freshly loaded tables
    empList.Constraints.Add("PK_empList",
                    empList.Columns["EmpID"],
                    true);
    bonus.Constraints.Add("PK_bonus",
                    bonus.Columns["BonusID"],
                    true);
    // Add a foreign key constraint to the foreign key table
    ForeignKeyConstraint fkc =
            new ForeignKeyConstraint("FK_EmpList_Bonus",
                                empList.Columns["EmpID"],
                                bonus.Columns["EmpID"]);
    // Add the new tables to the DataSet
    m_ds.Tables.Add(empList);
    m_ds.Tables.Add(bonus);
    }
    // If any errors occured, discard them for now
    // but have the function return false to indicate
    // that an error occurred
```

Catch and discard any errors:

```
    catch(Exception e)
    {
        rc = false;
    }
    return rc;
    }
```

`_ViewDataSet` creates a view on top of the `DataTable` m_dt. This view allows us to view the data sorted by the employee's last name, and to trim off any records where the employee has not earned any bonus. The private function `BuildTable` actual creates the m_dt `DataTable`.

```
    // Create a view over the merge-to data table
    private bool _ViewDataSet()
    {
        // Load up the merge table
        BuildTable();

        // Create a view of the merge table that
        // filters of anybody who has gotten a bouns
        // and then sort the rows into alphabetical
        // order by last name. Show only the current rows.
        m_dv = new DataView(m_dt,
                        "TotalBonus > 0.0",
                        "Last",
```

```
                          DataViewRowState.CurrentRows);
        return(true);
    }
```

BuildTable creates a `DataTable` for storing the employee IDs, last names, and bonus amounts. We need to do this because there is no way for a single `DataView` or `DataViewManager` to combine columns from multiple `DataTables` into a view or single `DataTable`. Thus we get to dynamically build a `DataTable` with the data we want. We just saw how the view was overlaid on this table.

```
// Builds a merge-to table from EmpList and BonusInfo
// Both of those tables are already in the dataset
private bool BuildTable()
{
    // drw is the current row in the EmpList DataTable
    // id is current EmployeeID
    DataRow drw;
    string id;
    decimal total_bonus = 0;
```

The first step is to create an empty table called `Bonus` to work with. Don't worry about the name possibly colliding with the `Bonus` `DataTable` in the `DataSet`, as these two `DataTables` will not be added to the same `DataSet`.

```
// Create a merge-to table called BonusInfo
m_dt = new DataTable("Bonus");
```

Next, we define the columns we want to use, specifying the data types desired and defining a primary key based on the employee ID.

```
// Create a new column called EmpID of type string
// and make it the primary key for this table
m_dt.Columns.Add("EmpID");
m_dt.Columns["EmpID"].DataType = System.Type.GetType("System.String");
m_dt.Constraints.Add("PK_BonusInfo",m_dt.Columns["EmpID"],true);
// Create another string-based column to hold
// the employee's last name
m_dt.Columns.Add("Last");
m_dt.Columns["Last"].DataType = System.Type.GetType("System.String");

// Add a column to hold the total
// bonuses paid and integer
m_dt.Columns.Add("TotalBonus");
m_dt.Columns["TotalBonus"].DataType =
                            System.Type.GetType("System.Int32");
```

All that is left to do is add the rows to the `DataTable`. We do this by walking through each of the rows of the employee, adding the employee ID and last name to the working row. We then need to iterate through each of the rows of the bonus table to find rows where the employee IDs match. When they are found, they are added to an accumulator. Finally, we just roll the total bonus into a row and add the row to the `DataTable`.

```
// Iterate through the rows of the EmpList table
foreach(DataRow dre in m_ds.Tables["EmpList"].Rows)
{
    // Create a new working row
    drw = m_dt.NewRow();
    // Get the EmpID of the currently iterated employee
    // Put that value into our working row, then also insert
    // that employee's last name into the working row
    id = dre["EmpID"].ToString();
    drw["EmpID"] = id;
    drw["Last"] = dre["Last"].ToString();

    // Reset the total bonus
    total_bonus = 0.0M;
    // Iterate through the rows of the bonus table
    foreach(DataRow drb in m_ds.Tables["Bonus"].Rows)
    {
        // was this bonus paid to the current employee?
        // If so, add it to the total_bonus amount, or
        // add zero if no bonus was paid
        if(drb["EmpID"].ToString() == id)
            total_bonus += (drb["BonusMoney"] != DBNull.Value ?
                            Convert.ToDecimal(drb["BonusMoney"]) : 0);
    }
    // Insert the total bonus into the current working row
    drw["TotalBonus"] = total_bonus;
    // Add the working row to the merge table
    m_dt.Rows.Add(drw);
}
return(true);
}
```

When executed, all of this code produces a run-time form like this:

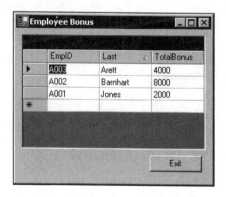

Granted, the code behind this Windows form could have been much simpler if we were not using it to demonstrate how to use almost all of the objects of ADO.NET. We have seen how to create a `DataTable` from `DataRows` and `DataColumns`. We have also seen how to load into a `DataTable` using a `DataAdapter`. Finally, we have seen how to create and use a `DataView` as a way to sort and filter data down to meet business requirements. However, there is more left to discuss.

117

XML, Schemas, and ADO.NET

Unless you are still programming on punch cards, chances are good that you have at least heard of XML – the Extensible Markup Language. Simply put, XML is a flexible, self-describing way to communicate and persist information. XML strives to be completely platform-neutral, meaning that if an XML file is generated on a PC we should be able to expose that file on an Solaris Web Server and perhaps let it be read by a IBM/390 mainframe as input for some process. The important thing is not what platform does the work, rather, that they can all use and "understand" the data in exactly the same way. Once that data is exposed, any process that can load and parse the file should also be able to use it. If you can imagine how many times you have written programs to load up comma-delimited or otherwise formatted files, you can understand just how useful XML can be.

It would fair to say that without XML and Schemas, ADO.NET probably would be much different from how we have come to know it today. In fact, ADO.NET was designed from the ground up to unify database access with XML from the data access point of view. In the past, developers and architects had to make a choice between using ADO or XML as their data media (or least, you had to either write a lot of code or work with awkwardly structured XML if you wanted to use both).

In Chapters 7 and 8, we take a more in-depth look at XML and the interplay between XML and ADO.NET in the .NET Framework. What we will cover here is:

❑   A brief introduction to Schemas, in particular the World Wide Web Consortium (W3C) standard for XML schemas commonly know as XSD

❑   Persisting a `DataSet` as an XML stream

❑   Loading a `DataSet` from an XML stream

❑   Using the `XSD.exe` tool to generate a data access class

Schemas and XSD

Psychologists frequently define a schema as "a pattern imposed on complex reality or experience to assist in explaining it, mediate perception, or guide response". Schemas in the XML context have almost the same meaning. In that context, a schema can be used to answer the question "How is this data structured, what does it mean, and how does it interrelate?" This kind of information is absolutely critical if XML is going to be used by any process on any system, because if you do not know how the data should be presented or how the data should be interpreted, you are probably doomed to struggle to use it. But, by referencing and validating an XML document against its schema, you can be assured that the data structure is as expected.

A problem, however, is that it took a while for the Internet community to agree on exactly what the schema for XML schemas should be and how it should work. The culmination of that work to date is something known as the "XML Schemas recommendation". This work defines a standard format on how a schema for XML should be. That specific format for a schema is commonly known by its file extension – XSD.

Both XML and XSD are commonly though of as being generalized tree structures. A well-formed XML document contains exactly one root element and as many child elements as needed. Both the root and the child nodes may also contain attributes, which act as informational nodes on an element. In an XML document, data is represented as elements and attributes. In a schema, the data type, occurrences, limitations, and names of elements in the XML document are represented as elements. An example should make this a bit clearer.

An XML representation of the of `EmpList` table from the `ProTest` database would be:

```xml
<?xml version="1.0" encoding="UTF-8"?>
<employees>
    <employee empID="A001" last="Jones" dept="IT" salary="5000"/>
    <employee empID="A002" last="Barnhart" dept="Sales" salary="4000"/>
    <employee empID="A003" last="Arett" dept="Marketing" salary="3000"/>
    <employee empID="A004" last="Shinohara" dept="Clerical" salary="2000"/>
</employees>
```

While the schema for this file would be:

```xml
<?xml version="1.0" encoding="UTF-8"?>
<xs:schema xmlns:xs="http://www.w3.org/2001/XMLSchema">
    <xs:element name="employee">
        <xs:complexType>
            <xs:attribute name="empID" type="xs:string" use="required"/>
            <xs:attribute name="last" type="xs:string" use="required"/>
            <xs:attribute name="dept" type="xs:string" use="required"/>
            <xs:attribute name="salary" type="xs:positiveInteger"
                                                    use="required"/>
        </xs:complexType>
    </xs:element>
    <xs:element name="employees">
        <xs:complexType>
            <xs:sequence>
                <xs:element ref="employee" maxOccurs="unbounded"/>
            </xs:sequence>
        </xs:complexType>
    </xs:element>
</xs:schema>
```

ADO.NET is rather ingenious about using XML and schemas. Internally, a `DataRow` can be considered as being an element in an XML document, while a `DataColumn` holds schema information. One of the ways ADO.NET exposes XML functionality is with XML generating and consuming methods on the `DataSet` class. These methods include:

❑ `GetXML`: Provides the `DataSet` as a string

❑ `GetSchema`: Provides the XSD schema of the `DataSet` in a string

❑ `InferXmlSchema`: Computes an XSD schema from a given file

❑ `ReadXml`: Loads an XML file or a string into a `DataSet`

❑ `ReadXmlSchema`: Loads a schema from a file or string into a `DataSet`

❑ `WriteXml`: Persists the `DataSet` into an XML file to a stream, `TextWriter`, or `XmlWriter`

❑ `WriteXmlSchema`: Persists the schema for the `DataSet` into an stream, `TextWriter`, or `XmlWriter`

Persisting XML to a Stream

Let us take a quick look at saving a `DataSet` out to file for future use. This will get us into some new C# features. The `WriteXML` method has seven interesting overloaded signatures.

Method Signature	Description
`WriteXml(Stream)`	Saves the current data and schema for the `DataSet` using the given `System.IO.Stream`
`WriteXml(string)`	Saves the current data and schema for the `DataSet` to a file using the path and file name in the string parameter
`WriteXml(TextWriter)`	Saves the current data and schema for the `DataSet` to a file using the given `TextWriter`
`WriteXml(XmlWriter)`	Saves the current data and schema for the `DataSet` to a file using the given `XmlWriter`
`WriteXml(Stream, XmlWriteMode)`	Saves the current data and/or schema for the `DataSet` using the given `System.IO.Stream`, determined by the `XmlWriteMode`
`WriteXml(string, XmlWriteMode)`	Saves the current data and/or schema for the `DataSet` to a file using the path and file name in the string parameter, determined by the `XmlWriteMode`
`WriteXml(TextWriter, XmlWriteMode)`	Saves the current data and/or schema for the `DataSet` to a file using the given `TextWriter`, determined by the `XmlWriteMode`

- ❑ Streams are instances of `System.IO.Stream`. The stream abstract class provides a generic sequence of bytes. Streams are the base class for `NetworkStreams` (copies a stream for network access), `FileStreams` (writes to a disk file), and `CryptoStreams` (copies a stream to an encrypted stream).

- ❑ `TextWriter` is an instance of a character-oriented stream. Such streams can be directed to strings, HTTP Responses, and `HTMLTextWriters` to ASP.NET Server controls.

- ❑ `XmlWriter` is a fast, generator of streams or files of XML.

`XmlWriteMode` is an enumeration providing behaviors for the `WriteXml` method. The members of this enumeration include:

Enumeration Value	Description
`DiffGram`	Writes the entire `DataSet`, including original and current values, as a `DiffGram`
`IgnoreSchema`	Writes the all of the existing current rows of the `DataSet` as an XML document without an embedded XSD schema
`WriteSchema`	Writes the all of the existing current rows of the `DataSet` as an XML document with the relations as an embedded XSD schema

> **DiffGrams are XML serializations that include the original and current data of an element, and a unique key. This key ties the original and current versions of the data to each other. DiffGrams are primarily used for transmitting the changed data in a `DataSet` over network connection it can be updated and persisted. SQL Server 2000 can consume DiffGrams as well.**

Let us take a quick look at an example of some code that uses the `WriteXml` method to persist a `DataSet` to a file. We will start with yet another Console Application. To keep things simple, we will copy the `LoadDataSet()` from the `DataAccessClass.cs` file, used in the `DataView` example, into this file. Our `Main` function can be as simple as:

```
static void Main(string[] args)
{
    Console.WriteLine("Starting...");

    // Load the data from the server into the DataSet
    m_ds = new DataSet("EmpInfo");

    if(LoadDataSet())
    {
        // Show the row count for each table
        foreach(DataTable dt in m_ds.Tables)
        {
            Console.WriteLine("There are {0} rows in table {1}.",
                                            dt.Rows.Count,dt.TableName);
        }

        // write just the data out from the data set
        m_ds.WriteXml(@"c:\inetpub\wwwroot\protest.xml",
                                        XmlWriteMode.IgnoreSchema);

        // write out the schema for schema for the data set
        m_ds.WriteXmlSchema(@"c:\inetpub\wwwroot\protest.xsd");

        // write out the schema for schema for the data set
        m_ds.WriteXml(@"c:\inetpub\wwwroot\protest_complete.xml",
                            XmlWriteMode.WriteSchema);
    }
    // Let the user see the row count
    Console.WriteLine("Files created, press Enter to continue.");
    Console.ReadLine();
}
```

You might be asking, "Why are we writing the XML files to that location – into the typical root of the the default Web site?" Easy enough: so we can demonstrate how to pull a saved `DataSet` over the network and into a client application. It is "cool" that generating XML and XSD files is so easy. But what is really helpful is that you can just as easily rebuild a `DataSet` using these files.

> You might be thinking about using the XSD file generated by the `WriteXmlSchema` method as a validation schema for the XML file generated by the `WriteXmlMethod`. Be careful – the XSD file generated is not always complete enough to be considered standalone! If the `DataSet` you are creating from contains primary keys, `WriteXmlSchema` will create the selector xpath such that it selects nodes improperly. To address this, just remove the "../" from the `xpath` attribute's value.

Loading XML from a Stream

Its should be fairly easy to correctly deduce that the `ReadXml` and `ReadXmlSchema` methods load up XML files into a `DataSet`.

Method Signature	Description
`ReadXml(Stream)`	Reads the data and schema in an XML document from a `System.IO.Stream` into the `DataSet`
`ReadXml(string)`	Reads the data and schema in an XML document from the given path and file into the `DataSet`
`ReadXml(TextReader)`	Reads the data and schema in an XML document from a `TextReader` into the `DataSet`
`ReadXml(XmlReader)`	Reads the data and schema in an XML document from an `XmlReader` into the `DataSet`
`ReadXml(Stream, XmlReadMode)`	Reads the data and schema in an XML document from a `System.IO.Stream` into the `DataSet` using the technique set by the `XmlReadMode` enumeration value
`ReadXml(string, XmlReadMode)`	Reads the data and schema in an XML document from the given path and file into the `DataSet` using the technique set by the `XmlReadMode` enumeration value
`ReadXml(TextReader, XmlReadMode)`	Reads the data and schema in an XML document from a `XmlReader` into the `DataSet` using the technique set by the `XmlReadMode` enumeration value

The `XmlReadMode` is a bit more complex than the `XmlWriteMode`, but is still fairly easy to grasp.

Enumeration Value	Description
Auto	Selects the most appropriate from DiffGram, ReadSchema or InferSchema, as described in the following sections.
DiffGram	Treats the XML document as a DiffGram and applies updates. It is strongly suggested that you use this mode when XML documents generated using the WriteXml function.
Fragment	Used with XDR schemas fragements, like those generated by the various FOR XML SQL statements.
IgnoreSchema	Reads data into the existing DataSet schema, ignoring any schemas explictly or implicity defined by the XML document.
InferSchema	Infers a schema from the data, and loads the data, ignoring any schema embedded into the XML document. Any existing schema for the DataSet is extended to best fit the presented data.
ReadSchema	Reads and loads the data, and any inline schemas.

For our sample client application (LoadXML.sln in the downloads), we have started with a C# Windows application with a single DataGrid and two buttons. One of the buttons will be used to exit the application, while the other button allows us to scroll through the DataTables of the downloaded DataSet. When running, it looks like this:

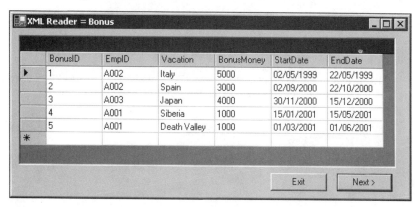

Assuming that you are using Visual Studio .NET, start a new C# Windows Form project, then complete the following tasks:

❑ Resize the form, drag a DataGrid and two buttons on the form, and shape them as seen above

❑ Rename the form frmMain and change its Text property to XML Reader

❑ Rename the left-hand button btnExit and change its Text property to Exit

❑ Rename the right-hand button btnNext and change its Text property to Next >

❑ Rename the DataGrid to dgViewer

❑ Add using System.Net; before the first namespace declaration

Following the frmMain class declaration, add the following variable declarations:

```
private int currentTable = 0;
DataSet ds = new DataSet("EmpInfo");
```

The currentTable variable tracks which table is currently being reviewed, while the ds instance of DataSet accommodates our working DataSet.

Here is the frmMain_Load event handler. It does most of the work for this little application.

```
private void frmMain_Load(object sender, System.EventArgs e)
{
    // temporary file name to hold the downloaded XML
    string filename;
```

We create an instance of the System.Net.WebClient class to use. This object provides a simple, easy-to-use HTTP client for programmatic use. In this case, we will take advantage of its DownloadFile method to fetch the complete DataSet XML document we created in the previous example program. To use it, we need to provide a file name to write to and the address of the desired URL to download. For our purpose, a temporary file will be just fine. We use an instance of the Guid class to generate the filename using the NewGuid method.

```
    // Create a new instance of WebClient to work with
    WebClient wc = new WebClient();
    // Get a temporary download file name
    filename = Guid.NewGuid() + ".xml";
    // Download the complete dataset file into the temporary file
    wc.DownloadFile("http://localhost/protest_complete.xml",filename);
```

Once we have downloaded the file, we can use the ReadXML method of our local DataSet to load up the data. We can then dispose of the temporary file and bind the first table to the DataGrid.

```
    // Load up the complete data set from the downloaded file
    ds.ReadXml(filename,XmlReadMode.ReadSchema);
    // purge the downloaded file
    System.IO.File.Delete(filename);
    // bind the downloaded file to the data grid
    dgViewer.DataSource = ds.Tables[currentTable];
}
```

Now double-click btnNext, and add the following code:

```
private void btnNext_Click(object sender, System.EventArgs e)
{
    // If we haven't seen all of the tables, show the next one
    // otherwise, show the first table
    if(currentTable < ds.Tables.Count -1) {
        currentTable++;
    } else {
        currentTable = 0;
    }
```

```
    // Update the data table binding and refresh it
    dgViewer.DataSource = ds.Tables[currentTable];
    dgViewer.Refresh();
    // Update the form caption and refresh it
    frmMain.ActiveForm.Text = "XML Reader = " +
                        ds.Tables[currentTable].TableName.ToString();
    frmMain.ActiveForm.Refresh();
}
```

This will enable the user to page through the tables in the DataSet. Finally, btnExit:

```
private void btnExit_Click(object sender, System.EventArgs e)
{
    // Exit the application
    Application.Exit();
}
```

As you can see, ADO.NET makes it easy to generate an XML document from a DataSet and to generate a DataSet from an XML document. Other parts of the .NET Framework make it very easy to do this with applications scaled over the Internet; powerful stuff indeed. There is one last tool we need to look at to round off our tour of how ADO.NET and XML function together.

The XML Schemas/DataTypes Support Utility Tool (xsd.exe)

An amazingly useful tool ships with the .NET Framework SDK – the XML Schemas/DataTypes support utility (commonly called by its filename, xsd.exe). This tool provides:

❑ XML-Data-Reduced Schema (XDR) to XSD schema conversions

❑ Schema inference from an XML data file

❑ Schema generation from an assembly

❑ Class sourcecode from an XSD file

For developers, all of these options are helpful, but the last one particularly so because it generates what is known as a strongly-typed DataSet. These amount to class files that provide an object-oriented rather than DataSet-specific way to work with data. An example will probably help make that clear, so we will demonstrate one in a moment. The XDR to XSD feature is handy if you made use of the early XDR standard for schemas. The schema inference feature works as does DataSet.ReadXmlSchema using the XmlReadSchema.InferSchema enumeration, followed by a call to the WriteXmlSchema method. The schema generation process is a bit more complex as it uses reflection to analyze the assembly, but the result is generally the same.

If you want to use this tool to generate a class file for a "strongly-typed" DataSet class, all you need do is "feed" xsd.exe a valid W3C schema file, specify that you want a strongly-typed DataSet class (in C#, of course) and a namespace. The option for DataSet output is "/d," for C# is "/l:cs" and "/n:" followed by the namespace desired. So, if we wanted a strongly-typed DataSet for the ProTest database generated by the WriteXmlSchema method previously seen, and we want to that use the namespace "," all we would need to do is:

```
xsd /d /l:cs /n:StronglyTypedDemo
```

You can do this same thing by adding the schema file to your project, then opening it in the XML Schema Editor. Once you have the file opened, right-click in any empty area of the edit window and choose **Generate DataSet**. Could it get much simpler?

Putting It All Together

To close up this chapter, let us take a look a fully-featured application that:

❑ Loads data into a strongly-typed `DataSet` using `DataAdapters`. If an `SqlException` occurs, the application captures the error information to a file for future use. This also gives us a chance to look at `XmlTextWriter`.

❑ Binds Windows Forms controls to a table within the strongly-typed `DataSet`. We will be using the `EmpList` table from `ProTest` for this example.

❑ Uses other Window Forms controls (namely, the button control) to navigate about the bound `DataSet`.

❑ Allows the addition, updating, and removal of data in the `DataSet` with some validation built in.

❑ Persists the final state of the `DataSet` back to its data source, also catching any errors.

All of the code for this example can be found in the download code available from www.wrox.com. We will review the more interesting aspects here.

SqlErrorPersister.cs

We start by defining a class for the capture of `SqlExceptions` to an XML file. We do this for a couple of reasons:

❑ It allows us to persist the record for future use in troubleshooting

❑ It gives us a chance to look at the `XmlTextWriter` class

The `XmlTextWriter` is an easy way to write information to a stream (such as a file) using XML, without having to construct a Document Object Model instance, add nodes to that, and persist to a file. Using an `XmlTextWriter` to dump information to disk file as an XML document is great, providing the information is written sequentially; catching and recording information about errors fits that description nicely. The file `SqlErrorPersister` defines the `Util.SqlErrorPersister` namespace. There are two classes in that namespace:

❑ `SqlErrorPersister`, where the code to write the file exists

❑ `SqlErrorPersisterAppInfo`, a property-bag class that holds information about the run-time enviroment of the application that we want to persist

As classes should, `SqlErrorPersister` starts off by defining the imported classes to be used and the namespace for the embedded classes:

```
using System;
using System.Data;
using System.Data.SqlClient;
using System.Xml;
using System.IO;
using System.Windows.Forms;


namespace Util.SqlErrorPersister
{
```

The first class we define holds information about the application using it and its run-time context. These are the same properties that System.Windows.Forms.ActiveForm holds.

```
public class SqlErrorPersisterAppInfo
{
    private string _CompanyName;
    private string _CurrentCulture;
    private string _CurrentInputLanguage;
    private string _ExecutablePath;
    private string _ProductName;
    private string _ProductVersion;
    private string _StartUpPath;

    public string CompanyName
    {
        set { _CompanyName = value; }
        get { return _CompanyName; }
    }
    public string CurrentCulture
    {
        set { _CurrentCulture = value; }
        get { return _CurrentCulture; }
    }
    public string CurrentInputLanguage
    {
        set { _CurrentInputLanguage = value; }
        get { return _CurrentInputLanguage; }
    }
    public string ExecutablePath
    {
        set { _CurrentInputLanguage = value; }
        get { return _CurrentInputLanguage; }
    }
    public string ProductName
    {
        set { _ProductName = value; }
        get { return _ProductName; }
    }
    public string ProductVersion
    {
        set { _ProductVersion = value; }
        get { return _ProductVersion; }
```

```
        }
    public string StartUpPath
    {
        set { _StartUpPath = value; }
        get { return _StartUpPath; }
    }
}
```

The next class, `SqlErrorPersister`, defines a single method called `SaveErrorToFile`. This method expects a `SqlException` to be passed in, along with a completed instance of `SqlErrorPersisterAppInfo`:

```
public void SaveErrorToFile(SqlException sqle,
                            SqlErrorPersisterAppInfo App)
{
```

Creating an `XmlTextWriter` object is fairly easy, as you simply put the path and filename where you want your results to go, along with an enumeration that describes the data encoding within the document. In this case, we find out where the application is running, and work back up to the top-level directory for our file location. We also use the standard UTF-8 encoding for this file.

```
// Create a new XmlTextWriter that writes an
// XML file containing the encountered errors.
// Create this file in the root of the drive where
// this application was run from and call it sqlerror.xml
XmlTextWriter xtw =new XmlTextWriter(
                Directory.GetDirectoryRoot(
                Directory.GetCurrentDirectory()) +
                "sqlerrors.xml",
                System.Text.Encoding.UTF8);
```

The `WriteStartDocument` actually writes the standard `<?xml version="1.0" ?>` heading to the file. The standard `standalone` attribute is controlled by the boolean value passed to the function.

```
// Write what we know about the application runtime
// including then the exception occurred.
xtw.WriteStartDocument(true);
```

Now we can write the root node element and use its attributes to record the information passed along about the run-time context. The `WriteAttributeString` makes this very easy to do.

```
xtw.WriteStartElement("errors");
xtw.WriteAttributeString("companyName", App.CompanyName);
xtw.WriteAttributeString("currentCulture", App.CurrentCulture);
xtw.WriteAttributeString("currentInputLanguage",
                    App.CurrentInputLanguage);
xtw.WriteAttributeString("executablePath", App.ExecutablePath);
xtw.WriteAttributeString("productName", App.ProductName);
xtw.WriteAttributeString("productVersion", App.ProductVersion);
xtw.WriteAttributeString("startupPath", App.StartUpPath);
```

One hairy bit is that we probably should record when the error occurred. The following bit of code writes the current system time to the XML file in a format consistent with the W3C Schema definition for xs:dateTime.

```
// Save the time the event occured using the
// current system time using universal time format
xtw.WriteAttributeString("occurredAt",
                System.DateTime.Now.GetDateTimeFormats('u')[0]);
```

Now we can start walking through each of the exceptions nested into the SqlException we have been handed. Each instance of an exception found starts a new element called instance.

```
// Walk through first exception and all of
// exceptions nested with it.
while(sqle != null)
{
    // Put each exception in an instance
    xtw.WriteStartElement("instance");
```

Recall that the actual errors provided by SQL Server are stored in the Error collection of the SqlException. It is rather easy to iterate through these adding them to our error file. Each error generates a new error element and the details about that error are written as attributes.

```
// For each SQL error collected in the exception
foreach(SqlError err in sqle.Errors)
{
    // Create an attribute for field in
    // in the error caught
    xtw.WriteStartElement("sqlerror");
    xtw.WriteAttributeString("lineNumber",
                            err.LineNumber.ToString());
    xtw.WriteAttributeString("message", err.Message.ToString());
    xtw.WriteAttributeString("number",err.Number.ToString());
    xtw.WriteAttributeString("procedure",
                            err.Procedure.ToString());
    xtw.WriteAttributeString("server",err.Server.ToString());
    xtw.WriteAttributeString("source",err.Source.ToString());
    xtw.WriteAttributeString("state",err.State.ToString());
```

To keep the document well formed, we need to close the current error element; this is done with WriteEndElement.

```
    xtw.WriteEndElement();
}
```

And then we can close off the current instance and move on to the next.

```
    // Close off the current instance
    xtw.WriteEndElement();
    // Get the next exception
    sqle = (SqlException)(sqle.InnerException);
}
```

Finally, we can close the errors element and finish up the document. Calling the `Close()` method causes the document to be written to disk.

```
        // Close the errors element and then the document
        xtw.WriteEndElement();
        xtw.WriteEndDocument();
        xtw.Close();
    }
  }
```

If we mistakenly refer to "EmpID" as "EmpList", the XML file generated is (here formatted for readability):

```
<?xml version="1.0" encoding="utf-8" standalone="yes"?>
<errors companyName="StronglyTypedDemo" currentCulture="en-US"
        currentInputLanguage="System.Windows.Forms.InputLanguage"
        executablePath="C:\Documents and Settings\kent\Desktop\592x\chap4
                       \StronglyTypedDemo\bin\Debug\StronglyTypedDemo.exe"
        productName="StronglyTypedDemo" productVersion="1.0.670.40820"
        startupPath="C:\Documents and Settings\kent\Desktop\592x\chap4\
                                      StronglyTypedDemo\bin\Debug"
        occurredAt="2001-11-01 22:42:35Z">
    <instance>
        <sqlerror lineNumber="1" message="Invalid column name 'EmpList'."
            number="207" procedure="" server="ORAC"
            source=".Net SqlClient Data Provider" state="3"/>
    </instance>
</errors>
```

ProTest.cs

This file is generated by either the Visual Studio UI or by the `xsd.exe` tool. We did not need to make any customizations to this file, so we will not review any of it here.

frmMain.cs

This is a rather lengthy file, just over 700 lines, so we will not look at all of it here. We will, however, look at the parts we had to add or otherwise customize.

Since this is a standard Windows Forms project, the only additional namespaces we need to import are:

```
using System.Data.SqlClient;
using Util.SqlErrorPersister;
```

In the `frmMain` class, we need to define the following items as they are used throughout the class:

```
// Letter starting all EmpID fields
const string EmpIDPrefix = "A";
// Working storage for the strongly-typed dataset
private EmpInfo empInfo;
```

```
// Stack of EmpIDs to be deleted
private System.Collections.Stack deletes;
// DataBinding manager for the form
private BindingManagerBase bmEmpList;
// Tracks the last EmpID value value used.
private int lastBaseEmpID = -1;
```

One of the things we need to manually keep track of is what value of `EmpID` should be used for newly added records. In order to make sure we are starting off in the right place, we need to find the highest numeric portion of the employee's ID. This function walks through each of the IDs looking for that. When a higher value that the current value is found, the class level tracker for that value is updated.

```
private bool FindNextEmpID()
{
    int current;
    string working;

    foreach(DataRow dr in empInfo.EmpList.Rows)
    {
        working = dr["EmpID"].ToString();
        working = working.Substring(1,3);
        current = Convert.ToInt16(working);
        lastBaseEmpID = (current > lastBaseEmpID ? current : lastBaseEmpID);
    }
    return true;
}
```

The movement of data from the server into the strongly-typed `DataSet` is accomplished by the `LoadDataSet` function.

```
private bool LoadDataSet(EmpInfo empInfo)
{
```

To start with, we use some well-worn code based on a `DataAdapter` to load up the current recordset. When it comes time to update the data source later, we will actually not use a `DataAdapter`. Instead, we will scroll sequentially through the records and execute individual SQL commands. We do this purely for the purposes of demonstration:

```
    try
    {
        // Create a DataAdapter instance to load up the EmpList table
        // then fill the empList.EmpList table with the results.
        SqlDataAdapter daEmpInfo = new SqlDataAdapter(
                "SELECT EmpID,Last,Dept,Salary FROM EmpList",
                "Integrated Security=SSPI;Initial Catalog=ProTest;" +
                "Data Source=localhost;" );
        daEmpInfo.Fill(empInfo.EmpList);
        // Create a DataAdapter instance to load up the Bonus table
        // then fill the empList.Bonus table with the results.
        SqlDataAdapter daBonus = new SqlDataAdapter(
            "SELECT BonusID,EmpID,Vacation,BonusMoney,StartDate,EndDate " +
```

```
        "FROM Bonus", "Integrated Security=SSPI;" +
        "Initial Catalog=ProTest;Data Source=localhost;" );
    daBonus.Fill(empInfo.Bonus);
}
```

Hopefully, all will go well in the loading process, but if it does not, we should gracefully catch any exceptions and record them. Once recorded, we can explain to the user why our application is ending.

```
    // Catch any errors that might occur
catch(SqlException sqle)
{
    // Save them to a file
    SqlErrorPersister sqlep = new SqlErrorPersister();
    SqlErrorPersisterAppInfo appInfo = new SqlErrorPersisterAppInfo();

    appInfo.CompanyName = Application.CompanyName;
    appInfo.CurrentCulture = Application.CurrentCulture.ToString();
    appInfo.CurrentInputLanguage =
                        Application.CurrentInputLanguage.ToString();
    appInfo.ExecutablePath = Application.ExecutablePath;
    appInfo.ProductName = Application.ProductName;
    appInfo.ProductVersion = Application.ProductVersion;
    appInfo.StartUpPath = Application.StartupPath;
    sqlep.SaveErrorToFile(sqle,appInfo);

    // Show an error error message to the user
    MessageBox.Show("An error occured loading data. " +
                "See the sqlerrors.xml file in your system's " +
                "root directory for details.", "Aborted",
                MessageBoxButtons.OK, MessageBoxIcon.Error);
    return false;
}
```

If the data successfully loads, we can find the highest numeric part of an EmpID to work with.

```
    FindNextEmpID();
    return true;
}
```

Now let's spend a few moments looking at the code behind the actual form itself. When this program is run and the data is successfully loaded, we are presented a form that looks like the screenshot opposite. The texboxes are named, from top to bottom, EmpID, Last, Dept, and Salary. The Exit button will give the user the option to save changes:

The following function updates the navigation control buttons based on what row is currently being referenced.

```
private void UpdateButtons(object sender, EventArgs e)
{
    // Assume no buttons should be active
    btnRewind.Enabled = false;
    btnBack.Enabled = false;
    btnNew.Enabled = true;
    btnDelete.Enabled = false;
    btnNext.Enabled = false;
    btnEnd.Enabled = false;

    // If not at the initial row of the table,
    // we can allow a backwards scroll
    if(bmEmpList.Position > 0)
    {
        btnBack.Enabled = true;
        btnRewind.Enabled = true;
    }
    // If there are records left, we can
    // scroll forward
    if(bmEmpList.Position <   empInfo.EmpList.Rows.Count -1)
    {
        btnNext.Enabled = true;
        btnEnd.Enabled = true;
    }
    // If there are rows left in the table we can offer
    // the ability to delete the current row, but don't
    // the user remove all of the records
    if(empInfo.EmpList.Rows.Count > 1)
    {
        btnDelete.Enabled = true;
    }
}
```

The following functions are set up as event handlers for the click events on each button.

```
private void btnNext_Click(object sender, System.EventArgs e)
{
    // If not at the last row, scroll to the next
    bmEmpList.Position += (bmEmpList.Position < bmEmpList.Count -1 ? 1 : 0);
}

private void btnBack_Click(object sender, System.EventArgs e)
{
    // If not at the first row, scroll back
    bmEmpList.Position -= (bmEmpList.Position > 0 ? 1 : 0);
}

private void btnRewind_Click(object sender, System.EventArgs e)
{
    // Go to the first row
    bmEmpList.Position = 0;
}

private void btnEnd_Click(object sender, System.EventArgs e)
{
    // Go to the last row
    bmEmpList.Position = empInfo.EmpList.Rows.Count -1;
}
```

The click events for the **OK**, delete, and add buttons are a bit more complex. The **OK** click handler prompts the user if they want to save the data. If so, the handler calls the `SaveDataSet` function, which we'll see in a bit. Finally, it ends the application.

```
private void btnOK_Click(object sender, System.EventArgs e)
{
    // Check of see if the user wants to update the
    // the database with the current DataSet or not.
    // If so, show a progress bar of that process
    if(DialogResult.OK == MessageBox.Show(frmMain.ActiveForm,
                                "Save changes first?",
                                "Exiting",
                                MessageBoxButtons.OKCancel,
                                MessageBoxIcon.Question))
    {
        bntOK.Visible = false;
        SaveDataSet();
    }
    // End
    Application.Exit();
}
```

The delete button click handler prompts the user before removing the current record. To make sure the record is also removed from the database (if the user choses to save their changes), we push the current `EmpID` onto the `deletes` stack. We also reposition the bound data to the first element, or if available, the previous element.

```
private void btnDelete_Click(object sender, System.EventArgs e)
{
    // Verify that the user wants to expunge this record and if
    // so, push the EmpID onto the deletes stack for processing
    // at exit, then drop the current row from the DataSet
    // ScrollBack as appropriate.
    if(DialogResult.OK == MessageBox.Show(frmMain.ActiveForm,
                        "Are you sure you want to delete this record?",
                        "Delete",
                        MessageBoxButtons.OKCancel,
                        MessageBoxIcon.Stop))
    {
        deletes.Push(empInfo.EmpList[bmEmpList.Position].EmpID);
        empInfo.EmpList.Rows[bmEmpList.Position].Delete();
        bmEmpList.Position = (bmEmpList.Position == 1 ? 0 :
                                        bmEmpList.Position - 1);
    }
}
```

Finally, our new button click handler just calls the NewRow function we will see shortly. There is no sense in writing the same code twice:

```
private void btnNew_Click(object sender, System.EventArgs e)
{
    // Just clone the record
    NewRow();
}
```

Let us now look at some of the code taking care of the data in the strongly-typed DataSet. The NewRow function asks the user to confirm that the new row to be added should be based on current data. If so, it detemines what the appropriate EmpID should be. We use the AddEmpListRow function from the strongly-typed DataSet to actually add the row. AddEmpListRow is essentially a sub-classing of the AddRow method of the regular DataRow method of a regular DataRow. Of course, our efforts to add a new EmpID might go awry, so just in case we try to add a value already in use, the user gets a warning.

```
private void NewRow()
{
    // Ask the user if they want to the current record
    // to the dataset.
    if(DialogResult.OK == MessageBox.Show(frmMain.ActiveForm,
                                "Use current data as a new record?",
                                "New",
                                MessageBoxButtons.OKCancel,
                                MessageBoxIcon.Question))
    {
        try
        {
            // Make sure the empID record is valid by generating it
            tbEmpID.Text = EmpIDPrefix +
                        (++lastBaseEmpID).ToString().PadLeft(3,'0');

            // Add the current textboxes as a new row
```

```
            // then make the new row the current row
            empInfo.EmpList.AddEmpListRow(tbEmpID.Text,
                                    tbLast.Text,tbDept.Text,
                                    Convert.ToInt16(tbSalary.Text));
            bmEmpList.Position = empInfo.EmpList.Rows.Count -1;
        }
        catch(ConstraintException ce)
        {
            // If this exception occurs, it probably means
            // that the user tried to add a new record wih
            // a primary that was already in use
            MessageBox.Show("That ID is already in use.",
                        "Error : cannot add record",
                        MessageBoxButtons.OK,
                        MessageBoxIcon.Hand);
        }
    }
    frmMain.ActiveForm.Refresh();
}
```

The NewRowEvent method is called when the EmpID is changed. We will see how this is done in a moment. It saves enough about the current EmpID to restore the record being cloned back to its original state once the flow is completed.

```
private void NewRowEvent(object sender, ConvertEventArgs cevent)
{
    int saveRow;
    string saveID;

    // Make sure not to overwrite the EmpID record on the current record
    // saving that information, then adding the new row, then updating
    // the cloned record
    saveRow = bmEmpList.Position;
    saveID = empInfo.EmpList[saveRow].EmpID;
    NewRow();
    empInfo.EmpList[saveRow].EmpID = saveID;
}
```

Finally, we can show how the DataSet is persisted back to the DataSource. We start by displaying a progress bar pbStatus.

```
private bool SaveDataSet()
{
    // Show the progess bar
    pbStatus.Visible = true;
    pbStatus.Minimum = 0;
    pbStatus.Maximum = empInfo.EmpList.Count + deletes.Count;
```

Here we create a connection back to the data source and a command to operate on it:

```
    // Prepare a new connection and command for use
    SqlConnection conn = new SqlConnection(
```

```
                    "Integrated Security=SSPI;Initial Catalog=ProTest;" +
                    "Data Source=localhost;");
    SqlCommand cmd = new SqlCommand();
```

Then we open the connection, bind our command to it, and set the command type to dynamic SQL:

```
    // Open the connection and bind it the command.
    // Define that we will be using text commands.
    conn.Open();
    cmd.Connection = conn;
    cmd.CommandType = CommandType.Text;
```

Next we set the up a transaction that will prevent other processes from updating our data while we are working with it. We then can bind that transaction to the current command set.

```
    // Create a serialized transaction. This prevents
    // concurrent updates to the data we want to update,
    // then bind our command to that tranaction
    SqlTransaction trns = conn.BeginTransaction(IsolationLevel.Serializable);
    cmd.Transaction = trns;
```

Now we can look at each row in the `DataTable` in series. If it is new row, we will set up and issue a SQL INSERT command to add it to the table. If it is changed data, it's simply a matter of using an SQL UPDATE command instead.

```
    try
    {
        // examine each of rows in the table
        foreach(EmpInfo.EmpListRow row in empInfo.EmpList.Rows)
        {
            switch(row.RowState)
            {
                // If the row is a new row, try add it to the datatatbase
                case DataRowState.Added :
                    cmd.CommandText =
                        "INSERT INTO emplist(empid,last,dept,salary) VALUES (" +
                        "'" + row.EmpID.ToString() + "'," +
                        "'" + row.Last.ToString() + "'," +
                        "'" + row.Dept.ToString() + "'," +
                        row.Salary.ToString() + ")";
                    cmd.ExecuteNonQuery();
                    break;
                // If the row is an update row, try to update it in the db.
                case DataRowState.Modified :
                    cmd.CommandText = "UPDATE emplist SET " +
                        "last='" + row.Last + "'," +
                        "dept='" + row.Dept + "'," +
                        "salary=" + row.Salary + " " +
                        " WHERE empid = '" + row.EmpID + "'";
                    cmd.CommandType = CommandType.Text;
                    cmd.ExecuteNonQuery();
```

```
              break;
          default :
              break;
      }
      // Update the progress bar
      pbStatus.Value += 1;
  }
```

Next, we can issue a SQL DELETE command for each of the deleted IDs. Yes, we may be trying to remove IDs that were created and removed from our DataSet – remember this is just an example!

```
      // process the stack of deletes
      while(deletes.Count > 0)
      {
          cmd.CommandText = "delete from emplist where EmpID = '" +
                                                deletes.Pop() + "'";

          cmd.ExecuteNonQuery();
          pbStatus.Value += 1;
      }
```

With all of the records added, updated, or removed, we can commit them to the data source through the transaction.

```
      // All done, so commit these changes
      trns.Commit();
  }
```

Since errors might occur, let us catch them if they do, and save them to a file for future analysis.

```
  catch(SqlException sqle)
  {
      // Save them to a file
      SqlErrorPersister sqlep = new SqlErrorPersister();
      SqlErrorPersisterAppInfo appInfo = new SqlErrorPersisterAppInfo();

      appInfo.CompanyName = Application.CompanyName;
      appInfo.CurrentCulture = Application.CurrentCulture.ToString();
      appInfo.CurrentInputLanguage =
                          Application.CurrentInputLanguage.ToString();
      appInfo.ExecutablePath = Application.ExecutablePath;
      appInfo.ProductName = Application.ProductName;
      appInfo.ProductVersion = Application.ProductVersion;
      appInfo.StartUpPath = Application.StartupPath;
      sqlep.SaveErrorToFile(sqle,appInfo);

      // Show an error error message to the user
      MessageBox.Show("An error occured saving data. " +
                  "No changes were saved. See the sqlerrors.xml file " +
                  "in your system's root directory for details.",
                  "Aborted",
                  MessageBoxButtons.OK,
```

```
                        MessageBoxIcon.Error);
        return false;
    }
```

Lastly, we need to close the relatively resource-expensive database connection.

```
    finally
    {
        // Close the connection so that the resources it uses
        // can be returned for use elsewhere
        conn.Close();
    }
    return true;
}
```

In the `ChangeSalaryEvent`, we need to implement a couple of business rules:

❑   Nobody can have a negative salary

❑   The salary amount must be a valid integer

If the user enters a non-numeric character into the salary control textbox, the value will not be converted to an integer and a `FormatException` is thrown. We also need to check and prevent the user from entering too high a salary amount (more than 65,535).

```
// Capture any changes to the salary
private void ChangeSalaryEvent(object sender, ConvertEventArgs cevent)
{
    // Save the current salary... just in case
    int salary_was = empInfo.EmpList[bmEmpList.Position].Salary;

    // Did the textbox value change
    try
    {
        if(Convert.ToInt16(tbSalary.Text) < 0)
        {
            tbSalary.Text = "0";
        }
    }
    catch(FormatException fe)
    {
        // If this exception occurs, the user probably
        // entered a text value for a salary
        MessageBox.Show("Sorry, thats not a valid salary.",
            "Error : Invalid salary",
            MessageBoxButtons.OK,
            MessageBoxIcon.Hand);
        tbSalary.Text = salary_was.ToString();
    }
    catch(OverflowException ofe)
    {
        // If this exception occurs, the user probably
```

```
        // entered a bad value for a salary
      MessageBox.Show("Sorry, thats not a valid salary.",
                     "Error : Invalid salary",
                     MessageBoxButtons.OK,
                     MessageBoxIcon.Hand);
      tbSalary.Text = int.MaxValue.ToString();
   }
   finally
   {
      empInfo.EmpList[bmEmpList.Position].Salary =
                                   Convert.ToInt16(tbSalary.Text);
      tbSalary.Refresh();
      frmMain.ActiveForm.Refresh();
   }
}
```

Finally, we can define our data bindings. We need an instance of the binding class to work with for some of the more complex bindings, where we need to take a validation action if the value changes.

```
private void EstablishDataBindings()
{
   // Working data bind
   Binding b;
```

For the Last Name and Department values, we really do not need to worry about the values the user may enter, so we can use simple bindings for these values. The constructor for a `DataBinding` asks for the type of control to bind to, the `DataSet` in which the data resides, and the column where the field is.

```
   // Add simple bindings for the last name and department
   tbLast.DataBindings.Add(new Binding("Text",empInfo,"EmpList.Last"));
   tbDept.DataBindings.Add(new Binding("Text",empInfo,"EmpList.Dept"));
```

When an employee ID changes, we want to treat that as a command to clone the current record. To accomplish that, we first bind the control to the data field, and then add an event handler for our function that codes the actual cloning. Once the binding is completely defined, we can add it to the collection of bindings on that control.

> **You must define any handlers for events before adding the binding to its host control or the handler will not be bound to the control.**

```
   // Add a binding that when the EmpID is changed,
   // a new row is added to the table (cloning)
   b = new Binding("Text",empInfo,"EmpList.EmpID");
   b.Parse += new ConvertEventHandler(NewRowEvent);
   tbEmpID.DataBindings.Add(b);
```

And the same process for the salary change to make sure we get valid data:

```
// Add an event to make a valid salary is entered.
b = new Binding("Text",empInfo,"EmpList.Salary");
b.Parse += new ConvertEventHandler(ChangeSalaryEvent);
tbSalary.DataBindings.Add(b);
```

We can associate the whole `BindingContext` between the strongly-typed `DataSet` and the `BindingManager`. The `BindingManager` is, in effect, the glue that holds records and controls together. Also, our function that updates the navigation control buttons needs to be assosciated to the `PositionChanged` event. This event occurs whenever we move between rows in the strongly-typed table. To make sure the buttons are in the right state when we first show the form, we call `UpdateButtons` before exiting.

```
// Bind the list of bindings the form
bmEmpList = this.BindingContext[empInfo,"EmpList"];
bmEmpList.PositionChanged += new EventHandler(UpdateButtons);
UpdateButtons();
}
```

To provide the users with some idea of how to use the form, we will add a number of tool tips to the controls on the form.

```
private void CreateTips()
{
    // Create the ToolTip and associate with the Form container.
    ToolTip tip1 = new ToolTip();

    // Set up the delays for the ToolTip.
    tip1.AutoPopDelay = 5000;
    tip1.InitialDelay = 1000;
    tip1.ReshowDelay = 500;
    // Force the ToolTip text to be displayed whether or not the
    // form is active.
    tip1.ShowAlways = true;

    // Set up the ToolTip text for the Button and Checkbox.
    tip1.SetToolTip(this.btnRewind, "First Record");
    tip1.SetToolTip(this.btnBack, "Previous Record");
    tip1.SetToolTip(this.btnEnd, "Last Record");
    tip1.SetToolTip(this.btnNext, "Next Record");
    tip1.SetToolTip(this.btnNew, "Add as new record");
    tip1.SetToolTip(this.btnDelete, "Remove this record");
}
```

Last but certainly not least, we can write the form's load event handler. It starts by creating an instance of the strongly-typed `DataSet` and our stack of employee IDs to delete at exit. It then attempts to load the data from the data source to the `DataSet`. If that goes well, it binds the controls on the form to the data, and adds our tool tips.

```
private void frmMain_Load(object sender, System.EventArgs e)
{
    // Create a new instance of the typed DataSet
    // and a stack to track any deleted records
    empInfo = new EmpInfo();
```

```
      deletes =   new System.Collections.Stack();
      // Load the data from the server. If that fails, abort
      if(!LoadDataSet(empInfo))
      {
         Application.Exit();
      }
      // Establish DataBindings
      EstablishDataBindings();

      // Create tool tips.
      CreateTips();
   }
```

Summary

In this chapter you have seen the basics of working with data using ADO.NET. We discussed the differences between working with connected and disconnected data, using `DataReader` and `DataSet` respectively. We also discussed how XML is the underlying format for data within the `DataSet`, which can be saved to and read from an external file.

In addition, we discussed displaying data using data binding, which binds controls to a data source.

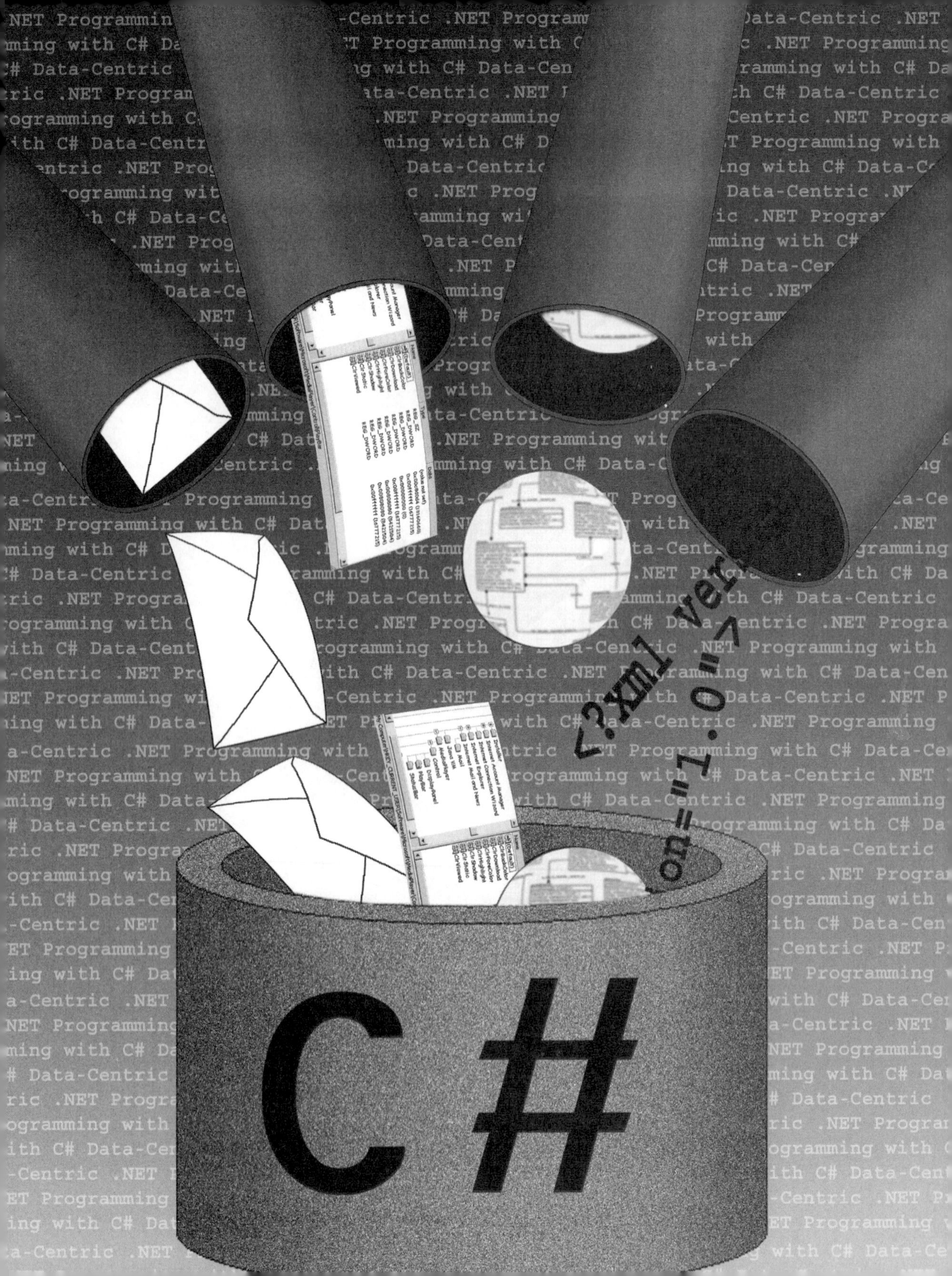

Data-Centric .NET Programming with C#
<?xml ver
on="1.0"?>
C#

ADO.NET and C# III: Data and VS

In the previous chapters, we went through the basics of connecting to data. In this chapter, we will be using those basic principles to build larger applications, using both Windows Forms and Web Forms.

Windows Forms provide an easy way to build GUI-based desktop applications. As you probably know, Web Forms are an extremely logical way to develop client browser-independent, server-side applications using a standard IDE, in this case, Visual Studio .NET.

The chapter concludes with an exploration of the Visual Studio .NET data environment, in order to see how quickly data-aware applications can be developed using the Visual Studio .NET tools.

Using the .NET DataGrid

Let's go ahead and take a look at the `DataGrid` control, a control re-engineered fresh for the .NET Framework. This control is based on previous data-bound grid controls. In the following example, we will explore many facets of using this control including:

- ❑ Data binding
- ❑ Setting the styles
- ❑ Adding and updating records

The `DataGrid` control also allows relations between tables to be defined and exposed. To be more precise, it is the `DataSet` that provides this functionality and that the `DataGrid` control binds to the `DataSet`. Thus the `DataGrid` benefits from the `DataSet`'s ability to define and allow relationhips between tables.

Like many other .NET controls, there are two variants of the `DataGrid` control. One class is found in the `System.Windows.Forms` namespace, and the other in the `System.Web.UI.WebControls` namespace. We will look at both classes.

As you undoubtedly know, the Windows Forms `DataGrid` class is for programming standard executable programs, whereas the Web Controls `DataGrid` class will be rendered into HTML and is populated on the server side.

Getting Started with the Windows Forms DataGrid

Let's get started with the Windows Forms `DataGrid`. First off, we need to know how to actually make a simple connection to a data source. The `DataGrid` only has the default constructor, which takes no parameters. All properties are set and all methods are called after instantiation of the `DataGrid`.

Displaying Data from a Table

A `DataGrid` can be bound to several different data sources, including:

❑ `DataTable`, and a `DataTable` in a `DataSet`. Tables in a strongly-typed `DataSet` can also be used.

❑ `DataView`, which is used for sorting and filtering a `DataTable` without actually altering the underlying data.

❑ Single dimension arrays.

❑ Classes that implement `IListSource`, the actual interface that allows data binding to work.

❑ Classes that implement the `IList` interface, such as the `ArrayList`, the `ComboBox.ObjectCollection`, collections in the `ListBox`, `ListItem`, and `ListView` classes, `MenuItems`, `StringCollections`, and `TreeNodeCollections`.

A `DataGrid` has a number of style and formatting properties we can tweak programmatically to get the look we desire.

Property	Description
AlternatingBackColor	Alternating row's background color.
BackColor	The background color used for alternating rows.
BackgroundColor	The color between rows of the `DataGrid`.
BackgroundImage	A background image on the `DataGrid`.
BorderStyle	The `DataGrid`'s border style. Accepts a member of the `BorderStyle` enumeration. The choices are `Fixed3D`, `FixedSingle`, or `None`, and the default is `FixedSingle`.
CaptionBackColor	The background color of the `DataGrid`'s caption.
CaptionFont	The font of the `DataGrid`'s caption.

Property	Description
CaptionForeColor	The foreground color of the DataGrid's caption area.
CaptionText	Obviously the actual text of the caption in the DataGrid's window.
CaptionVisible	Lets you choose if the DataGrid's caption is visible or not.
ColumnHeadersVisible	Controls if the column headings are visible or not.
FlatMode	Allows you to choose if the DataGrid's display is flat.
Font	Chooses a font for the DataGrid.
ForeColor	The text color of the DataGrid.
GridLineColor	The color of the grid lines.
GridLineStyle	The style of the grid lines. This property takes a value from the DataGridLineStyle enumeration. The choices are None and Solid, where the default is Solid.
HeaderBackColor	Gets or sets the background color of all of the row and column headers.
HeaderFont	The font used for the DataGrid's headers.
HeaderForeColor	Text color for the DataGrid's headers.
LinkColor	The color for links in the DataGrid.
LinkHoverColor	The hover color for links in the DataGrid.
SelectionBackColor	The background color of selected cells.
SelectionForeColor	The text color of selected cells.

We will now look at a simple Windows Form application that fetches the authors table from the ubiquitous pubs database. In this example, we will be using the SQL Server version of this database to further demonstrate the use of the SQL Server .NET Data Provider. It also gives us an opportunity to see how to use Visual Studio .NET to create this application.

We will give the users the ability to view a table, or a view, and to sort the data of the authors table. We will also allow the user to filter the list by state, and to apply some styles. Here are the steps for creating this application. Please follow along, or download the source code from www.wrox.com for review.

Start by creating a new Windows Application called Wrox .ProCSharpData Chapter 5 Author Grid in the Visual Studio .NET and then follow these steps:

❑ In the Solutions Explorer, add the SqlErrorPersister.cs file from the example code of Chapter 4, and rename Form1.cs to frmMain.cs. In the code view of frmMain.cs, find and replace all instances of Form1 with frmMain and resave. Now add:

```
using Util.SqlErrorPersister;
```

as the last of the imported namespaces in that file. As we have detailed this class in the last chapter, we will not review it here again.

❑ Switch over to the design view of the form, and resize the form to be about 775 pixels wide by 300 pixels high.

❑ In the tool box, select the **Windows Forms** pallet.

❑ Add a `Main Menu` control to the form, and call it `menuMain`.

❑ In the first menu slot, add an item labelled **Connect** and change its name to `menuConnect`.

Under this menu, we will add the following items:

Name	Text
menuConnectTable	To Table
menuConnectView	To View
menuQuit	Quit

❑ Next to the **Connect** menu item, add a new menu item, **Sort**, and name it `menuSort`. Set its **Enabled** property to `false`.

Under the **Sort** menu, we will add the following items:

Name	Text
menuSortLast	By Last Name
menuSortFirst	By First Name
menuSortState	By State

❑ Next to the **Sort** menu item, add a new menu item as **Style** and name it `menuStyle`. Set its default **Enabled** property to `false`.

Under the **Style** menu, we will add the following items:

Name	Text
menuStyleGreenbar	Greenbar
menuStyleExecutive	Executive
menuStylePaper	Paper

❑ About five grid lines under the bottom edge of the main menu, add a `DataGrid` control to the form, about 750 wide by 200 pixels tall, then change the name of this to `gridMain` using the **Properties** sheet in the Visual Studio IDE.

❑ Add a `Label` to the form between the main menu and the data grid, and set its text property to **State:**, name this control `lbStateFilter`, and set **TextAlign** to `TopRight`. Set its default **Visibility** to `false`.

❑ Next to the label, add a `ComboBox` to the form and name it `cbStateFilter`. Again, set its default **Visibility** to `false`. Also set the `DropDownStyle` property to `DropDownList`.

We should now have a form that looks like this:

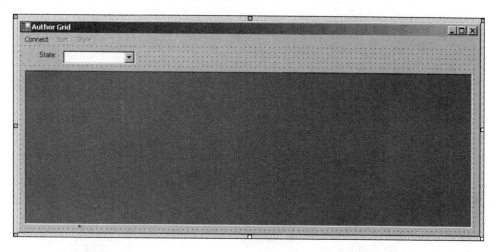

❑ Using the Solution Explorer, create a new **XML Schema (XSD)** file called `authors.xsd`, and add the following XML document as the contents of that document.

```xml
<?xml version="1.0" standalone="yes" ?>
<xs:schema id="AuthorsSet" xmlns=""
          xmlns:xs="http://www.w3.org/2001/XMLSchema"
          xmlns:msdata="urn:schemas-microsoft-com:xml-msdata">
   <xs:element name="AuthorsSet" msdata:IsDataSet="true">
      <xs:complexType>
         <xs:choice maxOccurs="unbounded">
            <xs:element name="Authors">
               <xs:complexType>
                  <xs:sequence>
                     <xs:element name="au_id" type="xs:string"
                                 minOccurs="0" />
                     <xs:element name="au_lname" type="xs:string"
                                 minOccurs="0" />
                     <xs:element name="au_fname" type="xs:string"
                                 minOccurs="0" />
                     <xs:element name="phone" type="xs:string"
                                 minOccurs="0" />
                     <xs:element name="address" type="xs:string"
                                 minOccurs="0" />
                     <xs:element name="city" type="xs:string"
                                 minOccurs="0" />
                     <xs:element name="state" type="xs:string"
                                 minOccurs="0" />
```

```
                            <xs:element name="zip" type="xs:string"
                                       minOccurs="0" />
                            <xs:element name="contract" type="xs:boolean"
                                       minOccurs="0" />
                        </xs:sequence>
                    </xs:complexType>
                </xs:element>
            </xs:choice>
        </xs:complexType>
    </xs:element>
</xs:schema>
```

❏   In the Visual Studio IDE, select **Generate DataSet** from the **Schema** menu. We now have a strongly-typed `DataSet` called `AuthorsSet` with a single `DataTable` called `Authors` to work with.

Note that you may find the code generated by **Generate DataSet** *does not actually appear in the Solution Explorer, check the Class View.*

Now comes the code! Add a new class file called `DataAccess.cs`; we'll walk through the code for the class in this file.

DataAccess.cs

We start this file with these imports:

```
using System;
using System.Data;
using System.Collections;
using System.Data.SqlClient;
using Util.SqlErrorPersister;
```

And we will change the namespace to:

```
namespace Wrox.ProCSharpData.Chapter5.AuthorGrid
{
    public class DataAccess
    {
```

This class will encapsulate a strongly-typed `DataSet` for the `authors` table of the `pubs` database, a view on that table for sorting and filtering, and an array list that will hold the list of distinct states in the table.

```
// Use the strongly-typed AuthorsSet DataSet
private AuthorsSet au_set;
// Announce that we will have a DataView called dv_authors,
// an array list called states_list and a string to hold
// the current state the dv_authors view will be filters on
// the string filter_state
private DataView dv_authors;
private ArrayList states_list;
private string filter_state;
```

This property provides access to the list of distinct states. We will eventually bind this to the cbStatesFilter on the main form.

```
// Returns the list of distinct states in the authors table
// This is bound to the cbStatesFilter on the frmMain
public ArrayList StatesList
{
    get { return states_list; }
}
```

This property provides access to the Authors table in the AuthorsSet. We will bind to this if **Connect | To Table** is requested.

```
// Returns the DataTable from the AuthorsSet
// This is bound to the gridMain if "To Table" is selected
public DataTable authors
{
    get { return au_set.Authors; }
}
```

This property provides access to the DataView superimposed on the Authors table. We will bind to this if **Connect | To View** is requested.

```
// Returns the DataView imposed on the authors table
// This is bound to the gridMain if "To View" is selected
public DataView authors_view
{
    get { return dv_authors; }
}
```

This function sets the sorting order for the DataView to the author's last name. This will be called when the **By Last Name** option is selected from the **Sort** menu.

```
// Orders the DataView by the Author's last name column.
// This function is called when the menuSortLast menu is selected
public void SortViewByLastName()
{
    dv_authors.Sort = "au_lname";
}
```

This function sets the sorting order for the DataView to the author's first name. This will be called when the **By First Name** option is selected from the **Sort** menu.

```
// Orders the DataView by the Author's first name column.
// This function is called when the menuSortFirst menu item is select
public void SortViewByFirstName()
{
    dv_authors.Sort = "au_fname";
}
```

This function sets the sorting order for the DataView to the author's state name. This will be called when the **By State** option is selected from the **Sort** menu.

```
// Orders the DataView by the Author's state column.
// This function is called when the menuSortState menu item is select
public void SortViewByState()
{
    dv_authors.Sort = "state";
}
```

This function sets the filtering for the `DataView` to the given state. This will be called when the state filter combobox option changes.

```
// In the DataView, filter out any state not matching the state
// passed into the function. If state was "*," no filtering occurs
public string SetStateToFilterOn(string FilterOnState)
{
    filter_state =   FilterOnState;
    if(filter_state != "*")
    {
        dv_authors.RowFilter = "state='" + filter_state.Trim() + "'";
    }
    else
    {
        dv_authors.RowFilter = "";
    }
    return(filter_state);
}
```

The bulk of the work in this class is done in the `LoadDataSet` function. It takes an instance of `SqlErrorPersisterAppInfo` as a parameter for use if needed.

```
// Loads data into the strongly type dataset
// the AppInfo parameter passed in provides information
// about the application at run time.
public bool LoadDataSet(SqlErrorPersisterAppInfo AppInfo)
{
```

Next, we define and create a few ADO.NET objects to work with. We will use a `DataReader`, `SqlConnection`, and `SqlCommand` to load a list of the distinct states into an `ArrayList`. We will also use a `DataAdapter` to fill the `Authors` table of the `Authors` set. We also set the default filtering to none.

```
// Announce that we will be using a DataReader called dr
SqlDataReader dr;

// Create a new data adapter to load the authors table from
// pubs into strongly-typed DataSet
SqlDataAdapter authors_da = new SqlDataAdapter(
    "SELECT au_id,au_lname,au_fname,phone,address," +
    "city,state,zip,contract " +
    "FROM authors",
    "Integrated Security=SSPI;Initial Catalog=pubs;Data Source=localhost;");

// Create an new SqlConnection to use for getting this list of states
SqlConnection conn = new SqlConnection(
    "Integrated Security=SSPI;Initial Catalog=pubs;Data Source=localhost;");
```

```
// Create a new SqlCommand to use for getting the list of states
SqlCommand cmd = new SqlCommand(
    "SELECT DISTINCT(state) FROM authors ORDER BY state",conn);

// Add an entry to the list of states to represent "all states"
states_list.Add("*");
```

Now we can fill the `DataSet` from the `authors` table, and load the list of distinct states into the `ArrayList`.

```
try
{
    // Load the pubs.authors table into the dataset, then associate
    // that table with the dataview
    authors_da.Fill(au_set.Authors);
    dv_authors.Table = au_set.Authors;

    // Open a connection to the database and execute the
    // command which sends back a list of the distinct states
    // in the authors table. Add each state to the states_list,
    // then close the connection to free its resources.
    conn.Open();
    dr = cmd.ExecuteReader(CommandBehavior.CloseConnection);
    while(dr.Read())
        states_list.Add(dr["state"].ToString());
    dr.Close();
}
```

If any errors occur, save them off to a file using the familiar `SqlErrorPersister` class.

```
    // Catch any errors durring the database reads
    catch(SqlException sqle)
    {
        // If an error occurs, capture it to a file and return false,
        // indicating that an error has occurred.
        SqlErrorPersister sqlep = new SqlErrorPersister();
        sqlep.SaveErrorToFile(sqle,AppInfo);
        return false;
    }
    // Return true indicating a successful load
    return true;
}
```

Finally, we have the constructor. Other classes call this to get the data ready to use. It simply creates instances of the classes used in the class, and then sets the default filter to none.

```
    // Constructor for the DataAccess class. This creates
    // instances of the strongly typed data set, the DataView
    // and the list of distinct states. It also sets the default
    // state filter to not exclude any state
    public DataAccess()
```

```
    {
        au_set = new AuthorsSet();
        dv_authors = new DataView();
        states_list = new ArrayList();
        filter_state = "*";
    }
}
} // End of namespace
```

frmMain.cs

Now let us look at the `frmMain.cs` code. This class glues the user interface we have previously designed, to the `DataAccess` class we have just looked at.

As the start of the class definition, add the following declarations:

```
DataAccess da;
SqlErrorPersisterAppInfo AppInfo;
```

We will take the opportunity to populate a `SqlErrorPersisterAppInfo` instance in this constructor for class `frmMain`. In the code, look for:

```
// TODO: Add any constructor code after InitializeComponent call
```

and then add the following:

```
AppInfo = new SqlErrorPersisterAppInfo();

AppInfo.CompanyName = Application.CompanyName;
AppInfo.CurrentCulture = Application.CurrentCulture.ToString();
AppInfo.CurrentInputLanguage = Application.CurrentInputLanguage.ToString();
AppInfo.ExecutablePath = Application.ExecutablePath;
AppInfo.ProductName = Application.ProductName;
AppInfo.ProductVersion = Application.ProductVersion;
AppInfo.StartUpPath = Application.StartupPath;
```

We won't be discussing the `Dispose()`, `InitializeComponent()`, and `Main()` methods, as we won't be touching them.

Now we need to write our own event handlers, so let's look at them next.

Connect to Table

The click event handler for the `menuConnectTable` checks to see if the data has been loaded into the strongly-typed `DataSet`. If not, it loads the data. In either case, it binds the `authors` table in the strongly-typed `DataSet` to the main `DataGrid`. It also disables any features that are only available if the grid is bound to the `DataView` instead.

```
// Respond to the Connect to table menu event
private void menuConnectTable_Click(object sender, System.EventArgs e)
{
    // Have we loaded the data yet? if da or da.authors are null,
    // then we have not but need to. While the data loading is occurring,
    // change the cursor to "busy."
```

```
   if((da == null)||(da.authors == null))
   {
      Cursor.Current = Cursors.WaitCursor;
      LoadDataSet();
      Cursor.Current = Cursors.Default;
   }
   // Bind the DataGrid to the authors table
   gridMain.DataSource = da.authors;
   // Disable the option to connect the table
   menuConnectTable.Enabled = false;
   // Allow connections the view instead
   menuConnectView.Enabled = true;
   // Disable the sort menu and all of its options
   menuSort.Enabled = false;
   // Disable and hide the state filter
   lbStateFilter.Visible = false;
   cbStateFilter.Enabled = false;
   cbStateFilter.Visible = false;
   cbStateFilter.DataSource = null;
   // Uncheck the menu option for Connect to view
   menuConnectTable.Checked = true;
   menuConnectView.Checked = false;
   // Enable styling
   menuStyle.Enabled = true;
}
```

Connect to View

We can handle any Connect To | View menu click events with this next piece of code. It tests to make sure the data is loaded and the user interface is properly configured for use with the view.

```
// Respond to the Connect to view menu event
private void menuConnectToView_Click(object sender, System.EventArgs e)
{
   // Have we loaded the data yet? if da or da.authors are null,
   // then we have not but need to. While the data loading is occurring,
   // change the cursor to "busy."
   if((da == null)||(da.authors == null))
   {
      Cursor.Current = Cursors.WaitCursor;
      LoadDataSet();
      Cursor.Current = Cursors.Default;
   }
   // Bind the DataGrid to the authors view
   gridMain.DataSource = da.authors_view;
   // Enable the connect to table option,
   // but disable the connect to view.
   menuConnectTable.Enabled = true;
   menuConnectView.Enabled = false;
   // Enable the sort menu and all of its options
   menuSort.Enabled = true;
   menuSortLast.Enabled = true;
   menuSortFirst.Enabled = true;
```

```
        menuSortState.Enabled = true;
        // Enable the state filter combo box
        // and bind it to the unique list of states
        lbStateFilter.Visible = true;
        cbStateFilter.Enabled = true;
        cbStateFilter.Visible = true;
        cbStateFilter.DataSource = da.StatesList;
        // Disable connect to view, enable connect to table
        menuConnectTable.Checked = false;
        menuConnectView.Checked = true;
        // Enable styling
        menuStyle.Enabled = true;
    }
```

The Sort Menu

The next four functions are reasonably self-explanatory, involving the Quit option of the Connect menu, and the options on the Sort menu:

```
// Handle any clicks of the connect menu, quit option
private void menuConnectQuit_Click(object sender, System.EventArgs e)
{
    Application.Exit();
}


// Handle any requests to order the view by last name from the sort menu
private void menuSortLast_Click(object sender, System.EventArgs e)
{
    da.SortViewByLastName();
    menuSortLast.Checked = true;
    menuSortFirst.Checked = false;
    menuSortState.Checked = false;
}


// Handle any requests to order the view by first name from the sort menu
private void menuSortFirst_Click(object sender, System.EventArgs e)
{
    da.SortViewByFirstName();
    menuSortLast.Checked = false;
    menuSortFirst.Checked = true;
    menuSortState.Checked = false;
}


// Handle any requests to order the view by state from the sort menu
private void menuSortState_Click(object sender, System.EventArgs e)
{
    da.SortViewByState();
    menuSortLast.Checked = false;
    menuSortFirst.Checked = false;
    menuSortState.Checked = true;
}
```

When the user changes the value of the cbStateFilter control, we want to automatically update the DataGrid to show only those rows where the state matches. This is actually fairly simple to do, and is accomplished with the following event handler.

```
// When a different state is selected in the state filter combo
// box, update the state filter on the data view with the current state
// and then repaint the data grid
private void cbStateFilter_SelectedIndexChanged(object sender,
                                                System.EventArgs e)
{
    da.SetStateToFilterOn(cbStateFilter.Text);
    gridMain.Refresh();
}
```

The Style Menu

We also need to write some event handlers for changing Style menu choices. These are fairly simple:

```
// The "Greenbar Style" grid should look like it was printed
// on old fashioned green-bar paper.
// The alternating rows should be light green,
// the currently selected row should be light green,
// no caption and show in 3D form.
private void menuStyleGreenbar_Click(object sender, System.EventArgs e)
{
    gridMain.AlternatingBackColor = Color.LightGreen;
    gridMain.CaptionVisible = false;
    gridMain.SelectionBackColor = Color.Green;
    gridMain.FlatMode = false;
    gridMain.GridLineStyle = DataGridLineStyle.Solid;
    menuStyleExecutive.Checked = false;
    menuStyleGreenbar.Checked = true;
    menuStylePaper.Checked = false;
    menuStyleGreenbar.Enabled = false;
    menuStyleExecutive.Enabled = true;
    menuStylePaper.Enabled = true;
}

// The "Executive Style" look "high-tech"
// The alternating rows should be light gray,
// the currently selected row should have a navy-colored background,
// there should be a caption and it shown in 3D form.
private void menuStyleExecutive_Click(object sender, System.EventArgs e)
{
    gridMain.CaptionVisible = true;
    gridMain.CaptionText = "AUTHORS";
    gridMain.AlternatingBackColor = Color.LightGray;
    gridMain.SelectionBackColor = Color.Navy;
    gridMain.FlatMode = false;
    gridMain.GridLineStyle = DataGridLineStyle.Solid;
    menuStyleExecutive.Checked = true;
    menuStyleGreenbar.Checked = false;
    menuStylePaper.Checked = false;
```

```
        menuStyleGreenbar.Enabled = true;
        menuStyleExecutive.Enabled = false;
        menuStylePaper.Enabled = true;
    }


    // The "Paper Style" formats the grid to look like
    // plain paper with a caption, and pink highlighting
    // used to show the current row. Hide the lines and
    // display in flat mode to made the grid look like paper.
    private void menuStylePaper_Click(object sender, System.EventArgs e)
    {
        gridMain.CaptionVisible = true;
        gridMain.CaptionText = "AUTHORS";
        gridMain.AlternatingBackColor = gridMain.BackColor;
        gridMain.SelectionBackColor = Color.LightPink;
        gridMain.FlatMode = true;
        gridMain.GridLineStyle = DataGridLineStyle.None;
        menuStyleExecutive.Checked = false;
        menuStyleGreenbar.Checked = false;
        menuStylePaper.Checked = true;
        menuStyleGreenbar.Enabled = true;
        menuStyleExecutive.Enabled = true;
        menuStylePaper.Enabled = false;
    }
```

Loading the Data

The last function in this class is the `LoadDataSet` function. It creates an instance of the data access class and then attempts to have it load the data. If that fails for some reason, the application is ended.

```
    private bool LoadDataSet()
    {
        da = new DataAccess();

        if(!da.LoadDataSet(AppInfo))
        {
            MessageBox.Show("Unable to load data and cannot continue.\n"+
                            "Check the sqlerror.xml file for more information.",
                            "Fatal Error",
                            MessageBoxButtons.OK,
                            MessageBoxIcon.Stop);
            Application.Exit();
        }
        return true;
    }
```

The last thing we need to do is register our event handlers for each of the events we are interested in. To do this, simply select each of the following controls. In the property sheet for that control, select the events by clicking on the "lighting bolt" icon (the tooltip says "Events"); find the event name from the second column of the following table, then select the event handler from the third column.

Control	Event	Set To
menuConnectView	Click	menuConnectView_Click
menuConnectTable	Click	menuConnectTable
menuConnectQuit	Click	menuSortLast_Click
menuSortLast	Click	menuSortLast_Click
menuSortFirst	Click	menuSortFirst_Click
menuSortState	Click	menuSortState_Click
cbStateFilter	Selected IndexChanged	cbStateFilter_SelectedIndexChanged
menuStylePaper	Click	menuStylePaper_Click
menuStyleExecutive	Click	menuStyleExecutive_Click
menuStyleGreenbar	Click	menuStyleGreenbar_Click

In effect, this adds the named function as a delegate to the event list for each control. If you now look through the code of the `InitializeComponent()` function, you will see this implemented as:

```
this.menuConnectTable.Click +=
    new System.EventHandler(this.menuConnectTable_Click);
```

At this point, we have a Windows Form application that will display the contents of the `authors` table from the `pubs` database, and allow us to sort this data or view by state.

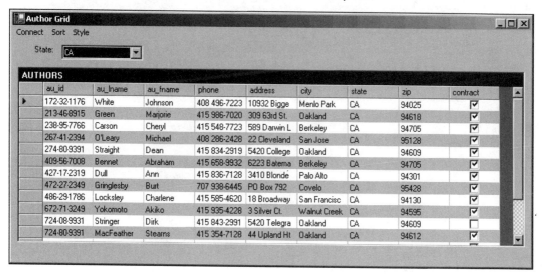

Let's take this a step further, and develop a browser-based version of this data editor grid, complete with the ability to save our changes, using the ASP `DataGrid` control.

Getting Started with Web Forms

Using the `DataGrid` control in this example, we will examine an ASP.NET-based application for editing the `authors` table. In particular, this application will feature:

- ❑ Row filtering by an author's state of residence
- ❑ Pagination of a `DataView`
- ❑ Filtering by row-version
- ❑ Sorting by column
- ❑ Editing, deleting, and updating data
- ❑ Persistence of current data back to the server

When compiled and executed, our application looks somewhat like this. We have added some annotations to clarify the description that follows.

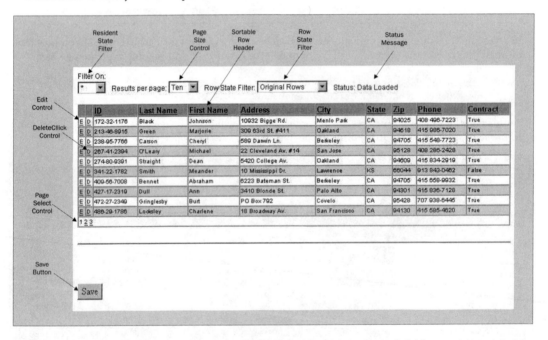

Getting started, go ahead and create a new C# Web Application in the web folder `AuthorWebGrid`, and follow these initial steps:

- ❑ Add the XML schema file `authors.xsd` from earlier in the chapter
- ❑ Add a class file called `DataAccess.cs`
- ❑ Rename `WebForm1.aspx` to `default.aspx`
- ❑ Add a stylesheet called `standard.css`

Having done this, your **Solution Explorer** view should look similar to this:

Authors Schema File

As with the previous example, we use the **Generate DataSet** option from the **Schemas** menu to generate the strongly-typed `DataSet` from the `authors.xsd` file. The files `authors.cs` and `authors.xsx` files will be created under the `authors.xsd` file.

The `Authors` class must be in the same namespace as the rest of the project. If the `authors.cs` file is not listed in the **Solution Explorer**, click the **Class View** tab. Double-click `authors.cs` and change the namespace to `Wrox.ProCSharpData.Chapter5.AuthorWebGrid`. This will enable us to reference the typed dataset elsewhere in our application.

DataAccess.cs

As in our previous examples, this class encapsulates and hides the strongly-typed `DataSet` that we use throughout the application; an example of using the Façade design pattern. This particular `DataAccess` class starts with some fairly common imported namespaces from the .NET Framework

```
using System;
using System.Collections;
using System.Data;
using System.Data.SqlClient;
```

We also make sure that this class can be seen throughout our application by adding it to the `Wrox.ProCSharpData.Chapter5.AuthorWebGrid` namespace.

```
namespace Wrox.ProCSharpData.Chapter5.AuthorWebGrid{
```

The class itself has some shared constants, objects, and variables that it uses, so we define them next. The constants allow us to fix the SQL statements and connection string properties we will be using. The object instances include the strongly-typed `DataSet`, and `ArrayList` used for holding an array of the distinct states in the `authors` table, a `DataView`, and `DataAdapter`, and a `DataRowViewState` to keep track of the user's selected `RowState` view filter. We have a few simple variables to track the currently used state filter and sort order.

```
public class DataAccess
{
   // The connection string used to communicate with the database
   private const string CONNECTIONSTRING =
       "Integrated Security=SSPI;Initial Catalog=pubs;" +
       "Data Source=localhost;";
   // The SQL statement that we use for loading the table into the grid
   private const string SELECTSTATEMENTFORAUTHORSTABLE =
       "SELECT au_id,au_lname,au_fname,phone,address," +
       "city,state,zip,contract " +
       "FROM authors";
   // The SQL statement used to populate the state drop-down list
   private const string SELECTSTATEMENTFORSTATELIST =
       "SELECT DISTINCT state FROM authors";
   // The strongly-typed dataset used hold the authors table
   private AuthorsSet auSet;
   // An array to hold the list of states used for the by-state row filter
   private ArrayList statesList;
   // A view of the strongly-typed dataset
   private DataView dvAuthors;
   // The DataAdapter that bridges the database and the application
   private SqlDataAdapter daAuthors;
   // Which state is currently selected. "*" means none.
   private string _currentFilter = "*";
   // Which column is the DataGrid sorted on.
   private string _currentSort = "au_id";
   // Which RowState are we currently displaying
   private DataViewRowState _currentRowStateFilter =
           DataViewRowState.OriginalRows;
```

The `DataAccess` class has a fair number of properties to look at first. The first set of these properties provides data encapsulation for variables controlling certain aspects of how the grid renders. The `DataAccess` class holds only the grid configuration variables that affect the `DataView` on which the grid is based.

```
// Property controlling the author's resident state filter
public string currentFilter
{
   set{ _currentFilter = value; }
   get{ return _currentFilter; }
}
// Property controlling the column sorted on
public string currentSort
{
   set{ _currentSort = value; }
   get{ return _currentSort; }
}
// Property controlling the current RowState filter
public DataViewRowState currentRowStateFilter
{
   set{ _currentRowStateFilter = value; }
   get{ return _currentRowStateFilter; }
}
// Read-only property providing the state list
```

```
public ArrayList StatesList
{
    get { return statesList; }
}
// Read-only property providing the DataView of the DataSet
public DataView AuthorView
{
    get { return dvAuthors; }
}
```

Next, we have the meaty functions involved in maintaining the strongly-typed DataSet. In this group, we have a simple function that returns a DataRow where the table's primary key (au_id) matches a given string. We use this function later on, when we figure out what to do when a row is edited.

```
// Returns the DataRow, if any, where the primary key of au_id
// matches an ID provided to the function. Returns an null
// DataRow if that ID is not matched.
public DataRow FindByAuID(string au_id)
{
    return auSet.Authors.Rows.Find(au_id);
}
```

The SaveData function writes the current strongly-typed DataSet to a given table and database. It starts simply enough, creating instances of the Connection, DataAdapter, and CommandBuilder classes for the SQL Server .NET Data Provider.

```
// Saves the current DataSet back to the database
// using the SqlCommandBuilder class.
public bool SaveData()
{
    // Create new instances Connection class
    SqlConnection connWorking = new SqlConnection(CONNECTIONSTRING);
    SqlDataAdapter daWorking = new
            SqlDataAdapter(SELECTSTATEMENTFORAUTHORSTABLE,connWorking);
    SqlCommandBuilder cbWorking = new SqlCommandBuilder(daWorking);
```

The CommandBuilder

Let us stop for a moment and re-introduce the CommandBuilder. As you will probably recall from previous chapters, instances of the CommandBuilder analyze a SQL SELECT statement and attempt to construct matching INSERT, UPDATE, and DELETE statements from that. It uses a DataAdapter, which in turn uses a Connection to the target database to gather some information about the schema of the table. With that information, and a few assumptions it can make, it generates appropriate statements. An example of what it generates for our application may help with your understanding:

Our SELECT statement looks like this:

```
SELECT au_id,au_lname,au_fname,phone,address,city,state,zip,contract
FROM authors
```

The DELETE statement is considerably more complex. At a simplistic level, it deletes all rows exactly matching the values held in the current row. The parameters used in this statement are internally generated.

```
DELETE FROM authors
WHERE
(
(au_id = @p1)
AND ((au_lname IS NULL AND @p2 IS NULL) OR (au_lname = @p3))
AND ((au_fname IS NULL AND @p4 IS NULL) OR (au_fname = @p5))
AND ((phone IS NULL AND @p6 IS NULL) OR (phone = @p7))
AND ((address IS NULL AND @p8 IS NULL) OR (address = @p9))
AND ((city IS NULL AND @p10 IS NULL) OR (city = @p11))
AND ((state IS NULL AND @p12 IS NULL) OR (state = @p13))
AND ((zip IS NULL AND @p14 IS NULL) OR (zip = @p15))
AND ((contract IS NULL AND @p16 IS NULL) OR (contract = @p17))
)
```

The generated `INSERT` command is fairly simple:

```
INSERT INTO authors( au_id , au_lname , au_fname , phone ,
                     address , city , state , zip , contract )
VALUES ( @p1 , @p2 , @p3 , @p4 , @p5 , @p6 , @p7 , @p8 , @p9 )
```

The `UPDATE` statement is even more complex that the `DELETE` statement, just to make sure that exactly the desired recorded is updated.

```
UPDATE authors
SET au_id = @p1 , au_lname = @p2 , au_fname = @p3 , phone = @p4 ,
    address = @p5 , city = @p6 , state = @p7 , zip = @p8 , contract = @p9
WHERE
(
(au_id = @p10)
AND ((au_lname IS NULL AND @p11 IS NULL) OR (au_lname = @p12))
AND ((au_fname IS NULL AND @p13 IS NULL) OR (au_fname = @p14))
AND ((phone IS NULL AND @p15 IS NULL) OR (phone = @p16))
AND ((address IS NULL AND @p17 IS NULL) OR (address = @p18))
AND ((city IS NULL AND @p19 IS NULL) OR (city = @p20))
AND ((state IS NULL AND @p21 IS NULL) OR (state = @p22))
AND ((zip IS NULL AND @p23 IS NULL) OR (zip = @p24))
AND ((contract IS NULL AND @p25 IS NULL) OR (contract = @p26))
)
```

With the `DELETE`, `INSERT`, and `UPDATE` commands known to the `DataAdapter`, we can make use of the `Update` method of a `DataTable` to automatically take care of all of the details of the update for us. The code to set up the command builder, and then take advantage of the `DataTable`'s `Update` method is straightforward:

```
try
{
    // Open a connection to the database
    connWorking.Open();
    // Call the update method on the dataset, this will
    // make the appropriate insert, updates and deletes
    daAuthors.DeleteCommand = cbWorking.GetDeleteCommand();
    daAuthors.InsertCommand = cbWorking.GetInsertCommand();
```

```
        daAuthors.UpdateCommand = cbWorking.GetUpdateCommand();
        daAuthors.Update(auSet.Authors);
    }
```

The rest of this should seem fairly familar now. Of course, you could use a much more elegant error handling routine if desired. We will refresh the state list just in case any states have been added or removed since our last update.

```
    catch(SqlException sqle)
    {
        // if any SqlErrors occur, just return false
        return false;
    }
    finally
    {
        // If the connection is still open,
        // close it to free up our resources
        if(connWorking.State != ConnectionState.Closed)
            connWorking.Close();
    }
    // Update the state filter list, just to be sure it's correct.
    return LoadStatesList();
}
```

Loading the Data

The next function we have is the `LoadDataSet` function. It should seem reasonably familiar from the previous examples.

```
public bool LoadDataSet()
{
    // Create a new data adapter to load the authors table from
    // pubs into a strongly-typed DataSet
    SqlConnection connWorking = new SqlConnection(CONNECTIONSTRING);
    daAuthors = new
                SqlDataAdapter(SELECTSTATEMENTFORAUTHORSTABLE,connWorking);
    try
    {
        // Connect to the database
        connWorking.Open();
        // Use the fill method of the DataSet to push
        // the data from the connection into the DataSet
        daAuthors.Fill(auSet.Authors);
        // Add a primary key to the Authors virtual table
        auSet.Authors.Constraints.Add(
                        "PK_AUTHORS",auSet.Authors.Columns[0],true);
    }
    catch(SqlException sqle)
    {
        // Return false if an error occurs
        return false;
    }
    finally
```

```
        {
            // Force the connection closed either way
            if(connWorking.State != ConnectionState.Closed)
                connWorking.Close();
        }
        // Return true if data was successfully loaded
        return true;
    }
```

Next, we have a function that loads a list of the distinct states. It uses a `DataReader` instance to stream the results into an `ArrayList` instance.

```
public bool LoadStatesList()
{
    // Create a new Connection, Command and DataReader class
    // instance to work with
    SqlConnection connWorking = new SqlConnection(CONNECTIONSTRING);
    SqlCommand cmd = new SqlCommand(SELECTSTATEMENTFORSTATELIST, connWorking);
    SqlDataReader dr = null;

    // Add an "all states" option to the list
    statesList.Add("*");

    try
    {
        // Open a connection to the Database
        connWorking.Open();

        // Create and execute a data reader that
        // bridges the state list to our application
        dr = cmd.ExecuteReader(CommandBehavior.CloseConnection);

        // While data remains in the DataReader's stream,
        // pump each statement element (as a string) into
        // the array of author resident states
        while(dr.Read())
            statesList.Add(dr["state"].ToString());

        // Cleanup the DataReader
        dr.Close();
    }
    catch(SqlException sqle)
    {
        // If any errors occurred, return false
        return false;
    }
    finally
    {
        // Clean up the connection as appropriate,
        // the close the DataReader to free its resources
        if(connWorking != null)
            if(connWorking.State != ConnectionState.Closed)
```

```
              connWorking.Close();
    }
    // if all went well, return true
    return true;
}
```

The DataAccess Constructor

The last function in this class is the constructor. It creates an instance of the strongly-typed `DataSet`, and an `ArrayList` to hold the list of distinct states. It then loads the `authors` table and the list of distinct states. If both of those operations succeed, the constructor creates a view of that table to work with.

```
// Class constructor
public DataAccess()
{
    // Initialize the strongly-typed DataSet
    auSet = new AuthorsSet();

    // Initialize the array of states
    statesList = new ArrayList();

    // Load the data into the grid now
    if(LoadDataSet())
    {
        // If successful, create a view on the DataSet
        // and enable deletes and edits.
        dvAuthors = new DataView(auSet.Authors);
        dvAuthors.AllowDelete = true;
        dvAuthors.AllowEdit = true;
    }
}
```

Default.aspx

Now let's look at how to lay out the `default.aspx` page. When you open this page, you should be in the page designer view. Here are the steps you should to follow:

❑ From the HTML pallet of the toolbox, drag a table onto the page, anchored at the top left corner of the form.

❑ Select the table, and from the Table menu, select Insert | Column to the right. Use Table | Delete | Rows to make the table's dimensions one row and four columns. Using Table | Select to select the table, from its Properties dialog, make the table width 100%, with a border width of zero pixels.

❑ Toggle over to the HTML view of the page, then insert width=25% into each of the <TD> elements, then toggle back to the Design view.

❑ From the WebForms pallet, select and drag a Literal control into each cell. Using the Properties of each control, change the Text and ID as follows:

Column Number	Text	ID
1	Filter On:	lbStateFilter
2	Results per page:	lbPageSize
3	Row State Filter:	lbRowStateFilter
4	Status:	lbStatusCaption

where Column Number 1 is the left hand column, and so on.

❑ Drag and drop a DropDownList into the first cell, next to the Literal control. Use the Properties sheet of that list to change its ID to ddlStateFilter and its AutoPostBack property to true. Click on the "lighting bolt" icon on the property sheet to bring up the control events. Enter StateListClick for the action SelectedIndexChanged. We will see the code behind that event shortly.

❑ Repeat the process to create a DropDownList in the next cell with the ID of ddlPageSize and a SelectedIndexChanged event of PageSizeClick.

❑ Repeat the process to create a DropDownList in the next cell with the ID of ddlRowStateFilter and a SelectedIndexChanged event of RowStateFilterClick.

❑ Drag and drop another Literal control into the last cell. Name that lbStatus and set its Text property to loading.

❑ Under the table, drag and drop a DataGrid from the WebForms pallet. Using its Properties sheet, make the following changes to the DataGrid:

Property	Value
ID	gridMain
AllowSorting	true
AllowPaging	true
DataSource	da.AuthorView
Font	Arial
Name Font Size	X-Small
Width	100%.

❑ Return to the HTML control tab, and drag and drop a horizontal rule under the grid, then add a lable with the following text:

Use E to start an edit on a row or D to delete; U to save or C to cancel changes.

❑ Finally, drag and drop a WebForms Button onto the form after the line of text you have just entered. Use the Properties of that control to set the ID to btnSaveChanges, its Text to Save, and its Click event to btnSaveChanges_Click.

Visually, the design view of your your form should look like this now:

While this form is functional, it is far from complete. There are a number of changes that need to be made, so let us look at the completed code behind this form to see what those changes are:

The directives line should not require any changes, but do make sure the `AutoEventWireup` is set to `true`.

```
<%@ Page language="c#" Codebehind="default.aspx.cs"
    AutoEventWireup="true" Inherits="AuthorWebGrid.WebForm1" %>
```

The next section of the page should not require changes, other than setting an appropriate page title.

```
<!DOCTYPE HTML PUBLIC "-//W3C//DTD HTML 4.0 Transitional//EN" >
<html>
    <head>
        <title>Author Edit Grid</title>
        <meta content="True" name="vs_showGrid">
        <meta content="Microsoft Visual Studio 7.0" name="GENERATOR">
        <meta content="C#" name="CODE_LANGUAGE">
        <meta content="JavaScript" name="vs_defaultClientScript">
        <meta content="http://schemas.microsoft.com/intellisense/ie5"
            name="vs_targetSchema">
        <link href="standard.css" type="text/css" rel="stylesheet">
    </head>
    <body>
```

We have changed the `id` for the form to `frmMain` to be consistent with other forms we have used in previous chapters.

```
<form id="frmMain" method="post" runat="server">
```

We have a good amount of work with the elements we have inserted into the table. We've changed the formatting here a bit to make it easier to read in printed form; you don't actually need to make any changes here. For example, we've changed `<asp:literal></asp:literal>` to `<asp:literal />` to simplify our presentation. You will want to insert the `class="menu"` elements in the `<td>` tags.

169

```
<table width="100%" border="0">
   <tr>
      <td class="menu" width="25%">
      <asp:literal id="lbStateFilter" runat="server"
                Text="Filter On:" />
      <asp:dropdownlist id="ddlStateFilter" runat="server"
                    AutoPostBack="True"
                    OnSelectedIndexChanged="StateFilterClick" />
      </td>
      <td class="menu" width="25%">
      <asp:literal id="lbPageSize" runat="server"
                Text="Results per page:" />
      <asp:dropdownlist id="ddlPageSize" runat="server"
                    AutoPostBack="True"
                    OnSelectedIndexChanged="PageSizeClick">
```

Now add the following list items to the page size drop-down list:

```
<asp:ListItem Value="5">Five</asp:ListItem>
<asp:ListItem Value="10" Selected="True">Ten</asp:ListItem>
<asp:ListItem Value="25">25</asp:ListItem>
<asp:ListItem Value="50">50</asp:ListItem>
<asp:ListItem Value="100">100</asp:ListItem>
```

Returning to the code, we do not need to make any changes to the next few lines:

```
      </asp:dropdownlist>
      </td>
      <td class="menu" width="25%">
         <asp:literal id="lbRowStateFilter" runat="server"
                   Text="Row State Filter:" />
         <asp:dropdownlist id="ddlRowStateFilter" runat="server"
                       AutoPostBack="True">
```

Add the following ListItems for the row state filter:

```
   <asp:ListItem Value="Added">Added</asp:ListItem>
   <asp:ListItem Value="CurrentRows">Current Rows</asp:ListItem>
   <asp:ListItem Value="Deleted">Deleted</asp:ListItem>
   <asp:ListItem Value="ModifiedCurrent">Modified Current</asp:ListItem>
   <asp:ListItem Value="ModifiedOriginal">Modified Original</asp:ListItem>
   <asp:ListItem Value="None">None</asp:ListItem>
   <asp:ListItem Value="OriginalRows" Selected="True">
      Original Rows</asp:ListItem>
   <asp:ListItem Value="Unchanged">Unchanged</asp:ListItem>
```

Returning to the code, we do not need to make any changes to next few lines:

```
      </asp:dropdownlist>
      </td>
      <td class="menu" width="25%">
         <asp:literal id="lbStatusCaption" runat="server" Text="Status:" />
         <asp:literal id="lbStatus" runat="server" Text="Loading" />
```

```
        </tr>
    </table>
```

Next comes the `DataGrid` itself. The first part of the table was set up during the visual design process.

```
<asp:datagrid id=gridMain runat="server"
              Width="100%" DataSource="<%# da.AuthorView %>"
              AllowSorting="True" Font-Names="Arial"
              Font-Size="X-Small"
```

You need to add the following attributes to the grid:

```
AutoGenerateColumns="False"
AllowPaging="True" PageSize="10" OnPageIndexChanged="PageClick"
OnCancelCommand="CancelClick"
OnDeleteCommand="DeleteClick" OnEditCommand="EditClick" OnSortCommand="SortClick"
OnUpdateCommand="UpdateClick">
```

To make the grid a bit easier to read, we set a styling background for each alternating row, by inserting the following:

```
<AlternatingItemStyle BackColor="Gainsboro"></AlternatingItemStyle>
```

To make the column headers stand out, we also give them a specific style, by inserting the following:

```
<HeaderStyle Font-Size="X-Small" Font-Names="sans-serif"
             Font-Bold="True" BackColor="DarkGray" />
```

Finally, we define the columns that appear on the grid. The following information needs to be entered into the page:

```
<Columns>
<asp:EditCommandColumn ButtonType="LinkButton" UpdateText="U"
                       CancelText="C" EditText="E" />
<asp:ButtonColumn Text="D" CommandName="Delete" />
<asp:BoundColumn DataField="au_id" SortExpression="au_id"
                 HeaderText="ID" />
<asp:BoundColumn DataField="au_lname" SortExpression="au_lname"
                 HeaderText="Last Name" />
<asp:BoundColumn DataField="au_fname" SortExpression="au_fname"
                 HeaderText="First Name" />
<asp:BoundColumn DataField="address" SortExpression="address"
                 HeaderText="Address" />
<asp:BoundColumn DataField="city" SortExpression="city" HeaderText="City" />
<asp:BoundColumn DataField="state" SortExpression="state"
                 HeaderText="State" />
<asp:BoundColumn DataField="zip" SortExpression="zip" HeaderText="Zip" />
<asp:BoundColumn DataField="phone" SortExpression="phone"
                 HeaderText="Phone" />
<asp:BoundColumn DataField="contract" SortExpression="contract"
                 HeaderText="Contract" />
</Columns>
```

We use three types of columns in the grid. The `EditCommandColumn` allows us to provide text for each of the essential commands needed for editing, and also a way to indicate how they should be rendered on the control. We have chosen to render them as text, but you could make them clickable buttons by changing the `ButtonType` to **PushButton**. The next type of column, the `ButtonColumn`, allows us to add a delete command. Finally, we have nine `BoundColumns`, one for each column in the view we want to bind to.

> **You do not need to bind to all columns in a table or view, but you must bind to any column that you want to edit through the grid.**

Next, we set up the page select control. The `Mode` attribute controls whether a "back-forward" or a set of numbered pages will be shown.

```
<PagerStyle HorizontalAlign="Justify" Mode="NumericPages"></PagerStyle>
```

Now we simply have to finish off the form:

```
    </asp:datagrid>
  <hr noShade>
  <P>Use E to start an edit on a row or D to delete; U to save
      or C to cancel changes.</P>

  <P><asp:button id="btnSaveChanges" runat="server"
                  Text="Save">
  </asp:button></P>
</form>
```

And finally finish the HTML document:

```
    </body>
  </html>
```

Now let's look at the code behind this form that makes it work.

Default.aspx.cs

Given that this is a code-behind file for a WebForm, all of the following namespaces are automatically imported:

```
using System;
using System.Collections;
using System.ComponentModel;
using System.Data;
using System.Drawing;
using System.Web;
using System.Web.SessionState;
using System.Web.UI;
using System.Web.UI.WebControls;
using System.Web.UI.HtmlControls;
```

As usual, we will change the namespace so this code can be seen throughout our project:

```
namespace Wrox.ProCSharpData.Chapter5.AuthorWebGrid
{
   public class WebForm1 : System.Web.UI.Page
   {
```

The visual design process should have created the following variable declarations for us:

```
// objects defined by drag-and-drops
protected System.Web.UI.WebControls.DataGrid gridMain;
protected System.Web.UI.WebControls.DropDownList ddlStateFilter;
protected System.Web.UI.WebControls.DropDownList ddlPageSize;
protected System.Web.UI.WebControls.DropDownList ddlRowStateFilter;
protected System.Web.UI.WebControls.Literal lbRowStateFilter;
protected System.Web.UI.WebControls.Literal lbStatus;
protected System.Web.UI.WebControls.Button btnSaveChanges;
protected System.Web.UI.WebControls.Literal lbPageSize;
protected System.Web.UI.WebControls.Literal lbStatusCaption;
protected System.Web.UI.WebControls.Literal lbStateFilter;
```

We need to declare a shared instance of the `DataAccess` class as most of the functions in this class will use that to manipulate the strongly typed `DataSet`:

```
// Shared instance of the DataAccess class
// which holds an instance of the strongly typed dataset
protected DataAccess da;
```

Next, we have a short function that makes sure the grid will display properly. This uses values held in the `DataAccess` instance persisted in the user's session.

```
// Refreshes the current grid
private void UpdateGrid()
{
   // Uodate the current row ordering
   da.AuthorView.Sort = da.currentSort;

   // Update the state row filter
   if(da.currentFilter != "*")
      da.AuthorView.RowFilter = "state='" + da.currentFilter + "'";
   else
      da.AuthorView.RowFilter = "";

   // Update the current row state filter
   da.AuthorView.RowStateFilter = da.currentRowStateFilter;

   // Refresh the data grid
   gridMain.DataSource = da.AuthorView;
   gridMain.DataBind();
}
```

Event Handlers

Now we have the event handlers for the events set up in the `default.aspx` page for the `DataGrid`. For the most part, these are fairly self-explanatory:

```
// handle any EditClicks (the E in the first grid column)
// by settings the grid's edit item index to the selects row
// as described by the event arguments.
protected void EditClick(Object sender, DataGridCommandEventArgs e)
{
    gridMain.EditItemIndex = e.Item.ItemIndex;
    lbStatus.Text = "Row in Edit";
    UpdateGrid();
}

// handle any EditClicks (the D in the second grid column)
// by filtering down to the selected row, then calling the
// delete method on the view.
protected void DeleteClick(Object sender, DataGridCommandEventArgs e)
{

    string au_id = e.Item.Cells[2].Text;

    da.AuthorView.RowFilter = "au_id='" + au_id + "'";
    if (da.AuthorView.Count > 0)
        da.AuthorView.Delete(0);
    da.AuthorView.RowFilter = "";
    lbStatus.Text = "Row Deleted";
    UpdateGrid();
}
```

Updating the Data

Handling updates is a bit trickier. In the code that follows, we have set up some logic, resembling a business rule. If the user doesn't change the author ID (`au_id`) field, we assume that the user wants to update just that author. If the user changes or creates a new ID, we assume that they want to create a new author element.

In a production-quality application, we would have checked to see if any newly entered information for the resident state was already in the state drop-down filter, adding it if was not. We would also need to check that all of the states in the drop-down filter are still in our actual data, removing those that are not. We should also take the opportunity to validate any data; for example, checking that no alphabetic characters were entered in a purely numeric field. Ideally, it is best to code such rules as methods in the `DataAccess` class and use those methods here.

Here is the `UpdateClicks` event handler:

```
// Handle UpdateClicks (when in edit, the U in the 1st column)
protected void UpdateClick(Object sender, DataGridCommandEventArgs e)
{
    // A working Data Row
    DataRow drWorking;

    // Extract the text boxes with the changed values from
```

```csharp
// the event arguments.
TextBox tb_au_id = (TextBox)e.Item.Cells[2].Controls[0];
TextBox tb_au_lname = (TextBox)e.Item.Cells[3].Controls[0];
TextBox tb_au_fname = (TextBox)e.Item.Cells[4].Controls[0];
TextBox tb_address = (TextBox)e.Item.Cells[5].Controls[0];
TextBox tb_city = (TextBox)e.Item.Cells[6].Controls[0];
TextBox tb_state = (TextBox)e.Item.Cells[7].Controls[0];
TextBox tb_zip = (TextBox)e.Item.Cells[8].Controls[0];
TextBox tb_phone = (TextBox)e.Item.Cells[9].Controls[0];
TextBox contract = (TextBox)(e.Item.Cells[10].Controls[0]);

// See if this row already exists.
// If it does, the FindByAuID function will
// return that row, if not it returns null
drWorking = da.FindByAuID(tb_au_id.Text);

// Does this row already exist?
// if the drWorkng is known, then it does,
// so we can just update the found row.
if(drWorking != null)
{
    drWorking["au_lname"] = tb_au_lname.Text;
    drWorking["au_fname"] = tb_au_fname.Text;
    drWorking["address"] = tb_address.Text;
    drWorking["city"] = tb_city.Text;
    drWorking["zip"] = tb_zip.Text;
    drWorking["state"] = tb_state.Text;
    drWorking["phone"] = tb_phone.Text;
    drWorking["contract"] = Convert.ToBoolean(contract.Text);

    lbStatus.Text = "Row Updated";
}
else
{
    // treat this as a new row...
    // Get a new, empty row to work with.
    drWorking = da.AuthorView.Table.NewRow();

    // Populate values into that row
    drWorking["au_id"] = tb_au_id.Text;
    drWorking["au_lname"] = tb_au_lname.Text;
    drWorking["au_fname"] = tb_au_fname.Text;
    drWorking["address"] = tb_address.Text;
    drWorking["city"] = tb_city.Text;
    drWorking["zip"] = tb_zip.Text;
    drWorking["state"] = tb_state.Text;
    drWorking["phone"] = tb_phone.Text;
    drWorking["contract"] = Convert.ToBoolean(contract.Text);

    // Add the new row
    da.AuthorView.Table.Rows.Add(drWorking);
    lbStatus.Text = "Clone Added";
}
```

```
        // Clear the edit row, as that process should now be done.
        gridMain.EditItemIndex = -1;
        UpdateGrid();
    }
```

The `Cancel`, `Sort`, `StateFilter`, and `Pagination` click events are fairly straightforward:

```
// Handle any Cancel Clicks (the letter C in the first column in edits)
// All we need to do here is just cancel the view's EditItemIndex
protected void CancelClick(Object sender, DataGridCommandEventArgs e)
{
    gridMain.EditItemIndex = -1;
    lbStatus.Text = "Edit Cancelled";
    UpdateGrid();
}

// Handle any clicks to changing the sorting
// These events raise when the users clicks on a column header
protected void SortClick(object sender, DataGridSortCommandEventArgs e)
{
    da.currentSort = e.SortExpression.ToString();
    lbStatus.Text = "Sort Column Changed";
    UpdateGrid();
}

// Handle any clicks to the changes of the resident state
// These arise from the drop-down list. Finding the selected
// state is just a matter of getting it from the passed-in
// event arguments.
protected void StateFilterClick(object sender, EventArgs e)
{
    da.currentFilter = ddlStateFilter.SelectedItem.Text.ToString();
    lbStatus.Text = "State Filter Changed";
    UpdateGrid();
}

// Handle changes to paging sizes
protected void PageSizeClick(object sender, EventArgs e)
{
    gridMain.PageSize = Convert.ToInt32(ddlPageSize.SelectedItem.Value);
    lbStatus.Text = "Page Change";
    UpdateGrid();
}

// Handle page change clicks
protected void PageClick(object sender, DataGridPageChangedEventArgs e)
{
    gridMain.CurrentPageIndex = e.NewPageIndex;
    lbStatus.Text = "Page Size Changed";
    UpdateGrid();
}
```

The `RowStateFilter` click event is a bit more complex, due to the number of options that the list has:

```
// Handle changes of the RowStateFilter
protected void RowStateFilterClick(object sender, EventArgs e)
{
    switch(ddlRowStateFilter.SelectedItem.Text.ToString())
    {
        case "Added":
            da.AuthorView.RowStateFilter = DataViewRowState.Added;
            break;
        case "CurrentRows":
            da.AuthorView.RowStateFilter = DataViewRowState.CurrentRows;
            break;
        case "Deleted":
            da.AuthorView.RowStateFilter = DataViewRowState.Deleted;
            break;
        case "ModifiedCurrent":
            da.AuthorView.RowStateFilter = DataViewRowState.ModifiedCurrent;
            break;
        case "ModifiedOriginal":
            da.AuthorView.RowStateFilter = DataViewRowState.ModifiedOriginal;
            break;
        case "None":
            da.AuthorView.RowStateFilter = DataViewRowState.None;
            break;
        case "OriginalRows":
            da.AuthorView.RowStateFilter = DataViewRowState.OriginalRows;
            break;
        case "Unchanged":
            da.AuthorView.RowStateFilter = DataViewRowState.Unchanged;
            break;
        default:
            da.AuthorView.RowStateFilter = DataViewRowState.None;
            break;
    }
    da.currentRowStateFilter = da.AuthorView.RowStateFilter;
    lbStatus.Text = "RowVersion Filter Changed";
    UpdateGrid();
}
```

Now we can look at the **Save** button click handler. It simply calls the `SaveData` method of the `DataAccess` class.

```
// Handle clicks of the save button
private void btnSaveChanges_Click(object sender, System.EventArgs e)
{
    lbStatus.Text = "Staring Save";
    if(da.SaveData())
        lbStatus.Text = "Successfully saved";
    else
        lbStatus.Text = "Save failed";
}
```

Our handler for the `Page_Load` event tries to pull an instance of the `DataAccess` class from the user's session. If it cannot, which would occur the first time the page is run or if a session timed-out, the function creates a new instance of it and adds it to the user's session. It then checks to see if this is a fresh page load or not. If it is the first view of the page, an attempt is made to load the data and read the grid for use.

```
private void Page_Load(object sender, System.EventArgs e)
{
    // Try to retrieve a current instance of DataAccess from the
    // user's current session. If that is null, create a new
    // instance of that class and save it to the session area.
    da = (DataAccess)Session["daPersisted"];
    if(da == null)
    {
        da = new DataAccess();
        this.Session.Add("daPersisted",da);
    }

    // If this is not the first time the page has been loaded
    if(!IsPostBack)
    {
        // If the load of the state list works, continue
        // and bind to the drop down list.
        lbStatus.Text = "Starting Data Load";
        if(da.LoadStatesList())
        {
            ddlStateFilter.DataSource = da.StatesList;
            ddlStateFilter.DataBind();
            lbStatus.Text = "Data Loaded";
            UpdateGrid();
        }
        else
            lbStatus.Text = "Data Load failed";
    }
}
```

Within the page, there is some further code generated by the visual design process, but we have no need to review that here.

Let's stop and summarize how this page works:

❑   The user requests the page, causing ASP.NET to start processing the page.

❑   The `Page_Load` event fires, creating an instance of the `DataAccess` class, and loading the desired data.

❑   The user clicks on various links and controls on the page. When these events occur, the code in the `default.aspx.cs` file fires in reaction. This may modify the strongly-typed `DataSet` held in the `DataAccess` class.

We conclude the discussion of creating our ASP.NET page by looking at the stylesheet for the page.

Standard.css

This is just a very simple stylesheet file

```
body
{
    font-family:Sans-Serif;
    font-size:smaller;
    background-color:white;
    color:Black;
    text-align:left;
}

p,td
{
    vertical-align:baseline;
    text-align:left;
}

.menu
{
    font-size: x-small;
}
```

We have come a long way in terms of using ADO.NET and Visual Studio .NET to build great data-centric applications. We have seen how the use of a strongly-typed `DataSet`, the `DataGrid`, and good object-oriented design can quickly and easily develop .NET applications.

We finish this chapter with a tour of the Visual Studio .NET data environment.

Visual Studio .NET Data Environment

The Visual Studio .NET data environment includes many tools that are similar to other tools you may have come across with previous versions of Visual Studio and SQL Server. Tools are included that permit programmers to view and modify data from the data source. In addition, the environment provides a point-and-click interface for instantiating and putting to use classes like `SqlConnection`, `SqlDataAdapter`, and `DataSet`.

Examining the Server Explorer

The Server Explorer window of Visual Studio .NET displays, among other things, connections to databases, tables, and data itself.

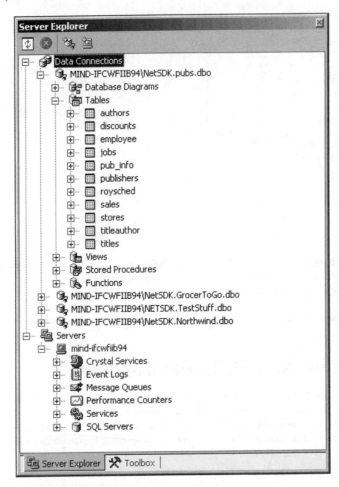

Setting up a Connection

Under the Tools menu, you should see Connect to Server; since the menus are context-sensitive, you may need to select View | Server Explorer, then select Tools | Connect to Server. This option is used to connect, obviously, to a server. When you installed the .NET Framework, a desktop version of SQL Server may also have been installed. If you are connecting to that version of SQL Server, simply put in the name of your computer or click on the server's name under the Servers section of Server Explorer.

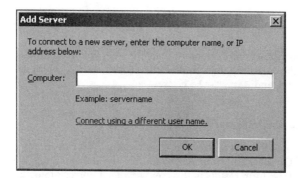

By clicking on the link Connect using a different user name you have the option to add a new username and password. When connecting to the desktop version of SQL Server, you can use the name sa with no password. This is rarely a good idea, however – the sa password should be as strong as reasonably possible.

Once you have established a connection with a server, you will need to make a connection to the individual database on that server, by selecting Tools | Connect to Database, or by right-clicking clicking Data Connections in Server Explorer, and choosing Add Connection.

The .NET framework includes several sample databases: pubs, Northwind, GrocerToGo, and Portal. For this example, make a connection to the pubs database.

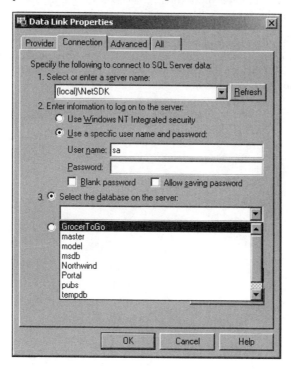

Once you have successfully connected to the database, you should be able to see all the tables, stored procedures, views, and database diagrams in the database.

Creating this connection, however, does more than allowing you to analyze the data, it also will actually help you to create all the necessary objects in your program, such as instances of the `DataConnection`, `DataAdapter`, `DataSet`, and `DataTable` classes.

Using the Data Environment

Creating a `SqlConnection` and `SqlDataAdapter` is easy. You can simply drag the desired table name from the Server Explorer and drop it onto the Windows form. Dragging a table from the Server Explorer into the Windows form results in the creation of six objects: four `SqlCommand` objects (named `SqlSelectCommandX`, `SqlInsertCommandX`, `SqlUpdateCommandX`, and `SqlDeleteCommandX`), a `SqlConnection` object (`sqlConnectionX`) and a `SqlDataAdapter` object (`sqlDataAdapterX`). Underneath your Windows Form you will see a list of the elements:

By clicking on these icons, their properties will appear in the Properties window.

Go ahead and start a new Windows Application project. Let's begin by opening the connection to the pubs database, and drag the `authors` table onto the blank C# form.

You should see a `SqlConnection` and a `SqlDataAdapter` object displayed underneath the form, as we just saw above. If you click on the `sqlDataAdapter1` icon, you should notice its properties appear in the Properties window. Click on the Generate Dataset link, found below the list of properties, at the bottom of the Properties dialog.

The window that appears allows you to name your DataSet, and choose the tables that will be added to it. In our case, we will give it the name ds. By keeping the checkbox Add this dataset to the designer checked, you will be able to modify the properties of the DataSet from the Properties window in the Visual Studio .NET IDE.

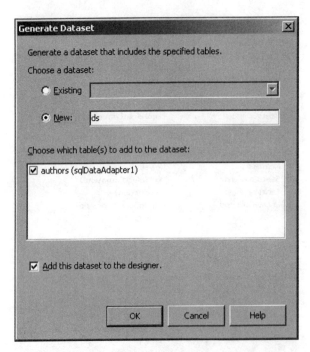

Let's take a look at the code that is generated by Visual Studio .NET. Not only has it created the SqlConnection, SqlDataAdapter, and the DataSet, but it actually created the InsertCommand, UpdateCommand, and DeleteCommand as well, in addition to defining all the parameters involved for defining the INSERT, UPDATE, and DELETE commands, as discussed in the last chapter.

```
this.SqlSelectCommand1 = new System.Data.SqlClient.SqlCommand();
this.SqlInsertCommand1 = new System.Data.SqlClient.SqlCommand();
this.SqlUpdateCommand1 = new System.Data.SqlClient.SqlCommand();
this.SqlDeleteCommand1 = new System.Data.SqlClient.SqlCommand();
this.SqlConnection1 = new System.Data.SqlClient.SqlConnection();
this.SqlDataAdapter1 = new
    System.Data.SqlClient.SqlDataAdapter();
this.ds1 = new dataEnvironment.ds();
this.dataGrid1 = new System.Windows.Forms.DataGrid();
```

Again, Visual Studio .NET has done all the menial work of defining the parameters for the INSERT, UPDATE, and DELETE statements.

Let's look at the SELECT command first:

```
//
// sqlSelectCommand1
//
this.sqlSelectCommand1.CommandText = "SELECT au_id, au_lname," +
    "au_fname, phone, address, city, state, zip, contract FROM" +
    " authors";
this.sqlSelectCommand1.Connection = this.sqlConnection1;
```

Next we have the INSERT command. After this, the UPDATE and DELETE parameters are very similar.

```
//
// sqlInsertCommand1
//
this.sqlInsertCommand1.CommandText = @"INSERT INTO authors" + "(au_id, au_lname,
au_fname, phone, address, city, state, zip, " + "contract) VALUES (@au_id,
@au_lname, @au_fname, @phone, " + "@address, @city, @state, @zip, @contract);
SELECT au_id, " + "au_lname, au_fname, phone, address, city, state, zip, " +
"contract FROM authors WHERE (au_id = @Select_au_id)";

this.sqlInsertCommand1.Connection = this.sqlConnection1;
this.sqlInsertCommand1.Parameters.Add(new
    System.Data.SqlClient.SqlParameter("@au_id",
    System.Data.SqlDbType.NChar, 11,
    System.Data.ParameterDirection.Input, false,
    ((System.Byte)(0)), ((System.Byte)(0)), "au_id",
    System.Data.DataRowVersion.Current, null));
this.sqlInsertCommand1.Parameters.Add(new
    System.Data.SqlClient.SqlParameter("@au_lname",
    System.Data.SqlDbType.NVarChar, 40,
    System.Data.ParameterDirection.Input, false,
    ((System.Byte)(0)), ((System.Byte)(0)), "au_lname",
    System.Data.DataRowVersion.Current, null));
this.sqlInsertCommand1.Parameters.Add(new
    System.Data.SqlClient.SqlParameter("@au_fname",
    System.Data.SqlDbType.NVarChar, 20,
    System.Data.ParameterDirection.Input, false,
    ((System.Byte)(0)), ((System.Byte)(0)), "au_fname",
    System.Data.DataRowVersion.Current, null));
this.sqlInsertCommand1.Parameters.Add(new
    System.Data.SqlClient.SqlParameter("@phone",
    System.Data.SqlDbType.NChar, 12,
    System.Data.ParameterDirection.Input, false,
    ((System.Byte)(0)), ((System.Byte)(0)), "phone",
    System.Data.DataRowVersion.Current, null));
this.sqlInsertCommand1.Parameters.Add(new
    System.Data.SqlClient.SqlParameter("@address",
    System.Data.SqlDbType.NVarChar, 40,
    System.Data.ParameterDirection.Input, true,
    ((System.Byte)(0)), ((System.Byte)(0)), "address",
    System.Data.DataRowVersion.Current, null));
this.sqlInsertCommand1.Parameters.Add(new
    System.Data.SqlClient.SqlParameter("@city",
    System.Data.SqlDbType.NVarChar, 20,
    System.Data.ParameterDirection.Input, true,
    ((System.Byte)(0)), ((System.Byte)(0)), "city",
    System.Data.DataRowVersion.Current, null));
this.sqlInsertCommand1.Parameters.Add(new
    System.Data.SqlClient.SqlParameter("@state",
    System.Data.SqlDbType.NChar, 2,
    System.Data.ParameterDirection.Input, true,
    ((System.Byte)(0)), ((System.Byte)(0)), "state",
    System.Data.DataRowVersion.Current, null));
```

```
this.sqlInsertCommand1.Parameters.Add(new
    System.Data.SqlClient.SqlParameter("@zip",
    System.Data.SqlDbType.NChar, 5,
    System.Data.ParameterDirection.Input, true,
    ((System.Byte)(0)), ((System.Byte)(0)), "zip",
    System.Data.DataRowVersion.Current, null));
this.sqlInsertCommand1.Parameters.Add(new
    System.Data.SqlClient.SqlParameter("@contract",
    System.Data.SqlDbType.Bit, 1,
    System.Data.ParameterDirection.Input, false,
    ((System.Byte)(0)), ((System.Byte)(0)), "contract",
    System.Data.DataRowVersion.Current, null));
this.sqlInsertCommand1.Parameters.Add(new
    System.Data.SqlClient.SqlParameter("@Select_au_id",
    System.Data.SqlDbType.NChar, 11,
    System.Data.ParameterDirection.Input, false,
    ((System.Byte)(0)), ((System.Byte)(0)), "au_id",
    System.Data.DataRowVersion.Current, null));
```

Here is the UPDATE command, minus the parameters. The UPDATE command can be modified if you wish to customize it.

```
//
// sqlUpdateCommand1
//
this.sqlUpdateCommand1.CommandText = @"UPDATE authors SET " +
    "au_id = @au_id, au_lname = @au_lname, " +
    "au_fname = @au_fname, phone = @phone, " +
    "address = @address, city = @city, state = @state, " +
    "zip = @zip, contract = @contract WHERE " +
    "(au_id = @Original_au_id) AND " +
    "(address = @Original_address OR " +
    "@Original_address1 IS NULL AND address IS NULL)" +
    " AND (au_fname = @Original_au_fname) AND " +
    "au_lname = @Original_au_lname) AND " +
    "(city = @Original_city OR @Original_city1 IS NULL " +
    "AND city IS NULL) AND (contract = @Original_contract) " +
    "AND (phone = @Original_phone) AND " +
    "(state = @Original_state OR @Original_state1 IS NULL " +
    "AND state IS NULL) AND (zip = @Original_zip OR " +
    "@Original_zip1 IS NULL AND zip IS NULL); SELECT au_id, " +
    "au_lname, au_fname, phone, address, city, state, zip, " +
    "contract FROM authors WHERE (au_id = @Select_au_id)";
```

Finally the DELETE command, again without generated parameters:

```
//
// sqlDeleteCommand1
//
this.sqlDeleteCommand1.CommandText = @"DELETE FROM authors " +
"WHERE (au_id = @au_id) AND (address = @address OR @address1 " +
"IS NULL AND address IS NULL) AND (au_fname = @au_fname) AND " +
"(au_lname = @au_lname) AND (city = @city OR @city1 IS NULL " +
```

```
"AND city IS NULL) AND (contract = @contract) AND (phone = " +
"@phone) AND (state = @state OR @state1 IS NULL AND state IS " +
"NULL) AND (zip = @zip OR @zip1 IS NULL AND zip IS NULL)";
```

The `DataSet` itself is described in a generated W3C-style schema XSD file, shown below. Thus the application has a record of the data type for each of the fields.

```xsd
<xsd:schema id="ds"
    targetNamespace="http://www.tempuri.org/ds.xsd"
    xmlns="http://www.tempuri.org/ds.xsd"
    xmlns:xsd="http://www.w3.org/2001/XMLSchema"
    xmlns:msdata="urn:schemas-microsoft-com:xml-msdata"
    attributeFormDefault="qualified"
    elementFormDefault="qualified">
    <xsd:element name="ds" msdata:IsDataSet="true">
        <xsd:complexType>
            <xsd:choice maxOccurs="unbounded">
                <xsd:element name="authors">
                    <xsd:complexType>
                        <xsd:sequence>
                            <xsd:element name="au_id" type="xsd:string" />
                            <xsd:element name="au_lname" type="xsd:string" />
                            <xsd:element name="au_fname" type="xsd:string" />
                            <xsd:element name="phone" type="xsd:string" />
                            <xsd:element name="address" type="xsd:string"
                        minOccurs="0" />
                            <xsd:element name="city" type="xsd:string"
                        minOccurs="0" />
                            <xsd:element name="state" type="xsd:string"
                        minOccurs="0" />
                            <xsd:element name="zip" type="xsd:string"
                        minOccurs="0" />
                            <xsd:element name="contract" type="xsd:boolean" />
                        </xsd:sequence>
                    </xsd:complexType>
                </xsd:element>
            </xsd:choice>
        </xsd:complexType>
        <xsd:unique name="Constraint1" msdata:PrimaryKey="true">
            <xsd:selector xpath=".//authors" />
            <xsd:field xpath="au_id" />
        </xsd:unique>
    </xsd:element>
</xsd:schema>
```

At this point, let's go ahead and link the data to the `DataGrid`. From the toolbox, drop the `DataGrid` onto the form. In the **Properties** window, set the data source equal to our `DataSet`, ds1. Then set the `DataMember` property to the `authors` table from within the `DataSet`.

At this point, the field headers should appear in the `DataGrid`. Finally, we need to supply the code to actually fill the `DataSet`. Let's jump into the form load event and actually fill the `DataSet` using the `DataAdapter`. Simply double-click on the form in design mode, and you should be put into code view, in the `Form1_Load` event. Add the single line of code as seen overleaf.

```
private void Form1_Load (object sender, System.EventArgs e)
{
    sqlDataAdapter1.Fill(ds1, "authors");
}
```

At this point run the program. As you can see, in almost no time at all, the `DataSet` is filled with consumate ease.

au_id	au_lname	au_fname	phone	address	city	state	zip	contract
172-32-1176	White	Johnson	408 496-7223	222 s. street	Menlo Park	CA	94025	☑
213-46-8915	Green	Marjorie	415 986-7020	309 63rd St.	Oakland	CA	94618	☑
238-95-7766	Carson	Cheryl	415 548-7723	589 Darwin L	Berkeley	CA	94705	☑
267-41-2394	O'Leary	Michael	408 286-2428	22 Cleveland	San Jose	CA	95128	☑
274-80-9391	Straight	Dean	415 834-2919	5420 College	Oakland	CA	94609	☑
341-22-1782	Smith	Meander	913 843-0462	10 Mississipp	Lawrence	KS	66044	☐
409-56-7008	Bennet	Abraham	415 658-9932	6223 Batema	Berkeley	CA	94705	☑
427-17-2319	Dull	Ann	415 836-7128	3410 Blonde	Palo Alto	CA	94301	☑
472-27-2349	Gringlesby	Burt	707 938-6445	PO Box 792	Covelo	CA	95428	☑
486-29-1786	Locksley	Charlene	415 585-4620	18 Broadway	San Francisc	CA	94130	☑
527-72-3246	Greene	Morningstar	615 297-2723	22 Graybar H	Nashville	TN	37215	☐
648-92-1872	Blotchet-Halls	Reginald	503 745-6402	55 Hillsdale B	Corvallis	OR	97330	☑
672-71-3249	Yokomoto	Akiko	415 935-4228	3 Silver Ct.	Walnut Creek	CA	94595	☑
712-45-1867	del Castillo	Innes	615 996-8275	2286 Cram Pl	Ann Arbor	MI	48105	☑
722-51-5454	DeFrance	Michel	219 547-9982	3 Balding Pl.	Gary	IN	46403	☑
724-08-9931	Stringer	Dirk	415 843-2991	5420 Telegra	Oakland	CA	94609	☐
724-80-9391	MacFeather	Stearns	415 354-7128	44 Upland Ht	Oakland	CA	94612	☑
756-30-7391	Karsen	Livia	415 534-9219	5720 McAule	Oakland	CA	94609	☑
807-91-6654	Panteley	Sylvia	301 946-8853	1956 Arlingto	Rockville	MD	20853	☑
846-92-7186	Hunter	Sheryl	415 836-7128	3410 Blonde	Palo Alto	CA	94301	☑
893-72-1158	McBadden	Heather	707 448-4982	301 Putnam	Vacaville	CA	95688	☐
899-46-2035	Ringer	Anne	801 826-0752	67 Seventh A	Salt Lake City	UT	84152	☑
998-72-3567	Ringer	Albert	801 826-0752	67 Seventh A	Salt Lake City	UT	84152	☑

Summary

In the previous chapters you learned how to create database applications "by hand". This chapter was meant to teach you how to take advantage of some of the productivity features provided by Visual Studio .NET.

Visual Studio increases the productivity of the developer by allowing them to concentrate on the logic of the application, while automatically generating code for typical (sometimes unpleasant and boring) tasks. The automatically generated code is quality code that is generally very efficient and does not require intensive testing. By reading this chapter, you have seen see how easily the Visual Studio .NET data environment allows you to create a data-aware application with just a few mouse clicks.

Along with the code generation features, Visual Studio also provides tools and components with the same purpose of helping the programmer to quickly create fast, quality code: `DataGrid`, and data-bound controls. A description with short, clear examples was given.

You are now ready for the next chapter, which presents advanced topics about programming database applications with C# and ADO.NET.

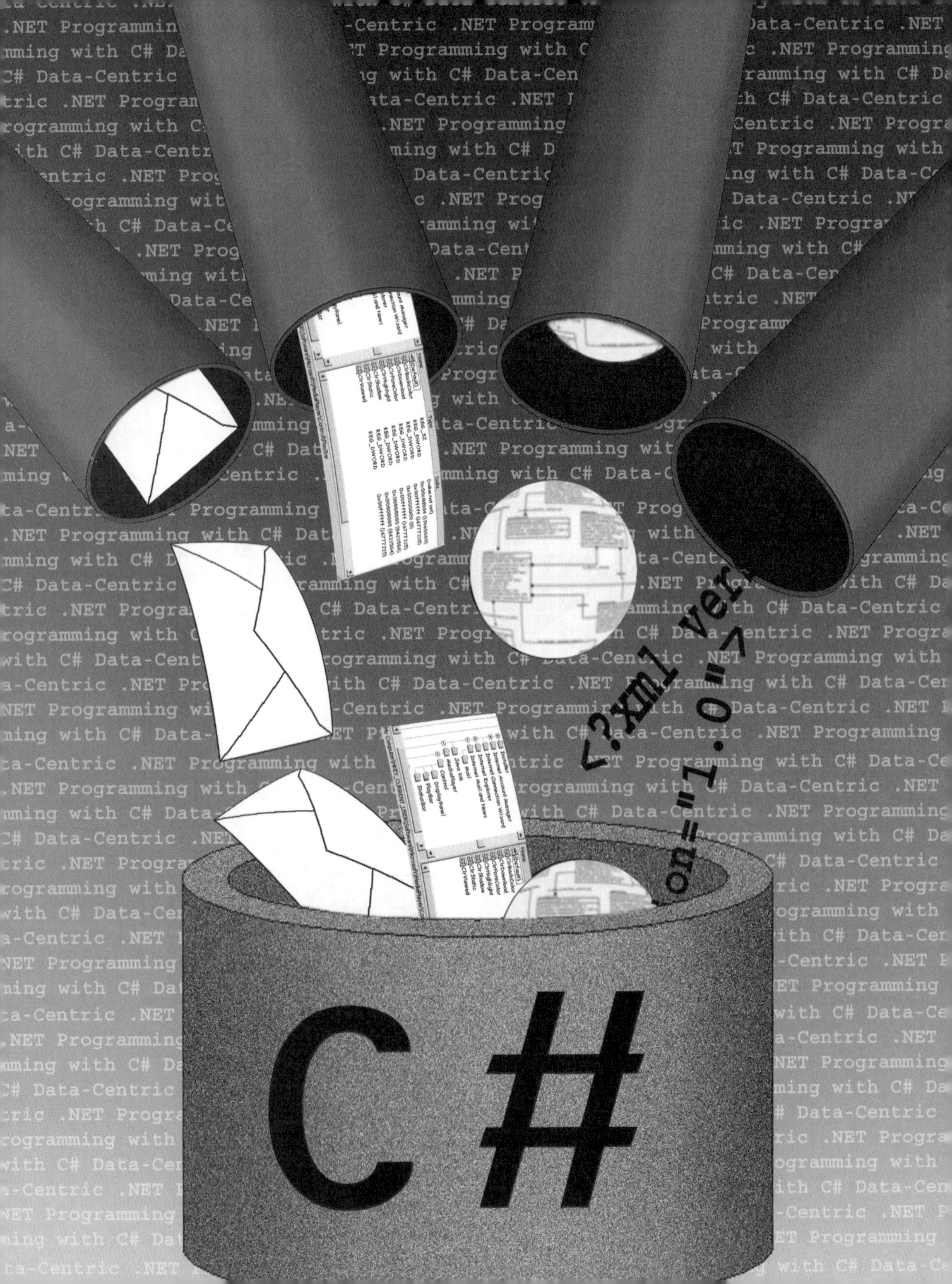

Data-Centric .NET Programming with C#
<?xml ver
on="1.0"?>
C#

6

ADO.NET and C# IV: Advanced .NET Topics

Ever since Microsoft released the first beta of the .NET Framework, people have been wondering whether .NET spells the end of COM+. Some argue that since .NET and COM+ represent two different application development frameworks, COM+'s days are numbered. Once the .NET Framework has been officially released, developers will use it exclusively for creating new applications. While it's often not viable to upgrade all existing COM+ applications to .NET, they will simply become legacy applications, much like DOS and Win16 applications.

Others argue that, while COM+ is not perfect, it represents a solid application development framework and infrastructure. Unless .NET incorporates all COM+ features, COM+ is here to stay for a long time. In the last few years, application developers have created proven architectures and applications based on COM and COM+. It will take time for .NET to catch up.

Both arguments are valid. It has become apparent that, instead of replacing COM+ completely, .NET actually uses many well-designed and proven COM+ features in order to provide a better application development platform.

In this chapter, we will take a look at some advanced .NET techniques that either originated from, or are related to, the familiar COM+ architecture. In particular, we will examine the following features:

❑ Connection Pooling

❑ Integration of .NET and COM+

❑ Implementing Serviced Components with .NET

We will create several small and focused sample applications to illustrate concepts such as connection pooling, implementing serviced components, object pooling, and transactions.

> **Please note, that, for some of the code in this chapter, there appears to be significant implementation differences between the Beta 2 and Release Candidate 1 versions of the .NET Framework. Furthermore there are issues that are likely to change in the final version of the framework. We have attempted to note the differences and issues where possible, and will provide further information at www.wrox.com when the final release version becomes available.**

Connection Pooling

Many applications need to access data stored in databases and other sources. In order to access data, an application needs to establish a connection to the database. The application can then use the connection to perform data access operations.

It can take a relatively long time to establish a database connection because the database server and the application must negotiate during the process. A database connection also consumes precious system resources such as the CPU power, memory, and network bandwidth. Therefore, it is well worth the effort to investigate and apply techniques that reduce the need to establish database connections and the number of live connections.

What is Connection Pooling?

Because establishing a database connection takes time, it is a common practice to keep the connection open till the application is finished with it. This allows the application to perform better and be more responsive.

On the other hand, when the number of connections increases, system resources may be stretched, so the overall performance suffers. While this may not be critical when the application is only used by a limited number of users, it can cause problems when the application needs to support a large number of users concurrently. In database-driven web applications with heavy traffic, it is not uncommon to have thousands of users connected simultaneously.

To solve this problem, applications use **connection pooling** to both speed up the connection process and conserve system resources. In a nutshell, connection pooling works as follows:

1. When an application requests a database connection for the first time, a data provider program intercepts the request, creates a new connection to the database, and hands it over to the application.

2. The application uses the connection to perform a sequence of database operations.

3. The application releases the connection when it no longer needs it.

4. The data provider intercepts the connection release request. Instead of actually destroying the connection, it caches it in a connection pool.

5. When the application needs a connection again, the data provider again intercepts the request. This time, instead of creating a new connection, it picks up an idle connection from the pool and passes it to the application. If there is no connection available in the pool because other instances of the application or other applications are using all available connections, the data provider will create a new connection and pass it to the application requesting the connection.

6. The application uses the connection to perform another sequence of database operations.

Back in the days of ADO and ODBC, Microsoft provided connection pooling to help enterprise application developers create scalable applications. Microsoft has since also offered connection pooling in OLE DB.

With .NET, Microsoft has introduced the concept of **managed data providers**, which conform to the .NET Framework. As we've seen in previous chapters, at the present time, there are two managed data providers; the OLE DB .NET data provider provides access to data sources through their specific OLE DB providers and the SQL Server .NET data provider provides optimized access to Microsoft SQL Server 7.0 and 2000. Both data providers offer connection pooling.

Before going any further to see how we can take advantage of connection pooling, let's take a look at an example demonstrating connection pooling.

Connection Pooling in Action

This sample application will allow us to create any number of database connections to the sample `Northwind` database shipped with SQL Server 2000. We'll be able to specify whether or not we wish to use connection pooling when creating the connections.

Firstly create a C# Windows Application, `ConnectionPooling`, and rename the automatically generated Windows Form class `PoolingTester`.

On the Pooling Test form, add the following controls with the properties as listed in the table below:

Control Type	Property	Property Value
Form	Text	ADO.NET Connection Pooling Test Form
Label	Text	Number of Connections:
Textbox	Name	txtNumberOfConnections
	Text	[Blank]
CheckBox	Name	chkPooling

Table continued on following page

Control Type	Property	Property Value
	Text	Pool Connections
Button	Name	btnConnect
	Text	Connect
Button	Name	btnDisconnect
	Text	Disconnect

In the `PoolingTester` form Code Window, add the following code:

```
using System;
using System.Drawing;
using System.Collections;
using System.ComponentModel;
using System.Windows.Forms;
using System.Data;

using System.Data.SqlClient;

namespace ConnectionPooling
{
    public class PoolingTester : System.Windows.Forms.Form
    {
        public PoolingTester()
        {
            //
            // Required for Windows Form Designer support
            //
            InitializeComponent();

            // Enable the Connect button and
            // disable the Disconnect button
            EnableButtons(false);
        }

        // Enable the Connect and Disconnect buttons depending on
        // whether or not it is connected to the database
        private void EnableButtons(bool Connected)
        {
            btnConnect.Enabled = !Connected;
            btnDisconnect.Enabled = Connected;
        }

        // The basic connection string
        private const string mcConnString =
                            "Data Source=(local);" +
                            "Integrated Security=SSPI;" +
                            "Initial Catalog=Northwind";
```

In this example, we'll use the SQL Server .NET data provider to connect to a SQL Server, so we need to import the `System.Data.SqlClient` namespace to simplify the code. The `mcConnString` data member stores the basic connection string to the local `Northwind` database.

The EnableButtons() method enables and disables the Connect and Disconnect buttons based on the connection state. It accepts one parameter, Connected, that represents whether or not the program is currently connected to the database. If it is connected, this method disables the Connect button and enables the Disconnect button. Otherwise, it enables the Connect button and disables the Disconnect button.

When the form is loaded, it is not connected to the database. Therefore its constructor calls the EnableButtons() method and passes in false.

Now, double-click the Connect button and add the following code in the code window to create an array of connections:

```
// The connection array
private ArrayList mConnectionArray = null;

// Connect to database
private void btnConnect_Click(object sender, System.EventArgs e)
{
    Connect(Convert.ToInt32(txtNumberOfConnections.Text),
            chkPooling.Checked);
    EnableButtons(true);
}

// Create a number of connections to the database.
// Explicitly specify the connection pooling property
private void Connect(int NumberOfConnections, bool PoolConnections)
{
    string ConnString = mcConnString + ";Pooling=" + PoolConnections;

    mConnectionArray = new ArrayList(NumberOfConnections);
    for (int Idx = 0; Idx < NumberOfConnections; ++Idx)
    {
        SqlConnection cn = new SqlConnection(ConnString);
        cn.Open();
        mConnectionArray.Add(cn);
    }
}
```

The mConnectionArray data member stores a number of connections according to the value specified in the txtNumberOfConnections textbox. The Connect() method actually creates those connections. It accepts two parameters, NumberOfConnections and PoolConnections, which specify the number of connections to be created and whether it should instruct the SQL Server data provider to use connection pooling, respectively.

The Connect() method first builds the connections by concatenating the basic string defined in mcConnString and the pooling requirement. For instance, if the PoolConnections parameter is true, the connection string will be:

```
Data Source=(local);Integrated Security=SSPI;
Initial Catalog=Northwind;Pooling=true
```

Next, it instantiates mConnectionArray, to create the required connections, and adds them to mConnectionArray.

The `Connect` button's `Click` event handler, `btnConnect_Click`, reads in the number of connections and the pooling requirement. It then passes them to the `Connect()` method. Once the `Connect()` method returns, that is, it has created the connections, `btnConnect_Click` calls the `EnableButtons` to disable the `Connect` button and enable the `Disconnect` button.

Clicking the `Disconnect` button will disconnect all connections. Just double-click the `Disconnect` button and add the following code snippet in the code window:

```
// Disconnect from the database
private void btnDisconnect_Click(object sender, System.EventArgs e)
{
    Disconnect();
    EnableButtons(false);
}

// Close all connections
private void Disconnect()
{
    foreach (SqlConnection cn in mConnectionArray)
    {
        cn.Close();
    }
}
```

The `Disconnect` button's `Click` event handler, `btnDisconnnect_Click`, calls the `Disconnect()` method, which simply loops through `mConnectionArray` and closes each connection. It then calls the `EnableButtons()` method to enable the `Connect` button and disable the `Disconnect` button.

Testing the Sample

To see the number of live connections, you can use the Windows Performance Monitor. It is accessible through Administrative Tools in the Control Panel. In Administrative Tools, open the **Add Counters** dialog. In the dialog, find **SQLServer:General Statistics** in the **Performance object** drop-down box and select the **User Connections** counter.

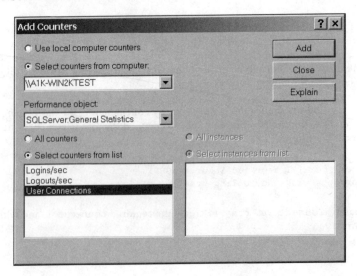

You can then click the **Add** button and then the **Close** button. The Performance Monitor should now display a diagram showing the number of transactions. The figure you will be interested in is the **Last value**, which shows the number of currently opened connections.

Now compile and run the `ConnectionPooling` application. First, try to create one connection without connection pooling by leaving the **Pool Connections** checkbox unchecked. You will see in the Performance Monitor that a connection is created when you click the **Connect** button, and removed when you click the **Disconnect** button. You can try to create more than one connection, and watch the number of live connections in the Performance Monitor. That number should match that entered in the **Number of Connections** textbox.

Next, try to create one connection with connection pooling. You should see that one connection is created when you click the **Connect** button, as you would expect.

> *Beta 2/RC1 notes: In the .NET Framework and Visual Studio pre-releases, the SQL Server data provider creates an extra connection due to a threading timing issue. So you will see that two connections have been created even though you only asked for one.*
>
> *Also, connection pooling is disabled when running the project in debug mode inside the Visual Studio .NET IDE. Therefore you must run the program either using the* **Start Without Debugging** *option, or outside the Visual Studio .NET IDE as a standalone application.*

When you click the **Disconnect** button, you will notice that the number of connections remains unchanged in the Performance Monitor. As described previously, that is because the connection is not destroyed, but just returned to the connection pool.

If you click the **Connect** button again without entering a different number of connections, no new connection is created and the Performance Monitor will again show the same number of connections. The SQL Server data provider simply reuses the pooled connection.

When you close the application, the connection pool is closed and all connections are released.

You can play with this little program with different numbers of connections, with or without connection pooling, and mix pooled and un-pooled connections to see how the SQL Server data provider manages those connections.

Connection Pooling is Bound to Process

An important characteristic of connection pooling is that a pool is associated with a process. In the above example, if you run multiple instances of the `ConnectionPooling` program, you will notice that each instance maintains its own connection pool. That is, when one instance executes, the SQL Server data provider creates one connection pool for it. When the second instance then executes, the SQL Server data provider creates another pool for it. The two instances do not share the same pool.

When you terminate one instance, its connection pool is destroyed. Other instances cannot reuse the pool. This may seem to somehow negate the primary advantage of connection pooling where many clients can share a finite number of connections in a pool. However, we need to look beyond the face value to examine how we design the architecture of scalable applications.

In a scalable application, we typically partition it into several tiers. Data access functionality is encapsulated into a set of data access tier components that perform database access operations. Those components manage database connections internally in order to execute requests from client objects. In the COM+ world, where sets of components are packaged in a COM+ server application, COM+ component services (DLLHost) hosts the data access tier components. Each instance of DLLHost is a process that hosts all instances of data access components in a COM+ application package.

Connection pooling works perfectly within this architecture. From the data provider's perspective, all instances of the data access components run in the same process. Therefore, all clients using the same data access components will share just one connection pool.

Another scenario is when data access components are used from a web application. Because IIS itself is installed as a COM+ application, all web pages in the same web application run in one process as far as COM+ is concerned. Therefore, they can also share the same connection pool. We will see how this works in a moment.

Using Connection Pooling

The key to the successful use of connection pooling is that an application should acquire connections as late as possible and release them as soon as possible. For instance, suppose a typical flow of an application is as follows:

1. The user starts the application

2. The application loads data from the database and displays it to the user

3. The user examines the data and modifies it

4. The application saves the changes to the database

5. The application again waits for user input

The most scalable and high-performance solution for this application is then to:

❑ Acquire a connection in Step 2, before loading data from the database

❑ Release the connection in Step 2, either after loading the data or after displaying the data, depending on whether or not the disconnected DataSet object or the connected DataReader object is used

❑ Acquire another connection in Step 4, before saving the changes to the database

❑ Release the connection in Step 4, after saving the changes

Doing this ensures that the application never holds a connection when it isn't actually performing data access operations. For instance, in Step 3, when the application waits for user input, there is no need to hold on to the connection.

Using Connection Pooling in a Web Application

This example shows how connection pooling works in a typical web application. It has only one page, which lists all customers from the Customers table in the sample Northwind database. Following the principle of separating data and presentation, we will partition it into two assemblies: a data access class library and a web ASP.NET project.

The Data Access Code

Firstly, create a C# Class Library project named ConnPoolingLib and change the automatically created class name from Class1 to PoolingServer. In the PoolingServer class, add these two using statements to import data access namespaces:

```
using System;
using System.Data;
using System.Data.SqlClient;
```

This class has only one method, ReadCustomers(), which simply connects to the Northwind database and returns a disconnected DataSet object containing all customer records:

```
public DataSet ReadCustomers(bool PoolConnections)
{
    string ConnString =
            "Data Source=(local);" +
            "Integrated Security=SSPI;" +
            "Initial Catalog=Northwind;" +
            "Pooling=" + PoolConnections;
    SqlConnection cn = new SqlConnection(ConnString);
    DataSet         ds = new DataSet();

    cn.Open();
    SqlDataAdapter da = new SqlDataAdapter(
        "SELECT CustomerID, CompanyName FROM Customers", cn);
    da.Fill(ds);
    cn.Close();
    return ds;
}
```

It accepts one parameter, PoolConnections, which specifies whether it should use connection pooling for the database operations. The first statement builds a connection string including the pooling property based on the PoolConnections parameter value. The rest of the code in this method is very straightforward. It uses a DataAdapter object, da, to read data from the database and populate a DataSet object ds, and then returns ds.

That's the data tier – compile it and build the library for use in the next step.

The Web Interface Code

Next, create an ASP.NET Web Application project and name it ConnPoolingWebClient. As usual, we need to add a reference to the ConnPoolingServer assembly in order to use the PoolingServer class. You can either use the default WebForm1.aspx or, if you prefer explicit naming of ASP pages, remove it and add a new Web Form named PoolingClient.

Drop a `DataGrid` control on to the `PoolingClient` form and rename it `grdCustomers`. Then open the code window for the `PoolingClient` form class and add the following code to the `Page_Load()` method:

```
private void Page_Load(object sender, System.EventArgs e)
{
    // Populate the grdCustomers DataGrid control
    ConnPoolingLib.PoolingServer svr = new ConnPoolingLib.PoolingServer();
    DataSet ds = null;
    for (int i = 0; i < 100; ++i)
    {
        ds = svr.ReadCustomers(true);
    }
    grdCustomers.DataSource = ds;
    grdCustomers.DataBind();
}
```

This method instantiates a `PoolingServer` object and invokes its `ReadCustomers()` method to retrieve a `DataSet` object, `ds`, containing all customer records. Note that it passes `true` to the `PoolConnections` parameter in the `ReadCustomers()` method to indicate to the server that it should enable connection pooling. It then binds the `grdCustomers` `DataGrid` control to `ds` so that the customer records will be displayed on the page. The `for` loop simulates many database operations performed in a page. Note that it only binds the customer record grid to the `DataSet` returned in the last iteration.

The `DataSets` returned from the first 99 iterations are simply thrown away. While we wouldn't want to do this in a real application, it's fine here as the purpose of this application is to just simulate a long operation.

The above code shows how connection pooling works. You can change the parameter passed to the `ReadCustomers` method from `true` to `false` to see what happens when connection pooling is disabled. This helps you to see the difference with and without connection pooling in a web application.

The last step is to build the project.

Running the Example

As shown previously, the **SQL Server User Connections** counter in the Performance Monitor can be used to monitor the number of database connections.

Now load the page in Internet Explorer. The Performance Monitor should show that just one database connection is created (two in Beta 2, as explained before). The connection stays even after the page has been successfully loaded because the IIS process is still up. If you load the page again, no new connection is created because the pooled connection will be used instead.

If you change the `PoolConnections` parameter in the `ReadCustomers` call to `false`, rebuild the web application, and load the page again, you will see several, or perhaps many more, connections showing up in the Performance Monitor while the page is being loaded.

This is because when connection pooling is not enabled, each connection waits to be destroyed by the garbage collector after it is closed. With the .NET garbage collection mechanism, closed connections stay in the memory until the garbage collector cleans them up. Before the garbage collector gets around to destroying the connection, the connection still shows up in the Performance Monitor. The second call to `ReadCustomers()` will create a new connection since it can't reuse the old ones without connection pooling. Therefore you will see a number of connections in the Performance Monitor while loading the page.

The exact number of connections created will depend on your machine configuration. On a fast machine, the number may be very small because the garbage connector may start to reclaim the discarded connections a lot quicker. You can explicitly destroy the connection by calling the static `Collect` method of the system garbage collector, GC. However since such a heavy-handed approach has other implications, you should restrict the use of this to situations where it is absolutely necessary.

For a good introduction to the concept and issues of garbage collection, please read the MSDN article *Programming Essentials for Garbage Collection*

> *In Visual Studio .NET Beta 2, you may need to remove the User Connections counter from the Performance Monitor and add it in again after changing the connection pooling setting in order for it to display the correct number of connections. You may even have to stop and restart the SQL Server as well.*

This example shows that in a high-volume web application, using connection pooling can significantly reduce the number of database connections. Consequently, you can develop scalable, high-performance web applications without having to invest vast amounts of money on expensive system hardware.

By default, both SQL Server and OLE DB .NET data providers enable connection pooling. For most applications, you will use this feature as provided. In some cases, however, you might want to modify the connection pooling settings to fine-tune your data access subsystems. Detailed descriptions on those settings are beyond the scope of this book – and the interested reader is referred to the MSDN Library for more information on this subject.

Integration with COM+

In the last section, we saw that .NET provides the connection pooling capability by implementing it in managed data providers. To develop high-performance, scalable distributed applications, we need more tools like connection pooling.

If you have created distributed applications using COM+, you know that you need to use other facilities such as object pooling, just-in-time activation, distributed transaction processing, and so forth. COM+ provides those facilities as integrated parts of the COM+ component services. So how does .NET implement those services?

Unlike the way .NET provides connection pooling, which does not use existing COM+ services, .NET uses COM+ as the foundation for providing the other services mentioned to application developers. .NET implements COM+ services as managed components to provide native Enterprise Services support to .NET components. To understand how we can take advantage of this approach in our applications, let's briefly review how COM+ implements those services.

A Brief Review of COM+ Services

COM+ provides a set of run-time services to facilitate the development and deployment of component-based distributed systems. Among them are:

- ❑ Contexts for providing services to objects
- ❑ Synchronization for managing concurrent access to configured objects

- Just-in-time activation for handling heavy object usage

- Object pooling for improving application performance

- Distributed transaction processing for supporting transactions across components and data sources

- Component services for application packaging and distribution

In this section, we will review these services briefly. We will discuss each of them in more detail in later sections when covering each service in .NET. There are other COM+ services such as security, queued components, and events that are not covered in this chapter.

Configured and Non-configured Classes

There are essentially two types of COM+ classes: **configured** and **non-configured**. A configured class has a set of COM+-specific declarative attributes, which specify the required COM+ services. At run time, COM+ ensures that it provides the required services to the COM+ objects. A non-configured class has no such attributes, and therefore does not require the COM+-specific services.

Contexts

COM+ provides its services through **contexts**, which are implemented as objects called the **object context**. All COM+ classes, configured and non-configured, are instantiated in a context. Each object lives in precisely one context.

COM+ provides services to configured classes at run time, when required, through contexts. Non-configured classes, on the other hand, ignore their associated contexts as they are not aware of such object contexts.

Just-In-Time (JIT) Activation

In COM, a client object holds a reference to a server object until it explicitly releases it. This presents a problem similar to holding a connection for a long time. Both consume precious system resources. In a large-scale application, this can have a big impact on system performance.

A common practice in COM is to release server object references often, and as soon as possible. This approach, however, puts the responsibility on client application developers to discover and understand how server classes work. They need to understand whether or not a server class consumes important system resources that need to be carefully managed, and if so, remember to release object references at critical points.

With JIT Activation, the server class developers specify whether an instance of a server class should be released early. They achieve this by indicating to COM+ whether the instance should be released after it returns the control to the client. It works as follows: the client object creates a server object and invokes one of its methods. When the method returns, COM+ may deactivate the server object even though the client object still holds a reference to it. When the client invokes another method, COM+ can re-activate the server object to execute the command.

As far as the client object is concerned, the server object is there to service its request all the time. How COM+ manages the server object is completely transparent to the client object. This approach conserves precious system resources, especially when we're developing high-volume transaction applications. There are overheads in object activation and deactivation, but they are marginal compared to the high demand on system resources caused by maintaining a large number of objects used by applications.

The most significant implication of this approach is that the client object cannot count on the server object to be able to maintain its state between two method calls because the server object will lose its state if it is deactivated after the first call. If the server object needs to maintain its state between calls, it can do so by saving its state to the Shared Property Manager provided by COM+, or to persistent data storage such as databases.

Object Pooling

To further improve the application performance, COM+ provides **object pooling** to cache deactivated objects in an object pool. This reduces the overhead associated with object creation and therefore greatly speeds up object reactivation. We can specify the object pool size to set aside a certain amount of memory for objects of the same type, thereby gaining more control in refining the balance of speed and memory consumption.

We exercise our control over the pool size by setting its minimum and maximum sizes. The minimum pool size specifies how many instances of an object should be created when it is created for the first time. For instance, if we set the minimum pool size to two, COM+ creates two instances with the first creation of an object. When the second client object creates another instance of the same server object, COM+ simply passes the idle instance from the pool to the client object.

The maximum pool size specifies how many instances at most can be maintained in the pool. If we set the maximum size to five, and five instances are being used by client objects, the sixth client object will have to wait for one of them to be released. This ensures that the memory is not overused by any single component.

You will probably ask how you should determine the maximum pool size. Unfortunately there is no definitive answer to this question. You need to test the possible uses of your applications to predict the statistics such as: typical and maximum concurrent usage; the expected object call duration; the total number of objects; and other system resource uses. Volume-testing your application often provides you with a good indication of the application performance, which allows you to fine-tune your application to achieve the best possible performance.

Distributed Transaction Processing

Database management systems typically provide transaction support to manage data integrity. For instance, when we need to update two tables in one transaction, we want both tables to be updated successfully. If for some reason we cannot update one table, we don't want the other to be updated either. Such a scenario is handled by wrapping the two updates in one database transaction. This guarantees that either both tables are updated, or neither of them is.

Beyond that, if we need the same ability to update two databases, single database-based transaction processing is not adequate. We need to coordinate the updates across databases. COM+ provides this functionality with distributed transactions through the Microsoft Distributed Transaction Coordinator (MS DTC). It guarantees that either both databases are updated or neither of them is.

Beyond cross-database updates, we may need distributed transactions across different components and data sources. For instance, one component may update a set of tables in one database while another component adds some messages to the message queue. MS DTC also manages such situations through distributed transaction processing.

.NET, COM+, and COM

As we've said, Microsoft has built capabilities into the .NET framework that allow interaction between .NET and COM/COM+ objects. It's important to understand that there are two quite different technologies; one provides interaction between .NET and COM and the other provides interaction between .NET and COM+.

Interaction between .NET and COM

The .NET Framework achieves .NET and COM interaction using **COM Interoperability** (**InterOp**). Again, there are two scenarios here. The first is when a .NET object needs to use a COM object. The second is when a COM object needs to use a .NET object.

Exposing COM Components to .NET

In the first scenario, we need to expose COM components to the .NET CLR. We can use one of the following three methods to make a COM component available to a .NET assembly.

❑ Using the Type Library Importer utility (`tlbimp.exe`). This utility converts a COM type library to .NET metadata. It can be run from the command line. The simplest form of using this utility is:

```
tlbimp MyComLib.dll /out:MyComLibA.dll
```

This converts the COM library `MyComLib.dll` to a .NET class library, `MyComLibA.dll`, with the necessary metadata. We can then use `MyComLibA.dll` in .NET assemblies just like we use any managed .NET libraries.

❑ Using Visual Studio .NET. We can add a reference to a COM library in Visual Studio .NET that automatically generates a wrapper library for us. You can find more details on this technique and an example in Chapter 15.

❑ Using the `TypeLibConverter` class. The .NET Framework provides the `TypeLibConverter` class in the `System.Runtime.InteropServices` namespace. This class defines methods to convert interfaces and classes in a COM library to .NET metadata at run time.

At run time, .NET intercepts calls from .NET clients to COM servers and invokes a **Runtime Callable Wrapper** (**RCW**). The RCW transparently translates .NET and COM messages so that a .NET client appears as a COM client to the COM server and a COM server appears as a .NET server to the .NET client.

Chapter 15 provides a case study on COM interoperability that demonstrates various techniques for using COM components in .NET assemblies.

Exposing .NET Components to COM

This scenario is less common than the above scenario where we use COM components within .NET assemblies. The .NET Framework uses a **COM Callable Wrapper** (**CCW**) that performs a similar task to the RCW, but in reverse. As this will be a fairly rare situation, we won't discuss it further (more details are available from the .NET Framework documentation on MSDN).

Interaction between .NET and COM+

As described previously, the .NET Framework essentially facilitates .NET and COM interaction through wrapper classes. While this approach works fine, it represents a relatively low level of integration.

.NET and COM+, on the other hand, are integrated at a much higher level. .NET still relies on COM+ to provide run time services to .NET components. The .NET Framework provides this integration with a comprehensive collection of classes in the `System.EnterpriseServices` namespace. From now on, we will use the following terms:

- ❑ **Enterprise Services** – COM+ services provided through the `System.EnterpriseServices` namespace in the `System.EnterpriseServices` library. Classes in this namespace provide application developers with useful tools to take advantage of those services.

- ❑ **Serviced component** – A .NET class designed to use Enterprise Services.

- ❑ **Serviced assembly** – A .NET assembly containing at least one serviced component.

The following sections explain how we can use .NET Enterprise Service classes in our applications.

Implementing Serviced Components with .NET

In order to use .NET Enterprise Services, serviced components must satisfy a set of requirements. We will create a couple of simple programs to get a feel for using these services in .NET applications. In the following sections, we will look at how to design, implement, and configure .NET assemblies and classes to use Enterprise Services.

Firstly, create a new C# Class Library application and name it `EntServLib`. The next thing we need to do is to add a reference to the `System.EnterpriseServices` library. This is required in any assemblies containing, or using, classes that require Enterprise Services.

Creating Serviced Assemblies

.NET requires that assemblies containing serviced components be **strongly named**. Serviced assemblies are generally public, meaning that they will be used by many client assemblies. The best place to install public assemblies is the **Global Assembly Cache** (**GAC**), because the GAC is where the .NET CLR will look for the referenced assemblies that are not in the same directory as the client assembly. Since the GAC will inevitably contain assemblies created by different vendors and applications, each assembly installed in the GAC must have a globally unique identifier so that it will not cause conflict with other assemblies. A strongly named assembly has a globally unique name that, among other benefits, allows the assembly to be installed in the GAC. To sign an assembly with a strong name, follow these two steps:

1. Create a strong name for the assembly using the **Strong Name** tool, `sn.exe`:

```
sn.exe -k EntServLib.key
```

This creates the key file `EntServLib.key`.

2. Sign the assembly with that key file. Open the generated `AssemblyInfo.cs` in the assembly and assign the `AssemblyKeyFile` attribute with the path and name of the key file:

```
[assembly: AssemblyDelaySign(false)]
[assembly: AssemblyKeyFile(@"..\..\EntServLib.key")]
[assembly: AssemblyKeyName("")]
```

This assumes that you have created the key file in the assembly project directory. As far as the Visual Studio .NET IDE is concerned, the current directory is the directory where the compiled DLL file resides. In most cases, this will be either the `bin\Debug` or the `bin\Release` subdirectory in the project directory. Therefore, the key file needs to be referenced by moving back up the directory tree.

That's all we need to do at the assembly level for now. There are other attributes we can set, as we'll see later.

Creating Serviced Components

All serviced components must inherit from the `ServicedComponent` class in the `System.EnterpriseServices` namespace, or other classes that derive from the `ServicedComponent` class. They must be public and concrete, and also define a public default constructor.

Now rename the generated `Class1` to `EntServClass` and modify it as shown below:

```
using System;
using System.EnterpriseServices;

namespace EntServLib
{
    public class EntServClass : ServicedComponent
    {
        public EntServClass()
        {}

        // Calculate n!
        public int CalcFactor(int n)
        {
            System.Threading.Thread.Sleep(n * 1000);
            int result = 1;
            while (n > 0)
                result = result * n--;
            return result;
        }
    }
}
```

As explained above, the `EntServClass` inherits from the `ServicedComponent` class to let the .NET CLR know that it intends to use Enterprise Services. It has only one method, `CalcFactor()`, which first waits n seconds and then calculates the factorial of the input parameter value n:

```
n! = n * (n - 1) * (n - 2) * ... * 2 * 1
```

This method uses the `Sleep()` method to suspend the current thread for a specified time, therefore simulating a long-lasting method. For instance, if n equals to 5, n! will wait for five seconds and then calculate the result as

```
5! = 5 * 4 * 3 * 2 * 1 = 120
```

This assembly now has all the basic elements of a serviced assembly. Once it's compiled, it's ready to be used.

Registering Serviced Components

But, wait a second, you say. Don't we need to install it as a COM+ application before we can use it just like we did in COM+? The answer is both yes and no.

In COM+, a component need not necessarily be registered in the Windows Registry. While registering a DLL in Windows makes it available as a normal COM server component (also called a **non-configured** COM+ server component) to client objects, it can act as a configured COM+ component if we simply add it to a COM+ application without registering it in Windows first. When we add a non-registered component to a COM+ application, the COM+ component services automatically creates COM+-specific entries to the Windows Registry. On the other hand, if we add a registered COM component to a COM+ application, COM+ automatically translates the COM-specific registry entries to COM+ specific ones.

The idea behind the above process is that, if we take COM out of the equation, registering a COM+ component is really a one-step process. Adding it to a COM+ application is all we need to do.

The process is the same in .NET. When we compile an assembly, it is not automatically registered. There are two ways to register a .NET serviced component. One is to register it manually. The other is to register it dynamically.

Manual Registration

Only system administrators, that is, users who are members of the Administrators group, can register .NET serviced components. Therefore, if you are not in the Administrators group, you need to either add yourself to the group, or log on as an administrator user. You can then manually register a serviced component using the .NET service installation utility, regsvcs.exe, from the command line:

```
regsvcs.exe EntServLib.dll
```

This installs a new COM+ application in the COM+ component services. By default, regsvcs assigns the application the same name as the assembly. You can use a command-line switch /appname to assign it a different name, for instance:

```
regsvcs.exe /appname:"Enterprise Service Library" EntServLib.dll
```

To verify that the application is correctly installed, use the COM+ Component Services MMC snap-in to check out the application. If you look at the settings of this application, you will see that it is created as a library application. This is the default setting if you have not specified the application type explicitly in the assembly. A library application always runs in process, that is, inside the client process memory space. There is no command-line switch to change the application type. You can specify the application type, among other settings such as the application name, in declarative attributes in the assembly. You will see how to do this in a moment.

To unregister a serviced component, you can either delete it in the COM+ Component Services snap-in or use regsvcs with the /u switch:

```
regsvcs.exe /u EntServLib.dll
```

Dynamic Registration

The other registration method is dynamic registration. When a client application instantiates an unregistered serviced component, the CLR registers the component on the fly. Because only administrators can register serviced components, either the client application user must be an administrator, or, if the client application itself is a serviced component, the client application is run under an administrator identity. While dynamic registration is handy in development, it's rarely used in a release version because typically application users are not granted administrator privileges.

Dynamic registration always installs the application using .NET Enterprise Services-specific settings specified in the assembly. If the assembly does not specify a setting, dynamic registration uses a predefined default value. In our EntServLib example, dynamic registration creates a library application with the name EntServLib, since the assembly does not specify an application name attribute.

With the server component ready to be used, it's time to write a simple client program to test it out.

Creating a Client Program

Create a C# Windows Application project named EntServClient and rename the automatically generated Form1 to ClientForm. Then add the following controls to the form:

Control Type	Property	Property Value
Label	Text	Enter a number:
Textbox	Name	txtNumber
	Text	[Blank]
Label	Text	Result:
Label	Name	lblResult
	BorderStyle	Fixed3D
	Text	[Blank]
Button	Name	btnCalc
	Text	Calculate Factor

Because this program will use the `EntServLib` application, we will need to add a reference to the `EntServLib.dll`. We should also add a reference to the `System.EnterpriseServices.dll` as `EntServClass` derives from the `ServicedComponent` class.

Double-click the **Calculate Factor** button to go to the code window and add the following code to the form:

```
public class ClientForm : System.Windows.Forms.Form
{
    ...

    public ClientForm()
    {
        //
        // Required for Windows Form Designer support
        //
        InitializeComponent();

        mServer = new EntServLib.EntServClass();
    }

    private void btnCalc_Click(object sender, System.EventArgs e)
    {
        lblResult.Text =
            mServer.CalcFactor(Convert.ToInt32(txtNumber.Text)).ToString();
    }

    private EntServLib.EntServClass mServer = null;
}
```

The private data member, `mServer`, is an instance of the `EntServClass` class. The `ClientForm` constructor instantiates it when the form is created. Clicking the **Calculate Factor** button will invoke the `CalcFactor()` method. Once the method returns, the result is displayed on the `lblResult` label.

If you have already manually registered `EntServLib`, just run the `EntServClient.exe` program to verify that it works as you expected. If you have not, start the `EntServClient.exe`. You will see in the COM+ Component Services snap-in that the CLR has automatically installed the `EntServLib` application for you. Either way, your client program will work.

You might expect to see the ball representing `EntServClass` spinning in the COM+ Component Services snap-in. It doesn't. The COM+ component services snap-in only displays the run-time status of server applications, but not that of library applications. So you will not see any other run-time statuses such as the number of activated objects or the number of objects in the call either.

In order to see the run-time status, you will need to configure the assembly as server applications. The next section will show how to create server applications and specify other run-time behaviors.

Configuration with Attributes

We can apply the attributes defined in the `System.EnterpriseServices` namespace at four levels: assembly, interface, class, and method.

Configuring Assemblies

In COM+, we can create a COM+ application package with any name we like. The package name can be different from the name of the DLL contained in the package. It is the same in .NET; we can provide an Enterprise Services application name that differs from our assembly name by adding an attribute, `ApplicationName`, to the assembly in `AssemblyInfo.cs`:

```
using System.Reflection;
using System.Runtime.CompilerServices;
using System.EnterpriseServices;

...

// Enterprise Service Application Attributes
[assembly: ApplicationName("Enterprise Service Application")]
```

Both manual and dynamic registration will now install the application with the specified name.

To specify the activation type of an application, that is, whether it's a server or library application, apply the `ApplicationActivation` attribute to the assembly as illustrated below:

```
// Enterprise Service Application Attributes
[assembly: ApplicationName("Enterprise Service Application")]
[assembly: ApplicationActivation(ActivationOption.Server)]
```

The following table lists some of the assembly-level attributes.

Attribute	Description
ApplicationAccessControl	Security settings. Its properties correspond to the settings on the **Security** tab in the COM+ Component Services application property dialog.
ApplicationActivation	Activation type, either server or library.
ApplicationID	GUID of the application.
ApplicationName	Name of the application.
ApplicationQueuing	MSMQ queuing support.
Description	Application description.

Server Application Considerations

> *It appears that due to changes in operation between Beta 2 and RC1, errors may not be generated at this point in RC1, but occur in Beta 2.*

If you assign the `ApplicationActivation` attribute with the `ActivationOption.Server` value and try to run the client program, either from within the Visual Studio .NET IDE or by executing the `EntServClient.exe` directly from the disk, an error will most likely occur. The client program starts fine but, if you try to invoke the `CalcFactor()` method by clicking the **Calculate Factor** button, you will get a **File Not Found** exception:

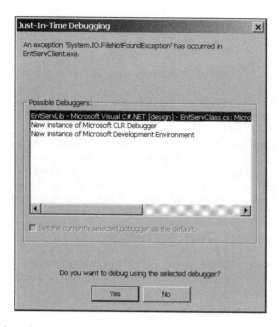

Why is this? If you look at the dialog box closely, you will see that it is complaining about not being able to find the `EntServClass` class. In fact, it just can't find `EntServLib.dll`, which contains metadata for the `EntServClass` class.

The rule the CLR uses to find a DLL at run time is to first look at the same folder where the client executable resides and, if it can't find it there, look in the global assembly cache (GAC). When a client creates an object in a server application for the first time, the COM+ component service starts a new instance of the component service runtime, `dllhost.exe`, and hosts the object in its memory space. Even though `EntServLib.dll` is copied to the folder where `EntServClient.exe` resides, `dllhost.exe` can't see it because `dllhost.exe` itself is installed in the `\WinNT\System32` folder.

Now that you know the problem, the solution is simple. There are two options:

❑ Copy `EntServLib.dll` to the `\WinNT\System32` folder

❑ Install `EntServLib.dll` in the GAC

The first option, while legitimate, is not a good solution. Copying your own DLL files to the `\WinNT\System32` folder is poor deployment practice for various reasons. First, it's a good idea to keep only operating system files in this important directory. Second, when other applications need to reference this DLL, they are more likely to look at the GAC rather than this folder to find shared files. In fact, if another client application is installed in any directory other than `\WinNT\System32`, it won't be able to find your DLL at all. Therefore, installing your own DLLs in the GAC is the better solution.

You can use the GAC installation utility, `GACUtil.exe`, to install DLLs in the GAC from the command line:

```
gacutil.exe /i EntServLib.dll
```

To uninstall it, you use GACUtil with the /u switch:

```
gacutil.exe /u EntServLib
```

Note that you must not specify the .dll extension when uninstalling it.

Once you have installed EntServLib.dll in the GAC, dllhost.exe can find it and your client program will be able to create objects and invoke their methods.

However, the ball is still not spinning, what's going on here? It turns out that the COM+ Component Services snap-in can only display the run-time status of serviced components if they support COM+ events and statistics. By default, a serviced component doesn't support this. So we will need to configure this setting in the serviced component property dialog in the snap-in. Or, as we will see in the next section, specify this and other serviced component settings using declarative attributes in code.

Configuring Serviced Components

We can also apply attributes to classes to specify the run-time behavior of each class. For instance, to enable support for COM+ events and statistics, we use the EventTrackingEnabled attribute. In EntServClass, we enable it as shown below:

```
[EventTrackingEnabled(true)]
public class EntServClass : ServicedComponent
```

The following table lists some of the most important attributes applicable to serviced components:

Attribute	Description
EventTrackingEnabled	Enables support for COM+ events and statistics
Description	Class description
Synchronization	Enables synchronization of serviced components
JustInTimeActivation	Enables just-in-time (JIT) activation of serviced components
ObjectPooling	Enables object pooling
Transaction	Enables declarative transactions
ConstructionEnabled	Enables object construction

We have seen what the EventTrackingEnabled attribute is used for. The Description attribute simply assigns a textual description of the class. In the following sections, we will see what each of the other five attributes means and how we can use them to enjoy the corresponding services provided by .NET enterprise services.

The Synchronization Attribute

A multi-threaded server object has to handle concurrency issues. If more than two client objects try to use an object simultaneously, we need to ensure that they don't interfere with each other. A common technique to manage such situations is to use object-level locking. When the first client object accesses the server object, we lock the server object to prevent the second client from using the same server object until the first client has finished with it.

Implementing this locking mechanism is not difficult, but it's cumbersome since the same thing has to be done for many multi-threaded objects. COM+ and .NET Enterprise Services provide the synchronization service to manage this automatically and transparently for us. All we need to do is to specify a synchronization level and let the synchronization service manage the problem.

By default, the CLR disables synchronization to reduce run-time overhead. We can turn it on explicitly by specifying a synchronization level:

```
[Synchronization(SynchronizationOption.Supported)]
```

We can also specify one of the five synchronization options shown in the following table.

Option	Description
Disabled	No synchronization. This is the default setting and produces exactly same behaviors as non-configured COM+ components.
NotSupported	This object will not participate in any synchronization.
Supported	This object will share its caller's synchronization and does not require its own synchronization. That is, if the client object is synchronized, this class instance will share the client object's synchronization. Otherwise, it is not synchronized, for instance, when the component is a single-threaded apartment component.
Required	This object requires synchronization. If its caller is synchronized, this object will share its synchronization. Otherwise, it needs its own synchronization.
RequiresNew	This object always requires its own synchronization.

In most cases, we don't need to specify this attribute explicitly. If a serviced component supports just-in-time activation or object pooling, the CLR will automatically set the synchronization level to Required.

The JustInTimeActivation Attribute

Normally, once we'veve instantiated a serviced component, it remains activated until we release it. To see this, run the sample client program, EntServClient.exe, and look at the COM+ Component Services snap-in.

Because it instantiates EntServClass in the ClientForm's constructor, you will see that once the client program is running, the number of activated objects is one. That means the object has been activated. The activated object count remains one as long as the client program is running. It becomes zero shortly after you close the client program. The slight delay is the time between when the program exits and when the garbage collector (GC) kicks in to actually release the object.

It's common for client objects not to release a server object until they no longer need it. For instance, the ClientForm object keeps the reference to the instance of EntServClass as a class-level object. So it won't release it until you close the program. Between the last invocation of its methods and the release of the object, the object sits idle waiting. In high-volume applications, the number of idle objects could be large, and so valuable system resources are effectively wasted.

COM+ and .NET provide the JIT activation service to solve this problem. Once the method invoked by the client object returns, the JIT activation service can deactivate the object even though the client object still holds a reference to the server object. The next time the client object invokes a method, the JIT service reactivates the object so that it can serve the client again. If, between the two method invocations, another client object tries to invoke a method of the server object, the JIT activation service can reuse the deactivated object by activating it. This approach helps to conserve system memory by effectively sharing a small number of server objects among a large number of client objects.

It's important that the JIT activation service knows when it can deactivate an object. It finds this information by querying a flag, normally called the **done bit**, in the object context. The server object therefore can set this flag to indicate whether or not it can be deactivated. If the serviced component also supports transactions, which will be discussed later, committing or aborting the transaction also sets the done bit to true. Otherwise, done bit needs to be set explicitly. The code snippet below shows how to do this in EntServClass:

```
[JustInTimeActivation(true)]
public class EntServClass : ServicedComponent
{
    ...
    // Calculate n!
    public int CalcFactor(int n)
    {
        System.Threading.Thread.Sleep(n * 1000);

        int result = 1;
        while (n > 0)
            result = result * n--;

        ContextUtil.DeactivateOnReturn = true;
        return result;
    }
}
```

The JustInTimeActivation attribute value true indicates that this serviced component is JIT activation-enabled. ContextUtil represents the context object in which the current instance of EntServClass lives. Setting its DeactivateOnReturn property to true effectively sets the done bit to true. This indicates that once this method returns, the JIT service can deactivate the current instance. You can rebuild the sample programs and verify that the JIT indeed deactivates this class as soon as CalcFactor() returns.

When the JIT activation service activates or reactivates an object, it calls the serviced component's Activate method to allow the component to perform necessary initializations. Similarly, when the JIT activation service deactivates an object, it calls the Deactivate() method to allow the component to perform necessary cleanup operations such as releasing database connections. A serviced component inherits those methods from the ServicedComponent class. By default, those methods do nothing. If we need to perform certain initialization or cleanup operations, we can override those methods to run our custom code.

For instance, if a serviced component performs database access operations, it may need to connect to a database when it's activated and release the connection when it's deactivated. We can code those operations as shown in the following code snippet:

```
public class DBAccess : ServicedComponent
{
    public override void Activate()
```

```
    {
        mConn = new SqlConnection("Integrated Security=SSPI;" +
                    "Initial Catalog=Northwind;Data Source=(local)");
        mConn.Open();
    }

    public override void Deactivate()
    {
        mConn.Close();
    }

    public void DoIt()
    {
        // Perform database access using mConn
    }
}
```

Please note that in RC1 the access modifiers for the `Activate()` *and* `Deactivate()` *methods have changed and you will need to use the lines:*

```
protected override void Activate()
protected override void Deactivate()
```

We'll see an example of this later when we investigate the transaction processing service.

The ObjectPooling Attribute

While the JIT activation service conserves system resources by deactivating objects while they are not in use, reactivating objects incurs slight overhead because deactivated objects may need to be loaded into the memory when reactivated. The .NET Enterprise Services provide object pooling to further increase the application performance by caching deactivated objects in an in-memory pool.

Object pooling is disabled by default. To turn it on and configure its settings, we use the `ObjectPooling` attribute. This attribute is slightly more complex than the `Synchronization` and `JustInTimeActivation` attributes.

The `ObjectPooling` attribute has four properties:

Name	Description	Default
Enabled	Specifies whether the instances of the class should be pooled.	false
MaxPoolSize	If object pooling is enabled, the maximum number of objects in the pool. If the number of activated objects reaches this limit, subsequent requests from client objects are queued.	1048576
MinPoolSize	If object pooling is enabled, the minimum number of objects in the pool. When a client object creates the first server object, Enterprise Services will create the specified number of server objects.	0

Table continued on following page

Name	Description	Default
CreationTimeout	The number of milliseconds client objects should wait for objects in the pool to be activated. If this timeout limit is reached, Enterprise Services will throw a `System.Runtime.InteropServices.COMException` exception. This timeout may happen when the number of client objects requesting the server object is more than the maximum number of server objects in the pool so that they have to wait for activated server objects to be released. However, if server objects need to perform activation operations that may take an undetermined length of time, for instance, trying to establish a connection to a remote server through an unreliable network, use this timeout to detect unsuccessful connection attempts.	60000

The `ObjectPooling` attribute defines constructors that only initialize the first three attributes. In order to initialize the `CreationTimeout` property, we can use named parameters:

```
[ObjectPooling(Enabled=true, MinPoolSize=2, MaxPoolSize=5,
               CreationTimeout=20000)]
```

Actually, the `Enabled` parameter is redundant here, as .NET Enterprise Services automatically enable object pooling if we provide any of the remaining parameters. It's good to make the intention clear though.

On the other hand, the default implementation of the virtual `CanBePooled()` method defined in the `ServicedComponent` class is to return `false`. Since the `EntServClass` now supports object pooling, it is necessary to override this method to return `true`. This really sounds a bit strange since the `ObjectPooling` attribute has indicated that this class can be pooled. However, if we don't explicitly override this method, we might encounter errors at run time in .NET Beta 2. This is likely to change by the final release of the .NET Framework.

To see how object pooling works, add the `ObjectPooling` attribute to `EntServClass` in `EntServLib`:

```
[ObjectPooling(Enabled=true, MinPoolSize=2, MaxPoolSize=5,
               CreationTimeout=10000)]
public class EntServClass : ServicedComponent
{
    public EntServClass()
    {}

    // Override the default
    public override bool CanBePooled()
    {
        return true;
    }
}
```

and add exception catching code to the `ClientForm`:

```
public ClientForm()
{
    //
    // Required for Windows Form Designer support
    //
    InitializeComponent();

    try
    {
        mServer = new EntServLib.EntServClass();
    }
    catch(Exception x)
    {
        MessageBox.Show(x.Message, x.GetType().ToString());
    }
}

private void btnCalc_Click(object sender, System.EventArgs e)
{
    try
    {
        lblResult.Text =
            mServer.CalcFactor(Convert.ToInt32(txtNumber.Text)).ToString();
    }
    catch(Exception x)
    {
        MessageBox.Show(x.Message, x.GetType().ToString());
    }
}
```

Please note that in RC1 the access modifies for the `CanBePooled()` *method has changed and you will need to use the line:*

```
protected override void CanBePooled ()
```

Running the Example

Compile and build both the `EntServLib` and `EntServClient` assemblies. Don't forget to add `EntServLib.dll` to the GAC every time you have rebuilt it. This is necessary because each time you rebuild an assembly, its version number increments. You should always ensure that the latest version is installed in the GAC. On the other hand, unlike in COM+ where you must register the component from its installed location, you can register a .NET enterprise component and then install it in the GAC. The CLR is smart enough to look into the GAC to find the registered assembly.

Now open the COM+ Component Services snap-in and change its view to Status View. When you run `EntServClient.exe` from Windows Explorer, you will see that there is one object activated and two pooled:

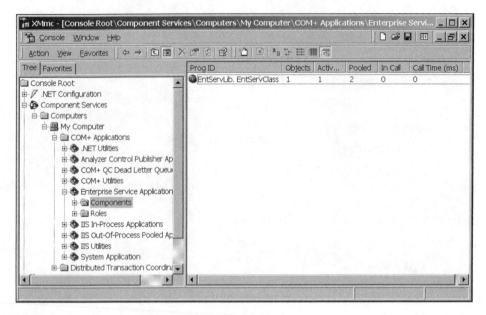

Even though the client program only activates one `EntServClass` instance, .NET Enterprise Services creates two objects in the pool to meet the `MinPoolSize` attribute setting. Now run four more instances of `EntServClient.exe`, you will see five objects activated and pooled. If you start one more instance of `EntServClient.exe`, you won't see it coming on the screen because the `MaxPoolSize` setting has been reached. If you wait long enough (about ten seconds, which is the `CreationTimeout` value), you will see a message box reporting the exception:

The sixth activation request waited for any available server objects and timed out because none of them became available within ten seconds. The program will continue to run after you click **OK** to dismiss the message box, but it has not created the `mServer` object. If you then enter a number and click on the **Calculate Factor** button, you will get a `null` reference exception.

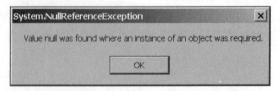

Now close the sixth instance of the client program. In the first instance of the client program, enter a number and press the **Calculate Factor** button. The activated object count decreases by one once the method returns. You can now start another instance of `EntServClient.exe` successfully because there is a deactivated server object in the pool. .NET Enterprise Services reactivates this object to serve the sixth client.

For client program instances two to five, enter a number and click the Calculate Factor button. Once all of them have completed, the activated count should be zero.

Now you have 6 client objects all containing a reference to the server object, even though there are only five instances in the pool. Enter the number 15, or a bigger number, in all six client forms, and then click the Calculate Factor buttons one at a time. If you click fast enough, the sixth instance will report the same activation failure exception because .NET Enterprise Services can't find a deactivated object for it before it times out.

The lesson here is that you need to think carefully about object pooling settings. If you can afford to have a large pool to serve potential clients, it's great. Otherwise, you will need to perform some stress testing to determine the best `MaxPoolSize` and `CreationTimeout` values.

Since object pooling requires JIT activation, the CLR will also enable JIT activation automatically if you enable object pooling. Therefore, if you specify the `ObjectPooling` attribute, there is no need to also explicitly specify the `JustInTimeActivation` attribute for the same class. If you enable object pooling while explicitly disabling JIT activation, the CLR will automatically enable JIT activation in order to provide object pooling properly.

Transaction Processing

.NET Enterprise Services is really an improved version of COM+ component services. Looking back a couple of years, COM+ component services was itself an improved version of the combination of COM and Microsoft Transaction Server (MTS). MTS 1.0 introduced distributed transaction processing to the Windows platform. Since then, MTS 2.0, COM+ 1.0, and COM+ 1.5 have all added feature enhancements and ease of use to transaction processing. Now .NET makes it even easier.

The Transaction Attribute

Turning on distributed transaction processing support in .NET is as simple as specifying a transaction option attribute for a serviced component. By default, the CLR disables transaction support to reduce run-time overhead. We can turn it on explicitly by specifying a transaction support level:

```
[Transaction(TransactionOption.Required)]
```

We can specify one of the five transaction options shown in the table below:

Option	Description
Disabled	Ignore transaction requirements. This is the default setting.
NotSupported	This object will not participate in any transactions.
Supported	This object will share its caller's transaction, but does not require its own transaction. For instance, if a class only performs SELECT queries in a database, there is no need to create its own transaction. However, its caller may perform database update and want to roll back the transaction based on the success of the SELECT query.
Required	This object requires a transaction. If its caller has created a transaction, this object will participate in it. Otherwise, it needs to create its own transaction.
RequiresNew	This object always requires creating its own transaction.

To see how .NET Enterprise Services manage transactions, let's create a sample application to insert an order into the `Orders` table and several items into the `Order Details` table in the `Northwind` database.

A Sample Application Using Distributed Transactions

As usual, we will partition this application into a server assembly and a client assembly. The server assembly performs the necessary database operations while the client assembly simply invokes the methods provided by the server.

Please note, as previously stated, that in RC1 the access modifiers for the `CanBePooled()`, `Activate()`, *and* `Deactivate()` *methods have been changed.*

NWServer Assembly

To begin with, create a class library assembly called `NWServer` and create a key file for the assembly in the project folder:

```
sn.exe -k NWServer.key
```

Next, add a reference to the `System.EnterpriseServices` library and change the `AssemblyInfo.cs` file as shown below:

```
using System.Reflection;
using System.Runtime.CompilerServices;
using System.EnterpriseServices;

...

[assembly: AssemblyDelaySign(false)]
[assembly: AssemblyKeyFile(@"..\..\NWServer.key")]
[assembly: AssemblyKeyName("")]

// Enterprise Service Application Attributes
[assembly: ApplicationName("Northwind Application")]
[assembly: ApplicationActivation(ActivationOption.Server)]
```

These changes look pretty familiar – they assign a strong-name key and an application name to the assembly, as well as specifying that it should run as a server application.

DBUtility Class

Next, change the name of the automatically created class from `class1` to `DBUtility`. In this application, this class simply stores a connection string to a database and provides it to other classes in the assembly. The following is a complete code listing for this class:

```
using System;
using System.Data;
using System.Data.SqlClient;
using System.EnterpriseServices;

namespace NWServer
{
    [EventTrackingEnabled(true)]
    [Transaction(TransactionOption.NotSupported)]
    public class DBUtility : ServicedComponent
    {
        public DBUtility()
```

```
    {}

    public static string DBConnString
    {
        get { return mcConnString; }
    }

    private const string mcConnString = "Integrated Security=SSPI;" +
        "Initial Catalog=Northwind;Data Source=(local)";
}
}
```

For now, the connection string is hard-coded. We will look at a better way that uses a construction string in a moment. In addition to the compulsory default constructor, this class provides only one read-only static property, DBConnString, to return the connection string.

Saving Orders Using a Stored Procedure

An important consideration when adding new order records into the database is that this method generally will also create new order item records. Because each item belongs to an order, an Order Details record must contain an OrderID value that references an Order record. The Northwind database implements this dependency by creating a foreign key in the Order Details table to reference the Order table, as illustrated in the figure below:

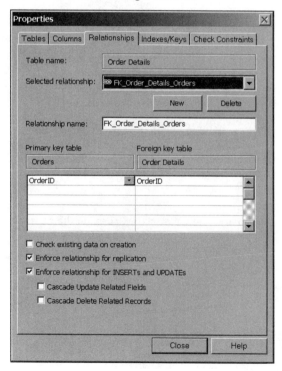

What this relationship means is that, when we create an `Order Details` record, we must assign it an `OrderID` value representing its parent `Order` record. However, the `OrderID` column in the `Order` table is an identity column, so SQL Server automatically generates an ID for each new order. The normal `SQL INSERT` statement does not return the newly assigned `OrderID` value, so we'll need to retrieve it using other methods.

One common way of achieving this is to use Transact SQL's `@@IDENTITY` global variable, which contains the value assigned to the identity field of the last created record. A good practice is to create a stored procedure that inserts the order record and returns its identity value.

Another issue is the `OrderDate` field in the `Order` table. To keep this sample application simple, we'll just store the date and time when the new order is saved to the database. This can be easily done using Transact SQL's `GetDate()` method, but we still need to get it back once the order has been created if we want to display it. This can be done in the stored procedure as well.

Let's take a look at the code for the stored procedure, named `spAddOrder`:

```
CREATE PROCEDURE spAddOrder
(
    @CustomerID char(5),
    @OrderDate  datetime OUTPUT
)
AS
    SELECT @OrderDate = GetDate()
    INSERT INTO Orders (CustomerID, OrderDate)
    VALUES (@CustomerID, @OrderDate)
    RETURN @@IDENTITY
GO
```

It takes two parameters. `@CustomerID` specifies the customer's ID. `@OrderDate` is marked as an `OUTPUT` parameter, which we will use to return the `OrderDate`.

Firstly, it calls the `GetDate()` method to obtain the current date and time and assigns it to `@OrderDate`. Next, it executes the `SQL INSERT` command to create a new `Order` record, passing it the `@CustomerID` and `@OrderDate` values. Finally, it retrieves the automatically generated `OrderID` value from the `@@IDENTITY` variable and returns it.

Order Class

With the stored procedure in place, add a new class, `Order`, to the assembly:

```
using System;
using System.Data;
using System.Data.SqlClient;
using System.EnterpriseServices;

namespace NWServer
{
    [EventTrackingEnabled(true)]
    [ObjectPooling(Enabled=true, MinPoolSize=2, MaxPoolSize=5,
                    CreationTimeout=20000)]
    [Transaction(TransactionOption.Required)]
    public class Order : ServicedComponent
    {
        public Order()
        {}
```

The above code snippet sets up the class as a serviced component and specifies various settings using attributes. In this sample application, we want to create a transaction to create both order header and item records. Therefore, we should set the `Transaction` attribute of the `Order` class to `Required`. If a client object runs in a transaction, the `Order` object will participate in its transaction. For instance, if the application needs to create a batch of orders, it can define an `OrderBatch` class that starts a transaction and calls the `Order` class' `Create()` method ten times to create ten new orders. If any of the orders fail to create, the whole transaction will roll back.

Since the `Order` class supports object pooling, it overrides the inherited `CanBePooled()` method to return `true`, indicating to .NET Enterprise Services that it can be pooled.

```
// Implements useful methods defined in ServicedComponent
public override bool CanBePooled()
{
    return true;
}
```

The `Order` class also overrides the `Activate()` and `Deactivate()` methods inherited from the `ServicedComponent` class:

```
public override void Activate()
{
    mConn = new SqlConnection(DBUtility.DBConnString);
}

public override void Deactivate()
{
    if (mConn.State == System.Data.ConnectionState.Open)
    {
        mConn.Close();
    }
}

private SqlConnection mConn = null;
```

The `Activate()` method creates the member `SqlConnection` object, `mConn`, using the connection string stored in the `DBUtility` class. Other class methods will use this connection object to access the database. The `Deactivate()` method closes the transaction and therefore returns the connection to the connection pool.

Note in this sample application, that the `Order` class only creates orders. So we could also create and release the transaction object in the `Create()` method. In a real-world application, however, a data access class generally defines several methods to perform different database operations such as querying, updating, and deleting orders. Defining transaction creation and release operations in the `Activate()` and `Deactivate()` methods simplifies the code and helps to improve the maintainability of the application.

The core part of this class is in the `Create()` method, which creates an order and several items in the database:

```
// Create a new order
public void Create()
{
    try
    {
        mConn.Open();
```

```
// Execute the spAddOrder stored procedure
SqlCommand cmd = new SqlCommand("spAddOrder", mConn);
cmd.CommandType = CommandType.StoredProcedure;

SqlParameter param =
     cmd.Parameters.Add("ID", SqlDbType.Int);
param.Direction = ParameterDirection.ReturnValue;

param = cmd.Parameters.Add("@CustomerID",
                              SqlDbType.Char, 5);
param.Direction = ParameterDirection.Input;
param.Value = "ANTON";

param = cmd.Parameters.Add("@OrderDate",
                              SqlDbType.DateTime);
param.Direction = ParameterDirection.Output;

cmd.ExecuteNonQuery();

// Retrieve the automatically generated order ID
param = cmd.Parameters["ID"];
int ID = Convert.ToInt32(param.Value.ToString(), 10);

// Add several order items
OrderItem item = new OrderItem();
for (int i = 1; i < 6; ++i)
{
     item.AddItem(ID, i, i * 10, i * 2);
}

ContextUtil.SetComplete();
}
catch (Exception x)
{
     ContextUtil.SetAbort();
     throw new Exception("Order.Create: " + x.Message);
}
}
}
}
```

This instantiates a `SqlCommand` object and binds it to the previously created connection. Because the stored procedure accepts two parameters and returns the newly created `OrderID`, we need to add three parameters to the command: the `OrderID` return value, the `CustomerID` input parameter, and the `OrderDate` output parameter. Calling the command object's `ExecuteNonQuery()` method executes the stored procedure, `spAddOrder`, to save the header record.

After the record has been created, the `ID` parameter stores the automatically generated `OrderID` value. This value is assigned to the `ID` property. Once the `OrderID` is there, this method goes on to create five items by passing in some arbitrary values to the `AddItem()` method of the `OrderItem` class. We'll see the `OrderItem` class definition in a moment.

If everything goes to plan, we want to commit the transaction. In .NET Enterprise Services, we never explicitly commit a transaction in a method. For a start, a method may just be a part of a transaction so we don't want to commit the transaction before it's ready. Rather, we opt for committing the transaction. Once all parties choose to commit the transaction, .NET Enterprise Services commits it. This approach enables us to focus on implementing functionality relevant to each class, without having to keep track on how it participates in transactions or exactly when you should commit the transaction.

To opt for committing the transaction, call the `SetComplete()` method of the `ContextUtil` object. Similarly, if anything goes wrong and throws an exception, we can catch the exception and decide to abort the transaction by calling the `SetAbort()` method of the `ContextUtil` object.

If you are familiar with COM+ component services, you can fine-tune your choices using the `EnableCommit()` and `DisableCommit()` methods. They both work exactly the same as in COM+.

That's all for the `Order` class. Next, add one more class, `OrderItem`, to the assembly.

OrderItem Class

The `OrderItem` class is responsible for creating order line items in the `Order Details` table. The listing below shows the complete code for the class:

```
using System;
using System.Data.SqlClient;
using System.EnterpriseServices;

namespace NWServer
{
    [EventTrackingEnabled(true)]
    [ObjectPooling(Enabled=true, MinPoolSize=2, MaxPoolSize=5,
                CreationTimeout=20000)]
    [Transaction(TransactionOption.Supported)]
    public class OrderItem : ServicedComponent
    {
        public OrderItem()
        {}

        public override bool CanBePooled()
        {
            return true;
        }

        public override void Activate()
        {
            mConn = new SqlConnection(DBUtility.DBConnString);
        }

        public override void Deactivate()
        {
            if (mConn.State == System.Data.ConnectionState.Open)
            {
                mConn.Close();
            }
        }

        private SqlConnection mConn = null;

        public void AddItem(int OrderID, int ProductID,
                    decimal UnitPrice, int Quantity)
        {
            string SQLString =
                    "INSERT INTO [Order Details] " +
                    "(OrderID, ProductID, UnitPrice, Quantity) " +
                    "VALUES " +
                    "(" + OrderID.ToString() + ", " +
                        ProductID.ToString() + ", " +
```

```
                              UnitPrice.ToString() + ", " +
                              Quantity.ToString() + ")";

          try
          {
              mConn.Open();
              SqlCommand cmd = new SqlCommand(SQLString, mConn);
              cmd.ExecuteNonQuery();
              ContextUtil.SetComplete();
          }
          catch(Exception x)
          {
              ContextUtil.SetAbort();
              throw new Exception("OrderItem.AddItem: " + x.Message);
          }
      }
  }
```

Creating an `OrderItem` often happens when the application creates a new order. It can also happen when we add a new item to an existing order. Either way the client object, which will be an `Order` object, will start a transaction. The `OrderItem` object will then be participating in the transaction. Therefore, this class supports transactions.

The `AddItem()` method is pretty simple. It takes four parameters; each passes in a value for a field in the new `Order Details` record, and executes a SQL INSERT query to add the record to the database. If it succeeds, it calls the `SetComplete()` method of the context object to opt for committing the transaction. If it fails for whatever reason, it calls `SetAbort` to roll back the transaction and throws an exception back to the client object to indicate the error.

Note that we don't have to throw an exception when there is an error. Once we call the `SetAbort()` method, the transaction is doomed and will be aborted when the `Create()` method in the `Order` class returns regardless what happens elsewhere. So there is no danger of .NET Enterprise Services inadvertently committing the transaction. However, without throwing an exception or using other methods to report the error, the client `Order` object does not know there is a problem. It will continue to execute the rest of the code even though the transaction is already doomed after this method calls the `SetAbort()` method. Throwing an exception helps the client object to detect the error condition early and thereby avoid unnecessary execution of the remaining code.

NWClient Assembly

To test this library out, build the assembly, register it, and add it to the GAC. Next, create a Windows Application assembly named `NWClient` and add references to both `NWServer.dll` and `System.EnterpriseServices.dll`. Then rename the automatically generated form `OrderClient`, add a button and change its `Name` and `Text` properties to `btnCreateOrder` and `Create Order`, respectively. Double-click this button and add the following code to the form:

```
public OrderClient()
{
    //
    // Required for Windows Form Designer support
    //
    InitializeComponent();
```

```
        mOrder = new NWServer.Order();
    }

    private void btnCreateOrder_Click(object sender, System.EventArgs e)
    {
        try
        {
            mOrder.Create();
            MessageBox.Show("Order Created!", "Create Order");
        }
        catch (Exception x)
        {
            MessageBox.Show(x.Message, x.GetType().ToString());
        }
    }

    private NWServer.Order mOrder = null;
```

There isn't much in this form, it simply instantiates the mOrder object in its constructor and calls its Create() method when the **Create Order** button is clicked.

You can now run this assembly and verify that it creates an order with five line items each time you click the **Create Order** button.

To see what happens if something goes wrong in the transaction, you can force an error yourself somewhere within the transaction. For instance, you can change the try block in the AddItem() method:

```
try
{
    if (ProductID == 3)
    {
        throw new Exception("Forced exception");
    }
    mConn.Open();
    SqlCommand cmd = new SqlCommand(SQLString, mConn);
    cmd.ExecuteNonQuery();
    ContextUtil.SetComplete();
}
```

This will always force an exception on the third item. You should see that the application will not create new records in the Order and Order Details tables.

The AutoComplete Attribute

When there is a problem during a transaction, it is quite common for a serviced component to raise an exception and return control to the client object. In that case, the serviced component typically wants to abort the transaction because it can't complete its tasks successfully. The Order.Create() and OrderItem.AddItem() methods do exactly that. If the catch statement in a method catches an exception, it aborts the transaction and throws an exception.

In such cases, we can further simplify those methods using the AutoComplete attribute provided by .NET. The AutoComplete attribute applies to methods only. At run time, .NET checks this attribute and automatically opts for committing the transaction on behalf of the method when the method returns normally. If the method throws an exception or returns an unhandled exception, .NET decides to abort the transaction.

In other words, by applying the AutoComplete attribute to a method, we delegate the responsibility for the transaction to .NET Enterprise Services. We instruct it to decide about committing the method according to the method's return status. We no longer need to explicitly call the context object's SetComplete() and SetAbort() methods.

We can apply this attribute to both the Order and OrderItem classes by making the following changes:

```
[AutoComplete]
public void Create()
```

```
[AutoComplete]
public void AddItem(int OrderID, int ProductID,
                    decimal UnitPrice, int Quantity)
```

We should also remove all SetComplete() and SetAbort() calls. To test it will commit the transaction when both methods return normally, comment out the if block in AddItem where we artificially throw an exception:

```
if (ProductID == 3)
{
    throw new Exception("Forced exception");
}
```

In .NET Beta 2, the AutoComplete feature works correctly in normal situations. It also cancels the transaction if any of the methods throws an exception, as you can test by uncommenting the above if block. However, instead of passing on the exception thrown in the Order.Create() method, it then throws its own exception indicating the problem instead of passing on the exception thrown by your objects:

This makes it a bit difficult for client objects to handle the exceptions thrown by the server objects. In addition to handling the documented application specific exceptions, they must also be able to catch this COMException. Furthermore, the message is confusing, as .NET should vote for canceling the transaction for both methods since they both return with an exception. This again shows the beta status of the .NET Framework as this chapter is written, and should be fixed in the release version.

Whether or not you use this AutoComplete feature depends on your application architecture. If your transactional components are simple and follow the same coding pattern, using AutoComplete will probably save you some development efforts. On the other hand, using explicit voting gives you more control over the transaction management process.

Object Construction

This sample application is pretty primitive. Many improvements should be made to make it a production-quality application. One such improvement is to change the way we specify the backend database.

The current implementation of the DBUtility class hard-codes the connection in a member constant. This means that it will always connect to a database in the same server where the component is installed. It's good enough to demonstrate .NET Enterprise Services' transaction process capability. In the real world, however, we often deploy serviced components in a server other than the dedicated database server. Therefore, we would not want to hard-code the connection string and recompile the assembly every time we change the component server or database server. There are many ways to solve this problem, one of which is to use a constructor string offered by .NET Enterprise Services.

The ConstructionEnabled Attribute

```
Please note, that in RC1 the access modifier for the Construct(string
ConstructString) and CanBePooled() methods have been changed.
```

To use the constructor string feature, we enable object construction by applying the ConstructionEnabled attribute to a serviced component:

```
[ConstructionEnabled(Enabled=true, Default="DefaultConstructorString")]
```

We then override the Construct() method inherited from the ServicedComponent class to retrieve the configured constructor string:

```
[ConstructionEnabled(Enabled=true, Default="DefaultConstructorString")]
public class MyClass : ServicedComponent
{
    // other class members

    public override void Construct(string ConstructString)
    {
        // uses ConstructString
    }
}
```

We can use the COM+ component services snap-in to administratively assign and modify the constructor string:

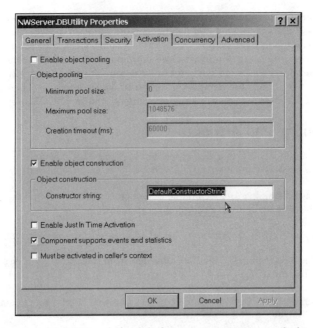

When the serviced component is registered, the default constructor string specified in the ConstructionEnabled attribute is assigned to the component. We can modify it dynamically at run time.

The ConstructString parameter passes in the assigned constructor string to the Construct() method. To see how to use it, modify the DBUtility class as shown below:

```
[EventTrackingEnabled(true)]
[Transaction(TransactionOption.Supported)]
[ObjectPooling(MinPoolSize=2, MaxPoolSize=10, CreationTimeout=20000)]
[ConstructionEnabled(Enabled=true,
                     Default="Integrated Security=SSPI;" +
                             "Initial Catalog=Northwind;" +
                             "Data Source=(local)")]
public class DBUtility : ServicedComponent
{
    public DBUtility()
    {}

    public override void Construct(string ConstructString)
    {
        mConnString = ConstructString;
    }

    public override bool CanBePooled()
    {
        return true;
    }

    public string DBConnString
    {
        get
        {
            ContextUtil.DeactivateOnReturn = true;
```

```
            return mConnString;
        }
//      get { return mcConnString; }
    }

    private string mConnString;
//  private const string mcConnString = "Integrated Security=SSPI;" +
//              "Initial Catalog=Northwind;Data Source=(local)";
}
```

The constructor string is only available to class instances; that is, .NET Enterprise Services calls the `Construct()` method only when the client object creates a `DBUtility` object. Therefore, the most significant change to this class is that the `DBConnString` should be changed to an instance property rather than a static property. When the `Construct()` method is called, it assigns the received `ConstructString` to an instance data member, `mConnString`. When the client object queries the `DBConnString` property, `mConnString` is returned.

Since the client object needs to instantiate this class in order to retrieve the `DBConnString` property, we should reconsider how this class uses .NET Enterprise Services. In this case, it now supports object pooling and transactions. While this class is simple and doesn't really need to be run as a part of the client's transaction, marking it as supported allows the object to be instantiated in the client object's context. This allows it to be deactivated when the call to `DBConnString` property returns.

Obviously, we will also need to change the client classes to instantiate the `DBUtility` class and retrieve the `DBConnString` property. All we need to do, in both the `Order` and `OrderItem` classes, is to replace this line:

```
mConn = new SqlConnection(DBUtility.DBConnString);
```

with:

```
DBUtility DBUtil = new DBUtility();
mConn = new SqlConnection(DBUtil.DBConnString);
```

Now we'll be able to use another database by simply changing the connection string in the COM+ component services snap-in.

Summary

.NET offers all services initially provided by COM+ in the `System.EnterpriseServices` namespace. A system assembly, `System.EnterpriseServices.dll`, provides the run-time support for .NET Enterprise Services. This chapter introduced some of the commonly used services.

In a large-scale application, providing high performance often means that we need to use limited system resources wisely. .NET provides just-in-time activation, object pooling, and connection pooling to enable systems to fully utilize limited resources to serve a large number of clients. In order to access multiple data sources such as database servers, or the Active Directory, application developers can also use the .NET distributed transaction process to manage complex data access operations in a well-defined framework.

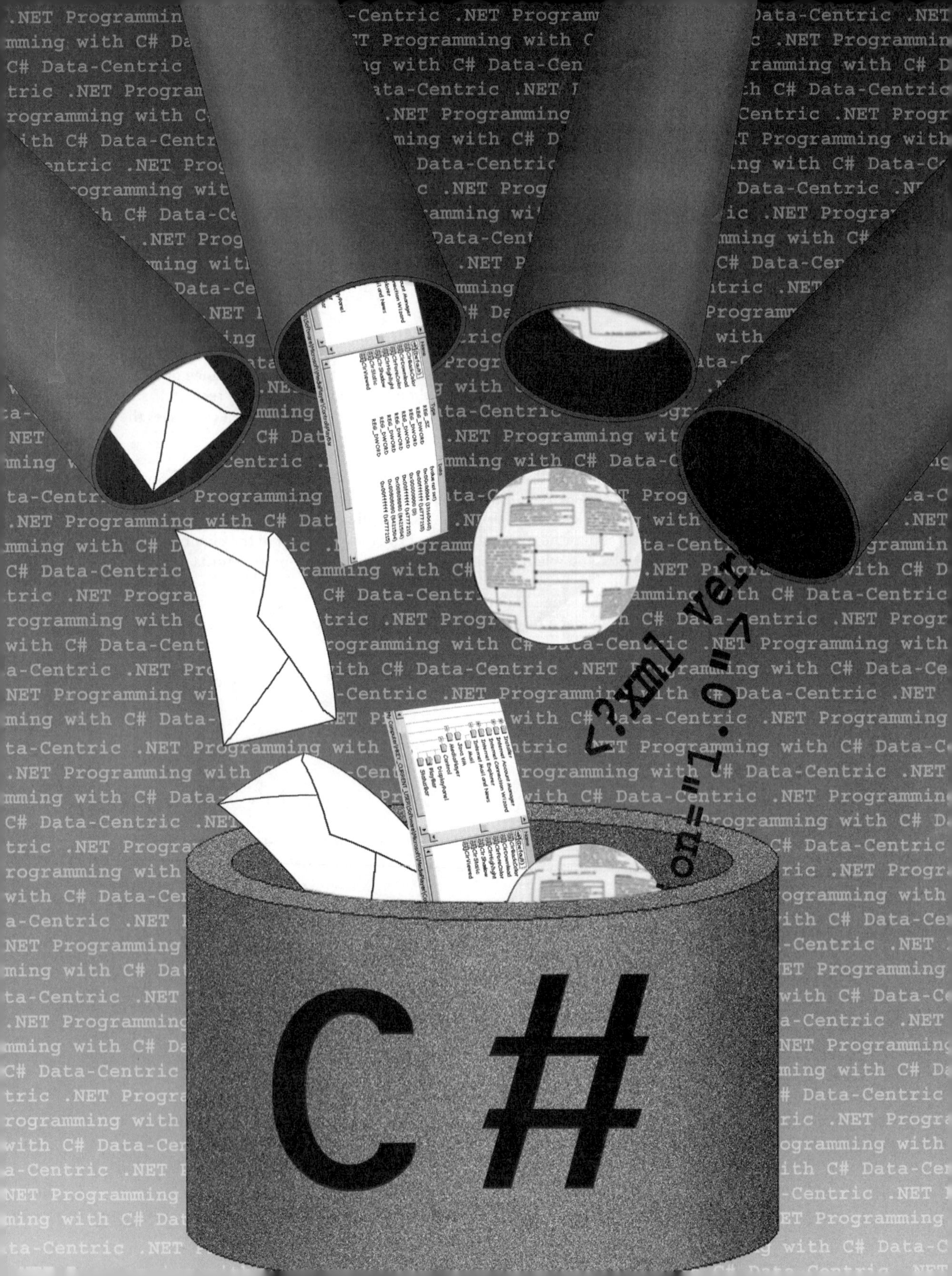
Data-Centric .NET Programming with C#
<?xml ver
on="1.0"?>
C#

7

XML

The speed at which XML has become so prevalent in today's world is staggering. Since the initial XML draft in 1996, XML has become a standard of data transportation and storage. XML is no longer just relegated to being part of web-based projects, and you can now find it performing all sorts of duties in a wide range of projects. The .NET Framework utilizes XML for several functions from configuration files and sourcecode documentation to SOAP and Web Services, not to mention ADO.NET, which relies on XML as the transport mechanism. Because of this extensive use by the framework, there is, as you would expect, very good support for developing applications that use XML. The System.Xml namespace is rich with classes for using XML. Note that this chapter assumes that you are already familiar with XML, and XML terms such as node, element, and attribute.

In this chapter, we will cover:

❑   The MSXML implementation, and see how it compares with the System.Xml namespace

❑   Exploring the XmlReader and XmlWriter classes

❑   Implementing the DOM through XmlDocument

❑   When it makes more sense to use XmlReader rather than using XmlDocument

Most importantly, we will see how XML and ADO.NET work together to give you the flexibility to deal with your data in a number of different ways.

Finally, we will look at validating the XML against a schema or DTD, and creating a schema from within Visual Studio .NET.

We begin the chapter by looking at the MSXML implementation.

Using MSXML

By using COM interoperability, you are still able to make use of MSXML in your .NET applications. Even though the `System.Xml` namespace is easy to learn and use, if you have spent a great deal of time using MSXML you may feel more comfortable using it instead of `System.Xml`. As you become more familiar with `System.Xml`, converting to it from MSXML is a fairly simple process. We'll see more about `System.Xml` later in the chapter.

Let's take a look at the code for using MSXML (in this case, version 3.0) in a C# application, which can be found in the `MSXML` folder of the download code, available from **www.wrox.com**.

Referencing MSXML

In order to run this sample you will have to add a reference to `MSXML3.dll` in the Visual Studio IDE. On the **Project** menu, select **Add Reference**, and on the **COM** tab look for **Microsoft XML, v3.0**. After selecting it and clicking **OK**, you may get a dialog box explaining that there isn't a primary interop assembly available. The IDE will make one for you and place it in the project's `bin` directory. In this case it will be named `Interop.MSXML2_3_0.dll`.

If you are using the command-line compiler you will have to use `tlbimp.exe` to create the wrapper DLL. At the command prompt enter `tlbimp msxml3.dll`. In the current directory you will now find `msxml2.dll`. The reason for the name change is that by default `tlbimp` will use the typelib name defined in the library. You can specify the `/out:` parameter of `tlbimp` and give the generated assembly any name you wish. Refer to the SDK documentation for more details on `tlbimp.exe`.

The MSXML Sample Project

Our sample project will demonstrate the use of a `TreeView` control to display the node names of an XML file called `books.xml`, which contains information about a selection of books available from a bookstore. The `books.xml` file is also included with the download code for this chapter, and is available from **www.wrox.com**.

```
using System;
using System.Drawing;
using System.Collections;
using System.ComponentModel;
using System.Windows.Forms;
using System.Data;
using System.Diagnostics;
using MSXML2;

namespace MSXML3
{
    /// <summary>
    /// Summary description for Form1.
    /// </summary>
    public class Form1 : System.Windows.Forms.Form
    {
        private System.Windows.Forms.TreeView treeView1;
        /// <summary>
        /// Required designer variable.
        /// </summary>
```

```
             private System.ComponentModel.Container components = null;


             public Form1()
             {
                //
                // Required for Windows Form Designer support
                //
                InitializeComponent();

                //
                // TODO: Add any constructor code after InitializeComponent call
                //
                LoadTree();
             }

             /// <summary>
             /// Clean up any resources being used.
             /// </summary>
             protected override void Dispose( bool disposing )
             {
                if( disposing )
                {
                   if (components != null)
                   {
                      components.Dispose();
                   }
                }
                base.Dispose( disposing );
             }

             #region Windows Form Designer generated code
             /// <summary>
             /// Required method for Designer support - do not modify
             /// the contents of this method with the code editor.
             /// </summary>

             private void InitializeComponent()
             {
                this.treeView1 = new System.Windows.Forms.TreeView();
                this.SuspendLayout();
                //
                // treeView1
                //
                this.treeView1.ImageIndex = -1;
                this.treeView1.Location = new System.Drawing.Point(16, 16);
                this.treeView1.Name = "treeView1";
                this.treeView1.SelectedImageIndex = -1;
                this.treeView1.Size = new System.Drawing.Size(192, 192);
                this.treeView1.TabIndex = 2;
                this.treeView1.AfterSelect += new
                            System.Windows.Forms.TreeViewEventHandler(
                                        this.treeView1_AfterSelect);
                //
```

```
            // Form1
            //
            this.AutoScaleBaseSize = new System.Drawing.Size(5, 13);
            this.ClientSize = new System.Drawing.Size(224, 266);
            this.Controls.AddRange(new System.Windows.Forms.Control[]
                                                    {this.treeView1});
            this.Name = "Form1";
            this.Text = "Form1";
            this.ResumeLayout(false);

        }
        #endregion

        /// <summary>
        /// The main entry point for the application.
        /// </summary>
        [STAThread]
        static void Main()
        {
            Application.Run(new Form1());
        }

        private void LoadTree() {

            DOMDocument30 doc=new DOMDocument30();
            //Load the xml file. Change path if needed
            doc.load(@"..\..\..\books.xml");
            //select the root node
            IXMLDOMNode node=doc.selectSingleNode("bookstore");
            //instantiate a new XmlTreeNode,
            //fill the node, and
            //load it into the TreeView
            XmlTreeNode rootNode=new XmlTreeNode(node);
            rootNode.FillTreeView();
            treeView1.Nodes.Add(rootNode);
        }

        private void treeView1_AfterSelect(object sender,
                            System.Windows.Forms.TreeViewEventArgs e)
        {
            MessageBox.Show(((XmlTreeNode)treeView1.SelectedNode).Value);
        }

        /// <summary>
        /// Our new TreeNode class. This will load the tree
        /// with our XML doc
        /// </summary>
        internal class XmlTreeNode : TreeNode
        {

            IXMLDOMNode node;

            internal XmlTreeNode()    : base(){}
```

```
            internal XmlTreeNode(IXMLDOMNode treeNode) :
                                        base(treeNode.nodeName)
      {

          node=treeNode;
          //Don't want the name of the node if it is null
          //or if the node is a text node
          if(node!=null && node.nodeType!=DOMNodeType.NODE_TEXT)
             this.Text=node.nodeName;

      }

      public string Value
      {
          get
          {
             return node.text;
          }
      }

      internal void FillTreeView()
      {

          if(node!=null)
          {
             this.Nodes.Clear();
             IXMLDOMNode cNode=node.cloneNode(true);

             if(cNode.hasChildNodes())
             {
                cNode=cNode.firstChild;

                while(cNode!=null)
                {
                   if(cNode.nodeType!=DOMNodeType.NODE_TEXT &&
                       cNode.nodeType!=DOMNodeType.NODE_ATTRIBUTE)
                   {
                      XmlTreeNode newTreeNode=new XmlTreeNode(cNode);
                      this.Nodes.Add(newTreeNode);
                      newTreeNode.FillTreeView();
                   }
                   cNode=cNode.nextSibling;
                }
             }
          }
      }
   }
}
```

This is the code for the entire form. It's included here so that you can see the "big picture". The first thing to look at is at the very top:

```
using System;
using System.Drawing;
using System.Collections;
using System.ComponentModel;
using System.Windows.Forms;
using System.Data;
using System.Diagnostics;
using MSXML2;
```

The important line is highlighted. Even though we are using version 3 of MSXML, the name we use here is MSXML2. This is the name of the typelib defined in the library. This is the same default name we saw when using `tlbimp`. It is important to remember this whenever you do any COM interop. Keeping this in mind will help eliminate confusion.

Let's jump down to the `LoadTree()` method. This is where we start everything off. If you have used MSXML before, this code will look familiar to you. We start by creating the XML document `DOMDocument30`. Then we load the XML file; in this case it is our bookstore file `books.xml`. Make sure that you change the path on the `doc.load` line to match your directory structure.

```
private void LoadTree()
{
    DOMDocument30 doc=new DOMDocument30();
    //Load the xml file. Change path if needed
    doc.load(@"..\..\..\books.xml");
```

Next, we use a simple `selectSingleNode()` statement to select the entire document. The bookstore node is the root node, so by selecting it, we select everything. Now we can start adding nodes to the `TreeView` control:

```
    //select the root node
    IXMLDOMNode node=doc.selectSingleNode("bookstore");
    //instantiate a new XmlTreeNode,
    //fill the node
    //load it into the TreeView
    XmlTreeNode rootNode=new XmlTreeNode(node);
    rootNode.FillTreeView();
    treeView1.Nodes.Add(rootNode);
}
```

The method that we are going to use to add the nodes to the `TreeView` control (`treeView1` is the instance of the `TreeView` class on our form) requires that we create our own node. We will do this by inheriting the `TreeNode` class and creating an `XmlTreeNode` class. When we instantiate the `XmlTreeNode` class, we pass in the node we just created with the `selectSingleNode` method. Here is the constructor that will be called when we do this:

```
internal XmlTreeNode(IXMLDOMNode treeNode)    : base()
{
    node=treeNode;
    //Don't want the name of the node is null
    //or if the node is a text node
    if(node!=null && node.nodeType!=DOMNodeType.NODE_TEXT)
        this.Text=node.nodeName;
}
```

We make sure that we call the constructor on the base class (TreeNode). Next we set the class variable node, which is of type IXMLDOMNode, to treeNode. We now have the reference to our XML node in the XmlTreeNode object. If node is not null, and if it is not a text node, we set the Text value of the XmlTreeNode object to the name of the node. We could have eliminated this by passing in treeNode.nodeName when we called the base class constructor.

Populating the TreeView Control

Now that we have an XmlTreeNode object instantiated (rootNode), we can call the FillTreeView() method on it. This is a recursive method that will fill the TreeView with all of the nodes in the XML document. The first thing to do is check to make sure we have a valid node to work with. Next we clone the node. We do this so that when we start to back out of the recursion, the original node will still be pointing to the correct node, and we can move to the next node in the list. Next we check for child nodes. If there are any, make the first child current. Then we can add the XML node to the XmlTreeNode nodes collection. We don't add attributes and we don't add text nodes; we don't want these node types to show in the TreeView. For each XmlTreeNode that we add, we have an associated XML node. Notice that so far, all we have done is add XmlTreeNodes to the Nodes collection of the parent XmlTreeNode. Here is the FillTreeView() method source:

```
internal void FillTreeView()
{
    if(node!=null)    {
        IXMLDOMNode cNode=node.cloneNode(true);

        if(cNode.hasChildNodes())
        {
            cNode=cNode.firstChild;

            while(cNode!=null)
            {
                if(cNode.nodeType!=DOMNodeType.NODE_TEXT &&
                    cNode.nodeType!=DOMNodeType.NODE_ATTRIBUTE)
                {
                    XmlTreeNode newTreeNode=new XmlTreeNode(cNode);
                    this.Nodes.Add(newTreeNode);
                    newTreeNode.FillTreeView();
                }
                cNode=cNode.nextSibling;
            }
        }
    }
}
```

When we finish with the recursions through the XML document and return to the LoadTree() method, we will have an XmlTreeNode (rootNode) with its Nodes collection filled with more XmlTreeNodes. We add this one node to the TreeView control, giving us the loaded TreeView. Here is a screenshot of the application during execution:

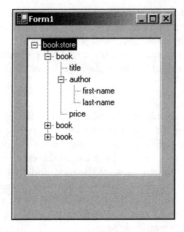

A couple of the nodes are expanded out to show that they're actually there. Notice that all we see are node names, not any data.

Here is the code for the `AfterSelect` event on the `TreeView` control:

```
private void treeView1_AfterSelect(object sender,
                        System.Windows.Forms.TreeViewEventArgs e)
{
    MessageBox.Show(((XmlTreeNode)treeView1.SelectedNode).Value);
}
```

We just show a message box with the value of the node. Notice that we have to cast the `TreeNode` that the `SelectedNode` property returns to the `XmlTreeNode` data type that we created. Here is the code for the `Value` property of our `XmlTreeNode` object:

```
public string Value
{
    get
    {
        return node.text;
    }
}
```

If you remember, `node` is the XML (`IXMLDOMNode`) node that we passed into the `XmlTreeNode` object when it was first created. Therefore, by associating an XML node with each `TreeView` node, we can just ask the XML node for whatever piece of information we need instead of trying to duplicate it. Here is a screenshot after selecting `price` from the `TreeView`:

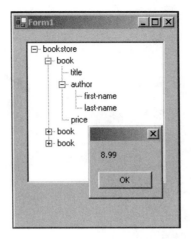

Once you have the XML nodes referenced by the `TreeView` nodes, there is a lot of functionality that can be provided. We'll see how to take advantage of this later in the chapter.

System.Xml

The `System.Xml` namespace has many useful tools. Let's take a quick look at the namespace, and how some of the classes relate to each other.

System.Xml Overview

`System.Xml` has three main classes:

❑ `XmlNode`

❑ `XmlReader`

❑ `XmlWriter`

Most of the remaining classes in the namespace are derived from one of these three. `XmlNode` is the base class for most of the classes. It is a representation of a single XML node, which could be one of several node types such as `entity`, `text`, `attribute`, or any of the other valid node types. `XmlDocument`, which is the DOM implementation in the framework, is derived from `XmlNode`.

`XmlReader` and `XmlWriter` are base classes for reading and writing XML data. `XmlReader` is the base class for three other classes, and `XmlWriter` is the base class for one class. These two base classes are the equivalent of the SAX API. `XmlReader` and `XmlWriter` use a streaming type method of reading and writing. They are both foward-only and the XML in each is not modifiable; because of this they are very efficient.

Here is what the class hierarchy model looks like. This will give you an idea of how the classes relate in terms of inheritance:

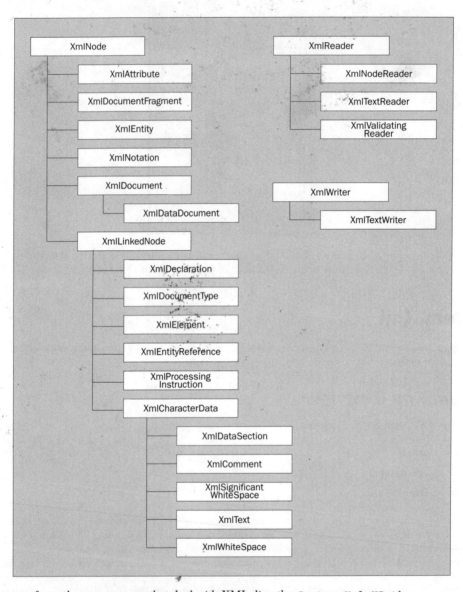

There are four other namespaces that deal with XML directly: System.Xml.XPath, System.Xml.Serialization, System.Xml.Xsl, and System.Xml.Schema. We will be taking a look at these namespaces in the next chapter.

XmlReader and XmlWriter are abstract classes in the System.Xml namespace that allow you to do very fast, foward-only parsing and writing of XML documents. XmlWriter has one concrete class, XmlTextWriter, in the framework. XmlReader has three concrete classes: XmlTextReader, XmlNodeReader, and XmlValidatingReader. We will look at the XmlWriter and XmlTextWriter classes first, then we'll take a closer look at the XmlReader-based classes.

XmlWriter

`XmlTextWriter` is the concrete class for `XmlWriter` in the framework. You can create a custom `XmlWriter` yourself by inheriting from either of these classes, but keep in mind that if you derive from `XmlWriter`, which is abstract, you will have to implement all of the abstract methods and properties, otherwise they will stay abstract. If you derive from `XmlTextWriter`, you only need to override the methods and properties that you need to customize.

Working with Delimited Files

Let's say that you have just received an inventory update from a book vendor, and it comes to you in a delimited file. You require that the data be in XML format. There are a couple of ways of achieving this, but since this section is about `XmlWriter`-based classes, that's what we will use.

Here is what your incoming data looks like:

```
computer|2001|1-861004-99-0|Professional C#|Wrox Author Team||49.99
computer|2001|1-861004-82-6|Expert One on One: Oracle|Thomas|Kyle|59.99
history|2001|0-357727-37-X|American Tabloid|James|Ellroy|8.99
```

This is the file `writer.psv`, and is included in the example download on the Wrox web site. As you can see, it is a basic pipe-delimited text file that contains the data for three new books. What we will do is open the pipe-delimited file, parse it, and create the XML from the data. Here is the first pass at doing this (the complete solution is called `WriterSample1` and can be downloaded from the Wrox web site). Here is the method that will do all of the work:

```
internal void CreateXmlFile(char delimiter, string filePath)
{
    //create the XmlWriter, sending the XML the specified file
    XmlTextWriter tw=new XmlTextWriter
                    (@"..\..\..\writer1.xml",System.Text.Encoding.UTF8);
    //set the formatting to indented
    tw.Formatting=Formatting.Indented;

    tw.WriteStartDocument();
    //root node
    tw.WriteStartElement("parsedTrx");
    //open the file to be parsed
    StreamReader sr=new StreamReader(filePath);
    string line;
    line=sr.ReadLine();

    while(line!=null)
    {
        //split the line into an array based on delimiter
        string[] parsedLine=line.Split(new char[]{delimiter});
        //new line element
        tw.WriteStartElement("line");
        //each element of the array is an element under <line>
        for(int i=0;i<parsedLine.Length;i++)
            tw.WriteElementString("col" +i.ToString(),
```

```
                                    parsedLine[i].ToString());

        tw.WriteEndElement();
        line=sr.ReadLine();
    }
    //clean up
    tw.WriteEndElement();
    tw.WriteEndDocument();
    //flush the XmlWriter
    tw.Flush();

    //tidy up and return
    tw.Close();
    sr.Close();
}
```

The first thing we do is to create a new instance of `XmlTextWriter`, tw, passing in the name of the output file and the text encoding that we want. In this case, we'll use `UTF8`, which is the default. `XmlTextWriter` has three constructor overloads, one that will take a `TextWriter`-based object, one that will take a `Stream`-based object, and one that takes a string representing a valid path and file name, which is the one that we will be using. Once we have the `XmlTextWriter` object created, we set the `Formatting` property to `Indented`. This will indent each child node from its parent node, making the resulting document a little easier to read. You can set the character used for indenting with the `IndentChar` property, and you can set the number of characters to indent with the `Indentation` property. The default is to use two space characters for indenting. The next line, `tw.WriteStartDocument()`, will create the XML declaration line with the version set to "1". This method will take an optional `Boolean` value that will add `standalone=yes` for a `true` value, or `standalone=no` for `false`. When `WriteStartDocument()` is called, the `XmlTextWriter` will make sure that what is being written is valid XML. For instance, it will check to make sure that only one root-level element exists and that the XML declaration exists. If `WriteStartDocument()` isn't called, then the `XmlWriter` will assume that an XML fragment is being written.

At this point we have the beginnings of a well-formed XML document. The next section of the code is going to open the delimited file and start parsing.

```
    StreamReader sr = new StreamReader(filePath);
    string line;
    line=sr.ReadLine();

    while(line!=null)
    {
        //split the line into an array based on delimiter
        string[] parsedLine=line.Split(new char[]{delimiter});
        //new line element
        tw.WriteStartElement("line");
        //each element of the array is an element under <line>
        for(int i=0;i<parsedLine.Length;i++)
            tw.WriteElementString("col" +
                                i.ToString(),parsedLine[i].ToString());

        tw.WriteEndElement();
        line=sr.ReadLine();
    }
```

We open up a `StreamReader` on the delimited file and start reading in a line at a time. We will use the handy `Split()` method on the string object line, parsing out on the pipe character, `delimiter`, that was passed into the method. We now have an array of all of the data elements in the line of data from the delimited file. The start tag named `line` is created by `tw.WriteStartElement("line")`. Now we iterate through the array, this time using `WriteElementString()` to create each element. `WriteElementString()` takes the element name and the element value as parameters, and optionally the namespace URI. We are creating the name "col" and the array index concatenated together for the element name, and using the data in the array as the value of the element.

> *It should be mentioned that element names cannot contain certain characters; we are not conducting a check for any illegal characters in this example, but in general, it is advisable to do so. If an illegal character is used, an* `InvalidOperationException` *is raised.*

The `tw.WriteEndElement` will close the line element we started earlier.

The `WriteEndElement` and `WriteEndDocument` outside the main loop close the root node and document element respectively. We then flush the `XmlTextWriter` and close up the streams:

```
//clean up
tw.WriteEndElement();
tw.WriteEndDocument();
//flush the XmlWriter
tw.Flush();

//tidy up and return
tw.Close();
sr.Close();
```

When the example is run, a form with an empty textbox will be presented to you, and the following XML document, `writer1.xml`, will be created:

```xml
<?xml version="1.0" encoding="utf-8"?>
<parsedTrx>
  <line>
    <col0>computer</col0>
    <col1>2001</col1>
    <col2>1-861004-99-0</col2>
    <col3>Professional C#</col3>
    <col4>Wrox Author Team</col4>
    <col5 />
    <col6>49.99</col6>
  </line>
  <line>
    <col0>computer</col0>
    <col1>2001</col1>
    <col2>1-861004-82-6</col2>
    <col3>Expert One on One: Oracle</col3>
    <col4>Thomas</col4>
    <col5>Kyle</col5>
    <col6>59.99</col6>
  </line>
  <line>
```

```
        <col0>history</col0>
        <col1>2001</col1>
        <col2>0-357727-37-X</col2>
        <col3>American Tabloid</col3>
        <col4>James</col4>
        <col5>Ellroy</col5>
        <col6>8.99</col6>
      </line>
  </parsedTrx>
```

As you can see, this isn't exactly the format we need it in; however, it is valid XML. Recall that the original books.xml had attributes on the book element. Also, the names were a little more descriptive than col1 and line.

The XmlTextWriter class can handle attributes. Here is the CreateXmlFile() method, modified to handle the correct node names and attributes. This is WriterSample2 in the examples download:

```csharp
internal void CreateXmlFile(char delimiter, string filePath)
{
    //create the XmlWriter, sending the XML the specified file
    XmlTextWriter tw=new XmlTextWriter
                            (@"..\..\..\writer2.xml",System.Text.Encoding.UTF8);
    //set the formatting to indented
    tw.Formatting=Formatting.Indented;

    tw.WriteStartDocument();
    //open the file to be parsed
    StreamReader sr=new StreamReader(filePath);
    string line;
    line=sr.ReadLine();
    //root node
    tw.WriteStartElement("bookstore");
    while(line!=null) {
        //split the line into an array based on delimiter
        string[] parsedLine=line.Split(new char[]{delimiter});
        //new line element
        tw.WriteStartElement("book");
        //each element of the array is an element under <line>
        for(int i=0;i<parsedLine.Length;i++)
        {

            switch(i)
            {
                case 0:
                    tw.WriteAttributeString("genre",parsedLine[i].ToString());
                    break;

                case 1:

                    tw.WriteAttributeString("publicationdate",
                                                parsedLine[i].ToString());

                    break;
```

```
            case 2:
                tw.WriteAttributeString("ISBN", parsedLine[i].ToString());
                break;

            case 3:
                tw.WriteElementString("title", parsedLine[i].ToString());
                break;

            case 4:
                tw.WriteStartElement("author");
                tw.WriteElementString("first-name",
                                            parsedLine[i].ToString());
                break;

            case 5:
                tw.WriteElementString("last-name", parsedLine[i].ToString());
                tw.WriteEndElement();
                break;

            case 6:
                tw.WriteElementString("price", parsedLine[i].ToString());
                break;

        }
    }
    tw.WriteEndElement();
    line=sr.ReadLine();

}
//clean up
tw.WriteEndElement();
tw.WriteEndDocument();
//flush the XmlWriter
tw.Flush();
//rewind

tw.Close();
sr.Close();

}
```

The changes are highlighted. Since we know, in this case, that the order of the data elements on each line is always going to be the same, we can take some liberties with our design. Without this knowledge you would need to determine which piece of data needs to be mapped to which element in the XML document. The first three data elements, or, after it has been parsed, the first three elements in the array parsedLine[], are always going to be the attributes genre, publicationdate, and ISBN. We use this bit of knowledge to set up the switch statement. For elements 0, 1, and 2, we use WriteAttributeString() to create the attribute. WriteAttributeString() will create the attribute on whatever the current element is; in this case it would be book. To go along with WriteAttributeString, there are the WriteStartAttribute() and WriteEndAttribute() methods. Each of these methods will create an attribute; however, with WriteAttributeString, the attribute is created and the data inserted in one line of code.

Look at the following section of code:

```
case 4:
    tw.WriteStartElement("author");
    tw.WriteElementString("first-name",parsedLine[i].ToString());
    break;

case 5:
    tw.WriteElementString("last-name",parsedLine[i].ToString());
    tw.WriteEndElement();
    break;
```

Under case 4 we added `WriteStartElement("author")`. author is the parent element for first-name and last-name. When you call `WriteStartElement()`, everything that is written before the `WriteEndElement()` will become children of that element. This is how we can get first-name and last-name as children of author.

The output of this code looks like this:

```
<?xml version="1.0" encoding="utf-8"?>
<bookstore>
    <book genre="computer" publicationdate="2001" ISBN="1-861004-99-0">
        <title>Professional C#</title>
        <author>
            <first-name>Wrox Author Team</first-name>
            <last-name />
        </author>
        <price>49.99</price>
    </book>
    <book genre="computer" publicationdate="2001" ISBN="1-861004-82-6">
        <title>Expert One on One: Oracle</title>
        <author>
            <first-name>Thomas</first-name>
            <last-name>Kyle</last-name>
        </author>
        <price>59.99</price>
    </book>
    <book genre="history" publicationdate="2001" ISBN="0-357727-37-X">
        <title>American Tabloid</title>
        <author>
            <first-name>James</first-name>
            <last-name>Ellroy</last-name>
        </author>
        <price>8.99</price>
    </book>
</bookstore>
```

Now this is more like it. We have taken the pipe-delimited text file and turned it into a valid XML document in the form that we require. The method that we used may not be the best, and it certainly isn't the most flexible. Whenever the form of the text file changes, the code will have to change, but it does serve the purpose of exploring the XmlTextWriter class.

Writing to Other Streams

Since the `XmlTextWriter` is a streaming model, it can use a stream instead of writing directly to a file. The advantage of this is that you can do things like write to a memory stream and chain to another stream to perform some other type of process. The streaming model allows you a great deal of flexibility on where you send the data. In the case of our sample, if you change the beginning of `CreateXmlFile()` to the following:

```
//create the XmlTextWriter
XmlDocument xmlDoc=new XmlDocument();
//create the streams for handling the data
MemoryStream streamMem=new MemoryStream();
StreamReader streamRead=new StreamReader(streamMem);
StreamWriter streamWrite=new StreamWriter(streamMem);

//create the XmlWriter, sending the XML to a memory stream
XmlTextWriter tw=new XmlTextWriter(streamWrite);
```

what you end up with is a memory stream that will be the receiver of `XmlTextWriter`'s output. Now as part of the cleanup, we do the following:

```
//rewind
streamMem.Seek(0,SeekOrigin.Begin);
//load the document, tidy up and return
xmlDoc.Load(streamRead);
```

This will create an `XmlDocument`, `xmlDoc`, in memory. Now if you need to traverse the document, or pass it to an ASP.NET page to display, you can. You can even write out to disk as a valid document by using the `XmlDocument.Save()` method.

Along with being able to write string data, there are several methods on the `XmlTextWriter` that can write other types of data. If you have a binary image of some type (such as a GIF or JPG file), you can use `WriteBase64`. The data needs to be in a byte array to be passed in to the method. There is also a `WriteBinHex` to use on binary data. `WriteCData` writes out a CDATA (or character data) section. CDATA is an element type that allows you to include what would normally be illegal characters. An example of its use would be to have a short JScript method that you want to save or display. If you have a large amount of data that needs to be written, you can do it a buffer at a time with the `WriteChars()` method. You can also write comments (`WriteComment()`), processing instructions (`WriteProcessingInstruction()`), entity refs (`WriteEntityRef()`) and the doctype declaration (`WriteDocType()`).

The one thing to remember is that `XmlTextWriter` does not append or edit a current document; it will only create new documents or fragments. You could merge the newly created documents with an existing document, but that could be more easily done by just editing the document with `XmlDocument`, which we will look at later in the chapter.

XmlReader

If you need to read an XML document quickly and you don't need editing capabilities, then an XmlReader-based class is the way to go. XmlReader is a fast, forward-only, and read-only pipe to your XML data. It is the .NET Framework replacement for SAX (Simple API for XML). Unlike SAX, which has a **push**-type architecture, XmlReader has a **pull**-based architecture. In SAX you set up event handlers to handle certain types of nodes and data as they are "pushed" to your application. With XmlReader you read in the data, or "pull" it from the XML document. As the data is read, you can write the code to process it accordingly. The pull model is a more natural and efficient way of dealing with data since with SAX you get the all of the data and then respond accordingly to the data. With XmlReader, you can limit the data that you see, thereby limiting the amount of data to process.

As was mentioned earlier in the chapter, there are three classes derived from XmlReader in the System.Xml namespace:

❑ XmlTextReader

❑ XmlNodeReader

❑ XmlValidatingReader

XmlTextReader has thirteen overloads on the constructor that take either a Stream object, a string object that contains a valid file name and path, or a TextReader object. You can also include a valid XmlNameTable object, a URI for referencing external resources, or an XmlParserContext. An XmlNameTable is a table of string objects that can be reused for names that are used many times during the processing of a document. An XmlParserContext is all of the context information for an XML fragment that may be used by an XmlReader.

Let's take a look at some examples to see how the XmlReader classes work.

Displaying Node Names

In the following example (ReaderSample1 in the download), we are going to read in the books.xml file and display the node names in a textbox. We will build on this in the following examples, displaying more meaningful and pertinent data.

```
using System;
using System.Drawing;
using System.Collections;
using System.ComponentModel;
using System.Windows.Forms;
using System.Data;
using System.Xml;

namespace Wrox.ProCSharpData.Chapter7.ReaderSample1
{
    /// <summary>
    /// Summary description for Form1.
    /// </summary>
    public class Form1 : System.Windows.Forms.Form
    {
        private System.Windows.Forms.RichTextBox richTextBox1;
```

```
/// <summary>
/// Required designer variable.
/// </summary>
private System.ComponentModel.Container components = null;

public Form1()
{
   //
   // Required for Windows Form Designer support
   //
   InitializeComponent();

   //
   // TODO: Add any constructor code after InitializeComponent call
   //
   LoadXml();
}

/// <summary>
/// Clean up any resources being used.
/// </summary>
protected override void Dispose( bool disposing )
{
   if( disposing )
   {
      if (components != null)
      {
         components.Dispose();
      }
   }
   base.Dispose( disposing );
}

#region Windows Form Designer generated code
/// <summary>
/// Required method for Designer support - do not modify
/// the contents of this method with the code editor.
/// </summary>
private void InitializeComponent()
{
   this.richTextBox1 = new System.Windows.Forms.RichTextBox();
   this.SuspendLayout();
   //
   // richTextBox1
   //
   this.richTextBox1.Anchor = ((
                        System.Windows.Forms.AnchorStyles.Top |
                        System.Windows.Forms.AnchorStyles.Left)|
                        System.Windows.Forms.AnchorStyles.Right);
   this.richTextBox1.Location = new System.Drawing.Point(4, 4);
   this.richTextBox1.Name = "richTextBox1";
   this.richTextBox1.Size = new System.Drawing.Size(284, 176);
   this.richTextBox1.TabIndex = 0;
   //
```

```
        // Form1
        //
        this.AutoScaleBaseSize = new System.Drawing.Size(5, 13);
        this.ClientSize = new System.Drawing.Size(292, 266);
        this.Controls.AddRange(new System.Windows.Forms.Control[]
                                            this.richTextBox1});
        this.Name = "Form1";
        this.Text = "Form1";
        this.ResumeLayout(false);

    }
    #endregion

    /// <summary>
    /// The main entry point for the application.
    /// </summary>
    [STAThread]
    static void Main()
    {
        Application.Run(new Form1());
    }

    internal void LoadXml() {
        //load the document
        XmlTextReader xmlRdr=new XmlTextReader(@"..\..\..\books.xml");
        //read in the nodes and display the node name
        while(xmlRdr.Read())
            richTextBox1.AppendText(xmlRdr.Name + "\r\n");

    }
  }
}
```

This is a pretty simple example showing the XmlTextReader. A new XmlTextReader, xmlRdr, is created passing in the file name and path for our XML document. The xmlRdr.Read() method will return false when there is nothing left to read, so we put that in as the test to the while loop and start reading. As you can see all we are accomplishing in this example is to load the name of the node into the RichTextBox.

If we knew what type of node we were looking at, then maybe we could make a decision as to what we need to do with the node. There may be certain node types that we want to ignore, or certain types of nodes that we want to display. The following modification to LoadXml(), made in ReaderSample2, gives us this information:

```
internal void LoadXml() {
    //open the document
    XmlTextReader xmlRdr=new XmlTextReader(@"..\..\..\books.xml");
    //column headings
    richTextBox1.AppendText("Node Name\tNode Type\r\n");
    //get the name and nodetype
    while(xmlRdr.Read())    {
        richTextBox1.AppendText(xmlRdr.Name + "\t\t");
        richTextBox1.AppendText(xmlRdr.NodeType.ToString() + "\r\n");
    }
}
```

Now we can see what type of node we are looking at. Here is a screenshot of the results from the code to this point:

Notice that we now have node names and node types. Notice that not all nodes have a name in the first column. Nodes of type `Comments`, `Whitespace`, and `Text` don't have a name associated with them. That's why we want to know the node type; all nodes have a type, and this is what you will base a major portion of your processing on.

Displaying Node Types

Without knowing what the values of the text nodes are, our example application is not very useful. After all, the data is what we are generally interested in. It just takes one more line of code and we can have the values. Here is the line in `ReaderSample3`:

```
internal void LoadXml() {
    //open the document
    XmlTextReader xmlRdr=new XmlTextReader(@"..\..\..\books.xml");
    //column headings
    richTextBox1.AppendText("Node Name\tNode Type\tValue\r\n");
    //get the name, nodetype and value
    while(xmlRdr.Read())    {
        richTextBox1.AppendText(xmlRdr.Name + "\t\t");
        richTextBox1.AppendText(xmlRdr.NodeType.ToString() + "\t");
        richTextBox1.AppendText("\t" + xmlRdr.Value + "\r\n");
    }
}
```

If you look at the output of this code, you will see that the title node doesn't have a value. It is actually the next node, a `Text` node, that has the value of the book title in it:

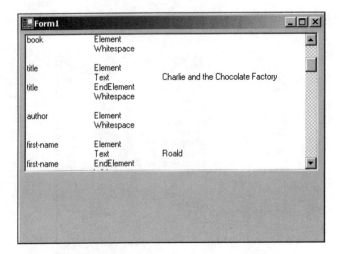

This can be a little confusing. The XML for this would look like this:

```
<title>Charlie and the Chocolate Factory</title>
```

You are looking at three nodes, not just one. The first node is `<title>`. It is of type `Element`. This is sometimes referred to as the start tag. The next node is a text node and contains the string `"Charlie and the Chocolate Factory"`. The last node is `</title>`, which is the end tag or as you can see in the screenshot, `EndElement`. The node types are members of the `System.Xml.XmlNodeType` enumeration. When using the `XmlReader`, you will generally read through the document, and based on node type, make a decision on what to do. In our sample we are interested in the `Element` and `Text` nodes. The rest of the nodes we can ignore. So let's rewrite the `LoadXml()` method to take this into account:

```
internal void LoadXml()
{

    XmlTextReader xmlRdr=new XmlTextReader(@"..\..\..\books.xml");

    while(xmlRdr.Read())
    {

        if(xmlRdr.NodeType==XmlNodeType.Element)
            richTextBox1.AppendText("\r\n"+xmlRdr.Name + ":");

        if(xmlRdr.NodeType==XmlNodeType.Text)
            richTextBox1.AppendText(xmlRdr.Value);


    }
}
```

Now we are checking to see what the node type is before we process it. If the node is an `Element` node, then we want the name to display. If the node is a `Text` node, then we want the node value.

Displaying Node Attributes

From a functionality standpoint we almost have something useful. We still haven't added the attributes, and the output still looks pretty anemic. Let's process the attributes and add some visual enhancements. Here is the changed code:

```csharp
internal void LoadXml() {
    //fonts for formatting the output
    Font fntBold=new System.Drawing.Font(richTextBox1.Font.FontFamily,
                        richTextBox1.Font.Size, FontStyle.Bold);
    Font fntNrm=new System.Drawing.Font(richTextBox1.Font.FontFamily,
                        richTextBox1.Font.Size, FontStyle.Regular);
    //create the reader
    XmlTextReader xmlRdr=new XmlTextReader(@"..\..\..\books.xml");
    //start reading
    while(xmlRdr.Read())
    {
        //we only want Elements and text nodes
        if(xmlRdr.NodeType==XmlNodeType.Element)   {

            richTextBox1.SelectionFont=fntBold;
            richTextBox1.AppendText("\r\n"+xmlRdr.Name + ":");
            richTextBox1.SelectionFont=fntNrm;
            //if we have attributes, process them also
            if(xmlRdr.HasAttributes)   {
                richTextBox1.SelectionFont=fntBold;
                richTextBox1.AppendText("\tAttributes:");

                for(int i=0;i<xmlRdr.AttributeCount;i++)
                {
                    xmlRdr.MoveToAttribute(i);
                    richTextBox1.SelectionFont=fntBold;
                    richTextBox1.AppendText(xmlRdr.Name + ":");
                    richTextBox1.SelectionFont=fntNrm;
                    richTextBox1.AppendText(xmlRdr.Value + " ");
                }
            }
        }

        if(xmlRdr.NodeType==XmlNodeType.Text)
            richTextBox1.AppendText(xmlRdr.Value);

    }
}
```

Now we have added a couple of new things. First let's talk about the attributes. If you look at the following section of code:

```csharp
if(xmlRdr.HasAttributes)
{
    richTextBox1.SelectionFont=fntBold;
    richTextBox1.AppendText("\tAttributes:");
```

```
for (int i=0;i<xmlRdr.AttributeCount;i++)
{
    xmlRdr.MoveToAttribute(i);
    richTextBox1.SelectionFont=fntBold;
    richTextBox1.AppendText(xmlRdr.Name + ":");
    richTextBox1.SelectionFont=fntNrm;
    richTextBox1.AppendText(xmlRdr.Value + " ");
}
}
```

Here we are checking to see if the current node has any attributes. This is an important point. We never noticed the attributes before when we were iterating through the nodes. This is because attributes are not part of the document structure. We have to check each node individually to see if it has any attributes. If it does we iterate through the `Attributes` collection of the current node using a `for` loop. For each attribute in the collection, we output the name and the value of the attribute. Since we are moving to each attribute with the `MoveToAttribute()` method, we can use the `Value` property just as we have done before. There are several other methods for processing attributes. If you know the attribute name, or its index in the `Attributes` collection, you can use the `GetAttribute()` method. There are also `MoveToFirstAttribute()` and `MoveToNextAttribute()` for iterating the attributes. These both return a Boolean depending on whether or not the move was successful.

The last addition we made to the sample was visual. We added the ability to make the node names bold. This will make it easier to read the document in the `RichTextBox` control. We create two fonts, one bold and the other normal. As we output the data, we can apply the fonts based on node types. The completed code is `ReaderSample5`, and here is what the output looks like now:

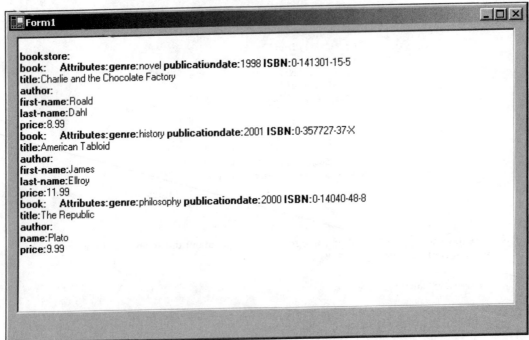

As you can see, this is much more readable, and we have all of the information that we want.

Other XMLReader Methods

There are several methods and properties that we have not covered. Some of the properties include: EOF (meaning end of file), which tells us if the reader is at the end of the stream; LocalName, which is the node name with any namespace prefix removed; ReadState, which returns the current state that the reader is in; and XmlLang, which returns a string with the current language. XmlTextReader adds properties such as LineNumber and LinePosition. These are both "1" based, meaning that the first line will start with "1" (one) and not "0" (zero), and are generally used for error reporting.

One of the methods that the XmlReader has is MoveToContent(), which will move to the next content node. Content nodes are nodes of type Element, EndElement, EntityReference, EndEntity, CDATA and non-whitespace Text nodes. MoveToContent() is used by a few of helper methods like IsStartElement(), ReadElementString(), and ReadStartElement(). ReadElementString() for example, makes a call to MoveToContent(), and then returns the text data from the element. So in the case of our sample data, when ReadElementString() hits the element:

```
<title>Charlie and the Chocolate Factory</title>
```

it will return "Charlie and the Chocolate Factory". Not only that, the current position will be on the node following the </title> EndElement. If the element does not have a text value or if the content node is not a start tag, then an XmlException is raised. Thus, if you were to use this method of reading in text values, you would need to handle the exception and continue reading.

The next example demonstrates one way of using ReadElementString(). This is taken from ReadSample6 in the download. It is based on ReaderSample3:

```
internal void LoadXml()
{
    //open the document
    XmlTextReader xmlRdr=new XmlTextReader(@"..\..\..\books.xml");
    //column headings
    richTextBox1.AppendText("Node Name\tNode Type\tValue\r\n");
    //get the name, nodetype and value
    while(!xmlRdr.EOF)
    {
        if(xmlRdr.MoveToContent()==XmlNodeType.Element)
        {
            richTextBox1.AppendText(xmlRdr.Name + "\t\t");
            richTextBox1.AppendText(xmlRdr.NodeType.ToString() + "\t");
            richTextBox1.AppendText("\t" + ReadValue(xmlRdr) + "\r\n");
        }
        else
        {
            xmlRdr.Read();
        }
    }
}
internal string ReadValue(XmlReader readerIn)
{
    try
```

```
    {
        return readerIn.ReadElementString();
    }
    catch(XmlException er)  {
        return "";
    }
}
```

You can see that this is a little more complex than the earlier examples. However, in this example we will only display element nodes, and not any of the other node types. Since `ReadElementString()` moves you to the next element after it reads the current one, we have to change the loop to check for the end of file (`EOF`) marker. We use the `MoveToContent()` method to find the element nodes. After we find one, we gather up some information from the node. Another change is that we put the `ReadElementString()` method call into another function. The reason is that if there isn't a text node associated with the element an `XmlException` is raised. If the exception were raised in the `LoadXml()` function, then we would fall out of the loop before we had a chance to read in all of the nodes. By putting into a separate function, we can handle the exception and return an empty string if need be and continue with reading the document.

Validating XML

Nothing in the previous section mentioned anything about validating XML against a schema or DTD. An XML document can be validated in two different ways. First you would validate that it is a well-formed XML document. This means that all of the start tags have end tags, there are no illegal characters, etc. When you load an XML document this check is performed by the parser. The other type of validation is to validate against a schema or DTD. This will validate that you have the proper type of data. We will look at creating a schema later in the chapter. In order to do this validation you must use the `XmlValidatingReader`. `XmlValidatingReader` is derived from `XmlReader` and can do most of the same things that `XmlTextReader` can do, in addition to the validation against a valid DTD, XSD, or XDR schema.

XmlValidatingReader

`XmlValidatingReader` adds three properties. They are the `Schemas`, `SchemaType`, and `ValidationType`. The `Schemas` property is a collection of schemas. The schemas are cached and can be reused many times. The `SchemaType` property returns an `XmlSchemaType` or `XmlSchemaDataType` object. If the type is user-defined, then the `XmlSchemaDataType` object is returned. The `ValidationType` property returns a `ValidationType` that describes what type of validation to do. The possible values are `None`, `Auto`, `DTD`, `XDR`, or `Schema`.

`XmlValidatingReader` does not always raise an exception when a validation error occurs. Instead, an event is raised. You set up a `ValidationEventHandler` just like you would any other type of event handler. When a validation error occurs, the `ValidationEventArgs` will contain the `XmlSchemaException`; `Message`, which is the text message of the event, and `Severity`, which is the severity of the event. `Severity` can be an `XmlSeverityType.Error` or `XmlSeverityType.Warning`. If a `ValidationEventHandler` has not been defined, then an exception will be raised of type `XmlException`.

Let's take a look at how this works. We'll change the code in our last example to do validation. Here is our new `LoadXml()` method, with the changes highlighted:

```
internal void LoadXml()
{
    //fonts for formatting the output
    Font fntBold=new System.Drawing.Font(richTextBox1.Font.FontFamily,
        richTextBox1.Font.Size,
        FontStyle.Bold);
    Font fntNrm=new System.Drawing.Font(richTextBox1.Font.FontFamily,
        richTextBox1.Font.Size,
        FontStyle.Regular);
    //create the reader
    XmlTextReader xmlRdr=new XmlTextReader(@"..\..\..\books.xml");

    XmlValidatingReader xmlValRdr=new XmlValidatingReader(xmlRdr);
    xmlValRdr.ValidationType=ValidationType.Schema;
    XmlSchemaCollection schemas=new XmlSchemaCollection();
    schemas.Add(null,@"..\..\..\booksBroke.xsd");
    xmlValRdr.Schemas.Add(schemas);
    xmlValRdr.ValidationEventHandler += new ValidationEventHandler
                                                (ValidationCallBack);


    //start reading
    while(xmlValRdr.Read())
    {
        //we only want Elements and text nodes
        if(xmlValRdr.NodeType==XmlNodeType.Element)    {
            //loop until we hit a text node.
            //this will accomodate nested nodes
            richTextBox1.SelectionFont=fntBold;
            richTextBox1.AppendText("\r\n"+xmlValRdr.Name + ":");
            richTextBox1.SelectionFont=fntNrm;
            //if we have attributes, process them also
            if(xmlValRdr.HasAttributes)
            {
                richTextBox1.SelectionFont=fntBold;
                richTextBox1.AppendText("\tAttributes:");

                for (int i=0;i<xmlValRdr.AttributeCount;i++)
                {
                    xmlValRdr.MoveToAttribute(i);
                    richTextBox1.SelectionFont=fntBold;
                    richTextBox1.AppendText(xmlValRdr.Name + ":");
                    richTextBox1.SelectionFont=fntNrm;
                    richTextBox1.AppendText(xmlValRdr.Value + " ");
                }
            }
        }

        if(xmlValRdr.NodeType==XmlNodeType.Text)
            richTextBox1.AppendText(xmlValRdr.Value);

    }

}
```

A new `XmlValidatingReader`, `xmlValRdr`, is created, passing in the `XmlTextReader` that we already have. `XmlValidatingReader` can also validate a fragment of XML. There are two other overloads on the constructor to handle this. One takes a `Stream` object, an `XmlNodeType`, and an `XmlParserContext` object. The other overload takes a string of XML instead of the `Stream` object.

After `xmlValRdr` is created, we set the `ValidationType` to `Schema`, create a new `XmlSchemaCollection`, `schemas`, and add a new schema to the collection called `booksBroke.xsd`. We add `schemas` to the `xmlValRdr` Schemas collection, and we are ready to go. Note that you can add several different schemas to this collection, and reuse them as often as needed. This way you would not need to reload each schema from disk every time you needed to validate a document.

The last thing we do is hook up the `ValidationEventHandler`. In this case, it is a method called `ValidationCallback()`, and the code for this is as follows:

```
public void ValidationCallBack (object sender, ValidationEventArgs args)
{
    MessageBox.Show(args.Severity.ToString() + " - " + args.Message);
}
```

All we are doing is displaying the `Severity` and the error message in a `MessageBox`. After the `MessageBox` is cleared, reading and validation continue. This gives you the flexibility to try to possibly correct an error when it occurs, instead of just killing the process.

We have looked at two of the three derived classes of `XmlReader`. The third class, `XmlNodeReader`, works very much like `XmlTextReader`, although it reads across an `XmlDocument`. `XmlDocument` is the DOM implementation in `System.Xml`. We'll look at `XmlDocument` next. The properties and methods are very similar to `XmlTextReader`. The only real difference is that the constructor will require an `XmlNode`-based object, since `XmlDocument` is derived from `XmlNode`.

XmlDocument (DOM)

`XmlDocument` is the DOM implementation for `System.Xml` and for the .NET Framework. If you are using MSXML for XML processing, then `XmlDocument` will have a familiar feel to it. `XmlDocument` is derived from `XmlNode`. It implements the `IXPathNavigable` interface, so it can be used to feed an `XslTransform`. We'll look at this in detail the next chapter.

`XmlDocument` is a tree representation of an XML document. Because of this, unlike the `XmlReader`-based classes, the document created with `XmlDocument` is editable and you also have the ability to navigate around in the document. There are several methods available to select single and multiple nodes for you to work with. Because of these features, `XmlDocument` is not as fast as an `XmlReader`-based object, but if you need the added flexibility, then it's a tradeoff worth taking.

The code snippet below is a simple example of an `XmlDocument`. It is taken from `DocSample1` in the examples download:

```
internal void LoadXml()
{

    XmlDocument xmlDoc=new XmlDocument();
    xmlDoc.Load(@"..\..\..\books.xml");
```

```
XmlNodeList nodes=xmlDoc.SelectNodes("/bookstore/book");
foreach(XmlNode node in nodes)    {
    richTextBox1.AppendText(node.Name + "\r\n");
}
}
```

Here is the `LoadXml()` method again, this time using an `XmlDocument` object. After `xmlDoc` is created, we use the `Load()` method to load up an `XmlDocument`. If the XML document is not well-formed, an exception will be raised when you try to load it.

Using XmlNodeList

The next line is where we are selecting the nodes that we want to work with:

```
XmlNodeList nodes=xmlDoc.SelectNodes("/bookstore/book");
```

The `XmlNodeList` object is not a snapshot or a copy of the `XmlDocument`'s selected nodes. Rather, it works by walking across the `XmlDocument`, showing only the nodes that match the `XPath` statement being passed to it; there is more on `XPath` in the next chapter. Walking across the document in such a way accomplishes two important things:

❑ Memory is not wasted by duplication of nodes

❑ Any changes that occur in the selected nodes will be seen immediately

In our example, we select the book nodes and display the name. Something else to notice is that `XmlNode` does implement the `IEnumerable` interface so we can use the `foreach` method of iteration.

If we extend our example a little, with the new code highlighted below, we can start to make it useful:

```
internal void LoadXml()
{

    XmlDocument xmlDoc=new XmlDocument();
    xmlDoc.Load(@"..\..\..\books.xml");

    XmlNodeList nodes=xmlDoc.SelectNodes("/bookstore/book");
    foreach(XmlNode node in nodes)
    {
        richTextBox1.AppendText(node.Name + "\r\n");
        foreach(XmlNode childNode in node.ChildNodes)
        {
            richTextBox1.AppendText("\t" + childNode.Name + ":");
            richTextBox1.AppendText(childNode.InnerText + "\r\n");
        }
    }

}
```

We added another `foreach` loop to take a look at the children of each of the nodes in the `nodelist`. The `ChildNodes` property returns another `XmlNodeList` of the current node's children. In this case, we look at each child node and return a name and the `InnerText`. The `InnerText` property will return the value of the current node concatenated with the values of all of its children. If the current node does not have any children (and is therefore a leaf node), then this is the same as the `Value` property. In this case, since the `author` node has two children, `first-name` and `last-name`, these values will be concatenated together with `author`. If there were other children, then these values would be added as well. To get around this we will need to keep checking to see if more children are present. The best way to do this is to use recursion. Here is our example with `LoadXml()` modified somewhat, and a recursive call to `XmlRecursive()`:

```
internal void LoadXml()
{

    XmlDocument xmlDoc=new XmlDocument();
    xmlDoc.Load(@"..\..\..\books.xml");

    XmlNodeList nodes=xmlDoc.SelectNodes("/bookstore/book");
    foreach(XmlNode node in nodes)
        XmlRecursive(node);
}

internal void XmlRecursive(XmlNode node)
{

    if(node.HasChildNodes)
    {
        foreach(XmlNode childNode in node.ChildNodes)
        {
            if(childNode.NodeType!=XmlNodeType.Text)
                richTextBox1.AppendText(childNode.Name + ": ");

            if(childNode.HasChildNodes)
            {
                if(childNode.NextSibling !=null &&
                        childNode.FirstChild.NodeType!=XmlNodeType.Text)
                            richTextBox1.AppendText("\r\n");

                XmlRecursive(childNode);

            }
            else
                richTextBox1.AppendText(childNode.InnerText + "\r\n");

            node=childNode.ParentNode;
        }
    }
}
```

In `LoadXml()` we still create the `XmlDocument` and load the XML document from file. We even still issue the `SelectNodes()` method to get the book nodes. After that, things start to change. We call the `XmlRecursive()` method with the book node as the parameter. In the `XmlRecursive()` method, the first thing we do is find out if there are any children. `HasChildNodes` returns `true` or `false` depending on whether any child nodes exist. If there are child nodes, then we use the `foreach` loop to iterate through them. Let's take a look at this code a little more closely:

```
if(childNode.NodeType==XmlNodeType.Element)
    richTextBox1.AppendText(childNode.Name + ": ");

if(childNode.HasChildNodes) {
    if(childNode.NextSibling !=null &&
        childNode.FirstChild.NodeType!=XmlNodeType.Text)
      richTextBox1.AppendText("\r\n");

    XmlRecursive(childNode);

}
else
    richTextBox1.AppendText(childNode.InnerText + "\r\n");

node=childNode.ParentNode;
```

The first check is to see if this is an `Element` node. If it is, then we want to display the name. Next we look to see if there are any child nodes. If we find child nodes here, we do another check to see if we want a carriage return-line feed combination inserted. We do this by making a call to the `NextSibling` property. `NextSibling` will return the very next node or `null` if there there are no further nodes. We also check to see if this is a `Text` node or not. If there is a sibling node and it is not a `Text` node, then we want a carriage return-line feed. Then we call `XmlRecursive()` again, passing in the current `childNode` object that we are working with. This can continue many levels deep if need be. If we didn't have any child nodes, we would display the current node's `InnerText` property and move back up to the current node's parent. We need to do this to get us back to the same level that the original `foreach` loop is on.

Here is the display from the recursive version of our program:

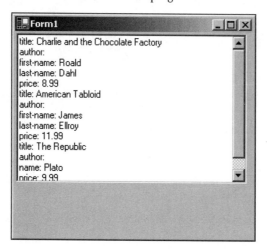

Remember in the MSXML section how we displayed the data in a `TreeView`, and how we derived our own `TreeViewNode`? Well, with just a couple of changes we can use almost the same code with `XmlDocument`. Here is the pertinent code. The complete project is `DocSample4` and it can be downloaded with all of the examples from the Wrox web site. The only real change is that there are two `RichTextBox` controls added. One will display the node value and the other will display the attributes. These are loaded when the `TreeView1_AfterSelect` event is fired:

```csharp
private void LoadTree()
{

    XmlDocument doc=new XmlDocument();
    //Load the xml file. Change path if needed
    doc.Load(@"..\..\..\books.xml");
    //select the root node
    XmlNode node=doc.SelectSingleNode("bookstore");
    //instantiate a new XmlTreeNode,
    //fill the node
    //load it into the TreeView
    XmlTreeNode rootNode=new XmlTreeNode(node);
    rootNode.FillTreeView();
    treeView1.Nodes.Add(rootNode);

}

private void treeView1_AfterSelect(object sender,
                                  System.Windows.Forms.TreeViewEventArgs e)
{
    richTextBox1.Clear();
    richTextBox2.Clear();
    richTextBox1.AppendText(((XmlTreeNode)treeView1.SelectedNode).Value);
    XmlAttributeCollection attributes=
                        ((XmlTreeNode)treeView1.SelectedNode).Attributes;
    if(attributes!=null)    {
        foreach(XmlNode attribute in attributes)    {
            richTextBox2.AppendText(attribute.Name + ": ");
            richTextBox2.AppendText(attribute.InnerText + "\r\n");
        }
    }
}


/// <summary>
/// Our new TreeNode class. This will load the tree
/// with our XML doc
/// </summary>
internal class XmlTreeNode : TreeNode
{

    XmlNode node;

    internal XmlTreeNode()    : base(){}

    internal XmlTreeNode(XmlNode treeNode)    : base()
    {
```

```
        node=treeNode;
        //Don't want the name of the node is null
        //or if the node is a text node
        if(node!=null && node.NodeType!=XmlNodeType.Text)
            this.Text=node.Name;

    }

    public string Value
    {
        get
        {
            if(node.HasChildNodes &&
                                node.FirstChild.NodeType==XmlNodeType.Text)
                return node.InnerText;
            return "";
        }
    }

    internal XmlAttributeCollection Attributes
    {
        get
        {
            if(node.Attributes.Count>0)
                return node.Attributes;

            return null;
        }
    }

    internal void FillTreeView()
    {

        if(node!=null)
        {
            this.Nodes.Clear();
            XmlNode cNode=node.CloneNode(true);

            if(cNode.HasChildNodes)
            {
                cNode=cNode.FirstChild;

                while(cNode!=null)
                {
                    if(cNode.NodeType!=XmlNodeType.Text &&
                        cNode.NodeType!=XmlNodeType.Attribute)
                    {

                        XmlTreeNode newTreeNode=new XmlTreeNode(cNode);
                        this.Nodes.Add(newTreeNode);
                        newTreeNode.FillTreeView();
                    }
                    cNode=cNode.NextSibling;
```

```
              }
          }
        }
      }
    }
```

We won't go into this line by line since it is almost identical to the previous MSXML example. There are a couple of items that do need to be pointed out. As before we are assigning an `XmlNode` to each `TreeView` node. One of the ways we take advantage of this is in the `Value` property of `XmlTreeNode`:

```
public string Value
{
    get
    {
        if(node.HasChildNodes && node.FirstChild.NodeType==XmlNodeType.Text)
            return node.InnerText;
        return "";
    }
}
```

`node` is the `XmlNode` that is associated with this particular instance of the `XmlTreeNode`. We check to see that `node` actually has a value by first looking to see if there is a child node, and then if the child node is a text node, and if it is, we return the node's `InnerText` property.

Something else to look at is how the attributes are loaded into the `RichTextBox`. If there are any attributes in the `Attributes` collection, we use a `foreach` loop and get each attribute name and attribute value.

Editing XML Documents

So far, all we have done is read in XML documents and display them, but what about editing an XML document? We stated before that the `XmlDocument` class was read/write. By adding a handful of `TextBoxes` and `Labels`, we can add the functionality to add new books to our catalog. The complete code is `DocSample5` in the examples download. Let's take a look at the method that actually adds the data to the document:

```
private void button1_Click(object sender, System.EventArgs e)
{
    XmlElement newBook=doc.CreateElement("book");

    //create and set the attributes on the 'book' element
    newBook.SetAttribute("genre",comboBox1.Text);
    newBook.SetAttribute("publicationdate",textBox6.Text);
    newBook.SetAttribute("ISBN",textBox2.Text);

    //create the 'title' element
    XmlElement newTitle=doc.CreateElement("title");
    newTitle.InnerText=textBox1.Text;
    newBook.AppendChild(newTitle);

    //create an author element
    XmlElement newAuthor=doc.CreateElement("author");
```

```
    newBook.AppendChild(newAuthor);

    //create the name element
    XmlElement newFirstName=doc.CreateElement("first-name");
    newFirstName.InnerText=textBox3.Text;
    newAuthor.AppendChild(newFirstName);
    XmlElement newLastName=doc.CreateElement("last-name");
    newLastName.InnerText=textBox4.Text;
    newAuthor.AppendChild(newLastName);

    //create the price element
    XmlElement newPrice=doc.CreateElement("price");
    newPrice.InnerText=textBox5.Text;
    newBook.AppendChild(newPrice);

    //append the 'book' element to the doc
    doc.DocumentElement.AppendChild(newBook);

    doc.Save(@"..\..\..\booksEdit.xml");
    LoadTree();
}
```

Writing XML with the XmlDocument is not very different from using the XmlWriter:

❑ First, we create a new XmlElement and name it book

❑ We use the SetAttribute method to add the genre, publicationdate, and ISBN
  attributes to the book element

❑ We create another XmlElement called title and set its InnerText property, and append
  the title element to the book element

❑ We create the author element and its two child elements, first-name and last-name

❑ We set the InnerText property of these child nodes, append them to the author element
  and append author to the book element

❑ Finally, we append the price element to the book element, save the document to disk, and
  reload the TreeView control

Here is what the sample looks like after adding a new book and displaying it in the `TreeView`:

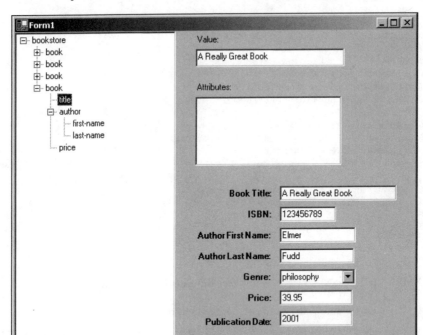

From this point, it probably wouldn't take a lot of work to take this example and make a useful XML viewer/editor out of it. The XML that was created from this example is shown below:

```xml
<?xml version="1.0" ?>
<bookstore>
    <book genre="novel" publicationdate="1998" ISBN="0-141301-15-5">
        <title>Charlie and the Chocolate Factory</title>
        <author>
            <first-name>Roald</first-name>
            <last-name>Dahl</last-name>
        </author>
        <price>8.99</price>
    </book>
    <book genre="history" publicationdate="2001" ISBN="0-357727-37-X">
        <title>American Tabloid</title>
        <author>
            <first-name>James</first-name>
            <last-name>Ellroy</last-name>
        </author>
        <price>11.99</price>
    </book>
    <book genre="philosophy" publicationdate="2000" ISBN="0-14040-48-8">
```

```
        <title>The Republic</title>
        <author>
            <name>Plato</name>
        </author>
        <price>9.99</price>
    </book>
    <book genre="philosophy" publicationdate="2001" ISBN="123456789">
      <title>A Really Great Book</title>
      <author>
        <first-name>Elmer</first-name>
        <last-name>Fudd</last-name>
      </author>
      <price>39.95</price>
    </book>
  </bookstore>
```

You can see that the book we entered is in the document. You can also see that it follows the same format that the other books use. You could very easily add the functionality that we looked at before to validate the new node prior to adding it to the document. Remember that `XmlValidatingReader` can validate document fragments.

XML and ADO.NET

XML is a key component in ADO.NET. In Chapter 4, we had an introduction to XML and ADO.NET, and now we shall look in more detail at the interplay between the two.

XML and `DataSets` are just two different views of potentially the same data. ADO.NET uses XML to move the data between the server and the `DataSet` and from component to component. ADO.NET does not keep the data in XML format in memory, but it will persist the data in XML. You can also create a `DataSet` from an XML document. This ability allows you to share your data with systems that are not even aware of ADO.NET. As long as the XML can be processed, you can send or retrieve data. The structure of a `DataSet` is essentially an XML schema; an XML schema is document that describes the structure and content of your XML data document. Given a schema, you can create a `DataSet` structure, and if you have a `DataSet` you can, in turn, create the schema. We'll take a more detailed look at schemas later in the chapter.

The `System.Xml` namespace has only one class that really ties directly with the `DataSet`, and that is `XmlDataDocument`. `XmlDataDocument` has a `DataSet` property that is a relational view of the data in the XML document. You can go back and forward, viewing the same data in either format. If the `DataSet` changes the data, the XML will reflect the changes immediately. The `DataSet` has a handful of methods and properties to deal with XML. The methods include:

- ❑   `ReadXml()`
- ❑   `ReadXmlSchema()`
- ❑   `WriteXml()`
- ❑   `WriteXmlSchema()`
- ❑   `GetXml()`
- ❑   `GetXmlSchema()`

The `ReadXml()` and `WriteXml()` methods deal with XML in a string or stream format. The `GetXml()` method retrieves the XML from a `DataSet` in a `string` object.

XML from a DataSet

Let's take look at an example of how to get the XML from a `DataSet`. The sample form has a `DataGrid` and that is all. The `ConnectToDatabase()` method is called once `InitializeComponent()` has executed. We'll just look at `ConnectToDatabase`. It will simply connect to the `Northwind` database in SQL Server and return the `customers` table. The entire project is called `ADOSample1` in the download.

```
internal void ConnectToDatabase()
{

    SqlConnection cn=new SqlConnection
      (@"data source=(local)\NETSDK;uid=sa;password=;database=northwind");

    SqlDataAdapter da=new SqlDataAdapter("SELECT * FROM customers",cn);

    DataSet ds = new DataSet("OrdersSample");

    da.Fill(ds,"custs");

    dataGrid1.DataSource=ds;
    dataGrid1.DataMember="custs";

    ds.WriteXmlSchema(@"..\..\..\customer.xsd");
    ds.WriteXml(@"..\..\..\customer.xml");

    cn.Close();

}
```

We make the connection and the `SqlDataAdapter` gets the `Customer` table from the `Northwind` database. We create a new `DataSet` called `OrdersSample`, and fill the `custs` table with the data from the `SqlDataAdapter`. Finally, we bind the `DataSet` to the `DataGrid` control. Up to this point, this is nothing new. The next two lines of code are what we are interested in:

```
ds.WriteXmlSchema(@"..\..\..\customer.xsd");
ds.WriteXml(@"..\..\..\customer.xml");
```

The `WriteXmlSchema()` method will infer the schema from the `DataSet` and create `customer.xsd`. `WriteXmlSchema()` has four overloads. You can write the schema to a file path and name as we have, or you can use a `Stream`, `TextWriter`, or `XmlWriter`-based object. The schema that is generated will contain table, constraint, and relation definitions. Here is the schema generated from this example, `customer.xsd`:

```
<?xml version="1.0" standalone="yes"?>
<xsd:schema id="OrdersSample"
            targetNamespace="" xmlns=""
            xmlns:xsd="http://www.w3.org/2001/XMLSchema"
            xmlns:msdata="urn:schemas-microsoft-com:xml-msdata">
```

```
            <xsd:element name="OrdersSample" msdata:IsDataSet="true">
              <xsd:complexType>
                <xsd:choice maxOccurs="unbounded">
                  <xsd:element name="custs">
                    <xsd:complexType>
                      <xsd:sequence>
                        <xsd:element name="CustomerID" type="xsd:string"
                                     minOccurs="0" />
                        <xsd:element name="CompanyName" type="xsd:string"
                                     minOccurs="0" />
                        <xsd:element name="ContactName" type="xsd:string"
                                     minOccurs="0" />
                        <xsd:element name="ContactTitle" type="xsd:string"
                                     minOccurs="0" />
                        <xsd:element name="Address" type="xsd:string"
                                     minOccurs="0" />
                        <xsd:element name="City" type="xsd:string"
                                     minOccurs="0" />
                        <xsd:element name="Region" type="xsd:string"
                                     minOccurs="0" />
                        <xsd:element name="PostalCode" type="xsd:string"
                                     minOccurs="0" />
                        <xsd:element name="Country" type="xsd:string"
                                     minOccurs="0" />
                        <xsd:element name="Phone" type="xsd:string"
                                     minOccurs="0" />
                        <xsd:element name="Fax" type="xsd:string"
                                     minOccurs="0" />
                      </xsd:sequence>
                    </xsd:complexType>
                  </xsd:element>
                </xsd:choice>
              </xsd:complexType>
            </xsd:element>
          </xsd:schema>
```

As you can see, this is a pretty standard schema document. This is in accordance with the current W3C standards, with one exception:

```
xmlns:msdata="urn:schemas-microsoft-com:xml-msdata">
```

This line defines a namespace to describe certain ADO.NET characteristics that cannot be represented by W3C standards. The W3C specification allows for these custom attributes, so if this document were to be processed by something that did not understand ADO.NET data sets, these custom attributes (qualified with msdata) would be ignored.

The following line in the example will output the XML document of the DataSet.

```
        ds.WriteXml(@"..\..\..\customer.xml");
```

WriteXml() has eight overloads; four are the same as the WriteXmlSchema() method, and the other four add a WriteXmlWriteMode parameter. There are three options in the WriteXmlWriteMode enumeration. The following table describes them:

Name	Description
DiffGram	Writes the DataSet as a DiffGram. A DiffGram is an XML document that includes the before and after data after an editing session; it includes the current and changed values for each row. The DiffGram can be applied to a SQL Server since it is a subset of the UpdateGram.
IgnoreSchema	Writes the data as an XML document without a schema.
WriteSchema	Writes the data, but includes a schema inline with the document.

Here is a sample of what the XML data document looks like.

```
<?xml version="1.0" standalone="yes"?>
<OrdersSample>
   <custs>
      <CustomerID>ALFKI</CustomerID>
      <CompanyName>Alfreds Futterkiste</CompanyName>
      <ContactName>Maria Anders</ContactName>
      <ContactTitle>Sales Representative</ContactTitle>
      <Address>Obere Str. 57</Address>
      <City>Berlin</City>
      <PostalCode>12209</PostalCode>
      <Country>Germany</Country>
      <Phone>030-0074321</Phone>
      <Fax>030-0076545</Fax>
   </custs>
   <custs>
      <CustomerID>ANATR</CustomerID>
      <CompanyName>Ana Trujillo Emparedados y helados</CompanyName>
      <ContactName>Ana Trujillo</ContactName>
      <ContactTitle>Owner</ContactTitle>
      <Address>Avda. de la Constitución 2222</Address>
      <City>México D.F.</City>
      <PostalCode>05021</PostalCode>
      <Country>Mexico</Country>
      <Phone>(5) 555-4729</Phone>
      <Fax>(5) 555-3745</Fax>
   </custs>
</OrdersSample>
```

Using More than One Table

This is easy enough with one table, but generally there is more then one table involved. What does the code look like when there are two or more tables in the DataSet. Let's make the change to the ConnectToDatabase() method and add the Orders table. The new lines of code are highlighted, and the complete code can be found in ADOSample2:

```
internal void ConnectToDatabase()
{

    SqlConnection cn=new SqlConnection(@"data source=
                  (local)\NETSDK;uid=sa;password=;database=northwind");
```

```
DataSet ds = new DataSet("OrdersSample");

SqlDataAdapter daCust=new SqlDataAdapter("SELECT * FROM customers",cn);
SqlDataAdapter daOrders=new SqlDataAdapter("SELECT * FROM orders",cn);

daCust.Fill(ds,"customers");
daOrders.Fill(ds,"orders");

ds.Relations.Add(ds.Tables["customers"].Columns["customerid"],
                     ds.Tables["orders"].Columns["customerid"]);

ds.WriteXmlSchema(@"..\..\..\custOrders.xsd");
ds.WriteXml(@"..\..\..\custOrders.xml");

dataGrid1.DataSource=ds;
dataGrid1.DataMember="customers";

cn.Close();

}
```

After we add the orders table to the DataSet, we add the relationship between the customers table and the orders table. We link the tables by CustomerID. This will have the effect of selecting all of the orders for each customer. Since we are selecting all of the customers we are effectively selecting all of the orders. Now if we look at the schema that is generated, it will become a bit more complex.

```
<?xml version="1.0" standalone="yes"?>
<xsd:schema id="OrdersSample"
                targetNamespace=""
                xmlns="" xmlns:xsd="http://www.w3.org/2001/XMLSchema"
                xmlns:msdata="urn:schemas-microsoft-com:xml-msdata">
    <xsd:element name="OrdersSample" msdata:IsDataSet="true">
        <xsd:complexType>
            <xsd:choice maxOccurs="unbounded">
                <xsd:element name="customers">
                    <xsd:complexType>
                        <xsd:sequence>
                            <xsd:element name="CustomerID" type="xsd:string"
                                        minOccurs="0" />
                            <xsd:element name="CompanyName" type="xsd:string"
                                        minOccurs="0" />
                            <xsd:element name="ContactName" type="xsd:string"
                                        minOccurs="0" />
                            <xsd:element name="ContactTitle" type="xsd:string"
                                        minOccurs="0" />
                            <xsd:element name="Address" type="xsd:string"
                                        minOccurs="0" />
                            <xsd:element name="City" type="xsd:string"
                                        minOccurs="0" />
                            <xsd:element name="Region" type="xsd:string"
                                        minOccurs="0" />
                            <xsd:element name="PostalCode" type="xsd:string"
```

```
                                          minOccurs="0" />
                    <xsd:element name="Country" type="xsd:string"
                                          minOccurs="0" />
                    <xsd:element name="Phone" type="xsd:string"
                                          minOccurs="0" />
                    <xsd:element name="Fax" type="xsd:string"
                                          minOccurs="0" />
                </xsd:sequence>
            </xsd:complexType>
        </xsd:element>
        <xsd:element name="orders">
            <xsd:complexType>
                <xsd:sequence>
                    <xsd:element name="OrderID" type="xsd:int"
                                          minOccurs="0" />
                    <xsd:element name="CustomerID" type="xsd:string"
                                          minOccurs="0" />
                    <xsd:element name="EmployeeID" type="xsd:int"
                                          minOccurs="0" />
                    <xsd:element name="OrderDate" type="xsd:dateTime"
                                          minOccurs="0" />
                    <xsd:element name="RequiredDate" type="xsd:dateTime"
                                          minOccurs="0" />
                    <xsd:element name="ShippedDate" type="xsd:dateTime"
                                          minOccurs="0" />
                    <xsd:element name="ShipVia" type="xsd:int"
                                          minOccurs="0" />
                    <xsd:element name="Freight" type="xsd:decimal"
                                          minOccurs="0" />
                    <xsd:element name="ShipName" type="xsd:string"
                                          minOccurs="0" />
                    <xsd:element name="ShipAddress" type="xsd:string"
                                          minOccurs="0" />
                    <xsd:element name="ShipCity" type="xsd:string"
                                          minOccurs="0" />
                    <xsd:element name="ShipRegion" type="xsd:string"
                                          minOccurs="0" />
                    <xsd:element name="ShipPostalCode" type="xsd:string"
                                          minOccurs="0" />
                    <xsd:element name="ShipCountry" type="xsd:string"
                                          minOccurs="0" />
                </xsd:sequence>
            </xsd:complexType>
        </xsd:element>
        </xsd:choice>
    </xsd:complexType>
    <xsd:unique name="Constraint1">
        <xsd:selector xpath=".//customers" />
        <xsd:field xpath="CustomerID" />
    </xsd:unique>
    <xsd:keyref name="Relation1" refer="Constraint1">
        <xsd:selector xpath=".//orders" />
        <xsd:field xpath="CustomerID" />
```

```
      </xsd:keyref>
   </xsd:element>
</xsd:schema>
```

Now you can see that both tables are included, and you can also see the constraints and relationships are also defined. The XML document for the data will look similar to the previous example, except that the orders will be displayed after all of the customers are listed. Here is a sample:

```
<?xml version="1.0" standalone="yes"?>
<OrdersSample>
   <customers>
      <CustomerID>ALFKI</CustomerID>
      <CompanyName>Alfreds Futterkiste</CompanyName>
      <ContactName>Maria Anders</ContactName>
      <ContactTitle>Sales Representative</ContactTitle>
      <Address>Obere Str. 57</Address>
      <City>Berlin</City>
      <PostalCode>12209</PostalCode>
      <Country>Germany</Country>
      <Phone>030-0074321</Phone>
      <Fax>030-0076545</Fax>
   </customers>
   <customers>
      <CustomerID>ANATR</CustomerID>
      <CompanyName>Ana Trujillo Emparedados y helados</CompanyName>
      <ContactName>Ana Trujillo</ContactName>
      <ContactTitle>Owner</ContactTitle>
      <Address>Avda. de la ConstituciÃ³n 2222</Address>
      <City>MÃ©xico D.F.</City>
      <PostalCode>05021</PostalCode>
      <Country>Mexico</Country>
      <Phone>(5) 555-4729</Phone>
      <Fax>(5) 555-3745</Fax>
   </customers>
   <orders>
      <OrderID>10248</OrderID>
      <CustomerID>VINET</CustomerID>
      <EmployeeID>5</EmployeeID>
      <OrderDate>1996-07-04T00:00:00.0000000-05:00</OrderDate>
      <RequiredDate>1996-08-01T00:00:00.0000000-05:00</RequiredDate>
      <ShippedDate>1996-07-16T00:00:00.0000000-05:00</ShippedDate>
      <ShipVia>3</ShipVia>
      <Freight>32.38</Freight>
      <ShipName>Vins et alcools Chevalier</ShipName>
      <ShipAddress>59 rue de l'Abbaye</ShipAddress>
      <ShipCity>Reims</ShipCity>
      <ShipPostalCode>51100</ShipPostalCode>
      <ShipCountry>France</ShipCountry>
   </orders>
   <orders>
      <OrderID>10249</OrderID>
      <CustomerID>TOMSP</CustomerID>
      <EmployeeID>6</EmployeeID>
```

```
        <OrderDate>1996-07-05T00:00:00.0000000-05:00</OrderDate>
        <RequiredDate>1996-08-16T00:00:00.0000000-05:00</RequiredDate>
        <ShippedDate>1996-07-10T00:00:00.0000000-05:00</ShippedDate>
        <ShipVia>1</ShipVia>
        <Freight>11.61</Freight>
        <ShipName>Toms Spezialitäten</ShipName>
        <ShipAddress>Luisenstr. 48</ShipAddress>
        <ShipCity>Münster</ShipCity>
        <ShipPostalCode>44087</ShipPostalCode>
        <ShipCountry>Germany</ShipCountry>
    </orders>
</OrdersSample>
```

Now if you need to have the orders for a customer nested inside the customer element, you will need to set the Nested property of the relationship to true. This is done by making the following modification to the code:

```
ds.Relations.Add(ds.Tables["customers"].Columns["customerid"],
                 ds.Tables["orders"].Columns["customerid"]);
ds.Relations[0].Nested=true;
```

If you do this, the orders data type in the schema will appear inside of the customer data type. The sample of the XML document will now look like this:

```
<?xml version="1.0" standalone="yes"?>
<OrdersSample>
    <customers>
        <CustomerID>ALFKI</CustomerID>
        <CompanyName>Alfreds Futterkiste</CompanyName>
        <ContactName>Maria Anders</ContactName>
        <ContactTitle>Sales Representative</ContactTitle>
        <Address>Obere Str. 57</Address>
        <City>Berlin</City>
        <PostalCode>12209</PostalCode>
        <Country>Germany</Country>
        <Phone>030-0074321</Phone>
        <Fax>030-0076545</Fax>
        <orders>
            <OrderID>10643</OrderID>
            <CustomerID>ALFKI</CustomerID>
            <EmployeeID>6</EmployeeID>
            <OrderDate>1997-08-25T00:00:00.0000000-05:00</OrderDate>
            <RequiredDate>1997-09-22T00:00:00.0000000-05:00</RequiredDate>
            <ShippedDate>1997-09-02T00:00:00.0000000-05:00</ShippedDate>
            <ShipVia>1</ShipVia>
            <Freight>29.46</Freight>
            <ShipName>Alfreds Futterkiste</ShipName>
            <ShipAddress>Obere Str. 57</ShipAddress>
            <ShipCity>Berlin</ShipCity>
            <ShipPostalCode>12209</ShipPostalCode>
            <ShipCountry>Germany</ShipCountry>
        </orders>
```

```
        <orders>
            <OrderID>10692</OrderID>
            <CustomerID>ALFKI</CustomerID>
            <EmployeeID>4</EmployeeID>
            <OrderDate>1997-10-03T00:00:00.0000000-05:00</OrderDate>
            <RequiredDate>1997-10-31T00:00:00.0000000-06:00</RequiredDate>
            <ShippedDate>1997-10-13T00:00:00.0000000-05:00</ShippedDate>
            <ShipVia>2</ShipVia>
            <Freight>61.02</Freight>
            <ShipName>Alfred's Futterkiste</ShipName>
            <ShipAddress>Obere Str. 57</ShipAddress>
            <ShipCity>Berlin</ShipCity>
            <ShipPostalCode>12209</ShipPostalCode>
            <ShipCountry>Germany</ShipCountry>
        </orders>
        <orders>
            <OrderID>10702</OrderID>
            <CustomerID>ALFKI</CustomerID>
            <EmployeeID>4</EmployeeID>
            <OrderDate>1997-10-13T00:00:00.0000000-05:00</OrderDate>
            <RequiredDate>1997-11-24T00:00:00.0000000-06:00</RequiredDate>
            <ShippedDate>1997-10-21T00:00:00.0000000-05:00</ShippedDate>
            <ShipVia>1</ShipVia>
            <Freight>23.94</Freight>
            <ShipName>Alfred's Futterkiste</ShipName>
            <ShipAddress>Obere Str. 57</ShipAddress>
            <ShipCity>Berlin</ShipCity>
            <ShipPostalCode>12209</ShipPostalCode>
            <ShipCountry>Germany</ShipCountry>
        </orders>
        <orders>
            <OrderID>10835</OrderID>
            <CustomerID>ALFKI</CustomerID>
            <EmployeeID>1</EmployeeID>
            <OrderDate>1998-01-15T00:00:00.0000000-06:00</OrderDate>
            <RequiredDate>1998-02-12T00:00:00.0000000-06:00</RequiredDate>
            <ShippedDate>1998-01-21T00:00:00.0000000-06:00</ShippedDate>
            <ShipVia>3</ShipVia>
            <Freight>69.53</Freight>
            <ShipName>Alfred's Futterkiste</ShipName>
            <ShipAddress>Obere Str. 57</ShipAddress>
            <ShipCity>Berlin</ShipCity>
            <ShipPostalCode>12209</ShipPostalCode>
            <ShipCountry>Germany</ShipCountry>
        </orders>
    </customers>
</OrdersSample>
```

As you can see, the orders for a particular customer are now inside the customers element. An example of the schema is included with the code download, and is named custOrdersNested.xsd. One reason why you may not want the relationship to be nested is if your application wants to display a classic parent-child type relationship. Displaying a parent-child relationship would be easier if the child elements were at the same level as the parent and you could link them by key. When a parent is selected, you issue a SelectNodes using the key as the criterion, and you will end up with an XmlNodeList object that has just the child nodes. The point is that you will have to think about what the use of the document will be before you automatically set the Nested property of the relationship. Sometimes it will make sense to have the elements nested, other times it may not make sense.

We can look at this a little more closely. The complete code for the following example is in the ADOSample3 folder of the code download.

We will explore the important parts of the code here. This example is actually a combination of some of the previous examples. We will be using the XmlTreeNode class we built earlier. There will be two TreeView components added to the form from the previous example. The ConnectToDatabase() method looks like this:

```
internal void ConnectToDatabase()
{

    SqlConnection cn=new SqlConnection(
        @"data source=(local)\NETSDK;uid=sa;password=;database=northwind");

    DataSet ds = new DataSet("OrdersSample");

    SqlDataAdapter daCust=new SqlDataAdapter("SELECT * FROM customers",cn);
    SqlDataAdapter daOrders=new SqlDataAdapter("SELECT * FROM orders",cn);
    ds.EnforceConstraints=false;
    daCust.Fill(ds,"customers");
    daOrders.Fill(ds,"orders");

    ds.Relations.Add(ds.Tables["customers"].Columns["customerid"],
                        ds.Tables["orders"].Columns["customerid"]);

    dataGrid1.DataSource=ds;
    dataGrid1.DataMember="customers";

    XmlDataDocument doc=new XmlDataDocument(ds);

    LoadTree(doc);

    cn.Close();

}
```

The highlighted lines are the only things that are different from past versions. We are creating a new XmlDataDocument from the DataSet of customer and order data. Keep in mind that this is the non-nested version of the XML document, since we have not set the Nested property of the relationship to true. Now that we have a valid XML document, doc, we can load the TreeView control just like we did before. This is the LoadTree method:

```
private void LoadTree(XmlDataDocument doc)
{
   XmlNodeList nodes=doc.SelectNodes("//customers");
   foreach(XmlNode node in nodes)
   {
      XmlTreeNode treeNode=new XmlTreeNode(node);
      treeNode.FillTreeView();
      treeNode.Text=node.FirstChild.InnerText;
      treeView1.Nodes.Add(treeNode);
   }
}
```

Instead of passing in one node to the XmlTreeNode class and loading it, this time, we will build an XmlNodeList of all of the customer nodes. We can pass in each customer node, one at a time. Now that we have customer data loaded, the next step is to get at the orders data. As each XmlTreeNode is clicked on treeView1, the following code is executed:

```
private void treeView1_AfterSelect(object sender,
                          System.Windows.Forms.TreeViewEventArgs e)
{
   if(e.Node.Parent==null)
   {
      XmlNodeList orders=((XmlTreeNode)e.Node).Orders;
      treeView2.Nodes.Clear();
      foreach(XmlNode node in orders)
      {
         XmlTreeNode ordTreeNode=new XmlTreeNode(node);
         ordTreeNode.FillTreeView();
         ordTreeNode.Text=node.FirstChild.InnerText;
         treeView2.Nodes.Add(ordTreeNode);
      }
   }
}
```

In the case of a TreeView control, the TreeViewEventArgs (e) contains the XmlTreeNode object. We can use this to see if the node has any orders attached to it. We have added one new property to the XmlTreeNode class, and that is Orders. The property returns an XmlNodeList of orders that have the same CustomerID as the current customer node. This is the Orders code:

```
public XmlNodeList Orders
{
   get
   {
      if(node==null)
         return null;

      return=node.OwnerDocument.SelectNodes(
              "//orders[CustomerID='"   + node.FirstChild.InnerText + "']");

   }
}
```

One thing to note here is that we don't have a reference to the `XmlDataDocument doc` object. This is the document that contains all of the orders and customers data that we started with. Remember we never pass in a reference to the document itself to the `XmlTreeNode` object. Fortunately the `XmlNode` object node has a property `OwnerDocument` that we can use to give us that reference. The section of the XPath query `node.FirstChild.InnerText` is just getting the `CustomerID` from the customer node. We know that this is the first node in the customer node, so we are making an assumption. For a more robust application we could use something like `node.SelectSingleNode("CustomerID").InnerText` in place of `node.FirstChild.InnerText`, but in this case the result is the same. The screenshot below shows the output for a couple of the nodes selected:

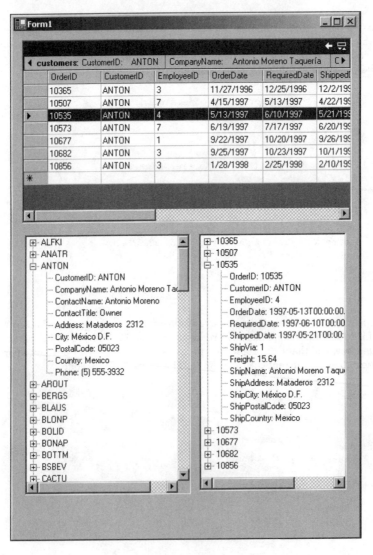

Notice that the same customer is selected in the grid and in the left `TreeView`. The orders are displayed in the grid, and the same orders are displayed in the right `TreeView`. If another customer is selected from the left `TreeView`, the right `TreeView` is cleared and a new list of orders is loaded and displayed. If any editing is done in the grid, the data is reflected in the `XmlDataDocument` immediately. However since the `TreeView` itself is static, the `TreeView` will need to be redisplayed or refreshed in some way.

If we had set the `Nested` property to `true` on the relationship, we would have had to parse through all of the `customer` and `orders` nodes immediately. Since the `orders` are nested inside the `customer`, it would have been difficult to pull them out. If we had to have the data in this form, we would not be able to realistically use this method to load the `TreeView`. We probably would need to use an `XmlReader`-based approach, which would allow faster loading, but may cost in the area of flexibility.

Loading a DataGrid from XML

What about loading a `DataGrid` from an XML document? We have seen how to get from the `DataSet` to XML. Getting from the XML to the `DataSet` is just as easy. Here is the `ConnectToDatabase()` method showing the easiest way to load a `DataGrid` with XML data:

```
internal void ConnectToDatabase()
{

    XmlDataDocument doc=new XmlDataDocument();
    doc.DataSet.ReadXmlSchema(@"..\..\..\custOrders.xsd");
    doc.Load(@"..\..\..\custOrders.xml");
    dataGrid1.DataSource=doc.DataSet;
    dataGrid1.DataMember=doc.DataSet.Relations[0].ParentTable.TableName;
}
```

Once again the `XmlDataDocument` shows off its flexibility. Since it has the `DataSet` property, we never even have to create a `DataSet` directly. We just assign the `DataSet` property to the grid's `DataSource` property and we are in business. Notice how we set the `DataMember` property. This is one way of letting the grid know the parent table in the relationship.

Schemas

An XML schema is a document that describes the structure and content of an XML data document. The schema defines the data by using the **XML Schema Definition Language** (**XSD**). XSD can define elements, attributes, types, and groups, as well as define default values and set relationships. Using XSD is very similar to defining the schema in a database. Schemas are important because they allow you to validate the data, checking to make sure that certain relationships are enforced. For example, you can't have an order detail without an order, and if you have an order you must have at least one order detail. Furthermore, you can enforce the use of the proper data type.

By defining a schema you are saying that your data is going to play by the rules. If you are developing for the enterprise, you can use schemas as a data dictionary. Any application that deals with any data that has a schema defined for it must use that schema. This makes exchanging data between applications easy. If you give your schema to a business partner, then you are asking that they play by the same rules. There are several industry-standard schemas starting to appear at places such as http://www.biztalk.org/. If you try to stay within the guidelines of an industry standard, then you will increase the chances that a future partner will be able to consume or provide data with much less effort.

XSD schemas in the .NET Framework conform to the current W3C standards as published at http://www.w3.org/. The `System.Xml.Schema` namespace includes classes that make it possible to create schemas from scratch that can be compiled and validated. Compiling a schema includes verifying that the schema is semantically correct. The compiler will verify that data types are defined properly, that the structure is correct and that complex types are defined properly. It will also check to validate that the document is well formed. Remember that an XSD schema is an XML document and is required to follow all of the same rules that any valid XML document must follow. If a schema is read in from a file, the syntax check happens at this point and the compiler will only check the semantics of the XSD. A `ValidationEventHandler` is used to deal with any `XmlSchemaExceptions` that are generated because of malformed XML, or because the structure is not valid.

When you create an XSD using the `System.Xml.Schema` namespace you are using the **Schema Object Model** (**SOM**). The SOM provides the following features:

❑ Loads and saves XSD schemas to and from disk

❑ Provides a model to build XSDs in memory

❑ Works with `XmlSchemaCollection` to cache schemas

❑ Interacts with `XmlValidatingReader` through the `XmlSchemaCollection` to validate a schema against an XML instance document

You can think of the SOM as the DOM for schemas. The two work very similarly to each other. The difference between the two is that the SOM is a much more detailed object model; there are more than sixty classes in the `System.Xml.Schema` namespace. There is a complete object model diagram in the help system of the framework.

Elements and Attributes

The basic building blocks of a schema are the **element** and **attribute**. Elements encapsulate the data while the attributes add further information about the data. Elements can contain simple or complex data types, while attributes can contain only simple data types. A simple data type can be either a built-in type or a user-defined type. A built-in type can be **primitive** or **derived**. Primitives are types such as `string` or `boolean`. Derived types are defined based on an existing type. An example would be `integer`, which is derived from the `decimal` data type.

A table comparing the W3C data types with the corresponding .NET data types can be found at the end of the chapter.

Another simple type is the user-defined type. A user-defined type is a built-in type with user-defined values called **facets** applied to it. A facet is a restriction or constraint of what the data can be. Here is a list of facets and the constraint that is applied.

facet	Description
enumeration	Constrains the data type to a list of specific values.
fractionDigits	Specifies the maximum number of decimal digits.
length	Number of units of length. Depends on data type.
maxExclusive	Upper bound, all values must be less then this value.

facet	Description
maxInclusive	The maximum value.
maxLength	Maximum units of length.
minExclusive	Lower bound. All values must be greater then this value.
minInclusive	The minimum value.
minLength	Minimum units of length.
pattern	Regular expression pattern that the value must match.
totalDigits	Maximum number of digits.
whiteSpace	Preserve, replace, or collapse.

As was mentioned, an element can also contain complex data. Complex data types can contain other simple or complex elements. A simple example of a complex element is the `author` element in the books.xml document that we have been using. `author` contains two other simple elements: `first-name`, and `last-name`.

Creating a Schema in Visual Studio .NET

Schemas can become very complex. Although you can create one with a simple text editor, using a tool with a graphical interface can make creating a schema much easier to do. Fortunately for us, there is such a thing built into the VS. NET IDE. So that we can see how some of this all fits together, let's look at creating the books.xsd using the Schema Editor in Visual Studio, and then we can look at how we would build the same schema in code. We won't get into a great amount of detail on using the XSD tool in Visual Studio, as there are a couple of detailed walkthroughs in the documentation.

Designing a schema for an XML document is a little like designing a database schema. We saw earlier in the chapter that a schema can be generated from a data set rather easily. One of the first things that you do is list all of the data elements that you will need to account for. For the books example this could be the following:

- ❑ Book
- ❑ Book Title
- ❑ Author first name
- ❑ Author last name
- ❑ Publication Date
- ❑ ISBN
- ❑ Selling Price
- ❑ Genre

The next step would be to arrange the data in a logical manner. One of the biggest philosophical differences in the world of XML is when to use attributes and when to use elements.

> **A rule of thumb is that elements contain and encapsulate data, whereas attributes add further data or describe the data.**

All of the data elements that we defined could be made into elements. However, it could be argued that the data elements Genre, Publication Date, and ISBN describe characteristics about the book, and should be attributes. Since the previous examples used them as attributes, we shall do that here as well, but keep in mind that there are other ways of defining the data. Author is an obvious candidate for a complex type. It would contain the first name and last name data elements.

We also need to look at data types. Attributes must always be of a simple type. All of the attributes will be of type `string`. Since the Publication Date attribute will only keep the year, a `string` type will be the best choice. If it were to keep month, day, and year, then we could have made it a `date` or `dateTime` data type. Book Title will be a `string`, as will the author information. Selling Price is a dollar amount, so using `decimal` would make the most sense. By doing this, only a number will work in that element. If someone tried to enter a string value, for example "20 bucks", the document would fail validation. Now that we have gathered this information, we can create the schema.

You will need to start a project to use the XSD editor. The example is `XsdSample2` in the sample code. To create a new schema, go to the **Project | Add New Item** menu and select **XSD Schema**. You will be presented with a blank screen. Under the **Schema** menu, select **Add**, and choose **New complexType**. When the new element is added to the diagram, you can edit the element. We want this to be the Author element. In the top-left edit box, enter `authorName`. In the line below, the first dropdown will be `element`, the second column will be `first-name`, and the last column will be `string`. This defines a new element named `first-name` that is of type `string`. Do the same on the next line for `last-name`.

Now add another new `complexType` from the menu. This one will be named `bookType`. We will add the Title element, the Price element, and an element named `author`. When you select the data type for `author`, one of the options in the list will be `authorName`. When you select `authorName` the IDE will draw a copy of the `authorName` element, giving it the name of `author`. Next, add the attributes to the `bookType`. In the first column, select **Attribute** from the list. The next column is for the name; we'll start by entering `genre`. The last column is the data type, `string` in this example. Your diagram should look something like this by now:

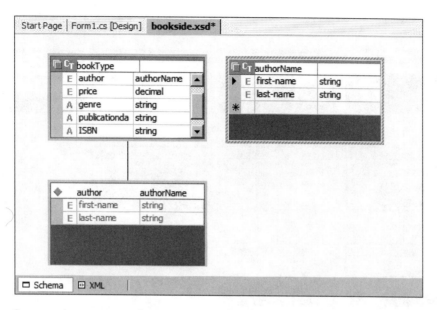

Add another complex type named `storeType`, and make a single element named `book`. It will be of type `bookType`. Finally, add a new element. This element will be named `bookstore`. In the top right corner select the data type of `storeType`. We now have the complete schema document finished. You can look at the XML by selecting the **XML** tab on the bottom left corner of the diagram. Here is what the output should look like:

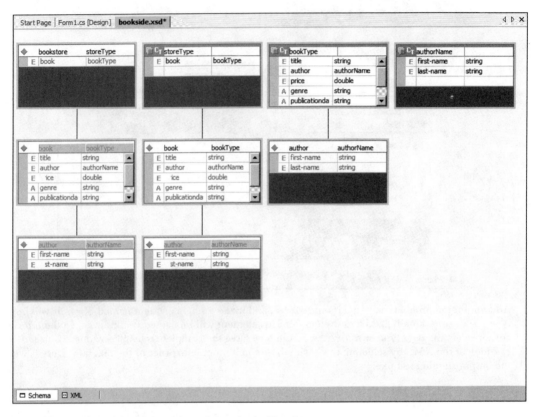

The XML that is produced from this schema looks like this:

```xml
<?xml version="1.0" encoding="utf-8" ?>
<xsd:schema id="bookside"
            targetNamespace="http://tempuri.org/bookside.xsd"
            elementFormDefault="qualified"
            xmlns="http://tempuri.org/bookside.xsd"
            xmlns:xsd="http://www.w3.org/2001/XMLSchema">

    <xsd:complexType name="authorName">
        <xsd:sequence>
            <xsd:element name="first-name" type="xsd:string" />
            <xsd:element name="last-name" type="xsd:string" />
        </xsd:sequence>
    </xsd:complexType>
    <xsd:complexType name="bookType">
        <xsd:sequence>
            <xsd:element name="title" type="xsd:string" />
            <xsd:element name="author" type="authorName" />
            <xsd:element name="price" type="xsd:double" />
        </xsd:sequence>
        <xsd:attribute name="genre" type="xsd:string" />
```

```
        <xsd:attribute name="publicationdate" type="xsd:string" />
        <xsd:attribute name="ISBN" type="xsd:string" />
    </xsd:complexType>
    <xsd:element name="bookstore" type="storeType"></xsd:element>
    <xsd:complexType name="storeType">
        <xsd:sequence>
            <xsd:element name="book" type="bookType" />
        </xsd:sequence>
    </xsd:complexType>
</xsd:schema>
```

Now let's take a look at building the same schema in code. The process is similar in that you will build each complex type and then combining them to make the complete schema. Here is the code for creating the bookscode.xsd schema. It is XsdSample1 in the examples download:

```
internal void CreateBookSchema()
{

    XmlSchema bookSchema=new XmlSchema();
    bookSchema.ElementFormDefault=XmlSchemaForm.Qualified;
    bookSchema.TargetNamespace="http://tempuri.org/bookscode.xsd";


    XmlSchemaComplexType authorNameType=new XmlSchemaComplexType();
    authorNameType.Name="authorName";
    bookSchema.Items.Add(authorNameType);

    XmlSchemaSequence authorSeq=new XmlSchemaSequence();
    authorNameType.Particle=authorSeq;

    XmlSchemaElement fname=new XmlSchemaElement();
    fname.Name="first-name";
    fname.SchemaTypeName=new
            XmlQualifiedName("string","http://www.w3.org/2001/XMLSchema");
    authorSeq.Items.Add(fname);

    XmlSchemaElement lname=new XmlSchemaElement();
    lname.Name="last-name";
    lname.SchemaTypeName=new
            XmlQualifiedName("string","http://www.w3.org/2001/XMLSchema");
    authorSeq.Items.Add(lname);

    XmlSchemaComplexType bookType=new XmlSchemaComplexType();
    bookType.Name="bookType";
    bookSchema.Items.Add(bookType);

    XmlSchemaSequence bookSeq=new XmlSchemaSequence();
    bookType.Particle=bookSeq;

    XmlSchemaElement bookTitle=new XmlSchemaElement();
    bookTitle.Name="title";
    bookTitle.SchemaTypeName=new
            XmlQualifiedName("string","http://www.w3.org/2001/XMLSchema");
    bookSeq.Items.Add(bookTitle);
```

```
XmlSchemaElement bookPrice=new XmlSchemaElement();
bookPrice.Name="price";
bookPrice.SchemaTypeName=new
        XmlQualifiedName("string","http://www.w3.org/2001/XMLSchema");
bookSeq.Items.Add(bookPrice);

XmlSchemaElement authorName=new XmlSchemaElement();
authorName.Name="author";
authorName.SchemaTypeName=new
      XmlQualifiedName("authorName","http://tempuri.org/bookscode.xsd");
bookSeq.Items.Add(authorName);

XmlSchemaAttribute genreAtt=new XmlSchemaAttribute();
genreAtt.Name="genre";
genreAtt.SchemaTypeName=new
        XmlQualifiedName("string","http://www.w3.org/2001/XMLSchema");
bookType.Attributes.Add(genreAtt);

XmlSchemaAttribute pubDateAtt=new XmlSchemaAttribute();
pubDateAtt.Name="publicationdate";
pubDateAtt.SchemaTypeName=new
        XmlQualifiedName("string","http://www.w3.org/2001/XMLSchema");
bookType.Attributes.Add(pubDateAtt);

XmlSchemaAttribute isbnAtt=new XmlSchemaAttribute();
isbnAtt.Name="ISBN";
isbnAtt.SchemaTypeName=new
        XmlQualifiedName("string","http://www.w3.org/2001/XMLSchema");
bookType.Attributes.Add(isbnAtt);

XmlSchemaComplexType bookStoreType=new XmlSchemaComplexType();
bookStoreType.Name="bookStoreType";
bookSchema.Items.Add(bookStoreType);

XmlSchemaSequence bookStoreSeq=new XmlSchemaSequence();
bookStoreType.Particle=bookStoreSeq;

XmlSchemaElement bookStore=new XmlSchemaElement();
bookStore.Name="book";
bookStore.SchemaTypeName=new
      XmlQualifiedName("bookType","http://tempuri.org/bookscode.xsd");
bookStoreSeq.Items.Add(bookStore);

XmlSchemaElement store=new XmlSchemaElement();
store.Name="bookstore";
store.SchemaTypeName=new
  XmlQualifiedName("bookStoreType","http://tempuri.org/bookscode.xsd");
bookSchema.Items.Add(store);

bookSchema.Compile(new ValidationEventHandler(ValidationHandler));

FileStream fs=new FileStream(@"..\..\..\bookscode.xsd",FileMode.Create);
```

288

```
        bookSchema.Write(fs);

    }
```

The first three lines create the `XmlSchema` object `bookSchema`:

```
    XmlSchema bookSchema=new XmlSchema();
    bookSchema.ElementFormDefault=XmlSchemaForm.Qualified;
    bookSchema.TargetNamespace="http://tempuri.org/bookscode.xsd";
```

We set the `ElementFormDefault` property to `XmlSchemaForm.Qualified`. This means that elements in the target namespace must be qualified with the namespace prefix. The next line is setting the target namespace for the schema.

The next section of code is where we start creating the complex types. We'll start with creating what will eventually be the `author` element. We need to create a data type that will encapsulate the author information, which is first name and last name. First, we create the complex type:

```
    XmlSchemaComplexType authorNameType=new XmlSchemaComplexType();
    authorNameType.Name="authorName";
    bookSchema.Items.Add(authorNameType);
```

The new data type object is `authorNameType`, and we give it the name `authorName`. We then add it to the `bookSchema` `Items` collection, which is a collection of elements. The `Items` collection can contain elements of the following types:

- ❑ `XmlSchemaAnnotation`
- ❑ `XmlSchemaAttribute`
- ❑ `XmlSchemaAttributeGroup`
- ❑ `XmlSchemaComplexType`
- ❑ `XmlSchemaSimpleType`
- ❑ `XmlSchemaElement`
- ❑ `XmlSchemaGroup`
- ❑ `XmlSchemaNotation`

The next thing that we do is create the `XmlSchemaSequence` object `authorSeq`:

```
    XmlSchemaSequence authorSeq=new XmlSchemaSequence();
    authorNameType.Particle=authorSeq;
```

This class is responsible for the **sequence element**. A sequence element is a **compositor**. A compositor creates a group of elements. In the case of the sequence compositor, it means that the elements must appear in the same order as they are declared in the schema. Other types of compositors are **choice** (`XmlSchemaChoice`) and **all** (`XmlSchemaAll`). Choice is used if you want only one of a list of elements to appear. In the example that we have with `authorName`, it would mean that either first name or last name could appear in the document, but not both. The all compositor means that elements can appear in any order, but they all must appear or none at all can appear. Any time you declare a complex type, you must use a compositor. The next line is setting the `Particle` property to the new compositor that we just created. The `Particle` property is used to contain the compositor for the complex type.

At this point we have a new data type. As it is now, the `authorName` data type won't do very much. What we need to do is add a couple of elements to it, so it will actually hold data. This is what the following lines of code do:

```
XmlSchemaElement fname=new XmlSchemaElement();
fname.Name="first-name";
fname.SchemaTypeName=new
          XmlQualifiedName("string","http://www.w3.org/2001/XMLSchema");
authorSeq.Items.Add(fname);
```

A new `XmlSchemaElement` object, fname, is created and given the name `first-name`. In the next line, we assign the data type for the element. `SchemaTypeName` sets the data type of any built-in data type defined in this schema or in an included schema. Note that we are adding the namespace as well. Finally, we add the element to the sequence compositor that we created.

We repeat the process for the last name and we now have a useful new data type. The next complex type that we need to build is the `bookType`. The process for creating this data type is similar to the `authorName`. However we do use `authorName` in the `bookType`, so let's look to see how that is done:

```
XmlSchemaElement authorName=new XmlSchemaElement();
authorName.Name="author";
authorName.SchemaTypeName=new
       XmlQualifiedName("authorName","http://tempuri.org/bookscode.xsd");
bookSeq.Items.Add(authorName);
```

We are using the `authorName` data type and since this is a data type that we created, we are using the target namespace that we declared at the beginning of the schema.

After adding the elements for `title`, `price`, and `author`, we need to add the attributes. This process is much like adding the elements:

```
XmlSchemaAttribute genreAtt=new XmlSchemaAttribute();
genreAtt.Name="genre";
genreAtt.SchemaTypeName=new

XmlQualifiedName("string","http://www.w3.org/2001/XMLSchema");
bookType.Attributes.Add(genreAtt);
```

The only difference from what we have seen before is that we are creating an `XmlSchemaAttribute` object. We give it the name `genre`, assign the data type (`string`) and add it to the `Attributes` collection of the `bookType` object, instead of to the sequence compositor.

The rest of the code pretty much follows the same pattern. At the end of the `CreateBookSchema()` method we compile the schema. You can see the `Compile()` method will want a `ValidationEventHandler`. The one we create is called `ValidationHandler`, and the code for it is listed below:

```
public static void ValidationHandler(object sender, ValidationEventArgs e)
{
    System.Diagnostics.Debug.WriteLine(e.Message);
}
```

This is simple enough. All we do is write the message out to the console if one is created. If we don't receive any messages, then we can assume that the schema compiled correctly. In this example, the last thing that we do is to write the schema out to a file, `bookscode.xsd`. The finished schema looks like this:

```
<?xml version="1.0"?>
<schema elementFormDefault="qualified"
        targetNamespace="http://tempuri.org/bookscode.xsd"
        xmlns="http://www.w3.org/2001/XMLSchema">
    <complexType name="authorName">
       <sequence>
          <element name="first-name" type="string" />
          <element name="last-name" type="string" />
       </sequence>
    </complexType>
    <complexType name="bookType">
       <sequence>
          <element name="title" type="string" />
          <element name="price" type="string" />
          <element name="author"
                   xmlns:q1="http://tempuri.org/bookscode.xsd"
                   type="q1:authorName" />
       </sequence>
       <attribute name="genre" type="string" />
       <attribute name="publicationdate" type="string" />
       <attribute name="ISBN" type="string" />
    </complexType>
    <complexType name="bookStoreType">
       <sequence>
          <element name="book"
                   xmlns:q2="http://tempuri.org/bookscode.xsd"
                   type="q2:bookType" />
       </sequence>
    </complexType>
    <element name="bookstore"
             xmlns:q3="http://tempuri.org/bookscode.xsd"
             type="q3:bookStoreType" />
</schema>
```

If you compare this version of the schema with the previous version you will see that there are some differences. However, if you validate the `books.xml` file with either version, you will discover that they both work. The differences are in how namespaces are handled.

Instead of writing the schema to disk, we can use it right away in validating an XML document, if we changed the code that created the `File Stream` and called the `Write` method to the following (this code is in the `XsdSample1` folder of the examples):

```
XmlSchemaCollection sc=new XmlSchemaCollection();
sc.Add(bookSchema);
XmlTextReader xr =new XmlTextReader(@"..\..\..\books.xml");
XmlValidatingReader vr=new XmlValidatingReader(xr);
vr.Schemas.Add(sc);
vr.ValidationEventHandler+=new ValidationEventHandler(ValidationHandler);
```

```
while(vr.Read()){
    //do your processing here
}
```

If you think back to the section on validation, this should be all very familiar. We create an `XmlTextReader` to read in the XML data file, pass that into an `XmlValidatingReader`, add the schema we just created to an `XmlSchemaCollection`, pass that collection to the `XmlValidatingReader`, hook up the `ValidationEventHandler` (reuse the one from the `compile` method), and then we start reading the document. If any validation errors exist, they would be caught and the `ValidationHandler` would write the message to the output window.

You can use the SOM to reverse-engineer a schema as well. There is a great example of how to do this in the SDK sample folder. The complete path is:

C:\Program Files\Microsoft.NET\FrameworkSDK\Samples\quickstart\howto
\samples\xml\xmlschemaobjectmodel\cs

Basically, what you have to do is iterate the `Items` collection of the `XmlSchema` object. Since this can be one of many objects, you will need to do this using `object` in the `foreach` statement. Then, you can check to see what type it is, and do what is appropriate from there. Remember the list of valid data types that can be in the `Items` collection? You will need to implement code for each data type. Some of the types will be recursive in nature, some won't be. Look at the example in the SDK to see what it is possible for you to do.

W3C and .NET Data Types

The table below shows each W3C data type and its corresponding .NET data type, and also indicates if it is a primitive or derived type.

XSD Type	Derived or Primitive	.NET Type
hexBinary	Primitive	System.Byte[]
base64Binary	Primitive	System.Byte[]
boolean	Primitive	System.Boolean
byte	Derived from short	System.SByte
normalizedString	Derived from string	System.String
date	Primitive	System.DateTime
duration	Primitive	System.TimeSpan
dateTime	Primitive	System.DateTime
decimal	Primitive	System.Decimal
double	Primitive	System.Double
ENTITIES	Derived from ENTITY	System.String[]

XSD Type	Derived or Primitive	.NET Type
ENTITY	Derived from NCName	System.String
float	Primitive	System.Single
gMonthDay	Primitive	System.DateTime
gDay	Primitive	System.DateTime
gYear	Primitive	System.DateTime
gYearMonth	Primitive	System.DateTime
ID	Derived from NCName	System.String
IDREF	Derived from NCName	System.String
IDREFS	Derived from IDREF	System.String[]
int	Derived from long	System.Int32
integer	Derived from decimal	System.Decimal
language	Derived from token	System.String
long	Derived from integer	System.Int64
gMonth	Primitive	System.DateTime
Name	Derived from token	System.String
NCName	Derived from Name	System.String
negativeInteger	Derived from nonPositiveInteger	System.Decimal
NMTOKEN	Derived from token	System.String
NMTOKENS	Derived from NMTOKEN	System.String[]
nonNegativeInteger	Derived from integer	System.Decimal
nonPositiveInteger	Derived from integer	System.Decimal
NOTATION	Primitive	System.String
positiveInteger	Derived from nonNegativeInteger	System.Decimal
QName	Primitive	System.Xml.XmlQualifiedName
short	Derived from int	System.Int16

Table continued on following page

XSD Type	Derived or Primitive	.NET Type
string	Primitive	System.String
time	Primitive	System.DateTime
timePeriod	Derived from recurringDuration	System.DateTime
token	Derived from normalizedString	System.String
unsignedByte	Derived from unsignedShort	System.Byte
unsignedInt	Derived from unsignedLong	System.UInt32
unsignedLong	Derived from nonNegativeInteger	System.UInt64
unsignedShort	Derived from unsignedInt	System.UInt16
anyURI	Primitive	System.Uri

Summary

It doesn't take much to see how powerful and flexible the System.Xml namespace is. Not only do you have the class structure to handle the XML, but you also have many options on how to handle it. You can use XmlReader or XmlWriter for very fast processing or creation of XML documents, and you have XmlDocument, that gives you a very flexible DOM implementation to work with. We will see in the next chapter that there are still more options available to the developer.

Microsoft has committed to keeping the System.Xml namespace compliant with all of the current W3C recommendations. Keep in mind that XML standards are a moving target, and that you should check in at the W3C site (http://www.w3c.org/) to see what may be coming up in the future. You can check the documentation of the .NET SDK to see the current levels of compliance by the framework. With System.Xml offering a high level of compliance, you can be sure that you will be able to share the XML documents that you generate using the .NET Framework with other platforms and environments. This is such a key point in e-business strategies that without W3C compliance the XML capabilities of .NET would have far less value.

The main point to note is how XML and ADO.NET work so closely together. Being able to take data from a relational model and view it in a hierarchical (XML) way, as well as taking hierarchical data and viewing it in a relational model, opens up all sorts of possibilities. It is this type of flexibility that will make it important that developers, architects, and designers learn the framework and understand the differences between the various ways of using XML.

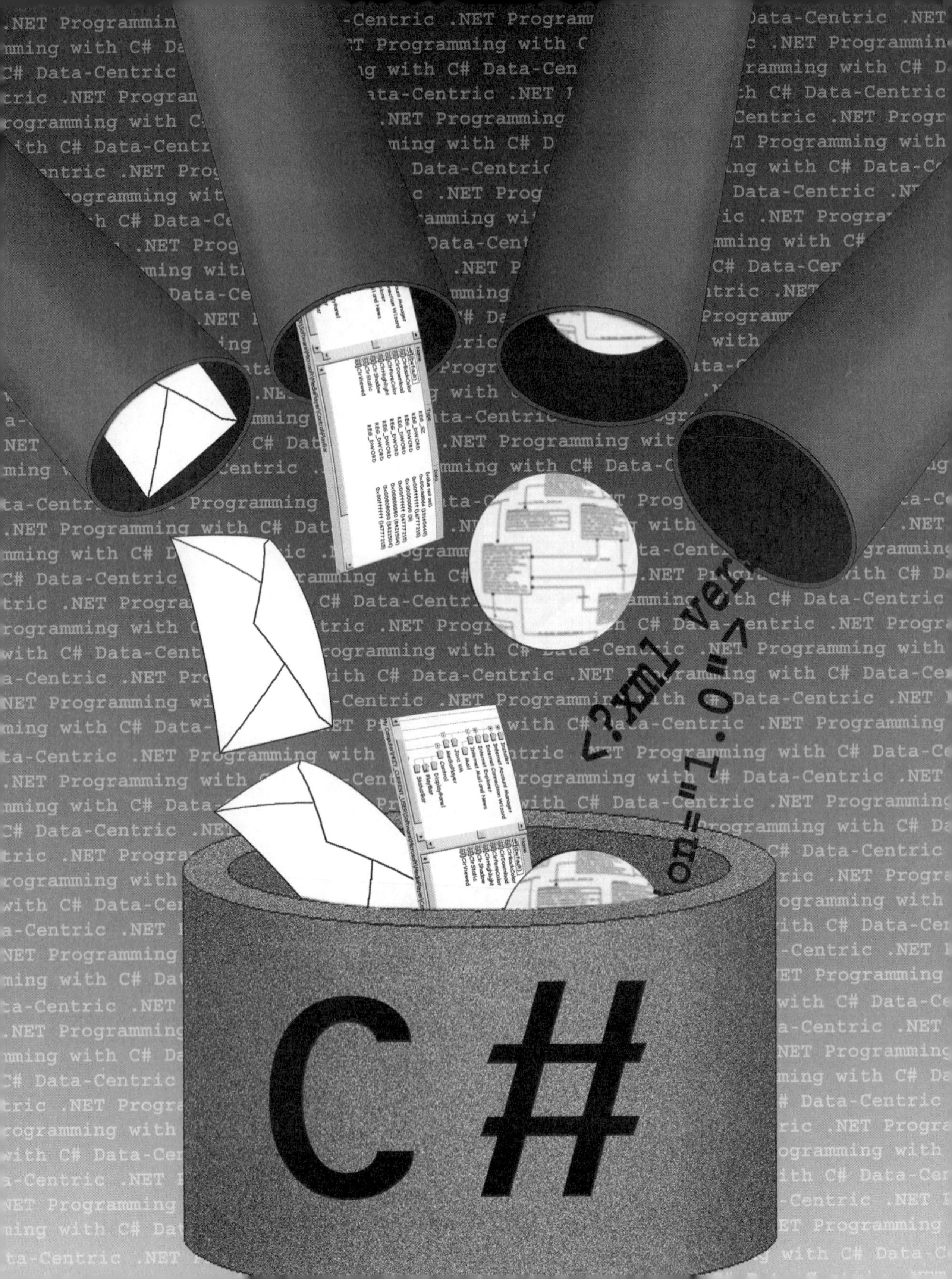
Data-Centric .NET Programming with C#
<?xml ver
on="1.0"?>
C#

Navigating and Transforming XML

In the last chapter we looked at how the .NET framework implements the DOM through `XmlDocument`, and how a SAX-like model exists in the form of `XmlReader`- and `XmlWriter`-based objects. In this chapter we will look at how the .NET framework implements **XPath** and **XSLT** support.

XPath is the query language for XML and is implemented in the `System.Xml.XPath` namespace. You would use XPath to select a subset of elements based on element text values or perhaps based on attribute values.

XSLT (or XSL Transforms) is implemented in the `System.Xml.Xsl` namespace. XSLT is used to transform a base document into another document of different structure or type. A simple example of this is the common practice of taking a valid XML document and transforming it into an HTML page for rendering. The XSLT stylesheet that would be used for this transform can contain HTML, scripting code, or calls to your own assemblies. The combination of XPath and XSLT is typically used, with the stylesheet using XPath syntax to process the elements of the original document. Along with transforming to HTML, you can transform to an XML document with a slightly different schema or perhaps transform to a delimited text file for processing by a legacy system. Since the stylesheet is also XML-based, everything has a similar look and feel to it.

In this chapter, we will:

❑ Explore the key classes for XPath support in `System.Xml.XPath` : `XPathNavigator` and `XPathNodeIterator`, and how an `XPathNavigator` object enables you to feed your data to the `System.Xml.Xsl` namespace and perform XSL transforms

❑ Explore the key classes for XSLT support in `System.Xml.Xsl` : `XslTransform` and `XsltArgumentList`

❑ Use XSL and scripting, which offers us access to the entire .NET Framework from within our XSLT stylesheet

We begin the chapter by looking at how the various classes for XPath and XSLT support are related.

XPath and XSLT in the .NET Framework

In the following figure, you can see that the data stores all implement the `IXPathNavigable` interface. As we will see later in the chapter, `IXPathNavigable` provides a `CreateNavigator` method. `CreateNavigator` will return an `XPathNavigator` for that particular data store. The `XPathNavigator` is fed into the XSL transform class, and the output document can either go to a `System.IO.Stream`, an `XmlWriter`, a `System.IO.TextWriter`, or an `XmlReader`. The `XmlReader` can be fed back into an `XPathNavigator` and the results chained back in for another transform. Here is a diagram that shows all of these relationships.

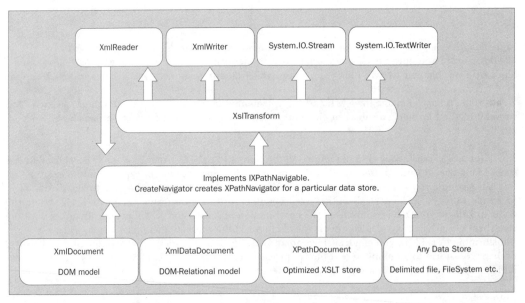

Since the output of a transform can be any of 4 different formats, there is quite a bit of flexibility with what you would do after the transform. Also notice one of the data sources is called *Any Data Store*. You are able to create a custom `XPathNavigator` on top of practically any data store. We'll take a closer look at this in the next section. The diagram above shows the `XPathNavigator` being fed into the `XslTransform`, but that isn't the only use for `XPathNavigator`. Since you have navigation capabilities you can use it much like you could use `XmlDocument`. The only difference is that `XPathNavigator` is read-only.

Whereas `XmlReader` was a streaming model to read-only data, `XPathNavigator` provides a random-access model on read-only data. `XPathNavigator` is a cursor model that sits on top of a data store that implements an `IXPathNavigable` interface. The .NET Framework has implemented this interface on `XmlDocument`, `XmlDataDocument`, and `XPathDocument`. We looked at `XmlDocument` and `XmlDataDocument` in the last chapter, but we have not yet seen `XPathDocument`.

XPathDocument is a cache for XML document processing. It does not maintain node identity. XPathDocument contains one method, and it is CreateNavigator. It should be noted that XPathDocument does not perform the same amount of rule checking as XmlDocument does. XPathDocument was built for speed. XPathDocument has six overloads on the constructor. You can pass in a Stream object, a TextReader object, a string with a valid path and file name, and an XmlReader-based object. If the XmlReader object is pointing to a node, that node and all of its children are loaded. This allows loading partial documents. The other two overloads are the XmlReader and the string object with an XmlSpace object that states namespace scope.

> *Once you have the XPathDocument created, about the only thing you can do with it is to call the* CreateNavigator *method.*

Note that System.Xml.Xsl is compliant with W3C XSL Transformations (XSLT) Version 1.0 recommendation located at http://www.w3.org/TR/xslt.

XPath – Navigating XML

XPath is the query language for XML and enables the selection of, or navigation to, chosen parts of an XML document. In this section, we will cover:

❑ Methods for random access navigation, and selecting various parts of an XML document using XPathNavigator

❑ Using the XPathNodeIterator object, which represents the set of nodes that matched the criteria used in our XPath query

❑ The possibility of using custom XPathNavigator and XmlReader objects to deal with the problem of incongruent data stores

XPathNavigator

XPathNavigator is the best way of navigating an XML document if you need read-only, random access. If you need to read sequentially, then an XmlReader, as we saw in the last chapter, may be a better option. XPathNavigator has fourteen different MoveTo methods and four separate Select variations. All but a couple of the MoveTo methods move you to an adjacent node. Unless otherwise noted, each of these methods returns true or false, depending on weather the move was successful or not. If a move was unsuccessful, the current node remains as the current node. Here is a table of the MoveTo methods, and a brief explanation of each one:

Method	Description
MoveTo(XPathNavigator other)	Moves to the same node in another XPathNavigator. If the other XPathNavigator has a different implementation, that is if the original is based on XPathDocument and the other is based on XmlDocument, then false is always returned.
MoveToAttribute(string localName, string namespaceURI)	Moves to the attribute with the matching localName and namespaceURI.
MoveToFirst()	Moves to the first sibling.
MoveToFirstAttribute()	Moves to the first attribute.
MoveToFirstChild()	Moves to the first child. Root and Element are the only two NodeTypes that can have children, all others return false.
MoveToFirstNamespace()	Moves to the first namespace node of the current element.
MoveToId(string id)	Moves to the first node with an attribute of type ID that matches the string id. A DTD or schema is needed to define the attribute as type ID.
MoveToNamespace(string name)	Moves to the namespace node with the matching name.
MoveToNext()	Moves to the next sibling of the current node.
MoveToNextAttribute()	Moves to the next attribute if one exists.
MoveToNextNamespace()	Moves to the next namespace node.
MoveToParent()	Moves to the parent of the current node.
MoveToPrevious()	Moves to the previous sibling of the current node.
MoveToRoot()	Moves to the root node that the current node belongs to. Always successful.

It would appear that you now have almost everything you need to move about an XML document. However, the real power comes with the Select methods. All of the Select methods return an XPathNodeIterator object. First, let's take a look at the Select methods, and then we'll discuss what an XPathNodeIterator is.

Select Methods

There are four Select methods:

❑   Select

❑   SelectDescendants

- ❑   SelectAncestors

- ❑   SelectChildren

Select can take a string or a precompiled XPath query (XPathExpression object). The XPathNodeIterator is returned that has the set of matching nodes. It is important to understand that the context of the XPath query is the current node. SelectDescendants has two overloads. The first one takes an XPathNodeType and a bool. The boolean value determines if the node should match itself. The second overload takes a string that represents the name of the descendant nodes, a string for the namespace, and the bool for matching itself. SelectDescendants will select all of the descendant nodes of the current node that match the criteria. SelectAncestors has the same overloads, but it will return all of the ancestors of the current node that match the criteria. SelectChildren also has similar overloads except that it does not include the boolean parameter to match itself, and returns the children of the current node that match the criteria.

You might think that SelectChildren and SelectDescendants are the same. The difference is that SelectChildren only returns the immediate children of the current node, while SelectDescendants returns the current children and all of their children.

XPathNodeIterator

The XPathNodeIterator object is a representation of the set of nodes that matched the criteria in the XPath query used by one of the Select methods. An XPathNodeIterator is not a copy of the nodes, but rather a list of pointers to the nodes that matched the criteria. The XPathNodeIterator has only three properties and two methods. The methods are:

- ❑   Clone

- ❑   MoveNext

Clone makes a copy of the current iterator. MoveNext simply moves to the next node in the selected node set of the XPathNodeIterator. The three properties are:

- ❑   Count

- ❑   Current

- ❑   CurrentPosition

Count returns the number of nodes that matched, Current returns an XPathNavigator pointing to the node that is currently being pointed at by the XPathNodeIterator, and CurrentPosition is a one-based index of the current node.

As you iterate through the node set that XPathNodeIterator has selected, at any time you can get another XPathNavigator object by using the Current property. With this XPathNavigator object you can make another call to one of the Select methods and return another XPathNodeIterator. This nesting of the XPathNavigator and XPathNodeIterator objects allows you to view the XML document in a number of different ways. Let's take a look at how the XPathNavigator and the XPathNodeIterator work. This sample is in the NavSample1 folder of the download code, available from www.wrox.com. It is a simple form with a single RichTextBox (richTextBox1), similar to some of the examples in the last chapter. Here is the LoadXml method.

```
internal void LoadXml ()
{
    //load the document - NavSample1

    XPathDocument doc=new XPathDocument(@"..\..\..\books.xml");
    XPathNavigator nav=doc.CreateNavigator();

    // Uncomment one of the following three lines
    // to see the difference in output.

    //XPathNodeIterator iterator=
                        nav.SelectDescendants(XPathNodeType.Element,true);
    //XPathNodeIterator iterator=nav.SelectChildren(XPathNodeType.Element);
    //XPathNodeIterator iterator=nav.Select("//book");

    while(iterator.MoveNext())
        richTextBox1.AppendText(iterator.Current.Name + ": " +
                                        iterator.Current.Value + "\r\n");
}
```

Depending on which line we uncomment, we can see how each of the Select statements work. The screen snapshots below will show the difference in what each Select statement will return, using the books.xml example from the previous chapter.

 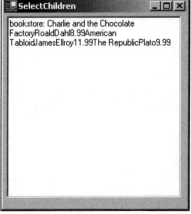

Let's look a little closer at the code and screenshots. The title of each screen will tell you which `Select` statement was uncommented in the example code. Now you can see the difference between `SelectDescendants` and `SelectChildren`. Since we were at the start of the document, `SelectDescendants` essentially selected the entire document. Now look closely at the `SelectChildren` screen, and you will see we have only one node, `<bookstore>`, but all of the data for the entire document is displayed. This is because the `Value` property of `XPathNavigator` returns the `InnerText` of the node. If you remember from the last chapter, `InnerText` returns the text value of the current node and all of its children concatenated together. You can also see the same effect on the `Select` screen, except it is only for each `<book>` node, since that was the selection criterion.

Take a look at the following couple of lines of code.

```
while(iterator.MoveNext())
    richTextBox1.AppendText(iterator.Current.Name + ": " +
                                    iterator.Current.Value + "\r\n");
```

This shows a use of the `Current` property of the `XPathNodeIterator` in action. As we do a `MoveNext` on each of the items in the `XPathNodeIterator` object's node set, we use `Current.Name` and `Current.Value` to load the textbox. This is the same as calling `XPathNavigator.Name` and `XPathNavigator.Value`, since `Current` returns an `XPathNavigator` object.

Nesting XPathNodeIterators

In the next example (`NavSample2` in the example download) we will demonstrate nesting of `XPathNodeIterators`. In the `SelectDescendants` example above, notice that the `<authors>` node contains the author first-name and last-name text values. Again this is because of the way the `Value` property works. One way to clean this up would be to change the code to the following:

```
internal void LoadXml()
{
    //load the document - NavSample2

    XPathDocument doc=new XPathDocument(@"..\..\..\books.xml");
    XPathNavigator nav=doc.CreateNavigator();
```

```
        XPathNodeIterator iterator=
                            nav.SelectDescendants(XPathNodeType.Element,true);

    while(iterator.MoveNext())
    {
        richTextBox1.AppendText(iterator.Current.Name);
        XPathNodeIterator childIter=
                        iterator.Current.SelectChildren(XPathNodeType.Text);
        while(childIter.MoveNext())
            richTextBox1.AppendText(": " + iterator.Current.Value);

        richTextBox1.AppendText("\r\n");
    }
}
```

This is the same as before, until we start iterating through the `iterator` nodes. The name of the current node is appended to the textbox, but then we create another `XPathNodeIterator`, basing it on `iterator.Current`. Notice the syntax; the line

```
    XPathNodeIterator childIter=
                        iterator.Current.SelectChildren(XPathNodeType.Text);
```

could have been written like this:

```
    XPathNavigator childNav=Iterator.Current;
    XPathNodeIterator childIter = childNav.SelectChildren(XPathNodeType.Text);
```

Also notice the parameter we are passing to the `SelectChildren` method. We want only nodes that are of type `Text`. We need to select the nodes this way; otherwise, when we query the `author` node, we will still get `first-name` and `last-name`, since they are children of `author`.

Another thing that should be mentioned is the next `while` loop. Even though there should only be one node in the `XPathNodeIterator childIter`, you have to do a `MoveNext` to actually get onto the node. When an `XPathNodeIterator` is first created, there isn't a current node, so calling `MoveNext` makes the first node current. After that, you are always on a node. If you reach the end of the list, another `MoveNext` will return `false`, and you will still be on the last node. The same applies for the `XPathNavigator Move` methods.

Remember the `TreeView`-based example from the last chapter. Can it use `XPathNavigator` instead of `XmlDocument`? The answer is yes. The only problem is that since `XPathNavigator` is read-only, we lose any editing capabilities, but we do gain a substantial increase in performance. The complete code example is in the `NavSample4` folder of the download code.

```
    private void LoadTree()
    {
        // load the document - NavSample4

        XPathDocument doc=new XPathDocument(@"..\..\..\custOrders.xml");
        XPathNavigator nav=doc.CreateNavigator();
        XPathNodeIterator iterator=nav.Select("//customers");

        while(iterator.MoveNext())
```

```
      {
         XmlTreeNode node=new XmlTreeNode(iterator.Current);
         node.FillTreeView();
         XPathNodeIterator custIter=
                           iterator.Current.SelectChildren("CustomerID","");

         while(custIter.MoveNext())
            node.Text=custIter.Current.Value;

         treeView1.Nodes.Add(node);
      }

}

private void treeView1_AfterSelect(object sender,
                                   System.Windows.Forms.TreeViewEventArgs e)
{
   if(e.Node.Parent==null)
   {
      treeView2.Nodes.Clear();
      XPathNodeIterator orderIter=((XmlTreeNode)e.Node).TreeNavigator.Select
                           ("//orders[CustomerID='" + e.Node.Text + "']");
      while(orderIter.MoveNext())
      {
         XmlTreeNode node=new XmlTreeNode(orderIter.Current);
         node.FillTreeView();
         XPathNodeIterator orderIdIter=
                           orderIter.Current.SelectChildren("OrderID","");

         while(orderIdIter.MoveNext())
            node.Text=orderIdIter.Current.Value;

         treeView2.Nodes.Add(node);
      }
   }
}

/// <summary>
/// Our new TreeNode class. This will load the tree
/// with our XML doc
/// </summary>
internal class XmlTreeNode : TreeNode
{

   XPathNavigator nav;

   internal XmlTreeNode() : base(){}

   internal XmlTreeNode(XPathNavigator treeNav) : base()
   {
      nav=treeNav;
      XPathNodeIterator iterTmp=nav.SelectChildren(XPathNodeType.Text);
      while(iterTmp.MoveNext())
         this.Text=nav.Name + ":" + iterTmp.Current.Value;
```

```
      }

      public XPathNavigator TreeNavigator
      {
         get
         {
            return nav;
         }
      }

      internal void FillTreeView()
      {
         if(nav!=null)
         {
            this.Nodes.Clear();
            XPathNodeIterator iterTmp=nav.SelectChildren(XPathNodeType.Element);
            while(iterTmp.MoveNext())
            {
               XmlTreeNode newTreeNode=new XmlTreeNode(iterTmp.Current);
               this.Nodes.Add(newTreeNode);
               newTreeNode.FillTreeView();
            }
         }
      }
   }
```

Making use of the `custOrders.xml` file we generated from the `Northwind` database in the previous chapter, the output of this code looks like:

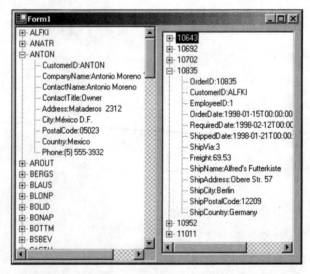

Using `XPathNavigator` not only makes the code a little more straightforward as you can see, but it also gives us better performance.

> *The reason for the performance boost is that `XPathNavigator` is just a list of pointers to the document. It is much quicker to navigate this list than it is to navigate the document itself.*

The LoadTree method starts off by getting the document opened with XPathDocument and creating an XPathNodeIterator with the <customers> nodes. As we iterate through the <customers> nodes, we create a new XmlTreeNode, this time passing in the XPathNavigator that the iterator is pointing to, and then call the FillTreeView method on the newly created XmlTreeView. The next section of code is to get the CustomerID value from the customer element. We want this to use as the text of the XmlTreeNode. Look at the code below:

```
XPathNodeIterator custIter=
                    iterator.Current.SelectChildren("CustomerID","");

while(custIter.MoveNext())
   node.Text=custIter.Current.Value;
```

Notice that we still need to do the custIter.MoveNext() or else we will not get the results that we are expecting. Even though there is going to be only one node in the custIter node set, the MoveNext is required.

When the new XmlTreeNode is created with the XPathNavigator as the parameter we do another Select statement to get the Name and Value pair for the node text. Here is the constructor code:

```
internal XmlTreeNode(XPathNavigator treeNav): base()
{
   nav=treeNav;
   XPathNodeIterator iterTmp=nav.SelectChildren(XPathNodeType.Text);
   while(iterTmp.MoveNext())
      this.Text=nav.Name + ":" + iterTmp.Current.Value;
}
```

We want to display only elements that have an associated text node, so by selecting the child nodes of type XPathNodeType.Text, we can use the newly created XPathNodeIterator and set the text to display the Name and Value. If there is no child node of type Text, then the iterTmp would skip over the Text assignment.

The FillTreeView method has simplified somewhat. We still use recursion in order to load all of the child nodes. We select all of the child elements of the current XPathNavigator, and use that XPathNodeIterator to initiate the recursion. If there are no children, then iterTmp would have a count of 0, and the recursive call would not be made. Notice that we didn't have to Clone the XPathNavigator, since iterTmp remembers where we are in the list. If there are any child nodes, iterTmp will cause the while loop to execute the call to create a new XmlTreeNode, and call FillTreeView.

The other thing to notice is that unlike the XmlDocument implementation, we don't assign an XML node to each XmlTreeNode. Since we can't edit the nodes, this really isn't an issue. We could clone the XPathNavigator to simulate the functionality, but there really wouldn't be much of a gain in doing that, and we would just waste memory. However, in order to fill the orders TreeView we still need access to the XPathNavigator that created the customer node. So we added a read-only property to return the XPathNavigator object that was passed in when XmlTreeNode was instantiated. When we load the orders in the treeView1_AfterSelect event, we use the XmlTreeNode.TreeNavigator to select the orders nodes. We use this because the XmlTreeNode.TreeNavigator will still be pointing to the current customer node and we can get the value of the CustomerID element to find the corresponding orders.

Custom XPathNavigator and XmlReader

By now, you should be able to see how powerful the XPathNavigator and XPathNodeIterator combination can be. It offers highly flexible selection methods with random access navigation, and it does this with a high degree of performance. Wouldn't it be nice to have this power over other types of data stores, such as the file system or that delimited text file that we used for input in the previous chapter? The .NET framework will allow you to build your own custom XPathNavigator.

What you have to do is inherit the XPathNavigator class and implement the methods and properties, and you will have a working XPathNavigator. The implementation of the methods and properties should map to the data store that you are working with. For example, if you are implementing on a delimited text file, MoveToNext should take you to the next delimited value. Keep in mind that whatever your data store, you will need to implement some sort of a state machine. What this means is that when you make the MoveToNext call, your data store will have to know where it is in order to know where to move to next. For some data stores, such as the file system or the registry, this will be inherent, since they are already in a hierarchical form.

Other data stores may not have this feature built-in for you. The delimited text file, for example, is not in a format that would be easy to hold state on. You have two options, a custom XmlReader or a custom XPathNavigator. If you don't need to be able to navigate in a random-access fashion on the resulting XML document, you could implement a custom XmlReader. Since the data is in a "stream" format, it would be an easier implementation to stay in the same model. However, if you want or need the functionality of an XPathNavigator, then you will need to implement your own state machine. In the case of the delimited text file you could construct a list of lists and have your state machine keep up with the index of the current location. Another idea is to implement the custom XmlReader and use it to generate an XML document, then take this resulting document, and pass it into an XPathDocument. Since all of these classes can handle streams, this could be done without creating a file on disk by feeding streams from one class to the other.

OK, this is starting to sound like a lot of work. Why would you want to do this? There are a couple of reasons. As we will see in the next section, once you have an XPathNavigator, you are able to feed the System.Xml.Xsl namespace your data and perform XSL transforms. As we shall see in the next section, XSL transforms can be a powerful tool, and that delimited text file could be displayed as a web page with very little effort. Another reason is if you have data coming in from various business partners in both XML and delimited format. The applications that use the data will need to be able to handle both formats. It may be easier from a maintenance standpoint to make the data consumer application handle XML data only. By implementing a custom XPathNavigator or XmlReader, the data consumer will never have to change if one of the partners decides to switch from delimited text to XML. Your application can be smart enough to see what format the data is in and use the appropriate XPathNavigator to parse out the data. Such an example would be too lengthy to present here, and there is a good example of implementing a custom navigator over the file system in the SDK documentation.

Other XPathNavigator Methods

There are a couple of other methods in the XPathNavigator class that should be mentioned:

- ❑ IsDescendant
- ❑ IsSamePosition
- ❑ Compile
- ❑ Evaluate

First, there are IsDescendant and IsSamePosition. Both take an XPathNavigator as a parameter and return a boolean. IsDescendant will tell you if the current navigator is a descendant of the passed-in navigator, and IsSamePostion determines if the current navigator is on the same node as the passed-in navigator. GetAttribute returns the attribute that matches the LocalName parameter passed into it.

The Compile method requires a little more explanation. The Compile method takes a string as a parameter. This string is a valid XPath expression. The return of the Compile method is an XPathExpression. An XPathExpression object, as you would imagine, is a compiled XPath expression. The expression should return a valid node set, a boolean, a floating-point number or a string. The data type that is returned will determine where the XPathExpression can be used. For example, if you remember, the Select methods can use an XPathXpression as a parameter. In order to use the XPathExpression object in a Select method, it must return a node set.

The last method that we need to look at is the Evaluate method. The Evaluate method takes an XPath statement or a compiled XPathExpression object as a parameter. The expression is evaluated and a typed result is provided. Looking back at our Select examples from earlier in the chapter, if we were to add the line:

```
richTextBox1.AppendText("Total: " +
                        nav.Evaluate("sum(/bookstore/book/price)"));
```

the sum of the price of all of the books in the XML document would be displayed. The Evaluate method will also take an XPathExpression as a parameter; however, it cannot return a node set. It must return a boolean, string, or number. Evaluate can use any of the XPath functions, however if you use the position() or last() functions, you must pass in an XPathNodeIterator. The reason is that these functions reference a node set, so one must be provided. If one is not available to these functions, a 0 is returned.

XSL Transforms – Transforming XML

XSLT is used to change or transform an XML document into another format. The other format could be another XML document, an HTML page, or a text file. The way this transformation takes place is by taking the original document, an XSL file, or stylesheet as it is sometimes called, and passing them to an XSL processor. The processor will then create the transformed document or file. The XSLT processor for the .NET framework is in the System.Xml.Xsl namespace.

Explaining the principles of XSLT or writing an XSL stylesheet is beyond the scope of this book. There are several book and resources that you can use to learn XSLT, such as:

❑ *XSLT Programmer's Reference 2nd Edition* (Wrox Press, ISBN 1-861005-06-7)

❑ *Professional* XSL (Wrox Press, 1-861003-57-9).

The System.Xml.Xsl namespace has two interfaces and five classes. In this section of the chapter, we will:

❑ Look at the XslTransform and XsltArgumentList classes

❑ Explore XSL and scripting, which puts the entire .NET Framework at our disposal from within our stylesheets

XslTransform

The XslTransform class is the XSLT processor class. It will take the XSL stylesheet and the XML document, and produce whatever results you want. The XslTransform class has only one property and two methods. The property is XmlResolver and we will talk about it shortly. The two methods are:

❑ Load

❑ Transform

Load has eight overloads and Transform has nine. The Load overloads take either an XPathNavigator object, an object that implements IXPathNavigable interface, an XmlReader, or a string containing the path and file name of the XSLT stylesheet. The other overloads add the XmlResolver as a parameter. All of these objects would contain a reference to, or the actual data from, an XSLT stylesheet. Once the stylesheet is loaded, you can call the Transform method. All of the Transform overloads use various combinations of an XPathNavigator object, and an XsltArgumentList object (we'll see this later in the section) and a stream of some type for the output.

First, we make a quick note about the examples in this section. Up until now, we have been looking at relatively simple Windows Form applications. In this section we will be using simple ASP.NET pages to show that the System.Xml namespaces can be used in any type of .NET application. Since it is the Web that gave XML its initial popularity, it seems only fitting to show some examples as web pages. It should be noted that while the code used to display the XML may be different, the code of interest to us, which processes the XML, will be the same, whether it's an ASP.NET application or a Windows Forms application. All of the code in these examples is contained in code download. We will show only what we need to.

> Please note that these examples will not be teaching ASP.NET; for a primer in ASP.NET, see Chapter 16 of Professional C# (Wrox Press, ISBN 1-8641004-99-0).

The first example we are going to look at is in the XslSample1 folder. Let's take a look at the code.

```
<%@ Page language="c#"
    AutoEventWireup="true"
    Inherits="XslSample26.WebForm1" %>

<%@ Import namespace="System.Data" %>
<%@ Import namespace="System.Data.SqlClient" %>
<%@ Import namespace="System.Xml" %>
<%@ Import namespace="System.Xml.XPath" %>
```

```
<%@ Import namespace="System.Xml.Xsl" %>
<html>
    <head>
        <script language="C#" runat="server">

            void Page_Load(Object sender, EventArgs e)
            {
                LoadXml();
             }

            private void LoadXml()
            {

                SqlConnection cn=new SqlConnection(
                @"data source=(local)\NETSDK;uid=sa;password=;database=northwind");

                SqlDataAdapter da=new SqlDataAdapter(
                    "SELECT CompanyName, ContactName, Phone FROM customers",cn);

                DataSet ds = new DataSet("CustList");

                da.Fill(ds,"custs");
                cn.Close();

                XmlDataDocument doc=new XmlDataDocument(ds);

                XslTransform xsl=new XslTransform();

                xsl.Load(Server.MapPath("") + "\\PhoneList.xsl");

                xsl.Transform(doc,null,Response.OutputStream);

            }

        </script>
    </head>
</html>
```

The first thing we do is to make sure that we import the proper namespaces to use. Since we are getting the data from a SQL Server database, we need to include the data access (ADO.NET) namespaces. On the `Page_Load` event, all we do is call the `LoadXml` method.

The next few line should look familiar by now. We establish the connection, create the `DataAdapter`, get the `customers` data into a new `DataSet`, and create a new `XmlDataDocument` doc with the `DataSet`. This is exactly as we did in the last chapter.

The next three lines of code are what we are interested in.

```
XslTransform xsl=new XslTransform();

xsl.Load(Server.MapPath("") + "\\PhoneList.xsl");

xsl.Transform(doc,null,Response.OutputStream);
```

The first line creates a new `XslTransform` object; there are no overloads on the constructor or `XslTransform`. The next line loads the XSLT stylesheet that we have created. In this case, it is the `Phonelist.xsl` file. The `xsl.Transform` line is what actually does the transform. As we mentioned before, the `Transform` method has several overloads. The one that we are using here takes the `XmlDataDocument` (doc) that we created from the SQL Server data, an `XsltArgumentList` null object which we will look at later in the chapter and the last parameter is a stream to send the output to. As you can see we are taking advantage of the stream by using the `Response.OutputStream` as the parameter.

Here is the `Phonelist.xsl` document:

```
<xsl:stylesheet xmlns:xsl="http://www.w3.org/1999/XSL/Transform"
                version="1.0">
<xsl:template match="CustList">
    <html>
          <body bgcolor="#FFFFE0">
          <h1>Customer List</h1>
          <table border="0" width="85%" cellspacing="4" cellpadding="4">
             <xsl:apply-templates select="custs"/>
          </table>
       </body>
    </html>
</xsl:template>
<xsl:template match="custs">
    <tr>
       <td colspan="3" bgcolor="lightblue">
          <font size="5">
             <xsl:value-of select="CompanyName"/>
          </font>
       </td>
    </tr>

    <tr>
       <td><xsl:value-of select="ContactName"/></td>
       <td><xsl:value-of select="Phone"/></td>
    </tr>
</xsl:template>
</xsl:stylesheet>
```

This is a fairly basic XSLT document. The output of this XSLT is HTML, which is why we are able to pass this into the `Response.OutputStream` and have it display in the client. This should give you an idea of how easy it is to get data straight from a database and display it in an HTML document. In this case it took only nine lines of code and an XSL stylesheet. Here is the output from this example:

Certainly quick and easy. Since the data is coming directly from the database, we are looking at current data. If a new customer is added or customer information is changed on a current customer then the new data will be displayed the next time the page is rendered. If all you need to do is display data, then this is a very viable and simple way to accomplish that. Keep in mind that once the page is rendered, you are looking at static data.

We can make this even more useful by adding order information. Since we are getting data straight from the database, we can add almost anything that we want. We can expand this a little and add the `freight` column from the `orders` table. The code for the `aspx` page (located in `XslSamples2` folder of the examples download) will look like this, with the new lines in bold:

```
private void LoadXml()
{

    SqlConnection cn=new SqlConnection(@"data source="+
                    "(local)\NETSDK;uid=sa;password=;database=northwind");

    SqlDataAdapter daCust=new SqlDataAdapter
    ("SELECT CustomerID, CompanyName, ContactName, Phone from customers",cn);
```

```
SqlDataAdapter daOrders=new SqlDataAdapter("select * from orders",cn);

DataSet ds = new DataSet("CustList");

daCust.Fill(ds,"custs");
daOrders.Fill(ds,"orders");

ds.Relations.Add(ds.Tables["custs"].Columns["customerid"],
                 ds.Tables["orders"].Columns["customerid"]);

ds.Relations[0].Nested=true;

cn.Close();

XmlDataDocument doc=new XmlDataDocument(ds);

XslTransform xsl=new XslTransform();

xsl.Load(Server.MapPath("") + "\\PhoneListOrders.xsl");

xsl.Transform(doc,null,Response.OutputStream);

}
```

This should look familiar. It is basically the same as the examples in the last chapter. We add a `DataRelation` to the `Relations` collection of the `DataSet`, which will link the `custs` table to the `orders` table using the `customerid` as the linking key. Notice that we set the `Nested` property to true, so that each child element will be nested inside the parent. We also have to make a small change to the XSL stylesheet that we are using. You will find this in the `XslSample2` folder, and it is the file `PhoneListOrders.xsl`. Here is the new code, with changes once again in bold:

```
<xsl:stylesheet xmlns:xsl="http://www.w3.org/1999/XSL/Transform"
                version="1.0">
<xsl:template match="CustList">
    <html>
        <body bgcolor=   "#FFFFE0">
        <h1>Customer List</h1>
        <table BORDER="0" width="85%" cellspacing="4" cellpadding="4">

            <xsl:apply-templates select="custs"/>
        </table>
    </body>
    </html>
</xsl:template>
<xsl:template match="custs">
    <tr>
        <td colspan="3" bgcolor="lightblue">
            <font size="5">
                <xsl:value-of select="CompanyName"/>
            </font>
        </td>
    </tr>
    <tr>
```

```
            <td colspan="2"><xsl:value-of select="ContactName"/></TD>
            <td></td>
            <td><xsl:value-of select="Phone"/></TD>
        </tr>
        <xsl:for-each select="orders">
            <tr>
                <td><xsl:value-of select="OrderID"/></td>
                <td><xsl:value-of select="Freight"/></td>
                <td></td>
            </tr>
        </xsl:for-each>
    </xsl:template>
</xsl:stylesheet>
```

As you can see, we added a `for-each` loop to process the `orders` child nodes of each customer. We output `OrderID` and `Freight`, the freight charge, for each child element. This is what the output looks like:

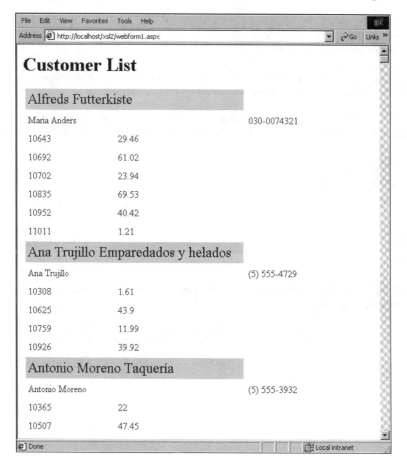

So we can display data pretty easily, but what if we have to do some calculations or execute other code based on the value of the data? There are a couple of ways to do this. The first way we cover, XSL and scripting, keeps all of the code in the XSL stylesheet, and the other way makes use of the `XsltArgumentList` class, allowing you to define methods in compiled code and execute them from the stylesheet.

XSL and Scripting

Scripting allows you to define and call functions in the XSL stylesheet. In order to use scripting you use the `<msxml:script>` element to wrap the scripting code. The full syntax is:

```
<msxml:script language="language-name" implements-prefix="your namespace">

        Insert your script code here...

</msxml:script>
```

`language-name` attribute can be `JScript`, `VB` or `C#`. The `implements-prefix` attribute is a user-defined namespace. It is used to associate the script block with the call to the method in the stylesheet. Both of these attributes are required.

`<msxml:script>` is part of the `urn:schemas-microsoft-com:xslt` namespace, so this must be included in the declaration of the stylesheet.

The scripting code that you write can call functions that you define in your scripts, and can call any of the functionality from the framework. The following list of namespaces is included by default:

- ❏ `System`
- ❏ `System.Collection`
- ❏ `System.Text`
- ❏ `System.Xml`
- ❏ `System.Xml.Xsl`
- ❏ `System.Xml.XPath`

You can use any classes you wish to use, but if they are not part of these namespaces, you must fully qualify them when you use them, for example:

```
System.Data.DataSet ds = new System.Data.DataSet();
```

Data types for function return types and parameters must be one of the following data types as defined by the W3C XPath Type:

W3C XPath Data Type	.NET Framework Data Type
String	System.String
Boolean	System.Boolean
Number	System.Double
Node Fragment	System.Xml.XPath.XPathNavigator
Node Set	System.Xml.XPath.XPathNodeIterator

If your script tries to pass or accept data not in one of these formats, an exception will be thrown.

Let's take a look at a simple stylesheet that creates a simple function and uses it. This will calculate a discount to the freight from the previous example. Since all of the changes are part of the XSL document, the aspx code is identical to the last example. This is PhoneListOrders.xsl located in the XslSample4 folder. In the code below, the changes are once again in bold.

```
<xsl:stylesheet xmlns:xsl="http://www.w3.org/1999/XSL/Transform" version="1.0"
                xmlns:msxsl="urn:schemas-microsoft-com:xslt"
                xmlns:user="http://wrox.com">

    <msxsl:script language="C#" implements-prefix="user">

        public double ReduceFreight(double currentFreight)
        {
            return currentFreight*.75;;
        }

    </msxsl:script>
<xsl:template match="CustList">
    <html>
        <body bgcolor=   "#FFFFEO">
        <h1>Customer List</h1>
        <table BORDER="0" width="85%" cellspacing="4" cellpadding="4">
            <xsl:apply-templates select="custs"/>
        </table>
        </body>
    </html>
</xsl:template>
<xsl:template match="custs">
    <tr>
        <td colspan="3" bgcolor="lightblue">
            <font size="5">
                <xsl:value-of select="CompanyName"/>
            </font>
        </td>
    </tr>
    <tr>
        <td colspan="2"><xsl:value-of select="ContactName"/></TD>
        <td><xsl:value-of select="Phone"/></TD>
    </tr>
    <tr>
```

```
            <td><b>Order ID</b></td>
            <td><b>Freight</b></td>
            <td><b>Disc Freight</b></td>
        </tr>
        <xsl:for-each select="orders">
        <tr>
            <td><xsl:value-of select="OrderID"/></td>
            <td><xsl:value-of select="Freight"/></td>
            <td><xsl:value-of select="user:ReduceFreight(Freight)"/></td>
        </tr>
        </xsl:for-each>
    </xsl:template>
</xsl:stylesheet>
```

We can see the namespace additions in the document declaration section.

```
xmlns:msxsl="urn:schemas-microsoft-com:xslt"
xmlns:user="http://wrox.com">
```

The first attribute makes the scripting element available. The second line is the user-defined namespace. We give this one the prefix user. You will see how this works shortly.

The code that we implemented is pretty simple; it takes the current Freight as a parameter, and returns the value of the Freight reduced by 25%. For a real-world scenario, we would want to add error handling and possibly some formatting to the return value.

Here you can see how we use the new ReduceFreight function:

```
<tr>
    <td><xsl:value-of select="OrderID"/></td>
    <td><xsl:value-of select="Freight"/></td>
    <td><xsl:value-of select="user:ReduceFreight(Freight)"/></td>
</tr>
```

This is part of the for-each loop that looks at each order child element. First we output the OrderID and Freight value. Then we take the Freight value and pass it into the ReduceFreight function. Notice that we have to use the user namespace prefix. This is the namespace that we defined earlier to identify the script block. The return value of ReduceFreight is placed in the output stream and displayed for the user.

Notice that it is inside the <msxml:script> element. We can add as many functions inside this element as we need. As a matter of fact you can add more than one namespace. This means you can have multiple versions of ReduceFreight and have them resolved by namespace. Here is the updated version of PhoneListOrders.xsl. Along with the namespace change and the addition of ReduceFreight, we made some changes to enhance the display as well.

```
<xsl:stylesheet xmlns:xsl="http://www.w3.org/1999/XSL/Transform" version="1.0"
                xmlns:msxsl="urn:schemas-microsoft-com:xslt"
                xmlns:user="http://wrox.com"
                xmlns:otheruser="http://mywebsite.com">

    <msxsl:script language="C#" implements-prefix="user">
```

```
            public double ReduceFreight(double currentFreight)
                {
                    return currentFreight*.75;;
                }
        </msxsl:script>

        <msxsl:script language="C#" implements-prefix="otheruser">

            public double ReduceFreight(double currentFreight)
                {
                    return currentFreight*.5;;
                }

        </msxsl:script>


<xsl:template match="CustList">
    <html>
            <body bgcolor=    "#FFFFE0">
            <h1>Customer List</h1>
            <table BORDER="0" width="100%" cellspacing="4" cellpadding="4">
                <xsl:apply-templates select="custs"/>
            </table>
        </body>
    </html>
</xsl:template>
<xsl:template match="custs">
    <tr>
        <td colspan="4" bgcolor="lightblue">
            <font size="5">
                <xsl:value-of select="CompanyName"/>
            </font>
        </td>
    </tr>
    <tr>
        <td colspan="2"><xsl:value-of select="ContactName"/></TD>
        <td colspan="2"><xsl:value-of select="Phone"/></TD>
    </tr>
    <tr>
        <td><b>Order ID</b></td>
        <td><b>Freight</b></td>
        <td><b>Disc Freight</b></td>
        <td><b>Big Disc Freight</b></td>
    </tr>
    <xsl:for-each select="orders">
<tr>
    <td><xsl:value-of select="OrderID"/></td>
    <td><xsl:value-of select="Freight"/></td>
    <td><xsl:value-of select="user:ReduceFreight(Freight)"/></td>
    <td><xsl:value-of select="otheruser:ReduceFreight(Freight)"/></td>
</tr>
    </xsl:for-each>
</xsl:template>
</xsl:stylesheet>
```

You can see the added namespace otheruser in the declaration section. Since it is a different namespace, we add another <msxml:script> element to wrap up the new ReduceFreight function. In this version, we reduce the Freight by half. Now if we look at the section of code that calls these functions, you can see how they differ.

```
<tr>
    <td><xsl:value-of select="OrderID"/></td>
    <td><xsl:value-of select="Freight"/></td>
    <td><xsl:value-of select="user:ReduceFreight(Freight)"/></td>
    <td><xsl:value-of select="otheruser:ReduceFreight(Freight)"/></td>
</tr>
```

You can see that even though we call the ReduceFreight in each case, the namespace causes the correct version of ReduceFreight to be called. You can verify this by looking at the output. If you look at the far right-hand column, you can see that the freight has indeed been cut in half.

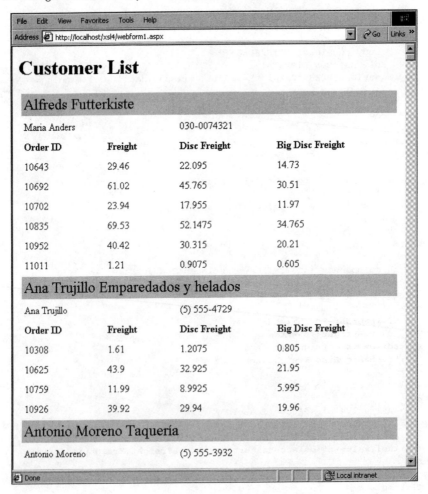

Since the entire .NET framework is at your disposal, the number of things that you could accomplish using this functionality is tremendous. This all works very well if you only have a couple of functions, or a limited amount of code to include. It may be better to keep the code in a managed assembly (DLL) and call it from the XSL stylesheet. This would improve the encapsulation as well as keeping the stylesheets smaller and a little easier to maintain. Also, since the code could be part of a shared assembly, the functionality could be called from several different stylesheets. At the moment, if we wanted to use the `ReduceFreight` function elsewhere, we would have to copy and paste it into the other stylesheet. If a change has to occur to the `ReduceFreight` function, that change would have to be manually propagated to all versions of `ReduceFreight`. This method of copy and paste is not what is meant by code reuse. We need to be able to take advantage of the shared assembly scenario. The way you do this is with the `XsltArgumentList` class.

XsltArgumentList

`XsltArgumentList` allows you to add parameters, and object extensions, and invoke them from within the stylesheet. This allows you to keep all of the logic in an assembly and only expose what the stylesheet will need. The complexity of the stylesheet is also reduced, if all of the code resides somewhere else. Using `XsltArgumentList` allows you to take advantage of existing code. Let's take a look at a couple of examples.

First we'll look at using parameters. This code can be found in `XslSample6`. When you use a parameter in an `XsltArgumentList` what you're basically doing is defining a value, storing that value in the `XsltArgumentList` object that you create, and making that value available for use in the XSL stylesheet. What makes this useful is that you can derive the value with the full resource of the .NET framework at you fingertips. All of the complexity of deriving the value is kept inside the application so that the stylesheet doesn't need to know about it. The parameter can be any of the W3C data types that we saw earlier, `String`, `Boolean`, `Number`, `Node Fragment`, `Node Set`. Any .NET data type that you use will be coerced into one of these types (more than likely either `Number` or `String`).

Let's look at the code for this example. We will add an effective date for future discounts. We'll make this effective date to be 30 days from today. Any orders placed will be able to take advantage of the discount.

```
private void LoadXml()
{

    SqlConnection cn=new SqlConnection
        (@"data source=(local)\NETSDK;uid=sa;password=;database=northwind");

    SqlDataAdapter daCust=new SqlDataAdapter
        ("SELECT CustomerID, CompanyName, ContactName, Phone " +
        "FROM customers",cn);
    SqlDataAdapter daOrder=new SqlDataAdapter("SELECT * FROM orders",cn);

    DataSet ds = new DataSet("CustList");

    daCust.Fill(ds,"custs");
    daOrder.Fill(ds,"orders");

    ds.Relations.Add(ds.Tables["custs"].Columns["customerid"],
                        ds.Tables["orders"].Columns["customerid"]);
    ds.Relations[0].Nested=true;
```

```
    cn.Close();
    XmlDataDocument doc=new XmlDataDocument(ds);

    DateTime d = DateTime.Now;
    TimeSpan ts=new TimeSpan(30,0,0,0);
    XsltArgumentList args=new XsltArgumentList();
    args.AddParam("effDate", "", d.Add(ts).ToString("D")) ;

    XslTransform xsl=new XslTransform();

    xsl.Load(Server.MapPath("") + "\\PhoneListOrders.xsl");

    xsl.Transform(doc,args,Response.OutputStream);

}
```

The changed code looks straightforward. First, we derive the value that we are going to add to
XsltArgumentList. In this case we are simply getting the date that is 30 days from now. Next, we
create a new XsltArgumentList and use the AddParam method to add the date. Notice that we use
one of the overloads of the ToString method on the DateTime object to format the date (string). The
empty string in the parameter list is for a namespace. If we wanted to include a namespace to identify
the parameter, we can. The empty string means that we will use the default namespace.

The last thing to look at is the call to xsl.Transform. Notice that we have added args as one of the
parameters. As we mentioned before, there are nine overloads to the Transform method, eight of
which can take an XsltArgumentList as a parameter. The XSL stylesheet looks like this:

```
<xsl:stylesheet xmlns:xsl="http://www.w3.org/1999/XSL/Transform" version="1.0"
                xmlns:msxsl="urn:schemas-microsoft-com:xslt"
                xmlns:user="http://wrox.com" >

    <msxsl:script language="C#" implements-prefix="user">

        public double ReduceFreight(double currentFreight)
        {
            return currentFreight*.75;
        }
    </msxsl:script>

<xsl:param name="effDate"/>

<xsl:template match="CustList">
    <html>
        <body bgcolor=    "#FFFFE0">
        <h1>Customer List</h1>
        <table BORDER="0" width="100%" cellspacing="4" cellpadding="4">
            <xsl:apply-templates select="custs"/>
        </table>
        </body>
    </html>
</xsl:template>

<xsl:template match="custs">
```

```
<tr>
    <td colspan="4" bgcolor="lightblue">
        <font size="5">
            <xsl:value-of select="CompanyName"/>
        </font>
    </td>
</tr>
<tr>
    <td colspan="2"><xsl:value-of select="ContactName"/></TD>
    <td colspan="1"><xsl:value-of select="Phone"/></TD>
</tr>
<tr>
    <td><b>Disc Effective Date: </b></td>
    <td><xsl:value-of select="$effDate"/></td>
</tr>
<tr>
    <td><b>Order ID</b></td>
    <td><b>Freight</b></td>
    <td><b>Disc Freight</b></td>

</tr>
<xsl:for-each select="orders">
<tr>
    <td><xsl:value-of select="OrderID"/></td>
    <td><xsl:value-of select="Freight"/></td>
    <td><xsl:value-of select="user:ReduceFreight(Freight)"/></td>

</tr>
    </xsl:for-each>
</xsl:template>
</xsl:stylesheet>
```

Changes in the stylesheet are minimal in this instance. The line

```
<xsl:param name="effDate"/>
```

defines the parameter effDate for the rest of the stylesheet. This parameter is used at a later point in the stylesheet:

```
<tr>
    <td><b>Disc Effective Date: </b></td>
    <td><xsl:value-of select="$effDate"/></td>
</tr>
```

Notice the $ in front of effDate. This is telling the XSL processor that what follows is a variable of some type, in this case a parameter. You can add several parameters to the XsltArgumentList to pass into your stylesheet. They could be values from a database, values based on user input or values that you derive directly, like we did with the effective date.

Passing a parameter value into the stylesheet can be a very useful tool, but to add real processing power to your stylesheets, setting object extensions in the `XsltArgumentList` is the way to go. Adding and passing object extensions is similar to using parameters. The difference is that instead of passing a value back to the stylesheet, you are passing a method name that can be invoked from inside the stylesheet. Unlike the scripting that we looked at before, the code stays in your application. This allows greater flexibility, not to mention better encapsulation. You can also make use of the entire .NET framework without any limitations.

The process of adding an object extension is simple. The first thing is to define the functionality that you wish to be able to call from your stylesheet. The example we have here is very simple and may not be the best way to accomplish the task, but it will serve to demonstrate the process. In this example we are using the code-behind feature of ASP.NET. The entire project is in the `XslSample5` folder; this code is in the `WebForm1.aspx.cs` file of the project.

```
private void LoadXml()
{

    SqlConnection cn=new SqlConnection(
            @"data source=(local)\NETSDK;uid=sa;password=;database=northwind");

    SqlDataAdapter daCust=new SqlDataAdapter
        ("SELECT CustomerID, CompanyName, ContactName, Phone " +
        "FROM customers",cn);
    SqlDataAdapter daOrder=new SqlDataAdapter("SELECT * FROM orders",cn);

    DataSet ds = new DataSet("CustList");

    daCust.Fill(ds,"custs");
    daOrder.Fill(ds,"orders");

    ds.Relations.Add(ds.Tables["custs"].Columns["customerid"],
                     ds.Tables["orders"].Columns["customerid"]);
    ds.Relations[0].Nested=true;

    cn.Close();

    XmlDataDocument doc=new XmlDataDocument(ds);

    XslTransform xsl=new XslTransform();

    XsltArgumentList args=new XsltArgumentList();
    args.AddExtensionObject("urn:ProCSharpData",this);

    xsl.Load(Server.MapPath("") + "\\PhoneListOrders.xsl");

    xsl.Transform(doc,args,Response.OutputStream);

}

public double ReduceFreight(double currentFreight)
{
    return currentFreight * .75;
}
```

```
public double TotalFreight(XPathNodeIterator iterator)
{

    double total=0;
    XPathNodeIterator freightIterator=
                            iterator.Current.Select("orders/Freight");
    while(freightIterator.MoveNext())
    {
        total+=Convert.ToDouble(freightIterator.Current.Value);
    }
    return total;
}

public double DaysToShip(string shipDate, string orderDate)
{

    if(shipDate.Length>0 && orderDate.Length>0)
    {
        DateTime ship=Convert.ToDateTime(shipDate);
        DateTime order=Convert.ToDateTime(orderDate);
        TimeSpan ts=ship-order;
        return Convert.ToDouble(ts.Days);
    }
    return 0;
}
```

We have created three methods that we will use from the stylesheet. The first method is the ReduceFreight method that we have seen before. The next method is TotalFreight. Take a look at the parameter and you can see we are passing in an XPathNodeIterator. In this case, iterator is expected to contain a list of orders elements. We use the MoveNext method to iterate through the node set to add up the total freight for that particular customer.

The DaysToShip method takes in the shipping date and the order date and calculates the number of days from the time of the order being placed it took to ship the product. We do a little string manipulation to get the date part of the order and ship date and subtract order date from ship date.

Notice these two lines of code in LoadXml:

```
XsltArgumentList args=new XsltArgumentList();
args.AddExtensionObject("urn:ProCSharpData",this);
```

Here we create the new XsltArgumentList args and add the extension to it. We don't add the methods individually; instead, we add the class that the methods are part of. In this case it is the keyword this which means the current object or class, which in this case would be WebForm1. The other parameter is the namespace that we will use to reference the method calls in the stylesheet. If you wish to use the default namespace, just use an empty string (" "), as we did for the parameters example.

Here is what the stylesheet looks like:

```
<xsl:stylesheet xmlns:xsl="http://www.w3.org/1999/XSL/Transform" version="1.0"
                xmlns:xslsample="urn:ProCSharpData">
```

```
<xsl:template match="CustList">
    <html>
        <body bgcolor=    "#FFFFEO">
        <h1>Customer List</h1>
        <table BORDER="0" width="100%" cellspacing="4" cellpadding="4">

            <xsl:apply-templates select="custs"/>
        </table>
        </body>
    </html>
</xsl:template>
<xsl:template match="custs">
    <tr>
        <td colspan="4" bgcolor="lightblue">
            <font size="5">
                <xsl:value-of select="CompanyName"/>
            </font>
        </td>
    </tr>

    <tr>
        <td colspan="2"><xsl:value-of select="ContactName"/></TD>

        <td colspan="2"><xsl:value-of select="Phone"/></TD>

    </tr>

    <tr>
        <td><b>Order ID</b></td>
        <td><b>Freight</b></td>
        <td><b>Disc Freight</b></td>
        <td><b>Days to Ship</b></td>
    </tr>

    <xsl:for-each select="orders">
        <tr>
            <td><xsl:value-of select="OrderID"/></td>
            <td><xsl:value-of select="Freight"/></td>
            <td><xsl:value-of select="xslsample:ReduceFreight(Freight)"/></td>
            <td><xsl:value-of select=
                        "xslsample:DaysToShip(ShippedDate,OrderDate)"/></td>
            <td></td>
        </tr>
    </xsl:for-each>
    <tr>
        <td><b>Total Freight</b></td>
        <td><xsl:value-of select="xslsample:TotalFreight(.)"/></td>
    </tr>

</xsl:template>
</xsl:stylesheet>
```

Notice the custom namespace declaration in the document declaration section. We are calling the namespace xslsample, and you can see that it maps to the name we used when we added the object extension to the XsltArgumentList in the code. Now whenever we call a method with that namespace prefix in front of it, it will look in the assembly that ProCSharpData was defined in. In this case it is XslSample5.dll, which is created by WebForm1.aspx.cs. You can see this when we call ReduceFreight and DaysToShip. Once again, the namespace helps to resolve naming issues. If we have another ReduceFreight method in another assembly, assigning them to different namespaces means that we can use each of them on the same stylesheet, without any naming conflicts.

The other interesting line of code is:

```
<td><xsl:value-of select="xslsample:TotalFreight(.)"/></td>
```

Notice what we are passing into the method; the "." notation in XSL means that we want to send in the current element, which in this case would be the customer element and all of its children. In the TotalFreight method, we use the XPathNodeIterator that was passed in, and from it we create another XpathNodeIterator, this time containing the freight element. It is this XPathNodeIterator that we use to calculate the total freight. Here is what the output looks like:

File	Edit	View	Favorites	Tools	Help

Address http://localhost/XslSample5/WebForm1.aspx

Customer List

Alfreds Futterkiste

Maria Anders		030-0074321	
Order ID	**Freight**	**Disc Freight**	**Days to Ship**
10643	29.46	22.095	8
10692	61.02	45.765	10
10702	23.94	17.955	8
10835	69.53	52.1475	6
10952	40.42	30.315	8
11011	1.21	0.9075	4
Total Freight	225.58		

Ana Trujillo Emparedados y helados

Ana Trujillo		(5) 555-4729	
Order ID	**Freight**	**Disc Freight**	**Days to Ship**
10308	1.61	1.2075	6
10625	43.9	32.925	6
10759	11.99	8.9925	14
10926	39.92	29.94	7
Total Freight	97.42		

Done — Local intranet

As you can see, the Days to Ship column has been added, as well as the Total Freight line item.

The System.Xml.Xsl namespace adds a great deal of power to the XSLT process. XsltArgumentList gives you the ability to use the entire .NET namespace in your stylesheets. For transforming XML into HTML, or delimited text files into XML, the System.Xml.Xsl namespace in combination with the System.Xml.XPath namespace is the tool that can do the job.

Summary

In this chapter we looked at three very powerful and useful namespaces for dealing with XML. The first two namespaces, System.Xml.XPath and System.Xml.Xsl, work very closely together. We saw how to harness the performance of XPathNavigator when we don't need the editing capabilities of the XmlDocument class, and explored how the XPathNodeIterator iterates over a set of nodes selected by an XPath query. XPathNavigator also is used to feed the System.Xml.Xsl namespace, giving a high performance boost in transformations. We used the Transform class to take the same basic set of data and display it a number of different ways.

Hopefully, the last couple of chapters will give you an idea of the importance of XML, and how instrumental it will be for applications developed in the future. The .NET framework uses it for a variety of housekeeping and configuration-setting chores. SOAP and the Remoting namespace use it extensively. And of course, the close tie with ADO.NET brings in all sorts of new possibilities. It shouldn't be difficult to come up with a number of different ways to use XML in your applications.

The System.Xml namespace is a large and complex set of classes. It will take a bit of study and work on your part to master all of the features. We have attempted to show a sample of what is possible; however, almost every example that was shown in the last two chapters has at least one other way of accomplishing the same thing. This is what makes the System.Xml namespace, and the .NET Framework in general, such a pleasure and challenge to work with.

9

Directory Services

Directory Services are specialized databases that make it quick and easy to look up information. We deal with Directory Services in our daily lives. Telephone books and television listings are available as paper-based Directory Services where we can search for phone numbers based on a region and a name, or for TV programs based on a day or a category. The Domain Naming Service (DNS) is an example of a Directory Service for the Internet where, for example, we can look up the IP address by using a host name.

In IT departments the need for centralized Directory Services has arisen from wanting to store user information in a single location, making it easier to manage users and lookup information such as names, addresses, or phone numbers. In such directory stores it is also possible to save other information like details of printers with their capabilities and locations, endpoint names, and capabilities of service processes, etc.

In this chapter we will see how to use the classes from the System.DirectoryServices namespace to access a Directory Service. In particular, we will look at:

❑   What is a Directory Service?

❑   The major classes of the namespace System.DirectoryServices

❑   Accessing Directory Services

❑   Using ADSI COM Objects

❑   Searching within Directory Services

❑   Publishing Using Directory Services

What is a Directory Service?

In a relational database, data is organized into tables where every row in a table has the same type of information. With a Directory Service we can store different types of data in a hierarchical way. In Directory Services, the term **object** is used for the data that is stored, and the term **container** for an object that can include other objects; **parent-child** is used to describe the relationship between containers and included objects.

The picture below shows how different object types can be organized in a hierarchy. In the diagram, there is a container object, Development Department, which includes the child objects Christian Nagel and Rainer Schmidt, another container object, Web Development, a File Share, and a Printer. The container object Web Development includes a user object, Oliver Kastner, and a mailing list.

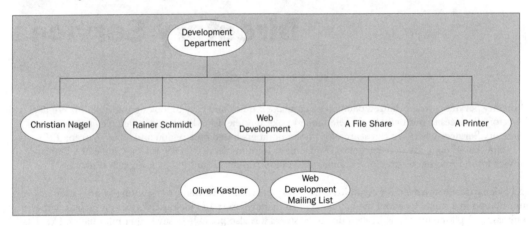

Objects and Attributes

An object in the Directory Service can have attributes that describe the object and are a way of identifying that object. For example, the attributes of a user object could be the account information including the logon name and hours, expiration date, address information with street, city, state, country, zip code, organization information, etc. Some of the attributes of a printer object are the network address, share name, maximum number of copies, and so on.

Searching for Objects

Unlike a database, a Directory Service is typically optimized for read-mostly access. We can write to the Directory Service to change attributes of objects and create new objects, but usually it will be used to read information and search for objects.

To search for objects, we can define attributes that should match the search. For example, we can search the complete directory store for a printer in a specific location with duplex support. Another example would be a search for all employees that are located in a specific city.

Because of the read-mostly nature, the directory store can be easily replicated across systems in different locations of the company.

Directory Servers

Using .NET Directory Services, we can access a lot of different directory providers. Because Directory Services is based on ADSI (Active Directory Services Interface), we need an ADSI provider. As part of Windows 2000 or Windows XP we get the following providers:

❑ **LDAP (Lightweight Directory Access Protocol) providers** to access the Windows 2000 Active Directory, the Exchange Server 2000, and any other Directory Service that supports LDAP.

❑ We get two providers for Novell services: **Novell Directory Services** and **Novell Netware 3.x**.

❑ A **Windows NT provider** can be used to access the account information from Windows NT 4 domains.

❑ The **IIS provider** can be used to read and configure the metabase from the Internet Information Server. The metabase of IIS holds the configuration data, such as virtual web sites and how these web sites are configured.

Usage Scenarios

What can Directory Services be used for? In the next sections we will look at some scenarios showing how the data from Directory Services can be used including:

❑ Information reuse

❑ Service publication

❑ Profile replication

Information Reuse

To begin with, Directory Services can be used for **information reuse**. With the previous release of Exchange, the system administrator had to enter the company's computer users into the operating system twice. Once to enable them to logon to the domain, and then to give them access to the Exchange Server store, where additional user information such as e-mail addresses, departments, and phone numbers was stored. The reason for this requirement was that the user information on Windows NT 4.0 was not extensible. The Exchange Server needed additional information for a user, so another information store was required.

With the release of Exchange Server 2000, Active Directory is used as the information store. The system administrator is no longer required to maintain user information in two independent stores. The information that can be stored for user objects within the Active Directory is very rich, and also extensible. Exchange Server 2000 exploits this extensibility mechanism, extending the available object types by using attributes that are required by this system, along with registering its own types.

In the picture overleaf, you can see how the Active Directory can be reused in different scenarios. The Active Directory can authenticate a user of a PC in the local network. You can also configure authentication for users that access resources over a web server to use the Active Directory; and when sending e-mails to users the Exchange Server can use the same information store.

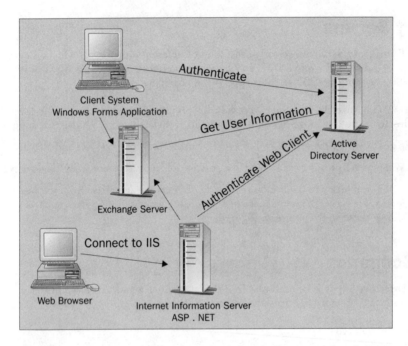

It is also possible that an application adds new types of objects that are used in the enterprise, locating information in the Active Directory instead of storing and maintaining its own copies. For example, you could extend the user object with an attribute *Knowledge* where knowledge-information about an employee can be entered. This way it would be an easier task to find employees when necessary. This scenario could be very advantageous to large companies with thousands of developers. Without this central store of information about the employees, the company may repeatedly fail to find a developer with some specific knowledge of a technology.

Service Publication

Application services can publish information in the directory about which services are available and at which hosts. Examples of such services that can be published could be a TCP socket server, a .NET Remoting server, or simply a printer. The client application can search in the Directory Service to find the service it wants, and use the information it reads from the object to bind to the service. For example, to use a TCP socket, the host name and port number are required to connect to it, or for .NET Remoting servers the protocol, host name, port number, server name, and object name are the necessary binding information for connecting to the server.

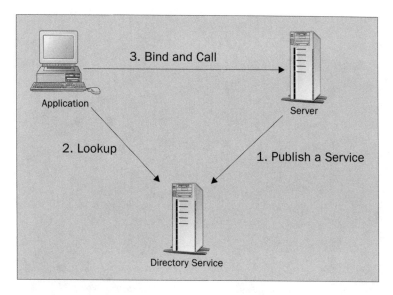

The picture above shows a service publication scenario. The server publishes binding information to the Directory Service. This can happen at the installation time of the service application. The client can then use the Directory Service to do a search on the service at run time, and use the binding information it reads to bind to the server and call methods.

By using service publication, we win **deployment flexibility**. In other words, we can change the host that offers a service without the need to reconfigure the client application.

> In the Publishing Services *section later in this chapter we will implement an example to publish and search for a service.*

Profile Replication

A third scenario is demonstrated in the following picture. We can store an application's configuration information using a Directory Service. With the Active Directory's replication mechanism, configuration is replicated across different domain servers that can reside in different locations. A roaming user (a user that changes their client system) can log on to any system in the company's network to get their application configurations.

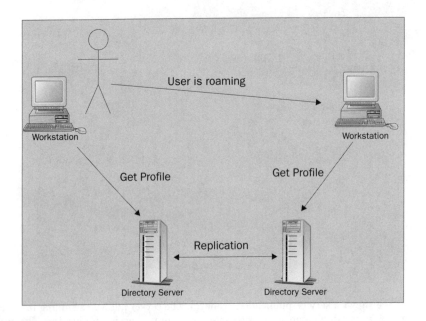

System.DirectoryServices Namespace

The .NET Framework provides us with some classes to access Directory Services in the `System.DirectoryServices` namespace. The classes from this namespace wrap the ADSI COM objects. The design goal of these .NET classes was to make it easy to use Directory Services for simple applications (ASP.NET pages as well as Windows applications). However, as the term *simple applications* implies, the .NET classes are not as powerful as the underlying COM objects. Still, it is easy to get access to the underlying COM objects and to use them directly as we will see in the *Using ADSI* section later in the chapter.

The classes in the namespace `System.DirectoryServices` primarily serve two purposes:

❑ **Read and write objects** in a Directory Service. We can read and write the properties of the objects using the `DirectoryEntry` class.

❑ **Search for objects** in a Directory Service. We can search a complete tree for objects that have some specified properties. The primary class needed for searching is `DirectorySearch`.

The classes from the `System.DirectoryServices` namespace are listed in the following tables. The first table shows the more important classes to read and write objects from the tree.

Classes	Description
DirectoryEntry	Encapsulates a directory object. With this class we can read and write properties of the object.
DirectoryEntries	`DirectoryEntries` is a collection of `DirectoryEntry` objects. With this class we can add and remove objects.

Classes	Description
PropertyCollection	PropertyCollection can be used to enumerate the properties of an object.
PropertyValueCollection	The indexer of the PropertyCollection returns a PropertyValueCollection that is used to access all values of a single property.

The second table shows the major classes that are used to find objects in the Directory Service.

Classes	Description
DirectorySearcher	The DirectorySearcher class is used to find objects in a directory tree
SearchResultCollection	Searching the Directory Service with the DirectorySearcher class returns a SearchResultCollection
SearchResult	A SearchResultCollection consists of SearchResult objects
ResultPropertyCollection	The ResultPropertyCollection represents the properties of a returned result collection
ResultPropertyValue Collection	The indexer of the ResultPropertyCollection returns an instance of ResultPropertyValueCollection that holds all values for a single property

Regarding the examples in this chapter, we have to reference the assembly System.DirectoryServices, and include the namespace System.DirectoryServices.

DirectoryEntry

The most important class in the System.DirectoryServices namespace is DirectoryEntry; this is the class that represents an object in the directory.

Caching

Before talking about properties and methods of the DirectoryEntry class we have to discuss one important detail regarding directory objects. An object that is offered in the Directory Service has a lot of properties. It is not useful to go through the properties one at a time, each time making a call across the network. As you know, every call to the network takes time. For performance reasons when calling across the network, it's better to perform fewer calls by passing more arguments, instead of having many calls passing fewer arguments. With the DirectoryEntry class, this happens automatically. As soon as we access a single property of the directory object, the object cache (which is implemented in the ADSI object used by DirectoryEntry) that stores all properties of the object is filled, and every following property access reads the data from the cache. To read the data from the directory object again, RefreshCache() must be called.

Caching is not only important for read access, but also for writing. Changing the property values only updates the cache. To update the object itself after changing the cache, CommitChanges() must be called to make the change permanent.

DirectoryEntry Properties

Properties that are common to all objects in Directory Services can be accessed directly by using properties of the DirectoryEntry class: Name, Path, Guid, NativeGuid, and SchemaClassName. The following table goes through each of the properties of the DirectoryEntry class and gives a short description of the action of each.

Property	Description
Children	If the object accessed is a container object that has children, a collection of type DirectoryEntries is returned from the Children property.
Parent	With the Parent property we go up the hierarchical tree to access the container object of the current DirectoryEntry.
Properties	Every directory object has different properties. The DirectoryEntry class must be flexible to allow access to all these properties. Properties return a PropertyCollection of all the properties of the DirectoryEntry object. Each of these properties has a name and a value that can be accessed with PropertyNames and Values.
SchemaClassName	The attributes of a directory object are defined in the schema. The property SchemaClassName returns the name of the schema class that defines the properties for a directory object.
SchemaEntry	We can use the SchemaEntry object to get more information about the attributes of a directory object. The property SchemaEntry returns an instance of DirectoryEntry as the schema objects themselves are stored within the Directory Service.
NativeObject	Because the classes of the namespace System.DirectoryServices put a layer above ADSI we can get direct access to the ADSI object with the NativeObject property.
UsePropertyCache	With this property we can turn off the object cache that we talked about earlier. Setting the value to false will result in a network call with every read and write of a property.
Name	Name is a read-only property that returns the name of the directory object.
Path	The Path property returns the path of the object. By reading the path we know the hierarchy in which the object is stored. Setting the Path property to a different value reads a different object from the Directory Service in the current DirectoryEntry instance.

Property	Description
Guid	Guid is a read-only property that returns a unique identifier of the object. Using an LDAP provider you should always use the NativeGuid property instead of the Guid property, as objects in LDAP providers are identified by X.500 unique names that cannot be represented in the Guid type that is returned from the Guid property.
NativeGuid	NativeGuid returns a string representation of the Guid. For LDAP providers this property should be used.

DirectoryEntry Methods

Method	Description
RefreshCache	If the cache is used with the default configuration UsePropertyCache = True, the cache is filled when the first property of the directory object is read. With the RefreshCache() method, the properties of the directory object are read again.
CommitChanges	If you change the values of properties, only the data of the cache is changed. To update the properties of the directory object in the Directory Service, CommitChanges() must be called after changing the values.
Close	The Close() method frees resources held by the DirectoryEntry instance. The Dispose() method can be used instead.
DeleteTree	DeleteTree() deletes the directory object to which DirectoryEntry points, and all of its child objects.
Rename	With Rename(), the name of the entry gets changed. CommitChanges() must be called to make the change permanent if the cache is used.
MoveTo	MoveTo() moves the entry to a new parent object in the tree. As with Rename(), CommitChanges() must be called to make the change permanent.
Invoke	With the Invoke() method, a method of the underlying COM object can be used. The classes from the System.DirectoryServices namespace are a small layer to COM components.

Accessing Directory Services

In our first sample application using the System.DirectoryServices class, we will use an IIS provider to access a Directory Service. Internet Information Server 5 has a metabase for its configuration. **IIS Admin Objects** can be used to create and configure web sites, to start and stop web services, etc. We can also use the .NET Directory Services classes to access this metabase.

Windows Client Application

What does IIS offer? We will build a Windows Forms application **IISBrowser** that uses the IIS provider to read all objects and properties of the objects that this provider offers to access the IIS metabase. This application should make it possible to see all objects of the metabase in a tree view, and to see the properties and values of selected objects in a list view.

You can see the design mode of the Windows application in the picture below. The white rectangle in the lower left side is a tree view that will display all objects in the directory tree. In the right-hand side we have some text fields to display some of the properties that every directory object offers, and a list view for the properties that differ from object to object. The Connect button initiates the initial connection to the Directory Service.

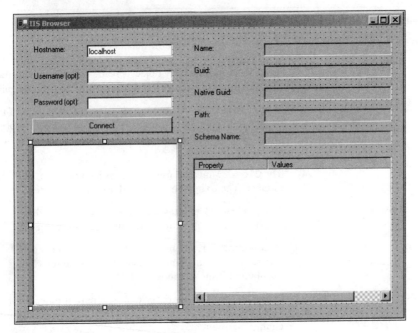

The Windows controls used in this application (with the exception of the labels) are summarized in this table:

Type	Property	Property Value
TextBox	Name	textHostname
TextBox	Name	textUsername
TextBox	Name	textPassword
TextBox	Name	textName
TextBox	Name	textGuid
TextBox	Name	textNativeGuid

Type	Property	Property Value
TextBox	Name	textPath
TextBox	Name	textSchema
Button	Name	buttonConnect
	Text	Connect
TreeView	Name	treeViewObjects
ListView	Name	listViewProperties

Binding

To get to an object in a Directory Service we have to specify binding information. With the `DirectoryEntry` class, the binding information can be passed into the constructor. When using the default constructor, the binding information is set by using the `Path` property. Both of these methods are shown in the following code example.

```
// Passing binding information in the constructor
DirectoryEntry entry1 = new DirectoryEntry("IIS://localhost/W3SVC/1");

// Using the Path property
DirectoryEntry entry2 = new DirectoryEntry();
entry2.Path = "IIS://localhost/W3SVC/1";
```

If the wrong binding string is assigned, we don't get an error at this time. Binding doesn't necessarily happen when the `Path` property is set because nothing is really needed from the Directory Service. The binding is delayed to reduce the number of calls across the network. The first time you will get an error message is when a wrong path is specified, properties of the native directory object are accessed, or methods are called.

So what are the parts of the binding string? The binding string that we're using is:

```
IIS://localhost/W3SVC/1
```

The following items specify the binding string:

❑ The **Protocol** defines the provider that is used. In our example we use `IIS:`.

❑ After the protocol the **host name** of the directory server is specified. We use `localhost` to access the IIS from the local system.

❑ The **Distinguished Name** that follows defines the name of the object in the directory tree in a unique way. In our example the distinguished name is `W3SVC/1`.

Protocol

The first part of the binding string specifies the provider used. The following table shows what protocol strings are required for the supported providers:

Protocol	Provider
LDAP:	LDAP Server like Microsoft's Active Directory and Exchange Server.
IIS:	Internet Information Server.
NWCOMPAT:	Novell Netware 3.x.
NDS:	Novell Directory Services.
GC:	The Active Directory supports a read-only cache called the Global Catalog to make fast searches. The string GC: is used to access this cache. GC uses the same LDAP provider as LDAP:
WinNT:	With the NT provider, it is possible to access the user database from Windows NT 4 domains.

Server and Port Number

The server is specified after the protocol in the binding string. Optionally, a port number can be added to the host name. If the port number is not specified, a default port that is defined by the provider is used; for example, the default port for the LDAP provider is 389.

Distinguished Name

Finally, the distinguished name is the last part of the binding string. Every object in the directory store can be selected by specifying its unique name in a way that is known by the provider. In the last example we used the distinguished name W3SVC/1. W3SVC is a container object that defines the WWW publishing service, 1 is another container object that defines the default web site of this publishing service. W3SVC/2 is the object name of the Administration Web site. An example of how a virtual directory of the default web site can be accessed with a distinguished name is: W3SVC/1/Root/IISSamples, which specifies the virtual directory IISSamples.

In the *LDAP Binding Information* section later in this chapter, we will see what the distinguished name for LDAP providers looks like.

Authentication

By default, the user that is associated with the current thread is used to access the Directory Service. If a different user is required, for example, the current user only has read privileges, but admin privileges are needed by the application, a different username and password can be passed. It is possible to pass the username and password in an overloaded constructor of the DirectoryEntry class, or these values can be set with the Username and Password properties.

How authentication happens is defined with the AuthenticationType property of the DirectoryEntry class. The AuthenticationTypes that need to be passed is an enumeration with the following values:

Enumeration value	Description
None	Setting the `AuthenticationType` to `None` means no authentication is requested.
Secure	With secure authentication, the LDAP provider will use Kerberos if it is available, or else it uses NTLM authentication.
Encription	Data that is sent across the network will be encrypted.
Delegation	With `Delegation` enabled, the security context can be sent across the network. This is necessary when moving objects across domains.
FastBind	With the `FastBind` option, the provider will only expose the base ADSI interfaces.
ReadOnlyServer	This value indicates that we just need read-only access to the Directory Service.
Signing	With the `Signing` option set, the sent and received data is verified.
Sealing	`Sealing` encrypts the data using Kerberos.
SecureSocketsLayer	Setting the option `SecureSocketsLayer` uses the SSL protocol for encryption.
ServerBind	When binding to an LDAP provider with this value, we indicate that the binding path includes a server name, so the provider may skip a few steps when binding.

Binding with the IIS Browser

Now that we know how to bind to a Directory Service, let's add this to our IIS Browser application. When we click the **Connect** button, we want to bind to the metabase with the option of setting the username and password.

The binding will be implemented in the `Click` event of the **Connect** button. First, we are going to create a new `DirectoryEntry` instance using the default constructor. The path to the directory object is set with the `Path` property. We bind to the IIS Directory Service provider using the IIS protocol. Appended to the protocol string is the hostname that was entered in the `textHostname` textbox. If the user of the IIS Browser application also enters a username and password, the properties `Username` and `Password` are also set.

```
private void buttonConnect_Click(object sender, System.EventArgs e)
{
    DirectoryEntry entry = new DirectoryEntry();
    entry.Path = "IIS://" + textHostname.Text;

    if (textUsername.Text == "")
    {
        entry.Username = null;
        entry.Password = null;
    }
    else
```

```
        {
            entry.Username = textUsername.Text;
            entry.Password = textPassword.Text;
        }
        //...
    }
```

As binding to the directory object doesn't happen until we try to access properties or call methods of the directory object, if the user enters the wrong hostname or username we won't get an error just yet.

We want to display this object as well as the child objects in the tree view so that's what we are going to do next.

Parents and Children

As was stated earlier, Directory Services represent a hierarchical object store. A container object can include other objects that are called children, and can be accessed using the `Children` property. The `Children` property returns a `DirectoryEntries` object that contains all the `DirectoryEntry` objects of the children. The class `DirectoryEntries` implements the interface `IEnumerable`, so that it is possible to enumerate all child objects with a `foreach` loop.

```
foreach (DirectoryEntry child in entry.Children)
{
    Console.WriteLine(child.Name);
}
```

Using the `Parent` property of the `DirectoryEntry` object we can walk up the tree again.

```
Console.WriteLine("Parent: " + child.Parent.Name);
```

Adding DirectoryEntry objects to the TreeView

So let's continue with the IIS Browser application and add the method to display the directory objects in the tree view. Because the `TreeView` class requires objects of type `TreeNode` to be added to the tree, but we want `DirectoryEntry` objects instead to be added to the view, we're creating a new class called `DirectoryEntryNode` that derives from `TreeNode`.

The constructor of the `DirectoryEntryNode` class accepts a `DirectoryEntry` object that will be stored in the private field `entry`. The `Text` property that is defined in the base class is set to the name of the `DirectoryEntry`. The `TreeView` class displays the elements in the tree by accessing the `Text` property.

The `DirectoryEntryNode` class has a `DirectoryEntry` property that allows access to the embedded `DirectoryEntry` object.

```
    public class DirectoryEntryNode : System.Windows.Forms.TreeNode,
        IDisposable
    {
        private DirectoryEntry entry;

        public DirectoryEntryNode(DirectoryEntry entry)
        {
```

```
          this.entry = entry;
          this.Text = entry.Name;
      }

      public DirectoryEntry DirectoryEntry
      {
          get
          {
              return entry;
          }
          set
          {
              entry = value;
              this.Text = entry.Name;
          }
      }

      public override string ToString()
      {
          return entry.Name;
      }

      public void Dispose()
      {
          entry.Dispose();
      }
  }
```

How do we fill the tree view? In the `Click` event handler of the **Connect** button we will add directory objects to the tree. The `Click` event handler is implemented in the method `buttonConnect_Click()` that we started earlier. As a Directory Service can include millions of objects it is not useful to write all the objects to the tree as this could take a while, so we just add the topmost objects and their children. The tree view displays a + sign if child objects are available. If the user clicks the + sign, the tree view invokes the handler for the `BeforeExpand` and `AfterExpand` events. We will implement a handler for the `BeforeExpand` event to check for grandchildren that will display the + sign again if children of children are available.

We already implemented a handler for the `Click` event of the **Connect** button. Now we're adding code to this handler to create a `DirectoryEntryNode` object. This node is added to the tree view using `treeViewObjects.Nodes.Add()`. Before that, `BeginUpdate` is called on the tree view to prevent repainting before the tree update is finished. `treeViewObjects.Nodes.Clear()` removes all objects from the view that were inserted previously.

`AddChildren()` is the method that we will implement next. As this is where binding to the directory object really happens, we're adding a `try` block to catch an exception if the specified host doesn't exist.

```
      private void buttonConnect_Click(object sender, System.EventArgs e)
      {
          try
          {
              DirectoryEntry entry = new DirectoryEntry();
              entry.Path = "IIS://" + textHostname.Text;

              if (textUsername.Text == "")
              {
                  entry.Username = null;
                  entry.Password = null;
```

```
        }
        else
        {
            entry.Username = textUsername.Text;
            entry.Password = textPassword.Text;
        }

        DirectoryEntryNode node = new DirectoryEntryNode(entry);
        treeViewObjects.BeginUpdate();
        treeViewObjects.Nodes.Clear();
        treeViewObjects.Nodes.Add(node);

        AddChildren(node);

        treeViewObjects.EndUpdate();
    }
    catch (Exception ex)
    {
        MessageBox.Show(ex.Message, "IIS Browser Error",
            MessageBoxButtons.OK, MessageBoxIcon.Error);
    }
}
```

The AddChildren() method receives a DirectoryEntryNode object as argument. Using a foreach loop statement, all child objects of the DirectoryEntry object that are embedded in DirectoryEntryNode are enumerated to create new DirectoryEntryNode objects that will be added to the tree view using node.Nodes.Add().

It is tempting to call the method AddChildren() recursively, to walk down the entire tree and to add all grandchild objects to the view. The reason for not doing this is that a Directory Service can include millions of objects, and so this method could run for a really long time. Instead, only one level of children will be added automatically. As soon as the user accesses the child objects we will go one level deeper so that the user can see what objects can be expanded.

```
protected void AddChildren(DirectoryEntryNode node)
{
    foreach (DirectoryEntry child in node.DirectoryEntry.Children)
    {
        node.Nodes.Add(new DirectoryEntryNode(child));
    }
}
```

To make it possible for the user to read all the objects of the entire Directory Service tree we're adding an event handler to the BeforeExpand event of the tree view. This event occurs when the user presses the + of the tree node object before the tree is expanded. In this handler we are walking through all child objects of the selected tree node to add child objects by using the previously implemented AddChildren() method.

```
private void OnBeforeExpand(object sender,
            System.Windows.Forms.TreeViewCancelEventArgs e)
{
    treeViewObjects.BeginUpdate();

    foreach (TreeNode node in e.Node.Nodes)
    {
```

```
            if (node.Nodes.Count == 0)
                AddChildren((DirectoryEntryNode)node);
        }

        treeViewObjects.EndUpdate();
    }
```

Clicking the **Connect** button starts the application and connects to the IIS of the localhost. A dialog should appear, which displays the `Name` property of the root object, localhost. There will be a + sign on the left hand side of it, as we already enumerated the children of the root object in the first step.

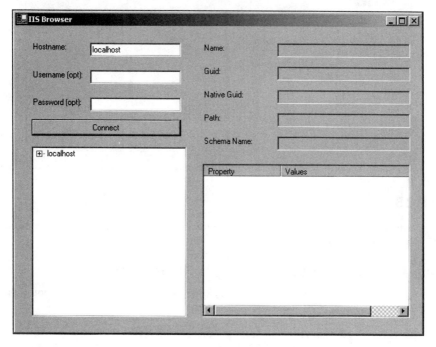

Pressing the + sign expands the tree so we can walk through the next level in the hierarchy of the tree in the `OnBeforeExpand()` handler. As you can see in the following screen, the + sign of the **Logging** object in the tree has also been clicked:

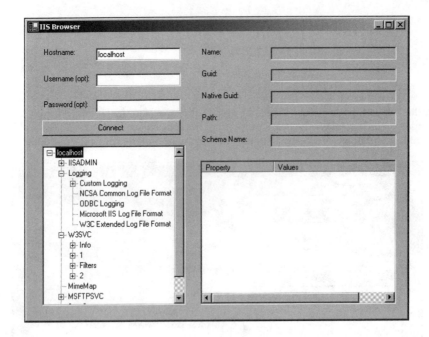

Properties

We not only want to walk through the hierarchy of the directory tree, but we also want to read the properties, and property values of the objects.

Displaying Properties for the IIS Browser Application

To display the properties of the `DirectoryEntry` class in our IIS Browser application we're adding an `OnSelectTreeItem` handler for the `AfterSelect` event of the tree view.

```
private void OnSelectTreeItem(object sender,
                    System.Windows.Forms.TreeViewEventArgs e)
{
    try
    {
        DirectoryEntryNode node = (DirectoryEntryNode)e.Node;

        DirectoryEntry entry = node.DirectoryEntry;
        this.textGuid.Text = entry.Guid.ToString();
        this.textNativeGuid.Text = entry.NativeGuid;
        this.textName.Text = entry.Name;
        this.textPath.Text = entry.Path;
        this.textSchema.Text = entry.SchemaClassName;

    }
    catch (Exception ex)
    {
        MessageBox.Show(ex.Message, "IIS Browser Error",
            MessageBoxButtons.OK, MessageBoxIcon.Error);
    }
}
```

PropertyCollection

By running the application now, we can see the path and type of the directory objects, as is shown in the following screenshot:

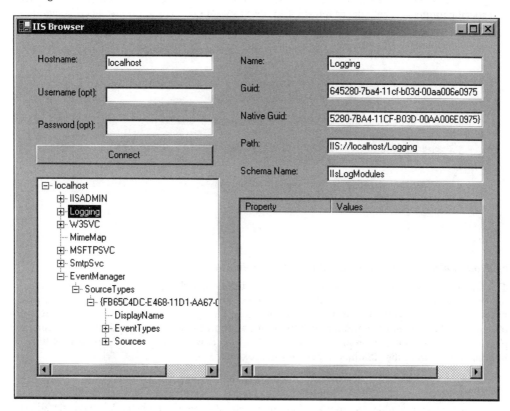

More interesting than the properties that can be accessed directly with the `DirectoryEntry` class are the object-type specific properties.

> **Don't confuse the properties of the `DirectoryEntry` class with the properties of the directory objects.** The properties of the `DirectoryEntry` class are defined in the class `DirectoryEntry`, but the properties of the directory objects are defined in the Directory Service. If we access a user object, a printer object, or a virtual web object, we will always use the `DirectoryEntry` class but each of these object types has different properties defined in the Directory Service.

The `DirectoryEntry` class returns a `PropertyCollection` by accessing the `Properties` property. A property of a directory object has a name and a value. Some of these properties are multi-valued; hence one property name can also have multiple property values. Using the `PropertyCollection` class we can access the property names and values with the `PropertyNames` and `Values` properties.

In the following sample code we display all properties and values of a directory entry object. We are going to use the `Properties` property to get a `PropertyCollection`. The `PropertyNames` in this `PropertyCollection` are used to enumerate all property names in the first `foreach` loop. The `PropertyName` will also be used with the indexer of the `PropertyCollection` class to get all values of a specific property. The indexer returns a `PropertyValueCollection` instance. As mentioned earlier, a single property can have multiple values; this is the reason why the indexer returns a collection instead of the value itself. This `PropertyValueCollection` class is used to enumerate all values in the inner `foreach` loop.

```
public void DisplayPropertiesAndValues(DirectoryEntry entry)
{
    PropertyCollection properties = entry.Properties;
    foreach (string propName in properties.PropertyNames)
    {
        PropertyValueCollection values = properties[propName];
        foreach (object val in values)
        {
            Console.WriteLine("Property: {0}, Value: {1}",
                propName, val.ToString());
        }
    }
}
```

Using PropertyCollections with the IIS Browser Application

The functionality of Directory Services providers is different, and depending on a provider some methods and properties are not available. The IIS provider doesn't support enumeration of the `PropertyNames`. Trying to do this results in the exception `System.NotSupportedException` with the message "The directory cannot report the number of properties." displayed. If we are using the IIS provider, we have to know the property names of the object we want to access. We can get this information by using the IIS objects that we will look at next.

IIS Objects

The properties that an object supports are defined with the type of the object. We have already read the object types with the `DirectoryEntry` property `SchemaClassName`. The type of the computer itself is `IIsComputer`. The W3SVC object has the type `IIsWebService`. In the hierarchy below the W3SVC object you find object of types `IIsWebInfo`, `IIsWebServer`, `IIsFilters`, `IIsWebDirectory`, `IIsWebVirtualDir`, and others.

> You can find documentation about the properties of these objects in the MSDN Library in the section **IIS Admin Object Reference**.

Next, we are going to create the helper function `GetPropertiesForSchema()` that returns a string array of properties for a specified type. The implementation of this method is not complete as some hundreds of property values are available for some of the object types.

```
protected static string[] GetPropertiesForSchema(string schema)
{
    string[] properties = null;
    switch (schema)
    {
        case "IIsLogModule":
```

```
                properties = new string[] { "LogModuleId","LogModuleUiId" };
                break;
            case "IIsComputer":
                properties = new string[] { "MaxBandWidth",
                                "MaxBandWidthBlocked", "MimeMap" };
                break;
            case "IIsWebDirectory":
            case "IIsWebVirtualDir":
                properties = new string[] { "AspBufferingOn",
                    "AppIsolated", "AppFriendlyName", "AspScriptLanguage",
                    "AppPackageName", "AspSessionMax", "AspThreadGateEnabled",
                    "LogonMethod", "CreateProcessAsUser" };
                break;
        }
        return properties;
    }
```

The `DisplayProperties()` method accepts a `DirectoryEntry` object as the first argument, and the second argument, `propertyNames`, passes the names of the properties, which are displayed in the list view. If no `propertyNames` are passed as an argument, we immediately return from this function after clearing the list view. With the `foreach` statement we enumerate the properties using the indexer of the `PropertyCollection` class that is returned by the `Properties` property. The returned `PropertyValueCollection` is used to get to all values (in most cases only one) of the property.

```
    protected void DisplayProperties(DirectoryEntry entry,
        string[] propertyNames)
    {
        listViewProperties.Items.Clear();

        if (propertyNames == null)
            return;

        foreach (string propertyName in propertyNames)
        {
            PropertyValueCollection values =
                entry.Properties[propertyName];
            foreach (object o in values)
            {
                string[] items = new string[2];
                items[0] = propertyName;
                items[1] = o.ToString();
                listViewProperties.Items.Add(new ListViewItem(items));
            }
        }
    }
```

`DisplayProperties()` itself is called in the method `OnSelectTreeItem()`:

```
    private void OnSelectTreeItem(object sender,
        System.Windows.Forms.TreeViewEventArgs e)
    {
        try
        {
```

```
DirectoryEntryNode node = (DirectoryEntryNode)e.Node;

DirectoryEntry entry = node.DirectoryEntry;
this.textGuid.Text = entry.Guid.ToString();
this.textNativeGuid.Text = entry.NativeGuid;
this.textName.Text = entry.Name;
this.textPath.Text = entry.Path;
this.textSchema.Text = entry.SchemaClassName;

DisplayProperties(entry,
    GetPropertiesForSchema(entry.SchemaClassName));
```

If we run the application now, we will see the properties for the selected objects that we specified in the method GetPropertiesForSchema():

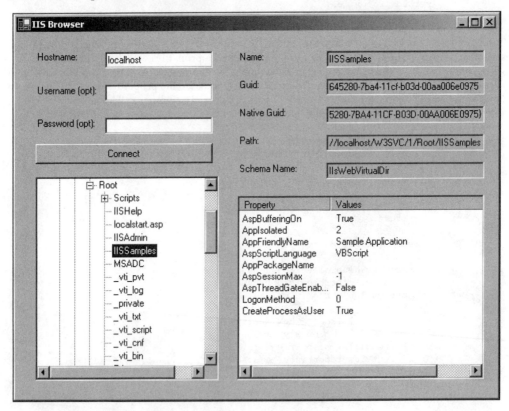

Accessing the Active Directory

In this next sample application, a few changes, but not many, are required to access the Directory Service of the Windows 2000 Active Directory instead of the IIS.

Instead of passing the hostname to the Path property prefixed with the string IIS:// we get the value completely from the Text property of the textObjectName textbox.

```
private void buttonConnect_Click(object sender, System.EventArgs e)
{
    try
    {
        DirectoryEntry entry = new DirectoryEntry();
        entry.Path = textObjectName.Text;
```

As with the LDAP provider we can now use the enumeration of the `PropertiesCollection`, and `OnSelectTreeItem()` can be changed to display all properties in the list view without the need to consult a different resource.

```
private void OnSelectTreeItem(object sender,
    System.Windows.Forms.TreeViewEventArgs e)
{
    try
    {
        DirectoryEntryNode node = (DirectoryEntryNode)e.Node;

        DirectoryEntry entry = node.DirectoryEntry;
        this.textGuid.Text = entry.Guid.ToString();
        this.textNativeGuid.Text = entry.NativeGuid;
        this.textName.Text = entry.Name;
        this.textPath.Text = entry.Path;
        this.textSchema.Text = entry.SchemaClassName;

        listViewProperties.Items.Clear();
        foreach (string propName in entry.Properties.PropertyNames)
        {
            foreach (object val in entry.Properties[propName])
            {
                string[] propValuePair = new String[2];
                propValuePair[0] = propName;
                propValuePair[1] = val.ToString();
                listViewProperties.Items.Add(
                    new ListViewItem(propValuePair));
            }
        }
    }
    catch (Exception ex)
    {
        MessageBox.Show(ex.Message, "AD Browser Error",
            MessageBoxButtons.OK, MessageBoxIcon.Error);
    }
}
```

So, with just a few changes we have an Active Directory browser to access the Active Directory. Entering `LDAP://sentinel`, which is the host name of one of my directory servers, I can access the objects in the Active Directory. By selecting a user object I can see all properties of the object and the values.

To display the value we use the `ToString()` method to get a string representation of the value. For some of the values, the `ToString()` method will just return `System.__ComObject`. The `System.Object` class implements the `ToString()` method so that it displays the name of the class. With classes that don't override the `ToString()` method, we get the implementation of the base class. As the class `__ComObject` indicates, COM objects are used behind the scenes of `System.DirectoryServices`. Later in this chapter we will look at how to access these COM objects from .NET.

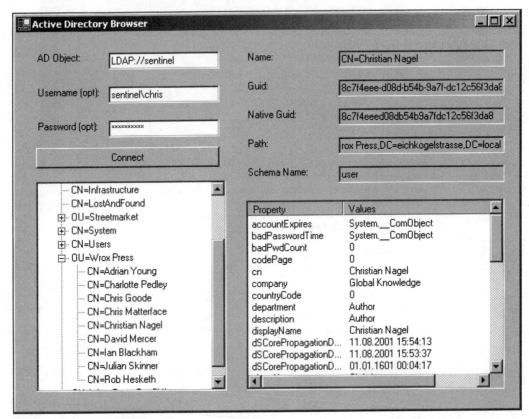

LDAP Binding Information

So far the binding string we have used to access the Active Directory looks similar to the binding string of the IIS provider: `LDAP://hostname`. Instead of just the `hostname`, we can specify the name of the object directly. This binding information looks very different from the IIS provider.

To access objects using the LDAP provider, an LDAP binding string can be used. The LDAP binding string uses a X.500 representation instead of using a directory-like syntax to access containers and objects. To reference a distinguished name in an LDAP provider the string can look like this:

```
CN=Christian Nagel, OU=Authors, DC=Wrox, DC=local
```

To walk through the tree to access the object we have to start with the last element on the right side and continue to the left. Object names are prefixed with a string attribute type. X.500 specifies the following string attribute types:

String	Attribute Type
CN	Common Name
L	Locality Name
ST	State or Province
O	Organizational Name
OU	Organizational Unit
C	Country Name
STREET	Street
DC	Domain Component
UID	User ID

To walk through the domain with the string we have seen earlier, DC=local is the topmost object followed by DC=Wrox. This domain is called Wrox.local. Inside this domain we access the container object OU=Authors, and finally the object with the common name CN=Christian Nagel.

The LDAP specification for the string representation of distinguished names can be found in RFC2253: http://www.ietf.org/rfc/rfc2253.txt.

The path that can be specified with the Path property of the DirectoryEntry class to access a specific object has this format:

```
DirectoryEntry entry = new DirectoryEntry();
entry.Path =
        "LDAP://server/CN=Christian Nagel, OU=Authors, DC=Wrox, DC=local";
```

> **With LDAP binding the server name is optional. If no server is specified, the fastest server in the domain is used to answer the request.**

Without changes in the application, we can specify the binding string to a specific object or container object directly in the textbox. With the LDAP binding string LDAP://OU=Wrox Press, DC=eichkogelstrasse, DC=local we get just the organizational unit in the tree view without having to expand the tree:

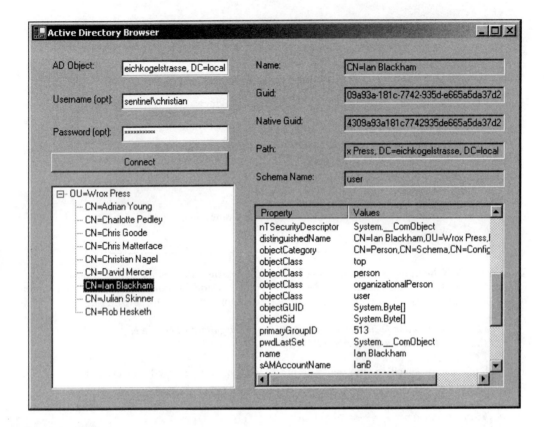

Using ADSI

The classes from the namespace `System.DirectoryServices` are a wrapper to the COM ADSI Library. With the .NET classes we have a very generic class `DirectoryEntry`, which has methods and properties that can be used on every directory object. With ADSI, we have a similar generic COM interface, `IADs`, but with ADSI we also have some object type-specific interfaces. Depending on the object type, some other interfaces are available with ADSI.

`IADsUser` is the interface that is available for user objects. With this interface, we have a lot of properties to access the last name, first name, phone numbers, etc. and methods to change the password. The interface `IADsService` can be used to configure Windows services, while `IADsContainer` is used to create and remove objects in a container. The ADSI interfaces have the advantage that we can use some early-bound interfaces that make development easier because the method names are known at compile time. ADSI objects are also required to access properties of type `System.__ComObject` that we have seen earlier.

You can read more about the ADSI interfaces and objects in "Professional ADSI Programming " (Wrox Press, ISBN 1-861002-26-2).

The `DirectoryEntry` class offers the property `NativeObject` that returns the underlying ADSI object. The object type that is returned by this property is `System.Object`. We can cast the returned object to an ADSI interface. To make the ADSI interfaces available from .NET applications, we have to reference the **Active DS Type Library**, `actaveds.tlb`.

Invoking Methods of ADSI Objects

The `DirectoryEntry` class is so flexible that methods of directory objects can be invoked without the need to use the ADSI interfaces. We just have to know the methods that are available with the selected object. The method can be passed as a string to the `Invoke()` method together with an array of arguments.

By opening a user object in the Active Directory, we have the methods `SetPassword()`, `ChangePassword()`, and `Groups()` as you can see in the documentation for the COM interface `IADsUser`.

The following code examples show how to set the password, how to change the password, and how to get the groups of a user by using the `Invoke()` method of the `DirectoryEntry` class. Because the object that is specified with the `Path` property is a **user object**, we can call the method `SetPassword()` to set the initial password. Of course, the user running this application must be a system administrator.

```
DirectoryEntry entry = new DirectoryEntry();
entry.Path =
  "LDAP://CN=Christian Nagel, OU=Wrox Press, DC=eichkogelstrasse, DC=local";
entry.Invoke("SetPassword", "somesecret");
```

The second code example uses the same directory object, this time to change the password instead of resetting it. To do this, we use the `ChangePassword()` method of the `IADsUser` interface that requires two parameters – the old and the new password. Because the second argument of the `Invoke()` method of `DirectoryEntry` is declared using the `param` keyword, we can pass a variable number of arguments and pass the old and the new password as the second and third arguments.

```
entry.Invoke("ChangePassword", "somesecret", "changingagain");
```

In the third example using the `Invoke()` method, we try to call the `Groups()` method of the `IADsUser` interface. Calling this method is simple, as the example shows; the challenge is to get access to the returned values from the `Groups()` method. The `Groups()` method returns references to the `IADsMembers` interface. The `Invoke()` method itself returns a reference to a `System.Object` instance. Indeed, a COM object can be found in this reference. Now we need to directly use the ADSI interfaces, which we will do next.

```
object groups = entry.Invoke("Groups");
```

Accessing ADSI Interfaces

Instead of calling the methods of the underlying ADSI interfaces by using the `Invoke()` method of the `DirectoryEntry` class, it is also possible to use the underlying interfaces directly. And as you have seen in the last example when calling `Invoke()`, sometimes it is also necessary to use the ADSI interfaces.

As already described earlier, to use the ADSI interfaces we have to reference the Active DS Type Library. Referencing this type library creates a .NET wrapper class with the `ActiveDS` namespace.

In the following code segment, we're carrying out the same action as previously when using the `Invoke()` method. The `NativeObject` property returns a reference to the underlying ADSI object. Because every object implements the `IADs` interface, casting to this interface will always work in the same way as is done here. The object being accessed is a user object, so casting to `IADsUser` also works. The `IADsUser` interface defines the `SetPassword()` method is called next.

```
DirectoryEntry entry = new DirectoryEntry();
entry.Path =
   "LDAP://CN=Christian Nagel, OU=Wrox Press, DC=eichkogelstrasse, DC=local";

ActiveDs.IADs ads = (ActiveDs.IADs)entry.NativeObject;
ActiveDs.IADsUser user = (ActiveDs.IADsUser)ads;

user.SetPassword("SomeSecret");
```

Now that we know how to use ADSI interfaces, let's get some useful information from the `Invoke()` method by calling the `Groups()` method of the ADSI object we created earlier. As has been said, the `Invoke()` method returns an object of type `System.Object`, while the `Groups()` method returns a reference to the `IADsMembers` interface. Using this interface, we can enumerate the groups of a user object as can be seen in the following code example.

Calling `Invoke()` on a `DirectoryEntry` object that represents a user object, and passing a request to call the `Groups` method on the underlying object, returns a reference to the `IADsMember` interface. With the `foreach` statement, we use the enumeration facility of this interface to access every object in this list. Every object in this list implements the interface `IADsGroup`. In the `foreach` code block, we use the `Name` and `ADsPath` property to output values to the console.

```
ActiveDs.IADsMembers members = (ActiveDs.IADsMembers)entry.Invoke("Groups");
foreach (ActiveDs.IADsGroup group in members)
{
   Console.WriteLine(group.Name);
   Console.WriteLine(group.ADsPath);
   Console.WriteLine();
}
```

By running the program, we can see that the specified user object belongs to the groups Domain Admins, Enterprise Admins, and Administrators.

Converting ADSI interfaces to DirectoryEntry objects

We have seen how we can get to the ADSI COM object by using a `DirectoryEntry` object. It is also possible to convert an ADSI interface back to a `DirectoryEntry` object, as a constructor of `DirectoryEntry` accepts an ADSI object. Changing the code from the earlier sample we convert the interface `IADsGroup` back to a `DirectoryEntry` and use this instead.

```
ActiveDs.IADsMembers members = (ActiveDs.IADsMembers)entry.Invoke("Groups");

foreach (ActiveDs.IADsGroup adsGroup in members)
{
    DirectoryEntry group = new DirectoryEntry(adsGroup);
    Console.WriteLine(group.Name);
    Console.WriteLine(group.Path);
    Console.WriteLine();
}
```

Searching

The IIS provider does not support searching for objects, but the LDAP provider does. We can search for objects in the tree by specifying property values for the objects we want to find. The major class used for searching is `DirectorySearcher`.

DirectorySearcher

With the `DirectorySearcher` class, we can search for objects in the tree. In the constructor of the class (as well as by specifying properties) we can restrict the search with these four major parts:

- ❑ The `SearchRoot` defines the `DirectoryEntry` object where the search should start.

- ❑ The `Filter` defines the search string, which defines the objects that should be searched for. We will look at the syntax of the filter in the next section.

- ❑ With `PropertiesToLoad` we define the list of properties that should be returned with the objects where the filter applies. Because a single object can define hundreds of properties, and we are only interested in a few of them, the result set can be reduced by setting `PropertiesToLoad`.

- ❑ `SearchScope` defines the scope of the search, or how deep into the object hierarchy the search should continue.

LDAP Filter

With the LDAP filter we can define the query string of the objects we want to find. In a filter string we define filter expressions enclosed within parentheses. A simple filter looking for all objects with a property sn (surname) set to `Nagel` would look like this:

```
(sn = Nagel)
```

Relational operators, such as <, <=, >, >=, or >, can be used in the filter expression. The following filter looks for all objects that have the property sn >= Nagel, so all objects that have a surname alphabetically equal to and following Nagel match the search.

```
(sn >= Nagel)
```

It is also possible to combine filters with prefix operators & and |. & stands for AND, so that all following filters must match with the object. | is an OR, so that one of the following filters must match.

The following filter looks for all objects where the objectClass=user, and the description=Author. The prefix operator & combines both filter expressions, so that both expressions must be valid for an object to match.

```
(&(objectClass=user)(description=Author))
```

It is also possible to combine the & and | operators in a single filter expression. The following filter specifies the prefix | to accept either building=42 or building=43. The result of the OR operator is combined with objectClass=printer, where the AND operator must match.

```
(&(objectClass=printer)(|(building=42)(building=43)))
```

The default filter is (objectClass=*), so that all objects match the search.

> *The LDAP filter syntax is defined in RFC 2254,* "The String Representation of LDAP Search Filters ". *This RFC can be found at http://www.ietf.org/rfc/rfc2254.txt.*

Active Directory Searcher Application

To start with, we need to create a form for the Active Directory Searcher sample application as shown opposite. The textboxes are going to be used to enter the Root Object in LDAP syntax, and the LDAP filter string. The Search Scope can be selected by using a combobox containing three values. Finally, property values that should be returned can be added to the property list. Clicking the Start the Search button starts the search using the DirectorySearcher class, and lists the returned objects in the Returned objects listbox. Selecting an object in this listbox displays the properties of this object in the Properties / Values listview.

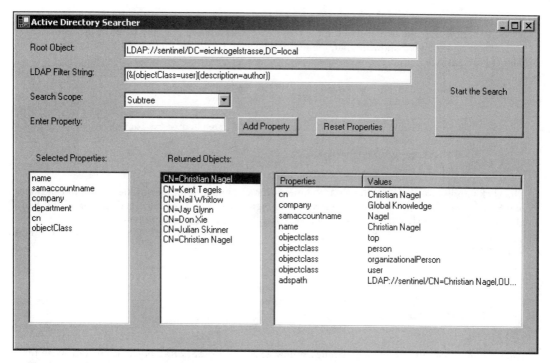

The names for the controls shown above are listed in the following table:

Type	Property	Property Value
TextBox	Name	textLDAPPath
TextBox	Name	textLDAPFilter
ComboBox	Name	comboBoxSearchScope
TextBox	Name	textProperty
Button	Name	buttonAddProperty
	Text	Add Property
Button	Name	buttonResetProperties
	Text	Reset Properties
Button	Name	buttonStart
	Text	Start the Search
ListBox	Name	listBoxProperties
ListBox	Name	listBoxObjects
ListView	Name	listViewProperties

With the form created, let's look at some of the code segments. The `Click` handler for the **Add Property** button adds the text entered in the textbox, `textProperty`, to the items of the listbox, `listBoxProperties`. Following that, the textbox is cleared and the focus is set back to the textbox so the user can easily enter additional properties.

```
private void buttonAddProperty_Click(object sender,
    System.EventArgs e)
{
    this.listBoxProperties.Items.Add(this.textProperty.Text);
    this.textProperty.Clear();
    this.textProperty.Focus();
}
```

The click handler for the **Start the Search** button first clears the objects from the listbox in case there had been a previous search. Also, the private field member `searchResults` is disposed of, if it had also been set previously with a search. `searchResults` is a private field of type `System.DirectoryServices.SearchResultCollection` that is kept after a search and is used to display the properties.

```
private void buttonStart_Click(object sender, System.EventArgs e)
{
    this.listBoxObjects.Items.Clear();
    if (searchResults != null)
        searchResults.Dispose();
```

After the resetting of the previous searches, a new `DirectorySearcher` object is created. With the `DirectorySearcher` object, the `SearchRoot` property is set to the value entered in the `textLDAPPath` textbox, the `Filter` property is set to the value entered in the `textLDAPFilter` textbox, and the `SearchScope` property is set to the value selected from the combobox. The properties that should be returned with the found objects are added to the `PropertiesToLoad` collection.

```
try
{
    using (DirectorySearcher searcher = new DirectorySearcher())
    {
        searcher.SearchRoot =
            new DirectoryEntry(this.textLDAPPath.Text);

        searcher.Filter = this.textLDAPFilter.Text;

        string scope =
            this.comboBoxSearchScope.SelectedItem.ToString();
        searcher.SearchScope =
            (SearchScope)SearchScope.Parse(typeof(SearchScope),
                                           scope);

        foreach (string prop in this.listBoxProperties.Items)
        {
            searcher.PropertiesToLoad.Add(prop);
        }
```

The `FindAll()` method returns all objects in the `searchResults` member variable. `searchResults` is of type `SearchResultCollection`, and includes all found objects with the defined properties. Because the `DirectorySearcher` object is no longer needed at this point, the `using` block is closed so that this object will be disposed of.

```
            searchResults = searcher.FindAll();
    }
```

In a `foreach` statement, the `SearchResultCollection` is now used to display all resultant objects. Every object is kept in an instance of the class `System.DirectoryServices.SearchResult`. We get to the `DirectoryEntry` instance by calling the method `GetDirectoryEntry()`. The `Name` property of the `DirectoryEntry` class is used as the value to display for the items in the listbox.

```
        foreach (SearchResult result in searchResults)
        {
            this.listBoxObjects.Items.Add(
                result.GetDirectoryEntry().Name);
        }
    }
```

We catch every exception thrown in the exception handler inside the `buttonStart_Click()` event handler. If the user enters a wrong LDAP binding string, or the LDAP filter string has a wrong syntax, we handle the exception here to display an error message:

```
        catch (Exception ex)
        {
            MessageBox.Show(ex.Message, "AD Searcher",
                    MessageBoxButtons.OK, MessageBoxIcon.Exclamation);
        }
    }
```

The last method of this sample application is the `SelectedIndexChanged` event handler of the object listbox. The first action taken within this method is to clear the listview that displays the properties that were displayed previously.

```
        private void OnSelection(object sender, System.EventArgs e)
        {
            this.listViewProperties.Items.Clear();
```

Then we get the selected index of the listbox for the use of the indexer in the `searchResults` member variable that was stored in the `buttonStart_Click()` method. The indexer of the `SearchResultCollection` class returns a `SearchResult`. The `SearchResult` represents a single object that is found in the tree. Compared to the `DirectoryEntry` class, we only have the properties that were specified with the search available with this class.

```
            int sel = this.listBoxObjects.SelectedIndex;

            SearchResult result = searchResults[sel];
```

363

The `Properties` property of the `SearchResult` class returns a `ResultPropertyCollection` that includes all properties that were specified with the search and are available with the object. We use this `ResultPropertyCollection` to get to all names of the properties by using the `PropertyNames` property in a `foreach` statement. The indexer of the `ResultPropertyCollection` passes a `PropertyName` to get to all the `values` of a single property represented in the class `ResultPropertyValueCollection`. All the values of the property are displayed in the listview.

```
ResultPropertyCollection properties = result.Properties;

foreach (object prop in properties.PropertyNames)
{
   ResultPropertyValueCollection values =
      properties[prop.ToString()];
   foreach (object val in values)
   {
      string[] items = new string[2];
      items[0] = prop.ToString();
      items[1] = val.ToString();
      this.listViewProperties.Items.Add(
         new ListViewItem(items));
   }
}
}
```

Search Limits

In addition to the search restrictions that can be set with the constructor, we have additional search restrictions that can be set with properties of the `DirectorySearcher` class.

With the `SizeLimit` property you can set the maximum number of objects returned by a search. The default server limit is 1000 objects, and you cannot set this value any higher.

Another way to restrict the search result is by specifying the time the server takes to carry out the search. By setting the `ServerTimeLimit` property to a `TimeSpan` value, you can restrict the time the server takes to return the objects. When the limit is reached, the objects found so far are returned to the client. Unfortunately, it is not possible to continue the search if it was ended by a time or size limit. To continue the search, you need to start the second search without accessing the objects that were already returned. To do this, you can use a paged search.

Paged Search

With a paged search, the server searches until either a maximum number of objects are found, or a time out is reached. The objects found up to this point are returned to the client. Unlike the `ServerTimeLimit` property, with a paged search the search can continue where it left off.

To do a paged search, you can set the `PageSize` property of the `DirectorySearcher` class to the value of how many objects should be returned. The first call to `FindAll()` returns the maximum number of objects that is specified with `PageSize`; a second call to `FindAll()` continues where the first call finished to return the next objects.

Instead of doing a count limit page search, you can do a time limit page search. Here you have to set the `ServerPageTimeLimit` property instead of `PageSize`.

Paged Search does not work with the Beta 2 version of Visual Studio .NET.

Global Catalog

If a search for an object spans multiple domains, the search can take quite a long time. For faster searches, the Active Directory has a **global catalog** that consists of copies of all the objects and selected properties of all the domains in an enterprise. When defining a property in the Active Directory schema, whether the property should be included in the global catalog can be set. This is useful for properties that are often used in searches.

Instead of hopping from one server to the next when searching in multiple domains, you can use the global catalog to search by replacing `LDAP` in the binding string with `GC`. However, the global catalog is a read-only cache, so changing objects inside this cache is not possible.

You can read more about the Global Catalog and the replication features of the Active Directory in "Professional C# " *(Wrox Press, ISBN 1-861004-99-0).*

Publishing Services

The remainder of this chapter will demonstrate further sample applications of how the Active Directory can be used. The first example shows how and why it can be useful to publish connection information from a remoting service. We will not elaborate on writing a remoting service, as you can read about creating such services in "*Professional C# Web Services*" (Wrox Press, ISBN 1-861004-39-7), but will discuss where such a service can take advantage of the Directory Service.

A remoting service offers remote objects that can be called across the network. A remote object defines the public methods that can be called across a TCP, HTTP, or custom channel as defined by the remoting server. The client that connects to the remoting object must know the necessary URL for the remote object. An example looks like this: `TCP://CNagel/ServerName/RemoteObject` where `TCP:` defines the protocol used, followed by the host name (`CNagel`), the application name (`ServerName`), and the endpoint name of the remote object.

The remote server can offer the endpoint name that the client needs to connect to by writing it to the Active Directory. However, before we attempt to extend the schema of the Active Directory, we should always check if the type already exists. **Service connection points** that can be used by RPC servers and socket servers are already defined. We can use these existing types without a need to define new schema types.

Service Connection Points

Service connection points can store information about service names and connection information in the Active Directory. `connectionPoint` is the base type for service connection points defined in the Active Directory. The following diagram illustrates the class hierarchy of connection point types.

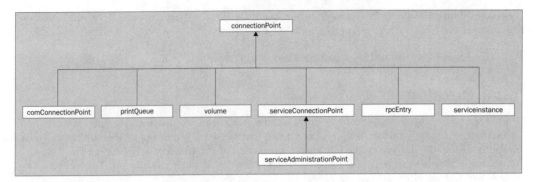

The diagram shows the connection point types derived from the `ConnectionPoint` type.
`comConnectionPoint` can be used from COM servers. `printQueue` makes it possible to search for a
printer with specific capabilities like double sided or color printing. `volume` defines disk drives for a
RAID system. RPC servers that write binding information to a naming server use the `rpcEntry` type.
We will use the `serviceConnectionPoint` for a .NET remoting server.

In order to make use of the type `serviceConnectionPoint`, two programs need to be created:

❑ The installation program of the service that will create the service connection point to write
the binding information to the Directory Service

❑ The client application that can search the Directory Service to get the binding information
from the server

Registering the Service

The service shouldn't be registered in the service program when it is started the first time, because the
account that is used to run the service may not have the required privileges to write entries to the Active
Directory. Instead, the registration should be the job of the installation program. A requirement of the
installation program is that the user starting this application must have rights to write new entries to the
Active Directory (such as the Domain Administrator). We will write a small helper class that will be
invoked from the installation program to register the endpoint of the service into the Active Directory.

The `RemoteServiceInstaller` class writes the name of the remote object to a service connection
point object in the Active Directory using the `CreateServiceConnectionPoint()` method.

The `CreateServiceConnectionPoint()` method has some arguments: the name of the directory
entry object, the endpoint of the remote object, and an array of keywords that can be used for searching
this directory entry instance. The endpoint of the remote object is made up of the following items:
protocol, host name, port number, remote application name, and the remote object name.

```
using System;
using System.Net;
using System.DirectoryServices;

namespace Wrox.ProCSharpData.Chapter9.RemoteServiceExample
{
    class RemoteServiceInstaller
```

```
{
    public string CreateServiceConnectionPoint(string name,
        string protocol, string hostname, string port,
        string application, string remoteObject, object[] keywords)
    {
```

In this method we first get the domain name of the Directory Service where the user is logged on. The LDAP name of the Directory Service is a property of the `rootDSE` object. LDAP 3.0 defines the binding name `rootDSE` as the root of a directory tree. The property `defaultNamingContext` returns the LDAP name of the Directory Service; in my case it is `DC=eichkogelstrasse, DC=local`. This property value is stored in the variable `namingContext`.

```
// get the default naming context
DirectoryEntry root = new DirectoryEntry("LDAP://rootDSE");
string namingContext =
    root.Properties["defaultNamingContext"].Value.ToString();
```

Now this domain name can be used to connect to the computer object. The name of the host where the remote object is running is passed with the variable `hostname`. We use this variable to bind to the computer object that is inside the container `Computers`. The connection string can look like this if the host name is, for example, `celticrain`: `LDAP://CN=celticrain, CN=Computers, DC=eichkogelstrasse, DC=local`.

```
// connect to the computer object
DirectoryEntry computerEntry = new DirectoryEntry();
string path = "LDAP://CN=" + hostname + ",CN=Computers, " +
                                                namingContext;
computerEntry.Path = path;
```

In the container object, a new service connection point can be created. The `Children` property of the `computerEntry` object returns a `DirectoryEntries` collection. We use the `Add()` method to create a new directory object with a name that is set in the variable name, and we use the type `serviceConnectionPoint` that is defined in the schema. Now we can fill the properties of the `serviceConnectionPoint` object. `ServiceDNSName` defines the host name of the service.

```
// create a new serviceConnectionPoint object
DirectoryEntry serviceEntry =
    computerEntry.Children.Add("CN=" + name,
                               "serviceConnectionPoint");
serviceEntry.Properties["serviceDNSName"].Add(hostname);
```

The heart of the `serviceConnectionPoint` object is the `serviceBindingInformation` property. This is a multi-valued property where the complete binding information can be defined. How the binding information looks depends on the type of the service. To connect to a simple socket server we have to know the host name and the port number. With a .NET Remoting server, additional information, like the type of the remote object, the application name, and the remote object name, must be set. How we add the information to this property is not defined, the only requirement we have is that the client of the service must know how to interpret the information.

Next, we specify the protocol, port number, and server, application, and object names using the
`serviceBindingInformation` property.

```
        // write binding information
        PropertyValueCollection bindingInformation =
            serviceEntry.Properties["serviceBindingInformation"];
        bindingInformation.Add("protocol=" + protocol);
        bindingInformation.Add("port=" + port);
        bindingInformation.Add("server=" + hostname);
        bindingInformation.Add("application=" + application);
        bindingInformation.Add("object=" + remoteObject);
        serviceEntry.Properties["serviceClassName"].Add(
                                    ".NET Remoting Service");
```

The `keywords` property is another multi-valued property of the `serviceConnectionPoint` object.
The values of this property are written to the global catalog, so the client can use these values for a fast
search to get the `serviceConnectionPoint`. You can enter all the information that you think may be
useful to find the service; for example, this could be the company name of the service publisher, or
keywords that tell about the functionality of the service. We are going to use the `AddRange()` method
to write the object array `keywords` that was defined with the declaration of the method
`CreateServiceConnectionPoint()`.

```
        serviceEntry.Properties["keywords"].AddRange(keywords);
```

No information is written to the Active Directory until we call `CommitChanges()` to flush the cache.
After flushing the cache we return the dynamically created GUID of the directory object to the caller of
the method.

```
        // write the object to the store
        serviceEntry.CommitChanges();

        return serviceEntry.NativeGuid;
    }
```

The `Main()` method of this installation application does nothing more than call
`CreateServiceConnectionPoint()` to create a new directory object. We use the static method
`GetHostName()` of the class `Dns` to get the host name of the local host where the service is going to be
installed. Then, we define keywords that are going to be passed to the
`CreateServiceConnectionPoint()` method that can be used to search for the service. Instead of
searching for the service it would also be possible to write the GUID that is returned from the method to a
configuration file to have fast access to the connection point object without the necessity to do a search.

```
    [STAThread]
    static void Main(string[] args)
    {
        try
        {
            // get hostname of localhost
            string hostname = Dns.GetHostName();

            string[] keywords = {"Wrox Press", "Math"};
```

```
                    // create the service connection point
                    RemoteServiceInstaller installer =
                                          new RemoteServiceInstaller();

                    string guid = installer.CreateServiceConnectionPoint(
                          "MyRemoteService", "tcp", hostname, "9000",
                          "MyRemoteServer", "MyRemoteObject", keywords);

                    Console.WriteLine("Created object: " + guid);

                }
                catch (Exception ex)
                {
                    Console.WriteLine(ex.Message);
                }
            }
        }
    }
```

Deleting the Service

The uninstall program of the service must also remove the directory entry for the service connection point in the Active Directory. For this purpose, we add the method RemoveServiceConnectionPoint() to the class RemoteServiceInstaller. This method gets the name of the directory entry and the host name as parameters. As in the previous methods we have implemented, we obtain the name of the Directory Service by using the rootDSE object. Next, we connect to the computer object, and use the Remove() method of the DirectoryEntries class to remove the child of the computer object that corresponds to our service connection point.

```
        public void RemoveServiceConnectionPoint(string name,
                                                 string hostname)
        {
            // get the default naming context
            DirectoryEntry root = new DirectoryEntry("LDAP://rootDSE");
            string namingContext =
                root.Properties["defaultNamingContext"].Value.ToString();

            // connect to the computer object
            DirectoryEntry computerEntry = new DirectoryEntry();
            string path = "LDAP://CN=" + hostname + ",CN=Computers, " +
                namingContext;
            computerEntry.Path = path;

            DirectoryEntry serviceEntry = new DirectoryEntry();
            serviceEntry.Path = "LDAP://CN=" + name + ",CN=" + hostname +
                ",CN=Computers, " + namingContext;
            computerEntry.Children.Remove(serviceEntry);

            computerEntry.CommitChanges();
        }
```

Searching for the Service

The client application that wants to access the remoting object can now use a search in the Active Directory to find the name of the server and the endpoint name of the remote object. To make a fast search, the global catalog can be used as all properties we want to access are written to this catalog.

We'll create a method `GetConnectionString()` in the class `SearchService` to be used in a .NET Remoting client application that returns a `NameValueCollection` with the binding information needed.

As in the previous example we use the `rootDSE` binding string to the default naming context. If the user of the client system is not logged on to the domain, we may have to get the domain name in a different way, such as through a configuration file. Then we connect to the `Computers` object in this domain, as we will start our search for the binding information below this object. It is not necessary to search the complete domain tree, as the binding information is the child of a `Computer` object.

```
using System;
using System.DirectoryServices;
using System.Collections.Specialized;

namespace Wrox.ProCSharpData.Chapter9.RemoteClientExample
{
    class SearchService
    {
        public NameValueCollection GetConnectionString(string keyword)
        {
            // get the default naming context
            DirectoryEntry root = new DirectoryEntry("LDAP://rootDSE");
            string namingContext =
                root.Properties["defaultNamingContext"].Value.ToString();

            DirectoryEntry rootEntry =
                new DirectoryEntry("GC://CN=Computers," + namingContext);
```

Next, we create a `DirectorySearcher` object and set the `SearchRoot` property to the object that was returned in the previous call. The `Filter` property defines that we are only interested in objects of type `serviceConnectionPoint`, and the `keywords` property must be set to a value that is passed by calling the method `GetConnectionString()`. We are only interested in the values of the property `serviceBindingInformation`, so this property is added to `PropertiesToLoad`. The search should go into all children of the `Computers` object, so the scope is set to `Subtree`. Calling `FindOne()` returns a `SearchResult` object that matches the request.

```
            DirectorySearcher searcher = new DirectorySearcher();
            searcher.SearchRoot = rootEntry;
            searcher.Filter =
                "(&(objectClass=serviceConnectionPoint)(keywords=" +
                    keyword + "))";

            searcher.PropertiesToLoad.Add("serviceBindingInformation");
            searcher.SearchScope = SearchScope.Subtree;
            SearchResult result = searcher.FindOne();
```

The `Properties` property of the `SearchResult` class returns a `ResultPropertyCollection`. We can use the indexer of this class to get the values that are stored in the directory object property `serviceBindingInformation`. The indexer returns a `ResultPropertyValueCollection` so that we can get all the values of this directory object property.

```
ResultPropertyCollection serviceProperties = result.Properties;

ResultPropertyValueCollection bindingInformation =
    serviceProperties["serviceBindingInformation"];
```

Finally, we need to create a new `NameValueCollection` object that stores all keys and values of the binding information. The binding information is stored with an = sign between the key and the value, for example `port=9000`, so we can split the string returned using the `Split()` method of the string class.

```
NameValueCollection bindingKeysAndValues =
    new NameValueCollection();
foreach (string binding in bindingInformation)
{
    string[] s = binding.Split('=');
    bindingKeysAndValues.Add(s[0], s[1]);
}

return bindingKeysAndValues;
        }
    }
}
```

The client can now use the binding information inside the `NameValueCollection` class to connect to the remote server. If for some reason the host name of the server changes, no changes are required in the client code or configuration. The client will get the host name from the Directory Service at run time.

Summary

In this chapter we have seen how to use the classes from the `System.DirectoryServices` namespace to access Directory Services. These classes are a small wrapper to the underlying ADSI COM objects, so we also looked at how to access these underlying objects. The `DirectoryEntry` class allows direct access of the ADSI COM objects.

The classes from the namespace `System.DirectoryServices` are used to read, write, and search objects in a Directory Service. The most important classes for these tasks are `DirectoryEntry` and `DirectorySearcher`.

With the `DirectoryEntry` and `DirectoryEntries` classes we walked through the hierarchy of a Directory Service and read the properties. We used the `DirectorySearcher` class to search for objects with a specified filter.

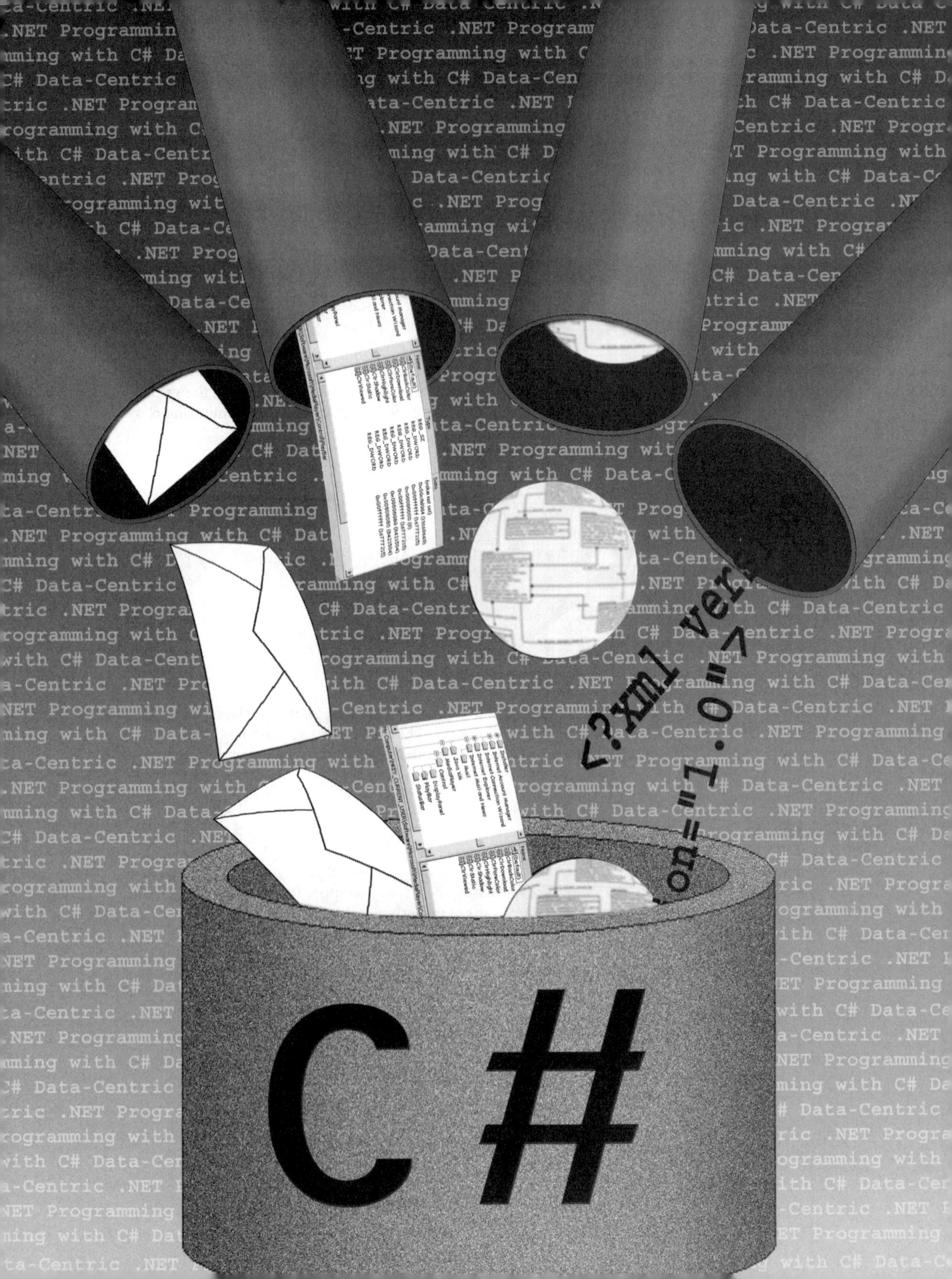
Data-Centric .NET Programming with C#
<?xml ver
on="1.0"?>
C#

Messaging Services

In this chapter we'll discuss how to use **Message Queuing 2.0**, the messaging services that are part of the Windows 2000 operating system, from the .NET Framework. As we'll elaborate below, messaging is used for **asynchronous**, **disconnected** environments and offers great services for enterprise applications.

In particular, we will look at:

❑ Messaging services in general, and Message Queuing 2.0 for Windows 2000 – including the different versions available, the underlying architecture, and some of the associated tools

❑ How to use Message Queuing with the classes in the `System.Messaging` namespace to send and to receive messages, and to control message queues

❑ How to use **Queued Components**, a feature of COM+ that abstracts Message Queuing

To demonstrate the use of messaging services we'll look at a Windows Forms-based simple book ordering application, which will allow us to send orders to a messaging queue and then to retrieve them.

> *Please note that at the time of going to press, there were issues with the support of Queued Components in Visual Studio .NET RC1. In light of this, users of RC1 may experience difficulties will the latter sections of the chapter that deal with Queued Components. Updates to this chapter will be available from www.wrox.com.*

Messaging Services

Before we dive into programming, let's first discuss the basic concepts of this chapter.

When we call a method, the program usually waits until the method is completed before continuing. This is called **synchronous programming**. With **asynchronous** programming, the client can call a method on a server, and then continue with other processing while it waits for the server to complete the call. Messaging services are not required for asynchronous programming, since the .NET Framework already provides a lot of support – for example, classes in the `System.IO` and `System.Net` namespaces that have methods like `BeginRead()` and `BeginReceive()` start an asynchronous operation. It is also possible to call any method asynchronously with the help of delegates. You can read more about delegates in "*Professional C#*" (Wrox Press, ISBN 1-861004-99-0).

Although messaging services operate asynchronously, as the client (sender) does not wait for the server (receiver) to read the data that is sent to it, there is a crucial difference between messaging services and asynchronous programming: message queuing can be done in a disconnected environment. At the time we send data, the receiver can be offline. Later, when the receiver goes online, it receives the data without the sending application intervening.

We can compare connected and disconnected programming with the example of a phone and a fax machine. When talking to someone on the phone, both participants must be connected at the same time. The communication is **synchronous**. When sending a fax, the sender isn't sure if the message will be dealt with immediately, as the fax could be read sometime after it was sent; people using this technology are working in a disconnected mode. Of course, the fax message may never be dealt with – it may be ignored. That's in the nature of disconnected communication. To avoid this problem we can ask for a reply to confirm that the message has been read. If the answer doesn't arrive within a time limit, we need to deal with this 'exception'. The same is true with message queuing.

In some ways, message services are e-mail for application-to-application communication, instead of person-to-person communication. However, this gives us a lot of features that are not available with mailing services, such as guaranteed delivery and transactions. As we see in the next section, messaging services have a lot of features useful for communication between applications.

With Message Queuing we can send, receive, and route messages in a connected or disconnected environment. Looking at Message Queuing from a very distant viewpoint we can describe it with the next picture. The sending application creates a message and sends it to the message queue; the receiving application reads messages by receiving it from the queue:

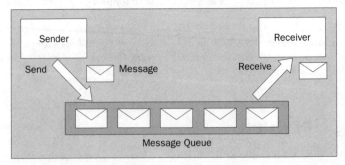

The COM+ Service **Queued Components (QC)** is an abstraction layer to Message Queuing. With QC the client can call a method on the component and return immediately, but behind the scenes a message is created that is passed into the message queue. At a later time when the queue is read, the method is called at the real component. Queued Components have the advantage that we no longer have to deal with messages – we can treat them as regular method calls. We will talk about Queued Components in the second part of this chapter.

Where to Use Messaging Services

One case where Messaging Services can be used is in this example environment. A sales person is at a customer's site with a notebook and inputs a customer's order. The notebook is not connected to the company's network. But that's not a problem: the application sends the order as if it were online. As soon as the sales person is back in the office and connects the notebook to the network, the order will be transferred to the target system. There is no need for the application to keep running and check for a network connection to send the messages as soon as it is possible, because this is a service of the operating system.

Besides using a notebook, the sales person could also use a Pocket Windows device. Message Queuing is available on this device, too. Here's a diagram of what's happening: potentially both the notebook and the server queue up messages, to be exchanged when the connection is established:

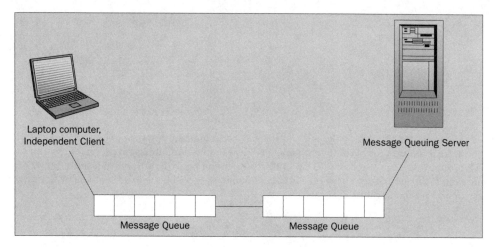

Laptop computer,
Independent Client

Message Queuing Server

Message Queue   Message Queue

Messaging Services can also be useful in connected environments. Imagine an e-commerce site where the server is fully loaded with order transactions at certain times, say early evening and weekends, but the load is low at night times. A solution could be to buy a faster server or add additional servers to the system so that the peaks can be handled. But there's a cheaper solution: flatten the peak loads by moving transactions from the times with high loads to the times with lower loads. In this scheme, we would send the orders to the message queue, and the receiving side reads the orders at the rates that are useful for the database system. The load of the system is now flattened over time so that the server dealing with the transactions can be a less expensive than upgrading the database server(s).

The following figure shows a web server that is using a message queue to store received orders:

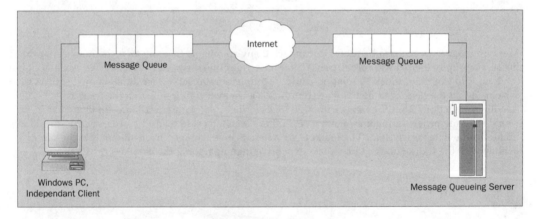

If systems or networks occasionally fail and there is no immediate response required, messaging services can be a great solution for partner companies. With Windows XP, messaging services can run using the HTTP protocol. On the Windows PC on the left side of the figure below, messages can be sent to the queue even if the network or the server is not available; they will be delivered at a later time when the server can be reached again.

Message Queuing can also be used to communicate with IBM's messaging services product **MQSeries**. Microsoft offers a Message Queue–MQSeries Bridge for the Host Integration Server (former SNA Server) to address IBM's queues so that they can be accessed like Microsoft Message Queues:

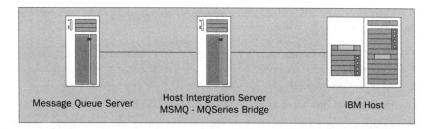

Message Queue Server   Host Intergration Server   IBM Host
MSMQ - MQSeries Bridge

Turning around from the IBM host to the small devices, Pocket Windows also has Message Queuing support built in. A Pocket Windows device can act as a client to messaging services.

Message Queuing Features

Message Queuing is part of Windows 2000. The main features of this service are:

❑ Messages can be sent in a **disconnected** environment; it's not necessary that the sending and receiving application are running at the same time.

❑ With the **express mode,** messages can be sent very fast. Recoverable messages are stored within files; express messages only use memory.

❑ Using recoverable messages we have **guaranteed delivery**. The message will be delivered even if the server crashes.

❑ Message Queues can be **secured** with access control lists to restrict which users can send or receive messages from a queue. You can also encrypt the messages to be sent, so that it is not possible for network monitors to read the data.

❑ Messages can be sent with **priorities** to handle high priority items faster.

❑ With **transactional** message queues, messages can take part in a COM+ Transaction.

We will discuss these features and how they are dealt with programmatically later in this chapter.

Product Versions and Installation

Message Queuing 2.0 is part of Windows 2000, and is the successor to Microsoft Message Queuing (MSMQ) 1.0. Some articles use the term MSMQ to refer to Message Queuing 2.0.

We can install Message Queuing 2.0 with Add / Remove Programs in Control Panel or with Start | Programs | Administrative Tools | Configure your Server, and choosing the Advanced options.

MSMQ 1.0 was delivered with the Option Pack for Windows NT 4.0. MSMQ 1.0 used SQL Server to store its message queues. A Message Queuing server in Windows 2000 uses Active Directory instead, which we saw in the previous chapter.

If Active Directory isn't installed, we can still install Message Queuing in a Workgroup environment. Working this way creates the following restrictions:

❑ We can only use private queues. This means that you cannot search for a queue, but must always access it only by knowing the queue and server name. We will explore searching for queues later in the chapter.

❑ We cannot secure the queue with an access control list (ACL).

With Active Directory, you must first install the Message Queuing Server on a Windows 2000 domain controller.

> **In this chapter we will use Message Queuing in an Active Directory configuration. If you don't have the Active Directory installed, nearly all the code samples run with minor changes using private queues.**

Installing Message Queuing with Windows 2000 gives you the following three product options depending on the target platform, as you can see in this table:

Message Queuing Component	Windows 2000 Platform
Message Queuing Server	Windows 2000 Server, Windows 2000 Advanced Server
Dependent Client	Windows 2000 Professional, Windows XP Professional, Windows 2000 Server, Windows 2000 Advanced Server
Independent Client	Windows 2000 Professional, Windows XP Professional

The message queuing client is also supported on Windows 98 and Windows ME operating systems, but not for Windows XP Personal Edition.

Message Queuing Server

Message Queuing Server requires a Server edition of Windows 2000. To use queuing, the network must have at least one Message Queuing Server.

The Message Queuing Server can:

❑ Send and receive messages

❑ Store messages in local queues

❑ Route messages to other servers

Furthermore, the Message Queuing Server has a client proxy server to support dependent clients.

Dependent Client

A dependent client always needs a connection to a Message Queuing server. It cannot work in a disconnected environment because it has no message store. The Message Queuing dependent client sends and receives messages to and from a server.

The dependent client has the API calls to send and receive messages to a Message Queuing Server. Part of the product of the dependent client is a client proxy. A client proxy connects to its server counterpart, the client proxy server. The client proxy server is running on the Message Queuing Server.

Independent Client

The independent client can send messages without being connected to a server.

The Message Queuing independent client can:

❑   Send and receive messages

❑   Store messages in local queues

❑   Operate in a disconnected environment

The independent client has no support for dependent clients.

> *When installing Message Queuing on a Notebook with Windows 2000 Professional, you should go for the independent client because it can work in a disconnected environment.*

Message Queuing Architecture

A .NET application can use the `System.Messaging` namespace, in which we find a lot of classes such as `Message` and `MessageQueue` necessary to program using Message Queuing. The classes from this namespace make use of the **Message Queuing API** calls to create and to control messages. The Message Queuing API is the programming interface to the Message Queuing Library where the main tasks that can be done are opening and closing queues, and sending and receiving messages. The Message Queuing Library sends requests to the **Message Queuing Service** that you can see in the MMC-snap in Services in the picture below. You can start the Administrative tool by selecting Start | Settings | Control Panel | Administrative Tools | Services on a Windows 2000 Server system. The Message Queuing Service can communicate with other Message Queuing Services across the network to route messages, and it also writes and reads messages from message queues.

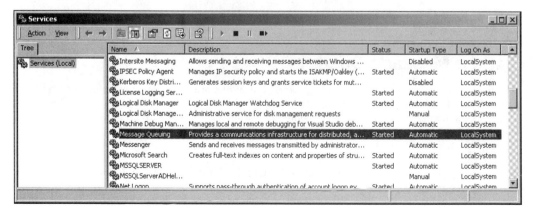

So while we only need to worry about using .NET System.Messaging namespace, there's a lot more going on behind the scenes. The following image shows these underlying layers:

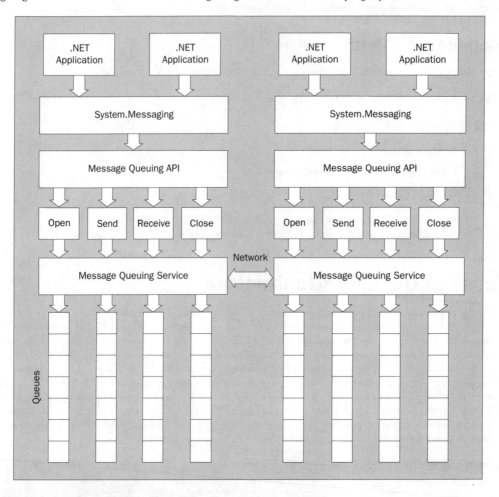

What's a Message Queue?

The message queue is a temporary message store. For public queues, the names of the queues are stored in the Active Directory, but the messages are stored in the file system or just in memory. Thus the messages can be persistent or volatile, depending on whether they are stored in the file system or in memory. The default location for the messages that are stored in the file system is C:\Winnt\System32\msmq\STORAGE.

We can secure a queue with access control lists (ACL). With the ACL we can define the permissions of a user or user group. For message queues we have permissions to receive and peek messages (read messages without removing it from the queue), to write messages, to get and set properties, and more.

Message Queue Types

To send and receive messages we usually use public and private queues. But there are a lot more queue types available:

- ❏ Public
- ❏ Private
- ❏ Journal
- ❏ Dead-letter
- ❏ Administration
- ❏ Response
- ❏ Report
- ❏ System

Let's look into the purposes of these queue types.

- ❏ A **public queue** is published in the Active Directory. Information about these queues is replicated across a Windows 2000 domain. We can use browsing and searching features to get information about these queues. A public queue can be accessed without knowing the name of the computer where it is placed. It's also possible to move such a queue from one system to another without the client knowing it. It's not possible to create public queues in a workgroup environment because public queues are published in the Active Directory. We saw how to access the Active Directory programmatically in the previous chapter.

- ❏ **Private queues** are not published in the Active Directory. These queues can only be accessed knowing the full path name to the queue. It is possible to use this queue type in a workgroup environment.

- ❏ A **journal queue** keeps copies of the messages after they are received. Enabling journaling for a public or private queue automatically creates a journal queue. If a journal queue is enabled, copies of the messages are stored within this queue. We have to differentiate between source and target journaling. **Source journaling** is turned on with the properties of a message; the journal messages are stored in the source system. **Target journaling** is turned on with the properties of a queue; these messages are stored in the journal queue of the target system.

- ❏ If a message doesn't arrive at the target system before the specified timeout is reached, the message is stored in the **dead-letter queue**. You can check the dead-letter queue for messages that didn't arrive.

  For transactional messages that didn't arrive, there's a separate **transactional dead-letter queue**. We will talk about transactional messages later.

- ❏ **Administration queues** contain acknowledgements for messages sent. The sender can specify an administration queue from which it receives notification whether if the message was sent successfully or not.

- ❏ If more than a simple acknowledgement is needed as answer from the receiver, a **response queue** can be used, where the receiving application can send a response message back to the sending application.

❑ A **report queue** is used for test messages. You can create a report queue by changing the type (or category) of a public or private queue to the predefined ID {55EE8F33-CCE9-11CF-B108-0020AFD61CE9}. Report queues are useful as a testing tool to track messages on their route.

❑ **System queues** are private queues that are used by the message queuing system. These queues are used for administrative messages, storing of notification messages, and to guarantee the correct order of transactional messages.

What's in a Message?

A message is defined by its properties. Included in these properties is the **label** that corresponds to the title of the message, and a **body** that is the data sent. In this body we can put information of any type – there's just the requirement that we know how to read it again. In addition to the label and the body the message describes further data such as information about the sender, timeout configurations, transaction ID, or priority.

Message Types

We have to differentiate messages into the following types that Microsoft messaging services define:

❑ A **normal message** is one that's sent by an application. Such a message doesn't hold status information.

❑ An **acknowledgement message** reports the status of a normal message. These messages are sent to administration queues, reporting success or failure of sending normal messages.

❑ The sending application can specify a response queue to get an answer from the receiving application. The receiver sends a **response message** to this queue.

❑ A **report message** is generated by the Message Queuing system. Test messages and route-tracking messages belong to this category.

Message Priority

A message can have a priority that defines the order in which the messages will be read from the queue. The messages will be sorted in the queue according to their priority; so by reading the next message from the queue you will get the message with the highest priority.

Message Delivery

The delivery mode defines how the message is sent to the queue. There are two different delivery modes:

❑ With **express mode,** messages are transmitted very fast because only memory is used for a message store.

❑ With the **recoverable mode,** the messages are stored in files at every step along the route until they are delivered. This way delivery of the messages is assured, even with a computer crash or network failure.

More guarantees are given with a special version of recoverable mode: transactional messaging. Using transactional messaging, it is guaranteed that messages arrive only once, and in the same order that the messages were sent, regardless of the priority.

Message Queuing Administrative Tools

As we now know about the principles of message queuing, let's see how we can create and configure queues using administrative tools.

Creating Message Queues

With the Computer Management MMC snap-in we can create and configure message queues. On a Windows 2000 System, Computer Management can be started with Start | Settings | Control Panel | Administrative Tools | Computer Management. In the Tree View pane, you can open Services and Applications. If Message Queuing is installed, you can see a Message Queuing entry. Selecting Public Queues, with Action | New | Public Queue, the following dialog comes up to create a new queue:

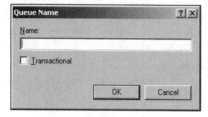

Set the name to WroxTest and press the OK button.

Message Queue Properties

After a queue is created, we can modify the queue's properties with the Computer Management snap-in by selecting the queue in the tree pane, and selecting Action | Properties:

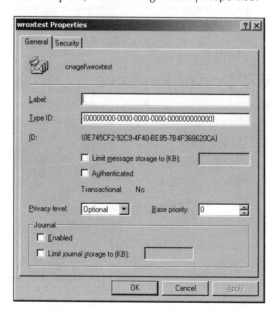

We can configure several options:

❑   We can define a Label, a string used to identify the queue during a search.

❑   We can set a Type ID to group multiple queues to one category. With programmatic interfaces, we can search for all queues of a specific type. Report queues use a specific type ID as we have seen earlier. A Type ID is a universal unique ID (UUID).

> *To create our own type IDs we can use the* uuidgen.exe *or* guidgen.exe *tools.* uuidgen.exe *is a command-line utility to create UUIDs,* guidgen.exe *is the graphical version to create UUIDs where the UUID can be easily used with copy and paste. Both tools can be optionally installed as part of the Platform SDK, and can be found in the directory* <Program Files>\Microsoft Platform SDK\bin.

❑   So as not to fill the disk with messages, we can specify a maximum size for the message store, using the Limit the message storage to (KB) option. On Windows 2000 the maximum size of the message store is 2GB, but this limit is removed with Windows XP. Setting this limitation is a good way to avoid filling up the disk if a program sends excessive messages in a loop.

❑   By selecting Authenticated, messages from non-authenticated users will not be accepted. We can define the users that are allowed to write messages to the queue in the Security tab of this administration tool.

❑   The Privacy Level can be set to None, Optional, or Body. The privacy level defines if the queue accepts messages that are encrypted. Setting the value None means that no encrypted messages are accepted, Body accepts *only* encrypted messages, and the default Optional accepts both.

❑   The Base Priority specifies how routing between queues is done. Message Queuing allows setting up routes between different queues in a large network. We will not discuss this in this book, as this is mainly a task for the System Administrator.

❑   With the Journal options, journaling can be turned on and the size of the journal queue can be restricted by setting the option Limit journal storage to (KB).

With this MMC tool we can also read and purge the messages in the queue.

Visual Studio .NET Server Explorer

You can also use the Server Explorer in Visual Studio .NET to create and manage queues if you are using the Active Directory. If the Server Explorer is not shown, you can open it with the menu View | Server Explorer. In the Properties window you can see and change the properties of the queue:

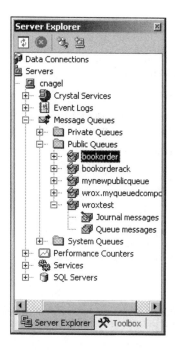

Programming Message Queuing

Now that we understand the architecture of Message Queuing, we can look into the programming. In the next sections we will see how to create and control queues, and how to send and receive messages.

We will also build a small book order application that consists of a sending and a receiving part. In the first application we create, we send messages (book orders) to a message queue. Then we will write an application to receive and process those messages.

The tasks that are before us are listed here:

❑ `System.Messaging` namespace – we will look into the main classes of this namespace.

❑ We already know how to create message queues with administrative tools, but here we will look at how to create queues programmatically.

❑ If it is not known on what host a queue is installed, we will look at ways to find queues by using a label or a format number.

❑ After finding and opening queues we can send messages to the queue. Here we will start our Book Order sending application where we pass a .NET object that contains other objects in a message to the queue.

❑ Following the sending part we look into how to receive messages. Here we build the second part of our book application to receive book orders.

❑ After sending and receiving we discuss some more features that can be used for error handling. With acknowledgement queues we can receive success or failure messages.

- ❏ Information can be returned from the server to the client application by the use of response queues. We discuss how using response queues can be implemented.

- ❏ Recoverable messages are required in a disconnected environment, and sometimes they are also useful in a connected environment.

- ❏ Message Queuing supports transactional queues. We will look at how these are to be programmed.

- ❏ Message Queue Installation is also a part we have to discuss as the user running the application probably doesn't have administrator privileges.

- ❏ The final part in programming with `System.Messaging` is to look at how tracing can be set up up to find out which routes a message takes in a big enterprise environment using multiple sites.

System.Messaging

The namespace `System.Messaging` defines a lot of classes, interfaces, and enumerations. We will group them to get a better overview of this namespace. But before looking into the groups let's discuss the most important classes from this namespace: `MessageQueue` and `Message`.

Core Classes

The core classes for Message Queuing in the `System.Messaging` namespace are `MessageQueue` and `Message`. These classes are shown in the following diagram:

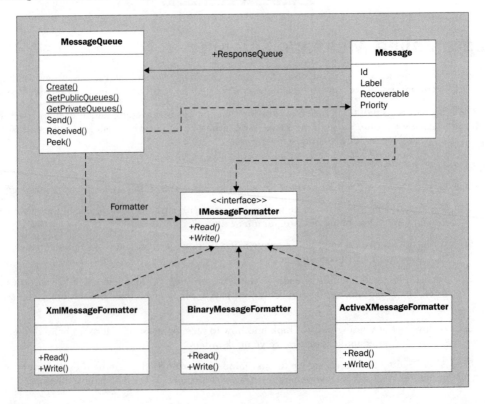

MessageQueue represents a queue into which we can send and from which receive messages with the Send(), Receive(), and Peek() methods. With static methods of the MessageQueue class (these methods are underlined in the diagram) we can search for public or private message queues depending on the category, label, machine, or with search criteria defined using the MessageQueueCriteria class.

The messages sent are represented with the Message class. The Message class has several properties to change the label and the priority, to send the message express or recoverable, to define response and acknowledgement queues, among others things.

The message also defines a formatter that is responsible for the transformation of the data of an object to a format that can be transferred through a queue. With the System.Messaging namespace, we get three formatter classes that all implement the interface IMessageFormatter:

- ❑ XmlMessageFormatter
- ❑ BinaryMessageFormatter
- ❑ ActiveXMessageFormatter

System.Messaging Groups

The System.Messaging namespace provides a lot more classes besides Message, MessageQueue, and the formatting classes. We can group these classes into five categories for a better overview: classes for finding message queues, sending messages, receiving messages, configuring security, and handling errors.

Finding Message Queues

To find message queues we have some static methods in the MessageQueue class, and the MessageQueueCriteria class where a filter can be defined for the message queue we want to find.

Sending Messages

Of course the classes MessageQueue and Message play an important part when sending messages. But there's one class more: DefaultPropertiesToSend can be used to specify message properties when sending .NET objects.

Receiving Messages

To receive messages we can enumerate all messages in the queue using a forward-only cursor, the MessageEnumerator class. To select properties to read when receiving a message the MessagePropertyFilter class plays a useful role.

Configuring Security

To configure the security of the queue we have a lot of classes in the System.Messaging namespace. We will discuss these classes later.

Handling Errors

If there's an error with messaging services, an exception of type MessageQueueException will be thrown.

In all programs in this chapter where we use classes from the System.Messaging namespace, the assembly System.Messaging must be imported.

Creating a Message Queue Programmatically

We've already seen how to create queues with the Computer Management administrative tool. We can also easily create a queue programmatically using the static `Create()` method of the `MessageQueue` class, as we shall see in this section.

With the `Create()` method we have to pass the path of the new message queue. The path consists of the host name where the queue is located and the name of the queue. In this example we'll be creating a public queue on the local host with the name `MyNewPublicQueue`:

```
using System;
using System.Messaging;

namespace Wrox.ProCSharpData.Chapter10.CreateMessageQueue;
{
    class Class1
    {
        [STAThread]
        static void Main(string[] args)
        {
            MessageQueue queue = MessageQueue.Create(@".\MyNewPublicQueue");
            Console.WriteLine("Created this public queue: ");
            Console.WriteLine("Path: " + queue.Path);
            Console.WriteLine("FormatName: " + queue.FormatName);
        }
    }
}
```

After creating the queue, the properties `Path` and `FormatName` of the queue are displayed with `Console.WriteLine()`. As we can see in the following picture the `Path` displays the name we assigned to the queue; the `FormatName` is automatically created with a UUID that we can use to get access to this queue without the name of the server. The path and format name can be used to identify the queue:

We can change the attributes of the queue by setting the properties of the returned `MessageQueue` instance. As we can see in the following example where we set the `Label` property of the `MessageQueue` class to define the label of the queue:

```
MessageQueue queue = MessageQueue.Create(@".\MyNewPublicQueue");
queue.Label = "MyLabel";
```

We have seen that using the Create() method of the MessageQueue class to create message queues is straightforward. However, there is one big drawback for using this way to create queues: the user creating the queue must have administrative privileges. Usually you can't expect that the user of your application has administrative rights, but the user installing the application has them. Later in this chapter we will see how message queues can be created programmatically using the class MessageQueueInstaller.

Creating a Private Queue

To create a private queue, Private$ must be included in the path name, as shown:

```
MessageQueue queue =
            MessageQueue.Create(@".\Private$\MyNewPrivateQueue");
Console.WriteLine("Created this private queue: ");
Console.WriteLine("Path: " + queue.Path);
Console.WriteLine("FormatName: " + queue.FormatName);
```

Finding a Queue

As we have seen earlier, the path name and the format name can be used to identify queues. To find queues we have to differentiate between public and private queues. Public queues are published in the Active Directory. For these queues it's not necessary to know the system where these queues are located. Private queues can only be found if we know the name of the system where they are located.

Looking for public queues in the domain we can search by the queue's label, category, or for all queues on a machine, with static methods of the class MessageQueue: GetPublicQueuesByLabel(), GetPublicQueuesByCategory(), and GetPublicQueuesByMachine(). With the static method GetPublicQueues() we get an array of all public queues of the domain.

```
using System;
using System.Messaging;

namespace Wrox.ProCSharpData.Chapter10.ListPublicQueues;
{
    class Class1
    {
        [STAThread]
        static void Main(string[] args)
        {
            MessageQueue[] queues = MessageQueue.GetPublicQueues();
            foreach (MessageQueue queue in queues)
            {
                Console.WriteLine(queue.Path);
            }
        }
    }
}
```

This application could give this output:

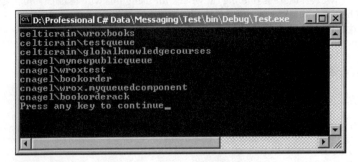

```
D:\Professional C# Data\Messaging\Test\bin\Debug\Test.exe
celticrain\wroxbooks
celticrain\testqueue
celticrain\globalknowledgecourses
cnagel\mynewpublicqueue
cnagel\wroxtest
cnagel\bookorder
cnagel\wrox.myqueuedcomponent
cnagel\bookorderack
Press any key to continue_
```

There are more ways to look for queues besides looking for a label, a category, or a machine. Next we will look at:

❑   Using the MessageQueueCriteria to define searches for public queues

❑   The purpose of the MessageQueueEnumerator

❑   How to get private queues

MessageQueueCriteria

The GetPublicQueues() method is overloaded. One version allows us to pass an instance of the MessageQueueCriteria class. With this class we can search for queues that are created or modified before or after a certain time, and we can also look for a category, label, or machine name.

MessageQueueEnumerator

MessageQueue.GetMessageQueueEnumerator() returns a MessageQueueEnumerator object that is a dynamic forward-only cursor. Using this enumerator is slower than the methods returning an array, because every call to the MoveNext() method is a call to a domain controller to get actual information. But the enumerator has the advantage that newly created queues or deleted queues can be automatically detected. Because of the replication latency of the Active Directory the information may not be really up to date.

Locating Private Queues

To locate a private queue we have to pass the server name where the queue is located. MessageQueue.GetPrivateQueuesByMachine() returns all private queues for a specified computer.

Opening Known Queues

If you know the name of the queue it is not necessary to search for it – we can open it using the path or format name. We can set the path or format name by calling the constructor of the MessageQueue class. Let's look at the differences between the path and the format name.

Path

The path specifies the machine name and the queue name to open the queue. This code example opens the queue WroxTest on the local host. To be sure that the queue exists, we will check with MessageQueue.Exists():

```
using System;
using System.Messaging;

namespace Wrox.ProCSharpData.Chapter10.OpenMessageQueue;
{
    class Class1
    {
        [STAThread]
        static void Main(string[] args)
        {
            if (MessageQueue.Exists(@".\WroxTest"))
            {
                MessageQueue queue = new MessageQueue(@".\WroxTest");
            }
            //...
        }
    }
}
```

Depending on the queue type, we have to add some identifier when opening queues. The following table shows the syntax of the queue name for specific types:

Queue Type	Syntax
Public queue	MachineName\QueueName
Private queue	MachineName\Private$\QueueName
Journal queue	MachineName\QueueName\Journal$
Machine journal queue	MachineName\Journal$
Machine dead-letter queue	MachineName\DeadLetter$
Machine transactional dead-letter queue	MachineName\XactDeadLetter$

With the syntax used to open public queues it now looks as if the machine name is required to access public queues, but this is only necessary if we choose to use the path name. If you don't want to pass the machine name you can use the format name of the queue instead. We will do this next.

Format Name

In the MessageQueue constructor we can also pass the format name of the queue instead of the path name we have seen earlier. The format name has the advantage that the queue can be specified independent of the hostname where the queue is installed; this will be found automatically.

> *In a disconnected environment where the queue is not available at the time when the message is sent, it's necessary to use the format name.*

Passing FormatName:PUBLIC=UUID to the constructor opens a public queue. The UUID of a queue is generated when the queue is created. You can use the Server Explorer or the Computer Management tool to read the UUID of queues.

```
MessageQueue queue = new MessageQueue(
    "FormatName:PUBLIC=0e745cf2-92c9-4f40-be85-7b4f368620ca");
```

391

The `FormatName` has some different uses. It can also be used to open private queues, and to specify a protocol that should be used.

❑   Accessing a private queue, the string that has to be passed to the constructor is: `FormatName:PRIVATE=MachineGUID\QueueNumber`. The queue number for private queues is generated when the queue is created. You can see the queue numbers in the directory `<windows>\System32\msmq\STORAGE\LQS`.

❑   With `FormatName:DIRECT=Protocol:MachineAddress\QueueName` we can specify the protocol that should be used to send the message. The SPX protocol is supported on Windows NT 4 and Windows 2000, but this support has been removed from Windows XP. TCP is supported with all Message Queuing versions. Windows XP has a greater integration of Message Queuing with the Internet Information Server and supports accessing queues with the HTTP protocol.

❑   `FormatName:DIRECT=OS:MachineName\QueueName` is another way to specify a queue using a format name. This way we don't have to specify the protocol but still can use the machine name with the format name.

Sending a Message

To send a message to the queue we can use the `Send()` method of the `MessageQueue` class. The object passed as an argument of the `Send()` method will be serialized to the associated queue. The `Send()` method is overloaded, so that a label and a `MessageQueueTransaction` object can be passed. We will talk about the transactional features of message queues later in this chapter.

We'll be using a C# Console Application project for this example. First, we will check if the message queue with the name `WroxTest` already exists on the localhost using `MessageQueue.Exists()`. If it doesn't exist, then the `MessageQueue.Create()` method will create it.

After the `if` statement, the message queue is opened by using the `MessageQueue` class constructor. `queue.Send()` sends the message "Message to the queue", with the label "Hi, there" to the queue.

```
using System;
using System.Messaging;

namespace Wrox.ProCSharpData.Chapter10.HiThereQueue;
{
    class Class1
    {
        [STAThread]
        static void Main(string[] args)
        {
            try
            {
                if (!MessageQueue.Exists(@".\WroxTest"))
                {
                    MessageQueue.Create(@".\WroxTest");
                }

                MessageQueue queue = new MessageQueue(@".\WroxTest");

                queue.Send("Message to the queue", "Hi, there");
            }
            catch (MessageQueueException ex)
```

```
    {
        Console.WriteLine(ex.Message);
    }
catch (Exception ex)
    {
        Console.WriteLine(ex.Message);
    }
```

After running the program we can see in the Computer Management tool that the queue `WroxTest` was created, and a message is in the queue as the following screenshot shows. We can see the label Hi, there that we have set when sending the message:

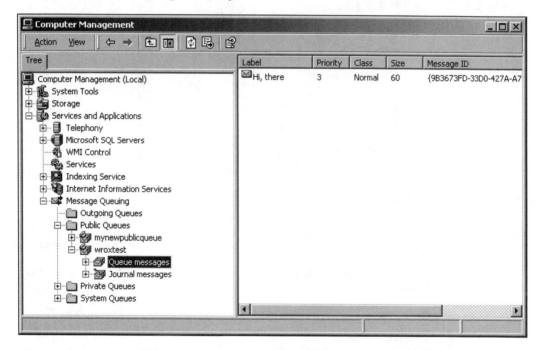

Opening the message and selecting the **Body** tab of the dialog we can see that the message was formatted using an XML format. How the message is formatted is the function of the formatter that's associated with the message queue. The label is not part of the body, but we can see that the label is displayed in the title bar of this dialog:

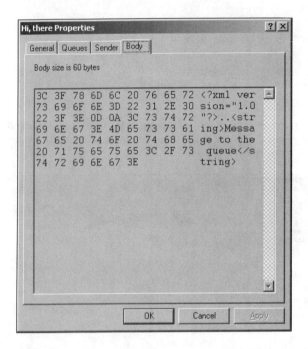

Formatting Messages

The format in which messages are transferred to the queue depends upon the formatter. The MessageQueue class has a Formatter property, through which a formatter can be assigned. The default formatter, XmlMessageFormatter, will format the message in XML syntax, as we saw in the last example.

A message formatter implements the interface IMessageFormatter. With the System.Messaging namespace we get three formatters:

- ❑ The XmlMessageFormatter is the default formatter. It serializes objects using XML.

- ❑ With the BinaryMessageFormatter, messages are serialized in a binary format. These messages are shorter than messages formatted using XML.

- ❑ The ActiveXMessageFormatter is a binary formatter for compatibility with COM objects that were used to read and write messages from the message queue.

The Hi, there message with the message body Message to the queue using the binary formatter is shown in the picture opposite. The body now has 44 bytes compared to the 60 bytes before with the XmlMessageFormatter:

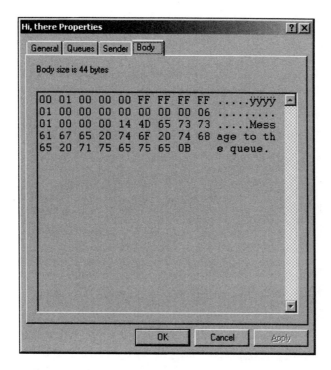

Sending Complex Messages

We could package a lot of data into a string, and send quite complex messages this way. But there is an easier way to do this. The object passed to the Send() method of the MessageQueue is of type Object. We can pass instances of any class to the method MessageQueue.Send(), as long as the class meets some basic some requirements. The object passed will be serialized into the queue.

Class Requirements for Complex Messages

The compiler will give you no errors if you pass an object of any class derived from Object, but there are some more requirements for objects sent to a message queue:

❏ The class must have a default public constructor. If you use a class without a default public constructor, you'll see this exception message: There was an error reflecting '<ClassName>'. If you access the InnerException to get to the exception that was thrown the first time you see the reason why: <ClassName> cannot be serialized because it does not have a default public constructor.

❏ Properties must be read/write. If you have a read-only property the value of this property will not be serialized. You don't get a run time error – the value just isn't sent with the message.

Book Order Sending Application

To demonstrate the use of messaging services, we shall create an application for ordering books. In the first part we will create an application that sends messages (book orders) to a message queue, later we will write the second application to receive the book orders from the message queue. The assemblies of these applications are shown in the component diagram overleaf:

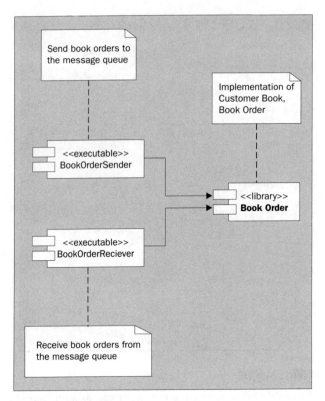

We implement one component library, BookOrder, with the classes BookOrder, Book, and Customer. Two Windows Forms applications (the executable assemblies in the diagram) will be used to send and receive messages.

Creating the Book Order Class Library

Both the sending and the receiving application need the order information. For this reason, I've put the classes that handle the order information into a single assembly. The order information is kept in the class BookOrder.

This UML class diagram shows all the properties and classes of the assembly BookOrder. The class BookOrder is composed of a Book and a Customer to define an order. With a single order a number of books can be ordered; the class BookOrder defines the property Quantity. The Book class has the Title property the Customer class has the properties Company and Contact:

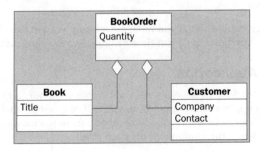

For a real order application, these classes wouldn't have all the required properties; we could add an ISBN to the Book class, and address information to the Customer, and build up the BookOrder of multiple BookOrderLines. But for now, the properties we have are sufficient to get the idea how message queuing works with complex objects.

In the file Customer.cs we define the class Customer with its properties Contact and Company:

```
// Customer.cs
using System;

namespace Wrox.Books
{

    public class Customer
    {
        private string companyName;
        private string contactName;

        public Customer(string company, string contact)
        {
            companyName = company;
            contactName = contact;
        }

        public Customer()
        {
        }

        public string Company
        {
            get
            {
                return companyName;
            }
            set
            {
                companyName = value;
            }
        }

        public string Contact
        {
            get
            {
                return contactName;
            }
            set
            {
                contactName = value;
            }
        }
    }
}
```

In the file `Book.cs` we define the `Book` class with a `Title` property:

```
// Book.cs
using System;

namespace Wrox.Books
{
    public class Book
    {

        private string title;

        public Book(string title)
        {
            this.title = title;
        }

        public Book()
        {
        }

        public string Title
        {
            get
            {
                return title;
            }
            set
            {
                title = value;
            }
        }
    }
}
```

In the file `BookOrder.cs` we see the class `BookOrder`. `BookOrder` contains fields of the classes `Book` and `Customer`, and makes these available as properties. In addition to that the property `Quantity` is defined:

```
// BookOrder.cs
using System;

namespace Wrox.Books
{
    public class BookOrder
    {
        public BookOrder()
        {
        }

        private Book product;
        private int quantity;
        private Customer customer;

        public Book Product
        {
            get
            {
                return product;
```

```
         }
         set
         {
            product = value;
         }
      }

      public int Quantity
      {
         get
         {
            return quantity;
         }
         set
         {
            quantity = value;
         }
      }

      public Customer Customer
      {
         get
         {
            return customer;
         }
         set
         {
            customer = value;
         }
      }
   }
}
```

Creating the Sending Application

The second part of this application is a Windows application BookOrderSender where books can be ordered. In this application references to the assemblies System.Messaging and BookOrder are required.

The user interface of the application looks like this:

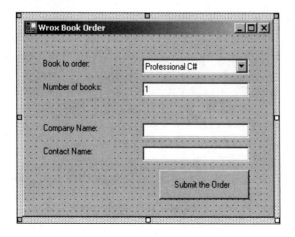

The user interface elements of this application, with their names, are:

System.Windows.Forms Control	Name
ComboBox	comboBoxBooks
TextBox	textNumberBooks
TextBox	textCompany
TextBox	textContact
Button	buttonSubmitOrder

The Items property of the control comboBoxBooks is set to the strings" Beginning C#", "Professional C#", "Professional C# Web Services", "Professional ASP.NET", and "Data Centric .NET Programming with C#", so that it is possible to select one of these books for the order.

When the **Submit the Order** button is clicked, a book order should be sent to the message queue. So in the click event handler of this button we create a new instance of the BookOrder class, and set the properties to the values the user enters with the form:

```
using System;
using System.Drawing;
using System.Collections;
using System.ComponentModel;
using System.Windows.Forms;
using System.Data;
using System.Messaging;
using Wrox.Books;

namespace Wrox.Messaging
{
    public class BookOrderSender : System.Windows.Forms.Form
    {

//...

        private void buttonSubmitOrder_Click(object sender,
                                        System.EventArgs e)
        {
          try
          {
            BookOrder bookOrder = new BookOrder();
            bookOrder.Count = Convert.ToInt32(textNumberBooks.Text);
            bookOrder.Product =
                    new Book(comboBoxBooks.SelectedItem.ToString());
            bookOrder.Customer = new Customer(textCompany.Text,
                                        textContactName.Text);
```

Next, we create a new instance of the MessageQueue class to connect to the public queue with the format name 3abdfb36-76f3-401d-973c-b52685bc3d3f. We can get the format name by using the Computer Management snap-in we used earlier to read the ID of the message queue. Here we use the format name because this makes the application independent of the server where the queue is installed:

```
MessageQueue orderQueue = new MessageQueue(
    "FormatName:Public=3abdfb36-76f3-401d-973c-b52685bc3d3f");
```

With the `Send()` method of the `MessageQueue` class, we pass the `bookOrder` object:

```
orderQueue.Send(bookOrder, "Book Order (" +
                bookOrder.Customer.Contact + ")");

MessageBox.Show("Order submitted");
}
```

The exception handler for the exception `FormatException` is responsible for dealing with wrong inputs in the **Number of Books** textbox, and the `MessageQueueException` handler will deal with all queuing problems:

```
catch (FormatException ex)
{
    MessageBox.Show(ex.Message, "Conversion Error");
}
catch (MessageQueueException ex)
{
    MessageBox.Show(ex.Message, "Error sending message");
}
    }
  }
}
```

> As mentioned earlier, read-only properties of a class are not serialized. The class to be serialized must have a public default constructor and read/write properties.

Sending Prioritized Messages

You can prioritize messages in the queue so that the high priority messages will be read before the low priority messages. The class `Message` has the property `Priority` where the priority can be specified using the `MessagePriority` enumeration.

With the `MessagePriority` enumeration we have the following priority values for the messages:

MessagePriority Enumeration	Priority Value
Highest	7
VeryHigh	6
High	5
AboveNormal	4

Table continued on following page

MessagePriority Enumeration	Priority Value
Normal (default)	3
Low	2
VeryLow	1
Lowest	0

Fast Book Orders with the Sending Application

For our book order application it should be possible to do fast orders that are delivered by FedEx. The customer has to pay an additional price to handle fast orders. The receiving application should handle these orders before the other ones. That's an ideal use of message priorities.

We'll add a checkbox button to the dialog that the user can select for fast orders. To set the priority of the message we have to pass an instance of the class `Message` instead of the class `BookOrder`.

As you can see in the following code segment an instance of the `Message` class is created. Since the type `Message` is ambiguous in a Windows application because of the structure `System.Windows.Forms.Message`, we use the full name of the class `System.Messaging.Message` for unique identification. In the constructor the `order` instance is passed to set the `Body` property. `fastOrderCheckBox.Checked` checks the `boolean` value to see if the user selected a fast order, and sets the `Priority` property of the `Message` class accordingly. Then the instance of the `Message` class is passed to the `MessageQueue.Send()`. With the `Send()` method we set the label to `Book Order` appended with the contact name of the `Customer` class. This will make it easy to differentiate the orders when reading the messages:

```
BookOrder bookOrder = new BookOrder();
bookOrder.Count = Convert.ToInt32(textNumberBooks.Text);
bookOrder.Product =
    new Book(comboBoxBooks.SelectedItem.ToString());
bookOrder.Customer = new Customer(textCompany.Text,
                                  textContactName.Text);

MessageQueue orderQueue = new MessageQueue(
    "FormatName:Public=3abdfb36-76f3-401d-973c-b52685bc3d3f");

System.Messaging.Message message =
                    new System.Messaging.Message(bookOrder);
if (checkBoxFastOrder.Checked)
{
    message.Priority = MessagePriority.High;
}
orderQueue.Send(message, "Book Order (" +
                         bookOrder.Customer.Contact + ")");
```

Running the Book Order Sender

Starting the book order sender application we can write book orders to the message queue. We can select a book from the combo box, enter the number of books to order, the company and contact names, and also select a fast order. Pressing the Submit the Order button writes a new order to the message queue. You can easily verify that messages are sent by using the Computer Management snap-in:

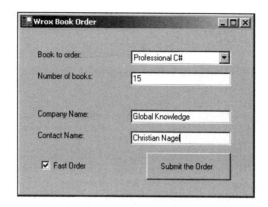

Receiving Messages

Now knowing how to send messages, let's continue to the receiving side. Before we create the Book Order receiving application we will look into receiving messages overall.

To read messages, again the `MessageQueue` class is used. With `Receive()` we read a single message from the queue. After calling this method the message is removed from the queue. The message that's taken is the one with the highest priority. With similar priorities we read the message with the oldest arrival time, but this message may not be that one sent the longest time ago, because without transactional messages the order in the queue is not guaranteed. You can compare this with sending a letter. If letter A is sent on 1-June, and letter B is sent on 3-June letter B may arrive before letter A.

In the following example we read a message from the queue `.\WroxTest`. Earlier we have sent simple string messages with the `XmlMessageFormatter` that is by default associated with the `MessageQueue` class. To read the message we have to associate an `XmlMessageFormatter` explicitly to the `MessageQueue` that accepts messages of type `System.String`. By default the `XmlMessageFormatter` is associated with the `MessageQueue` class, but on the receiving side we have to define the class types that may be read. The `Receive()` method returns a `Message` object where the `Body` property returns the string we have sent:

```
using System;
using System.Messaging;

namespace Wrox.Messaging
{
   class Class1
   {
      [STAThread]
      static void Main(string[] args)
      {
         MessageQueue queue = new MessageQueue(@".\WroxTest");
         queue.Formatter = new XmlMessageFormatter(
             new string[] {"System.String"});

         Message message = queue.Receive();
         Console.WriteLine(m.Body);
      }
   }
}
```

If there's no message in the queue, `Receive()` will wait for a message to arrive. If you don't want to wait that long you can pass a maximum time to wait with a `TimeSpan` to the `Receive()` method. If a time out occurs, `Receive()` raises a `MessageQueueException`.

`GetAllMessages()` returns an array of `Message` objects corresponding to every message in the queue at that time. With this method the messages are also removed from the queue.

To only read the messages without removing them from the queue, use `MessageQueue.Peek()`.

> **A message will be removed from the queue if it is read. If multiple applications read messages from the queue, the application reading first will get the message. To avoid this, you can deny other applications read access to the queue by setting the property `MessageQueue.DenySharedReceive` to true.**

Enumerating the Messages

There's another easy way to walk through all messages in the queue: using an enumerator. With the `foreach` statement the method `GetEnumerator()` of the `MessageQueue` gets called, which returns a reference to the interface `IEnumerator`. Using this interface we can dynamically walk through all messages:

```
MessageQueue queue = new MessageQueue(@".\WroxTest");
queue.Formatter = new XmlMessageFormatter(
        new String[] {"System.String"});
```

```
foreach (Message message in queue)
{
    Console.WriteLine(message.Body);
}
```

Using the MessageEnumerator

The `MessageEnumerator` has some more features than the simple `IEnumerator` interface. While with the `IEnumerator` interface the messages are never removed from the queue, we can do this with the method `RemoveCurrent()` of the `MessageEnumerator`. Both enumerators are dynamic, which means that we will get the messages that are sent to the queue after we started the enumeration. Using a `foreach` statement with the `IEnumerator` interface we will leave the `foreach` as soon as there are no more messages in the queue. Instead of leaving a loop to receive messages from the queue we can also wait until a new message arrives. This can be done by using the method `MoveNext()` of the `MessageEnumerator`.

In this following code example we use a 30 minutes time out value for the `MoveNext()` method of the `MessageEnumerator` class, which means if the queue is empty let's wait up to 30 minutes for a new message to arrive. If a new message doesn't arrive in this time slot, `MoveNext()` returns `false` which ends the `while` loop. The `Current` property is used to get access to the message without removing it from the queue:

```
MessageQueue queue = new MessageQueue(@".\WroxTest");
queue.Formatter = new XmlMessageFormatter(
        new String[] {"System.String"});
```

```
MessageEnumerator messages = queue.GetMessageEnumerator();
while (messages.MoveNext(new TimeSpan(0, 30, 0)))
```

```
    {
        Message message = messages.Current;
        Console.WriteLine(message.Body);
    }
}
```

Asynchronous Read

As we have seen, the `Receive()` method waits until a message arrives. To avoid blocking the thread a timeout can be specified using an overloaded method of `Receive()` that allows passing a `TimeSpan`. To read messages again from the queue you have to call `Receive()` again. But when is the best time to do this? How can you know when a message arrives? To avoid this kind of problem, we could start a new thread that is waiting in the `Receive()` method. But there is an easier way: using asynchronous reads.

Asynchronous reads depend on the `BeginReceive()` method that initiates the receive. This method doesn't block the thread, but returns immediately. The `EndReceive()` method completes the receive, and returns an instance of `Message` for the received message. With asynchronous reads the `ReceiveCompletedEventHandler` will be called when a new message arrives. Let's look at a simple code example.

Before we call the `BeginReceive()` method we have to associate an event handler with the `ReceiveCompleted` event. We create a delegate instance `ReceiveCompletedEventHandler()` where we define that the method `MessageArrived()` should be called when a new message arrives:

```
static void Main(string[] args)
{
    MessageQueue queue = new MessageQueue(@".\WroxTest");
    queue.Formatter = new XmlMessageFormatter(
        new String[] {"System.String"});

    queue.ReceiveCompleted +=
        new ReceiveCompletedEventHandler(MessageArrived);
    queue.BeginReceive();

    // now you can do something else...
}
```

The `ReceiveCompletedEventHandler` defines the signature of our `MessageArrived()` method. In the first argument we receive the message queue where the message arrived, in the second argument, `ReceiveCompletedEventArgs`, we have access to the asynchronous result and the message. To complete the operation that `BeginReceive()` initiated we call `EndReceive()`. `EndReceive()` returns the message from the queue. The last method of our event handler invokes `BeginReceive()` again so that the next message can be dealt with:

```
public static void MessageArrived(object source,
                                ReceiveCompletedEventArgs result)
{
    MessageQueue queue = (MessageQueue)source;
    try
    {
        Message message = queue.EndReceive(result.AsyncResult);

        Console.WriteLine(message.Label);
```

```
            Console.WriteLine(message.Body);
        }
        catch (Exception e)
        {
            Console.WriteLine(e.Message);
        }

        queue.BeginReceive();
    }
```

Similar to `BeginReceive()` *and* `EndReceive()` *if we only want to peek messages asynchronously we can use* `BeginPeek()` *and* `EndPeek()`.

Book Order Receiving Application

Knowing how to receive and peek messages we can again concentrate on our book application. Now let's move to the receiving part, the Book Order receiving application.

The user interface of the book order receiving application is shown in the following picture. This application displays labels of all the open orders in a listbox on the left side of the dialog. If an order line is selected, the textboxes on the right side display information that is in the body of the message like the book title, the number of books ordered, the company, and contact of the ordering person. The label **FAST ORDER** by is not visible by default; this label is set to visible only if a high priority message is selected.

As long as the message is only displayed, it should not be removed from the queue. The removal of the message in the queue only happens if the **Process Order** button is pressed. Here's the form:

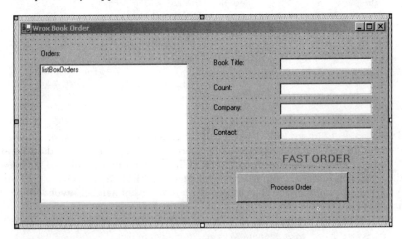

The following table shows the classes and properties of the Windows controls in the dialog:

System.Windows.Forms Control	Name
ListBox	listBoxOrders
TextBox	textBookTitle
TextBox	textBookQuantity

System.Windows.Forms Control	Name
TextBox	textCompany
TextBox	textContact
Label	labelPriorityOrder
Button	buttonProcessOrder

In the constructor of the `BookOrderReceiver` class the message queue is set up with the `XmlMessageFormatter` to read the `BookOrder` objects. Because a `BookOrder` class contains `Book` and `Customer` classes we have to set all these types in the `Type` array that is passed to the `XmlMessageFormatter` constructor. Then a thread that fills the listbox is started. The property `IsBackground` of this thread is set to `true`, so that the thread exits as soon as the user ends the application.

```
using System;
using System.Drawing;
using System.Collections;
using System.ComponentModel;
using System.Windows.Forms;
using System.Data;

using System.Messaging;
using System.Threading;
using Wrox.Books;

namespace Wrox.Messaging
{
    public class BookOrderReceiver : System.Windows.Forms.Form
    {
        private System.Messaging.MessageQueue orderQueue;
        //...

        public BookOrderReceiver()
        {
            //
            // Required for Windows Form Designer support
            //
            InitializeComponent();

            // setup the message queue
            orderQueue = new MessageQueue(
                "FormatName:Public=3abdfb36-76f3-401d-973c-b52685bc3d3f");
            System.Type[] types = new Type[3];
            types[0] = typeof(BookOrder);
            types[1] = typeof(Book);
            types[2] = typeof(Customer);
            orderQueue.Formatter = new XmlMessageFormatter(types);

            // start the thread that fills the
            // ListBox with messages
            Thread t1 = new Thread(new ThreadStart(PeekMessages));
            t1.IsBackground = true;
            t1.Start();

        }
```

The thread function `PeekMessages()` uses the `MessageEnumerator` to walk through the messages in the message queue. `MoveNext()` is set to a two hour timeout if no messages are in the queue. If the queue is empty, the thread will wait here. With a message a new instance of `LabelIdMapping` is created where the `Label` and `Id` of the message are associated. This instance is added to the `Items` list of the listbox:

```
protected void PeekMessages()
{
    MessageEnumerator messageEnum = orderQueue.GetMessageEnumerator();

    while (messageEnum.MoveNext(new TimeSpan(2, 0, 0)))
    {
        LabelIdMapping labelId = new LabelIdMapping(
            messageEnum.Current.Label, messageEnum.Current.Id);
        listBoxOrders.Items.Add(labelId);
    }

    MessageBox.Show("No message arrived in the last 2 hours. " +
                    "Ending the thread");
}
```

The `LabelIdMapping` class is used to associate the `Label` with the `Id` of the message. The `Label`, which is not necessarily unique, will be displayed in the listbox because the `ToString()` method is overridden to return the `label`. The listbox uses strings to display the values in the list, so `ToString()` will be called to get the string representation of an object. The property `Id` in the class `LabelIdMapping` is used to uniquely identify the message.

This class is only used inside the `BookOrderReceiver` class; it is created as private nested class:

```
private class LabelIdMapping
{
    private string label;
    private string id;

    public LabelIdMapping(string label, string id)
    {
        this.label = label;
        this.id = id;
    }

    public override string ToString()
    {
        return label;
    }

    public string Label
    {
        get
        {
            return label;
        }
    }

    public string Id
    {
        get
        {
```

```
                  return id;
            }
      }
}
```

For the `SelectedIndexChanged` event of the listbox an event handler is implemented. With `listBoxOrders.SelectedItem` we get the `labelId` of which the `Id` is used to get the message with `orderQueue.PeekById()`. `PeekById()` reads the specified message without removing it from the queue. We read the `Body` property to get to the `BookOrder` instance. Then the textboxes of the form are filled with the values we read in the message. The **Process Order** button will be enabled now because the order can be processed now:

```
private void OnSelectionChanged(object sender, System.EventArgs e)
{
    LabelIdMapping labelId =
          (LabelIdMapping)listBoxOrders.SelectedItem;
    // nothing selected
    if (labelId == null)
        return;

    System.Messaging.Message message = orderQueue.PeekById(labelId.Id);

    if (message.Body is BookOrder)
    {
        BookOrder bookOrder = message.Body as BookOrder;

        textBookTitle.Text = bookOrder.Product.Title;
        textBookQuantity.Text = bookOrder.Quantity.ToString();
        textCompany.Text = bookOrder.Customer.Company;
        textContact.Text = bookOrder.Customer.Contact;
        buttonProcessOrder.Enabled = true;
    }
    else
    {
        MessageBox.Show("The selected item is not a book order");
    }
}
```

If the user presses the **Process Order** button, the handler `buttonProcessOrder_Click` for the `Click` event gets invoked. Here we finally remove the message from the message queue by calling `orderQueue.ReceiveById()`, and of course it will be removed from the listbox items:

```
private void buttonProcessOrder_Click(object sender,
                                      System.EventArgs e)
{
    LabelIdMapping labelId =
          (LabelIdMapping)listBoxOrders.SelectedItem;
    System.Messaging.Message message =
          orderQueue.ReceiveById(labelId.Id);

    listBoxOrders.Items.Remove(labelId);
    listBoxOrders.SelectedIndex = -1;
    buttonProcessOrder.Enabled = false;
    textBookQuantity.Text = "";
    textBookTitle.Text = "";
```

```
        textCompany.Text = "";
        textContact.Text = "";

        MessageBox.Show("The order was shipped");

    }
```

Using Properties When Reading Messages

The dialog of the receiving book order application has a red label **FAST ORDER**. The `Visible` property of this label is set to `false`; it should only be enabled when a high priority order is displayed. If you try to access the property `Priority` of the `Message` class you will get the exception `InvalidOperationException` because by default this property is not readable. We can change what message properties should be read by assigning a `MessagePropertyFilter`.

The default constructor of the `MessagePropertyFilter` initializes all the Boolean properties to `false`. Calling the method `SetDefaults()` sets most common properties to `true`. In addition to the most common properties we want to read the value for the `Priority` property, so we set this property to `true`:

```
    private void OnSelectionChanged(object sender, System.EventArgs e)
    {
        LabelIdMapping labelId =
            (LabelIdMapping)listBoxOrders.SelectedItem;
        // nothing selected
        if (labelId == null)
            return;

        MessagePropertyFilter filter = new MessagePropertyFilter();
        filter.SetDefaults();
        filter.Priority = true;
        orderQueue.MessageReadPropertyFilter = filter;
        System.Messaging.Message message = orderQueue.PeekById(labelId.Id);
```

Now we can access the `Priority` property of the `Message` class. If the value is higher than `Normal`, the **Fast Order** label will be visible:

```
        if (message.Body is BookOrder)
        {
            if (message.Priority > MessagePriority.Normal)
            {
                labelFastOrder.Visible = true;
            }
            else
            {
                labelFastOrder.Visible = false;
            }

            BookOrder bookOrder = message.Body as BookOrder;
        }
    }
```

Running the Book Order Receiver

Running the receiving application (as shown in the picture below), displays all messages that are in the queue and that are put into the queue while the application is running in the list view on the left side of the application. Selecting one of the messages the data of the message is displayed in the right part of the application. Pressing Process Order receives the message from the queue, and the message is also removed.

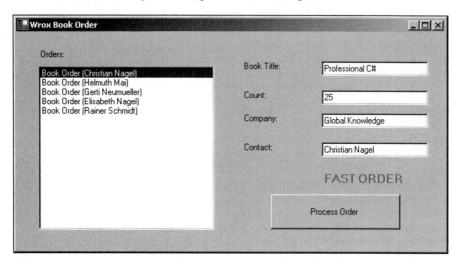

Acknowledgement Queues

Now we have Book Order sending and receiving applications. In the current phase of development, the sending application will never know if the receiving application has received the message. With an acknowledgement queue the application sending the message could get information about the status of the message. To set the required acknowledgement, the Message class has the properties AdministrationQueue and AcknowledgeType. The AdministrationQueue needs to be set to the queue that receives the acknowledgements; the AcknowledgeType defines the acknowledgements we are interested in.

The property AcknowledgeType can be set to one of the values of the enumeration AcknowledgeTypes that are shown in the following table:

Member Name	We get this information
None (default)	Default value. We get no acknowledgement at all.
FullReachQueue	We receive an acknowledgement message if the queue was reached, or it couldn't be reached because of time-out values or denied access.
PositiveArrival	The message arrived in the destination queue. Arrival in the queue happens before it is received. Arrival doesn't say if it is received from an application at all.

Table continued on following page

Member Name	We get this information
NotAcknowledgeReachQueue	The message didn't reach the queue. The error can occur because one of the timers time-to-reach-queue or time-to-be-received expired.
FullReceive	We receive an acknowledgement message if the message was received or the time-out happened.
NegativeReceive	With this value we just get the information when the message couldn't be read.
PositiveReceive	This is the opposite of NegativeReceive. We get an acknowledgement only if the message was read.
NotAcknowledgeReceive	The message wasn't read before the time-to-be-received timer expired.

The following code example shows how we can set the AdministrationQueue and AcknowledgeType to receive acknowledgements in the queue BookOrderAck:

```
System.Messaging.Message message =
                    new System.Messaging.Message(order);

message.AdministrationQueue =
    new MessageQueue(@".\BookOrderAck");
message.AcknowledgeType  = AcknowledgeTypes.FullReachQueue;

orderQueue.Send(message, "Book Order (" +
    order.Customer.Contact + ")" );
```

Depending on the AcknowledgeType that is set, we get messages in the acknowledgement queue. To see the result of the message transfer we have to receive the messages from this queue and read the value of the Acknowledgement property. This property has a value from the Acknowledgement enumeration. This enumeration gives us the information about the result, such as Receive, ReceiveTimeout, AccessDenied, ReachQueue, and ReachQueueTimeout.

Correlation ID

On the sender side we can read messages from the administration queue just as we can from any other message queue. But how do we know what acknowledgement message belongs to which sent message? The label of the acknowledgement message will be the same as from the sent message, but the label is not necessarily unique to identify messages.

Whenever a message is sent, a unique message identifier is created that can be read by accessing the Id property of the Message class. An acknowledgement message defines the **correlation ID** to be the same as the ID of the message to which the acknowledgement belongs. So, to get to an acknowledgement message that belongs to a specific message sent, we can use MessageQueue.ReceiveByCorrelationId() to receive the correct acknowledgement.

> Another check if messages are sent successfully is by using the dead-letter queue. By setting the **UseDeadLetterQueue** property of the **Message** class to **true**, we can define that the message should be copied to the dead-letter queue if it didn't arrive at the target queue in the specified time.

Response Queues

We may want to receive more information from the receiving application than a message acknowledgment provides. In our book ordering application, we may be interested in whether the book was in stock or at what date we can expect the order to arrive.

The design to do this can be completely independent of the message queue architecture. If the book ordering takes place from a web site and the ASP.NET application puts messages into the ordering queue, you can send automatic e-mails to the user that ordered the book, providing actual information about the order. In that case message queues are not used to send answers.

On the other hand, if the book ordering application is designed as a Windows application where the client system has a message queue, we can use response queues to send answers.

For the sending application, response queues are very similar to administration queues. The sending application defines the response queue where the receiver should send messages with the `ResponseQueue` property of the `Message` class. Responses are not automatically sent to the receiving application as we have seen with acknowledgements, we have to explicitly send a response from the receiving application. The receiving application has to create a response `Message` object where the `CorrelationId` property must be set to the `Id` of the received messages, and the message must be sent into the queue where `ResponseQueue` points. As with acknowledgement message, the client application can use the correlation ID to identify the response message that corresponds to a sent message.

Recoverable Messages

If we want messages to be available when the sending or receiving system crashes, or to use messages in a truly disconnected environment such as on a notebook that is not connected to the network when the message will be sent, we need to use **recoverable messages**. To send recoverable messages, the `Recoverable` property of the `Message` must be set to `true`. The default value for `Recoverable` is `false`, which means that **express messages** will be sent. Recoverable messages are stored in a file, express messages just in memory. So express messages are a lot faster compared to recoverable messages.

One important scenario where recoverable messages are required is a disconnected environment. Using messages with a Notebook, the message should still be available after the Notebook is turned off and on again. So let's look at all the requirements for disconnected environments.

Messages in a Disconnected Environment

If you want to use a Notebook system where the message should be delivered in a disconnected environment, you have to be aware of some issues sending messages:

❑ The message must be sent in recoverable mode, as the message must be stored within a file to route it to a different message queue as can be seen in the following code segment:

```
msg.Recoverable = true;
```

❑ You may not use the label and server name of the queue to connect to a specific queue as this queue and the Active Directory are not available at the time you send the message. Instead you have to use the format name of the queue. This way the message is stored in the message store of the local message queue until the network is connected and the message can be routed to the queue where it belongs.

413

> You cannot use the dependent client in a disconnected environment. On a Windows 2000
> Professional system you have to install the independent client for disconnected environments.

Transactional Queues

With recoverable messages, it's not guaranteed that the message arrives only once. If both the sending
and the receiving application have multiple transport protocols installed, the same message can arrive
two or more times. It's also not guaranteed that the messages arrive in the same order they have been
sent. To get this guarantee, we can use transactional messages with transactional queues.

Transactional queues ensure that

❑   Messages arrive in the same order they have been sent

❑   Messages will arrive only once

For message queuing, a transaction doesn't mean that the message is sent and received in a single
transaction. For the sender a single transaction just means that all messages are put into the queue or
none at all. For the receiver it means that messages are read in order.

Another important point with transactions is about the message priority. Setting the Priority property of
the Message class doesn't affect transactional messages. Setting priorities for transactional messages is
ignored because transactions guarantee the order of the messages.

Creating a Transactional Queue

To create a transactional queue programmatically you can set the `transactional` parameter of the
`MessageQueue.Create()` method to `true`. To create a transactional queue with an administrative
tool, select the checkbox to define the queue as transactional. In the picture below you can see the
dialog of the Computer Management snap-in to create a new transactional queue. We have already used
the Computer Management administration tool at the beginning of this chapter:

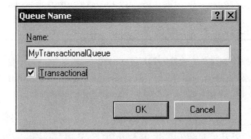

> You cannot change a non-transactional queue to a transactional queue after it has been created.

Transaction Management

To manage transactions the class `MessageQueueTransaction` can be used. `Begin()` starts a transaction, `Commit()` completes it and puts the messages into the queue. Calling `Abort()` aborts the transaction and no message will be put into the queue:

```
using System;
using System.Messaging;

namespace Wrox.ProCSharpData.Chapter10.TransactionalMessages
{
    class Class1
    {
        [STAThread]
        static void Main(string[] args)
        {
            if (!MessageQueue.Exists(@".\MyTransactionalQueue"))
            {
                MessageQueue.Create(@".\MyTransactionalQueue", true);
            }
            MessageQueue queue = new MessageQueue(@".\MyTransactionalQueue");
            MessageQueueTransaction transaction =
                new MessageQueueTransaction();
            try
            {
                transaction.Begin();
                queue.Send("one", transaction);
                queue.Send("two", transaction);
                queue.Send("three", transaction);
                transaction.Commit();
            }
            catch
            {
                transaction.Abort();
            }
        }
    }
}
```

Message Queue Installation

We can create queues with a simple call to `MessageQueue.Create()`, but be aware that the user running the application may not have the administrative privileges required to create queues.

A different way to create queues is using an installation program. The System Administrator usually starts application installations, so creating queues in the installation program is the best way to do this task.

In the installation program it is better to use the `MessageQueueInstaller` component than `MessageQueue.Create()`. A `MessageQueueInstaller` included in the application can be used from a Microsoft Installer Package, or from the `installutil.exe` command-line tool.

Visual Studio .NET makes adding a `MessageQueueInstaller` to a Windows application easy. Dropping a message queue from the Server Explorer to the Windows application creates a new instance of the `MessageQueue` class in the method `InitializeComponent()`. In the **Properties** window of the `MessageQueue` you will see a link to **Add Installer**. Selecting this link creates a project installer class that is derived from `System.Configuration.Install.Installer`. This project installer class uses the `MessageQueueInstaller` to create a new message queue. We can configure the options of the message queue by setting the properties of the `MessageQueueInstaller` class.

415

Security

We can configure the message queue so that only specific users can access it. An access control list about users and user groups that can use the message queue can be configured at installation time by setting the property `Permissions` of the `MessageQueueInstaller` class, or by calling the method `SetPermissions()` of the `MessageQueue` class after it is installed.

The best way learn about setting message queue permissions is to look at the class diagram below, and see the associations of the relevant classes in the `System.Messaging` namespace:

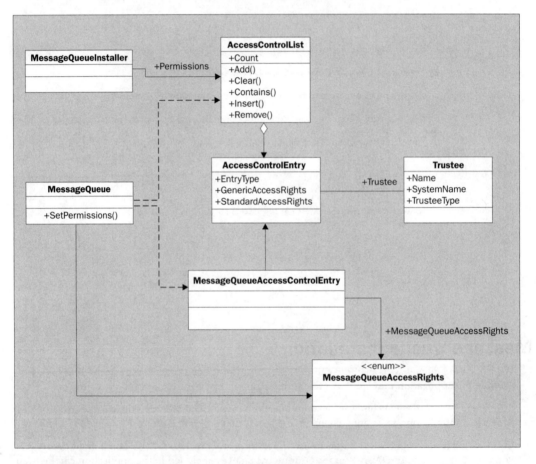

To set the access control list at installation time we set the `Permissions` property of the `MessageQueueInstaller` class. The `Permissions` property needs an `AccessControlList`. The `AccessControlList` is a collection of `AccessControlEntry` objects that define the access rights and the trustee. The class `MessageQueueAccessControlEntry`, derived from `AccessControlEntry`, can define specific `MessageQueueAccessRights` that are defined in an enumeration. With the `MessageQueueAccessRights` enumeration, other permissions like `ReceiveMessage`, `WriteMessage`, and `DeleteMessage` can be set.

To change the permissions after installation, use the `SetPermissions()` method of the `MessageQueue` class. `SetPermissions()` is overloaded, so that we can set the permissions by passing one or more of `AccessControlList`, `MessageQueueAccessControlEntry`, or `MessageQueueAccessRights`. To have the authority to change permissions, the permission **Set Permissions** must be set for the user account. By default system administrators have this permission.

Instead of setting permissions programmatically this also can be done from the Computer Management administration tool as can be seen in the screenshot below:

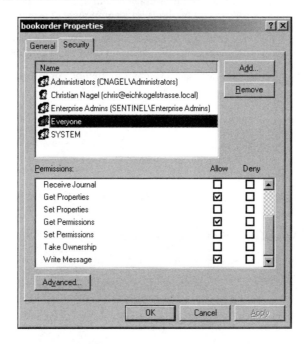

Encryption

We can encrypt messages so that they are better protected. The `EncryptionRequired` property of the `MessageQueueInstaller` class accepts an `EncryptionRequired` enumeration that can have the values `Body`, `None`, or `Optional`. With `None` only non-encrypted messages are accepted, `Body` means that encrypted messages are required. The default `Optional` means that the sender can choose to send encrypted or non-encrypted messages. To send encrypted messages the sender can set the `UseEncrypted` property of the `Message` class to `true`.

Tracing

We might use messaging services in a large enterprise with multiple sites. Messages can be routed from one site to another. We did not talk about the routing configuration of Message Queuing in this chapter because this is primarily an administrative task. But for the programming part it can be interesting to get reports of how a message is routed and where it arrives. This can be achieved with **tracing**. We turn on message tracing to get reports of where a message arrives. Setting the property `Message.UseTracing` to `true` turns tracing on, so a message to the report queue gets generated when a message arrives on a system. This can be very helpful for troubleshooting especially if the messages are routed between message queue servers.

Queued Components

Queued Components were introduced with COM+ services to make it easier to call methods across a message queue. At the time of writing, there's no native implementation of Queued Components for the .NET Framework, but of course we can use the COM+ features from within .NET applications. In a future release of the .NET Framework a concept similar to Queued Components may become available natively.

Queued components are an abstraction of the Message Queuing service. Instead of dealing with messages and message queues we can call methods on a component. The component will not be called directly from our client application, but some COM+ services intercept the method calls.

The advantages of Queued Components over the classes in the `System.Messaging` namespace are:

❑ We don't have to deal with messages. We can call methods of the queued component instead.

❑ Queued Components can take part in a COM+ transaction.

But there are also some disadvantages of Queued Components that may lead us to stay with `System.Messaging`:

❑ We have to use the COM+ facility for Queued Components. This makes the installation and configuration more complex.

❑ To pass classes as arguments we have to implement the COM interface `IPersistStream`.

Queued Components Architecture

With queued components some new terms come into play: recorders, listeners, and players as you can see in the following figure.

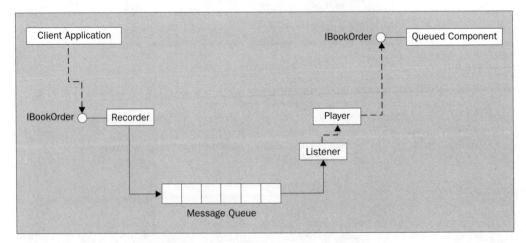

The queued component is a COM+ component that supplies methods that a client can call. The client doesn't call the methods directly, it uses a **recorder** instead. The recorder puts all method calls the client into the message queue as messages. To compare it with the architecture of the Message Queuing application we've seen before in this chapter, the recorder is the sender. The listener waits for messages to arrive and reads the messages from the queue. The **player** is responsible for calling the methods on the queued component.

Requirements of a Queued Component

The queued component has some specific requirements. All queue-able methods may only have input parameters. Output or reference parameters are not allowed, as the client and server can run at different times.

When we used the `System.Messaging` classes earlier in this chapter, it was possible to pass serializable object types within messages. Such classes can't be used as parameters for queued components because the queued components are based on COM technologies. Here the class passed as parameter must implement the COM interface `IPersistStream`.

COM+ Services

Queued components are part of the COM+ services come with the Windows 2000 operating system. A managed component can make use of COM+ services by configuring the component library in a COM+ application. This way managed code is using COM+ services running in unmanaged code. To use the COM+ services and the inception mechanism there is an unmanaged context object for every .NET object, as shown in the following figure:

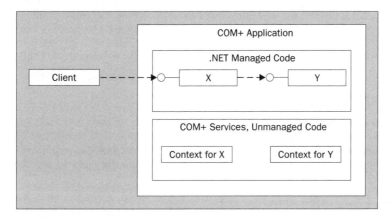

To get an overview of what services are available to .NET applications running inside a COM+ application here is a list showing the features:

❑ **Automatic Transactions** was already a feature of the Microsoft Transaction Server in NT4. With this service it's not necessary for the application to deal with problems where a database update to one database succeeded, but failed to another one. Transactions can be automatically managed across different systems, and across different resource managers. Message Queuing can take part in such a transaction.

❑ **Just-in-time (JIT) Activation** creates an object not when the client calls new, but when the client first needs the object, when a method is called. With JIT Activation fewer server resources are required as the object creation can be delayed.

❑ **Loosely Coupled Events** is a component-based event system that uses publishers and subscribers and so reduces the complexity of programs using network events as the publisher and subscriber no longer need to be directly connected.

419

❏ With **Object Pooling**, the time the client is waiting for the creation of an object can be reduced, because an already initialized object can be used from a pool of objects. This feature is useful for object types where the initialization takes some time.

❏ **Synchronization** is another feature of COM+ services. If you don't implement locking to synchronize multiple threads calling the object, COM+ can create a logical thread of execution to do it for you.

❏ **Queued Components** is the COM+ service that we will use in this chapter.

To use queued components from within .NET we have to reference the assembly `System.EnterpriseServices`, *and include the namespace* `System.EnterpriseServices`.

Queued Component Server

We'll implement a similar application to that before where we used the messaging classes from the `System.Messaging` namespace with queued components. Instead of dealing with messages we can call methods.

First, we create a C# Class Library project called `BookOrderQC`, because the queued component will be configured with COM+ services, and so such a library is needed.

COM+ Assembly Attributes

To configure the component with COM+ services it must be shared. Shared assemblies need a strong name. The strong name consists of the name of the assembly, the version number, a culture, and a public key. We will create a public key file (or use one that already exists) with the strong name utility `sn -k mywroxkey.snk`. In the file `AssemblyInfo.cs`, we reference this key file to put the public key into the assembly:

```
[assembly: AssemblyDelaySign(false)]
[assembly: AssemblyKeyFile(@"..\..\..\keys\mywroxkey.snk")]
[assembly: AssemblyKeyName("")]
```

The Book Order class library that we created previously will be used from the queued component. The classes that are used by a shared assembly must be shared, so we will change the implementation of the Book Order class library to use the same shared-key file. We add the same `AssemblyKeyFile` attribute pointing to the file `mywroxkey.snk` into the file `AssemblyInfo.cs` of the Book Order class library.

In addition to the key file, some more assembly attributes are required for the COM+ application configuration:

```
[assembly: ApplicationActivation(ActivationOption.Server)]
[assembly: ApplicationID("442DA2F1-7953-46ff-A3C5-F39694C38BA9")]
[assembly: ApplicationName("Wrox.BookOrder")]
[assembly: Description("Book Order Queued Component")]
[assembly: ApplicationQueuing(Enabled=true, QueueListenerEnabled=true)]
```

❏ The attribute `ApplicationActivation` is about how the COM+ application should be started – as library in the client process (`ActivationOption.Library`), or run in its own process (`ActivationOption.Server`). For queued components, the only possible option is `ActivationOption.Server`.

❑ The attribute `ApplicationID` specifies the GUID of the application where the component should be installed. We create a new GUID using `guidgen.exe`. If you specify an existing application ID, the component will be installed in the existing application.

❑ The `ApplicationName` attribute defines a name of the COM+ application that can be remembered more easily than the GUID. This name can be seen in the Component Services snap-in, and an automatically generated public queue will get the same name.

❑ The `Description` is just information that will show up in the Component Services snap-in.

❑ An important attribute for queued components is `ApplicationQueuing`. The named property `Enabled` sets the `Queued` option of the COM+ application to `true`. This option creates a public message queue on the system. The named property `QueueListenerEnabled` creates a thread that reads messages from the queue as soon as the COM+ application is started. With the named property `MaxListenerThreads` it is possible to set the maximum number of threads that should be started reading messages from the queue.

If you use the message queue in a workgroup environment, or if you want to access it from accounts outside the Active Directory domain, the attribute `ApplicationAccessControl` is also needed to set the authentication of the queued component to none:

```
[assembly: ApplicationAccessControl(Value=false,
Authentication=AuthenticationOption.None)]
```

Queued Component

The class that implements the queued component must be derived from `ServicedComponent`, and the `InterfaceQueuing` attribute must be specified. The `InterfaceQueuing` attribute can be applied either to the interface, or to the class that derives from `ServicedComponent`. I'm defining the interface `IBookOrder` that the queued component implements:

```
[InterfaceQueuing()]
public interface IBookOrder
{
    void OrderABook(Customer customer, Book book, int count);
}
```

The class `BookOrderQC` derives from `ServicedComponent` and implements the interface `IBookOrder`. The implementation of `OrderABook()` just shows a message box to demonstrate that the queued component has been called. A useful implementation could be to write the order to a database using ADO.NET.

```
public class BookOrderQC : ServicedComponent, IBookOrder
{

    public void OrderABook(Customer customer, Book book, int count)
    {
        MessageBox.Show("The book " + book.Title + " was ordered by "
        + customer.Contact + " " + count + " times");
    }
}
```

ServicedComponent

Every .NET component that should be configured in a COM+ Services application must be derived from this class. This class has methods that can be overridden to react to activation, deactivation, and object pooling requests.

InterfaceQueuing attribute

For queued components, the class must be marked with the attribute `InterfaceQueuing`. This enables queuing support for the interface that is specified with the `Interface` property. Registration of the component will fail if this property is not set to the name of the interface, because the interface does not exist in the `System.EnterpriseServices` assembly.

Supported Argument Types

It's not possible to pass simple .NET classes with the method of a queued component as we have done earlier with message queuing. The object doing the serialization is a COM object, and therefore only simple data types and classes implementing the COM interface `IPersistStream` can be passed to the queued component.

> Passing unsupported data types results in a `System.Runtime.InteropServices.COM` `Exception` with the message `Catastrophic failure`. You may think that this message is not very helpful, but reading the event log gives a nice explanation of the failure: an unsupported object reference was used during a method call to a QC component. The object reference should either be a QC recorder or support `IPersistStream`.

Registration of the Queued Component

A component that uses COM+ services has the following registration and configuration:

- ❑ The assembly must have a strong name
- ❑ The assembly must be configured in the Registry like all COM components
- ❑ The definitions of the library must be installed in a COM+ application
- ❑ COM+ services that are used for the component must be configured in the COM+ catalog

We will discuss two ways to register and configure our COM+ service:

- ❑ Dynamic COM+ Registration
- ❑ Manual COM+ Registration

Dynamic COM+ Registration

Dynamic COM+ Registration is an easy, but limited, way to configure assemblies in the COM+ catalog. The assembly just needs to be copied to the server. If the component is used from an ASP.NET application, the assembly has to be copied to the `/bin` directory of the web application. As soon as an application uses the assembly, it's installed in the COM+ catalog.

The disadvantages of dynamic configuration is that COM clients cannot make use of assemblies that are dynamically configured, because the assemblies are not installed in the global assembly cache, and as such will not be found from the COM client. Additionally, the first application to access the .NET component must run with administrator privileges.

> During development, dynamic COM+ registration is a great feature that makes testing of application easier. For production systems you should use manual registration instead because it is not certain that the first user running the application has administrative privileges.

Manual COM+ Registration

For a manual registration, we have to install the assembly of the queued component in the global assembly cache. This can be done using the command line utility `gacutil -i`. Wrox's *Professional C#* (ISBN 1-861004-99-0) gives more information about shared assemblies and the global assembly cache.

> **Pay attention that every time you do a new build of the component library, you must re-register the assembly in the global assembly cache.**

For the sample application we'll install the assembly `BookOrderQC` in the global assembly cache:

```
gacutil -i BookOrderQC.dll
```

Now we can register the .NET assembly manually using the .NET Services Installation tool, `Regsvcs.exe`. We register the assembly `BookOrderQC` to generate and register a type library, and to create and configure a COM+ application with the attributes this tool finds in the assembly:

```
regsvcs BookOrderQC.dll
```

After registration of the assembly `BookOrderQC` the application `Wrox.BookOrder` and the interface `IBookOrder` can be found in the Component Services administration tool:

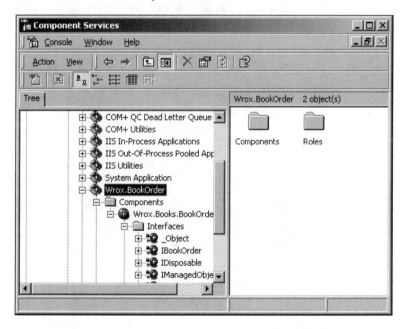

We can see from the application's properties that the `Queuing` properties `Queued` and `Listen` are already set. This is because the assembly attribute `ApplicationQueuing` was set:

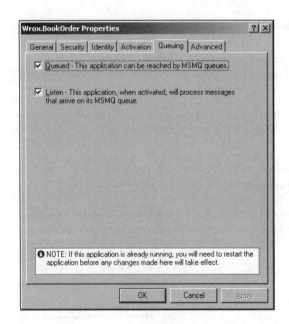

With the COM+ option Queued automatically, some private message queues and a public message queue are generated, and they are named after the COM+ application.

Selecting the properties of the interface IBookOrder in the Component Services tool, we can see that this interface is queue-able. The **Queued** checkbox is selected because of the attribute InterfaceQueuing:

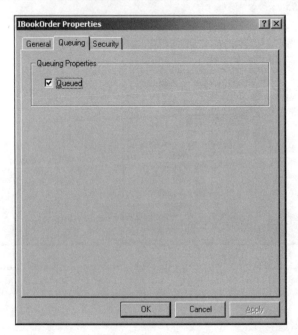

Message Queue for the COM+ Application

Because the COM+ application has the property Queues – This application can be reached by MSMQ queues set, a message queue was created automatically. If you use the Visual Studio .NET Server Explorer, you can see the public queue `wrox.bookorder`. The queue has the same name as the COM+ application:

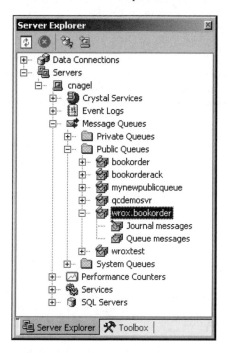

Queued Component Client

The server is configured as a COM+ application; now we have to write a client that calls the methods of the queued component. If the client calls the component directly the message queue wouldn't be used. The client has to call the recorder to pass the method call in a queue. The recorder can be instantiated with the queue moniker.

Moniker

Before we look at the queue moniker maybe this question arises: what is a moniker? A moniker was introduced for the first time in the days of OLE. With a link to a document, a file moniker was stored in the containing document. A moniker knows something about how to instantiate a COM object, and how to initialize it with data. If a link to an Excel sheet is placed in a Word document, the created file moniker stores the CLSID of Excel, and the filename of the Excel sheet. Instantiating the linked Excel sheet activates the moniker, which in turn activates Excel, as it knows the CLSID, and initializes the Excel application by passing the file.

Internet Explorer uses a different moniker when you enter a web address in the address box. Here the URL moniker is instantiated that knows the URL to pass this data to the web browser control.

To summarize, a moniker is itself a COM object that knows how to instantiate and initialize a COM object (or a .NET object).

With the .NET Framework we can use the static `BindToMoniker()` method of the `System.Runtimer.InteropServices.Marshal` class to instantiate and bind a moniker.

For queued components we need a queue and a new moniker.

New Moniker

With the new moniker we can create a COM object passing a prog-ID or a CLSID. The new moniker calls the Windows API call to create COM objects: `CoCreateInstanceEx()` if it is not left-prefixed. Prefixing the new moniker with the queue moniker passes the CLSID of the component to the queue moniker:

```
IBookOrder qc =
        (IBookOrder)Marshal.BindToMoniker("new:Wrox.Books.BookOrderQC");
```

Queue Moniker

The queue moniker must be left-prefixed with the new moniker. In this example `queue:/` represents the queue moniker:

```
"queue:/new:Wrox.Books.BookOrderQC"
```

With the queue moniker we start the recorder that records the method calls.

It is not necessary to create a new application for the client as we already built a Windows application to send messages for message queuing. We can use the same application and change the click handler method for the **Submit Order** button.

In the `buttonSubmitOrder_Click()` handler we now bind to the queue moniker and call the method `OrderABook()` of the queued component. The recorder that is started from the queue moniker puts the call to the method in the message queue that is associated with the COM+ application. `Marshal.ReleaseComObject()` releases the recorder and frees the memory:

```
        private void buttonSubmitOrder_Click(object sender,
                                        System.EventArgs e)
    {
        Cursor c = this.Cursor;
        IBookOrder qc = null;
        try
        {
            this.Cursor = Cursors.WaitCursor;
            string moniker = "queue:/new:Wrox.Books.BookOrderQC";

            qc = (IBookOrder)Marshal.BindToMoniker(moniker);

            string company = textCompany.Text;
            string contact = textContactName.Text;
            string bookTitle = comboBoxBooks.SelectedItem.ToString();
            int count = Convert.ToInt32(textNumberBooks.Text);

            qc.OrderABook(company, contact, bookTitle, count);
        }
```

```
        catch (Exception ex)
        {
            MessageBox.Show(ex.Message);
        }
        finally
        {
            if (qc != null)
                Marshal.ReleaseComObject(qc);
            this.Cursor = c;
        }
    }
```

Running the client and submitting some book orders we can see that the book orders are sent to the message queue by looking at the queue with the Computer Management tool (or Server Explorer in Visual Studio .NET) as you can see in the picture below:

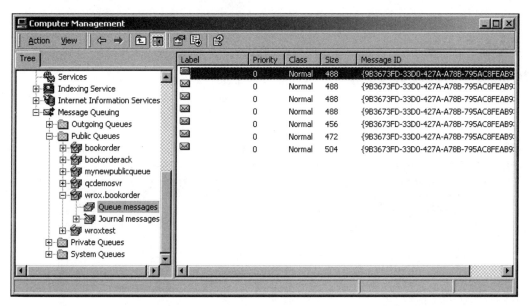

There is an interesting aspect from a performance point of view: if you use the same queue moniker object to call more than one method, instead of creating a single message for every call, all method calls will be put into the same message. This also means that you have to call
Marshal.ReleaseComObject() to have the message sent.

Queue Moniker Parameter

With the queue moniker it's also possible to specify parameters to select a different message queue using a computer name, queue name, path, or format name. Message parameters can be specified to select express or recoverable mode, to encrypt the messages, and to define a journal queue and timeouts.
To change the queue the parameters ComputerName, QueueName, PathName, and FormatName can be specified. To change the message we can use the parameters AppSpecific, AuthLevel, Delivery, EncryptAlgorithm, HashAlgorithm, Journal, Label, MaxTimeToReachQueue, MaxTimeToReceive, Priority, PrivLevel, and Trace. We've already seen what these parameters mean in previous discussions.

427

Now we'll change the example, so that if the checkbox for fast orders is checked, we send high priority messages to the queue with the message parameter `Priority=5` in the queue moniker:

```
Cursor c = this.Cursor;
IBookOrder qc = null;
try
{
    this.Cursor = Cursors.WaitCursor;
    string moniker;

    if (this.checkBoxFastOrder.Checked)
    {
        moniker = "queue:Label=BookOrder," +
                        "Priority=5/new:Wrox.Books.BookOrderQC";
    }
    else
    {
        moniker = "queue:Label=BookOrder/new:Wrox.Books.BookOrderQC";
    }
    qc = (IBookOrder)Marshal.BindToMoniker(moniker);
```

Running the Queued Component

The messages are written to the queue. How can the queued component read the messages from the queue? The COM+ application that has the process for the queued component must be started. This can be done either administratively or programmatically.

We can use the Component Services tool, select the COM+ application in the tree view, and start the application with the menu Action | Start as you can see in the screenshot below:

As soon as the application is started, we see the message boxes that are shown by the queued component when messages are received:

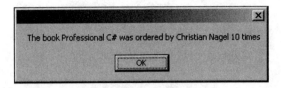

The book Professional C# was ordered by Christian Nagel 10 times

OK

Programmatically we can start the COM+ application by accessing the COM+ catalog API's.

Summary

In this chapter we've seen how Messaging Services can be used. In an environment where notebooks play important roles, messaging has the advantage that the application itself need not deal with disconnected environments as this is done from the system service. Messaging can also be used to move the peak-loads of database servers to night shifts. For connected environments messaging also has its use, where priorities should be used to classify the importance of messages.

With the classes from the System.Messaging namespace, message queuing can be used directly from managed code. MessageQueue is the class that represents a message queue. The second most important class is Message, which encapsulates the properties of a message and the message itself.

Another way to use message queuing is by using Queued Components. With this COM+ service we no longer have to deal with messages, but instead can call methods with the help of a recorder. The disadvantage of using queued components within a .NET application is that there is not such a nice integration as with the System.Messaging classes, as we have to deal with COM objects.

11

Files, Serialization, and Registry Operations

In this chapter we're going to broaden our coverage of data sources even further, as we look at reading and writing data to both files and the Registry, and examine how .NET uses streams to facilitate all input/output (IO) tasks.

We will also examine how to serialize data and objects to streams and how to deserialize data back into objects. This can facilitate transferring objects from application to application, or allow you to persist objects to a file for later use.

Most modern applications will require the use of some or all of the topics discussed in this chapter. Configuration files can be used to store application settings, order and transaction files can be generated and sent to external systems, and raw network communication could be required to interact with a remote client. User preferences often need to be stored in the Registry, and remote systems need a fast and efficient way to transport objects through serialization. All these opportunities involve reading from or writing to streams. By the end of this chapter you will understand how to accomplish all of these tasks easily and efficiently in the .NET Framework.

In this chapter we'll cover:

❑   What the major classes of the System.IO namespace are and why they are used

❑   What streams are, and how the .NET Framework uses them extensively

❑   How to read and write any data in a file

❑   How to utilize isolated storage to store information protected and maintained at a user level

❑   Reading delimited data from a file

❑   Serializing objects to a stream in XML, SOAP, and Binary formats

❑   Storing and retrieving data in the Windows Registry

System.IO

All of the classes used to manipulate the file system are located in the System.IO namespace. This namespace contains classes that manage the reading and writing of data to and from files, as well as classes that query and update information about the files and directories in the file system itself. There are classes for file IO, file and directory modification, file system information, and even in-memory IO.

> *We will not be concentrating on specific file system manipulation issues in this chapter; an in-depth coverage of the details of file system manipulation can be found in Chapter 14 of* Professional C#, Wrox Press (ISBN 1-861004-99-0).

This chapter will examine the major classes used to manipulate the file system, but will primarily focus on streaming input and output in .NET.

The following diagram shows the major classes in the System.IO namespace that we will be concentrating on in this chapter.

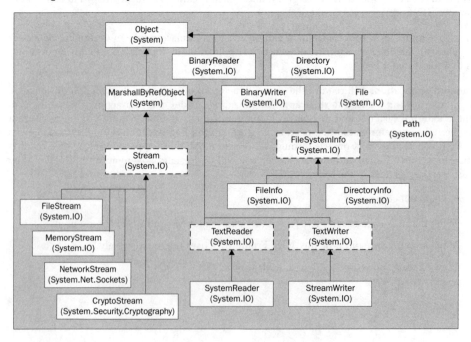

Note that the classes outlined with a dotted line are abstract. These cannot be instantiated directly, but provide methods and properties for their derived classes. The classes in the diagram that are of interest to us in this chapter are the following:

Class	Description
File	A utility class, which exposes many static methods for moving, copying, and deleting files.
Directory	A utility class, which exposes static methods for moving, copying, and deleting directories.
Path	A utility class used to manipulate path names.
FileInfo	Represents a physical file on disk, and exposes methods to manipulate this file. For any reading from or writing to the file, a Stream object must be created.
DirectoryInfo	Represents a physical directory on disk, and has methods to manipulate this directory.
FileStream	Represents a file that can be written to or read from, or both. This file can be written to and read from asynchronously or synchronously. We will cover both methods in this chapter.
StreamReader	Reads character data from a stream.
StreamWriter	Writes character data to a stream.
BinaryReader	Reads primitive data types from a stream.
BinaryWriter	Writes primitive data types to a stream
MemoryStream	Represents a memory location that can be written to and read from exactly like a FileStream. Used for caching data in memory.
NetworkStream	Represents a network socket connection. Since it derives from the stream class, you can read and write data using the same interface as the stream class.
CryptoStream	The output of this stream can be piped into another stream, thereby effectively encrypting any stream. This way the NetworkStream, FileStream, MemoryStream, and StreamReader/StreamWriter classes can all be strongly encrypted.
IsolatedStorageFileStream	Represents a file within isolated storage, a protected and user-isolated private data store.

To begin we'll take a look at the File, Directory, FileInfo, and DirectoryInfo classes.

The File and Directory Classes

As utility classes, both the `File` and `Directory` classes expose methods for manipulating the file system and the files and directories within it. These are static methods that involve moving files, querying and updating attributes, and creating `FileStream` objects.

Some of the most useful static methods of the `File` class are:

Method	Description
Copy()	Copies a file to the specified location.
Create()	Creates a file in the specified path.
Delete()	Deletes a file.
Open()	Returns a `FileStream` object at the specified path.
Move()	Moves a specified file to a new location. You can specify a different name for the file in the new location.

Some useful static methods of the `Directory` class are:

Method	Description
CreateDirectory()	Creates a directory with the specified path.
Delete()	Deletes the specified directory and all the files within it.
GetDirectories()	Returns an array of `strings` representing the directories below the current directory.
GetFiles()	Returns an array of `strings` representing the files in the current directory.
Move()	Moves the specified directory to a new location. You can specify a new name for the folder in the new location.

The FileInfo Class

Unlike the `File` class, the `FileInfo` class does not have static methods, and can only be used as an instantiated object. The `FileInfo` object represents a file on a disk or network location. Note that it is not a stream, which means that to do any reading or writing to a file, a `Stream` object has to be created. The `FileInfo` object aids you in doing this by exposing several methods that return `Stream` objects. First, to create a `FileInfo` object, you must supply a path to a file.

```
FileInfo aFile = new FileInfo("C:/Log.txt");
```

Note that if the file C:\Log.txt does not exist, an exception is not thrown: the FileInfo object simply points to a non-existent file. Methods are available that can test for the existence of the file, and to create the file. Many of the methods exposed by the FileInfo class are similar to those of the File class; however, because File is a static class, it requires a string parameter specifying the file location for every method call. Therefore, the following two calls are functionally identical:

```
FileInfo aFile = new FileInfo("Data.txt");
if (aFile.Exists)
    Console.WriteLine("File Exists");

if (File.Exists("Data.txt"))
    Console.WriteLine("File Exists");
```

Most of the FileInfo methods mirror the File methods in this manner. It makes sense to use the static File class if you are only making a single method call on the object. In this case, the single call will be faster because the .NET Framework will not have to go through the process of instantiating a new object and then calling the method.

Security checks are performed on the file every time a File method is called; the file security is only checked when the FileInfo object is created. Therefore, if your application is performing several read/write operations on the same file it will be more efficient to instantiate a FileInfo object and use its methods. This will provide a performance advantage, because the object will already be referencing the correct file on the file system, whereas the static class will have to locate it every time and perform the security checks.

The FileInfo class also exposes the following properties about the underlying file, which can be manipulated to update the file:

Property	Description
Attributes	Gets or sets the attributes of the current file
CreationTime	Gets the creation date and time of the current file
DirectoryName	Returns the path to the file's directory
Exists	Determines whether a file exists
FullName	Retrieves the full path of the file
Length	Gets the size of the file
Name	Returns just the name of the file, not the full file location path
Directory	Returns a Directory object representing the parent directory of FileInfo object
Extension	Returns the extension of the file
LastAccessTime	Gets or sets the time this file was last accessed
LastWriteTime	Gets or sets the time this file was last written to

The DirectoryInfo Class

The `DirectoryInfo` class works exactly like the `FileInfo` class. It is an object that represents a single directory on a machine. Like the `FileInfo` class, many of the method calls are duplicated between `Directory` and `DirectoryInfo`. The same rule as above applies as to when to use each. If you are making a single call, use the static `Directory` class. If you are making a series of calls, use a `DirectoryInfo` object.

The `DirectoryInfo` class shares almost all of the same properties as the `FileInfo` class, except that it operates on directories, not files.

Streams

The .NET Framework uses streams to facilitate all input and output operations. A stream is an abstract representation of a serial device that stores and accesses data one byte at a time. The underlying device can be a disk file, a printer, a memory location, a network socket, or anything else that is accessed in this manner. This creates a level of abstraction that allows practically any device to be accessed via the same process. Therefore, similar code can be transferred and reused when the application is reading from a file input stream or a network input stream. In addition, the physical mechanics of the device are hidden, meaning the programmer does not need to worry about hard disk heads or TCP/IP packets when writing to a file stream or a network stream.

This same principle applies to input streams. You can write code to read from an input stream, and that stream can come from the keyboard, a network socket, or a file. This section will cover how the .NET Framework makes use of streams to facilitate all IO, and how you can design flexible stream-based applications. To do this we'll be looking in detail at the following classes:

❑   `FileStream`

❑   `StreamReader` and `StreamWriter`

❑   `BinaryReader` and `BinaryWriter`

❑   `MemoryStream`, `NetworkStream`, and `CryptoStream`

FileStream

The `FileStream` class allows for synchronous and asynchronous random access to files. An important consideration is that the `FileStream` class operates on bytes, not characters. To write a string to a file using this class requires you to convert the string into an array of bytes (later, we'll examine the `StreamWriter` and `StreamReader` classes, which are better suited for character IO because they operate on character data natively).

The `FileStream` class provides overloaded constructors to facilitate the various ways you will want to access the underlying file. Specifically, the `FileAccess`, `FileMode`, and `FileShare` properties must be configured when a new `FileStream` object is created. The `File` and `FileInfo` classes also provide the ability to set these properties in their `Open` methods.

The `FileAccess` enumeration specifies how the `FileStream` object can access the file. The options are `Read`, `Write`, and `ReadWrite`. This determines what rights the `FileStream` object will have to the underlying file. If a `FileStream` object is created with `Read` access, any attempt to write to the file will throw an `IOException`. You might decide to open a file in read-only mode based on user configuration settings.

The `FileMode` enumeration determines how the file should be opened or created. The following table lists the options available for the `FileMode` enumeration:

FileMode Enumeration Members	Description
`Append`	Opens the file if it exists and moves the file position to the end of the file, or creates a new file. `FileMode.Append` can only be used in conjunction with the `FileAccess` enum value `FileAccess.Write`.
`Create`	A new file is created; if one already exists, the contents are destroyed.
`CreateNew`	A new file is created, but if one already exists an exception will be thrown.
`Open`	Opens an existing file. If the file specified does not exist, an exception is thrown.
`OpenOrCreate`	Specifies that the file should be opened if it exists, otherwise a new file is created. If it exists, the data in the file is retained.
`Truncate`	An existing file is opened and its contents erased. The file must exist or an exception is thrown.

Therefore, to create a new file that does not already exist, the following code could be used:

```
FileStream fs = new FileStream("Data.txt",FileMode.ReadWrite,FileAccess.Create);
```

To open an existing file in read-only mode, the following code would be needed:

```
FileStream fs = new FileStream("Data.txt",FileMode.Read,FileAccess.Open);
```

Finally, the `FileShare` enumeration property specifies how other processes can access this file while you have it open. The following table lists the options:

FileShare Enumeration Members	Description
`None`	No other process can access this file until you explicitly close it
`Read`	Allows other processes to open this file for read-only access
`ReadWrite`	Allows other processes to open this file for both reading and writing
`Write`	Allows other processes to open this file for writing

By default, the `FileStream` sets the `FileAccess` property to `ReadWrite` and sets the `FileShare` property to `Read`, meaning that other processes can read the file, but cannot write data to it while it is open. The `FileMode` property must be explicitly set, otherwise the .NET Framework will not know what to do with the supplied file name: open it; create a new one, truncate the data, etc.

When creating a `FileStream` object, the constructor can throw the following exceptions:

Exception	Condition
ArgumentException	The supplied path is an empty string ("").
ArgumentNullException	The supplied path is null.
SecurityException	The user does not have the required permission to access this file.
FileNotFoundException	The file cannot be found when a `FileMode` has been set that requires a file to exists, such as `FileMode.Truncate` or `FileMode.Open`. The file must already exist in these modes.
IOException	Some sort of I/O error occurred, such as a hard drive failure or a file already existing when a `FileMode`, such as `FileMode.CreateNew`, is used that requires the file specified not to exist already.
DirectoryNotFoundException	The supplied path contains a directory path that does not exist.

Reading Data

The `FileStream` class exposes two methods to read data from a file: one to read blocks of bytes and one to read single bytes. These methods are explained below.

```
public int Read(byte[] data, int offset, int count)
```

This method reads up to `count` bytes of data, starting at the `offset` position within the file, and stores the data within the `data` byte array. If the `count` parameter is larger than the remaining bytes in the file, the method will simply read the data until the end of the file is reached. The method always returns the number of bytes read from the file.

This method allows random access to the file, meaning you can read data at any position within the file. This can be very useful in situations where you know the exact size of the records stored in the file and you need to access a specific record. By setting `offset` to the size of a record multiplied by the number of records to skip, and `count` to the size of a record, the exact record you want will be returned in the `byte[]` data, without having to progress sequentially through the file. The `Seek()` method can also be used to move the read/write position in a file.

This process is used in fixed positional files. Many files use a delimiter, such as a comma, to break apart the data fields. We will look at one of the most common formats of this, the comma-separated file, later in this chapter. Another way to store data is to use a fixed size field. This allows the program to instantly read or write in the correct location, without having to parse the file for the delimited text. The downside is the wasted space and lesser human readability of the files created, as well as the explicit limit on field lengths. For example, here is a sample price listing in comma-separated values format:

```
110.20,5.50,1.20,10.50
```

As you can see, each field is separated from the previous by a comma. Here is the same file in a fixed format, with each record being fixed at 6 characters long:

```
110.20  5.50  1.20 10.50
```

Note that, because every record is exactly six characters in length, some of the records must be padded with whitespace. The upside is that the code to grab the third record in the row is very simple:

```
int nRecordLength = 6;
int nRecord = 3;
aFile.Read(arBytes,(nRecordLength * nRecord),nRecordLength);
```

To accomplish the equivalent task in a delimited format would involve reading the row of data into memory and iterating through each field. We will look at how this is done later. As in most things, it is a tradeoff between portability, speed, and ease of use.

```
public int ReadByte()
```

This method reads the next byte from the file and returns it to the caller, or it returns −1 if the end of the stream is reached. Note that the return type is not byte, as one would expect. This is because −1 is outside the range of a byte, so the .NET Framework casts the return value to an integer. This can result in some interesting ways of reading the file. Since we cannot simply read the return value into a byte and check if it is negative (because that will never be true with a byte), we must first get the integer value, use it to compare to −1, and then cast it to a byte:

```
int nTemp;

try
{
    nTemp = fs.ReadByte();

    while(nTemp != -1)
    {
        Byte byByte = (Byte)nTemp;
        //Do processing of by Byte variable
        nTemp = fs.ReadByte();
    }
}
catch(IOException ex)
{
    //Some form of error occurred.
}
```

Writing Data

The `FileStream` class also exposes several methods to facilitate writing data to files. These methods mirror those provided for reading data.

The `Write` method:

```
public void Write(byte[] array, int offset, int count)
```

writes a `byte` array to the underlying file, starting at position `offset` (in bytes) in the file, and writes `count` bytes to the file.

The `WriteByte` method:

```
public void WriteByte(byte value)
```

writes a `byte` to the file at the current file position.

Let's look at an actual example of some of these methods in action. The following code writes the bytes 1 to 100 to a local file. This code can be found in the `/FileStreamOutput` directory in the code download:

```
using System;
using System.IO;

namespace FileStreamOutput-Wrox. ProCSharpData Chapter 11 FileStreamOutput
{
    class WriteBytes
    {
        static void Main(string[] args)
        {
            try
            {
                //Open or create file
                FileStream aFile = new FileStream(
                        "Log.dat",FileMode.OpenOrCreate,FileAccess.ReadWrite);

                //Write bytes 0-99 to file
                for(byte b=0;b<100;b++)
                    aFile.WriteByte(b);

                //Close file
                aFile.Close();
            }
            catch(IOException e)
            {
                //Error occurred
                Console.WriteLine("An IO Exception has occurred!");
                Console.WriteLine(e.ToString());
                Console.ReadLine();
            }
        }
    }
}
```

As an exercise, open the resulting file Log.dat in Notepad. You will see an incomprehensible garble of data. If you open the Log.dat file in Visual Studio .NET, you will see the following screen:

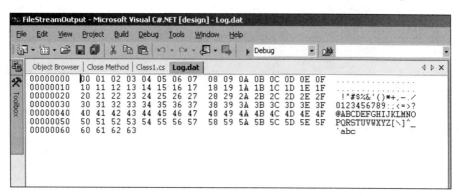

This behavior is normal, and it is a result of writing bytes, rather than character data, to the file. In the sample program we wrote the **values** 0 to 99 to the file, not the **characters** 0 to 99. Therefore, the actual data in the file is the numbers 0 to 99. We can see that in the screenshot above, but note that the data points are represented in hexadecimal, which is why it counts from 00 to 63. Note that when the numbers reach the ASCII character range for printable characters, starting at decimal 33 (the ! character), we begin to see readable output in the file.

Asynchronous Data Access

The FileStream class provides the ability to read and write data asynchronously. The file access methods we have seen so far have been synchronous, meaning that an application waits while the file IO process occurs. This is not always what you want in your applications – sometimes you may want to begin reading a large data file in the background, but continue to do other processing in the foreground. It is possible to do this with multiple threads. A background processing thread could be created that managed the read or write IO process. In .NET, this process is not difficult, but fortunately for us it is even easier to create asynchronous file access with the asynchronous methods of the FileStream object.

The basic idea with asynchronous data access is the ability to start a file IO process, and then continue to do other processing while it is occurring. The IO process will notify your application when it has completed. Thus it can actually take longer to complete the IO process, since it is a background process and much of the computer's resources will be aimed at providing a fluid user interface. However, in terms of the user experience, using asynchronous methods provides a much friendlier alternative. By allowing the user to continue working during costly file or network IO, the user is not forced to wait and can continue to get their work done. This results in happier end users and a more stable and robust application overall.

To accomplish this task, there are pairs of methods that can be used in tandem. To read data asynchronously requires the use of BeginRead() and EndRead(). When writing data, the BeginWrite() and EndWrite() methods are used.

```
IAsyncResult BeginRead(byte[] array, int offset, int numBytes,
        AsyncCallback userCallback, object stateObject);
```

The first three parameters are identical to the `FileStream.Read()` method. The `userCallback` parameter is a delegate method you write that the .NET Framework will call back in your application when the reading is completed: this is how your application can continue processing, but still respond to the end of the read request. The `stateObject` parameter is a user-supplied object that is used to distinguish this asynchronous read request from others in your application. This object is available as a property of the `IAsyncResult` object that is returned from the method call.

The `IAsyncResult` object returned is an abstract representation of the reading process. It contains many properties and methods to allow you to query the status of the process, as well as determine if it is completed.

The `AyschCallback` method is very simple. It is just a method that returns `void` and accepts a single `IAsyncResult` parameter. The following is an example of a simple implementation of this delegate method:

```
private void HandleRead(IAsyncResult ar)
{
    Console.WriteLine("Reading file complete…");
}
```

We pass this to the `BeginRead()` method by creating a new `AsyncCallback` object, passing in the address of this method. The code to do this looks like this:

```
System.AsyncCallback cb = new AsyncCallback(HandleRead);
```

After this, the `cb` variable is passed to the `BeginRead()` method as the fourth parameter.

`EndRead()` is called when you want to forcibly end the asynchronous data read, or you wish to discover the number of bytes read from the file. `EndRead()` is called with the `IAsyncResult` object returned from the corresponding `BeginRead()` method call.

Asynchronous File Reader Example

Let's see an example of how this will work. The following example opens up a file specified as a command-line argument, and asynchronously reads the entire contents into memory. Meanwhile it writes data to the console, simulating processing that can continue uninterrupted while the IO process continues. The result will be something like this, with a simple text file specified:

Obviously, in a real application we would be doing more significant processing than echoing out to the console, but this example shows you how to write code that reads data from a file without blocking your application synchronously.

Create a new C# Console Application project in Visual Studio .NET. Change the name of the default class to ReadAsync. The code for this project can be found in the \ReadAsync directory in the online code.

First we need to add the required namespaces. We will be using the System.IO namespace for the majority of the classes, but we will also need the System.Text namespace for the conversion from bytes to characters. Add the following two lines to the top of the file:

```
using System;
using System.IO;
using System.Text;
```

Add the following private member variables to the ReadAsync class:

```
class ReadAsync
    {
        private byte[] byData;
        private char[] charData;
        private FileStream aFileStream;
```

Now add the following text to the Main method. This will check for the existence of a filename as a command line argument, and create an instance of the ReadAsync class:

```
static void Main(string[] args)
{
    if (args.Length == 0)
    {
        Console.WriteLine("You must supply a file name " +
                                        "for this application.");
        Console.ReadLine();
        return;
    }

    //Create ReadAsync object with command line argument
    ReadAsync aRead = new ReadAsync(args[0]);

}
```

Create the following constructor for the ReadAsync class. This is where most of the work in the application occurs:

```
public ReadAsync(string strFile)
    {
        //Create FileInfo object pointing to file
        FileInfo aFile = new FileInfo(strFile);

        //Check if the file exists
        if(aFile.Exists)
        {
            //Get length
```

443

```
            byData = new byte[aFile.Length];

            try
            {
                //Open FileStream object
                aFileStream = aFile.OpenRead();

                //Create the callback delegate method
                System.AsyncCallback cb = new
                        AsyncCallback(HandleRead);

                //Begin the asynchronous reading
                System.IAsyncResult aResult =aFileStream.BeginRead(
                            byData,0,(int)aFile.Length,cb,"Read Data");

                //Loop -> Performing other processing
                for(int x=0;x<300;x++)
                    Console.WriteLine("Reading data from file - " +
                                    "performing other processing...");

                Console.ReadLine();
            }
            catch(IOException e)
            {
                //Error occurred
                Console.WriteLine("Failed to start asynchronous read.");
                Console.WriteLine(e.ToString());
                Console.ReadLine();
            }
        }
        else
            Console.WriteLine("No file with that name exists.");
}
```

After checking to see if there really is a file with that name, this code instantiates a `FileStream` object, using the `OpenRead()` method of `FileInfo`. It then sets up the parameters for reading the data from the file asynchronously, and begins the read operation. Note that we pass in the callback method and the `state` object, which in this example is the string **Read Data**. Recall that this object could be used to differentiate multiple read requests occurring simultaneously. In the `HandleRead` method, we will extract the state object to show how this would be accomplished. Finally, to simulate other processing that can occur simultaneously, the application writes data to the Console in a loop.

Now, add the following code:

```
private void HandleRead(IAsyncResult ar)
{
    //Convert byte array from raw bytes into character array
    Decoder d = Encoding.ASCII.GetDecoder();
    charData = new char[d.GetCharCount(byData,0,byData.Length)];
    d.GetChars(byData, 0, byData.Length, charData, 0);

    //Write state object and contents of file to console
    Console.WriteLine("Value of state object for this " +
```

```
                                          "operation: {0}", ar.AsyncState);
            Console.WriteLine("Data from file:");
            Console.WriteLine(charData);

    }
```

This is the callback method that the .NET Framework will call into the application when the file read operation is complete. This code must convert the byte array returned by the read operation into a character array for display to the user. The Decoding class manages converting between bytes and characters, based on a specific encoding. In this example we assume ASCII encoding. The other options available are: Unicode(UTF16), UTF7 and UTF8. Note that the StreamReader class automatically detects the correct encoding of the stream and reads the data accordingly. We will see how this works later. The state object passed to the BeginRead() method is echoed out to the user by accessing the IAsyncResult.AsyncState property. In this example it simply contains the string **Read Data**, but in an enterprise application it would be used to manage multiple asynchronous requests simultaneously.

With that, all the code required to run the sample is complete. Run the application with a text file as a command line argument to see asynchronous file reading in action!

Asynchronous File Writer Example

Writing data to files asynchronously uses the same basic process as reading data asynchronously. The BeginWrite()method is invoked on the FileStream object, passing in the byte array data to write to the file. This method processes the write request, and notifies the application when the operation is completed via a user supplied callback method.

The BeginWrite() method signature looks similar to the FileStream.Write() method, with the addition of the AsychCallback parameter and state object.

```
public void Write(byte[] array, int offset, int count, AsyncCallback userCallback,
object stateObject);
```

This method begins at position offset in the file and writes the data contained in array, up to count bytes. The userCallback method has the same signature as the callback method we looked at before. The stateObject is a user-supplied object to manage multiple asynchronous writes.

The following example writes a random block of data to a file. This example is very similar to the previous, and is included for comparison of how an asynchronous write operation is performed. This project can be found in the \WriteAsync directory in the online code:

```
using System;
using System.IO;

namespace WriteAsync
{
    class WriteAsync
    {
        private byte[] byData;
        private FileStream aFileStream;

        public WriteAsync()
        {
            Random aRnd = new Random();
```

```
        try
        {
           //Create random data
           byData = new Byte[10000];

           //Fill array with random byte data
           aRnd.NextBytes(byData);

           //Open FileStream object
           aFileStream = new FileStream(
                    "Output.dat",FileMode.OpenOrCreate,FileAccess.Write);

           //Create callback delegate
           AsyncCallback cb = new AsyncCallback(HandleWrite);

           //Begin asynchronous file write
           IAsyncResult aResult = aFileStream.BeginWrite(
                                        byData,0,10000,cb,"Write Data");

           //Perform other processing
           for(int x=0;x<300;x++)
              Console.WriteLine("Writing data to file - performing "
                                                + "other processing...");

           Console.ReadLine();
        }
        catch(IOException e)
        {
           //Error occurred
           Console.WriteLine("Failed to start asynchronous read.");
           Console.WriteLine(e.ToString());
           Console.ReadLine();
        }

     }

     private void HandleWrite(IAsyncResult ar)
     {
        //This method is called when the asynchronous process is complete
        // Simply echo out status to Console
        Console.WriteLine("Write operation complete.");
        Console.WriteLine("Value of state object for " +
                                "this operation: {0}", ar.AsyncState);
     }

     static void Main(string[] args)
     {
        //Create new WriteAsync object
        WriteAsync aRead = new WriteAsync();
     }
  }
}
```

This example creates the file `Output.dat` and writes 10,000 random bytes of data to it. While this relatively large IO operation is occurring, the application is busy with other processing. Hopefully this shows you how to maximize your application's performance when reading and writing data files.

Asynchronous processing will not always be useful for your application. If your application requires the contents of the file before it can continue processing, you might as well use a synchronous process. However, if the file needs to be saved in the background, or a large media file must be loaded from a slow network stream, giving the user the ability to perform other operations is very useful. Asynchronous file IO gives you this option, and it is very easy to use in the .NET Framework.

StreamReader and StreamWriter

Unlike the `FileStream` class, the `TextReader` and `TextWriter` classes do not derive from `Stream`. While the `Stream` class is designed to operate on bytes and byte arrays, the `Text` classes are designed to operate on character data. The actual `TextReader` and `TextWriter` classes are abstract, and the classes you will use in your applications are the `StreamReader` and `StreamWriter` classes. These provide a wrapper around a stream and allow you to read and write strings on the underlying stream without having to worry about byte data. The `StreamReader` and `StreamWriter` classes are very useful in a multitude of situations and will likely be used for the majority of the IO work you do.

The `StreamReader` and `StreamWriter` objects simply make it easier to read and write string or character data on an underlying stream. By sending the stream the raw byte data, or using conversion classes, it is entirely possible to use the basic stream classes, just as it is with a `FileStream` class. If you are writing an application that does not work with character data, this makes the most sense, but if you are reading and writing strings on any of these stream classes, using the `StreamReader` and `StreamWriter` classes saves time and energy.

StreamWriter

The `StreamWriter` class is used to write character data to streams. This class can be created around an existing stream to enable writing string and character data to that stream. The stream object is passed in as a parameter to the constructor, which allows us to access the underlying stream with the ease of use of the `StreamWriter`.

This allows us to create a `FileStream` object, using the `FileStream` constructor to specify the `FileMode`, `FileAccess`, and `FileShare` properties, while still leveraging the `StreamWriter` object to read and write character data to and from the file.

The following code uses the `FileMode.OpenOrCreate` parameter to open an existing file or create a new one if it doesn't exist. Then a `StreamWriter` object is created and wrapped around the `FileStream` object.

```
FileStream aFile = new
FileStream("Data.txt",FileMode.OpenOrCreate,FileAccess.ReadWrite);

StreamWriter sw = new StreamWriter(aFile);
```

Another method for creating a `StreamWriter` object is to simply specify the file name in Universal Naming Convention (UNC) format (for example: `//mycomputer/c_drive/chapter14/Data.txt`). This is an obvious option if the file already exists and you do not need to specify any special `FileAccess`, `FileMode`, or `FileShare` parameters. Creating a `FileStream` object is the only way to change these from the defaults. The default is `FileAccess.ReadWrite`, `FileMode.Open`, and `FileShare.Read`. If the file already exists, and you just want to write data to it, the following code will work fine:

```
StreamWriter sw = new StreamWriter("Data.txt");
```

Another convenient use of this class is to use it in combination with other forms of streaming IO. By wrapping a `StreamWriter` around any stream object, you can facilitate writing character data to that stream. This is obviously useful when dealing with `FileStream` objects, but can also be useful when working with a `NetworkStream` object to communicate over a network socket or a `CryptoStream` object to facilitate encryption of streams.

It is very simple to create a `StreamWriter` object wrapped around a `CryptoStream` object. The following code shows how to write encrypted strings to a file:

```
Public void EncryptFile(string FileName, string Text)
{
    //Key and Vector arrays used in encryption process
    // These need to match those used when the file is decrypted
    // In real application these would be supplied by the user or
    // some other external source like a database
    byte[] byKey = {1,2,3,4,5,6,7,8,9,10,11,12,13,14,15,16};
    byte[] byVec = {1,2,3,4,5,6,7,8,9,10,11,12,13,14,15,16};

    //Open the file
    FileStream fs = new FileStream(FileName, FileMode.OpenOrCreate,
                                   FileAccess.ReadWrite);

    //Create algorithm object
    SymmetricAlgorithm des = SymmetricAlgorithm.Create();

    //Create CyptoStream object from stream
    CryptoStream encStream = new CryptoStream(fs,
                              des.CreateEncryptor(byKey,byVec),
                              CryptoStreamMode.Write);

    //Create StreamWriter around CyptoStream
    StreamWriter sw = new StreamWriter(encStream);

    //Write the text out using the StreamWriter
    // all data is automatically encrypted through the CyptoStream
    sw.WriteLine(Text);

    //Close the stream
    sw.Close();

}
```

Note that the `System.Security.Cryptography` namespace is required to use such encryption methods.

This code creates a file and writes encrypted character data to the file. This data is encrypted using a symmetric algorithm that requires a `byte` array for the key and initialization vectors. Both these are specified in the method itself; in an enterprise application these would have to be application-or-user specific. After creating the `CryptoStream` object we create a `StreamWriter` object, passing in the `CryptoStream` as a parameter to the constructor. We can now write data to the file using the methods of the `StreamWriter` class, and the data is encrypted to the file.

The `StreamWriter` class exposes the `Write` and `WriteLine` methods for writing data to a stream. The `Write` method:

```
public void Write(string)
```

writes data to the underlying stream object, without a line breaking character after the string. Therefore the successive calls to this method will result in a single line of text being written to the stream. For example, the following block of code will write a single line to the file.

```
StreamWriter sw = new StreamWriter("Out.txt");
sw.Write("This ");
sw.Write("will ");
sw.Write("all ");
sw.Write("be on a single line. ");
```

This code will produce the output

This will all be on a single line

in the file `Out.txt`. The `Write()` method is overloaded and accepts many different data parameters. In each of these versions, the default `ToString()` method is called on the data passed in and the returned `string` value is written to the stream.

The `WriteLine` method:

```
public void WriteLine(string)
```

also writes data to the underlying stream object, but this time a line terminator is appended to the string. The default line terminator is a carriage return-line feed combination, but modifying the `NewLine` property can change this to a user-defined value.

The following code snippet writes several lines of text to `Out.txt`, using the `WriteLine()` method. Note that every call to `WriteLine()` causes a new line to be appended to the data.

```
StreamWriter sw = new StreamWriter("Out.txt");
sw.WriteLine("Hello World.");
sw.WriteLine("This string will be on another line.");
sw.WriteLine("So will this.");
```

This code will write the following data to the `Out.txt` file:

Hello World.
This string will be on another line.
So will this.

449

StreamReader

The StreamReader class is the companion of the StreamWriter class. StreamReader facilitates reading character and string data from an underlying stream. The StreamReader class handles all encoding issues and allows the developer to work at a higher level of abstraction than the stream-based classes.

Like StreamWriter, this class can be creating using an existing stream as a base, or pointing to an existing file. Using this class with an existing stream is convenient for reading character data from the underlying data source.

There are several ways of reading data using the StreamReader class. The three methods used to read data from a stream are:

- ❑ Read()
- ❑ ReadLine()
- ❑ ReadToEnd()

The following section explains these methods. We start with the Read method.

```
public int Read()
```

This method returns the next character from the stream, or -1 if the end of the stream has been reached. Note that the character value is returned as a integer, so a conversion must be done if you wish to use the data as a character. This is a simple matter accomplished by using the System.Convert class. Here is an example of how this could be done:

```
StreamReader sr = new StreamReader("Out.txt");
char chData = Convert.ToChar(sr.Read());
```

An overload of the Read method:

```
public int Read(char[] buffer, int index, int count)
```

retrieves up to count number of characters into the buffer array. It begins to retrieve the character as the position specified in the index parameter. The value returned is the number of characters read from the stream, or -1 if the end of the stream was reached. Like the FileStream's method, this can be used to perform random-access on the underlying stream. The major difference is that this method returns the data as a character array instead of a byte array. This makes it much more convenient to use with text files, but not very useful when working with any other format of file.

The ReadLine method:

```
public string ReadLine()
```

reads a line of data from the stream and returns it as a string variable. A line is defined as a sequence of characters ending in a line feed, or a carriage return followed immediately by a line feed. When the end of the stream is reached, the method returns a null value. Therefore the code to read the entire contents of a file would look like this:

```
StreamReader sr = new StreamReader("Out.txt");
string strLine = sr.ReadLine();
while(strLine != null)
{
    Console.WriteLine(strLine);
    strLine = sr.ReadLine();
}
```

The `ReadToEnd` method reads the entire contents of the stream into a string variable and returns the value to the caller.

```
public string ReadToEnd()
```

Therefore, the entire file could be read with a single call like this:

```
StreamReader sr = new StreamReader("Out.txt");
string strData = sr.ReadToEnd();
```

Creating the `StreamReader` class to read from a `NetworkStream` is very simple. The following code snippet shows how a simple TCP/IP server could use the `StreamReader` class to read the requests coming from a specific port and echo the data out to the console:

```
//Create a TcpListener object to listen to port 8080
TcpListener myListener = new TcpListener(8080);

//Start listening for incoming packets
myListener.Start();

Console.WriteLine("Server running...");

//Program blocks on AcceptTcpClient() until a client connects.
TcpClient myClient = myListener.AcceptTcpClient();

//Client has connected - get a NetworkStream object representing connection
NetworkStream myStream = myClient.GetStream();

//Wrap StreamReader object around NetworkStream for ease of use
StreamReader sr = new StreamReader(myStream);

//Use StreamReader methods to extract data from the network
String strRead = sr.ReadLine();
while(strRead != null)
{
    //Echo to console
    Console.WriteLine(strRead);
    strRead = sr.ReadLine();
}
```

Most of the code involves setting up the `TcpListener` object and waiting for a connection. Once a connection has been requested by a client, the `StreamReader` class is used to wrap the `NetworkStream` object returned by the `TcpClient.GetStream()` method call. Strings can now be read from the TCP request passed to this server.

To read the encrypted file we created earlier using the `StreamWriter` class, we could use the following code:

```
public void DecryptFile(string FileName)
{
    //Key and Vector arrays used in decryption process
    //These need to match those used when the file was encrypted
    byte[] byKey = {1,2,3,4,5,6,7,8,9,10,11,12,13,14,15,16};
    byte[] byVec = {1,2,3,4,5,6,7,8,9,10,11,12,13,14,15,16};

    //Open the file
    FileStream fs = new FileStream(FileName, FileMode.OpenOrCreate,
                                   FileAccess.ReadWrite);

    //Create algorithm object
    SymmetricAlgorithm des = SymmetricAlgorithm.Create();

    //Create a CryptoStream object around file, using algorithm
    CryptoStream encStream = new CryptoStream(fs,
                                  des.CreateDecryptor(byKey,byVec),
                                  CryptoStreamMode.Read);

    //Create StreamReader around CyptoStream
    StreamReader sr = new StreamReader(encStream);

    //Read string data from the Stream - automatically decrypted
    Console.WriteLine(sr.ReadToEnd());

    Console.ReadLine();
}
```

This code is the mirror of the previous example. It uses the same algorithm, but this time for decrypting purposes. It wraps the `CryptoStream` object in a `StreamReader` object, and calls the `StreamReader.ReadToEnd()` method to get all of the data from the file returned in a string object. The great thing is that this string is already decrypted by the time our application gets it, because it has already been through the `CryptoStream`.

Without the `StreamReader` and `StreamWriter` classes, this example would involve writing bytes to the `CryptoStream` class and having to convert between character and byte data. These classes make working with strings and character data very easy and manageable.

BinaryReader and BinaryWriter

If none of the other IO classes expose the functionality you need, you can always use a `BinaryReader` or `BinaryWriter` class. The `BinaryReader` and `BinaryWriter` classes provide the functionality for reading and writing binary data to and from a stream. Like the `StreamReader` and `StreamWriter` classes, they are created around an existing stream. Unlike those classes, however, the `BinaryReader` and `BinaryWriter` classes read and write primitive data types to a stream instead of character data, although one of the primitive types that can be used is `char`.

BinaryReader

Not all information an application needs is going to be in a text format. Often an application must be able to read and interpret binary data. The .NET Framework provides the ability to work with binary files in a simple manner with the `BinaryReader` class.

This class must be created around an existing stream. Therefore, using the class is a two-step process: create the stream pointing to the data store you wish to read, and then create a `BinaryReader` object based on that stream. Here is an example of opening up an image file using the `FileStream` class and then creating a `BinaryReader` object pointing to that file:

```
FileStream fs = new FileStream("ImageFile.bmp",FileMode.Open);
BinaryReader br = new BinaryReader(fs);
```

The `BinaryReader` class exposes many overloaded methods to read from the underlying stream. A `Read()` method exists for every primitive data type. Each method will read a certain amount of bytes from the underlying stream and return the data cast to the requested data type. The table lists the `Read()` method names, and how many bytes of data are read from the stream to return the value.

Method	Bytes Read From Stream
bool ReadBoolean	1
byte ReadByte()	1
byte ReadBytes(int count)	count
char ReadChar()	Depends on encoding used
decimal ReadDecimal()	16
double ReadDouble	8
short ReadInt16()	2
int ReadInt32	4
long ReadInt64	4
float ReadSingle	4
string ReadString	Depends on length of string

BinaryReader Example

Let's look at a simple example to see how the `BinaryReader` could be used for a common imaging task. The following code computes the number of times a color appears in an image. This can be used to generate a histogram of the image. A histogram displays the number of times each color pixel appears. Note that the application assumes that the file is 256 colors: therefore, each pixel color is represented by a single byte. It would not be a difficult task to modify the example to read a full (24 bit) color image (also called TrueColor, containing up to some 17 million colors in an image) and create a histogram, but that is left as an exercise for the reader.

Create a new C# Console Application in Visual Studio .NET and call it **Histogram**. The complete code project can be found in the \Histogram folder in the code download.

Since we are still dealing with IO classes, add the following namespace declaration at the top of the `Class1.cs` file.

```
using System;
using System.IO;
```

Now add the following code to the `Main` method:

```
static void Main(string[] args)
{
    const int HEADERSIZE = 1078;
    Byte aByte;
    long[] arHist = new long[256];
    FileStream fs;
    BinaryReader br;

    try
    {
        //Open file and wrap BinaryReader around stream
        fs = new FileStream("ImageFile.bmp",FileMode.Open);
        br = new BinaryReader(fs);
    }
    catch(IOException)
    {
        Console.WriteLine("IO Exception - Did you remember to place " +
                "an ImageFile.bmp in the same directory as this application?");
        Console.ReadLine();
        return;
    }

    try
    {
        //Move past Bitmap header information
        br.BaseStream.Seek(HEADERSIZE,SeekOrigin.Begin);

        //Loop through entire file
        while(true)
        {
            //Read next byte - update histogram array
            aByte = br.ReadByte();
            arHist[aByte]++;
        }
    }
    catch(EndOfStreamException)
    {
        //Reached end of file - stop processing
    }

    //Write out histogram array to console
     for(int x=0;x<256;x++)
    {
        Console.WriteLine("Color {0}: {1}",x,arHist[x]);
    }
```

```
        Console.ReadLine();
    }
```

To run this application, you must place a 256-color bitmap file called `ImageFile.bmp` in the same directory as the application. The download code contains a 256-color image that can be used as the input for this application. If you decide to use a different file name, make sure you update the code.

When you run this code you will get output similar to the following, displaying how many times each color appears in the image. Obviously, depending on the file specified you would get different results.

This application creates a `FileStream` object around the `ImageFile.bmp` file, and creates a `BinaryReader` object based on the `FileStream` object. We must skip past the Bitmap header information to get to the actual pixel data. The heart of the application is the `while` loop that continues to read the next byte of data from the `BinaryReader`. The application maintains an array of 256 values; this represents each of the colors possible in the image. The value of each of the points in the array represent, how many times that color appears in the image. Therefore, as a byte is retrieved from the image, that position in the array is increased by one, since that color value has been found.

When the end of the stream has been reached, the `BinaryReader` class throws an `EndOfStreamException` instead of returning an indicator value. Therefore, we have to catch the exception and use it to indicate that we are done reading from the stream. We then simply echo out the number of times each color appears in the image to the console.

BinaryWriter

The `BinaryWriter` class writes raw binary data to a stream. Like the `BinaryReader`, it is created around an existing stream. Since this can be any class that derives from `Stream`, you could use the `BinaryWriter` to write binary data to a `NetworkStream`, like this:

```
//Construct connection to a specific TCP address and port
TcpClient tcpClient = new TcpClient("10.4.0.1",8050);

//Get stream
```

```
NetworkStream myStream = tcpClient.GetStream();
//Wrap stream in a BinaryWriter
BinaryWriter binWrite = new BinaryWriter(myStream);

//Send data to the remote system
binWrite.Write(10);
binWrite.Write("username/password");
binWrite.Write(55.11);
binWrite.Write(123456789);
```

This code snippet might be an example of some custom networking protocol developed for a specific application. The NetworkStream is created pointing to the IP address 10.4.0.1 on port 8050. Then a BinaryWriter object is created to facilitate writing data to the NetworkStream. This is because various forms of data must be sent over the wire: integers, strings, floats, and longs. The BinaryWriter can handle writing all primitive data types to the underlying stream.

The BinaryWriter contains an overloaded Write() method that can take many different types of parameters. The following table lists the many versions of the Write() method. All of them write the primitive data type to the underlying stream. This is fundamentally not much different from what the FileStream class does, but the FileStream class only operates on bytes, while the BinaryWriter can write any data type to a stream.

Method	Number of Bytes Stream Position Advanced
public void Write(bool)	1
public void Write(byte)	1
public void Write(byte[]);	Length of array
public void Write(char);	Depends on encoding
public void Write(char[]);	Depends on encoding
public void Write(decimal);	16
public void Write(double);	8
public void Write(short);	2
public void Write(int);	4
public void Write(long);	8
public void Write(float);	4
public void Write(string);	Depends on encoding
public void Write(byte[], int, int);	Depends on encoding
public void Write(char[], int, int);	Depends on encoding

The BinaryWriter class is the choice for writing unformatted data types to a stream. This can be used for writing a specific proprietary file format, communicating over NetworkStreams, or other application-specific uses.

Other Stream Classes

Before we finish with streams let's quickly look at the `MemoryStream`, `NetworkStream`, and `CryptoStream` classes.

MemoryStream

The `MemoryStream` provides the same interface as a `FileStream`, but the information is stored in memory instead of on disk. This could be useful as a means to cache data in memory, while using the same method calls as on a `FileStream` object. Like the `FileStream` class, the `MemoryStream` class reads and writes byte data only. Note that it could be wrapped in one of the `StreamReader`/`StreamWriter` classes to facilitate reading and writing character data to and from memory.

NetworkStream

The `NetworkStream` class is not actually in the `System.IO` namespace, but it does derive from `Stream`. It provides the basic infrastructure for reading and writing bytes to a network location. The basic operations to read and write bytes to the stream are exactly the same as the `FileStream` class, which allows for some interesting design patterns, where your code can write to an underlying file or network stream without knowing the difference.

We have seen several examples of creating `NetworkStream` objects and wrapping them in other stream classes. The `NetworkStream` class supports the same methods as the `FileStream` class, because they both derive from the `Stream` class. Note that this also means it supports asynchronous reads and writes of data. This can be exceptionally useful in a network-programming environment.

CryptoStream

The `CryptoStream` class is another class that does not reside in the `System.IO` namespace, but derives from the `Stream` class. `CryptoStream` provides the ability to encrypt and decrypt byte arrays using a stream. This makes it possible to utilize sophisticated encryption techniques on sensitive data using the same stream operations we have already seen. Note that it is possible to chain the output of one stream, like a `FileStream`, though a `CryptoStream`, thus automatically encrypting the information! We saw an example of this earlier in the chapter using the `StreamWriter` and `StreamReader` classes to encrypt and decrypt the data passing into and out of a text file. This could also be combined with a `NetworkStream` to provide truly robust security on all transmissions over the network.

Delimited Data

Earlier in this chapter we saw how fixed width position files were useful for their speed and simple random access abilities. Another option for storing data in flat files is with a delimited data format. This format uses a delimiter, usually a comma, to separate the fields. A line terminator, usually a carriage return-line feed combination, is used to indicate the end of a row of data. Each row of data represents a single object or data for a single transaction. For example, the following lines might represent orders in an order processing system:

```
OrderNumber, CustomerID, ItemID, ItemQty, ItemPrice, LinePrice
1,100,50,2,300.00,600.00
2,101,3,1,50.00,50.00
3,57,42,5,5.00,25.00
```

As you can see, the first line contains the column names. This is useful to determine what the data actually means. Each row of numbers represents a single order, and each field is delimited with commas.

These types of files are definitely not the current standard for storing and transporting data, but many legacy systems use this format. It is also convenient to use when exporting or importing data to and from applications like Microsoft Excel and Data Transformation Services (DTS). If your application must interact with, or process the output of, a legacy system, it is likely that you will have to deal with a delimited data format like this. XML is a vastly superior method of data storage and transmission for modern systems because of its ease of use, readability, and flexibility to change. See Chapters 7 and 8 for full coverage of the benefits of XML data access and storage.

Reading Delimited Data

The String class provides a handy method for handling delimited data very easily. The method that makes parsing a delimited data stream possible is the String.Split() method. This method accepts an array of characters and the maximum number of fields to return. It parses the string data and returns each field as an element in an array of strings. The character array passed in the first parameter represents the characters that will act as field separators. This will often only be a single character, but could easily be multiple characters. Whenever any one of these characters is found in the string to be parsed, a new field is added to the returned array.

For example, suppose we create a character array containing the characters ',' and '|' and used it as the first parameter to the Split() method on the string: "To,be,or|not|to|be." The array returned would contain six elements, one for each word. However, if the same string was used, and the Split() method was called with only a comma character in the input array, the returned array would contain three elements: "To", "be", and "or|not|to|be." This is because the '|' character has not been defined as a field separator.

The following code reads the data.csv file that contains the above comma-separated value data. This project is located in the \ReadCSV directory in the code dowload.

```csharp
using System;
using System.IO;

namespace Wrox. ProCSharpData. Chapter 11 ReadCSV
{
    class ReadCSV
    {
        static void Main(string[] args)
        {
            char[] Separators = {','};
            string[] strData;
            string[] strHeaders;

            try
            {
                //Open StreamReader object on data file
                StreamReader sr = new StreamReader("data.csv");

                //Read first line
                string strLine = sr.ReadLine();

                if(strLine == null)
                    throw new Exception("No data found in file.");
```

```
                //Get header data - split string into array
                strHeaders = strLine.Split(Separators);

                //Grab the first line of data
                strLine = sr.ReadLine();

                //Begin retrieving data line by line
                //Loop until no more data found in file
                while(strLine != null)
                {
                    //Get data fields in line
                    strData = strLine.Split(Separators);

                    //Loop through and print data from line
                    for(int x=0;x<strData.Length;x++)
                        Console.WriteLine("{0}: {1}",strHeaders[x],strData[x]);

                    //Read next line
                    strLine = sr.ReadLine();
                }

                //Close the file
                sr.Close();
                Console.ReadLine();
            }
            catch(IOException e)
            {
                Console.WriteLine("An IO Exception has occurred!");
                Console.WriteLine("Did you forget to place the data.csv file "
                                    + "in the application directory?");
                Console.WriteLine(e.ToString());
                Console.ReadLine();
            }
        }
    }
}
```

This code reads the data file and produces the following output in the console:

This application uses a `StreamReader` object because it is reading string data from a text file, therefore the `StreamReader` provides the best interface to work with this format of data. We do not need to create a `FileStream` object, because the file already exists and we only need to have read-only access to it. We therefore create the `StreamReader` object directly from the file name.

We read in the first line of data into a separate headers array. This is done by calling the `Split()` method. Note that we pass in a character array with a single element; this element, the comma character, is our field delimiter.

After the headers have been loaded into the header array we loop through the file line by line with the `ReadLine()` method of the `StreamReader` class. With every line we parse the data, again using the `Split()` method and our single-element character array. The only thing we do with the data is echo it out to the console, but obviously this isn't what most applications will do. At this point you have the data from a single row in a string array, and you can process the data any way you need to. It can be passed to another object, written out as XML, or loaded into an object for manipulation.

Determining where to save data can be a difficult problem. Applications must save files in unique locations to ensure data is safe from accidental or purposeful corruption and destruction. In addition, in multiple user systems data must be isolated and secured while still allowing the current user to save and update any application and configuration data stored on the file system. An elaborate system would need to be developed to manage unique user data files as well as some form of protection scheme to ensure data safely and integrity. Fortunately, the .NET framework already contains this system for isolated user data storage. This system is called **isolated storage**.

Isolated Storage

Isolated storage is a mechanism for storing data in a unique and protected location based on the current user. Data can be written to and read from this data store using the same IO classes we have already examined in this chapter. The difference is that any directories and files created are stored in a data store containing a virtual file system unique to the current user. When a different user logs into the computer and accesses their isolated storage, only directories and files created by them will be found. This protects the user data, as well as providing a convenient and easy way to store user, application, and configuration data without worrying about the location on the file system to store data.

The files and directories in isolated storage are stored in protected data stores on the file system. The actual location of the data is dependent on the Operating System, but will exist in the user-specific location in each OS. For example, in Windows 2000 the data store will be located in: `<SYSTEMDRIVE>\Documents and Settings\<User Name>\Local Settings\Application Data`. Administrators can set size limits for each user's isolated storage data. In addition, if roaming profiles have been configured on the network, isolated storage data stores will roam with users, thus enabling the same data to be available to users regardless of their location.

Isolated storage data stores are not only unique for each user, but they are unique across applications as well. This means one application can safely create and manipulate files in isolated storage without overwriting or corrupting files required by another application. Each application has a unique isolated storage virtual file system to utilize. Because of this sandboxing, isolated storage allows untrusted applications the ability to store files on a client computer. Web applications and downloaded controls do not have permission to write data to the client's file system, thus making storing application and user configuration data a difficult task. However, these same applications can write to a user's isolated storage, because nothing can be destroyed in isolated storage that would destroy or corrupt the computer, unlike the 'real' file system.

Reading and writing data to isolated storage is exactly like the IO we have looked at so far. It is stream-based, and the same stream objects can be used to read and write data to isolated storage files. In addition, directories and files can be created, manipulated, and deleted like their counterparts in the standard file system. The key thing to remember is that you are operating within a virtual file system for this particular user. Standard file IO may not always work for every application. Having to hard-code file locations, and the inability to write files on remote clients, can be prohibitive in certain environments, such as downloadable components and web applications. In these scenarios, **isolated storage** may be the perfect answer. Isolated storage is a protected data store that enables data to be written to and read from a virtual file system. This virtual file system is scoped to a specific user and is protected from access by other users. It is also safe for the remote computer, because it cannot overwrite any existing files on the 'real' file system. It is analogous to the Common Language Runtime for a file system.

Using Isolated Storage

When should you use isolated storage in your applications? All application needs are unique, and only you can decide if isolated storage is the right tool for your application. However, Microsoft has identified five scenarios that benefit greatly from the use of isolated storage:

❑ **Roaming** – Isolated storage can be used with roaming profiles, thus enabling application settings and user preferences to follow users from machine to machine.

❏ **Persistent web application storage** – Web applications cannot use the standard IO because they have restricted access rights to the local computer; these applications can utilize isolated storage for the same reasons as downloaded components.

❏ **Shared component storage** – Components that are used by multiple applications can use isolated storage to provide persistent data storage at a per-user level.

❏ **Downloaded controls** – Controls that are downloaded from the Internet are not allowed to write to the file system, but they can use isolated storage to save user information and application configuration data.

❏ **Server storage** – Server applications can also provide cached data stores for users by using isolated storage. Since isolated storage is always segregated from the user, the server must impersonate the user to access and manipulate the data within their isolated storage data store.

The Isolated Storage Tool (`storeadm.exe`) is a command-line utility supplied with the .NET Framework. It can be found in the `FrameworkSDK\Bin` directory. This tool can be used for a variety of administration tasks, such as querying information about the data stores for the current user, removing all isolated storage data stores for the current user, and selecting a different current roaming data store, if this feature has been enabled on the network.

The System.IO.IsolatedStorage Namespace

The `System.IO.IsolatedStorage` namespace contains the classes required to manipulate and work with a user's isolated storage data file. Working with isolated storage is abstracted for the developer, and much of the complexity of managing unique data stores for each user is hidden by the .NET Framework. This is convenient, because the developer does not need to worry about where the physical data files are being stored, or if the data will be protected from access from other users. These tasks are handled by the .NET Framework and the isolated storage framework.

There are two classes that are required to work with data in isolated storage. These are:

❏ `IsolatedStorageFile`

❏ `IsolatedStorageFileStream`

IsolatedStorageFile

This class represents the isolated storage data store for the current user. It contains a host of methods for operating and enumerating the directories and files contained within this store. This class does not expose a constructor; instead it must be created by calling one of its static methods: `GetStore`, `GetUserStoreForAssembly`, or `GetUserStoreForDomain`. These each return an `IsolatedStorageFile` object representing the correct data store. The method to use depends on the isolation level required by the application.

The two methods `GetUserStoreForAssembly` and `GetUserStoreForDomain` each return an `IsolatedStorageFile` object, representing an isolated storage data store. The first method will return a shared data store for every instance of the current assembly. Therefore if the current user runs multiple instances of the application each will access the same isolated storage. The second method returns a unique data store for each instance of the assembly, as isolated by an application domain. Application domains are roughly analogous to process boundaries in the .NET framework. Therefore, if this user runs multiple instances of the application each will access a unique and isolated data store. The following diagrams demonstrate the difference between the two methods and the data stores accessed.

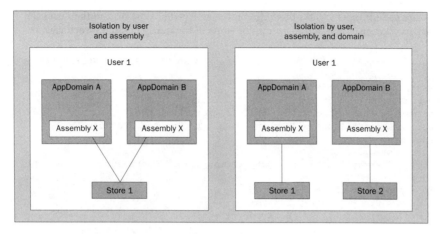

The picture on the left, which represents the GetUserStoreForAssembly method, shows that an isolated data store is shared for all instances of the assembly. The second picture shows the GetUserStoreForDomain method, demonstrating that a separate store can be used for each application domain, even when the same assembly is creating the isolated store.

The more generic GetStore method simply allows these settings to be specified in a more granular way. It also provides the ability to retrieve an isolated data store for a roaming user. This is the only way for roaming users to have their personal isolated storage data stores travel with them. This allows data to be associated with a user even when they move from computer to computer on the network.

To open a data store isolated to the current assembly, the following code would be used:

```
IsolatedStorageFile aIsoStore = IsolatedStorageFile.GetUserStoreForAssembly();
```

In addition to the previous three static methods, the IsolatedStorageFile class exposes the following methods for working with and manipulating the files and directories within a data store:

Method	Description
Close	Closes the current isolated storage data store.
CreateDirectory	Creates a directory in the isolated storage data store.
DeleteDirectory	Deletes a directory in the isolated storage data store.
DeleteFile	Deletes a file in the isolated storage data store.
GetDirectoryNames	Returns an array of string objects containing the names of directories matching a supplied search pattern. For example, "DirectoryName/*".
GetFileNames	Returns an array of string objects containing the names of files matching a supplied search pattern. For example, "DirectoryName/*.txt".
Remove	Permanently deletes the isolated storage data store and all the directories, files, and data contained within.

The following code snippet creates three directories in isolated storage, and then uses the `GetDirectoryNames()` method to search for some of the newly created directories:

```
IsolatedStorageFile aIsoStore = IsolatedStorageFile.GetUserStoreForAssembly();

//Create three directories
aIsoStore.CreateDirectory("TopLevelDirectory");
aIsoStore.CreateDirectory("TopLevelDirectory/NextLevel");
aIsoStore.CreateDirectory("TopLevelDirectory/AnotherDirectory");

//Search for directories
string[] DirArray = aIsoStore.GetDirectoryNames("TopLevelDirectory/*");

//Print out directories found
for(int x = 0;x < DirArray.Length;x++)
    Console.WriteLine("{0}",DirArray[x]);
```

This code would print out the following list:

```
AnotherDirectory
NextLevel
```

IsolatedStorageFileStream

This class is used to create and access data files within the isolated storage data store. It is derived from `FileStream`, and exposes all the same methods for reading and writing data that we examined in the `FileStream` class. A `StreamReader` or `StreamWriter` can also be wrapped around this class to provide an easier mechanism for manipulating the data within it. The same considerations that we examined earlier concerning when to use a `FileStream` object versus using a `StreamReader/StreamWriter` object apply here as well. If you are performing primarily character IO, using the `StreamReader/StreamWriter` classes makes working with the data easier and more manageable.

Creating and opening files within isolated storage is done through the `IsolatedStorageFileStream`'s constructor. The constructor is overloaded with many different versions, but essentially it accepts the name and location of the file within isolated storage, and the `FileMode`, `FileAccess`, and `FileShare` parameters that we examined for `FileStream`. These specify how to open or create the file, what access this application has to the file, and what access other applications have to the file. Another parameter that must be supplied is a previously opened `IsolatedStorageFile` object, which specifies the isolated storage data store to access and use. Remember that the file is not being created or opened in the physical file system of the computer; it is instead working within the current user's isolated data store.

To see how this all works in practice, let's create an application that utilizes isolated storage. Create a new C# Console Application titled **IsolatedStorage**. The code for this project can be found in the `IsolatedStorage` directory in the download code.

Add the following namespace declarations to the top of the file. We need to reference the `System.IO.IsolatedStorage` namespace to gain access to the new isolated storage classes:

```
using System;
using System.IO;
using System.IO.IsolatedStorage;
```

Now add the following code to the main method:

```
static void Main(string[] args)
{
    //Open isolated data store
    IsolatedStorageFile aIsoStore = IsolatedStorageFile.GetUserStoreForAssembly();

    //Create some directories within the data store
    aIsoStore.CreateDirectory("TopLevelDirectory");
    aIsoStore.CreateDirectory("TopLevelDirectory/AnotherDirectory");

    //Create new data file and wrap it in a StreamWriter object
    StreamWriter sw = new StreamWriter(new IsolatedStorageFileStream(
                        "TopLevelDirectory/AnotherDirectory/Data.txt",
                        FileMode.CreateNew, FileAccess.ReadWrite,
                        FileShare.Read, aIsoStore));
    //Write some data to the file
    sw.WriteLine("Hello Isolated World!");
    //Close file
    sw.Close();

    //Open the file up - this time with a StreamReader object
    StreamReader sr = new StreamReader(new IsolatedStorageFileStream(
                        "TopLevelDirectory/AnotherDirectory/Data.txt",
                        FileMode.Open, FileAccess.ReadWrite,
                        FileShare.Read, aIsoStore));
    //Read the data and print it to the console
    Console.WriteLine(sr.ReadToEnd());
    //Close file
    sr.Close();

    Console.ReadLine();
}
```

This application is very simple, and the output is only the text, "Hello Isolated World!" However, remember that all the file IO applications we have examined so far can be modified to utilize isolated storage instead of the file system. This example demonstrates how to open up a user's isolated storage data store and read and write data to it. If you check the physical file system you will notice that none of the directories or data files were created. They were created solely in isolated storage.

Isolated storage is a very powerful tool supplied with the .NET framework, and it can be used in many different ways. Explore its uses in your applications and discover how to utilize it effectively.

Object Serialization

In almost all applications data must be sent from one location to another. This could be as simple as the front-end interface sending data to the back-end database systems. It could also involve writing out a specific data file format in order to send transaction information to a mainframe system or other third-party enterprise. Another common requirement is the passing of objects between applications. A business object representing an Order running in a bank application might need to be sent over the network to another application that processes transactions. In order for this object to be sent to the remote application, it needs to be transformed from the in-memory representation to a form that can be sent over the network. This is done through a process called serialization. Serialization transforms objects into flat streams of data that can easily be sent to another application. Once there, the remote application can deserialize the incoming data and make use of the Order business object in its own processes.

The .NET Framework makes it very simple to send objects to other systems or store them in a file for later use. It does this by serializing the **state** data to a stream. State is what makes each object unique. You might have hundreds of customer objects, but each one has a different state, which is represented by values stored in object properties, and object data members. When an object is serialized this state data is extracted to a flat format and sent to some external stream for later use by the application or consumption by an entirely separate system.

Recalling what we have learned so far about stream IO, remember that this means that the state of an object can be saved to a `FileStream` or an `IsolatedStorageFileStream`, sent over a `NetworkStream` to another computer, or even encrypted using a `CryptoStream`. At the other end, the object can be completely recreated using similar methods of deserialization. Deserialization is a process whereby the flattened data is read and an object is recreated using the data. In the end you have an exact copy of the object, recreated from the file or network stream.

In this section we'll examine two aspects of object serialization:

❑   Serializing via XML

❑   Serializing via formatter objects

XML Serialization

Very little must be done to allow any object to be serialized via XML. Two simple rules must be followed:

❑   The class must support a default public constructor accepting no parameters. When the object is recreated via the deserialization process, the object is first instantiated with the default constructor, and then the public properties are set via the incoming data stream. If there is no default constructor, the .NET Framework will not know how to create the object.

❑   Only public properties that support both `get` and `set` operations and public data members are persisted. This is because the serialization process cannot access the private and read-only data members. There are ways to serialize this data, but it involves changes to the class itself. We will look at this in the next section.

To save all the public properties and data members of an object, nothing extra needs to be done to the class itself. All that is required is to create an `XmlSerializer` object based on the type of object you wish to serialize, and call the `Serialize` method.

To illustrate how simple this method is, let's create an example using the `XmlSerializer` class to serialize an object to XML format.

XmlSerializer Example

Create a new Console Application in Visual Studio .NET, and call it **XmlSerializer**. The complete code for this example can be found in the `\XMLSerializer` directory in the code download. Add the following namespace declaration to the top of the `Class1.cs` file:

```
using System;
using System.Xml.Serialization;
using System.IO;
using System.Xml;
```

We will need each of these namespaces to create our serializable object. Now add the following class to the namespace. Since this is a simple example you can just add this code to the same file, instead of creating a separate class file. For an enterprise application you would definitely want to separate your code modules as much as possible to facilitate code reuse.

```
public class OrderObject
{
    public int CustomerID;
    public int OrderID;
    public DateTime OrderDate;
    public string StoreName;

    private string InternalID;

    public OrderObject()
    {
    }

}
```

In our application, this class will represent a fictitious order. We will need to persist these orders to the file system and send them over the network to other applications. By using .NET we can serialize this object without much effort. Note that this object has a default constructor, even though it does nothing. The `XmlSerializer` class requires this. Also notice that this class contains a private data member, the `InternalID` variable. This data member will not be persisted to the final stream, as we will see.

Now add the following code to the `Main` method:

```
static void Main(string[] args)
{
    FileStream aFile;
    //Create XmlSerializer object based on the OrderObject object
    XmlSerializer aXML = new XmlSerializer(typeof(OrderObject));

    //Create new OrderObject
    OrderObject aObj = new OrderObject();

    //Fill OrderObject with data
```

```
    aObj.CustomerID = 1;
    aObj.OrderDate = DateTime.Now;
    aObj.OrderID = 1;
    aObj.StoreName = "Wrox Online Store";


    try
    {
    //Open file for writing out serialized object
        aFile = new FileStream("Order.xml",FileMode.Create);
    }
    catch(IOException e)
    {
        Console.WriteLine("An IO Exception occurred trying "
                                        + "to open the file.");
        Console.WriteLine(e.ToString());
        Console.ReadLine();
        return;
    }

    //Serialize object data to file
    aXML.Serialize(aFile,aObj);

    //Close file
    aFile.Close();
}
```

This code first creates the XmlSerializer object, passing in the Type of our OrderObject class. To do this it uses the typeof operator. This global method accepts any class and returns the System.Type object for that class. The XmlSerializer requires a System.Type object passed to it in its constructor. It uses this object to dynamically discover the data members to serialize to XML.

After this, an instance of the OrderObject is created and filled with data. Then a FileStream is opened pointing to the correct file, and the Serialize() method is called on the XmlSerializer object. This method is passed the stream to serialize the data to, as well as the object that contains the data to serialize.

The output of this program is the file Order.xml. If this file is opened with Internet Explorer, you should see the following text:

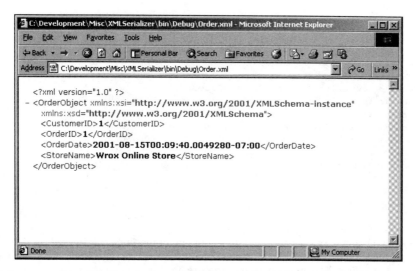

Note that the name of the class became the root XML node, and all the public variables became elements within the object. Another very important thing to note is that the private data member was not serialized.

Deserializing the Data

Deserializing the data into a new object is equally trivial. The `Deserialize()` method is called on the `XmlSerializer` object. This method accepts a stream that contains the serialized data, and returns an object that has been initialized with the serialized data.

The following example reads the file we created in the last example and instantiates a new object using that data. Before running this example make sure you place the XML file created in the last example in the same directory as this sample. This example uses the same `OrderObject`, but for space we are only showing the `Main` method. The complete project can be found in the `\XMLDeSerializer` directory in the download:

```
static void Main(string[] args)
{
    FileStream aFile;
    OrderObject aObj;
    //Create XmlSerializer object based on the OrderObject object
    XmlSerializer aXML = new XmlSerializer(typeof(OrderObject));

    try
    {
        //Open file containing serialized data
        aFile = new FileStream("Order.xml",FileMode.Open);
        //Deserialize file contents into an instantiated object
        aObj = (OrderObject) aXML.Deserialize(aFile);
    }
    catch(IOException e)
    {
        Console.WriteLine("An IO exception has been thrown!");
        Console.WriteLine("Did you forget to copy the XML file into the " +
                                        "application directory?");
        Console.WriteLine(e.ToString());
```

```
        Console.ReadLine();
        return;
    }

    //Write out properties of newly deserialized object
    Console.WriteLine("Object deserialized...");
    Console.WriteLine("Customer ID: {0}",aObj.CustomerID);
    Console.WriteLine("Order Date: {0}",aObj.OrderDate);
    Console.WriteLine("OrderID: {0}",aObj.OrderID);
    Console.WriteLine("Store Name: {0}",aObj.StoreName);

    Console.ReadLine();

    //Close file
    aFile.Close();
}
```

This code again creates a `XmlSerializer` object based on the `OrderObject` class. After reading the previously serialized data into a `FileStream` object, the `Deserialize()` method is called on the `XmlSerializer` object. This method accepts the stream that contains the data to deserialize, and returns an object. This object must be cast to the correct type, in this case the `OrderObject` class.

Once we have done this, we simply write the values to the console to show that the data has been persisted and successfully read back into a new object.

Shaping XML

If you want more control of the XML generated for a particular class, you can add attributes to the data members that the `XmlSerializer` class can interpret to create exactly the XML file you want to produce. These can include specifying if the created XML node is an element or an attribute, the data type, a new name for the XML node, or even the specific namespace of the node.

The most common of these attributes are the `XmlRoot`, `XmlAttribute`, and `XmlElement` attributes. The `XmlRoot` attribute specifies the root node of the XML document. The `XmlAttribute` attribute changes the generated XML from the default element-based to store the marked data member as an XML attribute. This attribute also allows you to specify additional changes, such as the name of the created XML attribute, the data type, and the namespace for the node. The `XmlElement` attribute supplies much of the same functionality, but creates an element in the serialized XML data.

The following example shows how these attributes can be used to modify the XML produced. This is the same `OrderObject` we have used in the example previously, but now we have modified the class itself to enable us to create exactly the type of XML we need in our application:

```
[XmlRoot("Order_Object_XML")]
public class OrderObject
{
    [XmlAttribute(AttributeName = "CustID", DataType = "int",
                Namespace = "www.Wrox.com")]
    public int CustomerID;

    [XmlAttribute(AttributeName = "Order_ID", DataType = "int",
                Namespace = "www.Wrox.com")]
    public int OrderID;
```

```
    [XmlAttribute(AttributeName = "Date_Of_Order", DataType = "date",
                Namespace = "www.Wrox.com")]
    public DateTime OrderDate;

    [XmlAttribute(AttributeName = "Store", DataType = "string",
                Namespace = "www.Wrox.com")]
    public string StoreName;

    private string InternalID;

    public OrderObject()
    {
    }
}
```

This class can be serialized using exactly the same code as the last example. In the code download in the \XMLSerializer directory, this OrderObject can be used instead of the previous one by simply uncommenting this OrderObject and commenting out the previous object. Doing so will result in the following XML output:

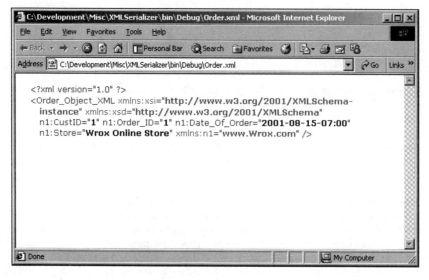

You can see the result of adding the attributes to the class and how it has changed the appearance of the XML generated. We have modified the default behavior and made the data members appear as attributes instead of elements. We also changed the names of the serialized data elements, and even added a custom namespace to the file.

As you can see, the XmlSerializer class can be very useful for serializing and deserializing public data members of a class. It can also be a useful tool for managing your XML data objects and transforming your XML data from streams into objects and back again. Using attributes to shape the generated XML to look exactly how you need is essential in this environment.

471

Serialization Formatter Objects

XML serialization is very convenient. While easy to implement, the inability to serialize non-public data members may be too restrictive. Serializing private data members is not difficult to do, but it does involve the use of serialization **formatter objects**.

Formatter objects translate an object into a flattened stream of data, much like the XmlSerializer class. The difference is that the formatter objects have access to all the public and private data members of a class. To permit this violation of encapsulation, you must mark the classes themselves as willing to be serialized. This is done with the [Serializable] attribute. For example:

```
[Serializable]
public class OrderObject
{
    public int CustomerID;
    public int OrderID;
    public DateTime OrderDate;
    public string StoreName;

    private string InternalID;

    public OrderObject()
    {
    }

}
```

Here is our trusty OrderObject again, but this time it has been marked as [Serializable]. This means that when the serialization formatter objects translate it into a stream, finally the private data member, InternalID, will be serialized.

An important consideration is that all members of a class must be serializable. This means that if a class contains an object as a private data member that is not marked as serializable, the serialization process will fail.

The two format options you have are SOAP and binary. The SOAP format is XML-based, and creates valid SOAP messages that can be sent to Web Services over the Internet. The binary format is much less verbose and faster to process and send, at the expense of human readability. Binary formatted objects cannot be sent over the Internet to Web Services. Also note that objects persisted in the binary format are not encrypted in any way; the data can still be seen in the file or sniffed during transit if it is sent over a network. Just because you can't read the binary format output in Notepad, do not let this lull you into a false sense of security.

To illustrate this, let's look at an example where an object is serialized in both binary and SOAP formats.

Formatter Objects Example

Create a new C# Console Application in Visual Studio .NET. Title it SOAPandBinarySerialize. This project can be found in the \SOAPandBinarySerialize directory in the code download. Add the following code to the top of the Class1.cs file. These namespaces are required for the serialization formatter objects:

```
using System;
using System.IO;

using System.Runtime.Serialization.Formatters.Binary;
using System.Runtime.Serialization.Formatters.Soap;
```

You will also have to add a reference in your project to the
`System.Runtime.Serialization.Formatters.Soap` assembly.

Once this has been completed, add our favorite `OrderObject` to the project. We will keep the
`[Serializable]` attribute, because this is needed for the formatter objects to gain access to the private
data members. We also add a simple method to set the value of the private data member:

```
[Serializable]
public class OrderObject
{
    public int CustomerID;
    public int OrderID;
    public DateTime OrderDate;
    public string StoreName;

    private string InternalID;

    public OrderObject()
    {
    }

    public void SetID(string ID)
    {
        InternalID = ID;
    }

}
```

Finally we get to the `Main` method, where the magic takes place:

```
static void Main(string[] args)
{
    FileStream aFileSoap, aFileBin;

    //Create new OrderObject
    OrderObject aObj = new OrderObject();

    //Create both types of formatter objects
    SoapFormatter aSoapFormatter = new SoapFormatter();
    BinaryFormatter aBinaryFormatter = new BinaryFormatter();

    //Add some data to the Order Object
    //This will be serialized
    aObj.CustomerID = 1;
    aObj.OrderDate= DateTime.Now;
    aObj.OrderID = 50;
```

```
aObj.StoreName = "www.Wrox.com";
//Set the private data member
//   By using the formatter objects even non-public
//   data members are serialized
aObj.SetID("123456789");

try
{
    //Create files
    aFileSoap = new FileStream("OrderSoap.xml",FileMode.OpenOrCreate);
    aFileBin = new FileStream("OrderBin.data",FileMode.OpenOrCreate);

    //Write output to files
    aSoapFormatter.Serialize(aFileSoap,aObj);
    aBinaryFormatter.Serialize(aFileBin,aObj);

    //Close the files
    aFileSoap.Close();
    aFileBin.Close();
}
catch(Exception e)
{
    //Display the error
    Console.WriteLine("An exception has been thrown!");
    Console.WriteLine(e.ToString());
    Console.ReadLine();
    return;
}

Console.WriteLine("File serialization complete.");
Console.ReadLine();

}
```

This code instantiates an OrderObject and sets the properties to various data values. Then BinaryFormatter and SoapFormatter objects are created, as well as two files to write the serialized data into. The Serialize() method of each formatter object is called, passing in the stream to serialize the data to and the object to serialize. If something goes wrong, the error handler catches it; otherwise the application closes without much happening on the screen except a brief message being displayed.

The real excitement is in the two files created. Open the resulting `OrderSoap.xml` file in Internet Explorer and you will see the following screen:

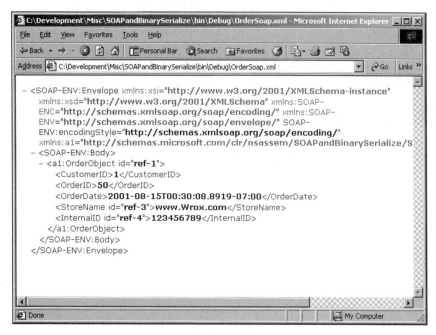

The `SoapFormatter` object has created a completely valid SOAP message that can be passed to any Web Service and operated on. The copious amounts of namespaces and elements are to make the message SOAP-compliant. We will learn more about Web Services in the next chapter.

Now open the `OrderBin.data` file in Visual Studio .NET. You will see the following screen:

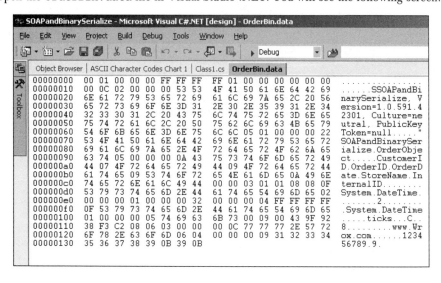

This is the binary output of the `OrderObject` that the `BinaryFormatter` object serialized to the file. As you can see, this format is much smaller, but far less readable. Note that much of the text data in the file is still readable, thus proving that this is not encrypting the data by any means.

Deserializing the Data

To perform the opposite operation, namely deserializing the data and creating a new object from the file stream, is relatively easy. The `Deserialize()` method is called on the formatter object, passing in the stream that contains the serialized data. This method returns an object containing the deserialized data.

Let's modify our application example to also read the files created, to demonstrate extracting the data out of the serialized format.

First, modify the `OrderObject` class to include the following method. We are adding this method so we can read the value of the private data member, thus proving that even the private data has persisted to the files:

```
public void SetID(string ID)
{
    InternalID = ID;
}
```

```
public string GetID()
{
    return InternalID;
}
```

Now add the following code at the end of the original `Main` method:

```
Console.WriteLine("File serialization complete.");
Console.ReadLine();

OrderObject aObjSoap, aObjBin;
Console.WriteLine("Begin deserialization process...");

try
{
    //Open files
    aFileSoap = new FileStream("OrderSoap.xml",FileMode.Open);
    aFileBin = new FileStream("OrderBin.data",FileMode.Open);

    //Read file data into objects
    aObjSoap = (OrderObject)aSoapFormatter.Deserialize(aFileSoap);
    aObjBin = (OrderObject)aBinaryFormatter.Deserialize(aFileBin);

    aFileSoap.Close();
    aFileBin.Close();
}
catch(Exception e)
{
    Console.WriteLine("An IO exception has been thrown!");
    Console.WriteLine(e.ToString());
    Console.ReadLine();
    return;
}
```

```
Console.WriteLine("Data object created from SOAP file:");
Console.WriteLine("CustomerID: {0}",aObjSoap.CustomerID);
Console.WriteLine("OrderDate: {0}",aObjSoap.OrderDate);
Console.WriteLine("OrderID: {0}",aObjSoap.OrderID);
Console.WriteLine("Store Name: {0}",aObjSoap.StoreName);
Console.WriteLine("InternalID: {0}",aObjSoap.GetID());
Console.WriteLine("");

Console.WriteLine("Data object created from Binary file:");
Console.WriteLine("CustomerID: {0}",aObjBin.CustomerID);
Console.WriteLine("OrderDate: {0}",aObjBin.OrderDate);
Console.WriteLine("OrderID: {0}",aObjBin.OrderID);
Console.WriteLine("Store Name: {0}",aObjBin.StoreName);
Console.WriteLine("InternalID: {0}",aObjBin.GetID());
Console.WriteLine("");

Console.WriteLine("File deserialization complete.");
Console.ReadLine();

}
```

This code creates objects based on the two data files created. It parses the data files using the same two formatter objects that were used to create them. After retrieving instantiated objects containing the data from the serialized files, the application writes the data in each object to the console.

The output should look something like this:

As a final note, if there is a data member that needs to not be persisted or serialized, it can be marked with the [NonSerialized] attribute. Any data members marked with this are not serialized when the formatter object serializes the object to a stream.

For example, here is our `OrderObject` with the `OrderDate` data member marked as
`[NonSerialized]`. When this class is written to a stream, this data member is not persisted. When the
object is recreated in the deserialization process, any values marked as `[NonSerialized]` will be filled
with either the values specified in the default constructor, or none at all.

```
[Serializable]
public class OrderObject
{
    public int CustomerID;
    public int OrderID;

    [NonSerialized]
    public DateTime OrderDate;
    public string StoreName;

    private string InternalID;

    public OrderObject()
    {
    }

}
```

Registry

The Registry is a hierarchical data store used by Windows to keep track of application data, user
preferences, and system information. An application can use the Registry to store information it needs
to perform its processing or successful operation.

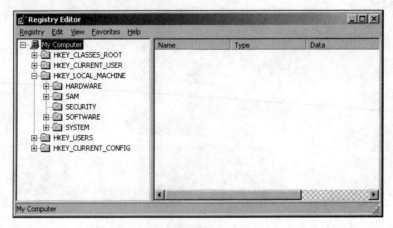

To edit the Registry, open the **RegEdit** application by navigating to **Start** | **Run** and typing in `regedit`.
The **RegEdit** application will appear on your screen, as shown above. This application allows you to
navigate through the Registry and examine the keys and values.

The Registry is very much like a file system, with keys representing folders. Keys can contain subkeys, much like a folder can contain subfolders within it. A key can have multiple values associated with it, similar to how a folder can contain multiple files within it. Each value contains one particular piece of information that can be retrieved or stored. Depending on the OS, the Registry can consist of seven root keys (sometimes referred to as **hives**); these are the very top keys to the system, and provide the seven general areas that information is stored in the Registry. The seven root keys are:

Root Key Name	Description
HKEY_CLASSES_ROOT	Defines the types (or classes) of documents and the associates between applications and COM servers
HKEY_CURRENT_CONFIG	Contains non-user-specific information about this machine configuration
HKEY_CURRENT_USER	Contains information about the current user preferences
HKEY_DYN_DATA	Contains dynamic registry data
HKEY_LOCAL_MACHINE	Contains non-user specific-information about the applications and servers for this machine
HKEY_PERFORMANCE_DATA	Contains performance information for Windows
HKEY_USERS	Contains information about all the users who use this computer and stores their configuration settings

As you would suspect, the .NET Framework makes working with the Windows Registry very simple. It provides several classes that facilitate access to the Registry and reading and writing keys and values.

Microsoft.Win32

The Registry classes are located within a namespace we have not looked at yet, the Microsoft.Win32 namespace. This namespace contains classes and delegates that relate to Windows-only operations, such as working with the Registry.

Registry class

The Registry class is a very simple, static-only class. It exposes seven public properties that relate to the seven root keys in the Registry data store. These are summarized overleaf; each property relates to a specific root key in the Registry. Each of these properties returns a RegistryKey object representing the requested root key.

Property Name	Root Key Name
ClassesRoot	HKEY_CLASSES_ROOT
CurrentConfig	HKEY_CURRENT_CONFIG
CurrentUser	HKEY_CURRENT_USER
DynData	HKEY_DYN_DATA
LocalMachine	HKEY_LOCAL_MACHINE
PerformanceData	HKEY_PERFORMANCE_DATA
Users	HKEY_USERS

The following code would return the RegistryKey object for the HKEY_LOCAL_MACHINE root key:

```
RegistryKey aRegKey = Registry.LocalMachine;
```

RegistryKey

The class used to manipulate and read the Registry is the RegistryKey class. This class represents a single key in the Registry. It contains methods to query its subkeys and the values contained within them. To navigate through the registry, the OpenSubKey() method is called on the current RegistryKey. This method returns another RegistryKey representing the newly opened key. This process can be used to navigate deeper and deeper into the Registry, like this:

```
RegistryKey aRegKey = Registry.LocalMachine;
RegistryKey aRegKeySoftware = aRegKey.OpenSubKey("Software");
RegistryKey aRegMS = aRegKey.OpenSubKey("Microsoft");
RegistryKey aRegWindows = aRegKey.OpenSubKey("Windows");
```

At the end of this code, the RegistryKey object called aRegWindows points to the Registry key HKEY_LOCAL_MACHINE\SOFTWARE\Microsoft\Windows. Note that the OpenSubKey() method is case insensitive.

Another, quicker way to navigate to a specified key in the Registry is to specify the entire address in a single call to OpenSubKey(). The same code could be rewritten as:

```
RegistryKey aRegKey = Registry.LocalMachine;
RegistryKey aRegWindows = aRegKey.OpenSubKey("Software\\Microsoft\\Windows");
```

So far, we have been opening RegistryKey objects in read-only mode. OpenSubKey() is actually an overloaded method that can be called with an additional Boolean parameter. If you need to modify a Registry key or add values, make sure you open the RegistryKey by passing in true as the second parameter, like this:

```
RegistryKey aRegKey = Registry.LocalMachine;
RegistryKey aRegWindows = aRegKey.OpenSubKey("Software\\Microsoft\\Windows",true);
```

Another operation that will be quite common as you work with the Registry in your application is adding keys. This will often need to be done the first time that an application runs. The .NET Framework provides us with a very convenient method for performing this task: the `CreateSubKey()` method.

This method creates the specified subkey under the current `RegistryKey` that it was called on. The convenient bit is that if the subkey already exists, it simply returns a `RegistryKey` object representing that subkey. This way, your code can always call the `CreateSubKey()` method. If it is the first time that this code is executed, the subkey will be created and a `RegistryKey` object will be returned. If it not the first time, a `RegistryKey` object will be returned for the existing key. Your code won't know the difference! We will see an example of using this in the Windows Form application we are going to build.

Once you have the correct `RegistryKey` object pointing at the correct key in the Registry, you will obviously want to read and write data to it. The `RegistryKey` class supports the `GetValue()` and `SetValue()` methods to do just these operations.

The `GetValue()` method contains two overloaded versions. The first simply accepts the name of the value to retrieve the data for. If no value exists, a `null` is returned. The second version accepts the name of the value to retrieve the data for, and another parameter specifying a default value if the value field is not found. Both methods return an `object` that must be cast to the correct type in order to extract the data. Note that by passing `null` for the name of the value, the default value for the key will be returned.

The `SetValue()` method will throw an `UnauthorizedAccessException` exception if the `RegistryKey` object is opened in read-only mode. This exception will also be thrown if you attempt to write values to one of the root keys in the registry. This method accepts two parameters: the name of the value to write to this key, and the actual data to store in the value field.

Registry Usage Example

Let's build a simple Windows Form application that remembers its settings by persisting them to the Registry and reading them on startup. This will demonstrate how to navigate through the Registry, retrieve and store values, and give a good example of how the Registry can be a powerful tool for building user-friendly .NET applications. This project can be found in the `\WinReg` directory in the code download.

Create a new C# Windows Application and title it **WinReg**. At the top of the **Form1.cs** file add the following namespace declaration:

```
using System;
using System.Drawing;
using System.Collections;
using System.ComponentModel;
using System.Windows.Forms;
using System.Data;
using Microsoft.Win32;
```

Modify the default Windows Form created for the application to look like the following screenshot. Add a single `TextBox` and a `Label`, shrink the form to a smaller size, and change the **StartPosition** property to **Manual**. We will be reading the start position for this form from the Registry, so we don't want Windows to place our form for us. Delete the text from the `TextBox` and set the text of the `Label` to **Form Name**:

Add the following code to the `Form1` constructor. This code reads the values from the Registry and sets the appropriate properties on the form:

```
public Form1()
{
    //
    // Required for Windows Form Designer support
    //
    InitializeComponent();

    RegistryKey aKey = Registry.CurrentUser;
    aKey = aKey.CreateSubKey("Software\\Wrox\\WinReg");
    this.Width = (int)aKey.GetValue("Width",this.Width);
    this.Height = (int)aKey.GetValue("Height",this.Height);
    this.textBox1.Text = (string)aKey.GetValue("FormText",this.Text);
    this.Left = (int)aKey.GetValue("Left",this.Left);
    this.Top = (int)aKey.GetValue("Top",this.Top);
}
```

This code first calls the method `CreateSubKey()`. The first time that this code is run, it will create the key in the Registry, but on subsequent calls it retrieves the `RegistryKey` object referencing the correct key. Once we have the correct `RegistryKey` object, we set the various properties of the form to the Registry values. Note that we pass in the current settings of the form as the default values. The first time that this code is run, there will be nothing in the Registry, so we simply use the current form's values as the default.

Now we need to add the code that will write the values to the Registry when the application exits. Add the `Closed` event to the form and add the following code to it:

```
private void Form1_Closed(object sender, System.EventArgs e)
{
    RegistryKey aKey = Registry.CurrentUser;
    aKey = aKey.OpenSubKey("Software\\Wrox\\WinReg",true);
    aKey.SetValue("Width",this.Width);
    aKey.SetValue("Height",this.Height);
    aKey.SetValue("FormText",this.textBox1.Text);
    aKey.SetValue("Left",this.Left);
    aKey.SetValue("Top",this.Top);
}
```

Ensure this code simply retrieves the same `RegistryKey` we have been using and writes the current values from the form to it. Note that the text you enter into the `Textbox` will be saved as the form's title; the next time that the application is run, the form will display the saved text.

Here is the window when the application is first launched. Since there is nothing in the Registry, the default values are preserved from Visual Studio .NET:

If you move the window to a different location on the screen, change the size, and enter the text Hello World into the text box, the next time that the application is run, you will see a drastically changed form.

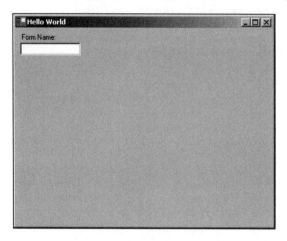

The Registry values have been saved to and retrieved from the Registry. This demonstrates how you can use the Registry to provide 'memory' for your applications. Modern desktop applications must create a user-friendly experience for the end user. One way to accomplish this is to remember the user's settings and configurations from session to session. By using the Registry, this type of information is easy to store. The Registry can be used for a variety of other purposes as well, such as storing component initialization strings, or middle-tier application settings. The .NET Framework makes working with the Registry very painless. Therefore it is easy to incorporate its usefulness into our own applications and components. A word of warning, however: the registry should be used for only limited amount of data. Significant data should be stored in configuration files, or even a database for faster and more secure access.

Summary

We have covered a lot of material in this chapter. We learned how the System.IO namespace classes help us to manipulate and manage files on the file system; we learned how to use the FileStream class for synchronous and asynchronous file access, and how the StreamReader and StreamWriter classes make reading and writing character data to and from streams simpler; we even examined the BinaryReader and BinaryWriter classes and saw how they can be used to provide-lower level file data manipulation. In addition, we saw how the .NET Framework uses streams for all input/output in the system, and examined several other stream classes like NetworkStream, MemoryStream, and CryptoStream.

We also saw how isolated storage can be used to write data in a safe and protected manner on any system. This information is isolated and protected at a user level. Even code that does not have permission to write to the file system can still store configuration settings or cache data locally for a user.

We also covered how .NET objects can be serialized to a stream and deserialized later to enable persisting and moving object data. .NET provides a very flexible architecture for these operations, and we saw how to serialize data in XML, SOAP, and binary formats. We learned how a class is flattened into a serial stream of data and how to control that process with formatter objects and attributes.

Finally we looked at using the Registry to store application configuration data. The .NET Framework enables the Windows Registry to be used to store and retrieve data easily and effectively. We saw how the Registry classes work and how a sample application could use the Registry to store user configuration data between instances of the running application.

After looking at how we can work with data in flat text files or the Registry let's move on to another, rather newer area, of data as we look at Web Services.

12

Web Services

Web services play a major role in the .NET application architecture. A significant part of the .NET vision revolves around building applications that consume Web services, which provide useful functions to client applications from a central location. Although we will discuss Web services in .NET, a Web Service is a very general model for building applications and can be implemented for any operating system that supports communication over the Internet. Furthermore, a Web Service interface is defined strictly in terms of messages that the Web service accepts and generates. Applications that consume Web Services can be implemented on any platform in any programming language, as long as they can create and consume the messages defined for the Web Service interface. The client application doesn't need to know anything about the internals of the Web Services it uses.

The true significance of Web services and their impact on application development is still to be seen, and given the size of the topic will be the subject of many books (see for example *Professional C# Web Services*, Wrox Press 1-861004-39-7 or *Professional ASP.NET Web Services*, Wrox Press, 1-861005-45-8). Hence in a book addressing data-centric application development we felt it appropriate to give at least a brief introduction to the terminology and concepts.

In this chapter we will look at:

- ❏ The definition of Web services and the need for Web services
- ❏ Protocols, contract languages, and standards used
- ❏ Implementing and consuming a simple Web service
- ❏ Creating and consuming Web services in Visual Studio .NET

Introducing Web Services

In the early days of the Internet, a web page displayed the same information regardless of when and by whom it was viewed. With the advent of technologies such as ASP, users could create dynamic web pages. However, these technologies had serious limitations, such as forcing us to use an HTML interface. Web services, in contrast, offer a direct means for applications to interact with other applications. Web services provide well-defined interfaces, called **contracts**, which describe the services provided. Applications hosted internally, as well as on remote systems, can communicate with Web services over the Internet via XML and SOAP messages.

What is a Web Service?

A Web service exposes functions over the Internet or another network, so that remote applications can use their application logic. Web services use standard Internet protocols, such as Hypertext Transfer Protocol (HTTP), Simple Object Access Protocol (SOAP), and Extensible Markup Language (XML), to transport their data, so that they work easily through firewalls. Thus Web services combine the best aspects of component-based development and the Web.

The idea is that if functions are called using standard HTTP based protocols over the Internet, then the component that calls them can be located anywhere on the Internet and there is no restriction on what platform it might be running on or what language it should be written in.

Thus a user at Location A can use remote function calls to invoke functions on Web service components at Location B and the output is packaged as XML and passed back to the user at Location A

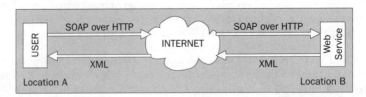

The client application at Location A must be aware of the interface that the Web service at Location B provides. The interface is defined in a Web Services Description Language (WSDL) document (as we discuss later WSDL is an XML-based standard for describing network services as sets of communication endpoints capable of exchanging messages).

Generic Architecture of Web Services

The architecture of a Web service usually broadly divides into four logical layers:

- ❑ Data layer
- ❑ Data access layer
- ❑ Business layer
- ❑ Listener

The listener layer is nearest to the client, and the layer furthest from the client is the data layer. The business layer is further divided in to two sub-layers:

❏ Business logic

❏ Business façade

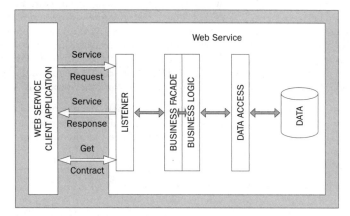

The data layer stores any physical data that the Web service requires. Above the data layer is the data access layer, which presents a logical view of the physical data to the business logic. The data access layer isolates business logic from changes to the underlying data stores and ensures the integrity of the data. The business façade provides a simple interface that maps directly to operations exposed by the Web service. The business façade uses services provided by the business logic layer. In a simple Web service, all the business logic might be implemented by the business façade, which would interact directly with the data access layer.

Web service client applications interact with the Web service listener. The listener is responsible for receiving incoming messages, which contain requests for services, parsing the messages, and dispatching the requests to the appropriate methods in the business façade. If the service returns a response, the listener is also responsible for packaging the response from the business façade into a message and sending that back to the client. The listener also handles requests for Web service contracts and other documents about the Web service. We will discuss the communication between client and Web service and the dynamic discovery process in more detail later in this chapter.

The generic Web service architecture presented in the above diagram is very similar to the *n*-tier application architecture encouraged in most modern application development. The listener layer in the takes the place of the presentation layer of a legacy Windows DNA application, in that both communicate with the business façade. It is straightforward to migrate a Windows DNA application to a Web service by adding a Web service listener parallel to the presentation layer and providing it the access to the existing business façade. Web service client applications will interact with the listener, while web browser clients can continue to use the presentation layer.

Protocols and Standards Used

For Web services to be truly useful businesses must be able to discover and use Web services offered by other organizations. For this to happen, Web services must obey certain standards and protocols for representing data, exchanging messages, providing service descriptions, advertising services on a particular site, and searching providers of Web services. These requirements currently rely on the following technologies:

❑ **XML** – The obvious choice for a standard way to represent data. XML can be easily transmitted over the Internet and it supports a wide variety of applications. The design of XML is formal and concise, and programs that process XML documents are easy to write. Most Web service-related specifications use XML for data representation, as well as XML Schemas to describe data types.

❑ **Simple Object Access Protocol** (**SOAP**) – A common, extensible, message format. SOAP provides a simple and lightweight mechanism for exchanging structured and typed information between peers in a decentralized, distributed environment using XML. Part of the SOAP specification defines a set of rules for how to use XML to represent data. Other parts of the SOAP specification define an extensible message format, conventions for representing remote procedure calls, and bindings to the HTTP protocol. Currently, the SOAP specification only defines bindings for HTTP and the HTTP Extension Framework, but SOAP can potentially be used in combination with a variety of other protocols.

❑ **Web Services Description Language** (**WSDL**) – A **WSDL document** (also known as WSDL file and WSDL contract) provides a standard way to describe Web services using XML. However, the WSDL needs to be provided in a contract language that the developers and developer tools understand. Web Services Description Language (WSDL) is the widely supported XML-based contract language for Web services.

❑ **Discovery Protocol** (**DISCO**) – A way to discover services located on a particular web site. Developers will also need some way to discover Web services located on a particular web site. The Discovery Protocol (DISCO) specification defines an XML-based discovery document format and a protocol for retrieving the discovery document, enabling developers to discover services available at a known URL.

❑ **Universal Description, Discovery, and Integration** (**UDDI**)– A way to discover service providers. Although DISCO is useful to discover services located on a particular web site, in many cases the developer will not know the URLs where services can be found. UDDI specifies a mechanism for Web service providers to advertise the existence of their Web services and for Web service consumers to locate Web services of interest. The UDDI specification describes an open framework to define, publish, and discover information about Web services.

In the following sections, we will start looking at SOAP, WSDL, DISCO, and UDDI in more detail, and then move on to see how they are used for Web services. Later, we will also discuss how to expose and consume Web services, and work through some examples.

Simple Object Access Protocol (SOAP)

Simple Object Access Protocol (SOAP) is a lightweight, XML-based protocol for exchanging information in a decentralized, distributed environment. It is rapidly gaining support and has been submitted to the W3C for consideration. SOAP is a messaging protocol that is not limited to Remote Procedure Calls (RPC). It does not require synchronous execution or request/response interaction, and SOAP messages can have multiple parts addressed to different parties. A SOAP message is the basic unit of communication between peer SOAP nodes. SOAP nodes along the message path process the message according to the formal set of conventions that the SOAP specification defines. SOAP defines an envelope formatting and processing mechanism for arbitrarily complex message structures. The W3C SOAP Specification Version 1.2 (Working Draft published on 9 July 2001) consists of four parts:

❑ The **envelope** defines an overall framework for expressing what is in a message, who should deal with it, and whether it is optional or mandatory

❏ The **encoding rules** defines a serialization mechanism that can be used to exchange instances of application-defined data types

❏ The **RPC representation** defines a convention that can be used to represent remote procedure calls and responses

❏ The **binding** defines a formal set of rules for exchanging SOAP envelopes between peers using an underlying protocol for transport

SOAP Messages

The SOAP message is an XML document that consists of:

❏ A mandatory SOAP envelope

❏ An optional SOAP Header

❏ A mandatory SOAP Body

A SOAP message is transmitted by the SOAP Sender node to the SOAP Receiver node through zero or more SOAP Intermediaries, which define the SOAP path.

Just as every HTTP message must be enclosed inside a HTTP header and body, each SOAP message must be delivered in an **envelope**. Inside this SOAP envelope must be contained one item, a message **body**.

The SOAP body is a collection of single logical computational units (blocks) targeted at the ultimate SOAP receiver within the SOAP message path. SOAP defines one element for the body, which is the Fault element (a special block) used for reporting errors. The message contained inside the envelope may, but does not have to, contain a **header** as well.

The SOAP header is a collection of SOAP blocks, which may be targeted at any SOAP receiver within the SOAP message path. SOAP messages are one-way transmissions from a SOAP sender to a SOAP receiver, but they may be combined to implement patterns such as request/response. However, SOAP messages do not require synchronous execution or request/response interaction, and it can have multiple parts addressed to different parties.

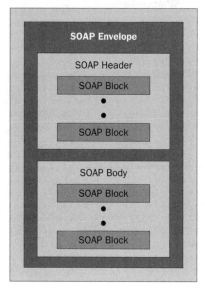

The `Envelope` node is the root element of the XML document representing the SOAP message. XML namespaces are used to make SOAP identifiers less ambiguous by using application-specific identifiers. The structure of a SOAP message containing a `header` block and a `body` block is shown below:

```
<env:Envelope xmlns:env="http://www.w3.org/2001/06/soap-envelope">
  <env:Header>
    <!--
      Header information.
    -->
  </env:Header>
  <env:Body>
    <!--
      Body
    -->
  </env:Body>
</env:Envelope>
```

The SOAP message must adhere to particular namespace conventions, and it must be a well-formed XML document. Proper SOAP namespaces are included on all elements and attributes defined by SOAP in messages. A SOAP application will process SOAP namespaces in messages that it receives. SOAP defines the following namespaces (note that the envelope and the encoding rules are defined in different namespaces):

❑ The SOAP envelope has the namespace identifier: http://www.w3.org/2001/06/soap-envelope

❑ The SOAP serialization has the namespace identifier: http://www.w3.org/2001/06/soap-encoding

❑ The SOAP must understand fault namespace identifier: http://www.w3.org/2001/06/soap-faults

❑ The SOAP upgrade namespace identifier: http://www.w3.org/2001/06/soap-upgrade

For detailed schema documents on these namespaces, visit the web site using the corresponding namespace identifier as the URL (for example, the URL http://www.w3.org/2001/06/soap-encoding to see the schema documents for SOAP encoding).

A SOAP message may be bound to different underlying protocols including, but not limited to HTTP. SOAP used along with HTTP as the underlying protocol takes advantage of the request/response mechanism that HTTP provides.

The following example shows what a SOAP Message embedded in an HTTP Request looks like:

```
POST /ItemPrice HTTP/1.1
Host: www.pricequoteserver.com
Content-Type: text/xml; charset="utf-8"
Content-Length: nnnn
SOAPAction: "http://example.org/2001/06/prices"

<env:Envelope xmlns:env="http://www.w3.org/2001/06/soap-envelope" >
  <env:Body>
    <m:GetPrice
        env:encodingStyle="http://www.w3.org/2001/06/soap-encoding"
        xmlns:m="http://example.org/2001/06/prices">
      <symbol>ITEM 1</symbol>
    </m:GetPrice>
  </env:Body>
</env:Envelope>
```

This example of a SOAP/HTTP request contains a `Body` block but no `Header` block. The `Body` block contains the actual notification message to be delivered. The `header` contains a SOAP block called `GetPrice`, enclosed within the `GetPrice` element pair, which is defined by the application, not the SOAP standard. This block in this example takes a single parameter, the ticker symbol for an item. The service's response to this request contains a single parameter, the price of the item.

The structure of a SOAP Message embedded in an HTTP Response is shown below:

```
HTTP/1.1 200 OK
Content-Type: text/xml; charset="utf-8"
Content-Length: nnnn

<env:Envelope xmlns:env="http://www.w3.org/2001/06/soap-envelope" >
 <env:Body>
  <m:GetPriceResponse
        env:encodingStyle="http://www.w3.org/2001/06/soap-encoding"
        xmlns:m="http://example.org/2001/06/prices">
   <Price>345</Price>
  </m:GetPriceResponse>
 </env:Body>
</env:Envelope>
```

The **datatypes** declared in the XML Schema specification may be used directly in element schemas (there is more information on XML datatypes at http://www.w3.org/TR/2001/REC-xmlschema-2-20010502/). Types derived from these may also be used. For example, a schema with simple types is shown below:

```
<!-- schema document -->
<xs:schema xmlns:xs="http://www.w3.org/2001/XMLSchema" >

  <xs:element name="age" type="xs:int" />
  <xs:element name="height" type="xs:float" />
  <xs:element name="color" >
    <xs:simpleType base="xsd:string">
      <xs:restriction base="xs:string" >
        <xs:enumeration value="Green"/>
        <xs:enumeration value="Blue"/>
      </xs:restriction>
    </xs:simpleType>
  </xs:element>

</xs:schema>
```

The modular packaging model and mechanisms for encoding application-defined data allows SOAP to be used in a large variety of systems ranging from messaging systems to remote procedure calls (RPC).

Web Service Description Language (WSDL)

Web Service Description Language is an XML-based language used to document the **WSDL** contract. The technical W3C specifications are available at http://www.w3.org/TR/2001/NOTE-wsdl-20010315. However, for now it's enough to know that it provides the following basic mechanisms:

- ❏ It describes the methods used for requests and responses; it defines how the method calls will be executed and what parameters are required for the execution to happen

493

❑ It defines the data types which each particular parameter, and function result should be (strings, longs, integers, dates, and arrays are all examples of data types supported by WSDL)

❑ It specifies the location of the service being exposed to SOAP (for example, a pointer to this URL)

❑ It provides the structure of the expected request and its resulting response (if any) in the form of XML Schema

❑ It defines the possible errors that can result from a particular service request

Later we will see how we can generate WSDL files automatically.

Discovery Protocol (DISCO)

To become a client of a Web service, you must first know that the Web service exists, and how you should interact with it; acquiring this information is done by performing a **discovery**. Web service discovery is the identification of Web service descriptions by a Web service client. A Web service may publish a DISCO file, an XML document that typically contains links to other resources that describe the Web service. However, web sites that implement a Web service need not support discovery – a Web service might be created for private use, where discovery would be inappropriate. We can use Microsoft Web services Discovery Tool, `Disco.exe` (a .NET Framework Tool) to create WSDL, XSD, and DISCO files. These files can in turn be used as input to the Microsoft Web services Description Language Tool, `Wsdl.exe`, to create Web service clients. The `disco.exe` tool can be invoked from the command prompt by typing the command `disco`.

The Web services Discovery tool searches and discovers the URLs of Web services located on a given web server and saves documents related to each Web service on a local disk.

The standard form of `disco` command is:

```
disco [options] URL
```

The following command searches the specified URL for discovery documents and saves them to the current directory:

```
disco http://www.xstreamindia.co.in/Webservice1.disco
```

The tool displays an error message if it cannot find discoverable resources at the specified URL.

The following command searches the specified URL for discovery documents and saves them to the specified output directory:

```
disco /out:myDir http://www.xstreamindia.co.in
```

Other options that can be used with the `disco` command include:

❑ `/d[omain]:domain` – Specifies the domain name to use when connecting to a proxy server that requires authentication

❑ `/p[assword]:password` – Specifies the password to use when connecting to a proxy server that requires authentication

❑   `/proxyusername:username` – Specifies the user name to use when connecting to a proxy server that requires authentication

❑   `/proxypassword:password` – Specifies the password to use when connecting to a proxy server that requires authentication

Universal Description, Discovery, and Integration (UDDI)

Until recently commerce between corporations over the Internet occurred only between known trading partners. In contrast, successful e-commerce requires businesses to be able to discover the services offered by others and integrate those services within their existing infrastructure. The first step towards achieving this is to provide information in a standard format that allows prospective trading partners to discover information about each other.

Universal Description, Discovery, and Integration (UDDI) addresses this challenge by providing a central repository and a standard way to categorize, and publish Web services that you offer and to locate Web services offered by corporations around the world. UDDI is itself a Web service that consists of a group of web-based registries that expose information about a business or other entity and its technical interfaces (or APIs). These registries are run by multiple **Operator Sites**, and can be used by anyone who wants to make information available about one or more businesses or entities, as well as anyone that wants to find that information. UDDI uses open standards such as HTTP, XML, Domain Name System (DNS), and SOAP. Therefore UDDI creates a platform-independent framework for various trading partners to undertake commerce anytime, anywhere over the network. XML provides a cross-platform approach to data encoding and formatting, while SOAP defines a simple way to package information for exchange across system boundaries.

The UDDI specifications are being developed by an industry initiative lead by several industry big names including Hewlett-Packard, IBM , and Microsoft. More than 300 other companies participate as Advisors of this UDDI Project. The UDDI version 1 final specification and an open draft of the UDDI version 2 specification were published in June 2001, and are available from http://www.uddi.org/specification.html. The UDDI Project has stated that the final UDDI specifications will be submitted to a standards group.

UDDI services are targeted at enabling *technical discovery* of services. The UDDI implementation is a Web service Registry that provides a mechanism to discover services – to advertise and find Web services. Service discovery is related to being able to advertise and locate information about different technical interfaces exposed by different parties. A program or programmer locates information about services exposed by a partner, or finds whether a partner has a service that is compatible with in-house technologies.

Services are interesting when you can discover them, determine their purpose, and then use them. The UDDI registry contains categorized information about businesses and the services they offer, and it associates those services with technical specifications of the Web service. Technical compatibility can be checked so that software companies can use the UDDI registries on the Web to automatically configure certain technical connections as software is installed or accounts are configured. The technical specifications are usually defined using WSDL, which describes what a Web service does, how it communicates, and where it lives. The ability to locate parties that can provide a specific product or service at a given price or within a specific geographic boundary in a given timeframe is not directly covered by the UDDI specifications, however. These kinds of advanced discovery features require further collaboration and design work between buyer and sellers. Instead, UDDI forms the basis for defining these services in a higher layer.

The teams working on the UDDI are, however, planning on features that will address the ability to locate products and services, define Web service implementation conventions, and provide the ability to manage hierarchical business organizations, communities and trade groups.

The UDDI Business Registry is available to everyone at no charge (see www.uddi.org). Using the UDDI discovery services, businesses can individually register information about the Web services that they expose for use by other businesses. This information can be added to the UDDI business registry either via a web site or by using tools that make use of the programmatic service interfaces described in the UDDI Programmer's API Specification. The UDDI business registry is a logically centralized, physically distributed service with multiple root nodes that replicate data with each other on a regular basis. Once a business registers with a single instance of the business registry service, the data is automatically shared with other UDDI root nodes, and becomes freely available to anyone who needs to discover what Web services are exposed by a given business.

This allows **register once, published everywhere** access to information about Web services. Organizations can also set a up private registry to support the requirements of their enterprise. The private registry can impose additional security controls to protect the integrity of the registry data and to prevent access by unauthorized users.

Information Provided in a UDDI Business Registry

Conceptually, the information provided in a UDDI business registration consists of three components:

❑ White pages – include address, contact, and known identifiers.

❑ Yellow pages – include industrial categorizations based on standard taxonomies.

❑ Green pages – include technical information about services that are exposed by the business. Green pages also include references to specifications for Web services, as well as support for pointers to various file and URL-based discovery mechanisms if required.

The data is represented using XML, which offers a platform-neutral view of data and allows hierarchical relationships to be described in a natural way. The core information model used by the UDDI registries is the XML schema standard, because of its support for rich data types as well as its ability to easily describe and validate information based on information models represented in schemas. The UDDI XML schema defines four core types of information that provide the kinds of information that a technical person would need to know in order to use a partner's Web services. These are:

❑ Business information

❑ Service information

❑ Binding information

❑ Information about specifications for services

The XML elements that are used to represent these four core types of information are:

❑ businessEntity – A business entity represents information about a business. The information stored in the businessEntity consists of a unique identifier, the business name, a short description of the business, some basic contact information, a list of categories and identifiers that describe the business, and a URL pointing to more information about the business.

❑ businessService – Associated with each business entity is a list of business services offered by that business entity. Each businessService entry contains a business description of the service, a list of categories that describe the service, and a list of pointers to references and information related to the service.

❑ bindingTemplate – Associated with each businessService entry is a list of bindingTemplate elements that point to specifications and other technical information about the service. For example, a binding template might point to a URL that supplies information on how to invoke the service. The specification pointers also associate the service with a service type.

❑ tModel – A tModel entry defines a service type. Multiple businesses can offer the same type of service, as defined by the tModel. Information stored in this entry consists of the tModel name, the name of the organization that published the tModel, a list of categories that describe the service type, and pointers to technical specifications for the service type such as interface definitions, message formats, message protocols, and security protocols.

The UDDI data types and their interrelationships can be represented as follows:

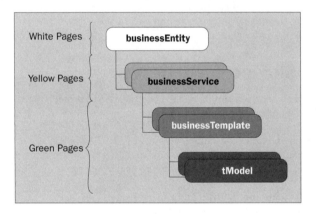

How to Use UDDI

We'll now discuss the steps involved in the process for discovery, lookup, and invocation of Web services using UDDI. Assume that there are a number of B2B auctioneers, who offer Web services that will process e-bids over the Web and provide up-to-date information on the current bid for a particular product. Any buyer planning to buy inventory through a B2B auctioneer can do so by placing a bid at their site. A software application written or deployed by the buyer will create a query that looks at the businessEntity element within UDDI and identify B2B auctioneers that offer auctioning Web services. If the query is successful, it will then look up the businessService element encapsulated by that businessEntity element. After obtaining the businessService element, the application will discover if the business publishes an e-bid Web service. If it does, the software application would access the bindingTemplate element to locate the address of the Web service stored in an accessPoint attribute of bindingTemplate element. However, finding the address of the Web service offered by an auctioneer is not enough. It is important to ensure that the technology implemented by the auctioneering firm is technically compatible with that of the buyer. The application can verify technical compatibility by analyzing the tModel element present in the selected bindingTemplate element. In short, this process can be described in the following steps:

❑   Use UDDI repository and locate a `businessEntity` element for the appropriate business offering Web services

❑   Locate the `businessService` element to identify all the Web services offered by the `businessEntity` located in the first step

❑   Select a `bindingTemplate` element to retrieve the address of the Web service and `tModel` element to ensure technical compatibility between the user's and the provider's systems

Implementing a Web Service

The Microsoft .NET architecture puts heavy emphasis on Web services. The Microsoft .NET framework is built from the ground up to meet the needs of Web services developers and consumers, with pervasive support for web standards such as XML and SOAP. Using the Microsoft Visual Studio .NET IDE, we can quickly create and include Web services using Visual Basic, C#, and native C++.

VS .NET will also enable us to create the WSDL and `.disco` files, without running the .NET Framework tools manually. However, the most thorough way to learn about Web services is to create one without even using the development environment. In this section, we will walk through the steps of creating a Web service without using VS.

Our First Web Service

The Web service we create here is a simple one – a Web service to provide the current date and the resulting date if we have added a number to today's date. We are going to use C# in Notepad to create the Web service. Web service files use an ASMX file extension as opposed to ASPX in an ASP.NET page. However, the Web service we write into the `.asmx` file is also an ASP.NET page and not only C# sourcecode. Similar to ASP.NET applications, we can copy the ASMX file to an IIS-controlled directory and the Web service is up and running. We can see things working by pointing our browser to the ASMX file.

Let's use Notepad and create the following text file and save it as `DateService.asmx` under the appropriate directory – the `inetpub/wwwroot/` folder. In this example the file is saved to a virtual directory called `murali` within the `/inetpub/wwwroot/` folder.

```
<%@ WebService Language="C#" class="DateService" %>

using System;
using System.Web.Services;

public class DateService : System.Web.Services.WebService
{
    [WebMethod]
    public string Today()
    {
        return DateTime.Now.ToLongDateString();
    }
    [WebMethod]
    public string AddToToday(int nDays)
    {
        DateTime NewDate = DateTime.Now.AddDays(nDays);
        return NewDate.ToLongDateString();
    }
}
```

The first line of the file, which is not in the normal C# syntax, looks like this:

```
<%@ WebService Language="C#" class="DateService" %>
```

The `<% WebService %>` tag in this line is to instruct the ASP.NET runtime to process this page as a Web service. When the browser requests this page for first time, the ASP.NET runtime will compile the file into a .NET class. As with ASP.NET pages, the runtime will cache the compiled executable so it can run faster during future executions. The language attribute to this tag specifies that we will use C# as the programming language. This code also defines the name of the Web service class as `DateService`.

The next two lines of code add a reference to namespaces required to build Web services and the `DateService` class in our Web service inherits its functionality from the `System.Web.Services.WebService` class.

The next step is to add methods that are accessible through the Web service. This requires that the methods be defined as public. Remember that we may be referring to sensitive business data in the code and wouldn't want it to fall into the wrong hands. The solution is to protect the business logic function and only have access to the presentation functions. This is achieved by giving the public functions the `WebMethod` attribute, which informs the compiler that the methods are callable over the Web and not just internally within the program.

Using the Web Service

Having saved the file as `DateService.asmx` under an Internet Information Service (IIS)-controlled directory, `/inetpub/wwwroot/murali/`, our Web service is now up and running. We will bring it up by requesting the page with the URL: http://localhost/murali/DateService.asmx.

Below is the returned web page rendered on Internet Explorer 6.0. We did not create this page – the .NET Framework generated it automatically. This ready-to-use functionality is quite adequate for simple Web services:

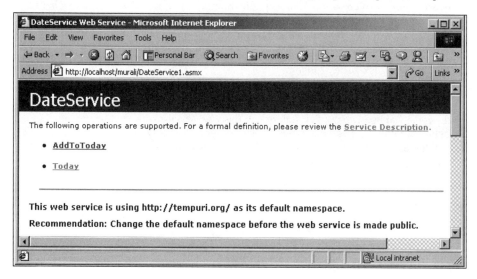

Notice the message displayed just below the AddToToday and Today links:

This Web service is using http://tempuri.org/ as its default namespace.

It's a good idea to change the default namespace before the Web service is made public. This is because each Web service needs a unique namespace to identify it so that client applications can distinguish it from other services on the Web. A default namespace `http://tempuri.org/` is available for Web services that are under development, but published Web services should use a more permanent namespace.

Since your Web service should be identified by a namespace that you control, the safest way is to use your company's Internet domain name as part of the namespace. Web service namespaces are called Uniform Resource Identifiers (URIs), though many Web service namespaces look like URLs. (For more information on the base URI `http://tempuri.org/` see the WSDL specification at http://www.w3.org/TR/2001/NOTE-wsdl-20010315).

For ASP.NET Web services, the default namespace can be changed using the `WebService` attribute's `Namespace` property. The `WebService` attribute is an attribute applied to the class that contains the Web service methods. For example, to set the namespace to `http://xstreamindia.co.in`, in the `DateService.asmx` file add the line above the name of the public function, as below:

```
[WebService(Namespace="http://xstreamindia.co.in")]
public class DateService : System.Web.Services.WebService
{
```

Once the name space is set to `http://xstreamindia.co.in`, the recommendation to change the namespace will disappear when you browse to the ASMX page.

You can do three things from this page:

❑   Click on the **Service Description** link to view the WSDL file, which basically gives an overview of the Web service and its public interface, that is, a description of what functions are available and what parameters they require. This description is useful to create a proxy object. In the WSDL file, you will only see the web-only methods being illustrated. All the private functions and attributes are not described in the WSDL file.

❑   Invoke the `AddToToday` function.

❑   Invoke the `Today` function.

First, click on the **Service Description** link or call the Web service with ?WSDL appended to the URL (http://localhost/murali/DateService.asmx?WSDL) to view the WSDL document (see the screenshot opposite). Note that this WSDL file is for a Web service that only includes the `Today` function:

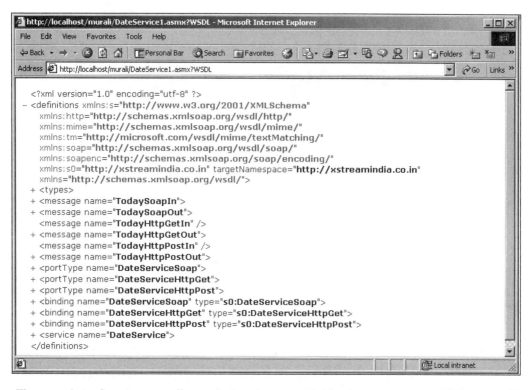

The second step here is to actually use the functions provided by the `DateService` Web service. We will try calling the `AddToToday` function. You can click on the link **AddToToday** or call the Web service with the URL http://localhost/murali/DateService.asmx?op=AddToToday. Now the dialog for entering the parameter appears:

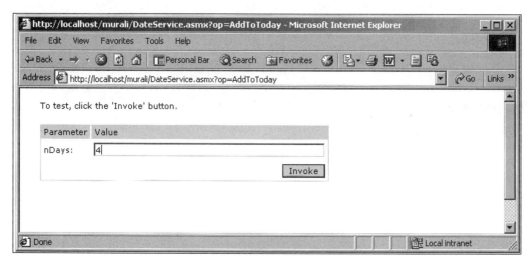

Let's check by entering 4 in the value field to get the date in four days time. Clicking the Invoke button will cause a new browser window to appear, with the results returned in SOAP format. So if we'd executed this program on August 19, 2001, we'd get:

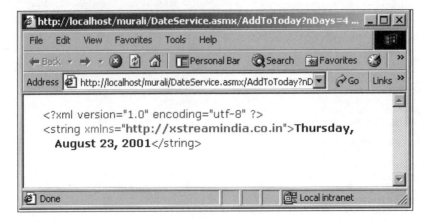

You can also call the Web service directly using the HTTP GET method. In this case, we will not be going through the above web page and clicking the Invoke button. The syntax for directly calling the Web service using HTTP GET is:

```
http://server/webServiceName.asmx/functionName?parameter=parameterValue.
```

Therefore, we can also accomplish the above action by directly calling the Web service using the URL:

```
http://localhost/murali/DateService.asmx/AddToToday?nDays=4
```

Now we know how to create a simple Web service and use it. But the work is only half done – we need to write applications to use the service. These clients could be web pages, Console or Windows applications, Wireless Markup Language (WML)/WMLScript programs to interact with mobile phones, or Palm or Win CE applications to use on PDAs. In addition, there should be a way for our clients to find our Web service.

Before we see how to consume the service we need to explore the process of creating a discovery file for our Web service.

Creating a Discovery File for the Web Service

The following command generates the discovery documents and saves them to the specified output directory:

```
D:\>disco /out:D:\inetpub\wwwroot\murali\
                          http://localhost/murali/DateService.asmx
```

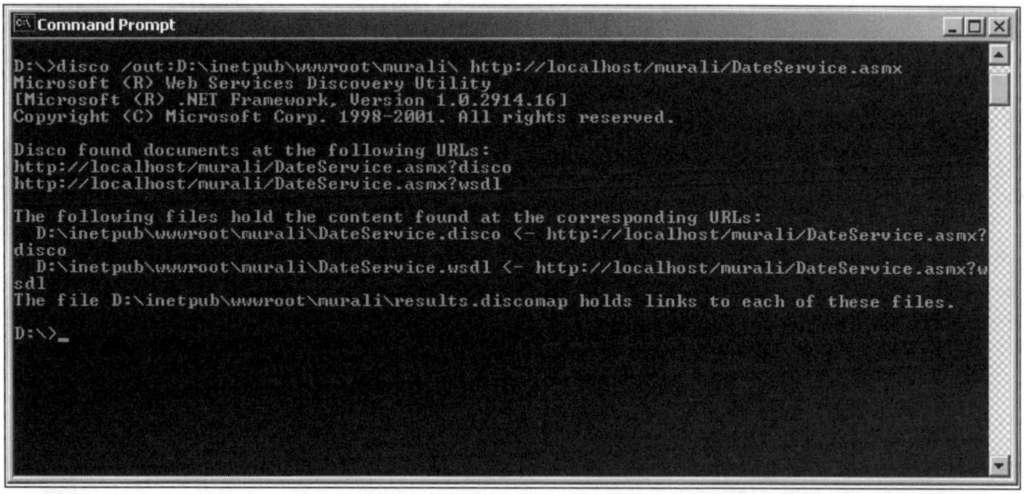

The discovery file will be automatically created and deployed since it's been created in the virtual directory (/out:D:\inetpub\wwwroot\) on the web server (if it hasn't, deploy the discovery document to the web server by copying it to a virtual directory). Here is the discovery file (DateService.disco) generated by Web service Discovery Tool (Disco.exe) for our DateService Web service:

```
<?xml version="1.0" encoding="utf-8"?>
<discovery xmlns:xsi="http://www.w3.org/2001/XMLSchema-instance"
                        xmlns:xsd="http://www.w3.org/2001/XMLSchema"
                        xmlns="http://schemas.xmlsoap.org/disco/">
    <contractRef ref="http://localhost/murali/DateService.asmx?wsdl"
                        docRef="http://localhost/murali/DateService.asmx"
                        xmlns="http://schemas.xmlsoap.org/disco/scl/" />
    <soap address="http://localhost/murali/DateService.asmx"
        xmlns:q1="http://xstreamindia.co.in" binding="q1:DateServiceSoap"
        xmlns="http://schemas.xmlsoap.org/disco/soap/" />
</discovery>
```

If we are creating any other Web services under the \inetpub\wwwroot\murali\ directory, it is wise to enable **dynamic discovery**. Dynamic discovery will scan for all the DISCO files in all the subdirectories of \inetpub\wwwroot\murali\ automatically. The code for our dynamic discovery file DateService.disco is shown below:

```
<?xml version="1.0" ?>
<dynamicDiscovery xmlns="urn:schemas-dynamicdiscovery:disco.2000-03-17">
    <exclude path="_vti_cnf" />
    <exclude path="_vti_pvt" />
    <exclude path="_vti_log" />
    <exclude path="_vti_script" />
    <exclude path="_vti_txt" />
    <exclude path="Web References" />
</dynamicDiscovery>
```

The named subdirectories, _vti_*, contain files to support Microsoft Front Page projects and not Web services, so they have to be excluded. The exclude path lines in the above XML document tell the dynamic discovery process to exclude these named groups of application subdirectories. Since the \bin subdirectory, the directory to which we deploy our Web service assembly, is not in the exclude list, our Web services will be discovered.

Deploying the Web Service

Deploying a Web service involves copying the .asmx file, and any assemblies used by the Web service that are not a part of the Microsoft .NET Framework, to the web server on which it will reside. For example, to deploy our sample Web service DateService, we have created a virtual directory on the web server and then placed the DateService.asmx file in that directory. A typical deployment would have the following directory structure:

```
\inetpub
  \wwwroot
    \murali
      DateService.disco
      DateService.asmx
      \Bin
```

The Bin folder contains various assemblies used by the Web service that are not in the Microsoft .NET Framework.

Items Published with a Web Service

When we publish a Web service, the following items are typically created on the server in a root directory for the project. In the above example the virtual directory called murali acts as the root directory for the Web service. All the remaining files are placed within this directory. This directory should be flagged as an Internet Information Services (IIS) application directory. This virtual directory typically contains the \bin directory and a number of files:

❑   The ASMX file – Acts as the base URL for clients calling the Web service.

❑   The DISCO file – Acts as a discovery mechanism for the Web service. The DISCO file hints about where to find Web services and their WSDL contracts.

❑   The Web.config file (optional) – Web services use the configuration file to allow customization and extensibility of the system. For example, you might supply a Web service-specific Web.config file if your Web service requires authentication and there are other web applications on the system that do not.

❑   The \bin directory – Contains the binary files for the Web service. If your Web service class is not in the same file as the ASMX, then the compiled DLL needs to be placed in the \bin directory (as we will see later in this chapter).

Consuming the Web Service

Applications usually communicate with a Web service using SOAP. But putting together SOAP calls every time we want to use a Web service can be a hassle. Web service proxies allow us to treat the Web service as a local class, with normal method calls – we don't need to worry about SOAP at all. The proxy converts our call into SOAP, and forwards the request to the Web service. It then receives the Web service's response, and then forwards that back to the application as a standard function result.

When we're writing an application that uses a given Web service, we use the Web services Description Language tool (`Wsdl.exe`) to generate a Web service client proxy class. The following command creates a client proxy class in C# for the `DateService` Web service:

```
Wsdl /language:Csharp /out:DateServiceProxy
http://localhost/murali/DateService.asmx
```

Here is the sourcecode for the `DateServiceProxy` file auto-generated by the Web services Description Language tool:

```
//------------------------------------------------------------------
// <autogenerated>
//     This code was generated by a tool.
//     Runtime Version: 1.0.2914.16
//
//     Changes to this file may cause incorrect behavior and will be
//     lost if the code is regenerated.
// </autogenerated>
//------------------------------------------------------------------
//
// This source code was auto-generated by wsdl, Version=1.0.2914.16.
//
using System.Diagnostics;
using System.Xml.Serialization;
using System;
using System.Web.Services.Protocols;
using System.Web.Services;

[System.Web.Services.WebServiceBindingAttribute(Name="DateServiceSoap",
                                  Namespace="http://xstreamindia.co.in")]
public class DateService :
                    System.Web.Services.Protocols.SoapHttpClientProtocol
    {

    [System.Diagnostics.DebuggerStepThroughAttribute()]
    public DateService()
    {
        this.Url = "http://localhost/murali/DateService.asmx";
    }

    [System.Diagnostics.DebuggerStepThroughAttribute()]
    [System.Web.Services.Protocols.SoapDocumentMethodAttribute
                            ("http://xstreamindia.co.in/Today",
                        RequestNamespace="http://xstreamindia.co.in",
                        ResponseNamespace="http://xstreamindia.co.in",
                Use=System.Web.Services.Description.SoapBindingUse.Literal,
    ParameterStyle=System.Web.Services.Protocols.SoapParameterStyle.Wrapped)]
    public string Today()
    {
        object[] results = this.Invoke("Today", new object[0]);
        return ((string)(results[0]));
    }

    [System.Diagnostics.DebuggerStepThroughAttribute()]
    public System.IAsyncResult BeginToday(System.AsyncCallback callback,
                                                    object asyncState)
    {
        return this.BeginInvoke("Today", new object[0], callback, asyncState);
```

```
    }

    [System.Diagnostics.DebuggerStepThroughAttribute()]
    public string EndToday(System.IAsyncResult asyncResult) {
        object[] results = this.EndInvoke(asyncResult);
        return ((string)(results[0]));
    }

    [System.Diagnostics.DebuggerStepThroughAttribute()]
    [System.Web.Services.Protocols.SoapDocumentMethodAttribute(
                        "http://xstreamindia.co.in/AddToToday",
                    RequestNamespace="http://xstreamindia.co.in",
                    ResponseNamespace="http://xstreamindia.co.in",
            Use=System.Web.Services.Description.SoapBindingUse.Literal,
ParameterStyle=System.Web.Services.Protocols.SoapParameterStyle.Wrapped)]
    public string AddToToday(int nDays) {
        object[] results = this.Invoke("AddToToday", new object[] {
                                                            nDays});
        return ((string)(results[0]));
    }

    [System.Diagnostics.DebuggerStepThroughAttribute()]
    public System.IAsyncResult BeginAddToToday(int nDays,
                    System.AsyncCallback callback, object asyncState)
    {
        return this.BeginInvoke("AddToToday", new object[] {
                                        nDays}, callback, asyncState);
    }

    [System.Diagnostics.DebuggerStepThroughAttribute()]
    public string EndAddToToday(System.IAsyncResult asyncResult) {
        object[] results = this.EndInvoke(asyncResult);
        return ((string)(results[0]));
    }
```

We can also create a proxy using the following command:

```
Wsdl http://localhost/murali/DateService.asmx?wsdl
```

This will create a proxy file with the name `DateService.cs`. In the next section, we will see how the client can be created in an easier way using VS .NET.

We can also use the discovery file to create the Client Proxy Class:

```
Wsdl /language:Csharp /out:DateServiceProxy
                        http://localhost/murali/DateService.disco
```

We have now created a proxy for our Web service. The classes in the proxy will be named after the Web service, in this case `DateService`, and contain methods that call identically named methods on the Web service. It's easy to instantiate this class and use it's methods, as if it were a local object:

```
DateService myService = new DateService();
String result = myService.Today();
```

The proxy object acts as a representative of the remote object and ensures that all calls made on the proxy are forwarded to the correct remote object instance.

Now let's see how to create Web services using the Visual Studio .NET IDE.

Web Services with Visual Studio .NET

Using Microsoft Visual Studio .NET, we can quickly create and include Web services using Visual Basic, C#, and native C++. Visual Studio .NET provides tools for creating Web services in both managed and unmanaged code. However, Web services created in managed code fully leverage the power of the .NET framework.

The Web services can take advantage of the fact that they are built on top of ASP.NET, which in turn is built on top of the .NET Framework and the common language runtime. The infrastructure for Web services is built using industry standards such as XML, SOAP, and WSDL, which allows clients from other platforms to interoperate with the Web services. As long as a client can create SOAP messages in a format that ASP.NET can handle and send across the Internet, that client can call a Web service, regardless of the platform on which it resides.

The default project setup for Web services in the VS .NET environment provides a slightly more complex structure than a single ASMX file, but using VS .NET will automatically generate a framework code that can further be expanded to build something complex.

Create a new ASP.NET Web service project and name it `WebService1`. Similar to creating ASP.NET Web Applications, this will create a new ASP.NET Web service project and add a new virtual directory called `WebService1` to our default web server. This virtual directory acts as the root directory for our Web service. All the remaining files are placed within this directory and it should be flagged as an IIS application directory.

After a few moments, Visual Studio .NET creates a `bin` directory and a number of associated files – let's just take a moment to look at these:

❑ `bin` directory – Contains the binary files for the Web service. Since your Web service classes are not written in the same file as the `.asmx` file, the compiled `.dll` needs to be placed in the `\bin` directory.

❑ `AssemblyInfo.cs` – General information about an assembly that is controlled through a set of attributes. Change these attribute values to modify the information associated with an assembly.

❑ `Service1.asmx` – The file that is invoked by the browser.

❑ `Service1.asmx.cs` – The code-behind page that contains the actual C# code.

❑ `WebService1.vsdisco` – The discovery file (VSDISCO extension when the Web service is created using VS.NET) that will return details of the Web services available on the site.

❑ `WebService1.csproj` – The C# project file, which enables VS.NET to open all files in the project.

❑ `Service1.asmx.resx` – .NET XML Resource Template.

❑ `WebService1.csproj.webinfo` and `WebService1.sln` – VS.NET Webinfo and solution files.

❑ `Global.asax` – Application global information and events. This file contains a single line of code, for example:

```
<%@ Application Codebehind="Global.asax.cs"
                        Inherits="WebService1.Global" %>
```

❑ Global.asax.cs – The code-behind file Global.asax.cs which contains the class Global inherited from System.Web.HttpApplication.

❑ Global.asax.resx – .NET XML Resource Template.

❑ Web.config – Allows customization and extensibility of the system by overriding the default configuration settings. For example, you might supply a Web service–specific Web.config file if your Web service requires authentication and other web applications on the system do not.

A typical deployment would have the following directory structure:

```
\inetpub
   \wwwroot
      \ WebService1
         AssemblyInfo.cs
         Service1.asmx
         Service1.asmx.cs
         Service1.asmx.resx
         WebService1.csproj
         WebService1.vsdisco
         WebService1.csproj.webinfo
         Global.asax
         Global.asax.cs
         Global.asax.resx
         Web.config
         \Bin
```

The Bin folder contains those assemblies that your Web service uses that are not in the Microsoft .NET Framework.

Using VS .NET, if we create a Web service WebService1, for example, then the Service1.asmx file will contain only a single line of code:

```
<%@ WebService Language="c#" Codebehind="Service1.asmx.cs"
                              Class="WebService1.Service1" %>
```

This file, when requested by the browser contains only a <% WebService %> tag, which defines the page characteristics. The language attribute of this tag specifies that we will use C# as the programming language throughout the program. The next two attributes are necessary, as the actual C# code driving the service has been set up by VS .NET in a separate file, Service1.asmx.cs. This file contains the definition of class Service1 that is used as the base class for the Web service. The code contained in the Service1.asmx.cs file can be viewed by right-clicking on Service1.asmx in the Solution Explorer and selecting View Code.

Let's look at the code generated for this file. Firstly we have the default references VS .NET uses for Web services:

```
using System;
using System.Collections;
using System.ComponentModel;
using System.Data;
using System.Diagnostics;
using System.Web;
using System.Web.Services;
```

This is followed by the namespace declaration of our Web service. These namespaces provide a way to group the web methods and other business logic together. This avoids name clashes between methods in different Web services, residing on the same server. Next we see the definition of `Service1`, the base class used for the Web service. This class inherits from the `System.Web.Services.WebService` class. It is up to the designer to add methods to this Web service class:

```
namespace WebService1
{
    /// <summary>
    /// Summary description for Service1.
    /// </summary>
    public class Service1 : System.Web.Services.WebService
    {
```

The following section of the code does some initialization tasks. The initialization method is contained in a `#region` block so that we can hide it using the outline view in VS .NET:

```
public Service1()
{
    //CODEGEN: This call is required by the
    //         ASP.NET Web services Designer
    InitializeComponent();
}

#region Component Designer generated code
/// <summary>
/// Required method for Designer support - do not modify
/// the contents of this method with the code editor.
/// </summary>
private void InitializeComponent()
{
}
#endregion

/// <summary>
/// Clean up any resources being used.
/// </summary>
protected override void Dispose( bool disposing )
{
}
```

Defining a public method and giving it the `WebMethod` attribute makes the Web service accessible to us. Visual Studio .NET adds a sample `HelloWorld` method, commented out, to illustrate how to write methods for Web services:

```
// WEB SERVICE EXAMPLE
// The HelloWorld() example service returns the string Hello World
// To build, uncomment the following lines then save and build the project
// To test this Web service, press F5

//      [WebMethod]
//      public string HelloWorld()
//      {
//          return "Hello World";
//      }
    }
}
```

Examining the code we understand that there is more code than is required for the simple `.asmx` file for performing this trivial function. However, the automatically generated framework code will help us get started if we want to do something more complex. We can see things working by compiling the project after uncommenting the `HelloWorld` method, and setting the namespace to, say, `http://xstreamindia.co.in` in our code as shown below:

```
namespace WebService1
{
   /// <summary>
   /// Summary description for Service1.
   /// </summary>
      [WebService (Namespace="http://xstreamindia.co.in")]
   public class Service1 : System.Web.Services.WebService
   {
      [WebMethod]
      public string HelloWorld()
      {
         return "Hello World";
      }
```

Rebuilding the project and checking the results yields:

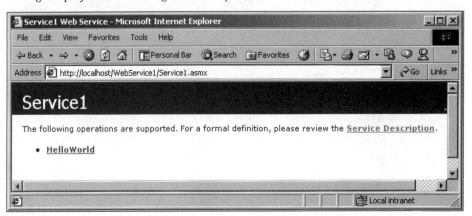

Clicking on the `HelloWorld` method name displays the sample request and response messages for SOAP, HTTP `GET`, and HTTP `POST` methods. The placeholders shown need to be replaced with actual values.

The following is the sample SOAP request and response:

```
POST /WebService1/Service1.asmx HTTP/1.1
Host: localhost
Content-Type: text/xml; charset=utf-8
Content-Length: length
SOAPAction: "http://xstreamindia.co.in/HelloWorld"

<?xml version="1.0" encoding="utf-8"?>
<soap:Envelope xmlns:xsi="http://www.w3.org/2001/XMLSchema-instance"
xmlns:xsd="http://www.w3.org/2001/XMLSchema"
xmlns:soap="http://schemas.xmlsoap.org/soap/envelope/">
  <soap:Body>
    <HelloWorld xmlns="http://xstreamindia.co.in" />
  </soap:Body>
</soap:Envelope>
```

```
HTTP/1.1 200 OK
Content-Type: text/xml; charset=utf-8
Content-Length: length

<?xml version="1.0" encoding="utf-8"?>
<soap:Envelope xmlns:xsi="http://www.w3.org/2001/XMLSchema-instance"
xmlns:xsd="http://www.w3.org/2001/XMLSchema"
xmlns:soap="http://schemas.xmlsoap.org/soap/envelope/">
  <soap:Body>
    <HelloWorldResponse xmlns="http://xstreamindia.co.in">
      <HelloWorldResult>string</HelloWorldResult>
    </HelloWorldResponse>
  </soap:Body>
</soap:Envelope>
```

The following is the sample HTTP GET request and response:

```
GET /WebService1/Service1.asmx/HelloWorld? HTTP/1.1
Host: localhost
HTTP/1.1 200 OK
Content-Type: text/xml; charset=utf-8
Content-Length: length

<?xml version="1.0" encoding="utf-8"?>
<string xmlns="http://xstreamindia.co.in">string</string>
```

The following is the sample HTTP POST request and response:

```
POST /WebService1/Service1.asmx/HelloWorld HTTP/1.1
Host: localhost
Content-Type: application/x-www-form-urlencoded
Content-Length: length

HTTP/1.1 200 OK
Content-Type: text/xml; charset=utf-8
Content-Length: length

<?xml version="1.0" encoding="utf-8"?>
<string xmlns="http://xstreamindia.co.in">string</string>
```

We can test the HelloWorld method by clicking on the Invoke button. (Since this method requires no parameters, there is no provision on the form to enter data.) The following XML output will be returned by the method:

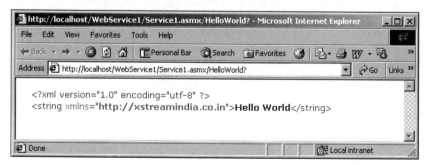

Clicking on the Service Description link (above the HelloWorld method link) on the first browser screen shown above displays the WSDL file of the Web service. The part of the file describing the element types for requests and responses is shown below (within the types block):

```
<?xml version="1.0" encoding="utf-8" ?>

<definitions xmlns:s="http://www.w3.org/2001/XMLSchema"
xmlns:http="http://schemas.xmlsoap.org/wsdl/http/"
xmlns:mime="http://schemas.xmlsoap.org/wsdl/mime/"
xmlns:tm="http://microsoft.com/wsdl/mime/textMatching/"
xmlns:soap="http://schemas.xmlsoap.org/wsdl/soap/"
xmlns:soapenc="http://schemas.xmlsoap.org/soap/encoding/"
xmlns:s0="http://xstreamindia.co.in" targetNamespace="http://xstreamindia.co.in"
xmlns="http://schemas.xmlsoap.org/wsdl/">

<types>
    <s:schema attributeFormDefault="qualified"
              elementFormDefault="qualified"
              targetNamespace="http://xstreamindia.co.in">
      <s:element name="HelloWorld">
        <s:complexType />
      </s:element>
      <s:element name="HelloWorldResponse">
        <s:complexType>
          <s:sequence>
            <s:element minOccurs="1" maxOccurs="1"
                       name="HelloWorldResult"
                       nillable="true" type="s:string" />
          </s:sequence>
        </s:complexType>
      </s:element>
      <s:element name="string" nillable="true" type="s:string" />
    </s:schema>
</types>
```

Creating an ASP.NET Client in Visual Studio .NET

In the previous section, we've seen how to create a proxy object and extract data from Web services. This proxy object will act on behalf of the original Web service and have the complete public interface for any sophisticated business logic functions. The proxy generator tool maps messages described in the WSDL file into methods on the generated class. The proxy hides all the network and marshaling plumbing from the application code, so using the Web service looks just like using any other managed code. The proxy will try to use SOAP to communicate with the Web service, but also supports the HTTP GET and HTTP POST mechanisms if necessary.

Now we need to compile the generated C# class, which will create a DLL under the Bin directory to link to our client projects. Now we are ready to use the proxy object and to extract data from the Web services. Remember, we didn't even register the DLL. We just compiled the sourcecode and stored the DLL in the bin directory. This is sufficient to get access to the DLL by the web server. The local bin directory and the .NET Framework will pick it up at run time. In order to create Web services clients we have to:

❑   Create an instance of a proxy object

❑   Execute method calls on the proxy object

❏   Capture the XML formatted data returned from the Web service

❏   Write client-specific controls to display the results

Now let's see how to build a web page client using VS .NET. We will write a client for a Web service similar to the `DateService` we created in the previous section with two methods, `CurrentDate()` and `AddToToday()`. The step-by-step instructions for achieving this are:

1.   Create a new ASP.NET Web Application using VS .NET in a virtual directory called `DateServiceClient`. A physical directory by the same name will be created under the `\inetpub\wwwroot\` directory.

2.   Now produce the form shown below using the Visual Studio .NET tools:

3.   In the Solution Explorer, right-click on the application and select the **Add Web References** option. Since we created the Web service on the local machine, we will click the **Web Reference** on the local server. We should get a discovery document where we select the desired Web service on the **Available References** box on the right pane. In our case we will select http://localhost/DateService/DateService.disco by clicking on that link.

4.   On the next screen, click the **Add Reference** button. This will result in adding the required entries to the Solution Explorer.

5.   In the Solution Explorer expand the **Web References** folder and rename the web reference from `localhost` to `ConvertDate`, which is the namespace we will use for accessing this web reference.

6.   Double-click on the **Current Date** and **Add Days To Current Date** buttons on the `WebForm1.aspx.cs` to add event handler code:

```
private void Button1_Click(object sender, System.EventArgs e)
{
   ConvertDate.DateService cService = new ConvertDate.DateService();
   Label2.Text = cService.Today();
}
```

```
private void Button2_Click(object sender, System.EventArgs e)
{
   ConvertDate.DateService cService2 = new ConvertDate.DateService();
```

```
        int daystobeadded= Convert.ToInt16(TextBox1.Text);
        Label5.Text = cService2.AddToToday(daystobeadded);
    }
```

7. After running the web application we can click on the buttons to get the current date and the date after adding a number to the current date.

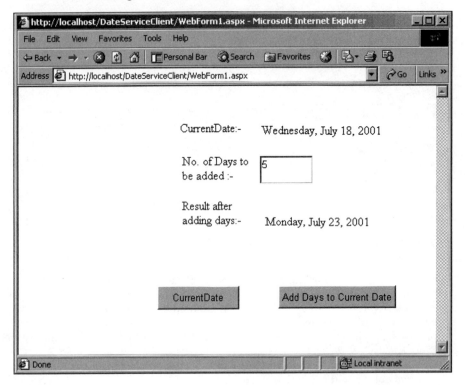

This Web service might change later, but we can still right-click on the web reference in the server explorer and select Update Web Reference. This will generate a new proxy class for us to use.

Summary

In this chapter we have looked briefly at creating Web services in C#. Web services are destined to play an extremely important role in future application developments and here we've taken a rapid run through of the major concepts and terminology related to this topic.

We started by looking at what Web services were, and why they are important – particularly the usefulness of exposing business logic to other client applications, regardless of the platforms involved.

Then we went on to explore the protocols and standards involved in Web services, including SOAP, WSDL, DISCO, and UDDI.

After this, we built Web services – both with and without the help of Visual Studio .NET. We looked at how to deploy and publish Web services.

Finally we used Visual Studio .NET to create a web page that consumed our Web service.

From here we'll move on to take a look at the Microsoft .NET Server family and take a birds eye view of the different products that can aid enterprise development on the Windows platform.

13

The Microsoft .NET Server Family

Over the past decade or so, our application development methodologies have changed drastically. We have seen a shift from monolithic single-executable applications to data-driven client-server systems to n-tier collaborative systems. As we've seen over the course of this book, the .NET framework works to facilitate the evolution of application development to an even more distributed, XML-based, device-aware set of services and components that can seamlessly integrate, communicate, and scale.

To support this onslaught of services, applications, and devices, Microsoft has released the .NET server family. Before we delve into a set of case studies, let's explore these products and briefly look at how they can be employed in large data-centric applications. If you're developing in a .NET environment you'll certainly encounter a situation where you will need to work with, implement, or evaluate these products.

The .NET server family extends previous server technologies that were grouped under Microsoft's now outdated DNA model. In the past, a DNA application may have used Site Server features to enhance security, manage order processing through pipelines, and provide document-searching support though an indexing service. The .NET Server platform now uses Commerce Server to support commerce-specific activities such as security, pipelines, profiling, and user targeting. For intranet, or content-specific features such as document indexing, SharePoint Portal Server is now used.

The .NET Server family has also extended its bricks-and-mortar-oriented applications such as SQL Server 2000, making adjustments for new demands such as rich XML support. The .NET Server platform also employs several new pieces such as BizTalk and Application Center Server to support scalability and flexibility.

Currently in Beta 3, the most awaited component of this puzzle – Microsoft .NET Server – will find itself serving as the cornerstone of the .NET framework, bringing Visual Studio .NET, XML, Web Services, and the .NET Server family of tools together.

This chapter aims to provide a rapid, but effective, review of the use of Microsoft's latest .NET server family to extend and enrich data-driven applications, particularly focusing on their use in the development of scalable, flexible, business-to-business (B2B) applications. Our approach here is to:

❑ Overview the .NET server range

❑ Identify some typical usage patterns

❑ Look at some application development scenarios, which can be solved using .NET servers

Hence we'll take both technology-centric and application-centric views on the products discussed and our starting point is to look at the servers themselves.

The .NET Server Range

The .NET Enterprise Server range currently consists of the following:

❑ Application Center Server

❑ BizTalk Server

❑ Commerce Server

❑ Content Management Server

❑ Exchange Server

❑ Host Integration Server

❑ Internet Security and Acceleration Server

❑ Mobile Information Server

❑ SharePoint Portal Server

❑ SQL Server

❑ Windows 2000 Server family

❑ ET Server/XP Server

Our first task is to provide a high-level view of each of these products (excepting SQL Server and the Windows 2000 Server family, which are fundamental to earlier parts of this book) and their role in the .NET Platform.

Application Center Server

Clustering, or the concept of grouping several servers to form a virtual server, helps achieve performance scalability and failover redundancy in an enterprise environment. Although clustering can be achieved using Windows 2000/XP, Application Center Server simplifies the implementation and maintenance of this task.

App Center Server is typically used in web or application farms for:

❑   Managing common **Network Load Balancing** (**NLB**) tasks on a web cluster

❑   **Component Load Balancing** (**CLB**) – a concept that allows deployment of COM+ objects and assemblies node by node on the cluster so that rebooting or downtime is seldom needed

❑   Component or content management

We will talk about App Center Server in more detail below.

BizTalk Server

Enterprise systems need to publish, process, and consume data regularly. Much of this book has discussed how to programmatically accomplish this task by writing to queues, sending, transforming and receiving XML, and interacting with a database such as SQL Server. BizTalk Server simplifies tasks such as these by taking out much of the arduous programming and data mapping involved.

To simplify and expedite process/data development, Microsoft has linked BizTalk with its Visio application/process modeling software, which creates a very powerful combination for producing, documenting, and developing file or data management applications using a technology that Microsoft calls **XLANG**, or XML language. If custom components are needed to hook into an application, a developer can write an Application Integration Component (AIC).

BizTalk in many ways attempts to accomplish what systems such as EDI and SAP have attempted to in the past, that is automate the sending, processing, and delivery of different standardized documents between different, usually dissimilar business. Thus BizTalk has had some big shoes to fill due to the high cost and difficulty in maintaining the aforementioned systems. Although the premise of BizTalk is very promising, the developer is still limited by the fact that documents must be standardized. Therefore, BizTalk should only be considered when the environment being developing in can be standardized and if the benefits of using a high-powered tool outweigh the cost of custom application/document integration.

Commerce Server

Commerce Server offers several features to expedite traditional e-commerce sites. It contains out-of-the-box solutions for product cataloguing and searching, profiling and personalization, consumer targeting, data mining, and warehousing. Commerce Server is tightly coupled with SQL Server, and integrates with BizTalk Server for document processing situations such as EDI.

Commerce Server has a rich SDK with many agile COM objects, pipelines, and modules that can be used to manage all the previously mentioned features as well as implementing solutions to integrate with existing .NET Server products.

Content Management Server

Content Management Server provides a quick, easy-to-implement solution for dynamic and data-driven web sites. Typically Content Management Server may be used at a company where site maintenance is crucial, but it isn't possible to provide a dedicated IT team. Web content publishing is then put in the hands of content managers who can publish advanced, data-driven pages from their desktops.

Such a scenario could be an environment where the content of a site changes frequently, but not the overall structure of the site, for example a news site, or a corporate intranet.

Exchange Server

Many companies use the Exchange Server platform for their dedicated e-mail/SMTP Server. Microsoft's Exchange Server also complements other .NET applications by providing a rich API to program or script against.

Host Integration Server

Host Integration Server is the next evolution of Microsoft's SNA Server; used primarily for integration with legacy systems such as Mainframe, or AS-400 platforms. We'll encounter this product during Chapter 16 when the topic of legacy integration is addressed in a case study.

Internet Security and Acceleration Server

Internet Security and Acceleration Server (ISAS) assists system administrators by offering VPN (virtual private network), Intrusion Detection, web-caching, and packet-filtering features to provide added security and enhanced performance at the connection/router/proxy level.

Mobile Information Server

Mobile Information Server provides security, management tools, and rich Outlook support for mobile devices such as cell phones, hand-helds, pagers, and other devices defined in the .NET Platform.

SharePoint Portal Server

SharePoint Portal Server is a product to be considered if you need to rapidly develop an intranet portal. Essentially, it's an extension of its predecessor Site Server, offering a stronger arsenal of intranet-geared features such as document searching and dashboard like pre-built navigation. SharePoint also works well with other .NET Server products offering full-blown data providers for Exchange Server, and documents.

.NET Server/XP Server

Formerly code named Whistler, and at the time of writing, currently in Beta 3, this sever line will come in four flavors (their applicability depending on your hardware platform and business needs):

- ❑   Windows .NET Web Server

- ❑   Windows .NET Standard Server

- ❑   Windows .NET Enterprise Server

- ❑   Windows .NET Datacenter Server

Most of these lines look familiar except the Web Server, which will probably be a stripped down version of the others, but focused on Web Services. The product features include full ADO.NET support and a new and improved version of IIS. .NET Server will handle much of the integration with the services that will be released with the .NET My Services platform (which will tie into many user-based services such as Messenger and Passport).

Now we've met the family let's see how they can be effectively used within the enterprise.

Enterprise Usage Patterns

Before we go much further, we should point out that many of these products are called, or considered, out-of-the-box solutions, meaning, that while most of the code to accomplish the chosen tasks is already written, you have the, sometimes not inconsiderable, task of configuring and integrating the product. These products also tend to link together well and, if you're thinking about using a .NET server product, you should take this into consideration. For example, Commerce Server's authentication features can easily be used to enhance applications using SQL Server and BizTalk.

In this section we're going to be looking at a number of different technical needs that the .NET server family can address, basing our coverage around the products themselves, before we take a business-centric view at the end of the chapter. We won't be looking at all the individual products, just highlighting those uses particularly appropriate to B2B scenarios; hence we'll cover:

- ❑ SQL Server including clustering, linking, and monitoring
- ❑ BizTalk Server including data mapping and transportation, validation, and process orchestration
- ❑ Application Server and clustering scenarios
- ❑ Commerce Server including security and data collection

In each case we'll identify the platforms that are involved in each scenario.

SQL Server

SQL Server will act as the cornerstone under the .NET Platform. To effectively manage any type of enterprise environment when dynamic or real-time data will be present, a strong enterprise-capable database is needed.

SQL Server is Microsoft's high-end server line for dealing with these types of needs. Below are some commonly used features that SQL Server can quickly implement.

SQL Clusters

> *Platforms: SQL Server 2000, Windows 2000 Server/Advanced Server*

SQL Clustering, also called **failover clustering**, is a widely used method to provide more uptime to a system. If one physical server goes down in the enterprise, another server can quickly take over, thus eliminating downtime. Failover clustering can also be used as a deployment and maintenance tool, allowing work or updates to be performed one server at a time, allowing the failover server to still process requests.

Failover clustering runs under the **Microsoft Clustering Service** (**MCS**). Under MCS, each physical server in the cluster is considered a node. These nodes can share system resources (typically disk drives) with each other. The nodes periodically send a special type of message called a **heartbeat message**, which tell the MCS service that everything is fine. If the MCS detects an absence of these heartbeats, then a failure is assumed and ownership of the cluster is simply transferred between nodes.

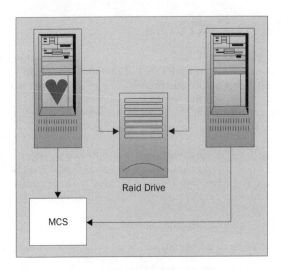

Raid Drive

MCS

SQL Partitioning/Shared Nothing Clustering

Platforms: SQL Server 2000, Windows 2000 Server/Advanced Server

There are historically two types of clustering:

❑ Failover clustering (as described above)

❑ Performance clustering

In performance clustering, resources are shared to boost performance. At the moment SQL Server does not support clustering for performance, only availability. True performance clustering supposedly will not come until Microsoft's next version of SQL Server, (code named Yukon). However, Microsoft was able to perform very well at the Transaction Processing Council's (TPC) most recent benchmarks (http://www.microsoft.com/sql/evaluation/compare/benchmarks.asp) using distributed partitioned views or **Shared Nothing Clustering**, which are essentially views of data, only the data exists on multiple physical servers to distribute server resources and processing load. Shared Nothing Clustering is not considered performance clustering however, because no resources are shared and each server performs autonomously.

Typically SQL partitions are formed by breaking extremely large tables up, and distributing them over several physical SQL Servers. For example, if a table called `Customer` contained six million records, it could be a good candidate for partitioning across a couple of SQL Servers with customers' names that begin with A-K on one machine and those beginning L-Z on another.

Linked Servers

Platforms: SQL Server 7/ SQL Server 2000, Windows 2000 Server/Advanced Server, NT

Most systems pull data from a data source. The problem is that this data source may not be in the format we expect. We may find ourselves needing to connect to anything ranging from a comma separated value flat file to an Oracle 8i database running on a Unix-based server. If we're running SQL Server, we can use its linked server feature, which allows us to effectively tap into any ODBC or OLE DB-compliant data source, or standardized file.

This feature is very useful when maintaining an enterprise application that needs to communicate with many different databases. Queries can be executed on the remote database using the OPENQUERY command. This allows us to break down database language and architecture barriers such as differences between T-SQL and PL/SQL, or the use of IDENTITY columns in SQL Server and Sequences in Oracle.

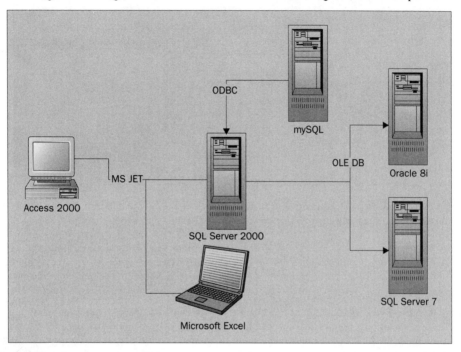

Monitor/Agent Services

Platforms: SQL Server 7/ SQL Server 2000

The .NET framework has several APIs, such as the System.ServiceProcess API, that allow Windows Services to be created for various jobs that may need to be run in an enterprise environment. SQL Server 2000 provides a fairly robust equivalent for creating long running, scheduled services through a utility called SQL Server Agent. The only difference between a SQL Agent job and a Windows Service is that SQL Server jobs run within the SQL Server process.

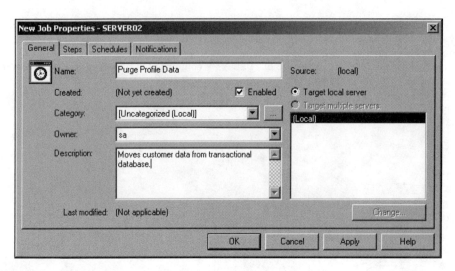

By setting up jobs using SQL Agent, data-oriented services can be created quickly and easily. Typically these services will follow either the monitor or agent pattern:

❑ **Monitor** – Under the Windows Service environment, the Monitor service pattern is typically used to monitor the status of system services, resources, or even clients. A common monitor implementation in the SQL Server 2000 environment might be to create a job to scan tables for number of records, concurrent users, or number of outstanding transactions.

❑ **Agent** – Typically, the Agent does background work that needs to get done without a client user. It can also do intensive processing work to prepare resources in advance of an incoming client. Common SQL Server implementations may include preparing temporary or worktables for processor-intensive activity, scanning error logs and taking appropriate action, or starting and controlling periodic batch jobs.

BizTalk Server

BizTalk Server provides a robust, high-level method of handling messaging, orchestration, and data transformation. Often businesses will need to modify their own internal documents or data to fit into a data consumer or provider's model – BizTalk Server provides tools such as the BizTalk Mapper to help the developer tackle this problem. BizTalk Server can also help to manage pipelines or business processes in the form of COM+ objects, which control decisions and actions needed to control the flow of business logic. The examples below cover common BizTalk Server data-centric tasks and implementations.

Data Mapper

Platforms: BizTalk Server, SQL Server 2000 (Optional), Windows 2000 Server/Advanced Server

Enterprise systems typically have to communicate with dissimilar or disparate systems. These systems may be dealing with the same data, but the interfaces for the data may be very different. For example, an e-commerce site may be talking XML, when a vendor can only talk in EDI.

Custom data mapping, such as that involved in the above example, can be very tedious to develop. BizTalk addresses this issue with an application called the BizTalk Mapper. This application uses XML and XSL to transform a document into its expected format at runtime.

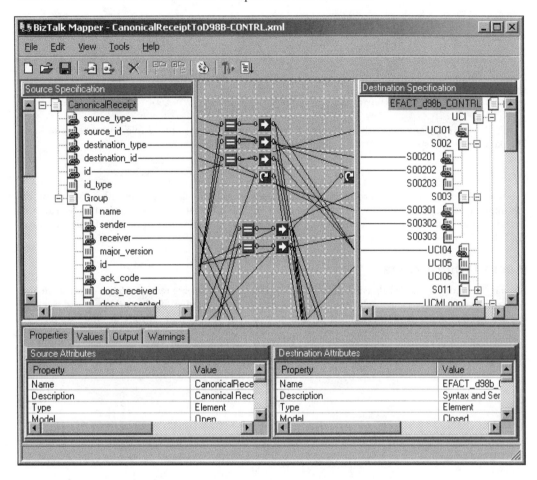

Transporter

Platforms: BizTalk Server, Windows 2000 Server/Advanced Server

To build on the problem of having dissimilar data formats and structures, data transportation is another burden most programmers would rather not deal with. Most companies for security reasons don't allow access to their internal networks except typically through port 80 (HTTP), or 21 (FTP). This often makes it difficult to automate the sending of data.

A common solution to this problem is to use BizTalk to take care of the dirty work of port mapping. Essentially BizTalk eases the data transportation problems of transforming data, then sending it off to specific ports over a chosen protocol, by taking care of most of the low-level programming.

Using BizTalk for this task allows data to be mapped from start to finish in the following protocols:

❑   HTTP

❑   HTTPS

❑   MSMQ

❑   FTP

❑   SMTP

❑   AIC (Application Integration Components – see below)

BizTalk essentially automates the delivery of documents mapping to the above ports. These tasks can be broken down into specific steps and scheduled using the XLANG Scheduler.

Validators

Data validation is a common problem faced by developers. Data validation algorithms are often difficult to implement programmatically for multiple companies or multiple documents. Most of BizTalk's data validation and transformation is done using XSL. Appropriate schemas can be used to check the validity of XML, EDI, fixed-width, comma-delimited, and other files.

Process Orchestrators

A very common use of BizTalk is for process orchestration. Processes are rarely isolated – they often are dependent on other processes, which in turn are dependent on a number of other processes and rules. This builds together into a workflow, or pipeline, of tasks in a business sense. In software this may also be termed a pipeline – here the pipeline will consist of a set of COM+ objects, which control process flow and business logic. BizTalk has features such as the XLANG Scheduler and the BizTalk Designer, which allow each step in these processes to be graphically modeled and appropriate actions for each stage to be defined.

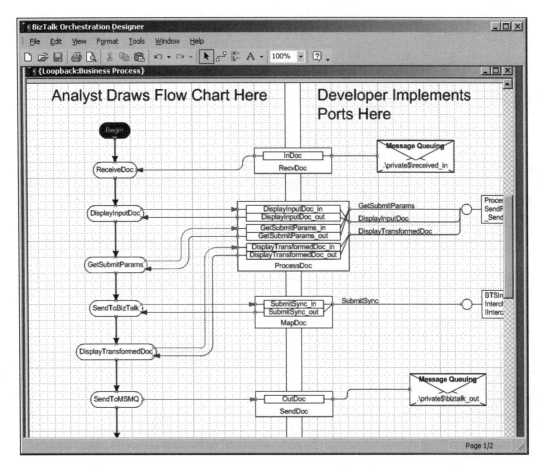

Listeners

Often it is necessary to listen for a specific event. This event could be a file arriving at a specific location, data being written to a remote queue, or an HTTP POST occurring. BizTalk can deal with these events programmatically using an XLANG schedule or custom code, then react and process these events depending on how the processes or pipelines have been defined in the BizTalk Application.

Custom Components (Application Integration Components)

Platform: BizTalk Server, SQL Server 2000 (Optional), Windows 2000 Server/Advanced Server

Although BizTalk provides quite a bit of high-level functionality, it may be necessary to write components to extend BizTalk's functionality to talk with specific applications. These components are COM+ objects called **Application Integration Components**. Examples of using AICs might include custom parsing, encryption, decryption, or document formatting.

Application Center Server

Application Center Server provides tools to enhance scalability and uptime to applications. Below are some common implementation scenarios for this product.

Web Farm/Web Cluster

Platforms: Windows 2000 Server/Advanced Server, Application Center Server

There are two common ways to reach scalability at the web-server level. One approach is to use massive servers. These servers typically have 32+ processors and many gigabytes of memory. Unfortunately, these computers usually cost millions of dollars, and have a fairly high maintenance and total cost of ownership (TCO) attached to them.

An alternative, and less expensive, approach is to use a **web cluster** or **web farm**. A web farm consists of several low-end servers, which essentially act as one virtual server. By dividing the work between multiple machines, scalability and failover can be achieved.

Application Center Server uses the latter approach. Using a wizard, clusters can be created and maintained using a graphical user interface. Clustering also allows software updates to be handled while still maintaining 100% uptime, since at least a single server, or node will be up while the others are being updated.

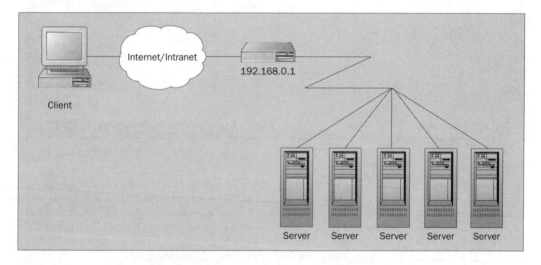

Single Node Cluster/Stager

Platforms: Windows 2000 Server/Advanced Server, Application Center Server

A common problem is that of promoting applications from a development environment to a production mirror (or staging environment), where they can be tested. To address this problem, Application Center Server can be used as a staging environment or **Stager**.

A Stager consists of a single server outside a cluster with an application server installed on it. When an application is ready to be promoted from the development environment, the application can move to the stager to be tested before it is finally moved into production.

Application Farm/Application Cluster

Platforms: Windows 2000 Server/Advanced Server, Application Center Server

An **application cluster** is similar to a web cluster in the sense that several servers can act as one virtual server to process client requests. Typically application clusters will run multiple mid-tier applications supporting web- or Windows-based clients. Using application clusters in this sense has advantages in that mid-tier applications are grouped in their own tier, where they can be behind an extra firewall for more security and can be updated or maintained easily with little or no downtime. The main drawback however, is that in most cases, a performance hit is taken due to the heavy marshaling involved with network Remote Procedure Calls (RPCs).

2-tiered Application Center Cluster

Platforms: Windows 2000 Server/Advanced Server, Application Server

A 2-tiered Application Center cluster uses both the web cluster and an application cluster to house COM+ objects/manifests. This solution is not as fast as the web server cluster, but offers more in the way of security, scalability, and failover.

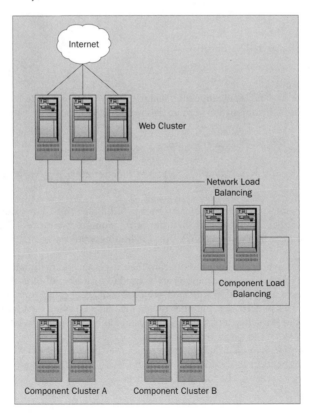

Network Load Balancing/NLB

Platform: Windows 2000 Server/Advanced Server

Network load balancing essentially provides the same service as web clusters, only at a lower level, – without a rich user interface or management tools. Network load balancing simply routes TCP/IP traffic to a virtual server or group of servers defined in a specified cluster. Network load balancing can be installed from the networking and dial up connections properties within the control panel.

Commerce Server

Commerce Server can be very useful when a flexible, proven security/authentication architecture or a solid foundation for reporting or document generation is needed. Commerce Server typically provides the front end for rapid Business to Consumer (B2C) architectures. Below are some more common Commerce Server implementations.

Gatekeeper/Security Portal

Platform: Windows 2000 Server/Advanced Server, SQL Server 2000 (Optional), Commerce Server

One of Commerce Server's strongest areas is its authentication features. Essentially three modes of authentication are supported:

❑ Windows

❑ Custom (similar to .NET's Form)

❑ Auto-cookie

All method's are similar to .NET's authentication features, however Commerce Server provides rich auditing features which, when used in conjunction with its rich reporting/data analysis features, can be very powerful.

Data Collector

Platform: Windows 2000 Server/Advanced Server, SQL Server 2000, Commerce Server, BizTalk Server (Optional)

Commerce Server has some very powerful customer profiling features. For example, information can be collected from users as they navigate, and then put into common data stores. This can be transferred to a data warehouse, then queried using OLAP, thus facilitating analysis and data-mining.

Many sites collect the same types of information from their users such as first name, last name, phone number, etc. This type of common information can be used in a number of different ways as it's captured. For example, if web site A has a partnership with web site B, A could replicate a user's profile information to web site B as it is received. This pattern has a number of benefits such as saving the user the headache of re-entering information, and providing a powerful way to share and track users and their activities.

A common way to carry this out is to use Commerce Server in conjunction with BizTalk Server. Using BizTalk Server, an Application Integration Component (AIC) can be created, that will automatically import profiles as they are received from BizTalk Server.

Data Warehousing/Data Mining

Platform: Windows 2000 Server, SQL Server 2000, Commerce Server

Data Warehousing is a very powerful data-analysis tool, which, when used correctly, can provide an accurate way to ask adhoc queries, examine trend analysis, and predict future events. Commerce Server allows data warehouses, enveloping vast amounts of information coming from sources such as web log files, customer databases, or other specified custom sources to be built quickly. Commerce Server has several tools that can then be used to mine, extrapolate, and report the data in a logical way that are already built and tuned for a commerce environment.

.NET Server Scenarios

As we've just seen, the .NET Server family provides some fairly robust, and powerful, solutions that can quickly integrate into a variety of platforms. The following section will look at real-world scenarios to try to understand the full picture and where the use of a .NET server product, or products, may be applicable.

The scenarios we'll look at are:

❑ Business process integration

❑ B2B communication

❑ Data preservation

In each case we'll identify a clear problem and an appropriate suggested solution.

Business Process Integration

A medium sized telecommunication company decides that it wants to offer Internet services with its base telecom package. To do so, it purchases a small internet service provider (ISP) with the aim of selling its phone package both online and through standard marketing channels. A sign-up process has been made for the telecom site, but there needs to be a way to simultaneously create an account with the ISP so the new customer can have instant Internet access.

When a customer signs up, a credit check needs to be run to make sure the customer's credit is in good standing. Also, data needs to be transferred to the ISP to load the customer into the system, and then process the customer for billing.

The telecom's web site currently runs IIS on a Windows 2000 Server with SQL Server 2000 running on a separate machine. The ISP exists on a different physical network, however, the RADIUS (or authentication) server is part of the telecom's virtual private network. The RADIUS server, due to its simplicity is running MySQL on a Linux Server for its database software. The change request document is standardized and requires specific customer information.

Problem

Here we have two particular issues:

❑ The need to merge two systems to allow the telecom web site to remotely update the ISPs RADIUS authentication database, which controls authentication.

❑ The need to send change request docs to the ISP after sign-up.

Suggestions

As with many situations, there are a several ways in which the problem could be addressed. Primarily the network structure and or platform issues usually influence business integration problems. In the above example, the RADIUS server, which we need to update to create an account, is running on non-Windows software.

The easiest solution for this example would be to add the RADIUS database as a **linked server**, then write stored procedures to handle the account management. However, if, due to networking restrictions, we cannot establish connectivity with the remote server, it may be a good idea to create a complete BizTalk solution involving a custom AIC that performs the necessary actions to inform the ISP that a customer has signed up for service.

Since the documents that need to be created are standardized, the XML documents can be translated using BizTalk's data mapper. Once the documents have been mapped to the appropriate fields, a document drop-off location should be determined. FTP in this case would be ideal because FTP is a platform-independent protocol. BizTalk can then use its **Orchestrator** functionality to fill in the gaps possibly using AICs.

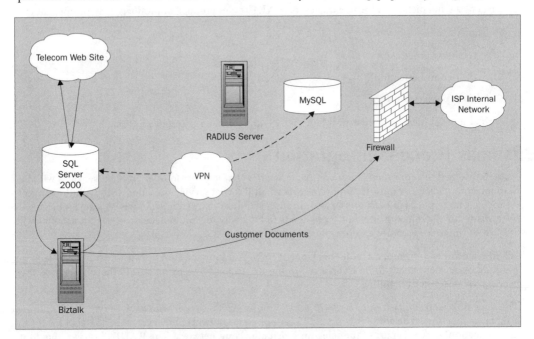

Business-to-Business Communication

Dot coms as we know them may be gone, but B2B commerce is still very much alive and growing. As a developer we may have the task of integrating data from an outside company into our company's native systems. This is often a very arduous task. Depending on the other company's systems, it may be using comma-delimited-or fixed width flat files coming from a mainframe computer to transport data or, if we're lucky, XML.

BizTalk server should be used when we have problems like the above situation. For example, let's say we're working for a company that sells magazine subscriptions online. Our company has multiple call divisions located in other geographic regions and run by several different companies. The telemarketing division consists of a call center and a large mainframe computer. To support the call center and provide details of the people to call, we need to transport our customer profiles from our databases at the magazine site to a repository located at the call center.

Problem

Moving customer data across network boundaries and resolving data into multiple data formats.

Suggestion

Use BizTalk as a data mapper and document transporter. BizTalk would be a good prospect for this situation since we have different data formats and geographic boundaries. Typically only port 80 (HTTP) or 21 (FTP) is open between most networks, so using SQL Server (which usually talks on port 1521) is most definitely out of the question. Since BizTalk is very protocol-agile, it would be appropriate for this situation. Furthermore, BizTalk could be used to map the data between native data structures and formats.

For example, while SQL Server typically takes advantage of relational databases, often in the mainframe world data is not very relational, but very flat and denormalized. BizTalk can be used to bridge the gap between these two systems by mapping to a common data format that the other system can handle such as EDI, XML, CSV, or fixed-width flat files.

`DataSets` could also be a very good solution to this problem. `DataSets` are now also a protocol since they are now XML based. If the receiving party could handle the XML `DataSet`, BizTalk could be used as the method of transport for each `DataSet`.

Data Preservation

Let's consider another scenario where our magazine site is actually the data consumer – here we'll receive data from another process. Let's say that one of our partners, company B, also has a magazine web site. One problem is that both sites refer customers to each other but, when a registered user from their site visits us, they have to register with us also, entering large amounts of profile data. It would be nice if we could share user profiles, thus meaning the user only has to register once before being able to use both sites.

Problem

Duplication of information – need to ensure data is entered once on each partner site.

Suggestion

Allow Commerce Server to control authentication and BizTalk to manage consumption of customer profiles. A BizTalk/Commerce Server/SQL implementation provides a potential solution for this problem. Using Microsoft's Passport authentication service, a feature supported by Commerce Server and BizTalk, we could easily move profile data between site A and B seamlessly without the user even knowing it. Since we are using Passport, we can be assured that a user will only have one identity, and all authentication schemes will be standardized.

The keys for this solution are:

❑ Having a unique way among sites to identify users, for example e-mail address and password

❑ Having a standardized format for representing customer profiles

This solution will only work effectively if the above requirements are met. BizTalk like any other system relies on standardized document formats to process data. E-mail addresses are usually a safe bet when trying to identify specific users. It is crucial that whatever key is used must be unique across systems.

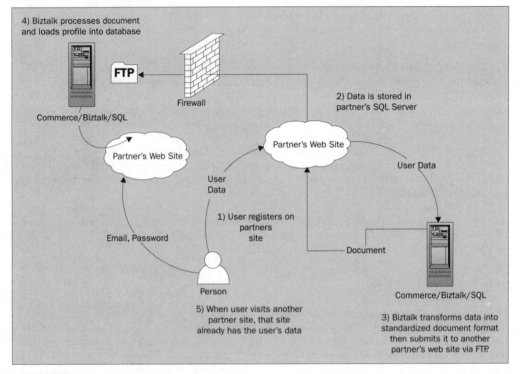

The above solution could potentially be replicated across many other partners provided the architecture was standardized and rules were followed.

Summary

Over the course of the chapter we've reviewed Microsoft's .NET Server family, and hopefully given some ideas of how they can be utilized in enterprise applications.

It is reasonable to say that the .NET Server products can be very effective at cutting costs, producing system synergy, and extending other applications given certain scenarios. However, they don't really do anything that can't be developed given time. They are in many cases "cookie cutter solutions". And just like anything these solutions, although powerful, do have costs and learning curves associated with them.

Now that we've looked at many aspects of .NET data-centric development from the point of view of the technologies, and in this chapter's case, the products that can be used, let's move on to the first of several case studies showing how to build a .NET data-centric application.

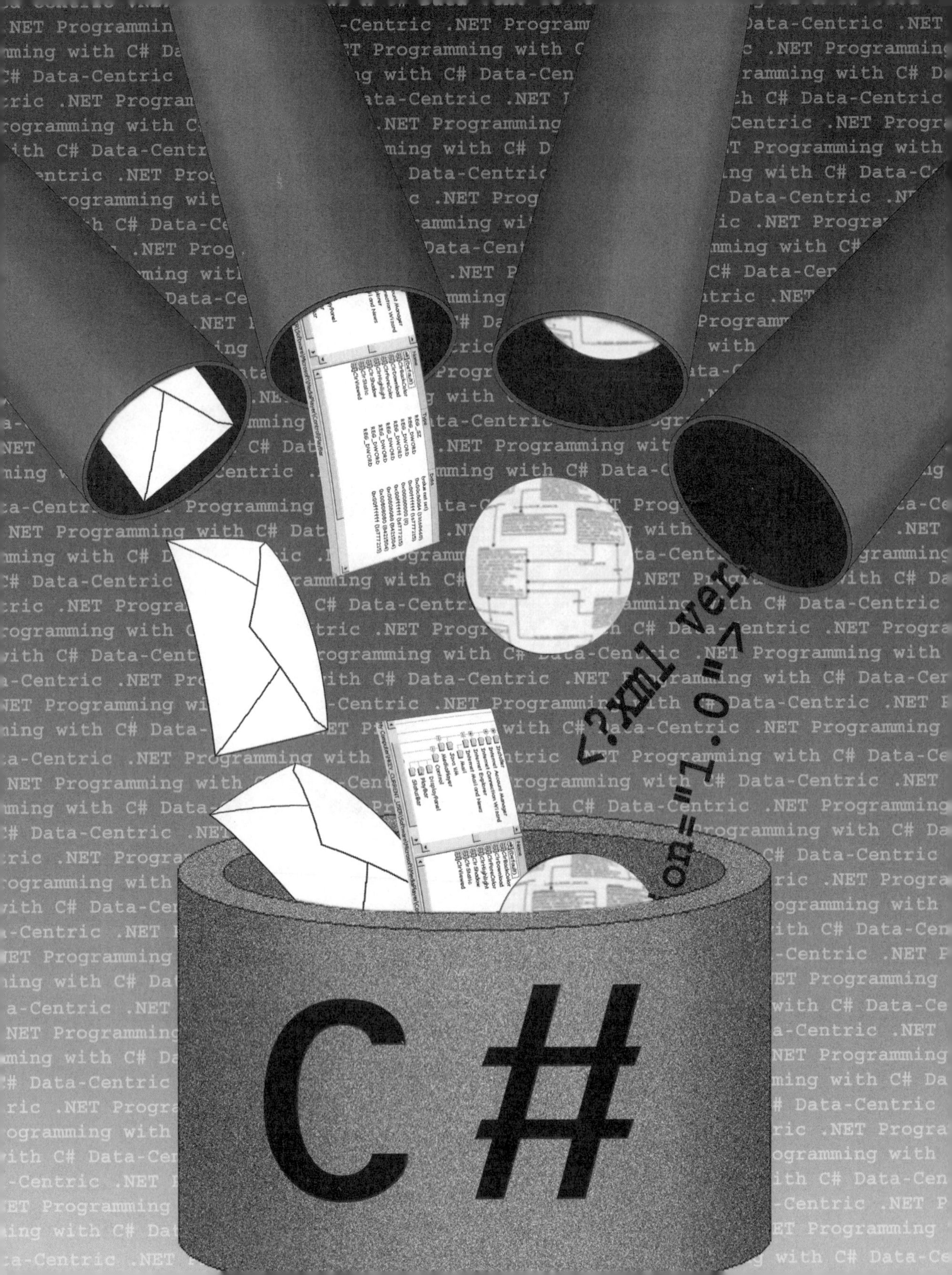
Data-Centric .NET Programming with C#
<?xml ver
on="1.0"?>
C#

14

Case Study I : A Scientific Data Center

Projects often use data from many disparate sources: SQL Server, Oracle, DB2, Sybase, Interbase, Access, dBase, Btrieve, MySQL, XML, and custom flat files to name but a few. Sometimes we are required to utilize entrenched legacy data in its current form, while at other times new data storage solutions are dictated by budgets, shop standards, licensing, politics, and other factors.

In this study we are going to build a sample application for an oceanographic monitoring organization that collects data from sensor buoys moored around the coast. Within our hypothetical scenario the programmer working on the project has decided to experiment with the new .NET Framework, but has decided to stick with an open source database – **MySQL**.

> *Please note that, at the time of writing the case study, the .NET Framework was at the Beta 2 stage, with the ODBC .NET data provider at the Beta 1 stage and that new releases of MySQL are regularly released. The experiences and strategies outlined below for using C# and the .NET managed OLE DB and ODBC providers with MySQL can be extrapolated to other data sources. The case study code is available from www.wrox.com.*

The case study is sub-divided into sections covering:

- ❑ A brief introduction to MySQL
- ❑ An overview of the application and details of the downloads required for the case study
- ❑ Configuration of the `Buoy` database
- ❑ Discussion of the `BuoyUpdate` Windows service (which watches for incoming data)

❏ Coding of a small application for probing performance of the MyOleDb provider and MyODBC driver and examination of their relative merits

❏ Development of a Windows Forms application for managing and viewing of the data

❏ Additional issues regarding improving the robustness of the application

Let's start with some background on the database we'll be working with.

MySQL

The MySQL founders and primary developers operate the Swedish company MySQL AB (http://www.mysql.com/). They own the MySQL trademark and the copyright to the MySQL server source code. MySQL is released under the **GPL** (GNU General Public License). You can consult the MySQL AB web site at http://www.gnu.org to determine how MySQL licensing fits in with your needs.

In addition to the documentation included with the MySQL binary distribution for Win32, the MySQL AB web site offers alternative document formats (PDF, PostScript) as well as numerous other resources. If you are unfamiliar with MySQL, http://www.mysql.com/documentation/ is definitely a great starting point.

The MySQL manual describes MySQL as a client-server relational database management system with a multi-threaded SQL server. Speed, stability, security, and ease of setup and use are the features most often cited by MySQL users as its chief strengths. MySQL supports most of the ANSI SQL 92 standard, although the documentation does list quite a few custom extensions.

This study was designed using the latest stable release of MySQL (3.23.X). While version 4.0 was in alpha release, it should be in beta by the time you are reading this according to MySQL AB's web site. The major features added in version 4.0 are performance tweaks, support for the UNION operator, support for SSL (secure socket layer) connections, and multi-table support for the UPDATE and DELETE commands.

The stable and soon-to-be beta versions still lack some features on which you may have come to rely. These include:

❏ **Views**. This is inconvenient at times, but not particularly distressing.

❏ **Subqueries**. MySQL does not support queries such as:

```
SELECT ProductId, Description FROM Products WHERE Price=(SELECT MAX(Price)
FROM Products);
```

You can work around this, but it will cost you two queries (round trips to the server) instead of one.

❏ **Foreign Key Constraints**. The server will not enforce referential integrity. You must handle enforcement in code, which produces even more network traffic. Since each consumer application is responsible, it only takes one irresponsible consumer to break the rules and invalidate the database.

❏ **Triggers**. You will not be able to rely on triggers to enforce business rules in the database. As we mentioned with constraints, you would have to replicate the business rules in each consumer application and rely on each application to implement the rules properly.

❑ **Stored Procedures**. Without stored procedures you won't be saving any server performance or network traffic on repetitive procedures. Instead you'll be sending line after line of SQL to the server so it can parse, optimize, and compile it each and every time.

❑ **Transactions**. This has got to be the ultimate missing feature of MySQL's default table type, **MyIsam**. Newer versions of MySQL actually do feature transaction support in the alternative table types **InnoDb** and **BDB** (**BerkeleyDB**). Be aware, however, that the MySQL manual notes that InnoDB and BDB tables should be considered beta features.

We won't be detailing workarounds for all of these issues in the limited scope of this chapter, but you can find a wealth of information online (see the list below). The MySQL faithful have been coping with these limitations for as long as MySQL has been around, so there are newsgroups, mailing lists, and web sites full of helpful examples in many languages. The MySQL development roadmap schedules subquery, foreign key constraint, stored procedure, and trigger support for version 4.1. Maybe we'll see some alpha releases of version 4.1 by the end of the year 2002.

Online sources for MySQL help include:

❑ The Database Talk and Windows Help forums at PHPBuilder: http://www.phpbuilder.com/

❑ The Yahoo Groups archives at http://groups.yahoo.com/group/mysql-win32/ and http://groups.yahoo.com/group/mysql-en/

❑ Developer Shed: http://www.devshed.com/

❑ The FAQTS knowledge base: http://www.faqts.com/knowledge_base/index.phtml/fid/52/

❑ The bitbybit.dk MySQL FAQ: http://www.bitbybit.dk/mysqlfaq/faq.html

Well, enough about features and limitations for now. Let's discuss the premise of our case study and how to acquire and install the necessary components. Then let's find out how well C# and the .NET managed providers work with MySQL.

Overview of the Applications

Our sample applications will revolve around a fictional scientific buoy data center. The premise is that the organization has moored several sensor buoys in various locations off the coast. These buoys transmit hourly meteorological data to one of several geostationary satellites, which then relay the information to the data center. The receiver at the data center decodes the incoming transmissions and assembles an ASCII flat file which is forwarded to the database server for processing:

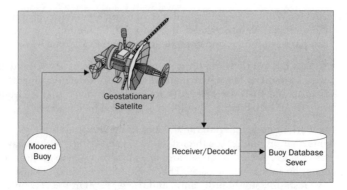

The inspiration for this study's database came from the National Data Buoy Center (NDBC), which is part of the National Weather Service (NWS) of the National Oceanic and Atmospheric Administration (NOAA). You can read about the real details of the Buoy Center at http://www.ndbc.noaa.gov/. Their FAQ provides some interesting information about the data collection issues they face. The example data elements we will be using only vaguely resemble a small subset of the real Buoy Center data. Also, the real-time transmissions they must decode are a bit more cryptic than the tidy little files we will be using.

We will create a Windows service named `BuoyUpdate` to watch for incoming transmissions of data from the buoys. When these hourly readings files arrive each day, the service will insert them into our database. We will also build a Windows Forms application to view the collected data, as well as allow for the addition of new buoys. This study will be more about discovering compatibility issues between .NET and MySQL than it will be about writing some production-ready, killer application for viewing, analyzing, and reporting on the fictional scientific data. I have frequently sacrificed robust features and good object-oriented design at the application level in favor of methods that show an entire process "start to finish" and are easy to dissect and analyze. For ease of setup and study, we'll also assume that the database and all programs will be running on the same physical machine.

Also, many methods have duplicates (both an OLE DB version and an ODBC version). This contrivance has, of course, added some extra code which would not really be necessary for these relatively simple applications were they written for production rather than instruction. As I break down these applications in the chapter, I will try to skip over the sections of code that exist merely to direct program execution to one data access method or the other.

While there are several options for connecting to MySQL, we will concentrate our efforts on two open source offerings: the **MyOleDb** provider and the **MyODBC** driver.

From this point, unless clearly specified, when I use the acronym OLE DB, I mean the .NET OLE DB managed provider connecting to MySQL via MyOleDb. Likewise, when I use the acronym ODBC, I mean the .NET ODBC managed provider connecting to MySQL via MyODBC.

Acquiring the Software

At the time this study was developed, the following Win32 binary versions of MySQL, MyODBC, MyOleDb, and ODBC .NET were the latest available. I cannot guarantee you will get the same results if you use any other versions. The following URLs were correct at the time of printing.

Component	Version	Location
MySQL	3.23.39-nt	http://www.mysql.com/downloads/mysql-3.23.html
MyODBC	2.50.37-nt	http://www.mysql.com/downloads/api-myodbc.html
MyOleDb	3.0.0	http://old.sw.com.sg/products/myoledb/
ODBC .NET Data Provider	1.0.2914.58 (Beta 1)	http://download.microsoft.com/download/dasdk/Beta/1.0.2914.58/W98NT42KMeXP/EN-US/odbc_net.exe

Since we will only be using MySQL's MyIsam table types for simplicity of study and ease of installation, you can download the regular MySQL 3.23 stable Win32 binary rather than the MySQL MAX 3.23 beta release.

Also, a word of caution about file collections that may become stagnant. You may notice a Win32 binary distribution of the MyOleDb provider in MySQL AB's download section. I discovered the hard way while preparing for this study that MySQL AB did not link to the latest version (3.0). Version 2.5 of the MyOleDb provider has serious compatibility issues with the .NET managed providers (hardly anything works). MyOleDb is actually a product of **SWSoft** instead of MySQL AB so you should definitely look to the actual developer of a component to find its latest incarnation. The table above should point you in the right direction to get the appropriate versions of each component.

Installation and Setup

Now that we've acquired the software, let's take a look at each component and how to properly configure it for our study.

ODBC .NET Data Provider

Just before this study was written, Microsoft released the ODBC .NET Data Provider Beta 1 add-on for the .NET Framework SDK Beta 2. This was very good timing, for it allows us to put both the MyODBC driver and the MyOleDb provider through their paces.

Running the ODBC .NET setup installs the proper files to allow the downloaded chapter code projects to use ODBC. Later, when you want to create projects from scratch that utilize the ODBC .NET data provider, you will have to add a reference to the System.Data.Odbc.dll in each project that will use the System.Data.Odbc namespace. In Visual Studio .NET, this is done via the Project | Add Reference dialog.

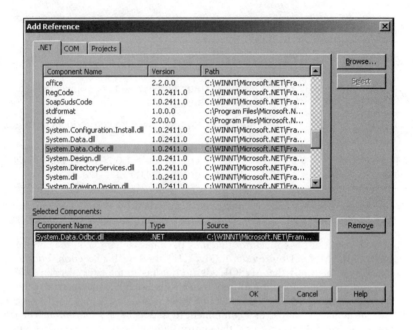

MySQL

Once you have downloaded the MySQL Windows 2000 binary package, extract the files and run `Setup.exe`, which installs MySQL into the default directory of `C:\mysql`. Now open a command prompt and execute the following command to install the MySQL server Windows service.

```
c:\mysql\bin\mysqld --install
```

Next you should copy all the files from the `\mysql\data\buoy` directory (found in the chapter code download) into a directory of the same name on your hard drive (`C:\mysql\data\buoy`). Each subdirectory under MySQL's `\data\` directory represents a database that the server will recognize once it is running.

Now that you have the database files in place, you are ready to start the service. Go into the services management console via Start Menu | Settings | Control Panel | Administrative Tools | Services. Find the MySql service line and right-click it. Select Start to get the MySQL server running. Also, if the Startup Type is Manual or Disabled, you might want to go into the Properties dialog and change it to Automatic for your convenience.

If you ever need to refresh the data from this study, you can take the following simple steps. Stop the MySQL service by selecting Stop from the right-click menu in the services management console mentioned above. Now just copy the original files from the chapter code download `\mysql\data\buoy` directory into the `C:\mysql\data\buoy` directory, then restart the service.

MyODBC

Once you have downloaded the MyODBC NT binary package, extract the files and run `Setup.exe`. While the MyODBC install adds a data source to a sample MySQL database, you will now need to configure a data source specifically for the buoy database. Select Settings | Control Panel | Administrative Tools | Data Sources (ODBC). After clicking the Add button on the User DSN tab, scroll down the list of drivers and select MySQL:

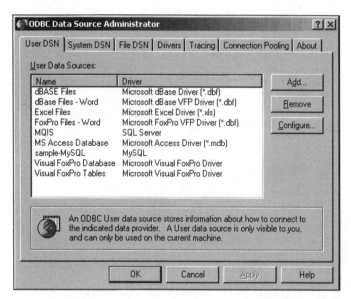

Once you click Finish, you will be presented with the following MySQL configuration screen. Since we are simply running this on the same computer as our applications, you can simply fill in Windows DSN name and MySQL database name with Buoy Database and buoy respectively, while leaving the MySQL host, User, and Password fields blank. In the "Options that affects the behaviour of MyODBC" (sic) section, be sure to check both the Return matching rows option and the Return table names in SQLDescribeCol option.

MyOleDb

Once you have downloaded the Windows binary package, simply run the setup program to install the MyOleDb provider at the default location \Program Files\MyOLEDB\MyProv.dll. No other configuration is required. It is worth noting that the help file installed in the directory with MyProv.dll goes into quite a bit of detail about the internals of the provider.

The Buoy Database

The BuoyUpdate service and the BuoyView application use a MySQL database that contains two MyIsam type tables (buoys and readings). Earlier, you installed fully-populated versions of these tables from the downloaded chapter code by simply copying the \mysql\data\buoy directory. For those interested in MySQL's dialect of SQL, the following statements would create the appropriate empty tables and related indexes (keys):

```
CREATE TABLE buoys (BuoyId INTEGER UNSIGNED NOT NULL
                         AUTO_INCREMENT PRIMARY KEY,
             Description varchar(40) NOT NULL,
             Latitude DOUBLE,
             Longitude DOUBLE,
             DeployDate DATETIME NOT NULL);
```

```
CREATE TABLE readings (BuoyId INTEGER UNSIGNED NOT NULL,
                       ReadingDate DATETIME NOT NULL,
                       ReadingHour INTEGER UNSIGNED NOT NULL,
                       WindSpeed DOUBLE,
                       AirTemp DOUBLE,
                       WaterTemp DOUBLE,
                       DewPoint DOUBLE,
                       PRIMARY KEY (BuoyId, ReadingDate, ReadingHour),
                       KEY BuoyKey (BuoyId),
                       KEY DateKey (ReadingDate));
```

The buoys Table

The buoys table contains a list of the deployed buoys and their characteristics. The table has the following structure:

Column Name	Type	Description
BuoyId	int(unsigned)	A unique ID for the buoy
Description	varchar	A descriptive name for the buoy; length of 40
Latitude	double	Latitude in decimal format
Longitude	double	Longitude in decimal format
DeployDate	datetime	Date the buoy was placed in service

The readings Table

The readings table contains the hourly readings reported by each buoy. The table has the following structure:

Column Name	Type	Description
BuoyId	int (unsigned)	A unique ID for the buoy
ReadingDate	datetime	Date of the readings (yyyy-mm-dd)
ReadingHour	int (unsigned)	Hour of the readings (0-23)
WindSpeed	double	Hourly average wind speed (miles/second)
AirTemp	double	Hourly average air temperature (Celsius)
WaterTemp	double	Hourly average sea surface temperature (Celsius)
DewPoint	double	Hourly average dewpoint temperature (Celsius)

A Few Words about Data Types

MySQL stores `real` and `double` types at the same level of precision, so there is no space saved by defining a column as `real` instead of `double`.

If we tried to use MySQL `DATE` column types in our tables instead of `DATETIME`, the `SELECT * FROM` operations via ODBC would generate `Unknown SQL type - 91` errors. When using OLE DB, `DATE` type columns would appear to cause no problems. If for some reason we absolutely had to use `DATE` type columns with ODBC, we could first specify each column by name rather than using the wildcard in our `SELECT` statements (which is good policy anyway). We could then wrap any `DATE` column in the `SELECT` statement with the MySQL `DATE_FORMAT` function to force a format:

```
SELECT BuoyId, DATE_FORMAT(DeployDate, '%m-%d-%Y') FROM buoys;
```

We would also get exceptions when retrieving MySQL `DECIMAL` column types via ODBC, although a peek at the schema returned in a .NET `DataSet` would show us that the type is directly defined as `System.Decimal`. This time, a null reference exception would be generated instead of an unknown SQL type. Looking at the schema returned if we used OLE DB instead, we would find a query returns the column as a `System.Double` type rather than producing an exception. Our sample tables will simply use the `DOUBLE` type to avoid the erratic behavior associated with the `DECIMAL` type.

These were the MySQL column types and conditions that threw outright exceptions. While there may be others, these are the only ones that came to light while compiling this study. Later we will see some possibly less catastrophic issues concerning how different providers return slightly different versions of some numeric types.

Hourly Readings File

We'll assume that the files transmitted by our fictional buoys are received in the following order: `BuoyId`, `ReadingDate`, `Reading Hour`, `WindSpeed`, `AirTemp`, `WaterTemp`, and `Dewpoint`. We'll also assume a delimiter of `"|"`.

Hence they'll look like this:

```
1|20010101|00|5.7|22.1|23.2|15.9
1|20010101|01|5.8|22.1|23.2|16.3
1|20010101|02|6.1|22.2|23.2|16.6
...
1|20010101|21|5.6|23.1|23.4|19.0
1|20010101|22|5.6|23.1|23.4|19.0
1|20010101|23|5.6|23.1|23.4|19.0
```

This format will make updating our `readings` table easy, since it matches that table, column for column. We'll also take a brief look at processing a less friendly alternative format of this file.

The BuoyUpdate Service

Since our database update process requires no user interface and will be running constantly in the background, waiting for incoming hourly readings files, we can implement it as a Windows service.

Our BuoyUpdate service will consist of three classes, all residing in the BuoyUpdate namespace (BuoyUpdate\ in the chapter code download):

❑   ProjectInstaller – Allows us to easily install the completed BuoyUpdate.exe with the installutil.exe utility

❑   BuoyServiceConfig – A small, internal class that handles Windows Registry access to configuration information used by the BuoyUpdate class

❑   BuoyUpdate – The service, derived from System.ServiceProcess.ServiceBase

Since we are going to be implementing a Windows service, rather than a Console or Windows Forms application, we'll go into a little more project detail than usual.

If you are unfamiliar with the Windows services namespaces within the .NET framework, Chapter 24 in Professional C#, Wrox Press (ISBN 1-861004-99-0) is an excellent starting point.

To begin creating a service, select **Windows Service** from the **New Project** wizard dialog:

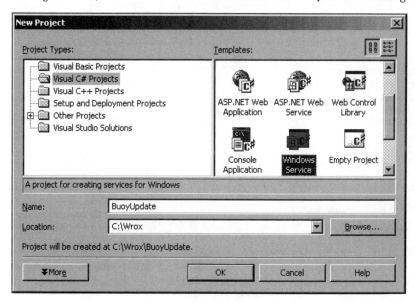

This will create a solution for us with a file called Service1.cs. Rename that file to BuoyUpdate.cs. Now, double-clicking on the BuoyUpdate.cs in the **Solution Explorer** will give us access to the **Properties Window** for the service. The Name and ServiceName properties are still set to Service1, so we need to change both values to BuoyUpdate:

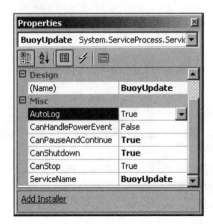

Since we are going to implement handlers for their events later, we should go ahead and take this opportunity to make sure the CanPauseAndContinue, CanShutdown, and CanStop properties are set to True. Also worth mentioning here is the AutoLog property. Leaving it set to True means that the ServiceBase class will automatically log start, stop, pause, and continue events for us. This also means that when we want to do our own event logging, we can easily use the static WriteEntry() method of the EventLog class rather than having to explicitly create an object of type EventLog.

The following namespaces are referenced in the BuoyUpdate service:

```
using System;
using System.Data;
using System.Diagnostics;
using System.ServiceProcess;
using System.IO;
using System.Data.Odbc;      //Don't forget to reference System.Data.Odbc.dll
using System.Data.OleDb;
using System.Text;
using Microsoft.Win32;
```

Remember that it was necessary to add a reference to System.Data.Odbc via the Project | Add Reference dialog.

ProjectInstaller Class

We should let Visual Studio .NET create the ProjectInstaller class for us (\BuoyUpdate\ProjectInstaller.cs). Select the Add Installer option either from the Properties Window or the context menu of the BuoyUpdate designer view. This adds the class with the appropriate ServiceInstaller and ServiceProcessInstaller components.

While this class was conveniently created for us, we must make certain that any subsequent changes we make do not cause an inconsistency between the ServiceName property of the ServiceInstaller and the ServiceName property in the constructor for the BuoyUpdate class.

```
private void InitializeComponent()
{
    this.serviceProcessInstaller1 = new
                    System.ServiceProcess.ServiceProcessInstaller();
```

```
    this.serviceInstaller1 = new System.ServiceProcess.ServiceInstaller();

    //
    // serviceProcessInstaller1
    //
    this.serviceProcessInstaller1.Account =
                        System.ServiceProcess.ServiceAccount.LocalSystem;
    //
    // serviceInstaller1
    //
    this.serviceInstaller1.ServiceName = "BuoyUpdate";

    //
    // ProjectInstaller
    //
    this.Installers.AddRange(new System.Configuration.Install.Installer[]
                            {this.serviceProcessInstaller1,
                             this.serviceInstaller1});
}
```

We can improve the way our service will appear in the Services Management Console by populating the DisplayName property of the ServiceInstaller component with a user-friendly name:

```
public ProjectInstaller()
{
    // This call is required by the Designer.
    InitializeComponent();
    this.serviceInstaller1.DisplayName = "Buoy Update Service";
}
```

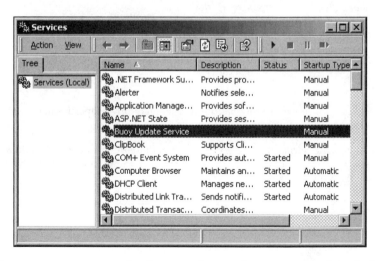

Sadly, the ServiceInstaller *class does not implement a description property for use by the Services Management Console. You can provide a description yourself by creating the appropriate registry entry.*

BuoyServiceConfig Class

As its name implies, this class holds configuration information about the `BuoyUpdate` service. The constructor queries the Windows Registry to fetch information specific to our service.

```
internal class BuoyServiceConfig
{
    private string mRegistryPath;
    private string mInputPath;
    private string mBackupPath;
    private string mExceptionPath;
    private string mInputFilter;
    private string mInputDelimiter;
    private string mConnectionType;

    public BuoyServiceConfig(string RegistryPath)
    {
        mRegistryPath = RegistryPath;
        RegistryKey WroxKey =
                Registry.LocalMachine.CreateSubKey(@"Software\WroxPress");
        RegistryKey BuoyUpdateKey = WroxKey.CreateSubKey(RegistryPath);

        mInputPath = BuoyUpdateKey.GetValue
                        ("InputPath", @"C:\mysql\wrox\datain\").ToString();
        mBackupPath = BuoyUpdateKey.GetValue
                        ("BackupPath",
                         @"C:\mysql\wrox\datain\backup\").ToString();
        mExceptionPath = BuoyUpdateKey.GetValue
                        ("ExceptionPath", @"C:\mysql\wrox\datain\exception\")
                        .ToString();
        mInputFilter = BuoyUpdateKey.GetValue
                        ("InputFilter", @"*.trx").ToString();
        mInputDelimiter = BuoyUpdateKey.GetValue
                        ("InputDelimiter", @"|").ToString();
        mConnectionType = BuoyUpdateKey.GetValue
                        ("ConnectionType", "MyOdbc").ToString();
    }
}
```

The rest of this class (not shown) simply defines public, read-only properties that expose each of the private string variables.

If you wish to change the settings for the service to something other than the default values given in the `GetValue()` methods, you can look to trusty `RegEdit` with the following image as a guide for adding values under the `BuoyUpdate` key.

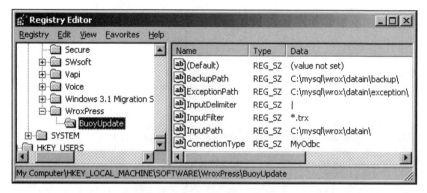

When changing values, just keep in mind that our simple example service relies on the various path values ending in the backslash character. Also, the ConnectionType property should be set to either MyOdbc or MyOleDb. Whether or not you change the default values for InputPath, BackupPath, and ExceptionPath, you will need to manually create the directories in order to test the BuoyUpdate service later.

> *It should be relatively simple to extend this class and reuse it as a component of a Windows Forms-based service controller application. See Chapter 24 in* Professional C# *(Wrox Press, ISBN 1-861004-99-0) for more information on using the* System.ServiceProcess.ServiceController *class to create such a helper application.*

BuoyUpdate Class

The BuoyUpdate class is the heart of our service as it is derived from the ServiceBase class:

```
public class BuoyUpdate : System.ServiceProcess.ServiceBase
{
    private BuoyServiceConfig myConfig;
    private FileSystemWatcher myWatcher;

    private string mOdbcConnString =   "DRIVER={MySQL};DATABASE=buoy";
    private string mOleDbConnString =
                            "Data Source=buoy;provider=MySQLProv";

    public BuoyUpdate()
    {
        this.ServiceName = "BuoyUpdate";
    }
```

Above, we declare the connection strings and the objects we will need throughout the class. Later we will see that the FileSystemWatcher object declared here is really our workhorse. The watcher will raise notification events for us based on criteria we specify.

> The **ServiceBase.ServiceName** property is the one whose value must match the **ServiceInstaller.ServiceName** property mentioned earlier in our discussion of the **ProjectInstaller** class.

Coding the Event Handlers

First let's see how we can override the `OnStart()` handler of the `ServiceBase` class:

```
/// <summary>
/// Set things in motion so your service can do its work.
/// </summary>
protected override void OnStart(string[] args)
{
    myConfig = new BuoyServiceConfig(this.ServiceName);

    StringBuilder myLogText = new StringBuilder
                      (this.ServiceName + " began starting with the " +
                                        "following options:\n");
    myLogText.Append("Input Path: " + myConfig.InputPath + "\n");
    myLogText.Append("Input Filter: " + myConfig.InputFilter + "\n");
    myLogText.Append("Input Delimiter: " + myConfig.InputDelimiter + "\n");
    myLogText.Append("Backup Path: " + myConfig.BackupPath + "\n");
    myLogText.Append("Exception Path: " + myConfig.ExceptionPath + "\n");
    myLogText.Append("Connection Type: " + myConfig.ConnectionType + "\n");
    EventLog.WriteEntry(myLogText.ToString(),
                           EventLogEntryType.Information, 0);

    myWatcher = new FileSystemWatcher
                        (myConfig.InputPath, myConfig.InputFilter);

    myWatcher.Created += new FileSystemEventHandler(onTrigger);
    myWatcher.EnableRaisingEvents = true;
}
```

We create our `FileSystemWatcher` object, passing it values via its constructor to designate the path and files to monitor. Next, we attach our event handler `OnTrigger()` to the watcher's `Created()` event. Now we simply set its `EnableRaisingEvents` property to `true` to have the watcher begin its vigil for hourly readings files from the buoys

After looking at the rest of the `BuoyUpdate` class, we will see that the object `myConfig` is only instantiated in the `OnStart()` handler (shown above). This means that any changes made to the appropriate Registry values will only be acknowledged by the `BuoyUpdate` service after it is restarted.

Debugging Windows services in the Visual Studio .NET development environment is problematic. While the core routines of our service could be written and initially tested as part of a regular Windows application project, we of course still eventually have to move them into our Windows service project to compile and test the service executable. It is possible to do some debugging by attaching to an already running service executable via the **Processes** option of the **Debug** menu. This, however, assumes that you already have the service running, which is of course not the case during the `OnStart()` event itself.

For our simple example, we can circumvent this problem by taking advantage of the Event Log to report on the state of some of our objects at important stages of execution. We will talk more about vent logging details and alternatives later. For now, just know that the above code culminating in ntLog.WriteEntry() will provide us with a helpful message in the log displaying the values of onfig() object properties at startup.

Before we talk about our OnTrigger() event handler, let's look at some more handlers for the ServiceBase class events. Below, we can see that in addition to the OnStart() handler, we want to override the OnStop(), OnShutdown(), OnPause(), and OnContinue() handlers. By utilizing the EnableRaisingEvents property of the FileSystemWatcher, we can turn the watcher on and off as the need arises.

```
/// <summary>
/// Stop this service.
/// </summary>
protected override void OnStop()
{
    myWatcher.EnableRaisingEvents = false;
    myWatcher.Dispose();
}

protected override void OnShutdown()
{
    OnStop();
}

protected override void OnPause()
{
    myWatcher.EnableRaisingEvents = false;
}

protected override void OnContinue()
{
    myWatcher.EnableRaisingEvents = true;
}
```

Now we'll discuss the OnTrigger() handler which we earlier attached to the watcher's Created event. We can be assured that the file is indeed a new arrival in our watched directory if we make sure that the ChangeType property of the eventargs object is of type WatcherChangeType.Created. Actually, this is overkill because when we attached the onTrigger event handler back in the OnStart() method, we only attached it to the FileSystemWatcher.Created event. This overkill simply demonstrates our ability to test the change type, which is handy to know if you wanted to have a single handler method attached to multiple FileSystemWatcher events (Changed, Renamed, Deleted).

```
private void onTrigger(object source, FileSystemEventArgs e)
{
    if (e.ChangeType == WatcherChangeTypes.Created)
    {
        FileInfo myFile = new FileInfo(myConfig.InputPath + e.Name);
        myFile.CopyTo(myConfig.BackupPath + myFile.Name, true);

        if (myConfig.ConnectionType.ToUpper() == "MYOLEDB")
        {
            AddNewOleDb(myFile);
        }
        else
        {
            AddNewOdbc(myFile);
        }
```

```
        myFile.Delete();
    }
}
```

Next we make a backup copy of our input file, just in case. We'll see later that the actual add methods may produce exception files for us that contain anywhere from one to all the original rows, depending on the number of exceptions. With a backup, however, we can be sure to get our hands on a complete, original file every time. The inner `if` checks the `ConnectionType` property from the `myConfig` object to call the method that utilizes the data access method we specified earlier in our `ConnectionType` registry key.

```
if (myConfig.ConnectionType.ToUpper() == "MYOLEDB")
```

Finally, we delete the input file since we now have a backup (and possibly an exception) version. This clears the directory being watched in preparation for the next day's file.

Database Input

Now let's dig into the two add methods (one for ODBC and one for OLE DB) that actually post our input file rows to the database.

ODBC Connection

Our default connection type is ODBC, so we'll cover the `AddNewOdbc()` method (shown below) first. After opening our connection, we then fetch a `StreamReader` object from our input file via the `OpenText()` method. Then we simply loop through the file using the reader, parsing each line into a string array. Finally, the string array is used to build a SQL `INSERT` command, which we subsequently execute against the database using the `ExecuteNonQuery()` method of the `OdbcCommand` object:

```
private void AddNewOdbc(FileInfo InputFile)
{
    bool HasException = false;

    OdbcConnection myConnection = new OdbcConnection(mOdbcConnString);

    myConnection.Open();

    StreamReader myReader = InputFile.OpenText();
    string NextLine;
    while ((NextLine = myReader.ReadLine()) != null)
    {
        string[] parsedLine=
                    NextLine.Split(myConfig.InputDelimiter.ToCharArray());

        StringBuilder myCommandText = new StringBuilder
                    ("INSERT INTO readings VALUES(");
        // element outside of loop, so there will be no comma
        // before first value
        myCommandText.Append(parsedLine[0].ToString());
        for (int j=1; j < parsedLine.Length; j++)
        {
            myCommandText.Append("," + parsedLine[j].ToString());
        }
        myCommandText.Append(");");
```

```
    OdbcCommand myCommand = new OdbcCommand
                (myCommandText.ToString(), myConnection);

    try
    {
        myCommand.ExecuteNonQuery();
    }
    catch (OdbcException myException)
    {
        HasException = true;
        LogOdbcErrors(myException);
        // Create line in exception file for possible retry
        StreamWriter myWriter = new StreamWriter
                (myConfig.ExceptionPath + InputFile.Name,
                 true, Encoding.ASCII);
        myWriter.WriteLine(NextLine);
        myWriter.Close();
    }
    catch (Exception e)
    {
        HasException = true;
        LogGenericException(e);
    }
}
myReader.Close();
myConnection.Close();
if (HasException)
{
    EventLog.WriteEntry(InputFile.FullName + "
            processed with exceptions!", EventLogEntryType.Error, 2);
}
else
{
    EventLog.WriteEntry(InputFile.FullName + "
            processed successfully!", EventLogEntryType.Information, 1);
}
}
```

We don't have the convenience of stored procedures with MySQL, but we can see how easily we can use the `ExecuteNonQuery()` method in conjunction with our custom-built `INSERT` command which would look something like:

```
INSERT INTO readings VALUES(1,20010101,0,5.7,22.1,23.2,15.9);
```

> *Just like in T-SQL, the MySQL `INSERT` statement allows us to omit the column names in the `VALUES` list as long as we are specifying a value for all columns in the table.*

In our example, we are assuming that the receiver that decodes the satellite signals and assembles our readings file also performs basic data validation for us. In a real-world application, you would probably want to validate each row before trying to insert it in the database.

When we look at the `BuoyView` application later, we will see an insert situation where MySQL's lack of stored procedures is a real inconvenience.

If we catch an OdbcException, we first call the LogOdbcErrors() method which we will look at in detail a little later. Next, we open up a StreamWriter object and create (or append to) an exception file in the specified directory. By writing the entire row to the exception file, we create a file containing data that identifies the incoming rows in need of scrutiny, as well as generate a file that can be easily re-submitted to the update service once the issues have been resolved.

Finally, after closing our reader and connection, we place an entry in the Event Log to either confirm the successful processing or to alert us that there were exceptions.

OLE DB Connection

If we had configured the Registry so the BuoyUpdate service would use OLE DB instead of ODBC, we would have been calling the AddNewOleDb() method instead of AddNewOdbc(). This method merely uses objects from the .NET OLE DB managed provider instead of from the .NET ODBC managed provider. Of course, the connection strings are provider-specific too. The differences are highlighted below:

```
private void AddNewOleDb(FileInfo InputFile)
{
    bool HasException = false;

    OleDbConnection myConnection = new OleDbConnection(mOleDbConnString);

    myConnection.Open();

    StreamReader myReader = InputFile.OpenText();
    string NextLine;
    while ((NextLine = myReader.ReadLine()) != null)
    {
        string[] parsedLine=
                    NextLine.Split(myConfig.InputDelimiter.ToCharArray());

        StringBuilder myCommandText = new StringBuilder
                        ("INSERT INTO readings VALUES(");
                    // element outside of loop so there will be no comma
                    // before first value
        myCommandText.Append(parsedLine[0].ToString());
        for (int j=1; j < parsedLine.Length; j++)
        {
            myCommandText.Append("," + parsedLine[j].ToString());
        }
        myCommandText.Append(@");");

        OleDbCommand myCommand = new OleDbCommand
                        (myCommandText.ToString(), myConnection);

        try
        {
            myCommand.ExecuteNonQuery();
        }
        catch (OleDbException myException)
        {
            HasException = true;
            ngOleDbErrors(myException);
```

```
        // Create line in exception file for possible retry
        StreamWriter myWriter = new StreamWriter
                (myConfig.ExceptionPath + InputFile.Name,
                true, Encoding.ASCII);
      myWriter.WriteLine(NextLine);
      myWriter.Close();
    }
    catch (Exception e)
    {
      HasException = true;
      LogGenericException(e);
    }
  }
  myReader.Close();
  myConnection.Close();
  if (HasException)
  {
    EventLog.WriteEntry(InputFile.FullName + "
            processed with exceptions!", EventLogEntryType.Error, 2);
  }
  else
  {
    EventLog.WriteEntry(InputFile.FullName + "
            processed successfully!", EventLogEntryType.Information, 1);
  }
}
```

Exception Logging

We won't be going into detail about OLE DB and ODBC errors just yet. For now, let's just look at how easily we can use the Windows system Event Logs to report exceptions. We only show the ODBC version of one of our three error logging methods here, since they all follow the same general format:

```
private void LogOdbcErrors(OdbcException myException)
{
  if (myException.Errors.Count == 0)
  {
    StringBuilder myLogText = new StringBuilder();
    myLogText.Append("Exception in [" + myException.Source + "]\n");
    myLogText.Append("Details: " + myException.Message + "\n");
    EventLog.WriteEntry(myLogText.ToString(), EventLogEntryType.Error, 2);
  }
  else
  {
    foreach (OdbcError myError in myException.Errors)
    {
      StringBuilder myLogText = new StringBuilder();
      myLogText.Append("Exception [");
      myLogText.Append(myError.NativeError.ToString());
      myLogText.Append("] in [" + myError.Source + "]\n");
      myLogText.Append("Details: " + myError.Message + "\n");
      myLogText.Append("SQL State: " + myError.SQLState);
```

```
        EventLog.WriteEntry(myLogText.ToString(), EventLogEntryType.Error, 2);
    }
  }
}
```

> Remember, we can simply use the static **EventLog.WriteEntry()** method since we
> are taking advantage of the automatic logging features of the **ServiceBase** class.
> However, this setting automatically directs all our entries to the Application Log.

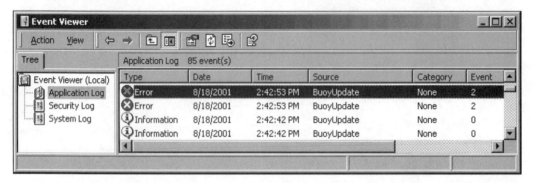

Our `LogOleDbErrors()` method is, not surpisingly, just a clone of our ODBC method except that it
uses `OleDb` exceptions. We also have a catch-all method called `LogGenericException()` that
handles any non-ODBC and non-OLE DB exceptions.

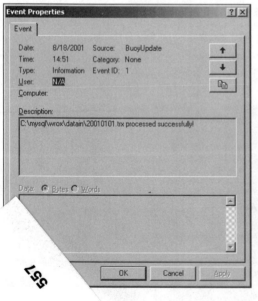

One thing you might want to strongly consider in a real-world Windows service would be to create a custom log. Since many programs write to the Application Log, we could really clutter it up with just one input file that generated numerous exceptions.

If you turn off the `AutoLog` property of the `ServiceBase` class, you can site your own custom `EventLog` component on the Service Designer in Visual Studio .NET. This way, you could create an Event Log with the name of your service, and write all your messages to that log rather than clutter up the common Application Log. If you choose this approach, you might still want to write one generic message to the common Application Log that gives an alert when there are detailed messages in the custom log file.

> Just remember, if you take this step to produce your own log, you will have to add your own calls to **WriteEntry()** in the **OnStart()**, **OnStop()**, **OnPause()**, and **OnContinue()** events if you wish those events to produce log entries.

Installing the Service

Once we have built a release configuration executable of our service, we can look in the `bin\Release\` directory of our solution to find BuoyUpdate.exe.

Since we instructed Visual Studio .NET to add the `ProjectInstaller` component to our project, we can now make use of the `installutil.exe` utility, using the following commands:

❑ **installutil BuoyUpdate.exe** installs the service

❑ **installutil /u BuoyUpdate.exe** uninstalls the service

Below we see the results of a successful installation:

Now, we will want to bring up the Services Management Console and start the `BuoyUpdate` service:

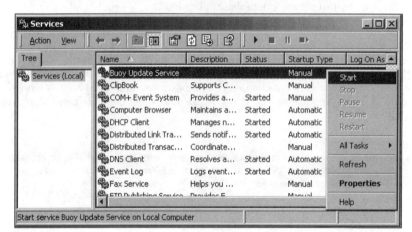

In a real-world application, once the service is tested and ready for production, we would also want to change the startup type to Automatic instead of Manual so we don't have to start it ourselves after every reboot.

Testing The Service

To simulate the delivery of the daily readings file from the buoys, simply copy the file `20010101.trx` to the input directory being watched (`C:\mysql\wrox\datain\` if you haven't changed the default `InputPath` setting in the `BuoyServiceConfig` class we discussed earlier).

> *Note that* `20010101.trx`*,* `20010102.trx`*, and* `error.trx` *can be found in the* `\mysql\wrox\delimit\` *folder of the code download.*

We can now check the Event Viewer to see what entries have been made to the Event Log file (noted in the Application Log unless you chose to implement a custom log).

If all goes well, we should be able to see the records for `01/01/2000` using the `BuoyView` application (discussed later). Alternatively, if you are comfortable with MySQL at the command line, you can submit the following query in the MySQL monitor:

```
SELECT * FROM readings WHERE ReadingDate="20010101";
```

> *If the processing was successful, but you would like to test the error logging too, you could copy the* `error.trx` *file (provided in the code download) into the specified input directory which, of course, forces the* `BuoyUpdate` *service to generate some errors.*

The specified backup directory (`c:\mysql\wrox\datain\backup\` if you haven't customized it) should now contain a copy of `20010101.trx`.

If the Event Log shows that there were exceptions, check the log details to find out more information about the particular error. Any input file rows that generated errors should be included in an exception file (residing in `C:\mysql\wrox\datain\exception\` if you haven't customized the exception directory).

Alternative Input File Format

The whole parsing process that built the INSERT command in our two add methods was actually quite easy, since our input file layout matched our target database table column for column. What if our input file, unlike in our straightforward case study, did not match our database table and we had no opportunity to change either the file or the table? For example, our format might be dictated by a huge installed base of relatively inflexible systems, such as medical equipment, cash registers, or other devices running embedded or proprietary operating systems.

Thinking about some oddball formats we all might have faced in the past, each day of the buoy file could very well be a single row with the four readings repeated 24 times left to right:

```
Buoy Id|  Date  |    Hour 0       |    Hour 1      |
      1|20010101|5.7|22.1|23.2|15.9|5.8|22.1|23.2|16.3|...
      2|20010101|6.4|22.8|23.3|19.4|6.8|22.8|23.2|19.5|...
```

In this case, the parsing, looping, and string-building code that really does the work would get a tiny bit more involved than the simple code we saw earlier. However, the basic idea of the method would remain the same. The code below (included in the chapter code download in MySQLMisc\ MySQLMisc.cs , not in the BuoyUpdate service project) shows an example of parsing such a file and building the same hourly INSERT statements.

```
private static void AlternateParse(FileInfo InputFile)
{
    StreamReader myReader = InputFile.OpenText();
    string NextLine;
    while ((NextLine = myReader.ReadLine()) != null)
    {
        string BuoyId = null;
        string ReadingDate = null;
        int RPH = 4;
        // RPH = Number of readings per hourly section
        string[] parsedLine=NextLine.Split("|".ToCharArray());

        // get the two pieces of data that go with every hour
        if (parsedLine.Length >= 2)
        {
            BuoyId = parsedLine[0].ToString();
            ReadingDate = parsedLine[1].ToString();
        }

        // now get each hourly section
        for (int i=0; i < 24; i++)
        {
            StringBuilder myCommandText = new StringBuilder
                                ("INSERT INTO readings VALUES(");
            myCommandText.Append(BuoyId + ",");
            myCommandText.Append(ReadingDate + ",");
            myCommandText.Append(i.ToString());

            // now get each reading within the hourly section
            for (int j=0; j < RPH; j++)
            {
```

```
                      myCommandText.Append("," +
                              parsedLine[j + ((i * RPH) + 2)].ToString());
            }
            myCommandText.Append(");");
            Debug.WriteLine(myCommandText.ToString());
        }
    }
    myReader.Close();
}
```

MyODBC Versus MyOledb

When comparing the MyOleDb provider and the MyODBC driver, one of the most fundamental issues for the .NET managed providers is the quality of the metadata provided by these two access options.

During the course of my compatibility testing, I wrote a small Windows Forms application to display the metadata we can retrieve from each access method. Let's talk about the pieces of this little application I named SchemaSnoop. I also took advantage of this test application to write a catch-all error handler that we will reuse in the BuoyView application later. We'll discuss that here as well.

The SchemaSnoop application consists of only two classes: one main Windows Form class that consumes the other class (both contained in SchemaSnoop\frmMain.cs):

- ❑ frmMain – To keep things simple and clear, all major functions of the application are members of this Windows Form class

- ❑ ErrorFormatter – Catch-all handler for displaying exceptions and errors

frmMain

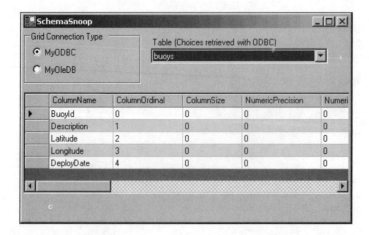

MySQL provides a number of native commands to retrieve metadata about a database, such as SHOW TABLES, SHOW COLUMNS, and SHOW INDEX. (see the MySQL manual for more information). Executing the MySQL command SHOW TABLES FROM buoy; returns a table containing a single string column named Tables_in_buoy. The value in each row is the name of a table in the database. In our case, we should see buoys and readings:

We can test the above SHOW command in code by retrieving a list of tables for binding to a ComboBox. This will allow us to select a table name to pass to the FillSchemaGridOdbc() and FillSchemaGridOleDb() methods. We can also create two radio buttons so we can select which managed provider we want to use.

```csharp
private void GetTableNames()
{
    OdbcConnection myConnection = new OdbcConnection(mOdbcConnString);
    try
    {
        string myCommandText = "SHOW TABLES FROM buoy;";
        DataTable myTables = new DataTable();
        OdbcDataAdapter myAdapter = new OdbcDataAdapter(myCommandText,
                                                        myConnection);
        myAdapter.Fill(myTables);

        // Bind the DataTable to the ComboBox, set the default choice,
        // then "enable" the ComboBox by hooking up an event handler
        this.cboTables.DataSource = myTables;
        this.cboTables.DisplayMember = myTables.Columns[0].ToString();
        this.cboTables.SelectedIndex = 0;
        this.cboTables.SelectedIndexChanged += new System.EventHandler
                            (cboTables_SelectedIndexChanged);
    }
    catch (Exception myException)
    {
        myErrorFormatter.DisplayException(myException);
    }
    finally
    {
        myConnection.Close();
    }
}
```

The `cboTables_SelectedIndexChanged` event handler simply checks which radio button has been selected, and calls the appropriate fill grid method based on your choice of data-access provider.

Below, we see a quick way to fetch metadata about a table through the `OdbcDataReader`, and then bind it to a grid for easy viewing. All of this should look quite familiar after reading the section on `DataReaders` in Chapter 4.

```
private void FillSchemaGridODBC(string TableName)
{
    DataTable myDataTable = new DataTable();
    ClearGrid();

    Cursor savedCursor = Cursor.Current;
    Cursor.Current = Cursors.WaitCursor;

    OdbcConnection myConnection = new OdbcConnection(mOdbcConnString);
    try
    {
        myConnection.Open();
        string myCommandText = "SELECT * FROM " + TableName + " LIMIT 0;";
        OdbcCommand myCommand = new OdbcCommand(myCommandText, myConnection);
        OdbcDataReader myReader = myCommand.ExecuteReader
                                            (CommandBehavior.SchemaOnly |
                                            CommandBehavior.KeyInfo);
        myDataTable = myReader.GetSchemaTable();

        grdSchemaView.SetDataBinding(myDataTable, null);
        myReader.Close();
    }
    catch (Exception myException)
    {
        myErrorFormatter.DisplayException(myException);
    }
    finally
    {
        myConnection.Close();
        Cursor.Current = savedCursor;
    }
}
```

First, we'll clear out the grid and change the cursor, just so we can get a clear visual sense of the execution time of the query. After creating and opening the obligatory connection, we create an `OdbcCommand`. This allows us to create an `OdbcDataReader` and direct it to retrieve schema and key information about the current select command by specifying the appropriate behaviors from the `System.Data.CommandBehavior` enumeration. Finally, the `GetSchemaTable()` method returns a `DataTable` of metadata that we can link to the grid.

According to the optimizations section of the `MySQL` manual (http://www.mysql.com/documentation/), adding the `LIMIT 0` clause to a `SELECT` command will quickly return an empty result set filled with column information. Common tricks such as adding a `WHERE` clause with impossible criteria, for example `WHERE 1=0`, would also achieve the same effect of returning zero rows, but only after incurring the full cost of a query. Since the designers of MySQL have built in an efficient short circuit with the MySQL specific `LIMIT 0` clause, it is definitely the preferred method for quickly fetching metadata about a `SELECT` command.

After binding the resultant `DataTable` object to the grid, we can now see just what kind of metadata the `MyODBC` driver makes available to the ODBC .NET Data Provider.

For now, let's ignore the custom exception handler in the `catch` statement, as it will be covered in the next section.

We also create a complementary method called `FillSchemaGridOleDb()` which does the same thing as `FillSchemaGridODBC()`, except it uses the .NET OLE DB provider. The differences are as follows:

```
private void FillSchemaGridOleDb(string TableName)
{
  DataTable myDataTable = new DataTable();
  ClearGrid();

  Cursor savedCursor = Cursor.Current;
  Cursor.Current = Cursors.WaitCursor;

  OleDbConnection myConnection = new OleDbConnection(mOleDbConnString);

  try
  {
    myConnection.Open();
    string myCommandText = "SELECT * FROM " + TableName + " LIMIT 0;";

    OleDbCommand myCommand = new OleDbCommand(myCommandText, myConnection);
    OleDbDataReader myReader = myCommand.ExecuteReader
                                  (CommandBehavior.SchemaOnly |
                                   CommandBehavior.KeyInfo);

    grdSchemaView.SetDataBinding(myReader.GetSchemaTable(), null);
    myReader.Close();
  }
  catch (Exception myException)
  {
    myErrorFormatter.DisplayException(myException);
  }
  finally
  {
    myConnection.Close();
    Cursor.Current = savedCursor;
  }
}
```

ErrorFormatter

The following simple routines are part of our `ErrorFormatter` class. The `DisplayException()` method of this class allows us to make one `catch` (see immediately below) no matter which .NET data provider we are using. While the methods merely display message boxes, that will suffice for our study. No matter where you finally display or log errors in a production application, these methods should at least show you how to extract the most information:

```
catch (Exception myException)
{
    ErrorFormatter myErrorFormatter = new ErrorFormatter();
    myErrorFormatter.DisplayException(myException);
}
```

Now, let's look at the methods in detail, starting with `DisplayException()`:

```
public void DisplayException(object myException)
{
    if (myException.GetType() == typeof(System.Data.Odbc.OdbcException))
    {
        DisplayOdbcErrors((OdbcException) myException);
    }
    else if (myException.GetType() ==
                typeof(System.Data.OleDb.OleDbException))
    {
        DisplayOleDbErrors((OleDbException) myException);
    }
    else
    {
        DisplayGenericException((Exception) myException);
    }
}
```

Once we receive the `Exception` object, we check its type and then call the appropriate detailed display method. The `DisplayGenericException()` method below is called to show non-ODBC and non-OLE DB exceptions.

```
public void DisplayGenericException(Exception myException)
{
    StringBuilder myLogText = new StringBuilder
                        ("Source: " +   myException.Source + "\n");
    myLogText.Append("Details: " +   myException.Message + "\n");
    myLogText.Append("Type: " +   myException.GetType().ToString() + "\n");
    MessageBox.Show(myLogText.ToString(), "Exception", MessageBoxButtons.OK,
                                        MessageBoxIcon.Error);
}
```

The following `DisplayOdbcErrors()` method is called to show ODBC-specific exceptions or errors. There is, of course, a `DisplayOleDbErrors()` method as well:

```
public void DisplayOdbcErrors(OdbcException myException)
{
    if (myException.Errors.Count == 0)
    {
        StringBuilder myLogText = new StringBuilder("Source: " +
                                        myException.Source + "\n");
        myLogText.Append("Details: " + myException.Message + "\n");
        myLogText.Append("Method: " + myException.TargetSite.ToString() +
                                        "\n");
        MessageBox.Show(myLogText.ToString(), "Odbc Exception" +
                        "(Sparse Information)", MessageBoxButtons.OK,
```

```
                                                        MessageBoxIcon.Error );
        }
        else
        {
            foreach (OdbcError myError in myException.Errors)
            {
                StringBuilder myLogText = new StringBuilder("Native Error:" +
                            myError.NativeError.ToString() + "\n");
                myLogText.Append("Source: " + myError.Source + "\n");
                myLogText.Append("Details: " + myError.Message + "\n");
                myLogText.Append("SQL State: " + myError.SQLState);
                MessageBox.Show(myLogText.ToString(), "Odbc Error",
                            MessageBoxButtons.OK, MessageBoxIcon.Error);
            }
        }
    }
```

If an exception object's `Errors` collection contains any error object members, those members are supposed to provide more detailed information. This means the individual errors should be extracted if they exist. You will find that the errors returned by the MyODBC driver are more helpful than those returned by the MyOleDb provider. The `OleDbException.Errors` collection is really never populated.

SchemaSnoop Results with MyODBC

By default, `SchemaSnoop` starts up with the `buoys` table selected and `MyODBC` as the chosen data access method. Let's leave the access method as `MyODBC` and select the `readings` table from the dropdown menu. The first item of interest is the lack of `ColumnSize`, `NumericPrecision`, and `NumericScale` information (see following screenshot). Also, note how the `BuoyId` and `ReadingHour` columns are returned as `System.Int32` even though these columns are defined in the database as the MySQL unsigned integer type.

ColumnName	ColumnOrdinal	ColumnSize	NumericPrecision	NumericScale	DataType	ProviderType
BuoyId	0	0	0	0	System.Int32	10
ReadingDate	1	0	0	0	System.DateTim	5
ReadingHour	2	0	0	0	System.Int32	10
WindSpeed	3	0	0	0	System.Double	8
AirTemp	4	0	0	0	System.Double	8
WaterTemp	5	0	0	0	System.Double	8
DewPoint	6	0	0	0	System.Double	8

Scrolling over to the right of the grid, we can see that the `BaseTableName` and `BaseColumnName` properties of each column are populated with the true names from the table.

BaseSchemaName	BaseCatalogName	BaseTableName	BaseColumnName
(null)	(null)	readings	BuoyId
(null)	(null)	readings	ReadingDate
(null)	(null)	readings	ReadingHour
(null)	(null)	readings	WindSpeed
(null)	(null)	readings	AirTemp
(null)	(null)	readings	WaterTemp
(null)	(null)	readings	DewPoint

The grid filling methods we constructed in our program create SELECT statements like the following:

```
SELECT * FROM readings LIMIT 0;
```

What if we created statements that use an alias for a table? The following example uses R as an alias for the readings table.

```
SELECT R.ReadingDate, R.ReadingHour, R.AirTemp FROM readings AS R
WHERE R.BuoyId=1 LIMIT 0;
```

Sadly, the BaseTableName is returned as R. All mappings to the readings table have been lost. Later, we'll discuss how this could become inconvenient to say the least.

SchemaSnoop Results with MyOleDb

Now, let's select the MyOleDb radio button to change the data access method and fetch the readings table metadata through the FillSchemaGridOleDb() method. We can see that the MyOleDb provider returns the size, precision, and scale information that MyODBC failed to provide. Also, note how the MySQL type of unsigned integer has been returned as System.Int64 instead of System.Int32, as was the case with MyODBC:

ColumnName	ColumnOrdinal	ColumnSize	NumericPrecision	NumericScale	DataType	ProviderType
BuoyId	1	4	4	0	System.Int64	19
ReadingDate	2	16	16	0	System.DateTime	135
ReadingHour	3	4	4	0	System.Int64	19
WindSpeed	4	8	8	31	System.Double	5
AirTemp	5	8	8	31	System.Double	5
WaterTemp	6	8	8	31	System.Double	5
DewPoint	7	8	8	31	System.Double	5

Scrolling to the right we would see that, unlike MyODBC, MyOleDb does not give its .NET provider any values for the IsUnique, IsKey, and IsAutoIncrement properties. At the far right of the grid, we can see the BaseTableName and BaseColumnName properties are not provided for us either.

	BaseSchemaName	BaseCatalogName	BaseTableName	BaseColumnName
▶	(null)	(null)	(null)	(null)
	(null)	(null)	(null)	(null)
	(null)	(null)	(null)	(null)
	(null)	(null)	(null)	(null)
	(null)	(null)	(null)	(null)
	(null)	(null)	(null)	(null)
	(null)	(null)	(null)	(null)

This means that we don't even have to use a table alias in a SELECT statement to lose our mapping back to the true table name. We get insufficient base metadata on even the simplest of queries. Another potential problem here would be for queries that join tables. If such queries retrieve more than one column with the same ColumnName value from different tables, there would be no BaseTableName qualifier to avoid ambiguity.

The help file packaged with the MyOleDb provider references the Microsoft article *OLE DB Leveling: Choosing the Right Interfaces* currently at http://www.microsoft.com/data/oledb/techinfo/oledbleveling2.htm. MyOleDb admittedly provides only the base consumer functionality as described in the article. As we will see later in the `BuoyView` application, this results in MyOleDb failing to return sufficient metadata to utilize some of the supposedly convenient features of the .NET OLE DB provider.

The Buoy Data Viewer

Since most people are probably more familiar with a Windows Forms application than a Windows service, we won't be going into nearly as much infrastructure detail with the viewer application as we did with the update service.

Here we're interested in what else (besides `InsertCommand` and `DataReader` objects and the `ExecuteNonQuery()` method) the OLE DB .NET and ODBC .NET managed providers can do properly with MyODBC and MyOleDb. Hence we won't be talking about `MenuItems` and `StatusBars` in this section. All the Windows Forms code I omit in the text is, of course, provided for you in the code download for this chapter (in `BuoyView\frmMain.cs`).

The Buoy Data Viewer application consists of three classes, with one main Windows Form class that consumes the other two:

❏ `frmMain` – To keep things simple and clear, all major methods of the application are members of this Windows Form class.

❏ `ErrorFormatter` – This is the same error handler class we used in `SchemaSnoop`. Since we covered it in detail earlier, we won't discuss it again here.

❏ `Options` – A small class that merely holds the choices from the `Options` menu. We'll skip discussing this class since it is so simple.

frmMain

First, take a look at the SQL statements we'll be using throughout `frmMain`:

```
private string mBuoysSQL = "SELECT * FROM buoys ORDER BY BuoyId;";
private string mReadingsSQL = "SELECT * FROM readings " +
                             "WHERE ReadingDate > '2000-11-30' " +
                             "ORDER BY BuoyId, ReadingDate, ReadingHour;";
// restrict by date for study performance
private string mOdbcConnString =   "DRIVER={MySQL};DATABASE=buoy";
private string mOleDbConnString = "Data Source=buoy;provider=MySQLProv";
```

Now let's see the menu choices we'll implement:

❏ File | Exit

❏ Edit | Buoys

❏ View | Raw Data

❏ Options | Connection Type (OleDb or Odbc) and AutoIncrement Columns (Hide or Show). Note: Changing the options will not automatically apply them to a currently filled grid. They will take effect on the next Edit or View.

View Raw Data

Let's talk about simply viewing our data first. We'll only discuss our ODBC viewing functions since the OLE DB versions are essentially the same. We will implement a very simple method here that will show off a handy feature of the `DataGrid`. The grid will allow us to specify relations in the `DataSet` and will give the user an easily navigable view of the data. It is necessary to set the `DataGrid`'s `AllowNavigation` property either at design time (as in our example) or at run time.

Below, we fill the `dsBuoyReadings DataSet` with both the `buoys` and `readings` tables. Then we add a style for each table to the grid. We will see that each style applies to its appropriate table rather than to the relationship itself:

```
private void DisplayOdbcRawData()
{
    OdbcConnection myConnection = new OdbcConnection(mOdbcConnString);
    DataSet dsBuoyReadings = new DataSet();
    try
    {
        // add rows from the buoy table into the DataSet
        OdbcDataAdapter myAdapter = new OdbcDataAdapter
                                          (mBuoysSQL, myConnection);
        myAdapter.Fill(dsBuoyReadings, "buoys");

        // also add rows from the readings table into the DataSet
        myAdapter = new OdbcDataAdapter(mReadingsSQL, myConnection);
        myAdapter.Fill(dsBuoyReadings, "readings");

        // specify the relation between the tables
        dsBuoyReadings.Relations.Add("BuoyReadings",
                dsBuoyReadings.Tables["buoys"].Columns["BuoyId"],
                dsBuoyReadings.Tables["readings"].Columns["BuoyId"]);

        // bind DataSet to grid then add styles
        grdMain.SetDataBinding(dsBuoyReadings, "buoys");

        grdMain.TableStyles.Add(CreateBuoyTableStyle());
        grdMain.TableStyles.Add(CreateReadingsTableStyle());
    }
    catch (Exception myException)
    {
        myErrorFormatter.DisplayException(myException);
    }
    finally
    {
        myConnection.Close();
    }
}
```

Now, let's take a closer look at the `CreateBuoyTableStyle()` method to see how we can control the appearance and behavior of the grid:

```
private DataGridTableStyle CreateBuoyTableStyle()
{
   DataGridTableStyle buoyStyle = new DataGridTableStyle();
   buoyStyle.HeaderFont = new System.Drawing.Font("Microsoft Sans Serif",
                          8.25F, System.Drawing.FontStyle.Bold,
                          System.Drawing.GraphicsUnit.Point,
                          ((System.Byte)(0)));

   buoyStyle.MappingName = "buoys";  // source table in DataSet
   buoyStyle.AlternatingBackColor = System.Drawing.Color.PaleTurquoise;
   buoyStyle.PreferredColumnWidth = -1;            // Autosize

   DataGridTextBoxColumn BuoyId = new DataGridTextBoxColumn();
   BuoyId.HeaderText = "Buoy ID";
   BuoyId.MappingName = "BuoyId";  // column in source table
   BuoyId.NullText = "(Next Id)";
   BuoyId.ReadOnly = true;

   DataGridTextBoxColumn Description = new DataGridTextBoxColumn();
   Description.HeaderText = "Description";
   Description.MappingName = "Description";

   DataGridTextBoxColumn DateDeployed = new DataGridTextBoxColumn();
   DateDeployed.HeaderText = "Date Deployed";
   DateDeployed.MappingName = "DeployDate";
   DateDeployed.Format = "MM/dd/yyy";  // leading zero, full date
                                       // example 01/01/2001

   DataGridTextBoxColumn Latitude = new DataGridTextBoxColumn();
   Latitude.HeaderText = "Latitude";
   Latitude.MappingName = "Latitude";
   Latitude.Format = "f2";  //fixed format, 2 decimal places

   DataGridTextBoxColumn Longitude = new DataGridTextBoxColumn();
   Longitude.HeaderText = "Longitude";
   Longitude.MappingName = "Longitude";
   Longitude.Format = "f2";

   if (mnuHideAutoIncColumns.Checked)
   {
      // don't add style for BuoyId column so it will be invisible
      buoyStyle.GridColumnStyles.AddRange(new DataGridColumnStyle[]
                     {Description, Latitude, Longitude, DateDeployed});
   }
   else
   {
      buoyStyle.GridColumnStyles.AddRange(new DataGridColumnStyle[]
                     {BuoyId, Description, Latitude,
                     Longitude, DateDeployed});
   }
   return buoyStyle;
}
```

Remember the `NullText` property we set on the `BuoyId` column, because we'll see what that does for us when we look at editing buoys later. Notice how we add the `BuoyId` column to the `GridColumnStyles` only if that option has been selected from the menu. By merely omitting a column from the column styles, it will not be shown in the grid. Below is a view of the data with the auto-increment column `BuoyId` hidden:

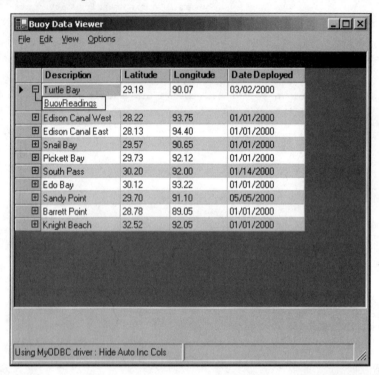

We can create a `DataGridTableStyle` for the `readings` table in much the same fashion as we did for the `buoys` table:

```
private DataGridTableStyle CreateReadingsTableStyle()
{
   DataGridTableStyle readingsStyle = new DataGridTableStyle();
   readingsStyle.HeaderFont = new System.Drawing.Font(
                                  "Microsoft Sans Serif",
                                  8.25F, System.Drawing.FontStyle.Bold,
                                  System.Drawing.GraphicsUnit.Point,
                                  ((System.Byte)(0)));

   readingsStyle.MappingName = "readings";  // source table in DataSet
   readingsStyle.AlternatingBackColor = System.Drawing.Color.PaleTurquoise;
   readingsStyle.PreferredColumnWidth = -1;  // Autosize

   DataGridTextBoxColumn ReadingDate = new DataGridTextBoxColumn();
   ReadingDate.HeaderText = "Date";
   ReadingDate.MappingName = "ReadingDate"; // column in source table
   ReadingDate.Format = "MM/dd/yyy"; // leading zero, full date
```

```
                    // example 01/01/2001
DataGridTextBoxColumn Hour = new DataGridTextBoxColumn();
Hour.HeaderText = "Hour";
Hour.MappingName = "ReadingHour";
Hour.Format = "00";
Hour.Alignment = HorizontalAlignment.Center;

DataGridTextBoxColumn WindSpeed = new DataGridTextBoxColumn();
WindSpeed.HeaderText = "Wind Speed";
WindSpeed.MappingName = "WindSpeed";
WindSpeed.Format = "f1";  // fixed format, one decimal place
WindSpeed.Alignment = HorizontalAlignment.Center;

DataGridTextBoxColumn AirTemp = new DataGridTextBoxColumn();
AirTemp.HeaderText = "Air Temperature";
AirTemp.MappingName = "AirTemp";
AirTemp.Format = "f1";
AirTemp.Alignment = HorizontalAlignment.Center;

DataGridTextBoxColumn WaterTemp = new DataGridTextBoxColumn();
WaterTemp.HeaderText = "Water Temperature";
WaterTemp.MappingName = "WaterTemp";
WaterTemp.Format = "f1";
WaterTemp.Alignment = HorizontalAlignment.Center;

DataGridTextBoxColumn DewPoint = new DataGridTextBoxColumn();
DewPoint.HeaderText = "DewPoint";
DewPoint.MappingName = "DewPoint";
DewPoint.Format = "f1";
DewPoint.Alignment = HorizontalAlignment.Center;

readingsStyle.GridColumnStyles.AddRange(new DataGridColumnStyle[]
            {ReadingDate, Hour, WindSpeed, AirTemp,
            WaterTemp, DewPoint});
return readingsStyle;
}
```

Overleaf is a view of the readings data we would see if we followed the **BuoyReadings** link under one of the buoy data rows. Note that the left-facing arrow at the top right of the grid will navigate back to the buoy view:

Edit Buoys

This function will allow the user to add and edit buoys, but not the data readings. In the `EditOdbcBuoyTable()` method below, we create an `OdbcDataAdapter` and fill a `DataSet`. Before we bind the `DataSet` to the `DataGrid`, we want to prepare the grid by giving it a table style and by turning off the `ReadOnly` property:

```
private void EditOdbcBuoyTable()
{
   ClearGrid();
   OdbcConnection myConnection = new OdbcConnection(mOdbcConnString);
   try
   {
      OdbcDataAdapter myAdapter = new OdbcDataAdapter
                                        (mBuoysSQL, myConnection);
      DataSet dsBuoys = new DataSet();
      myAdapter.Fill(dsBuoys, "buoys");
      grdMain.TableStyles.Add(CreateBuoyTableStyle());
      grdMain.ReadOnly = false;
      grdMain.SetDataBinding(dsBuoys, "buoys");

      // hookup event to alert us of possible changes
      grdMain.CurrentCellChanged += new
                                  System.EventHandler(this.GridChanged);
   }
   catch (Exception myException)
   {
```

```
            myErrorFormatter.DisplayException(myException);
    }
    finally
    {
        myConnection.Close();
    }
}
```

Finally, we attach the `GridChanged` event handler to the `CurrentCellChanged` event of the grid. This way, we can give the user access to a **Save** button at the appropriate time.

When we discussed the `CreateBuoyTableStyle()` method in the *View Raw Data* section, we set the `NullText` property of the `BuoyId` column to `(Next Id)`. If we choose the option to show auto-increment columns in the grid, we will see this text when adding a new row. The column is read-only, so we will be unable to edit it. Hopefully, the (Next Id) message will be a bit more informative than simply displaying (null). This at least informs the user that they are unable to enter a value in this column. Here is a view of adding a record with the applied style and the auto-increment column visible:

We still need to take a closer look at the event handler that fires when the user changes a row in the grid. In the following code, we cast the `sender` object into a `DataGrid`. Then we cast the resultant `DataGrid`'s `DataSource` property into a `DataSet`. Finally, we can test the resultant `DataSet`'s `HasChanges` property to determine if we need to make the **Save** button available:

```
private void GridChanged(object sender, System.EventArgs e)
{
    if (((DataSet)((DataGrid) sender).DataSource).HasChanges())
    {
        mUnsavedChanges = true;
        statusBar1.Panels[1].Text =    "Unsaved changes exist";
```

575

```
         btnSave.Visible = true;
      }
   }
```

The event handler for the **Save** button calls the `UpdateBuoys()` function below. The grid's `DataSource` property is cast into a `DataSet` object where it is used as the argument for the call to the appropriate provider-specific update method. We'll talk about the commented line later when we discuss the OLE DB methods.

```
private bool UpdateBuoys()
{
   bool NoExceptions = false;
   if (mnuODBC.Checked)
   {
      NoExceptions = UpdateOdbcBuoys((DataSet) grdSchemaView.DataSource);
   }
   else
   {
      NoExceptions = UpdateOleDbBuoys1((DataSet) grdMain.DataSource);
      //NoExceptions = UpdateOleDbBuoys2((DataSet) grdMain.DataSource);
   }
   if (NoExceptions)
   {
      btnSave.Visible = false;
      statusBar1.Panels[1].Text = "Changes saved";
      mUnsavedChanges = false;
   }
   else
   {
      statusBar1.Panels[1].Text = "Changes were not saved";
   }
   return NoExceptions;
}
```

ODBC Connection

In the following ODBC update method, we don't even attempt to manually determine the changes. The `CommandBuilder` object we create constructs commands to apply the changes we have made to the data set:

```
private bool UpdateOdbcBuoys(DataSet changedDataSet)
{
   OdbcConnection myConnection = new OdbcConnection(mOdbcConnString);
   try
   {
      OdbcCommand myCommand = new OdbcCommand(mBuoysSQL, myConnection);
      OdbcDataAdapter myAdapter = new OdbcDataAdapter(myCommand);
      OdbcCommandBuilder myBuilder = new OdbcCommandBuilder(myAdapter);
      myAdapter.Update(changedDataSet, "buoys");
      return true;
   }
   catch (Exception myException)
   {
      myErrorFormatter.DisplayException(myException);
```

576

```
        return false;
    }
    finally
    {
        myConnection.Close();
    }
}
```

CommandBuilder does a wonderful job if the query is straightforward. If you remember our discussion about the quality of the metadata from MyODBC, there are situations where a table alias in a query would render the CommandBuilder powerless. If, for instance, we had designated B as the alias for the buoys table, our update would fail with the following error:

OLE DB Connection

Let's get back to the straightforward query we originally defined. We'll try to execute the CommandBuilder logic in the UpdateOleDbBuoys1() method. Can you guess what kind of results we are going to have, even with no table alias involved?

```
private bool UpdateOleDbBuoys1(DataSet changedDataSet)
{
    OleDbConnection myConnection = new OleDbConnection(mOleDbConnString);
    try
    {
        OleDbCommand myCommand = new OleDbCommand(mBuoysSQL, myConnection);
        OleDbDataAdapter myAdapter = new OleDbDataAdapter(myCommand);
        OleDbCommandBuilder myBuilder = new OleDbCommandBuilder(myAdapter);
        myAdapter.Update(changedDataSet, "buoys");
        return true;
    }
    catch (Exception myException)
    {
        myErrorFormatter.DisplayException(myException);
        return false;
    }
    finally
    {
        myConnection.Close();
    }
}
```

The `myAdapter.Update()` line fails miserably, producing the following exception:

```
Exception                                                              [x]

        Source: System.Data
   X    Details: Dynamic SQL generation is not supported against a SelectCommand that does not return any base table information.
        Type: System.InvalidOperationException

                              [      OK      ]
```

If you remember back to our `SchemaSnoop` application, the OLE DB provider doesn't return key information to our data table. Possibly, we could add the following code to the `EditOleDbBuoyTable()` method where we first created and filled the `DataSet` and bound it to the grid:

```
DataTable myTable = dsBuoys.Tables[0];
DataColumn[] pk = new DataColumn[1];
pk[0] = myTable.Columns["BuoyId"];
myTable.PrimaryKey = pk;
```

Sadly, neither this approach nor setting the `DataAdapter`'s `MissingSchemaAction` property to `AddWithKey` helps. It is not the missing key designation, but rather the missing `BaseTableName` property that is thwarting the `CommandBuilder`. This invalidates our whole "convenient" update approach with MyOleDb.

It might not be as convenient, but we have an alternative method where we can handle all of our changes with OLE DB. We are forced to write more code, but we also have more control. Of course, we could write an ODBC version of the alternative code just as easily as we will for OLE DB. After considering the advantages of this alternative, we will find that not being able to use a command builder with MyOleDb is not a sufficient reason to choose ODBC over OLE DB.

To activate the alternative method, go back to the `UpdateBuoys()` method, comment out the call to `UpdateOleDbBuoys1()`, uncomment the call to `UpdateOleDbBuoys2()`, rebuild, and run. Now, if we try to add a valid record, the addition is successful.

We could definitely make use of stored procedures in the `UpdateOleDbBuoys2()` code below. However, we've already mentioned several times that they aren't supported in the current stable version of MySQL. In lieu of the stored procedures, we will just have to build our own SQL commands in code and process them with the `ExecuteNonQuery()` method. Thankfully, we have a `RowState` property for each `DataRow` in the buoy `DataTable` of our `DataSet`. By testing this property, we can create the appropriate command string.

While collecting all the following code in a single method as listed below may be fine for easily illustrating techniques in this study, for a real-world application you would probably want to encapsulate as much functionality as possible into a buoy data class. I would strongly suggest you also investigate the potential benefits of producing custom `DataSet`-derived classes via XML schema and the `XSD.exe` utility.

```
private bool UpdateOleDbBuoys2(DataSet changedDataSet)
{
    bool HasExceptions = false;

    // create a DataSet containing only changed rows
    DataSet dsChangesOnly = changedDataSet.GetChanges();
```

```
OleDbConnection myConnection = new OleDbConnection(mOleDbConnString);
myConnection.Open();
try
{
    for (int row=0; row < dsChangesOnly.Tables[0].Rows.Count; row++)
    {
        DataRow myDataRow = dsChangesOnly.Tables[0].Rows[row];
        StringBuilder myCommandText = new StringBuilder();

        // new row so insert into database
        if (myDataRow.RowState == DataRowState.Added)
        {
            myCommandText.Append("INSERT INTO buoys VALUES(null, ");
            myCommandText.Append("'" +
                        myDataRow["Description"].ToString() + "', ");
            myCommandText.Append(myDataRow["Latitude"].ToString() + ",");
            myCommandText.Append(myDataRow["Longitude"].ToString() + ",");
            myCommandText.Append("'" + Convert.ToDateTime
                (myDataRow["DeployDate"]).ToString("yyy/MM/dd") + "');");
        }

        // modified row so update database
        if (myDataRow.RowState == DataRowState.Modified)
        {
            myCommandText.Append("UPDATE buoys ");
            myCommandText.Append("SET Description='" +
                        myDataRow["Description"].ToString() + "', ");
            myCommandText.Append("Latitude=" +
                        myDataRow["Latitude"].ToString() + ", ");
            myCommandText.Append("Longitude=" +
                        myDataRow["Longitude"].ToString() + ", ");
            myCommandText.Append("DeployDate='" + Convert.ToDateTime
                (myDataRow["DeployDate"]).ToString("yyy/MM/dd") + "' ");
            myCommandText.Append("WHERE BuoyId=" +
                        myDataRow["BuoyId"].ToString() + ";");
        }

        // deleted row so look at original row version for BuoyId
        if (myDataRow.RowState == DataRowState.Deleted)
        {
            myCommandText.Append("DELETE FROM buoys WHERE BuoyId=");
            myCommandText.Append(myDataRow
                ["BuoyId", DataRowVersion.Original].ToString() + ";");
        }

        OleDbCommand myCommand = new OleDbCommand
                        (myCommandText.ToString(), myConnection);
        myCommand.ExecuteNonQuery();
    }
}
catch (Exception myException)
{
    myErrorFormatter.DisplayException(myException);
    HasExceptions = true;
```

```
    }
    myConnection.Close();
    if (HasExceptions)
    {
        // Maybe add some rollback code here
        return false;
    }
    else
    {
        // inform DataSet that its contents should now match database
        changedDataSet.AcceptChanges();
        return true;
    }
}
```

The addition and modification logic is pretty straightforward, simply accessing the current version and state of each `DataRow` to build `INSERT` or `UPDATE` commands. The delete logic, however, cannot retrieve the `BuoydId` value from the current version of a row marked for deletion. We can specify `DataRowVersion.Original` for the `DataRow` indexer's second parameter, thereby accessing the unchanged copy of the original row.

When we call the `AcceptChanges()` method, rows with a `DataRowState` of `Added` or `Modified` are reset to `Unchanged`. Rows with a state of `Deleted` are removed.

Food for Thought

Let's discuss some additional issues that are not covered in our sample edit/update code, but which should be considered for a production-ready application.

Since the current stable version of MySQL doesn't support constraints and thus does not afford us the option of cascading deletes, in order to maintain data integrity, we would need to go one step further than our example and also delete all the orphan `readings` rows that correspond to the deleted buoy master row. Of course, in a real-life situation involving historical scientific data, we would probably not allow anyone but an administrator to delete buoy master rows that already have associated `readings` detail rows. Preventing that elegantly would mean stopping the delete in the grid based on the user's authority (or better yet, not using a grid for editing at all).

Now let's discuss some additional integrity issues. We should never lose sight of the fact that we are applying changes to the database from a disconnected source `DataSet`.

Try the following in our viewer application. Make sure you have the options set to use ODBC and to show auto-increment columns. Select **Edit**, key in a new valid buoy row, and save it. Go right back to that new buoy row (which still shows (Next Id)), and change its latitude or longitude values. The row is properly marked as modified inside the `DataSet`, and you have the option to save again. Click the **Save** button and you'll get the following exception:

That time, we executed a method that used the `CommandBuilder`. We can test the reaction of the `UpdateOleDbBuoys2()` method by selecting **Options | OleDb** and **Edit | Buoys**, and then trying our exercise again. This will fail too, but this time with a pretty meaningless error message from MyOleDb.

What is wrong? When we called the `AcceptChanges()` method, we lied to the `DataSet` (the `CommandBuilder` unwittingly lies to the `DataSet` too). We told it that everything had been synchronized with the database; however, we never told it the new `BuoyId` value that was automatically generated by MySQL.

We need a way to get that new value back from our `INSERT` operation so we can update the `DataSet` to match the database. We must do this prior to calling the `DataSet`'s `AcceptChanges()` method. If we had the ability to use stored procedures, we could define one with an output parameter to return the new `BuoyId`, or the whole inserted row.

One solution to the synchronization problem would be to force a total re-query of all rows at the end of the method. This brute force approach just discards the `DataSet`, then fetches a new one. This might be fine for 100 rows, but what about 100,000? A better solution is to make use of the MySQL function `LAST_INSERT_ID()` (similar to `@@IDENTITY` in T-SQL), which returns the last automatically generated number that was inserted into an auto-increment column. Assume, for example, that we added an eleventh row to our buoys table as follows:

```
INSERT INTO buoys VALUES(null, "Pelican Isle", 27.34, 91.67, 2001/01/01);
```

Immediately after executing our `INSERT`, we can submit the following query to retrieve the complete new row:

```
SELECT * FROM Buoys WHERE BuoyId = LAST_INSERT_ID();
```

We can now update the `DataRow` with the complete row from the database. Then, when we execute the `AcceptChanges()` method, the row in our `DataSet` really will match the row in the database as it was immediately after the `INSERT`.

An issue we must contemplate for update operations is the possibility that another user may change a row in the database between the time we read it into our `DataSet`, and the time we attempt to post our changes.

Suppose we wanted to change the latitude and longitude of the Pelican Isle buoy we inserted in our earlier example. We could use the current version of our `DataRow` to populate the `UPDATE` part of our command and use the original version of the `DataRow` to populate the `WHERE` clause.

```
UPDATE buoys
SET    Description="Pelican Isle", Latitude=37.34,
       Longitude=81.67, DeployDate=2001/01/01
WHERE  BuoyId=11 AND Description="Pelican Isle" AND Latitude=27.34
       AND Longitude=91.67 AND DeployDate=2001/01/01;
```

This is merely one way to handle concurrency. Another method would be just to ignore the state of the database, embrace the "last in wins" approach, and post whatever changes exist in our `DataSet`.

Finally, another word about transactions. In real-world applications, you will often have a complex transaction that is stored across multiple tables. In this situation you want to update all of the involved tables or none of them. If one piece of the transaction update fails, you want to reverse any pieces you have already updated successfully.

If you are going to use MySQL and you must have transaction support, I would suggest you explore BDB or InnoDB table types instead of MyIsam. If you simply must use MyIsam and wish to try your hand at maintaining database integrity via your application code, we have at least discussed some of the tools you will need to use such as row states and the `DataRowVersion` enumeration. Be prepared for a lot of work and a lot of uncertainty, however. Before the newer table types were supported by MySQL, transaction support for ISAM table types was a hot topic in the MySQL developer community. As I mentioned at the beginning of this study, the MySQL resources on the Internet can offer many suggestions to help you, although the examples may be in Visual Basic, C++, Perl, PHP, or ASP.

In my opinion, transaction support is something best left to the database server.

For a production application, database backups are of vital importance. Such a topic is beyond the scope of this chapter, but if you are considering using MySQL in a production environment, you should certainly consult the MySQL manual for more information on backup and recovery options.

Summary

While we haven't had the space to cover all the possibilities, hopefully we've learned that it is feasible to connect to data sources other than SQL Server thanks to data connectivity standards such as OLE DB and ODBC. While the applications we've covered aren't production ready, they do demonstrate the essentials necessary to build solutions with C# and MySQL. We've also delved into limitations and workarounds for the MyOleDb provider and the MyODBC driver. We've even learned a bit more about Windows services, event logging, the `FileSystemWatcher` class, and `DataSet` metadata along the way.

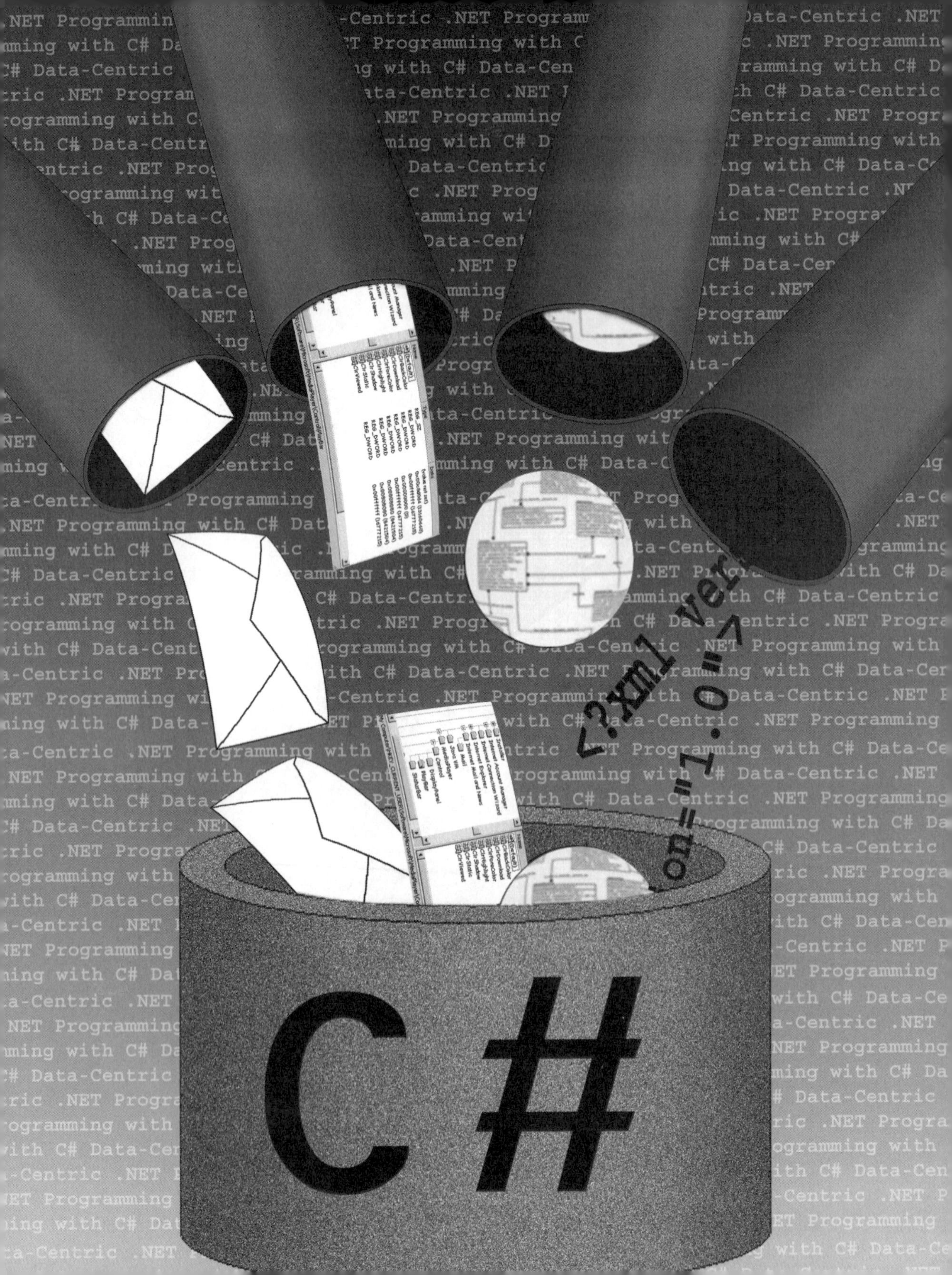
Data-Centric .NET Programming with C#
<?xml ver
on="1.0"?>
C#

15

Case Study II: Migrating to .NET

Programmers love jobs that provide opportunities to work with the latest technology without having to deal with legacy architecture and code. On the other hand, large, established companies usually run projects that must communicate with existing systems, or they will gradually migrate legacy systems to use new technologies. Developing a good understanding of both established and cutting-edge technologies is always going to be useful.

In this chapter, we're going to examine how to make .NET and Windows DNA applications work together by looking at how a Windows DNA application can be extended with .NET and C#. This is going to be a hands-on project – the best way to learn from it is to actually write code and configure the application.

The project starts as a simple ordering system using SQL Server as the backend data store, COM+ business classes in the middle-tier components, and a Windows Form-based user interface layer. By the end of the chapter we'll have looked at three versions of the project:

❑   A COM+ application written in VB 6

❑   A hybrid application using a .NET class library, and a Windows Form application (both written in C#) interoperating with the COM+ component

❑   A full .NET version of the application written in C#

> *Again all the code for the case study is available from www.wrox.com. Please note that there are a couple of places where code running under Visual Studio .NET RC1 differs from that which executes on the Beta release of the framework. We have highlighted these differences at the appropriate point. It appears some significant under-the-hood changes have been made between these releases – any further changes between RC1 and the final release version having impact on this study will be identified on www.wrox.com and an updated code download will be made available.*

Project Overview

We will create a simple ordering system that allows users to create new orders, and view and delete existing orders. Users can also use the system to maintain customer and product data. We will implement those features in three phases; each creates a version of the application.

❑ Firstly, we'll create a bare-bones COM+ application that allows users to retrieve existing orders, create new orders, and delete orders. They can also read customer data in order to enter orders. This version is written in Visual Basic 6.

❑ The second phase introduces interoperation between COM+ server and .NET client components. We'll extend the features implemented in version one to provide users with the ability to edit customer and product data. This version consists of a .NET class library and a Windows Form application. The .NET middle-tier component classes extend the customer and product COM+ classes using the .NET COM Interoperability features. The Windows Form application uses the .NET middle tier components. All new components will be written in C#.

❑ This final phase upgrades the application to .NET. We'll rewrite all COM+ components, including the middle-tier library component and the user interface application, completely in .NET.

The main objective of this project is to show ways of integrating COM+ applications with .NET applications. It focuses on introducing issues related to the interoperations between .NET and COM+ components. The simple ordering system is going to be reasonably functional, but not necessarily very user-friendly or bulletproof. By working on this case study, we'll see how to:

❑ Use COM+ components in .NET components

❑ Extend COM+ classes in .NET, by inheritance

❑ Extend COM+ components in .NET, by containment

❑ Handle COM+ errors in .NET components

❑ Handle COM+ events in .NET components

❑ Manage database transactions in .NET

Without further ado, let's get started.

Version One – Simple Order in COM+

We start by building the simple ordering system in COM+ and Visual Basic. It consists of two components: the user interface component and the business logic components. The diagram opposite illustrates the individual parts of the components and their relationships:

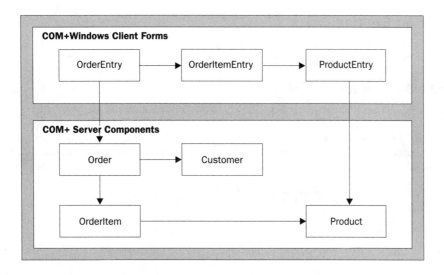

The User Interface

The user interface component contains just two forms, `OrderEntry` and `OrderItemEntry`. We will write code to implement its functionality later. For now, let's briefly describe how a user performs order maintenance tasks namely:

❑ Retrieving orders

❑ Creating new orders

❑ Deleting orders

The `OrderEntry` form is the starting point of the application, as illustrated in the figure below:

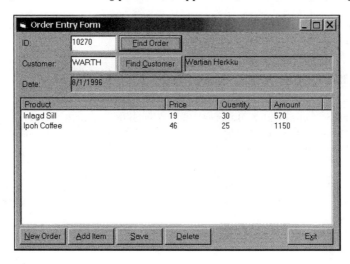

Retrieving an Existing Order

To retrieve an existing item, the user enters an order ID and clicks the Find Order button. The system will display the customer, order date, and all items ordered.

Creating a New Order

To create a new order, the user must first click the New Order button to clear the form.

The user can then enter a customer ID (if they wish to check the customer ID, they can click the Find Customer button to display the customer name). The user can add any number of product items to the order by clicking the Add Item button, which will display the OrderItemEntry form.

The user enters a product ID and order quantity. If the user clicks the OK button, the product will be added to the order. Clicking the Cancel button simply discards the new item.

Once all product items have been added to the order, the user can click the Save button to save the order. A new order ID will be automatically generated and displayed. The order date will be set to the date and time when the order is saved to the database.

Deleting an Existing Order

To delete an order, the user can simply enter an order ID and click the Delete button to delete it. Optionally, they can click the Find Order button to view the order so that they can decide whether or not it's the right order to be deleted.

We will now go through the database and business layers. Once we have built those layers, we will return to look at the code behind the user interface forms.

The Database

We will use Microsoft SQL Server 2000 as the database server. Specifically, we will use a subset of the Northwind database comes with SQL Server 2000. The code presented in this case study should work with other database products such as SQL Server 7.0, MSDE, and Access. But for simplicity, we will assume SQL Server 2000 throughout this chapter.

Among other objects, the Northwind database contains four tables: Customers, Products, Orders, and Order Details. Those tables contain data attributes for typical order management applications. We'll be using several columns from each table. The figure opposite shows the relevant database schema diagram.

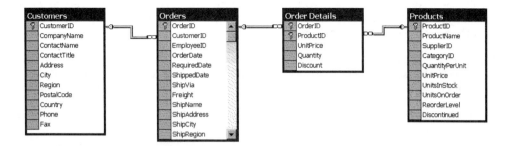

The Middle Tier – SOBizCom

From the descriptions of the user interface, it's quite logical to decide that we'll need to create four middle-tier classes to support the user interface. As we saw at the start of this section these will be:

- ❑   Customer
- ❑   Product
- ❑   OrderItem
- ❑   Order

We'll package them into just one COM+ DLL, SOBizCom.

To create the SOBizCom DLL, open Microsoft Visual Basic 6.0 and create a new ActiveX DLL. Then open the **Project Properties** dialog and change its name to SOBizCom. Enter a meaningful name in the **Project Description** textbox and check the **Unattended Execution** and **Retained In Memory** checkboxes, as illustrated:

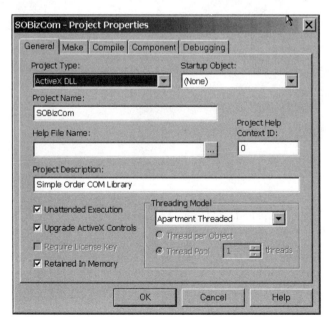

Since the application will be using ADO for database access, we need to add a reference to the ADO class library. Select the Project | References and check the Microsoft ActiveX Data Objects 2.6 Library (or whichever version you have) and click OK.

A common task in connecting to databases using ADO and OLE DB is to figure out the connection strings required to establish a database connection. In addition, code to open and release database connections is the same for all our middle-tier classes, so it's logical to put them in a common module.

Let's add a Module to the project and name it Common. Next, add the following code to the Common module:

```
Option Explicit

' Establish a database connection
' If DoShape is True, create a ADO shape enabled connection
' Otherwise, create a normal ADO connection
Public Sub OpenConnection(ByRef cn As ADODB.Connection, _
                                Optional ByVal DoShape As Boolean = False)
    Set cn = New ADODB.Connection
    With cn
        .CursorLocation = ADODB.adUseClient
        .Open ConnString(DoShape)
    End With
End Sub


' Close a database connection
Public Sub CloseConnection(ByRef cn As ADODB.Connection)
    If Not cn Is Nothing Then
        If cn.State = ADODB.adStateOpen Then
            cn.Close
        End If
        Set cn = Nothing
    End If
End Sub


' Build a connection string.
' If DoShape is True, use the MSDataShape provider
' Otherwise, use the native SQLOLEDB provider
Private Property Get ConnString(Optional ByVal DoShape As _
                                Boolean = False) As String
    If DoShape Then
        ConnString = "Provider=MSDataShape;Data Provider=SQLOLEDB;"
    Else
        ConnString = "Provider=SQLOLEDB;"
    End If

    ConnString = ConnString & "Data Source=(local);" & _
                        "Initial Catalog=Northwind;User ID=sa;Password="
End Property
```

The ConnString property method builds a connection string. It takes one argument, DoShape, which specifies whether or not the connection string should use a shaped data provider. The ADO data-shaping feature allows applications to create hierarchical recordsets that represent a parent-child relationships. For instance, you can create a recordset containing all orders and their items. The parent recordset contains all order header records. Each order header record contains a child recordset containing all items in the order. In this case study, the connection strings are hard-coded, but you can easily use the system Registry or other media to store them.

Remember to change the connection string to reflect your database setup.

The `OpenConnection` method takes two arguments, an ADO connection object to store the database connection, and an optional Boolean variable to specify whether or not the connection should be able to execute ADO shaped commands. It initializes the connection object and connects it to the database.

The `CloseConnection` method takes an ADO `Connection` object and closes the connection if necessary.

Creating the Customer Class

Now change the class module's name from `Class1` to `Customer`. Next, let's create an event, `Changed`. If a `Customer` object's state changes, it will fire this event to notify its client objects.

```
'**************************************************************
' Simple Order Customer business class
'**************************************************************
Option Explicit

' Event raised whenever the customer state has changed
Public Event Changed()

' Class constants for reporting errors
Private Const mcClassName   As String = "SOBizCom.Customer"
Private Const mcObjectError As Long = vbObjectError + &H1000
```

The two private constants, `mcClassName` and `mcObjectError`, specify the name of the class and its base custom error number. When a method raises an error, it uses those constants to report the error source to its client.

Next, create two private data members and the associated property methods:

```
' Private data members
Private mID     As String
Private mName   As String

' Customer ID property methods
Public Property Let ID(ByVal Value As String)
   mID = Value
End Property

Public Property Get ID() As String
   ID = mID
End Property

' Customer name property methods
Public Property Let Name(ByVal Value As String)
   mName = Value
End Property

Public Property Get Name() As String
   Name = mName
End Property
```

The property methods do not perform any data validation in order to keep the code simple. This class will also provide two public methods: `Read` and `Clear`.

Client objects can use the Read method to retrieve a customer record from the database:

```
' Retrieve a customer record from datastore
Public Sub Read(ByVal ID As String)
    On Error GoTo ErrHandler

    Const cMethodName    As String = mcClassName & ".Read()"
    Dim cn               As ADODB.Connection
    Dim rs               As ADODB.Recordset
    Dim SQLQuery         As String

    SQLQuery = "SELECT CustomerID, CompanyName FROM Customers " & _
                            " WHERE CustomerID = '" & ID & "'"

    OpenConnection cn
    Set rs = cn.Execute(SQLQuery)
    Set rs.ActiveConnection = Nothing

    Populate rs

FuncExit:
    ' Clean up after use
    If Not rs Is Nothing Then
        If rs.State = ADODB.adStateOpen Then
            rs.Close
        End If
        Set rs = Nothing
    End If

    CloseConnection cn
    Set cn = Nothing

    Exit Sub

ErrHandler:
    ' Raise error back to the client object
    Err.Raise mcObjectError + 1, cMethodName, Err.Description
End Sub
```

This class builds a SQL SELECT statement to read a record from the Customers table, opens a connection to the database, executes the query, populates object data members with the returned record using the Populate method, and then returns. The Populate method is shown below:

```
' Populate customer object data members from a recordset
' If a recordset is not passed, initialize the data members.
Private Sub Populate (Optional CustomerRS As ADODB.Recordset = Nothing)
    ID = ""
    Name = ""

    If Not CustomerRS Is Nothing Then
        With CustomerRS
            If Not (.BOF And .EOF) Then
                ID = .Fields("CustomerID").Value
                Name = .Fields("CompanyName").Value
            End If
        End With
    End If

    RaiseEvent Changed
End Sub
```

It takes an ADO `Recordset` object and assigns each data member with the corresponding field value in the recordset. If the `Recordset` object is not given, data members are set to blank. In both cases, it raises the `Changed` event to notify the client about the state change.

The `Clear` method simply calls the `Populate` method without passing in a recordset. As we've seen above, this clears the object state.

```
' Clear object data members
Public Sub Clear()
    Populate
End Sub
```

That's it for the first version of the `Customer` class.

Creating the Product Class

The `Product` class is almost identical to the `Customer` class, except that it has different data members. So, without boring you with the details, the code for this class is as follows:

```
'*********************************************************
' Simple Order Product business class
'*********************************************************
Option Explicit

' Event raised whenever the product state has changed
Public Event Changed()

' Class constants for reporting errors
Private Const mcClassName   As String = "SOBizCom.Product"
Private Const mcObjectError As Long = vbObjectError + &H1030

' Private data members
Private mID     As Long
Private mName   As String
Private mPrice  As Currency

' Product ID property methods
Public Property Let ID(ByVal Value As Long)
    mID = Value
End Property

Public Property Get ID() As Long
    ID = mID
End Property

' Product name property methods
Public Property Let Name(ByVal Value As String)
    mName = Value
End Property

Public Property Get Name() As String
    Name = mName
End Property

' Product price property methods
Public Property Let Price(ByVal Value As Currency)
    mPrice = Value
```

```
    End Property

    Public Property Get Price() As Currency
        Price = mPrice
    End Property

    ' Retrieve a product record from datastore
    Public Sub Read(ByVal ID As Long)
        On Error GoTo ErrHandler

        Const cMethodName   As String = mcClassName & ".Read()"
        Dim cn              As ADODB.Connection
        Dim rs              As ADODB.Recordset
        Dim SQLQuery        As String

        SQLQuery = "SELECT ProductID, ProductName, UnitPrice FROM Products" & _
                                        " WHERE ProductID = " & ID

        OpenConnection cn
        Set rs = cn.Execute(SQLQuery)
        Set rs.ActiveConnection = Nothing

        Populate rs

FuncExit:
        ' Clean up after use
        If Not rs Is Nothing Then
            If rs.State = ADODB.adStateOpen Then
                rs.Close
            End If
            Set rs = Nothing
        End If
        Exit Sub

ErrHandler:
        ' Raise error back to the client object
        Err.Raise mcObjectError + 1, cMethodName, Err.Description
    End Sub

    ' Populate product object data members from a recordset
    ' If a recordset is not passed, initialize the data members.
    Private Sub Populate(Optional ProductRS As ADODB.Recordset = Nothing)
        ID = 0
        Name = ""
        Price = 0

        If Not ProductRS Is Nothing Then
            With ProductRS
                If Not (.BOF And .EOF) Then
                    ID = .Fields("ProductID").Value
                    Name = .Fields("ProductName").Value
                    Price = .Fields("UnitPrice").Value
                End If
            End With
        End If

        RaiseEvent Changed
    End Sub
```

Creating the OrderItem Class

An order contains one or more items. One way of modeling this relationship is to define an `Order` class and an `OrderItem` class. The `Order` class encapsulates order properties and operations to manage order and item records in the database. We will see the definition of the `Order` class in a moment.

The `OrderItem` class simply encapsulates the properties for each individual item in the order. It is technically a subordinate class of the `Order` class, meaning an instance of it cannot live independently of an `Order` object. In fact, an `Order` object controls the life cycle of all child `OrderItem` objects. Because of this relationship, the `OrderItem` class is pretty simple:

```vb
'************************************************************
' Simple Order Item class
'************************************************************
Option Explicit

' Class constants for reporting errors
Private Const mcClassName   As String = "SOBizCom.OrderItem"
Private Const mcObjectError As Long = vbObjectError + &H1020

' Private data members
Private mProduct    As SOBizCom.Product
Private mQuantity   As Integer

' Assigning the product ID loads the product from database
Public Property Let ProductID(ByVal Value As Long)
    mProduct.Read Value
End Property

' Ordered product property methods
Public Property Get Product() As SOBizCom.Product
    Set Product = mProduct
End Property

' Ordered item price property methods
Public Property Get Price() As Currency
    Price = Product.Price
End Property

' Ordered item quantity property methods
Public Property Let Quantity(ByVal Value As Integer)
    mQuantity = Value
End Property

Public Property Get Quantity() As Integer
    Quantity = mQuantity
End Property

' Ordered item amount property methods
Public Property Get Amount() As Currency
    Amount = Quantity * Price
End Property

' Class initialization and termination methods
Private Sub Class_Initialize()
    On Error GoTo ErrHandler
    Set mProduct = CreateObject("SOBizCom.Product")
```

```
FuncExit:
    Exit Sub

ErrHandler:
    Err.Raise mcObjectError, mcClassName, Err.Description
    Resume FuncExit
End Sub

Private Sub Class_Terminate()
    Set mProduct = Nothing
End Sub
```

When the client object sets the ProductID property, the OrderItem object calls the Read method of the associated Product object to load the product record from the database. This provides clients with an intuitive way of assigning a product to an OrderItem object, as demonstrated later in the Order class.

The Price property is not strictly necessary here, as this project does not allow users to set prices. Therefore, it is always identical to the unit price of the associated product. However, it's common for ordering systems to offer the ability for users to change order price. For instance, good customers can get discounts on certain products. In such cases, it's important to provide a way of reporting the actual item prices that are different from the normal product prices. Therefore, this class also defines the Price property here, even though it always returns the product unit price.

Creating the Order Class

The final piece of the Simple Order business layer component is the Order class, which is the most complex class in version one:

```
'*************************************************************
' Simple Order business class
'*************************************************************
Option Explicit

' Event raised whenever the order state has changed
Public Event Changed()

' Class constants for reporting errors
Private Const mcClassName   As String = "SOBizCom.Order"
Private Const mcObjectError As Long = vbObjectError + &H1010

' Private data members
Private mID        As Long
Private mDate       As Date
Private mCustomer   As SOBizCom.Customer
Private mItems      As Collection

' Order ID property methods
Public Property Get ID() As Long
    ID = mID
End Property

' Order Date property methods
Public Property Get OrderDate() As Date
    OrderDate = mDate
End Property
```

```
' Assigning the customer ID loads the customer from database
Public Property Let CustomerID(ByVal Value As String)
    mCustomer.Read Value
End Property

' Order customer property methods
Public Property Get Customer() As SOBizCom.Customer
    Set Customer = mCustomer
End Property

' Return all items in the order
Public Property Get Items() As Collection
    Set Items = mItems
End Property

' Class initialization and termination methods
Private Sub Class_Initialize()
    On Error GoTo ErrHandler

    Set mCustomer = CreateObject("SOBizCom.Customer")
    Set mItems = New Collection

FuncExit:
    Exit Sub

ErrHandler:
    Err.Raise mcObjectError, mcClassName, Err.Description
    Resume FuncExit
End Sub

Private Sub Class_Terminate()
    Set mItems = Nothing
    Set mCustomer = Nothing
End Sub
```

This class provides a `Changed` event that will be raised whenever an `Order` object state has changed. An `Order` object associates with a `Customer` object, which represents the customer for whom the order is created. As in the `OrderItem` class, the `Order` class provides a `CustomerID` write-only property. When the client object sets this property, the `Order` object reads the customer record from the database.

The `mItems` collection contains all products ordered. While it's desirable to design a typed collection in a production system to provide a type-safe implementation and better VB IDE IntelliSense support, using the built-in Visual Basic 6 `Collection` object simplifies the code here. The `Items` read-only property returns the collection so that the client object can manipulate it directly.

When a client object instantiates the `Order` class, the `Class_Initialize` function initializes both the mCustomer and the mItems. The `Class_Terminate` function, on the other hand, destroys them when the client object releases the `Order` object.

As usual, we create a `Read` method to retrieve an order from the database:

```
' Retrieve a customer record from datastore
Public Sub Read(ByVal ID As Long)
    On Error GoTo ErrHandler
```

```
        Const cMethodName    As String = mcClassName & ".Read()"
        Dim cn               As ADODB.Connection
        Dim rs               As ADODB.Recordset
        Dim SQLQuery         As String

        SQLQuery = "SHAPE " & _
                "{" & _
                "    SELECT OrderID, CustomerID, OrderDate " & _
                "    FROM Orders WHERE OrderID = " & ID & _
                "} " & _
                "APPEND " & _
                "(" & _
                "    {" & _
                "        SELECT OrderID, ProductID, UnitPrice, Quantity " & _
                "        FROM [Order Details]" & _
                "    } " & _
                "    AS rsItems " & _
                "    RELATE OrderID TO OrderID" & _
                ")"

        OpenConnection cn, True
        Set rs = cn.Execute(SQLQuery)
        Set rs.ActiveConnection = Nothing

        Populate rs

FuncExit:
    ' Clean up after use
    If Not rs Is Nothing Then
        If rs.State = ADODB.adStateOpen Then
            rs.Close
        End If
        Set rs = Nothing
    End If

    CloseConnection cn
    Set cn = Nothing

    Exit Sub

ErrHandler:
    ' Raise error back to the client object
    Err.Raise mcObjectError + 1, cMethodName, Err.Description
End Sub
```

In order to load both the order header record and associated item records from the database, the Read method uses the ADO shape command to load both in one query. It achieves this by first establishing a connection supporting the shape command and then executing the query containing the shape command. Finally, the Populate method takes care of populating order header data members and items:

```
    ' Populate customer object data members from a recordset
    ' If a recordset is not passed, initialize the data members.
    Private Sub Populate(Optional OrderRS As ADODB.Recordset)
        Dim ItemRS      As ADODB.Recordset
        Dim Item        As SOBizCom.OrderItem
        Dim ItemIndex   As Integer
```

```
    mID = 0
    Customer.Clear
    mDate = Now
    For ItemIndex = 1 To mItems.Count
        mItems.Remove 1
    Next ItemIndex

    If Not OrderRS Is Nothing Then
        If Not (OrderRS.BOF And OrderRS.EOF) Then
            With OrderRS
                mID = .Fields("OrderID").Value
                CustomerID = .Fields("CustomerID").Value
                mDate = .Fields("OrderDate").Value

                Set ItemRS = .Fields("rsItems").Value
            End With

            With ItemRS
                Do While Not .EOF
                    Set Item = CreateObject("SOBizCom.OrderItem")
                    Item.ProductID = .Fields("ProductID").Value
                    Item.Quantity = .Fields("Quantity")
                    mItems.Add Item
                    .MoveNext
                Loop
            End With
        End If
    End If

    RaiseEvent Changed
End Sub
```

As in other classes, the `Populate` method accepts an optional ADO `Recordset` object containing both the order header and line items. If the recordset is not given, this method simply initializes the data members. Otherwise, it populates the header and item data members.

Note that the `Read` method does not read either the `Customer` record associated with the order, or the `Product` record associated with each order item. The `Populate` method makes it up by invoking the `Read` methods of the `Customer` and the `Product` class to do this. While this might seem to be less efficient, as it takes more database queries to complete the task, it decouples the `Order` and `OrderItem` classes from the `Customer` and `Product` classes. That is, the `Order` and `OrderItem` classes don't need to know the other classes; they simply use the other classes to perform the task. This design makes the application more extensible and easier to maintain.

The `Order` class also provides a `Clear` method for resetting all class data members to their default values.

```
' Clear object data members
Public Sub Clear()
    Populate
End Sub
```

Since the application needs to create new orders, the `Order` class provides the `Save` method to accomplish this. An important consideration of adding new order records into the database is that this method must also create new order item records. Because each item belongs to an order, an `OrderDetails` record must contain an `OrderID` value that references an `Order` record. The `Northwind` database implements this dependency by creating a foreign key in the `OrderDetails` table to reference the `Order` table (as we in fact saw in Chapter 6 in the section on *Transaction Processing*).

599

This relationship means that, when we create an `OrderDetails` record, we must assign it an `OrderID` value representing its parent `Order` record. However, since the `OrderID` column is an identity column, SQL Server automatically generates an ID for each new order. The normal SQL `INSERT` statement does not return the newly assigned `OrderID` value, so the `Save` method will have to manage it in code.

As in Chapter 6, we'll achieve this by using the T-SQL `@@IDENTITY` global variable inside a stored procedure. Another issue is the `OrderDate` field in the `Order` table. The Simple Order application does not want the user to manually enter it, but rather use the date and time when the new order is saved to the database. Here, we can use the T-SQL `GetDate()` function inside the same stored procedure.

So the code for our stored procedure (named `spAddOrder`) is:

```
USE Northwind
GO

CREATE PROCEDURE spAddOrder
(
    @CustomerID char(5),
    @OrderDate  datetime OUTPUT
)
AS
    SELECT @OrderDate = GetDate()
    INSERT INTO Orders (CustomerID, OrderDate)
        VALUES (@CustomerID, @OrderDate)
    RETURN @@IDENTITY
GO
```

Create the stored procedure by running the code in the Query Analyser against the `Northwind` database. This procedure takes two parameters. `@CustomerID` obviously specifies the customer's ID. `@OrderDate` is marked as an `OUTPUT` parameter, which we will use to return the `OrderDate`.

Firstly, it calls the `GetDate()` function to obtain the current date and time and assigns it to `@OrderDate`. Next, it executes the SQL `INSERT` command to create a new `Order` record, passing it the `@CustomerID` and `@OrderDate` values. Finally, it retrieves the automatically generated `OrderID` value from the `@@IDENTITY` variable and returns it.

The `Save` method uses this stored procedure to save the new order and obtain the `OrderID` and `OrderDate` values:

```
' Save a new order
Public Sub Save()
    On Error GoTo ErrHandler

    Const cMethodName   As String = mcClassName & ".Save()"
    Dim cn              As ADODB.Connection
    Dim cmd             As ADODB.Command
    Dim Item            As SOBizCom.OrderItem
    Dim SQLQuery        As String

    OpenConnection cn

    ' Create the order header record
    Set cmd = New ADODB.Command
    With cmd
```

```
        Set .ActiveConnection = cn
        .CommandType = ADODB.adCmdStoredProc
        .CommandText = "spAddOrder"
        .Parameters.Append .CreateParameter("OrderID", adInteger, _
                                            adParamReturnValue, 4)
        .Parameters.Append .CreateParameter("CustomerID", adChar, _
                                            adParamInput, 5, Customer.ID)
        .Parameters.Append .CreateParameter("OrderDate", ADODB.adDate,_
                                            ADODB.adParamOutput)
        .Execute Options:=ADODB.adExecuteNoRecords
    End With
    mID = cmd("OrderID").Value
    mDate = cmd("OrderDate").Value
```

The `Item` and `SQLQuery` objects will be used for creating order item records, as we'll see later. The above code snippet creates a new ADO `Command` object and links to the `spAddOrder` stored procedure by setting its `CommandType` and `CommandText` properties to the predefined ADO `adCmdStoredProc` constant and the stored procedure's name, respectively.

The snippet then creates three parameters. `OrderID` is a return value (ADO treats the return value of a stored procedure just as if it's a parameter with the `adParamReturnValue` type) and therefore doesn't need to specify its value. `CustomerID` is an input parameter with the customer's ID. `OrderDate` is an output parameter with no value.

The ADO `Command` object's `Execute` method executes the stored procedure. Once it's completed, the last two assignments assign the value stored in the `Command` object's `OrderID` and `OrderDate` parameters to the `mID` and `mDate` data members.

Now we have the ID of the new order, we can create all order item records:

```
    mID = cmd("OrderID").Value
    mDate = cmd("OrderDate").Value
```

```
    ' Create all order item records
    For Each Item In mItems
        SQLQuery = "INSERT INTO [Order Details] " & _
                "(OrderID, ProductID, UnitPrice, Quantity) " & _
                "VALUES " & _
                "(" & CStr(mID) & ", " & CStr(Item.Product.ID) & ", " & _
                CStr(Item.Price) & ", " & CStr(Item.Quantity) & ")"
        cn.Execute SQLQuery, , ADODB.adExecuteNoRecords
    Next

    RaiseEvent Changed

FuncExit:
    ' Clean up after use
    Set Item = Nothing
    Set cmd = Nothing
    CloseConnection cn
    Set cn = Nothing
    Exit Sub

ErrHandler:
    ' Raise error back to the client object
    Err.Raise mcObjectError + 2, cMethodName, Err.Description
End Sub
```

This time, simply executing the SQL INSERT commands is adequate.

While it is generally required for applications like this to provide the ability to modify existing orders, this case study implements only the order creation. This simplifies the state management of the Order and OrderItem classes.

The remaining data access method provided by the Order class is the Delete method, which is fairly straightforward and doesn't need to be discussed in detail. The code is listed below:

```
' Delete the selected order
Public Sub Delete()
    On Error GoTo ErrHandler

    Const cMethodName   As String = mcClassName & ".Delete()"
    Dim cn              As ADODB.Connection
    Dim SQLQuery        As String

    OpenConnection cn

    ' Delete all items first
    SQLQuery = "DELETE [Order Details] " & _
               " WHERE OrderID = " & ID
    cn.Execute SQLQuery, , ADODB.adExecuteNoRecords

    ' Then delete the order header
    SQLQuery = "DELETE Orders WHERE OrderID = " & ID
    cn.Execute SQLQuery, , ADODB.adExecuteNoRecords

    Populate

FuncExit:
    ' Clean up after use
    CloseConnection cn
    Set cn = Nothing
    Exit Sub

ErrHandler:
    ' Raise error back to the client object
    Err.Raise mcObjectError + 3, cMethodName, Err.Description
End Sub
```

The last function is AddItem, which allows the client objects to add a new item to the order.

```
' Add an item to the order
Public Sub AddItem(ProductID As Long, Quantity As Integer)
    On Error GoTo ErrHandler

    Const cMethodName   As String = mcClassName & ".AddItem()"
    Dim OrderItem       As SOBizCom.OrderItem

    Set OrderItem = CreateObject("SOBizCom.OrderItem")
    With OrderItem
        .ProductID = ProductID
        .Quantity = Quantity
    End With

    mItems.Add OrderItem
```

```
      RaiseEvent Changed

FuncExit:
    ' Clean up after use
    Set OrderItem = Nothing
    Exit Sub

ErrHandler:
    ' Raise error back to the client object
    Err.Raise mcObjectError + 4, cMethodName, Err.Description
End Sub
```

This function accepts two parameters, `ProductID` and `Quantity`, that specify the ID of the product to be ordered and the order quantity, respectively. It creates a new `OrderItem` object and assigns the two parameter values to the corresponding properties. Finally, it adds the newly created object to the `mItems` collection.

The business layer component is now completed. Once it's compiled, we can move on to create the user interface forms.

The User Interface – SOUICom

It's time to return to the user interface layer and complete the version one of our Simple Order application.

Follow the steps below to create the user interface project:

1. Open Microsoft Visual Basic 6.0 and create a new Standard EXE project with name SOUICom.

2. Select the Project menu and click Components. In the Components dialog box, check Microsoft Windows Common Controls 6.0 and click OK. This component provides a `ListView` control, which we will use to display order items in the order entry form.

3. Select the Project menu and click References. In the References dialog box, check Simple Order COM Library (or whatever description you gave to the SOBizCOM project) and click OK.

Creating the Order Entry Form

Change the name of the automatically created form from `Form1` to `OrderEntry` and its caption to Order Entry Form. Then add the following controls to the form and change their properties as listed overleaf:

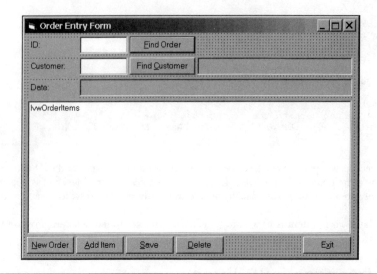

Control Type	Property	Property Value
Label	Caption	ID:
Textbox	Name	txtOrderID
	Text	[Blank]
CommandButton	Name	cmdFind
	Caption	&Find Order
Label	Caption	Customer:
Textbox	Name	txtCustomerID
	Text	[Blank]
CommandButton	Name	cmdFindCustomer
	Caption	Find &Customer
Label	Name	lblCustomerName
	Caption	[Blank]
Label	Caption	Date:
Label	Name	lblDate
	Caption	[Blank]
ListView	Name	lvwOrderItems
CommandButton	Name	cmdNew

Control Type	Property	Property Value
	Caption	&New Order
CommandButton	Name	cmdAddItem
	Caption	&Add Item
CommandButton	Name	cmdSave
	Caption	&Save
CommandButton	Name	cmdDelete
	Caption	&Delete
CommandButton	Name	cmdExit
	Caption	E&xit

Let's switch to the code window and create the code for our form. First, declare two object references, one for the `Order` class in the business component and the other for the `OrderItemEntry` class. The latter will be explained in the next section.

```
'*************************************************************
' Simple Order Order Entry Form
'*************************************************************
Option Explicit

' Reference to the Order class in the business component
Private WithEvents mOrder        As SOBizCom.Order

' Reference to the Order Item Entry form
Private WithEvents mItemEntry    As OrderItemEntry

' Form event handlers
Private Sub Form_Load()
    Set mOrder = CreateObject("SOBizCom.Order")

    With lvwOrderItems
        .ColumnHeaders.Add Text:="Product", _
                        Width:=lvwOrderItems.Width / 2 - 240
        .ColumnHeaders.Add Text:="Price", Width:=lvwOrderItems.Width / 6
        .ColumnHeaders.Add Text:="Quantity", Width:=lvwOrderItems.Width / 6
        .ColumnHeaders.Add Text:="Amount", Width:=lvwOrderItems.Width / 6
        .View = lvwReport
    End With
End Sub

Private Sub Form_QueryUnload(Cancel As Integer, UnloadMode As Integer)
    Set mOrder = Nothing
End Sub

Private Sub cmdExit_Click()
    Unload Me
End Sub
```

When the form loads, the `Form_Load` event handler instantiates mOrder and initializes the order item list. The user can click the Exit button to close the form, which triggers the `Form_QueryUnload` event handler that simply releases mOrder.

A user can enter an order ID and click the **Find Order** button to retrieve an existing order. The `cmdFind` button's `Click` event handler invokes the `Read` method of the `Order` class to read the specified order:

```
Private Sub cmdFind_Click()
    mOrder.Read OrderID
End Sub

Private Property Get OrderID() As Long
    On Error Resume Next
    OrderID = CLng(txtOrderID.Text)
End Property
```

Recall that whenever the order state has changed, the `Order` class raises the `Changed` event. We can catch this event and populate the form with the order data read from the database.

```
Private Sub mOrder_Changed()
    Populate
End Sub

Private Sub Populate()
    Dim OrderItem   As SOBizCom.OrderItem
    Dim ViewItem    As MSComctlLib.ListItem

    With mOrder
        txtOrderID.Text = .ID
        txtCustomerID.Text = .Customer.ID
        lblCustomerName.Caption = .Customer.Name
        lblDate.Caption = .OrderDate

        lvwOrderItems.ListItems.Clear
        For Each OrderItem In .Items
            Set ViewItem = _
                lvwOrderItems.ListItems.Add(Text:=OrderItem.Product.Name)
            ViewItem.SubItems(1) = OrderItem.Price
            ViewItem.SubItems(2) = OrderItem.Quantity
            ViewItem.SubItems(3) = OrderItem.Amount
        Next OrderItem
    End With
End Sub
```

The `Populate` function fills the textboxes and labels with order header data, and then enumerates order items to populate the item list.

The user can also enter an order ID and click the `Delete` button to delete an existing order, if it exists.

```
Private Sub cmdDelete_Click()
    With mOrder
        .Read OrderID
        .Delete
    End With
End Sub
```

There is a little trap here: if the user looks at an order with ID of 1 and then wants to delete the order with ID 2, they may simply enter the number 2 in the ID textbox and click the `Delete` button. Because entering an order ID doesn't automatically change the ID of `mOrder`, we must ensure that it refreshes before calling the `Delete` function. To ensure that the correct order be deleted, this `cmdDelete_Click` function loads the specified order to refresh `mOrder` before actually deleting it.

If the user wants to create a new order, they click the **New Order** button. This will invoke the `Clear` method of the `Order` class, which will in turn raises the `Changed` event. The `mOrder_Changed` event handler shown above will then clear the form for the user.

```
Private Sub cmdNew_Click()
    mOrder.Clear
End Sub
```

The user can then enter a customer ID and click the **Find Customer** button to display the name of the selected customer:

```
Private Sub cmdFindCustomer_Click()
    mOrder.CustomerID = txtCustomerID.Text
    With mOrder.Customer
        txtCustomerID.Text = .ID
        lblCustomerName.Caption = .Name
    End With
End Sub
```

In order to add product items to the new order, the user can click the **Add Item** button, which shows the `OrderItemEntry` form:

```
Private Sub cmdAddItem_Click()
    If mItemEntry Is Nothing Then
        Set mItemEntry = New OrderItemEntry
    End If
    mItemEntry.Show vbNormal, Me
End Sub
```

Let's look at the details of the Order Item Entry form in a moment. Briefly, it accepts a product ID and the order quantity. Once the user closes that form, it raises the `Completed` event. The Order Entry form will need to handle that event in order to update the underlying `Order` object:

```
Private Sub mItemEntry_Completed _
( _
    ByVal ProductID As Long, _
    ByVal Quantity As Integer _
)
    mOrder.AddItem ProductID, Quantity
End Sub
```

Again, the `mOrder` object will raise the `Changed` event, which will be captured to add the new item to the Order Entry form.

At last, the user can click the Save button to save the new order to the database:

```
Private Sub cmdSave_Click()
    With mOrder
        .CustomerID = txtCustomerID.Text
        .Save
    End With
End Sub
```

The Order Entry form is fairly straightforward, as the Order class does all the hard work. The Order Item Entry form is even simpler, let's quickly go through its design and code.

Creating the Order Item Entry Form

Add a new form to the SOUICom project and name it OrderItemEntry. Change its caption to Add Item and add the following controls to the form.

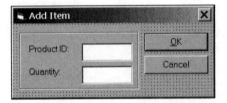

Control Type	Property	Property Value
Frame	Caption	[Blank]
Label	Caption	Product ID:
Textbox	Name	txtProductID
Label	Caption	Quantity:
Textbox	Name	txtQuantity
CommandButton	Name	cmdOK
	Caption	&OK
CommandButton	Name	cmdCancel
	Caption	Cancel

Now switch to the code window and enter the code as listed below:

```
'********************************************************
' Simple Order Item Entry Form
'********************************************************
Option Explicit

' Event to be raised when done
Public Event Completed(ByVal ProductID As Long, ByVal Quantity As Integer)
```

```
Private Sub Form_Activate()
    txtProductID.Text = ""
    txtQuantity.Text = 1
End Sub

Private Sub cmdOK_Click()
    RaiseEvent Completed( ProductID, Quantity)
    Me.Hide
End Sub

Private Sub cmdCancel_Click()
    Me.Hide
End Sub

Private Property Get ProductID() As Long
    On Error Resume Next
    ProductID = CLng(txtProductID.Text)
End Property

Private Property Get Quantity() As Integer
    On Error Resume Next
    Quantity = CInt(txtQuantity.Text)
End Property
```

When the form is activated, it initializes the product ID and order quantity. The user can enter the product ID and order quantity, and click the **OK** button. This raises the `Completed` event and passes the entered product ID and order quantity. The user may also click the **Cancel**, which simply hides the form.

That's it for version one and you should be able to compile and run it to verify that all the features are implemented correctly:

- ❑ To test the program will read and display those orders as expected try to load several orders with order ID from 10250 to 10255

- ❑ To create new orders, use customer ID ANTON, AROUT, or COMMI and product ID's from 1 to 100

You can also open SQL Server Enterprise Manager to verify the results and to see more details about existing customers, products, and orders.

Note that the application is merely meant for demonstrating key concepts, and doesn't have too much potentially confusing (for a demo application) error handling, so don't try too hard to break it!

Version Two – .NET Talking to COM+

While our Simple Order application version one satisfies basic requirements and works well, it lacks some features such as the ability to maintain customer and product data. This version will implement those missing features.

To demonstrate how existing components can be reused under .NET, version two will be based on the business components built in phase one. Specifically, we'll create a new .NET class library containing two classes, Customer and Product. These will extend the Customer and Product classes in the SOBizCom library, respectively.

We will also create a new .NET Windows Form application to use the new Customer and Product classes. The figure below illustrates the relationships between the .NET and COM+ components:

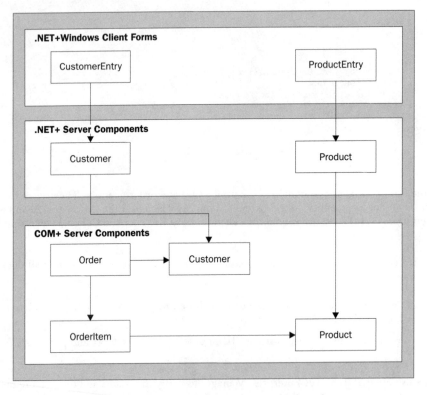

As we discussed, while building the new .NET components we will see how to:

- ❑ Use COM+ components in .NET components
- ❑ Extend COM+ classes in .NET by inheritance
- ❑ Extend COM+ components in .NET by containment
- ❑ Handle COM+ errors in .NET components
- ❑ Handle COM+ events in .NET components

Before looking into the implementation details, let's take a brief look at the theory behind the .NET and COM+ interoperations.

The Runtime-Callable Wrapper (RCW)

Chapter 6 introduced COM+ integration in .NET with the Enterprise Services library. However, that library doesn't provide the facility to use existing COM/COM+ components in managed .NET assemblies. The .NET Framework provides a class called the **Runtime-Callable Wrapper** (**RCW**). This class acts as a mediator between COM/COM+ server components and .NET client components, marshaling calls between them.

When a .NET client asks to create a COM+ object, the CLR creates an instance of the COM+ object and an instance of the RCW for that object. As far as the .NET client is concerned, it has created a .NET object and now has a reference to the created object. The CLR manages the interaction between the .NET client and the COM+ object through the associated RCW object. When the .NET client invokes a function in the COM+ object, the RCW translates the function call made by the .NET client to a call to the COM+ object and passes it on to the real COM+ object. After the COM+ object has completed the request by executing the function call, the RCW translates the result back to the .NET client.

If the COM+ object raises an event as a result of the request, the RCW also converts the COM+ event to a .NET event. The .NET client can then handle that event as a native .NET event.

COM+ does not support the concept of exception directly because exceptions are not binary compatible among COM+ components. COM+ components use the standard COM+ error reporting mechanism to process run-time errors. The RCW provides transparent translation between COM+ errors and .NET exceptions. If the COM+ object reports an error while processing the request, the RCW again converts the COM+ error to a .NET exception and throws it to the .NET client. The .NET client can catch these exceptions and decide how to manage them.

This is the theory. Now let's see how .NET clients work with COM+ servers with the help of the RCW.

The Middle Tier – SOBizNet

Open Visual Studio .NET and create a new Visual C# Class Library project named SOBizNet. In order to reuse the Customer and Product classes in the version one business component, we need to add a reference to SOBizNet.dll as we did before.

Some details of the next section – the appearance of the dialog box and the precise details appear to differ between RC1 and Beta 2. The underlying approach is the same, however.

If it has not been registered, click the Browse button and find the DLL file. Click the Select button and then the OK button to add the reference to the project.

At this point a dialog box may pop up, as shown in the figure below:

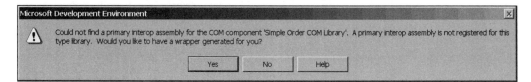

This means that Visual Studio .NET has discovered that the SOBizCom.dll is not a native .NET assembly, and that it must create a wrapper library in order to use it. Just click Yes to let Visual Studio .NET create the wrapper library for you. This wrapper library actually contains RCW instances for each public class in the original SOBizCom DLL, as well as other .NET metadata necessary for the CLR to use the COM+ DLL. You will now see SOBizCom appears in the project reference list in the Solution Explorer.

> **Alternatively, in RC1, it may be that a dialog box appears asking for the DLL to be registered (if it isn't already). In this case adding a reference to a registered DLL may generate the wrappers automatically.**

To see exactly what is happening under the hood, use the Windows Explorer to open the SOBizNet project's bin\Debug subdirectory:

Name ▲	Size	Type	Modified	
Interop.SOBizCom_3_0.dll	13 KB	Application Extension	8/13/2001 10:57 PM	
Interop.VBA_6_0.dll	10 KB	Application Extension	6/19/1998 12:00 AM	

The first file is the wrapper assembly of SOBizCom.dll. Since all COM+ libraries written in Visual Basic 6 require the Visual Basic 6 run-time library to run, a wrapper assembly for the Visual Basic 6 run-time library is also created.

The infrastructure is ready; let's look at the ways to extend COM+ components from .NET components.

First, we can extend a COM+ class in a .NET component using inheritance. When a C# class inherits a COM+ class, it is defined exactly the same as if it were inheriting from another C# class. That is, we use this syntax:

```
public class Derived : Base
{
    ...
}
```

The Derived class automatically inherits all public and protected members of the Base class. In addition to data members and methods, the Derived class also inherits events, since events are now first class members in C#.

There are advantages and disadvantages of extension by inheritance, as we'll see when you extend the COM+ Customer class by deriving the .NET C# class from it.

Extending COM+ Classes Using Inheritance

Change the name of the automatically created class in SOBizNet from class1 to Customer, the name of the constructor from class1 to Customer, and the file name from class1.cs to Customer.cs.

Now change the class definition by declaring it as derived from SOBizCom.Customer, as shown below:

```
using System;

namespace SOBizNet
{
```

```
/// <summary>
/// Summary description for Customer.
/// </summary>
public class Customer : SOBizCom.Customer
{
    public Customer()
    {
        //
        // TODO: Add constructor logic here
        //
    }
}
```

While the above code is correct for the Beta 2 release, in RC1 the definition needs to be:

```
public class Customer : SOBizCom.CustomerClass
```

We will add more methods to the derived `Customer` class later, but for now, we'll just compile it and test how it works by creating a new Windows Application project, `SOUINet`.

The CustomerEntry Class

After creating the `SOUINet` project, change the automatically created form name from `Form1` to `CustomerEntry` and add several controls to it as shown below:

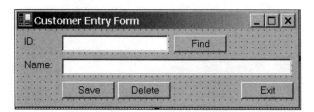

Control Type	Property	Property Value
Label	Text	ID:
Textbox	Name	txtID
	Text	[Blank]
Button	Name	btnFind
	Text	Find
Label	Text	Name:
Textbox	Name	txtName
	Text	[Blank]
Button	Name	btnSave

Table continued on following page

Control Type	Property	Property Value
	Text	Save
Button	Name	btnDelete
	Text	Delete
Button	Name	btnExit
	Text	Exit

Using the Derived .NET Class in .NET Clients

To be able to use the new C# Customer class, we should add a reference to the SOBizNet.dll.

Then switch to the code window of CustomerEntry.cs and add a reference to the Customer class as shown below:

```
private System.ComponentModel.Container components = null;

// Custom data members
private SOBizNet.Customer mCustomer = null;

public CustomerEntry()
{
    //
    // Required for Windows Form Designer support
    //
    InitializeComponent();

    mCustomer = new SOBizNet.Customer();
}
```

Add the event handler for the **Find** and **Exit** buttons as shown below:

```
private void btnFind_Click(object sender, System.EventArgs e)
{
    mCustomer.Read(txtID.Text);
    PopulateControls();
}

private void btnExit_Click(object sender, System.EventArgs e)
{
    Application.Exit();
}

private void PopulateControls()
{
    txtID.Text   = mCustomer.ID;
    txtName.Text = mCustomer.Name;
}
```

Using the Beta 2 release, VS IntelliSense doesn't seem to pickup any Customer class members. When the project is compiled, VS reports an error:

```
Referenced class 'SOBizNet.Customer' has base class or interface
'SOBizCom.Customer' defined in an assembly that is not referenced. You must add a
reference to assembly 'Interop.SOBizCom_3_0'.
```

The cause of this error is that while the new C# Customer class inherits from the COM+ Customer class; the interface of the base class is not statically linked into the SOBizNet assembly. In order for the C# compiler to pick up the interface, we must also add a reference to the COM+ library. Adding a reference to the COM+ library is exactly the same as for the SOBizNet project, including instructing VS to create a wrapper class. Once that's done, IntelliSense works as expected and the compiler is quite happy to build the executable for us.

If you run the project now, you will see that you can enter a customer ID and click the Find button to retrieve the customer record from the database. Inheritance works perfectly once we have figured out the little extra work to add the reference to both the .NET and COM+ libraries.

Handling Inherited COM+ Events

We saw earlier that data members, methods, and events are inherited. Therefore, we must be able to handle the Changed event defined in the base COM+ Customer class, and inherited in the derived C# Customer class. Unfortunately, while the events themselves are exposed through the derived class, the event handlers are not.

In order to implement a COM+ event handler in .NET clients, we must use a workaround. Add the following code snippets to the C# CustomerEntry class:

```
public CustomerEntry()
{
    //
    // Required for Windows Form Designer support
    //
    InitializeComponent();

    mCustomer = new SOBizNet.Customer();
    mCustomer.Changed += new
        SOBizCom.__Customer_ChangedEventHandler(OnCustomerChanged);
}

private void OnCustomerChanged()
{
    PopulateControls();
}
```

As we can see, while we can reference the Changed event through an instance of the C# Customer class, we can only reference the event handler through COM+ SOBizCom component (through RCW). VS IntelliSense helps us to find the event handler, but we can also use the .NET IL Disassembler to interrogate the Interop wrapper Interop.SOBizCom_3_0.dll. The double underscores prefixing the event handler name have to do with the way the Visual Basic 6.0 compiler generates COM+ interfaces for Visual Basic classes.

Since we are now using an event handler for the Customer object's Changed event, there is no need to explicitly call the PopulateControls function in the btnFind_Click event handler. So let's remove it from there.

If you compile and run the program at this point (commenting out the uncoded event handlers), it will show that the event handling works just fine.

Handling COM+ Errors

.NET has a completely different error handling mechanism from COM+. In COM+, components and methods report errors by returning an error code with HRESULT. In contrast, .NET components report errors by throwing exceptions. The RCW bridges this gap by wrapping up COM+ errors in System.Runtime.InteropServices.COMException objects. We can catch this exception to handle any errors raised by the COM+ components.

For the Customer class, there are two ways of capturing the errors raised by the COM+ base class. The first is the easiest – do nothing. What happens in the background is that it will simply pass the errors to the client object, for instance the CustomerEntry class, which can catch it. However, the client object then will have to be aware of the source of the error so that it can choose to catch either a COMException object or a normal .NET Exception object.

The better way is to catch any errors that might be raised by the COM+ base class in the Customer class itself. Depending on the nature of the error, we can then choose to either handle it in the Customer class itself, or throw a .NET Exception object to the client. We may also choose to throw a custom exception object according to system requirements. The C# Customer class can hide the Read method of the base class by declaring its own Read method, which calls the Read method of the base class, and decides how to handle COM+ errors. Let's take a look at how to implement this.

In the Customer class, add a new method, Read, as follows:

```
new public void Read(string ID)
{
   try
   {
      base.Read(ID);
   }
   catch (System.Runtime.InteropServices.COMException x)
   {
      throw new Exception("Error [" + x.ErrorCode.ToString() + "]
                           from " + x.Source + ": " + x.Message);
   }
}
```

Note the use of the new keyword here – it hides the Read() method in the base class. We could also override it by using the override keyword; however, the current C# compiler requires that if a derived class overrides one method in the COM+ base class, it overrides all of them including properties. For the sake of simplicity, we will just hide the Read() method.

The client object can then catch just the generic Exception object. Let's modify the btnFind_Click event handler to do this:

```
private void btnFind_Click(object sender, System.EventArgs e)
{
   try
   {
      mCustomer.Read(txtID.Text);
   }
   catch (Exception x)
   {
      MessageBox.Show(x.Message, "Application Error",
                      MessageBoxButtons.OK, MessageBoxIcon.Error);
   }
}
```

To cause an error in the COM+ Customer class' Read method, you can simply stop the SQL Server. When you run the application and click the Find button, you will see a message box showing the error:

Completing the C# Customer Class

We've seen how to extend COM+ components in .NET components by using C# inheritance. Let's complete the changes to the Customer class with two new methods, Save and Delete.

```csharp
using System;
using System.Data.SqlClient;
// ...
public void Save()
{
    SOBizCom.Customer Work = new SOBizCom.Customer();
    Work.Read(ID);

    string sqlString;
    if (Work.ID == "")
    {
        sqlString = "INSERT INTO Customers (CustomerID, CompanyName) " +
                    "VALUES ('" + ID + "', '" + Name + "')";
    }
    else
    {
        sqlString = "UPDATE Customers " +
                    "SET CompanyName = '" + Name + "' " +
                    "WHERE CustomerID = '" + ID + "'";
    }

    ExecuteSQLCommand(sqlString);
}

public void Delete()
{
    string sqlString = "DELETE Customers WHERE CustomerID = '" + ID + "'";
    ExecuteSQLCommand(sqlString);
    Clear();
}

private void ExecuteSQLCommand(string sqlString)
{
    SqlConnection cn = new SqlConnection(mcConnString);

    try
    {
        cn.Open();
        SqlCommand cmd = new SqlCommand(sqlString, cn);
        cmd.ExecuteNonQuery();
    }
    catch (SqlException e)
    {
```

```
        throw e;
    }
    finally
    {
        if (cn.State == System.Data.ConnectionState.Open)
        {
            cn.Close();
        }
    }
}

private const string mcConnString = "Integrated Security=SSPI;" +
                        "Initial Catalog=Northwind;Data Source=(local)";
```

The `ExecuteSQLCommand()` method performs necessary ADO.NET operations to execute a SQL command. Both the `Save()` and `Delete()` methods then simply build a SQL command string and invoke this method to run the query.

The `Save()` method first instantiates a temporary base `Customer` object to query the database. If it finds a customer record with the given customer ID, it will run a SQL update query. Otherwise it runs a SQL insert query.

More on Events

The `Delete()` method, defined above, seems to have a small flaw in it. Our design since version one has been that objects always raise a `Changed` event after state change. To follow this design principle, the `Delete()` method should raise the `Changed` event after it has executed the delete query. However it cannot, because the .NET Framework does not allow a derived class to raise an event defined in the base class.

We could work around this by declaring a new event in the `Customer` class, and raising it in the `Delete` method. The client object, however, must be aware of the fact that our class may raise two different events. This is another limitation of extension by inheritance.

However, we can actually do a lot better here. There is a simpler and better solution. The base COM+ `Customer` class defines a `Clear()` method, which resets the data members and raises the `Changed` event. The `Delete()` method can therefore simply call the `Clear()` method and let it handle the event raising. The client object can then handle this event to update the form display:

```
public void Delete()
{
    string sqlString = "DELETE Customers WHERE CustomerID = '" + ID + "'";
    ExecuteSQLCommand(sqlString);
    Clear();
}
```

Completing the CustomerEntry Class

The `Customer` class does all the hard work, so the changes to the `CustomerEntry` class are very simple:

```
this.btnSave.Click += new System.EventHandler(this.btnSave_Click);
this.btnDelete.Click += new System.EventHandler(this.btnDelete_Click);
this.btnExit.Click += new System.EventHandler(this.btnExit_Click);
//
```

```csharp
private void btnSave_Click(object sender, System.EventArgs e)
{
   UpdateCustomer();
   mCustomer.Save();
}

private void btnDelete_Click(object sender, System.EventArgs e)
{
   UpdateCustomer();
   mCustomer.Delete();
   PopulateControls();
}

private void btnExit_Click(object sender, System.EventArgs e)
{
   ApplicationExit();
}

private void UpdateCustomer()
{
   mCustomer.ID = txtID.Text;
   mCustomer.Name = txtName.Text;
}
```

The `btnSave_Click` and `btnDelete_Click` event handlers both update the `Customer` object's properties, and then call its `Save()` and `Delete()` methods, respectively, to update the database. The latter also explicitly calls the `PopulateControls()` method to refresh the form, because the `Delete()` method doesn't raise a `Changed` event. There is no need to do the same in the `Save` method though, because the customer ID and name shown in the form always match the underlying `Customer` object.

We've now completed the first part of upgrading the COM+ application to .NET using inheritance. The main advantage of this approach is that it allows us to reuse the functionality provided in the COM+ library without having to redo the work that has already been done. We have also seen some limitations, notably that the client object has to explicitly reference the COM+ library through the RCW, and that it's not possible to reuse the events defined in the COM+ library in new functions.

In the next section, we'll look at another approach – upgrading the COM+ application in .NET using containment.

Extending COM+ Classes Using Containment

This approach removes the limitations associated with the extension by inheritance. Let's see how it works by upgrading the COM+ `Product` class. The following code should be placed in a file called `Product.cs` in our .NET project.

```csharp
using System;

namespace SOBizNet
{
   public delegate void ProductChangedEventHandler();

   public class Product
   {
      public Product()
      {
```

```
      mProduct = new SOBizCom.Product();
      mProduct.Changed +=
         new SOBizCom.__Product_ChangedEventHandler(OnChange);
}

public event ProductChangedEventHandler ProductChanged;

public void OnChange()
{
   if (ProductChanged != null)
   {
      ProductChanged();
   }
}

// Properties
public int ID
{
   get
   {
      return mProduct.ID;
   }
   set
   {
      mProduct.ID = value;
   }
}

public string Name
{
   get
   {
      return mProduct.Name;
   }
   set
   {
      mProduct.Name = value;
   }
}

public decimal Price
{
   get
   {
      return mProduct.Price;
   }
   set
   {
      mProduct.Price = value;
   }
}

public void Read(int ID)
{
   try
   {
      mProduct.Read(ID);
   }
   catch (System.Runtime.InteropServices.COMException x)
```

```
        {
            throw new Exception("Error [" + x.ErrorCode.ToString() +
                            "] from " + x.Source + ": " +
                            x.Message);
        }
    }

    protected SOBizCom.Product mProduct = null;
    }
}
```

The new C# `Product` class contains the COM+ `Product` class by declaring a protected object reference to it and instantiating it in the constructor. Unlike the inheritance approach, which provides client objects ALL the base class's public properties and methods for free, we have to write our own wrapper properties and methods here. The three properties, `ID`, `Name`, and `Price`, and the `Read` method simply use their COM+ counterparts to do the real work.

Given that the C# `Product` class now isolates the client objects from the COM+ product class, it must also handle the COM+ events. It may capture the COM+ events and raise its own events, or it may handle the COM+ events in-house without alerting the client objects, or it may even ignore certain events completely. All those methods are reasonable. If we decided on the first two, we'll need to define an event handler in the `Product` class.

In the above class definition, the event handler is `OnChange`. The constructor registers it for the COM+ `Product` class' `Changed` event.

If we want the .NET `Product` object to simply re-raise an event to the client object after it receives the COM+ `Changed` event, we need to define an event in the `Product` class:

```
namespace SOBizNet
{
    public delegate void ProductChangedEventHandler();

    public class Product
    {
        public event ProductChangedEventHandler ProductChanged;
```

Then in the `OnChange` method, we simply raise the `ProductChanged` event.

```
        public void OnChange()
        {
            if (ProductChanged != null)
            {
                ProductChanged();
            }
        }
```

That's all we need to do at the class library to provide an existing COM+ class' functionality. Let's take a look at the client side to see what difference this approach makes.

621

The ProductEntry Class

In order to see the difference between these two approaches, either remove the `CustomerEntry` form and the reference to the `SOBizCom.dll` and `Interop.VBA_6_0.dll` from the `SOUINet` assembly or create a new, clean Windows Application. If you decide to create a new Windows Application, be sure to add a reference to the `SOBizNet` assembly.

Now either add a new Windows Form class named `ProductEntry`, or rename the automatically generated Windows Form from `Form1` to `Product`, depending on whether you reuse the `SOUINet` assembly or create a new Windows Application. It has the following controls:

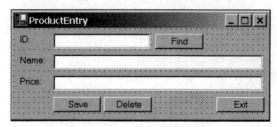

Control Type	Property	Property Value
Label	Text	ID:
Textbox	Name	txtID
	Text	[Blank]
Button	Name	btnFind
	Text	Find
Label	Text	Name:
Textbox	Name	txtName
	Text	[Blank]
Label	Text	Price:
Textbox	Name	txtPrice
	Text	[Blank]
Button	Name	btnSave
	Text	Save
Button	Name	btnDelete
	Text	Delete
Button	Name	btnExit
	Text	Exit

If adding a new form to an existing assembly, Visual Studio .NET will not automatically generate a `Main()` method as the application starting point for us and we need to add it ourselves (and remove that method from the existing class):

```
[STAThread]
static void Main()
{
    Application.Run(new OrderEntry());
}
```

Now add the code below to the `ProductEntry` class:

```
// Custom data members
private SOBizNet.Product mProduct = null;

public ProductEntry()
{
    //
    // Required for Windows Form Designer support
    //
    InitializeComponent();

    mProduct = new SOBizNet.Product();
    mProduct.ProductChanged +=
        new SOBizNet.ProductChangedEventHandler(OnProductChanged);
}
```

```
//

private void btnFind_Click(object sender, System.EventArgs e)
{
    mProduct.Read(ProductID);
}

private void OnProductChanged()
{
    PopulateControls();
}

private void PopulateControls()
{
    txtID.Text    = mProduct.ID.ToString();
    txtName.Text  = mProduct.Name;
    txtPrice.Text = mProduct.Price.ToString();
}

private int ProductID
{
    get
    {
        try
        {
            return System.Convert.ToInt32(txtID.Text, 10);
        }
        catch
        {
            return 0;
        }
    }
}
```

The `ProductEntry` class defines a private data member `mProduct` of type `SOBizNet.Product` and instantiates it in the constructor. It also defines a `ProductChanged` event handler, `OnProductChanged`, which simply populates the relevant controls to display the current product state. The `btnFind`'s `Click` event handler, `btnFind_Click`, just calls the `Product` class's `Read()` method to retrieve data from the database.

If we now compile and run the application (again comenting out the uncoded handlers), we can enter a product ID and click the Find button to retrieve the specified product data. There's a major difference here – we no longer need to reference `SOBizCom`, the COM+ library that contains the `Product` class in our client application. Event handling is also a lot easier that in the previous inheritance version.

It's good to decouple the client application from the COM+ library because if you later decide to rewrite the `Product` class entirely in .NET, you will not have to change the client application.

Completing the Product Class

Let's complete the new C# `Product` class by adding `Save()` and `Delete()` methods. First, import the `System.Data.SqlClient` namespace:

```
using System;
using System.Data.SqlClient;
```

It's also convenient to define a string constant for the connection string to the SQL server. Both the `Save` and `Delete` methods need to use it to connect to SQL server.

Again change the connection string to reflect your database's settings:

```
protected SOBizCom.Product mProduct = null;
private const string mcConnString = "Integrated Security=SSPI;" +
                        "Initial Catalog=Northwind;Data Source=(local)";
```

The `Save()` method is similar to its counterpart in the `Customer` class, where it queries the database to check whether a record with the same ID exists. If the record already exists, the `Save()` method updates it with the new product name and price. Otherwise it creates a new record. Since it will provide the client object with the new product ID that will be generated automatically by SQL Server, it needs to know the ID once the record is saved.

As we've seen in version one with the `Order` class, the best way to accomplish this task is to use a stored procedure that executes the `INSERT` command and returns the new ID. Here is the code for the stored procedure:

```
USE Northwind
GO

CREATE PROCEDURE spAddProduct
(
    @ProductName char(40),
    @UnitPrice   money
)
AS
    INSERT INTO Products (ProductName, UnitPrice)
    VALUES (@ProductName, @UnitPrice);
    RETURN @@IDENTITY
GO
```

Now add the `Save()` method to the `Product` class:

```
public void Save()
{
    SOBizCom.Product Work = new SOBizCom.Product();
    Work.Read(ID);

    string GoodName = Name.Replace("'", "''");
    string sqlString;
    if (Work.ID == 0)
    {
        // Create a new product record
        SqlConnection cn = new SqlConnection(mcConnString);
        cn.Open();

        SqlCommand cmd = new SqlCommand();
        cmd.Connection = cn;
        cmd.CommandText = "spAddProduct";
        cmd.CommandType = System.Data.CommandType.StoredProcedure;

        SqlParameter param = cmd.Parameters.Add("ID",
                                        System.Data.SqlDbType.Int);
        param.Direction = System.Data.ParameterDirection.ReturnValue ;

        param = cmd.Parameters.Add("@ProductName",
                            System.Data.SqlDbType.Char, 40);
        param.Direction = System.Data.ParameterDirection.Input;
        param.Value = GoodName;

        param = cmd.Parameters.Add("@UnitPrice",
                            System.Data.SqlDbType.Money);
        param.Direction = System.Data.ParameterDirection.Input;
        param.Value = Price;

        cmd.ExecuteNonQuery();
        ID = Convert.ToInt32(cmd.Parameters["ID"].Value.ToString(), 10);
    }
    else
    {
        // Update the existing product record
        sqlString = "UPDATE Products " +
                "    SET ProductName = '" + GoodName + "', " +
                "    UnitPrice = " + Price +
                " WHERE ProductID = " + ID;
        ExecuteSQLCommand(sqlString);
    }

    OnChange();
}
```

First, the `Save()` method uses a temporary `Product` object to check whether the given ID represents an existing product. If so, it will simply update the record. Otherwise, it will create a new record.

The `GoodName` string replaces any single apostrophe in the product name with a couple of apostrophes, so that any product names containing apostrophe will not cause any problems in SQL `INSERT` and `UPDATE` commands. When creating a new product, this method creates a `SqlCommand` object to call the stored procedure. It also adds parameters and return values to the command object.

Note that, as in ADO, we also attach the return value as a parameter of type `ReturnValue` to the command object in ADO.NET. Once the command object executes the query, the return value of the stored procedure is stored in this parameter. In the above code, the `Save()` method assigns the ID property with the new product ID returned in the return value parameter, `ID`.

When updating an existing record, the `Save()` method builds a SQL UPDATE command and invokes the helper function `ExecuteSQLCommand` to execute it, just as we did in the `Customer` class. The `ExecuteSQLCommand()` method is identical to the same method in the `Customer` class. It's reproduced here for convenience:

```
private void ExecuteSQLCommand(string sqlString)
{
    SqlConnection cn = new SqlConnection(mcConnString);

    try
    {
        cn.Open();
        SqlCommand cmd = new SqlCommand(sqlString, cn);
        cmd.ExecuteNonQuery();
    }
    catch (SqlException e)
    {
        throw e;
    }
    finally
    {
        if (cn.State == System.Data.ConnectionState.Open)
        {
            cn.Close();
        }
    }
}
```

The `Delete()` method looks very similar to the `Delete()` method in the `Customer` class:

```
public void Delete()
{
    string sqlString = "DELETE Products WHERE ProductID = " + ID;
    ExecuteSQLCommand(sqlString);

    ID = 0;
    Name = "";
    Price = 0;

    OnChange();
}
```

Now the `Product` class is complete, let's finish off the `ProductEntry` class.

Completing the ProductEntry class

The `ProductEntry` class handles the `Save` and `Delete` buttons' `Click` events, invoking the corresponding methods in the `Product` class:

```
private void btnSave_Click(object sender, System.EventArgs e)
{
    UpdateProduct();
    mProduct.Save();
}

private void btnDelete_Click(object sender, System.EventArgs e)
{
    UpdateProduct();
    mProduct.Delete();
}

private void UpdateProduct()
{
    mProduct.ID    = ProductID;
    mProduct.Name  = txtName.Text;
    mProduct.Price = System.Convert.ToDecimal(txtPrice.Text);
}
```

Both `Click` event handlers call the `UpdateProduct()` method to synchronize the `mProduct` object with the user input on the form, and then call the `mProduct` object's `Save()` and `Delete()` methods, respectively, to complete the database access work.

Adding the code for the Exit button rounds off the work for version two. Now let's take a look at migrating the whole system to .NET.

Version Three – Go All Out to .NET

The Simple Order version two added more functionality to version one. If it requires further improvements, it's natural to upgrade the whole application to .NET and take advantage of the full power of the .NET framework. Before going ahead, let's look back to the first two versions to see what we could have done better.

One notable flaw is the `Order` class, where the `Save` method creates an order header and several line items. This works well but its quality is not up to the standard we expect in a commercial product. What happens if something goes wrong after it has created the order header record, but before creating the line items or between creating two line items? It will end up creating the header record but not all the items. The common practice to solve this problem is to use a transaction to wrap the creation of all the header and item records. This approach ensures that either the complete order is saved, or no records are created at all. The same goes for the `Delete` method.

There are also other problems. For instance, one cannot use this application to modify an existing order and the user interface is fairly naive and error prone.

Since this is a book about data access, in our redevelopment we will concentrate on using transactions to improve database performance.

The figure below illustrates the relationships among the new .NET components:

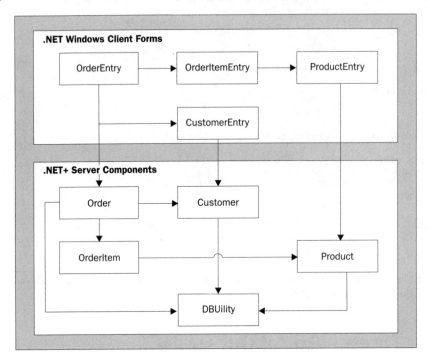

Upgrading Existing Classes

Now that we're moving the whole system to .NET, we can make architectural changes right across the system to benefit from of the framework.

The Middle Tier – SOBizNet

There is some duplicate code in the `Customer` and `Product` classes in version two. For instance, both classes define their own `ExecuteSQLCommand()` methods. Since they are identical, it would be more appropriate to define it in one place. Thinking ahead, there will be at least one other common task – executing SQL `SELECT` queries to retrieve records from the database. It sounds like we need a data access utility class.

Creating the Data Access Utility Class

Let's start by adding a new class called `DBUtility` to the `SOBizNet` assembly:

```
using System;
using System.Data;
using System.Data.SqlClient;

namespace SOBizNet
{
    internal class DBUtility
    {
```

```
        private DBUtility()
        {
            // Don't actually do anything, just to ensure that
            // this class can never be instantiated
        }
    }
}
```

Since only classes in the SOBizNet assembly will use this class, we should declare it as internal. Being a utility class, this class will provide only static methods. Therefore, the client objects don't have to instantiate it in order to use the methods. To help the client objects, we can define the constructor as private so the compiler will ensure that this class will not be instantiated.

Next, we define a constant holding the connection string to the database. In case the methods defined in this class do not provide all the operations required by other classes (as we will see later), it's also a good idea to expose it as a public property. Other classes can then use this property to connect to the database:

```
public static string DBConnString
{
    get { return mcConnString; }
}

private const string mcConnString = "Integrated Security=SSPI;" +
    "Initial Catalog=Northwind;Data Source=(local)";
```

The ExecuteSQLCommand() method will be exactly the same as defined in the Customer and Product classes:

```
public static void ExecuteSQLCommand(string SQLString)
{
    SqlConnection cn = new SqlConnection(DBConnString);

    try
    {
        cn.Open();
        SqlCommand cmd = new SqlCommand(SQLString, cn);
        cmd.ExecuteNonQuery();
    }
    catch (SqlException e)
    {
        throw e;
    }
    finally
    {
        if (cn.State == System.Data.ConnectionState.Open)
        {
            cn.Close();
        }
    }
}
```

There are different methods of retrieving data from a database. Since the DataSet class is always disconnected from the database, it is ideal for passing the retrieved data back to client objects:

```
public static DataSet Read(string SQLString)
{
   SqlConnection cn = new SqlConnection(DBConnString);
   DataSet        ds = new DataSet();

   try
   {
      cn.Open();
      SqlDataAdapter da = new SqlDataAdapter(SQLString, cn);
      da.Fill(ds);
   }
   catch (Exception e)
   {
      throw e;
   }
   finally
   {
      cn.Close();
   }

   return ds;
}
```

This method is simple. First it opens a connection to the database and binds a SqlDataAdapter object to the connection. Next, it uses the data adapter to fill the DataSet with records retrieved with the SQL query passed in with the SQLString argument. If there are any errors, it re-throws the exceptions to the client objects. Finally, it returns the DataSet object.

Upgrading the Customer Class

Recall that the C# Customer class in version two inherits from the COM+ Customer class. We will need to implement the data members, properties, methods, and the Changed event. First import the System.Data namespace to the class:

```
using System;
using System.Data;
using System.Data.SqlClient;
```

This makes it a bit easier to use the DataSet class. Then remove the inheritance declaration:

```
public class Customer    // : SOBizCom.Customer
```

To implement the two data members, mID and mName, and the corresponding public accessors, add the following code to the class:

```
public string ID
{
   set
   {
      mID = value;
   }
   get
   {
      return mID;
   }
```

```
}

public string Name
{
   set
   {
      mName = value;
   }
   get
   {
      return mName;
   }
}

protected string mID;
protected string mName;
```

The process of implementing the Changed event is quite straightforward as well:

```
public delegate void CustomerChangedEventHandler();

public class Customer    // : SOBizCom.Customer
{
   public Customer()
   {}

   public event CustomerChangedEventHandler CustomerChanged;

   public void OnChange()
   {
      if (CustomerChanged != null)
      {
         CustomerChanged();
      }
   }
}
```

Note that now the event is named CustomerChanged, just to make it consistent with the Product class, which names the event ProductChanged.

Next, let's re-work the Read() method to perform database read operation:

```
public void Read(string ID)
{
   string SQLQuery =
            "SELECT CustomerID, CompanyName " +
            "  FROM Customers " +
            " WHERE CustomerID = '" + ID + "'";
   try
   {
      DataSet ds = DBUtility.Read(SQLQuery);
      Populate(ds);
   }
   catch (Exception e)
   {
      throw e;
   }
}
```

```
private void Populate(DataSet ds)
{
    ID = "";
    Name = "";

    if (ds != null)
    {
        DataRowCollection Rows = ds.Tables[0].Rows;
        if (Rows.Count > 0)
        {
            ID   = Rows[0]["CustomerID"].ToString();
            Name = Rows[0]["CompanyName"].ToString();
        }
    }

    OnChange();
}
```

The `Read()` method calls the `DBUtility`'s `Read()` method and passes it the SQL SELECT query. It then assigns the record field values to the corresponding data members using the `Populate` method. If there are any unexpected errors, it just passes it on to the client object.

The `Clear()` method is even simpler, and requires no further explanation:

```
public void Clear()
{
    Populate(null);
}
```

At last, since the `DBUtility` class now defines the `ExecuteSQLCommand()` method, we can delete the `ExecuteSQLCommand()` method and the `mcConnString` constant definitions from the `Customer` class. The `Save()` and `Delete()` methods can call the `DBUtility` object's `ExecuteSQLCommand()` method to execute the relevant SQL commands:

```
public void Save()
{
    Customer Work = new Customer();
    Work.Read(ID);
    // ...
    DBUtility.ExecuteSQLCommand(sqlString);
}

public void Delete()
{
    string sqlString = "DELETE Customers WHERE CustomerID = '" + ID + "'";
    DBUtility.ExecuteSQLCommand(sqlString);
    Clear();
}
```

There is one more change in the `Save()` method: it now defines `Work` as an instance of the current `Customer` class, rather than the COM+ `Customer` class. This class no longer uses the COM+ class.

Upgrading the Product Class

Changes to the `Product` class are quite similar to those to the `Customer` class. Therefore, we won't go into details. The list below highlights the changes made to the `Product` class. The code in version two but not in this version is commented out:

```csharp
using System;
using System.Data;
using System.Data.SqlClient;

namespace SOBizNet
{
    public delegate void ProductChangedEventHandler();

    public class Product
    {
        public Product()
        {
        }

        public event ProductChangedEventHandler ProductChanged;

        public void OnChange()
        {
            if (ProductChanged != null)
            {
                ProductChanged();
            }
        }

        public int ID
        {
            get
            {
                return mID;
            }
            set
            {
                mID = value;
            }
        }

        public string Name
        {
            get
            {
                return mName;
            }
            set
            {
                mName = value;
            }
        }

        public decimal Price
        {
            get
            {
                return mPrice;
            }
            set
            {
                mPrice = value;
            }
        }
```

```csharp
public void Read(int ID)
{
    string SQLQuery =
                "SELECT ProductID, ProductName, UnitPrice" +
                "  FROM Products " +
                " WHERE ProductID = " + ID;

    try
    {
        DataSet ds = DBUtility.Read(SQLQuery);
        Populate(ds);
    }
    catch (Exception e)
    {
        throw e;
    }
}

public void Populate(DataSet ds)
{
    mID   = 0;
    Name  = "";
    Price = 0;

    if (ds != null)
    {
        DataRowCollection Rows = ds.Tables[0].Rows;
        if (Rows.Count > 0)
        {
            DataRow Row = Rows[0];
            mID   = Convert.ToInt32(Row["ProductID"]);
            Name  = Row["ProductName"].ToString();
            Price = Convert.ToDecimal(Row["UnitPrice"]);
        }
    }

    OnChange();
}


public void Save()
{
    Product Work = new Product();
    Work.Read(ID);

    string GoodName = Name.Replace("'", "''");
    string sqlString;
    if (Work.ID == 0)
    {
        // Create a new product record
        SqlConnection cn =
            new SqlConnection(DBUtility.DBConnString);
        cn.Open();

        // ...
    }
    else
    {
        // Update the existing product record
        sqlString = "UPDATE Products " +
```

```
                            "    SET ProductName = '" + GoodName + "', " +
                            "        UnitPrice = " + Price +
                            " WHERE ProductID = " + ID;
               DBUtility.ExecuteSQLCommand(sqlString);
           }

           OnChange();
       }

       public void Delete()
       {
           string sqlString = "DELETE Products WHERE ProductID = " + ID;
           DBUtility.ExecuteSQLCommand(sqlString);

           Populate(null);
       }

       protected int      mID;
       protected string   mName;
       protected decimal  mPrice;

   }
}
```

Now we've fully upgraded both the `Customer` and `Product` classes. The `SOBizNet` assembly no longer needs the references to both the `SOBizCOM` and, implicitly, the VBA run-time libraries. So remove them and rebuild the assembly. To verify that they work as expected, let's upgrade the UI assembly, `SOUINet`.

The User Interface

The two existing Windows Form classes, `ProductEntry` and `CustomerEntry`, were designed to work with middle-tier classes that use different COM+ component extension strategies. As we'll see, they require different modification approaches in order to work with the new C# classes.

Upgrading the ProductEntry Class

Recall that in version two, we designed the C# `Product` class that provided functionality available in its COM+ ancestor by containment. We wrote a bit more code for it, which resulted in cleaner client object, `ProductEntry`. This approach pays off well in this version – we need not modify the `ProductEntry` class at all!

If you followed the steps in developing version two, the `SOUINet` assembly should contain just the `ProductEntry` class with no reference to the `SOBizCom` library. Just rebuild and run it and you will be able to verify that it works well.

Upgrading the CustomerEntry Class

The change to the `CustomerEntry` class is minimal: we only need to change the event handler, `OnCustomerChange`, to subscribe to the `CustomerChanged` event. If you have a separate UI application assembly for the `CustomerEntry` class, open it up and make the following changes:

```
public CustomerEntry()
{
    //
    // Required for Windows Form Designer support
    //
```

```
    InitializeComponent();

    mCustomer = new SOBizNet.Customer();
//  mCustomer.Changed += new
//              SOBizCom.__Customer_ChangedEventHandler(OnCustomerChanged);
    mCustomer.CustomerChanged += new
        SOBizNet.CustomerChangedEventHandler(OnCustomerChanged);
}
```

We can now remove the references to SOBizCom and VBA.

If you use the same UI application assembly for both the ProductEntry and CustomerEntry classes, remove the ProductEntry.cs used in the last section. Then add the CustomerEntry class to it and change it accordingly.

Either way, you can now run it to verify that it works exactly the same as in version two.

Now we have fully upgraded all existing classes, it's time to implement the order entry functionality.

Creating .NET Components from Scratch

Since we've have already figured out how to do it in version one, we're not really starting from scratch. The challenge is to provide the same functionality in .NET, while using .NET's features effectively.

The Middle Tier – SOBizNet

Our task is simple here: simply migrate the two COM+ classes, Order and OrderItem, to C#.

Creating the OrderItem Class

Add a new class, OrderItem, to the SOBizNet assembly and enter the code as listed below:

```
using System;

namespace SOBizNet
{
    public class OrderItem
    {
        public OrderItem(int ProductID, int Quantity)
        {
            mProduct = new SOBizNet.Product();
            this.ProductID = ProductID;
            this.Quantity = Quantity;
        }

        public int ProductID
        {
            set
            {
                mProduct.Read(value);
            }
        }

        public SOBizNet.Product Product
        {
```

```
        get
        {
            return mProduct;
        }
    }

    public decimal Price
    {
        get
        {
            return mProduct.Price;
        }
    }

    public int Quantity
    {
        set
        {
            mQuantity = value;
        }
        get
        {
            return mQuantity;
        }
    }

    public decimal Amount
    {
        get
        {
            return this.Price * this.Quantity;
        }
    }

    protected SOBizNet.Product mProduct   = null;
    protected int                mQuantity = 0;
    }
}
```

The most significant change to the OrderItem class is that now it defines a constructor that accepts two parameters. This overcomes one Visual Basic limitation where it does not allow for defining constructors that have parameters.

Other changes are merely syntactical, the new code is simply the C# equivalent of the VB code we looked at in the first version

Creating the Order Class

Unlike the OrderItem class, which does not contain any methods, the Order class performs database access and order item management. Let's go through it step by step.

First up, the easy bits. Add a new C# class, Order, to the SOBizNet assembly and enter the code for properties and event handlers:

```
using System;
using System.Collections;
using System.Data;
using System.Data.SqlClient;
```

```
namespace SOBizNet
{
   public class Order
   {
      public Order()
      {
         mCustomer = new SOBizNet.Customer();
         mItems    = new ArrayList();
      }

      public int ID
      {
         set
         {
            mID = value;
         }
         get
         {
            return mID;
         }
      }

      public System.DateTime OrderDate
      {
         get
         {
            return mDate;
         }
      }

      public string CustomerID
      {
         set
         {
            mCustomer.Read(value);
         }
      }

      public SOBizNet.Customer Customer
      {
         get
         {
            return mCustomer;
         }
      }

      public ArrayList Items
      {
         get
         {
            return mItems;
         }
      }

      protected SOBizNet.Customer mCustomer = null;
      protected int               mID       = 0;
      protected System.DateTime   mDate     = System.DateTime.Now;
      protected ArrayList         mItems    = null;
   }
}
```

In addition to the syntax changes, there are two minor changes to the Visual Basic version. First, it defines `OrderDate` as `System.DateTime` because C# has no intrinsic date type. Second, it takes advantage of the C# data member initialization feature to initialize all data members.

Next, define a delegate for raising events:

```
namespace SOBizNet
{
    public delegate void OrderChangedEventHandler();

    public class Order
    {
        //...

        public event OrderChangedEventHandler OrderChanged;

        public void OnChange()
        {
            if (OrderChanged != null)
            {
                OrderChanged();
            }
        }
    }
```

One significant change to this class is in the `Read()` and `Populate()` methods. The Visual Basic version uses the ADO `Shape` command to retrieve both the order header and line items in one database query. A natural implementation here is to use the `OleDbDataReader` class that supports hierarchical rowsets. According to the .NET Framework documentation, we can achieve this with the following code.

```
using System.Data.OleDb;

public void Read(int ID)
{
    string OleDBConnString =
            "Provider=MSDataShape;Data Provider=SQLOLEDB;" +
            "Integrated Security=SSPI;" +
            "Initial Catalog=Northwind;Data Source=localhost";

    string SQLQuery =
            "SHAPE " +
            "{" +
            "    SELECT OrderID, CustomerID, OrderDate " +
            "    FROM Orders WHERE OrderID = " + ID.ToString() +
            "} " +
            "APPEND " +
            "(" +
            "    {" +
            "        SELECT OrderID, ProductID, UnitPrice, Quantity " +
            "        FROM [Order Details]" +
            "    } " +
            "    AS rsItems " +
            "    RELATE OrderID TO OrderID" +
            ")";

    OleDbConnection cn = new OleDbConnection(OleDBConnString);
    cn.Open();
```

```
    OleDbCommand cmd = new OleDbCommand(SQLQuery, cn);
    OleDbDataReader OrderReader = cmd.ExecuteReader();

    Populate(OrderReader);

    OrderReader.Close();
    cn.Close();
}

private void Populate(OleDbDataReader OrderReader)
{
    OleDbDataReader      ItemReader = null;
    SOBizNet.OrderItem Item         = null;

    mID = 0;
    Customer.Clear();
    mDate = System.DateTime.Now;
    mItems.Clear();

    if (OrderReader != null)
    {
        while (OrderReader.Read())
        {
            mID = OrderReader.GetInt32(0);
            CustomerID = OrderReader.GetString(1);
            mDate = OrderReader.GetDateTime(2);

            ItemReader = (OleDbDataReader)OrderReader.GetValue(3);
            while (ItemReader.Read())
            {
                Item = new SOBizNet.OrderItem(ItemReader.GetInt32(1),
                                              ItemReader.GetInt16(3));
                mItems.Add(Item);
            }
            ItemReader.Close();
        }
    }
    OnChange();
}
```

While this appears to work in the RC1 release, .NET Beta 2 has a bug that prevents the above code from working as expected, so if using Beta 2 a single SQL JOIN statement is needed to fetch the records as shown below:

```
public void Read(int ID)
{
    string SQLQuery =
        "SELECT Orders.OrderID, Orders.CustomerID, Orders.OrderDate," +
        "        OrderDetails.ProductID, OrderDetails.UnitPrice," +
        "        OrderDetails.Quantity" +
        "  FROM Orders INNER JOIN" +
        "        [Order Details] OrderDetails" +
        "        ON Orders.OrderID = OrderDetails.OrderID" +
        " WHERE (Orders.OrderID = " + ID.ToString() + ")";

    try
    {
        DataSet ds = DBUtility.Read(SQLQuery);
        Populate(ds);
```

```
        }
        catch (Exception e)
        {
            throw e;
        }
    }
```

Apart from the different query string, this method is the same as the `Read()` method in the `Product` class. The `Populate()` method is slightly different:

```
private void Populate(DataSet ds)
{
    mID = 0;
    Customer.Clear();
    mDate = System.DateTime.Now;
    mItems.Clear();

    if (ds != null)
    {
        DataRowCollection Rows = ds.Tables[0].Rows;
        if (Rows.Count > 0)
        {
            DataRow Row0 = Rows[0];
            mID = Convert.ToInt32(Row0["OrderID"]);
            CustomerID = Row0["CustomerID"].ToString();;
            mDate = Convert.ToDateTime(Row0["OrderDate"]);
            foreach (DataRow Row in Rows)
            {
                OrderItem Item =
                    new OrderItem(Convert.ToInt32(Row["ProductID"]),
                            Convert.ToInt16(Row["Quantity"]));
                mItems.Add(Item);
            }
        }
    }

    OnChange();
}
```

This gets the order header fields from the first row, and then loops through all rows to retrieve item records.

The `Clear()` and `AddItem()` methods are mostly simple conversions of the Visual Basic 6 versions:

```
public void Clear()
{
    Populate(null);
}

public void AddItem(int ProductID, int Quantity)
{
    SOBizNet.OrderItem Item =
        new SOBizNet.OrderItem(ProductID, Quantity);
    mItems.Add(Item);
    OnChange();
}
```

The next method is the `Save()` method, which saves a new order that consists of a header record and a set of item records. A common requirement for updating the database is that the operation must maintain data integrity. For instance, the complete order must be saved. Saving the order header but not the items is not acceptable. We get around this problem using **transactions**, which ensure that a whole set of operations succeed or fail as one operation – they are never partially fulfilled. We can also create **constraints** to ensure that relationships are maintained.

> There are two ways to ensure data integrity: transactions and constraints. Transactions treat several database operations as a single operation, that either suceeds or fails as a whole. Constraints can ensure that orphan records do not exist – for example that no order items exist without a corresponding order header.

ADO.NET offers two transaction classes, `System.Data.SqlClient.SqlTransaction` and `System.Data.OleDbClient.OleDbTransaction`, which provide methods to create, commit, and roll back transactions. For the Simple Order application that uses Microsoft SQL Server and therefore `SQLClient`, we use the `SqlTransaction` class. Let's have a look at how to implement transaction processing in the `Save()` method:

```
public void Save()
{
    SqlConnection cn = new SqlConnection(SOBizNet.DBUtility.DBConnString);
    cn.Open();

    SqlTransaction trans = cn.BeginTransaction();
```

The first step is to establish a database connection, and then invoke the connection object's `BeginTransaction()` method to create a transaction for this connection.

Once a transaction has begun, we perform a set of database operations. If everything goes to plan, we commit the changes to the database by calling the tranasaction's `Commit()` method. If anything goes wrong, calling the `Rollback()` method will roll back (undo) all changes.

One of the better ways of managing this process is to wrap all database operations in a `try` block. If all operations complete without error, we commit the change and exit the `try` block. Otherwise, the corresponding `catch` statement will catch any exceptions. We can then roll back the transaction:

```
try
{
    // perform database operations
    trans.Commit();
}
catch (Exception e)
{
    trans.Rollback();
}
```

In our class's `Save()` method, we create the order header record first using the same `spAddOrder` stored procedure used in version one. Next we create all item records. If both succeed, we commit the transaction:

```
try
{
    SqlCommand cmd = new SqlCommand("spAddOrder", cn, trans);
    cmd.CommandType = System.Data.CommandType.StoredProcedure;

    SqlParameter param = cmd.Parameters.Add("ID",
                                System.Data.SqlDbType.Int);
    param.Direction = System.Data.ParameterDirection.ReturnValue ;

    param = cmd.Parameters.Add("@CustomerID",
                                System.Data.SqlDbType.Char, 5);
    param.Direction = System.Data.ParameterDirection.Input;
    param.Value = mCustomer.ID;

    param = cmd.Parameters.Add("@OrderDate",
                                System.Data.SqlDbType.DateTime);
    param.Direction = System.Data.ParameterDirection.Output;

    cmd.ExecuteNonQuery();
    ID = Convert.ToInt32(cmd.Parameters["ID"].Value.ToString(), 10);
    mDate = Convert.ToDateTime(cmd.Parameters["@OrderDate"].Value);
```

The above code snippet instantiates a `SqlCommand` object and binds it to the previously created connection and the transaction. It then adds three parameters: the order `ID` return value; the `CustomerID` input parameter; and the `OrderDate` output parameter. Calling the command object's `ExecuteNonQuery()` method executes the stored procedure, `spAddOrder`, to save the header record.

After the record has been created, the `ID` parameter stores the automatically generated order ID value. The above code assigns this value to the `ID` property. Similarly, it assigns to the `mDate` variable the order creation time stored in the `@OrderData` parameter.

The next step is to save all item records.

```
foreach (OrderItem Item in mItems)
{
    string SQLQuery =
        "INSERT INTO [Order Details] " +
        "(OrderID, ProductID, UnitPrice, Quantity) " +
        "VALUES " +
        "(" + mID.ToString() + ", " +
            Item.Product.ID.ToString() + ", " +
            Item.Price.ToString() + ", " +
            Item.Quantity.ToString() +
        ")";

    cmd.CommandText = SQLQuery;
    cmd.CommandType = System.Data.CommandType.Text;
    cmd.ExecuteNonQuery();
}
```

The above code snippet loops through the item array and executes a SQL `INSERT` command for each item record. If all records are saved successfully, it will commit the transaction.

```
            trans.Commit();
            OnChange();
        }
```

Once the `Commit()` method has been completed, the `Save()` method calls the `OnChange()` method, which raises the `OrderChanged` event to inform all client objects about the order state change.

If any of the above operation fail, SQL Server will raise an error. The .NET CLR will then throw an exception for that error. The `Save()` method will catch such exceptions in the `catch` block as shown below.

```
        catch (Exception e)
        {
            trans.Rollback();
            throw e;
        }
```

The `catch` block rolls back the transaction to reverse any changes to the database. It then re-throws the exception to the client object. In a commercial quality application, the `Save` method typically tries to recover from such exceptions before giving in. In this program, simply re-throwing the exception is adequate.

Regardless of the outcome of the transaction, the `Save()` method closes the connection to release it in the `finally` block shown below.

```
        finally
        {
            cn.Close();
        }
    }
```

The `Delete()` method uses the same technique to delete an order:

```
public void Delete()
{
    SqlConnection cn = new SqlConnection(SOBizNet.DBUtility.DBConnString);
    cn.Open();

    SqlTransaction trans = cn.BeginTransaction();
    string SQLQuery;

    try
    {
        SQLQuery =
            "DELETE [Order Details] WHERE OrderID = " + ID.ToString();
        SqlCommand cmd = new SqlCommand(SQLQuery, cn, trans);
        cmd.CommandText = SQLQuery;
        cmd.ExecuteNonQuery();

        SQLQuery = "DELETE Orders WHERE OrderID = " + ID.ToString();
        cmd.CommandText = SQLQuery;
        cmd.ExecuteNonQuery();

        trans.Commit();
        Clear();
    }
    catch (Exception e)
```

```
    {
        trans.Rollback();
        throw e;
    }
    finally
    {
        cn.Close();
    }
}
```

The `Delete()` method first deletes all item records and then deletes the header record. If all operations complete successfully, it commits the transaction and calls the `Clear()` method to reset all data members and informs the client objects about the change. Otherwise, it rolls back the transaction.

We've now completed the `Order` and `OrderItem` classes. The last task is to create the user interface assembly, `SOUINet`.

The User Interface – SOUINet

As in version one, we need to provide two Windows Form classes to allow for displaying, creating, and deleting orders. The new `OrderEntry` form will be the startup form for the `SOUINet` assembly. It will load the other forms as required.

So, remove the `CustomerEntry` class from the assembly; we'll add it (and the `ProductEntry` class) back in after we've completed the `OrderEntry` and `OrderItemEntry` forms.

Creating the OrderItemEntry Class

Add a new Windows Form, `OrderItemEntry`, to the `SOUINet` assembly and the following controls to it:

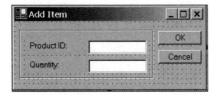

Control Type	Property	Property Value
Form	Text	Add Item
GroupBox	Text	[Blank]
Label	Text	Product ID:
Textbox	Name	txtProductID
	Text	[Blank]
Label	Text	Quantity:
Textbox	Name	txtQuantity

Table continued on following page

645

Control Type	Property	Property Value
	Text	[Blank]
Button	Name	btnOK
	Text	OK
Button	Name	btnCancel
	Text	Cancel

This form will raise an event, OrderItemChanged, when the user clicks the **OK** button:

```
namespace SOUINet
{
   public delegate void
      OrderItemChangedEventHandler(int ProductID, int Quantity);

   public class OrderItemEntry : System.Windows.Forms.Form
   {
      // ...
      public event OrderItemChangedEventHandler OrderItemChanged;

      public void OnChange()
      {
         if (OrderItemChanged != null)
         {
            OrderItemChanged(ProductID, Quantity);
         }
      }

      private int ProductID
      {
         get
         {
            return System.Convert.ToInt32(txtProductID.Text, 10);
         }
      }

      private int Quantity
      {
         get
         {
            return System.Convert.ToInt32(txtQuantity.Text, 10);
         }
      }
   }
}
```

The OnChange() method gets the product ID and order quantity from the textboxes, and raises the OrderItemChanged event.

When the client object, the OrderEntry form in this version, displays the OrderItemEntry form, both the ProductID and Quantity textboxes should be set to blank. We normally do this in the form's constructor. However, since the OrderEntry form may display and hide this form frequently, and loading and unloading forms is relatively time-consuming, it's better to load and unload this form only once.

After the `OrderEntry` form loads this form for the first time, we can hide it once the user clicks the **OK** or **Cancel** button. The next time the user clicks the **Add Item** button on the `OrderEntry` form, we can display the form by calling its `Show()` method without having to load it again. This makes the application more responsive.

We should therefore create a handler for the form's `Activated` event, which is raised each time the form is shown with the `Show()` method. To do so, click the **Events** button in the **Properties** window and type in OrderItemEntry_Activated in the field next to the **Activated** event, as shown in the figure below:

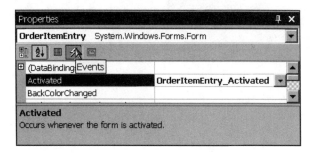

We can then add code to clear those textboxes in the following event handler:

```
private void OrderItemEntry_Activated(object sender, System.EventArgs e)
{
    txtProductID.Text = "";
    txtQuantity.Text = "";
}
```

Now double-click the **OK** and **Cancel** buttons and add the code below to their event handlers:

```
private void btnOK_Click(object sender, System.EventArgs e)
{
    OnChange();
    this.Hide();
}

private void btnCancel_Click(object sender, System.EventArgs e)
{
    this.Hide();
}
```

Clicking the **OK** button will raise the `OrderItemChanged` event and hide the form from view. Clicking the **Cancel** button simply hides the form.

Creating the OrderEntry Class

Now add a new Windows Form, `OrderEntry`, to the `SOUINet` assembly. As we're adding a new form to an existing assembly, we need to add the `Main()` method ourselves:

```
[STAThread]
static void Main()
{
    Application.Run(new OrderEntry());
}
```

The look and feel of this form will be very similar to its ancestor in version one, adding a couple of buttons to load the `ProductEntry` and `CustomerEntry` forms. In the form designer, add the following controls:

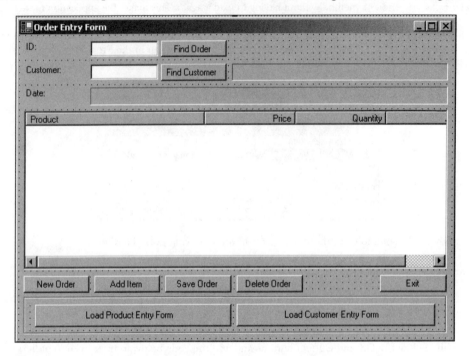

Here are the names and property values of the controls on the form:

Control Type	Property	Property Value
Label	Text	ID:
Textbox	Name	txtOrderID
	Text	[Blank]
Button	Name	btnFind
	Text	Find Order
Label	Text	Customer:
Textbox	Name	txtCustomerID
	Text	[Blank]
Button	Name	btnFindCustomer
	Text	Find Customer
Label	Name	lblCustomerName
	Text	[Blank]

Control Type	Property	Property Value
	BorderStyle	Fixed3D
Label	Text	Date:
Label	Name	lblDate
	Text	[Blank]
	BorderStyle	Fixed3D
ListView	Name	lvwItems
	View	Details
	Columns	
	Name	columnHeader1
	Text	Product
	TextAlign	Left
	Name	columnHeader2
	Text	Price
	TextAlign	Right
	Name	columnHeader3
	Text	Quantity
	TextAlign	Right
	Name	columnHeader4
	Text	Amount
	TextAlign	Right
Button	Name	btnNew
	Text	New Order
Button	Name	btnAddItem
	Text	Add Item
Button	Name	btnSave
	Text	&Save
Button	Name	btnDelete
	Text	Delete
Button	Name	btnExit

Table continued on following page

Control Type	Property	Property Value
	Text	Exit
GroupBox	Text	[Blank]
Button	Name	btnLoadProductEntryForm
	Text	Load Product Entry Form
Button	Name	btnLoadCustomerEntryForm
	Text	Load Customer Entry Form

First, we declare two references, mOrder and mOrderItemEntry, to the Order class and the OrderItemEntry form:

```
namespace SOUINet
{
    public class OrderEntry : System.Windows.Forms.Form
    {
        // ...

        private SOBizNet.Order          mOrder     = null;
        private SOUINet.OrderItemEntry mItemEntry = null;

        public OrderEntry()
        {
            //
            // Required for Windows Form Designer support
            //
            InitializeComponent();

            mOrder = new SOBizNet.Order();
            mOrder.OrderChanged +=
                new SOBizNet.OrderChangedEventHandler(OnOrderChanged);

            mItemEntry = new SOUINet.OrderItemEntry();
            mItemEntry.OrderItemChanged +=
                new SOUINet.OrderItemChangedEventHandler(OnItemChanged);
        }

        // ...
        private void OnItemChanged(int ProductID, int Quantity)
        {
            mOrder.AddItem(ProductID, Quantity);
        }

        private void OnOrderChanged()
        {
            PopulateControls();
        }
    }
}
```

When the `OrderEntry` form receives the `OnItemChanged` event from the `OrderItemEntry` form, it adds a new item to the `mOrder` object by calling its `AddItem()` method and passing in the `ProductID` and `Quantity` values. The `Order` class's `AddItem()` method will then raise an `OrderChanged` event, which triggers the `OnOrderChange()` method. This method in turn calls the `PopulateControls()` method listed below:

```
private void PopulateControls()
{
    ListViewItem    lvwItem    = null;

    txtOrderID.Text = mOrder.ID.ToString();
    txtCustomerID.Text = mOrder.Customer.ID;
    lblCustomerName.Text = mOrder.Customer.Name;
    lblDate.Text = mOrder.OrderDate.ToString();

    lvwItems.Items.Clear();
    foreach (SOBizNet.OrderItem orderItem in mOrder.Items)
    {
        lvwItem = lvwItems.Items.Add(orderItem.Product.Name);
        lvwItem.SubItems.Add(orderItem.Price.ToString());
        lvwItem.SubItems.Add(orderItem.Quantity.ToString());
        lvwItem.SubItems.Add(orderItem.Amount.ToString());
    }
}
```

The `PopulateControls()` method displays the order ID, customer ID, name, and order date controls on the form. It then loops through each order item to populate the list view.

Next, double-click on each command button to program their event handlers:

```
private void btnFind_Click(object sender, System.EventArgs e)
{
    mOrder.Read(OrderID);
}

private int OrderID
{
    get { return System.Convert.ToInt32(txtOrderID.Text, 10); }
}
```

The `Find` button's event handler calls the `mOrder` object's `Read()` method and passes in the order ID entered in the `txtOrderID` textbox. The `Order` class' `Read()` method reads the order records from the database and raises the `OrderChanged` event, which triggers the `PopulateControls()` method to display the order details in the form.

To create a new order, the user clicks the **New Order** button. The `OrderEntry` form will then call `mOrder`'s `Clear()` method to reset its data members. The `Clear()` method also raises the `OrderChanged` event, which is captured to clear the form controls:

```
private void btnNew_Click(object sender, System.EventArgs e)
{
    mOrder.Clear();
}
```

The user can enter a customer ID, and optionally gets the name of the specified customer by clicking the **Find Customer** button:

```
private void btnFindCustomer_Click(object sender, System.EventArgs e)
{
    mOrder.CustomerID = txtCustomerID.Text;
    txtCustomerID.Text = mOrder.Customer.ID;
    lblCustomerName.Text = mOrder.Customer.Name;
}
```

The user can then click the **Add Item** button to add products to the order:

```
private void btnAddItem_Click(object sender, System.EventArgs e)
{
    mItemEntry.Show();
}
```

This method displays the `OrderItemEntry` form for the user to specify the product ID and order quantity. If the user clicks the **OK** button on the `OrderItemEntry` form, the `OrderItemChanged` event is raised. As described previously, this adds the new item to the order and displays it in the list view, `lvwItems`.

After adding in all items, the user can save the order by clicking the **Save** button:

```
private void btnSave_Click(object sender, System.EventArgs e)
{
    mOrder.CustomerID = txtCustomerID.Text;
    mOrder.Save();
}
```

This method assigns the customer ID, in case the user has not done it by clicking the **Find Customer** button. It then calls the `mOrder` object's `Save()` method to save the order to the database.

If the user decides to delete an existing order, they can enter the order ID and then click the **Delete** button:

```
private void btnDelete_Click(object sender, System.EventArgs e)
{
    mOrder.Read(OrderID);
    mOrder.Delete();
}
```

This method reads in the order from the database and then calls `mOrder`'s `Delete()` method to delete it from the database.

Finalizing the UI

One of our last jobs is to add the `CustomerEntry` and `ProductEntry` forms back into the assembly and delete their static `Main()` methods, if there are any. This will give users the ability to maintain customers and products. The last two buttons, `btnLoadCustomerEntryForm` and `btnLoadProductEntryForm` do just that.

To ensure things work correctly we need to change the event handlers of the re-inserted forms' exit buttons as listed here:

```
    private void btnExit_Click(object sender, System.EventArgs e)
    {
// Application.Exit();
    this.Close();
    }
```

Thus instead of terminating the application, they simply close themselves.

That's it. Our Simple Order application version three is now complete. We can now build the assemblies and try them out.

Other Migration Issues

So far, we have seen how to migrate existing COM+ applications and components to .NET. This case study shows how .NET client objects can use existing COM+ server components. We haven't covered using .NET server components in COM+ clients.

Compared to using COM+ server components in .NET clients, this scenario is less common. If you find a need to improve an existing COM+ client application by using .NET components, you will want to take a look at another .NET facility called COM-Callable Wrapper (CCW). It plays a reverse role to the Runtime-Callable Wrapper (RCW). When a COM/COM+ client calls a .NET object, the CLR creates a CCW for the managed .NET object. This CCW transparently translates and marshals method invocations, exceptions, and events between the COM client and the .NET server object. The .NET framework documentation contains extensive information on this subject.

Summary

Moving to the .NET famework and Visual Studio .NET will allow us to integrate, reuse, and upgrade existing COM+ applications in new .NET applications. This case study has presented some useful techniques that we can use to perform those tasks.

We have seen the two techniques for using and extending COM+ components in .NET components. The first technique is to inherit a COM+ class in a .NET class. This makes it simple to reuse the existing functionality in the derived class. Very little code new needs to be written for the new .NET class. However, it has the drawback of requiring the client objects of the .NET class to know about the interface of the COM+ class. As we've seen, this means that we need to put in more effort to make the client objects work properly.

On the other hand, we can also design our new .NET class to contain a COM+ class in order to provide the existing functionality. This technique requires a bit more work in the .NET class, as we may need to create a wrapper method for each public function in the COM+ class. We will also need to catch the COM+ events and raise corresponding .NET events. Such efforts are generally offset by the reduction of work required in the client classes of the .NET classes. Usually, we only need to code the wrapper class once and use it in many client classes, so this technique will generally result in less overall development time.

We have also used many of the features of ADO.NET, including transactions, using stored procedures, and `DataSets`. While ADO already provides those features, ADO.NET has made performing such tasks more flexible.

16

Case Study III: Working with Legacy Systems

Recent years have seen the release of a number of technologies that facilitate integration of Internet solutions with mission-critical and other kinds of legacy systems. The challenge for developers consists in integrating old applications written using languages such as COBOL with Internet applications, while preserving the availability and scalability characteristics typical of the Internet solutions. The most common issues that need to be resolved are:

❑ **Availability** – An Internet application is on-line 24/7, unlike many legacy applications. We have to find a way to contact legacy systems even when they are not physically available (for example during nightly maintenance).

❑ **Performance**– An Internet application has many users that may require information using a lot of database connections. The majority of legacy systems don't allow many simultaneous connections.

❑ **Scalability** – Users of Internet applications expect rapid feedback. Legacy systems are usually connected through Wide Area Networks (WANs) so the information-querying phase is not necessarily as fast as desired.

There are also less obvious problems, other than those above, that could be raised by particular legacy systems. For example, some legacy applications still use flat files, comma-or tab-separated text files to store and exchange data. Also, some kinds of operations are still done manually.

In this case study we will examine some possible solutions to the above issues namely:

❑ The Microsoft Message Queuing service

❑ Microsoft Host Integration Server 2000

Our case study scenario is based around a store selling computer products, which wants to become Internet-enabled and improve communications with its warehouse. All the code is available for download from www.wrox.com, and the approach in this chapter is to highlight some of the important and interesting aspects of the code, rather than provide an exhaustive listing.

> *Please note the sample application is based around SQL Server 2000 and requires Message Queuing to be installed. The application was originally created using Visual Studio Beta 2.*

The Computer Products Store

Consider a computer product store that wants to use Internet e-commerce solutions to increase its sales. It uses a COBOL application to manage its central warehouse database installed on an IBM AS/400 system. The quantity of every product that has been sold is maintained in the warehouse database to keep the product inventory status current.

We will start by building a simple e-commerce site selling computer products such as monitors, hard disks and so on. The Internet application will contact the legacy application running in the company's warehouse to order a new stock of products when the local store is running low. We will look at how to use MSMQ, which allows us to send asynchronous requests. In this way, we can show the exact availability of the product and send a request for new products. We will use XML documents in both systems, to exchange ADO.NET `DataSets` filled with product data.

Our first solution will still involve some human interaction to mediate between the new and old systems. In our second section we will see how Microsoft Host Integration Server 2000 makes things easier by allowing developers to interface directly with legacy applications' databases, by providing specific OLE DB data objects. Also, Microsoft Host Integration Server 2000 contains all that is necessary to communicate with legacy systems through its own enhanced System Network Architecture (SNA) services and MSMQ bridges to IBM mainframe queues systems.

Before we build the computer products store, let's start by looking at its homepage:

Above you can see the screenshot of the ASP.NET application showing some offers in the center of the page and allowing customers to search for specific products as well. In order to display a more descriptive product page, we select the more--> link, as shown in the next screen:

This is the first page we encounter with some code working behind it. The original price and store price of the selected product will be inserted dynamically in the upper-right corner of the page. In the lower-left corner of the page the user can see how many units of the product are available in the store.

Now that we've had a quick look at the web site, let's go on to create it.

Creating the BLTStore Site

The BLTStore web site is a three-tier application using Microsoft SQL Server 2000 as a database server, Internet Information Server 5 and Microsoft Windows 2000 Server as web servers, and requires Microsoft Internet Explorer 5.x (or above) as the client application. Windows 2000 Server will use Message Queuing services to exchange product orders.

Our first step is to create the SQL Server database and the table that stores the product information. We will use SQL Server Enterprise Manager to accomplish this.

In the code download for this chapter, you will find the `BltStore.BAK` *and* `readme.txt` *files to create the BLTStore database and everything you need to run the web site.*

The following screenshot shows the `tabProducts` table used by the web application to manage every product sold by the store:

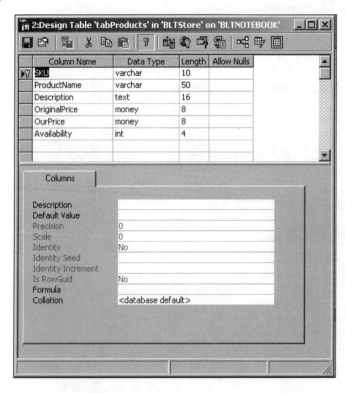

As can be seen, there are six columns in the `tabProducts` table, which are described in the following table:

Column Name	Description
SKU	The product unique code identifier – it is also the primary key
ProductName	Contains the name of the product
Description	Contains a product's description
OriginalPrice	Contains the manufacturer product's price
OurPrice	Contains the BLTStore product's price
Availability	Equal to the number of products available in the shop

The second step involves creating the web site application. Visual Studio was used to create a C# Web Application and the `default.aspx` and `hipzip.aspx pages.`

You can copy these pages along with the images and assemblies in the download code into the BltStore directory within the Inetpub\wwwroot directory. From the Control Panel | Administrative Tools menu, choose Internet Services Manager and create a new virtual site behind the default web site called BltStore. Now, by pointing your browser to http://localhost/BltStore you should see the BltStore's homepage.

Let's look at the code behind the ASPX pages to understand how the product availability counter is generated.

In the `hipzip.aspx` page (called by the more--> link) is the code that manages the product counter generation. The `Page_Init()` event, raised the first time that the ASP.NET page is loaded, is the best place to put some initializing code. The code starts by creating a `DataSet` object used to store the query result retrieved by the `Fill()` method of the `DataAdapter`, `daProducts`:

```
private void Page_Init(object sender, EventArgs e)
{
    // Connection to local database to retrieve
    // page information
    DataSet dsProduct = new DataSet("Product");
    daProducts.Fill(dsProduct);
```

Note: The daProducts object and the connection to the database object used in the page are Visual Studio .NET data components. They are declared and initialized in the #region #end region zone created by Visual Studio .NET.

The following query is used by the `Fill()` method of `daProducts` in order to fill the specified `DataSet` object. This query is very simple and it will only retrieve the record associated with the `SKU` of `HIPZIPS001`:

```
SELECT ProductName, Description, OriginalPrice, OurPrice, Availability, SKU
FROM tabProducts
WHERE (SKU = \'HIPZIPS001\')
```

Note: If you have correctly reproduced the database using the BltStore.BAK backup file, you will find this record in the tabProducts table.

The next piece of code simply inserts the product prices into the page. It uses two ASP.NET label controls, lbOriginalPrice and lbOurPrice, where we can specify the text to display dynamically, reading it from our DataSet. Because we have used a query that retrieves just a record, we can point to the zero-indexed row within the DataSet:

```
// Retrieves just the first row
// so we can use a fixed index.
lbOriginalPrice.Text = "$" +
dsProduct.Tables[0].Rows[0]["OriginalPrice"].ToString();
lbOurPrice.Text = "$" +
   dsProduct.Tables[0].Rows[0]["OurPrice"].ToString();
```

The final part checks the availability of the product, coloring the text of the third ASP.NET label control, lbAvailability, within the page in three different ways, the first of which is green for optimum product availability (greater than 100 units):

```
// Check the availability
int iAvailability = (int) dsProduct.Tables[0].Rows[0]["Availability"];

// If it is more than 100 pieces
if (iAvailability > 100)
{
   // Green text
   lbAvailability.ForeColor = Color.Green;
```

Then yellow for good availability (between 10 and 100 units),

```
}
else
{
   // If it is more than 10 pieces
   if (iAvailability > 10)
      // Yellow text
      lbAvailability.ForeColor = Color.Yellow;
```

Finally, the label is red for an insufficient availability (less than 10 units).

```
else
{
   // If it is more than 0 pieces
   if (iAvailability > 0)
   {
      // Red text
      lbAvailability.ForeColor = Color.Red;
```

When the selected product is not available in the local store, the code changes the appearance of the Add to my cart button so that it appears blurred and is disabled:

```
      // Send request to warehouse
      SendMessageForOrder("HIPZIPS001",100);
   }
```

```
        else
        {
            // Add to cart button disabled
            btnAddCart.Enabled = false;
            btnAddCart.ImageUrl = "images/add_cart_dis.gif";
            btnAddCart.AlternateText = "Sorry, the product is not
                                    + "available.";
        }
    }
}

    lbAvailability.Text = iAvailability.ToString();
}
```

The following screenshot shows how the web page would appear when the product is not available:

Message Queuing

When a product is running low, an automatic script will send a request to the warehouse, where an automated system will make provisions to send back more stock. The following diagram illustrates this scenario:

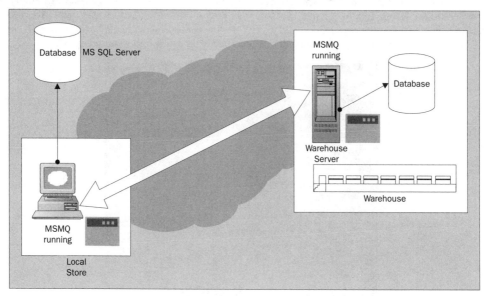

In the diagram we can see a hypothetical WAN where a .NET web server (for example Internet Information Server 5.0), in the bottom left corner, is connected to the warehouse server (for example, Windows 2000 server), in the top right corner. Each server has its own database for retrieving and managing the data, and a Message Queuing service to exchange information. By connecting to the web server, a user can purchase a specific product, thus reducing its availability in the local store. When the product amount drops to below 10 units, the ASP.NET page contacts the warehouse server requesting more units.

Here we stumble across the availability issue identified at the head of the chapter – what happens if the warehouse database is contacted during maintenance? Or worse, what happens if the WAN is overloaded and the warehouse server cannot be contacted? One possibility is that the request will be lost and the web application has to wait for another user requiring the same product. Clearly, this is not a viable solution.

In Chapter 10 we looked at the Microsoft Message Queuing service (MSMQ), which allows programs to exchange information in an asynchronous way. This provides a great way to address the problem.

Imagine that the warehouse server has been switched off for hardware upgrading operations and it is not contactable. Some customers buy the same product and a new message is queued requiring new product units. In this case MSMQ will store the product's supply request in the message queue. As soon as the warehouse server is restored, the messaging service will deliver the message, activating the product supply process.

Installing and Configuring the MSMQ Service

Working with MSMQ is not hard but involves some installation and configuration to establish communication between the servers.

First, we have to specify a primary domain controller where we configure the Active Directory services. I chose to install Windows 2000 Advanced Server on the store server (called BLTNOTEBOOK) as the primary domain controller, and Windows 2000 Server on the warehouse server (called BLTNET).

The second step is to add a computer and a user in the Active Directory database in order to connect the warehouse server to the domain. From Control Panel | Administrative Tools choose Active Directory Users and Computers. Then, to add BLTNET computer and the WAREHOUSE_SERVER user to the Active Directory database, firstly choose the New | Computer menu from the context menu that appears from right-clicking the Computers tree node. In the resulting dialog box specify the name of the computer to be added.

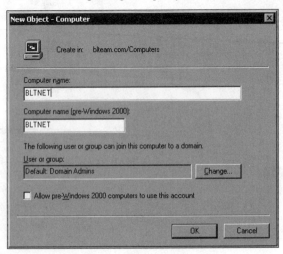

Next choose New | User from the same context menu and, in the resulting dialog box, specify user properties such as the First name, the Last name and so on. Full Name and User logon name are mandatory fields and must have the user's full name, and username to use when connecting to the server.

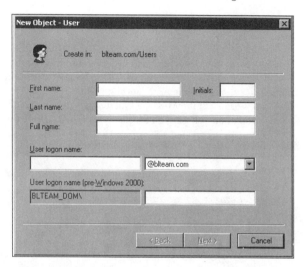

After the Next button is clicked, we are required to specify the user's first Password and choose options such as whether they have to change it after the first logon.

At this point a screen similar to that shown should be viewable, showing that the computer and user has been added.

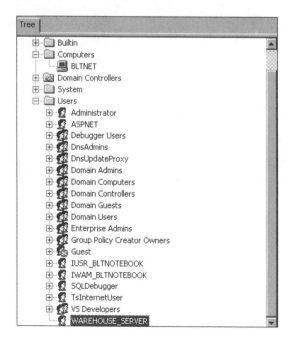

By default the Windows 2000 server installation doesn't include the messaging service so you have to add it in a second step. From the Control Panel choose Add/Remove Programs, then the Add/Remove Windows Components, and check the Message Queuing Services box

> *Please note that you have to use an account with administrator privileges in order to install the Message Queuing service.*

The store server will be configured as the Message Queuing server and the warehouse server as the dependent client. In this way, the warehouse server can check the store queue in order to retrieve the messages and manage them. You can choose the installation type in the second step of the Message Queue service installation (the first step is to install the Message Queuing service on the domain controller server, because the dependent client installation will ask you to specify a domain where the MSMQ is installed):

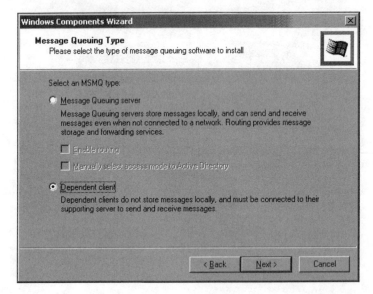

When installation is complete we will have to add two private queues in the primary domain controller's messaging services, where the messages will be exchanged between the store and warehouse servers. The private queue, as the name implies, is a private communication channel where the messages are only read by the users specified in the security dialog box.

Open the Active Directory Users and Computers management console, select the View menu and check the Users, Groups, and Computers as containers and Advanced Features items:

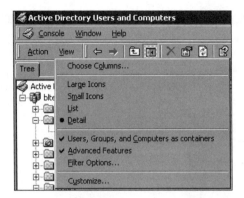

A new group of selectable tree nodes will appear; you can see the msmq node under the Domain Controllers parent node:

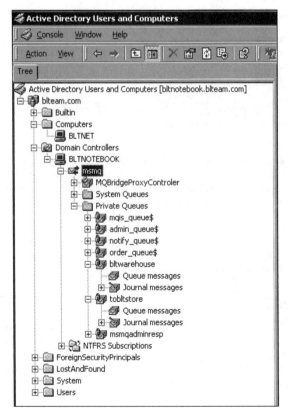

You can use this management console to customize some message queuing properties like limiting the storage space for the messages. However, from here you can't add a new private queue. To do that, run the Computer Management console from the Administration Tools and find the Message Queuing node under the Services and Applications parent tree node:

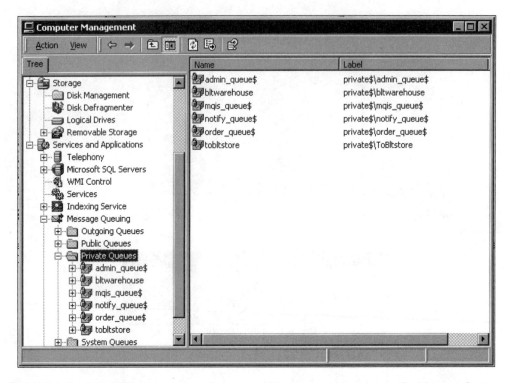

Right-click the **Private Queues** node and you can add a new private queue to the Message Queuing service queues. As you can see from the screenshot, the `bltwarehouse` and `tobltstore` private queues have been added to the private queues folder. The former will be used to store messages from the BLTStore web site when new product units are required. The latter will be used by the warehouse server to store messages confirming the shipping of new product units.

> **Remember to add the warehouse user to the queue security access list, otherwise you will encounter an error when you try to manage a message in the queue.**

The Applications

After installing and configuring the Message Queuing service on the two servers we can start to write the applications that will manage the communications between the servers and their respective queues. First, we have a Windows application running on the warehouse server that will show every request for new products. This application will have a **Send** button that will send a new message to the store confirming the shipping of the required quantity for that product. Naturally, this step will be accomplished after all the preliminary operations are done (passing the order to the storekeepers, product packing, and so on).

The second application is a Windows service running on the store server, listening for every new incoming message. The service will update the product availability number in the database.

ASP.NET Code

As we have seen in the first part of the chapter, the ASP.NET code will call the `SendMessageForOrder()` method when the number of available units falls below 10. Now, let's analyze the code in the `hipzip.aspx` page of the web site application.

The method starts by looking for the private queue called `bltwarehouse` used to store the messages used by the warehouse server. If the queue doesn't exist, the code creates a new one and then instantiates an object used to manage it. Note that the `MessageQueue` object used in the code is declared within the `System.Messaging` namespace:

```
private void SendMessageForOrder(string sku, string name, int qty)
{
    // If the queue doesn't exist, create a new one.
    if (!MessageQueue.Exists(@".\Private$\bltwarehouse"))
        MessageQueue.Create(@".\Private$\bltwarehouse");

    // Retrieve the queue object
    MessageQueue queue = new MessageQueue(@".\Private$\bltwarehouse");
```

The method retrieves all the messages in the queue to look for all the messages relating to the same product. This check is necessary because the method is called each time that users visit the ASP.NET page and the product quantity is low. If a message for the selected (but scarce) product has been already sent, the code will not send a new one:

```
    // Filter the messages to retrieve only the
    // Label property
    MessagePropertyFilter mpf = new MessagePropertyFilter();
    mpf.ClearAll();
    mpf.Label = true;
    queue.MessageReadPropertyFilter = mpf;

    // Retrieve all the messages within the
    // queue in order to check whether this
    // order has not already been dealt with.
    Message[] msg = queue.GetAllMessages();
    bool bFound = false;
```

Therefore, the `MessagePropertyFilter` class is used to define a filter in order to retrieve just the message label for every message in the queue. Since the product's `SKU` is used in the message label, we only need to retrieve this information to check whether a message concerning that product has been sent. In that way we will save a lot of server resources when the `GetAllMessages()` method is called to retrieve all the messages in the queue.

For each message in the queue, the code checks whether its label is equal to the `SKU` passed as a parameter to the method. If it finds a message having the same characteristics it exits from the loop and sets a `Boolean` value used to avoid the next code execution:

```
    foreach (Message m in msg)
    {
        if (m.Label == sku)
        {
```

```
                    // A message for this product already exists.
                    bFound = true;
                    break;
                }
        }
```

The final part of the code creates a `DataSet` object that will contain the product information that has to be sent to the warehouse.

> *The `DataSet` schema is contained in the `OrderSchema.xml` file that you have to copy to your hard disk in the D: partition or, better yet, use a relative path (http://localhost/BltStore/OrderSchema.xml). In the second case, you will have to copy the file to the same directory where you copied the web site files:*

```
            // Send a message to the queue only if
            // no messages associated with this product
            // have been found.
            if (!bFound)
            {
                DataSet dsOrder = new DataSet();
                dsOrder.ReadXmlSchema(@"D:\OrderSchema.xml");
                DataRow r = dsOrder.Tables[0].NewRow();
                r["SKU"] = sku;
                r["ProductName"] = name;
                r["QTY"] = qty;
                dsOrder.Tables[0].Rows.Add(r);

                Type[] type = new Type[1];
                type[0] = typeof(DataSet);
                queue.Formatter = new XmlMessageFormatter(type);
                queue.Send(dsOrder,sku);
                queue.Close();
            }
    }
```

The `DataSet`'s schema is loaded from the following XML schema:

```
<?xml version="1.0" standalone="yes"?>
<xsd:schema id="ProductOrder"
xmlns:xsd="http://www.w3.org/2001/XMLSchema" xmlns:msdata="urn:schemas-microsoft-
com:xml-msdata">
  <xsd:element name="ProductOrder" msdata:IsDataSet="true">
    <xsd:complexType>
      <xsd:choice maxOccurs="unbounded">
        <xsd:element name="Table">
          <xsd:complexType>
            <xsd:sequence>
              <xsd:element name="SKU" type="xsd:string" />
              <xsd:element name="ProductName" type="xsd:string" />
              <xsd:element name="QTY" type="xsd:integer" />
            </xsd:sequence>
          </xsd:complexType>
        </xsd:element>
      </xsd:choice>
    </xsd:complexType>
  </xsd:element>
</xsd:schema>
```

As you can see, the schema is very simple and defines three columns: SKU, ProductName, and QTY. The code adds a new row filled with the product SKU, the name, and the quantity required. Then, the code informs the queue that it will retrieve a message containing a DataSet object, which is accomplished by an object of the XmlMessageFormatter class. Finally, the message can be sent with the Send() method.

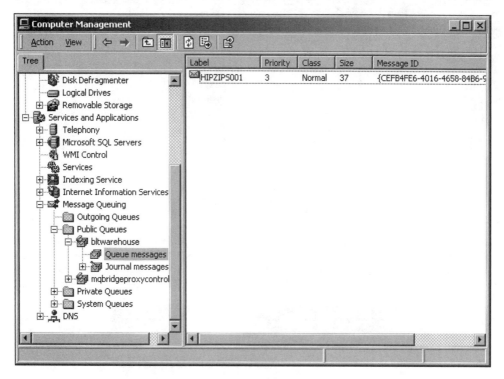

In the screen above you can see the new message stored in the queue ready to be read from the warehouse application.

The Warehouse Application

In the warehouse server we will create an application that will show a list of product orders. The content of the list will be refreshed at periodic intervals in order to determine whether new orders have been sent from the store. The initial stage is to create a Visual Studio .NET C# Windows Application project with a ListView control and two buttons on the main form:

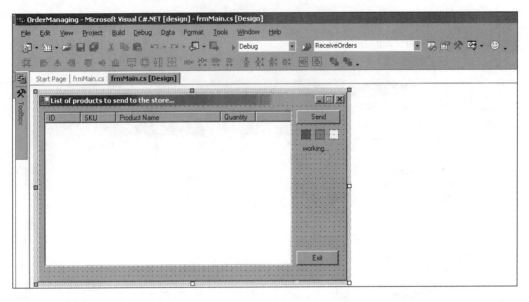

The above screen also shows three colored panels and a label used to create an animation effect that will inform the user that the application is working and searching for new orders. In order to set the ListView to show the columns, choose the Details value from the View property and add four columns by clicking the ellipsis(...) button in the Columns property. The following dialog box will appear:

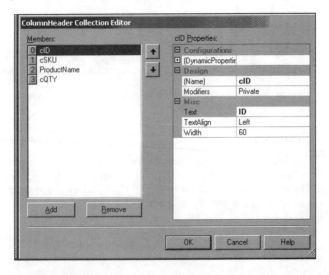

Clicking the Add button will insert a new item in the Members: list. The item's characteristics can be refined by setting the Properties on the right side of the dialog box.

The application is going to check the bltwarehouse private queue every ten seconds to refresh the ListView component with new messages. We have to define a timer that has to start when the application is started. The place to insert the code is in the form's constructor:

```
public frmMain()
{
    //
    // Required for Windows Form Designer support
    //
    InitializeComponent();

    // Starting a new timer to refresh the list
    // using a simple animating effect
    tmr = new System.Timers.Timer (10000);
    tmr.Elapsed += new ElapsedEventHandler(OnTimer);
    tmr.Enabled = true;
}
```

The snippet of code above creates a new timer, setting its ticking value to ten seconds (10000 milliseconds) and defining the `OnTimer()` event handler where we can add the code to refresh the list. The following method is called in the body of the timer event handler:

```
protected void FillListWithOrders()
{
    // Check if the queue exists
    if(MessageQueue.Exists(@".\Private$\bltwarehouse"))
    {
        // Retrieve the private queue
        MessageQueue q = new MessageQueue(@".\Private$\bltwarehouse");
```

The code starts retrieving an object to manage the private queue – the code will be processed only if the queue exists.

Next, we have to inform the queue that we will expect a `DataSet` within the message. We can use the `XmlMessageFormatter` class specifying a `DataSet` type in the constructor:

```
    // Format the message to retrieve a dataset
    System.Type[] type = new Type[1];
    type[0] = typeof(DataSet);
    q.Formatter = new XmlMessageFormatter(type);
```

Using the `GetMessageEnumerator()` method, exposed by the `MessageEnumerator` class, we can retrieve every message contained in the queue:

```
    // Retrieve the message enumerator
    MessageEnumerator msgEnum =
        q.GetMessageEnumerator();
```

We can go through each message simply using the `MoveNext()` method:

```
    // Clear all the items in the ListView
    lvOrders.Items.Clear();

    // Prepare to insert new items in the ListView
    DataSet dsOrder;
    string[] str = new string[4];
    System.Messaging.Message msg;

    // Loop through every message in the queue
    while(msgEnum.MoveNext(new TimeSpan(0,0,1)))
    {
```

The ListView content is cleared before the code inserts new items in it. A `DataSet` object is prepared to receive the message content, and a string array is defined to fill the ListView. The `MoveNext()` method accepts a `TimeSpan` object used to define a timeout beyond which the code exits from the loop.

The code retrieves the current message containing the `DataSet` object filled with the product information. The code casts the message's `Body` property to the `DataSet` class in order to retrieve the contained data:

```
// Add the item in the list
msg = msgEnum.Current;
dsOrder = (DataSet) msg.Body;

str[0] = msg.Id.ToString(); // Message ID
str[1] = dsOrder.Tables[0].Rows[0]["SKU"].ToString();
// Product SKU
str[2] = dsOrder.Tables[0].Rows[0]["ProductName"].ToString();
// Product Name
str[3] = dsOrder.Tables[0].Rows[0]["QTY"].ToString();
// Quantity

ListViewItem itm = new ListViewItem(str);
lvOrders.Items.Add(itm);

        }
        q.Close();
    }
}
```

As we have seen, the body of the message contains every parameter necessary to the warehouse to find and send a new stock of products. The content of the `DataSet` is split into the `String` array that is used with the `Add()` method of the `Items` collection exposed by the ListView class.

The screen below shows the application running and searching for a new order for the **HipZip** product:

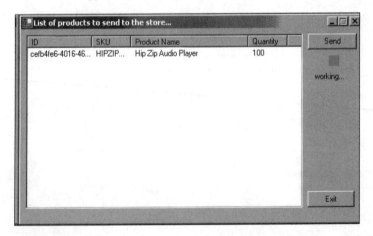

Now the operator passes the order to the storekeepers and waits for a phone call informing of the product supply. After that, the operator can select the row associated to the product and click the **Send** button in order to send a message to the store about the product supply.

Next, let's look at the code behind the **Send** button:

```
private void btnSend_Click(object sender, System.EventArgs e)
{
    // Check if the queue exists
    if(MessageQueue.Exists(@".\Private$\bltwarehouse"))
    {
        Cursor.Current = Cursors.WaitCursor;

        if (lvOrders.SelectedItems.Count > 0)
        {
```

The code executes a check to see whether the queue exists and if the user has selected a ListView row. Moreover the `Cursor` class is used to show the wait cursor when the user has to wait for the operation's completion.

In order to avoid multiple messages for the same product being sent to the warehouse, the message remains in the queue until the product supplying stage starts. The code simply deletes the message having the same ID as that retrieved from the first ListView column, because the operator is going to confirm that new stock of products has been sent to the store:

```
            // Retrieve the queue
            MessageQueue queue =
                new MessageQueue(@".\Private$\bltwarehouse");

            // Retrieve the message ID from the selected row
            ListViewItem item = lvOrders.SelectedItems[0];

            // Remove the message from the queue
            System.Messaging.Message msg = queue.ReceiveById(item.Text);

            queue.Close();
```

The code continues to send a private message to the `tobltstore` queue, providing the product quantity and product SKU.

```
            // Send a confirming message to the store
            if(MessageQueue.Exists(@".\Private$\tobltstore"))
            {
                // Retrieve the queue
                MessageQueue q = new
                MessageQueue(@".\Private$\tobltstore");
                string strQTY = item.SubItems[3].Text;
                q.Send(strQTY, msg.Label);

                q.Close();
            }
```

Finally, the list is refreshed in order to remove the product order message.

```
            // Refresh the listview
            FillListWithOrders();

            Cursor.Current = Cursors.Default;
        }
    }
}
```

> When you install the Message Queuing service as a dependent client you cannot use the asynchronous message receiving method because the operating system is not able to alert you when a new message has arrived.

The Store Windows Service

In addition to the ASP.NET application, a Windows Service runs on the store server that updates the database when it receives a confirmation message from the warehouse about the product supply. Here we use a Windows Service C# project, (which is renamed `BltStoreService`) to contain the code to manage the messages in the queue.

Let's start with the service class's constructor, the ideal place to insert our initialization code:

```
public BltStoreService()
{
    // This call is required by the Windows.Forms Component Designer.
    InitializeComponent();

    // Starting an asynchronous reading of messages
    MessageQueue queue = new MessageQueue(@".\Private$\tobltstore");

    // The message will contain a string type value
    // in the body, so I format the message
    Type[] type = new Type[1];
    type[0] = typeof(string);
    queue.Formatter = new XmlMessageFormatter(type);

    // Install the event handler
    queue.ReceiveCompleted +=
        new ReceiveCompletedEventHandler(OnProductArrived);

    // Begin the message receiving
    queue.BeginReceive();
}
```

In the constructor's body, above, we create a new `MessageQueue` object to manage the private queue. Then we have to inform the queue that we are going to receive a message having the body with only one `String` element. Finally, we can define an asynchronous method to read the messages declaring an event handler for the `ReceiveCompleted` event and starting the asynchronous process with the `BeginReceive()` method call.

When a new message is queued, the `ReceiveCompleted` event is fired by the operating system and this method is called:

```
public static void OnProductArrived(object source, ReceiveCompletedEventArgs args)
{
    try
    {
        // A new message arrived
        MessageQueue queue = (MessageQueue)source;
        Message msg = queue.EndReceive(args.AsyncResult);
```

The `source` event parameter will contain a reference to the queue that has generated the event. In order to use it we have to cast its value to the `MessageQueue` class. Then we can call the `EndReceive()` method retrieving a reference to the message contained in the queue.

This next piece of code is used to update the database with the product's new quantity available for the customer:

```
// Updating the database with the product's new unit number
SqlConnection dbConn = new SqlConnection
                        ("server=localhost;
                         database=BLTStore;uid=sa;pwd=;");

dbConn.Open();
SqlCommand cmm = new SqlCommand
                    ("UPDATE tabProducts SET
                     Availability=Availability+" + msg.Body.ToString()
                     + " WHERE SKU='" + msg.Label + "'", dbConn);
cmm.ExecuteNonQuery();
dbConn.Close();
```

After creating a new connection object, the code opens the connection to the database and executes the UPDATE SQL statement to add the quantity retrieved from the message to the current product availability.

Note: In the code I used the default Microsoft SQL Server username, sa, without defining a password. In real situations, for security implications, it is better to define a new administrator account with a valid password.

In the last part of the code we have to call BeginReceive() again in order to inform the message queuing service to wait again for a new message:

```
        // Wait for another message
        queue.BeginReceive();
    }
    catch (Exception ex)
    {
        // an error occurred, write its description
        // in the event log.
        EventLog e = new EventLog();
        e.WriteEntry(ex.Message,EventLogEntryType.Error);
    }
}
```

Finally, when an error occurs the instructions within the catch body will write a message in the event log. You can read these error messages with the Event Viewer within **Administrative Tools** in Windows Control Panel.

Now, the next user to choose the HipZip product will see that there are ample numbers of the product available, as shown below (**Current availability: 101**):

In order to install a Windows Service in the operating system you have to use the `InstallUtil.exe` program present in the .NET framework directory. This program looks for information contained in the `ProjectInstaller.cs` file that you have to add to the Windows Service project. This file defines some of the services characteristics like its name, default state (automatic starting, manual starting, disabled) and so on. You can find a copy of this file in the `BltStoreService` application that comes with the download code.

Testing the Application

Now you should have all that is necessary to test the application. Insert a product quantity value between 1 and 9 units and try to connect to the web site. A new message should be queued in the primary domain Message Queuing service. Launch the Windows application in the warehouse server in order to list the new order. Try to send a new product stock and launch the Windows Service in order to update the `BltStore` database. Now you should connect to the web site and see the new product quantity having the green color.

Using Microsoft Host Integration Server 2000

Legacy systems are often very complex. A lot of applications still in use have been written using languages like COBOL, which may use flat text files for data exchange. However, if still in use, they are likely to be proven, robust applications guaranteeing transactional operations and application stability. Trying to port them to other operating systems is not easy, or necessarily cost effective – it is often better to integrate these services with newer Windows applications.

Microsoft Host Integration Server 2000 (HIS) gives all the possible tools to integrate and then substitute the legacy systems. HIS has been created for improving the interoperability between Windows operating systems and legacy systems and covers three main areas:

❑ Application integration

❑ Data integration

❑ Network integration

The following figure illustrates these areas:

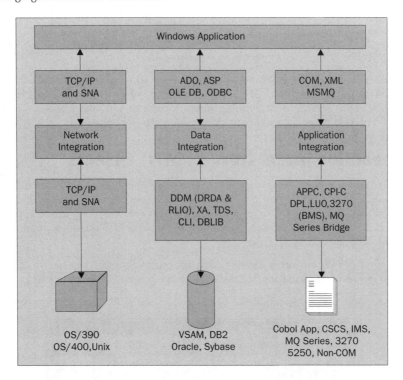

Let's look at how HIS deals with each area.

Application Integration

Microsoft HIS provides several services to integrate applications running on Windows with applications running on mainframes:

- ❑ COM Transaction Integrator for Customer Information Control System (CICS) and Information Management System (IMS) – This is a set of COM+ objects that manages IBM transaction processing program.

- ❑ The Microsoft Message Queuing service to IBM MQSeries message queuing service (MSMQ-MQSeries Bridge) – This is an external gateway between two otherwise incompatible message queuing systems.

- ❑ Application Integration Software Development Kit – This is used to create custom applications using the powerful Host Integration Server 2000's host connectivity services.

Data Integration

Microsoft HIS provides several OLE DB providers to interact with diverse data sources such as DB2 and VSAM.

Network Integration

❏ Microsoft HIS offers a complete compatibility of its services with the use of the TCP/IP protocol

❏ Microsoft HIS offers a complete compatibility of its services with the most diverse network protocols like X.25, SNA protocols, Synchronous Data Link Control (SDLC), and more

Ignoring network integration issues (which lie outside the scope of this book), let's look at the **COM Transaction Integrator COM+** (**COMTI**) objects and OLE DB providers supplied by HIS for managing legacy systems' databases. Here we won't get embroiled in the (significant) installation and configuration issues, which go along with using HIS, we'll just concentrate on the tools which developers will most likely work with.

COM Transaction Integrator (COMTI) Objects

COMTI objects enable a Windows client application to invoke mainframe transactional applications. The COM objects support IBM's Customer Information Control System (CICS) and IBM's Information Management System (IMS) mainframe transactional applications, providing data mapping between Intel-based architecture and OS/390-based architecture. Actually HIS doesn't support .NET assemblies and C# or Visual Basic .NET languages.

However, with the **COMTI Component Builder**, a developer can produce a type library (`.tlb`) file including methods and properties to call mainframe transactional applications that can be included in a .NET application.

Choosing New... from the application's File menu gives a prompt to insert some parameters:

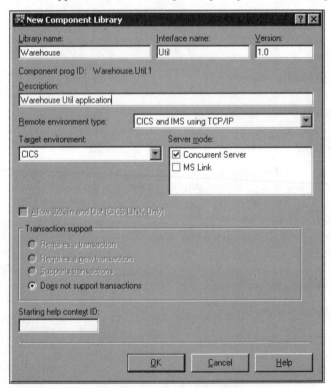

You can choose a type library identification name and an interface name plus the remote environment type and the target environment. The last two pieces of information are needed by the COMTI runtime engine, which works like a proxy for the mainframe. It intercepts object method calls and redirects them to the appropriate mainframe program. Also, it automatically converts the method's parameters from the Windows 2000 format to the selected mainframe format. Finally, the COMTI runtime engine returns every parameter from the mainframe application to the Windows application.

In our scenario, to facilitate the warehouse operator's tasks and to speed up the product-supplying phase, we can create a COMTI component running a mainframe application to return the actual product availability in the warehouse. If the warehouse can't send the required quantity to the store, the product will be declared out of stock and the store will inform every customer and insert an appropriate image on the web page.

From the COMTI component builder we can add a new method selecting the **Method** menu within the **Insert** main menu, and choose the **Return Type** from a list of possible data types:

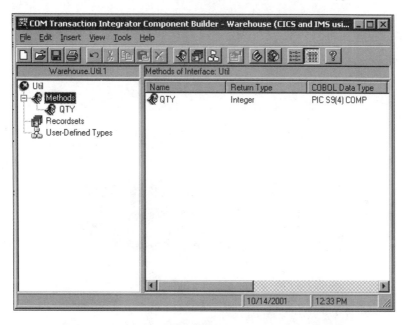

The product quantity is an integer data type, so we have to choose a method returning an integer equal to the PIC S9(4) COBOL data type. Now we can add a parameter in order to specify the product SKU. By right-clicking on the QTY method, we can select the **Insert Parameter** menu from the context menu and specify the string data type.

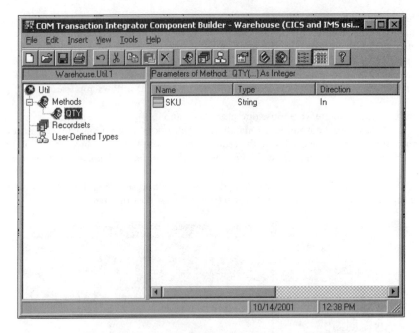

We have to refine the parameter's characteristics by specifying a ten-character string length and the input direction. To accomplish this task we have to select the Properties menu from the context menu that appears by right-clicking on the parameter name:

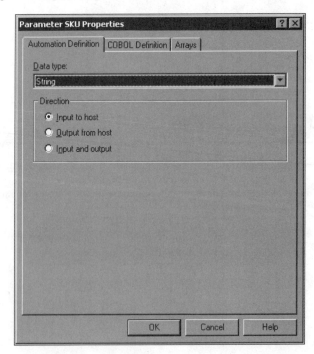

Choosing File | Save generates a new library.

The COMTI object is a transactional object component so it has to be registered into the COM+ or the Microsoft Transaction Server environment. From Windows 2000 open **Component Services** from the **Administrative Tools** menu in the Control Panel and expand the **Component Services, Computers, My Computers,** and **COM+ Applications** nodes and choose to create a new application from the **Action** menu. From the wizard choose the **Create an empty application** option:

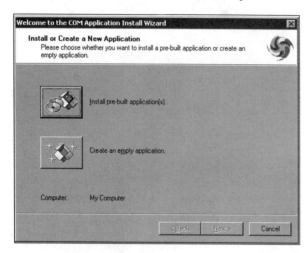

The wizard will ask you to insert a name for the application and to choose between library and server application type. The former allows components to run in the application process while the latter will run the components in a dedicated server process:

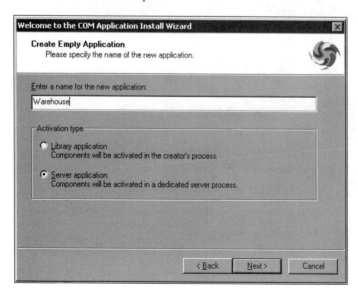

Finally you have to choose the Windows account used by the application when one of its components is run:

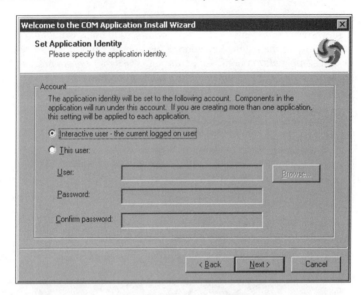

We have to insert the COMTI component within the new application COM+ environment. Simply drag the type library from Windows Explorer over the new COM+ application and it will be registered automatically:

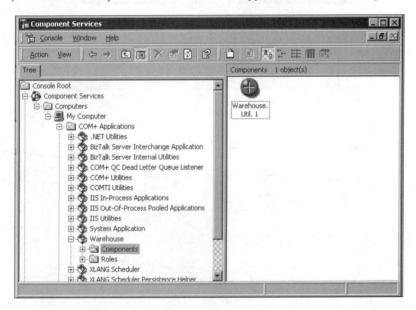

Warehouse Application Modification

After completing the installation and deployment of the new COMTI component, we can modify the OrderManaging warehouse application in order to instantly check the product availability in the warehouse database. First of all we have to add a reference to the type library (in our case labeled Warehouse Util application):

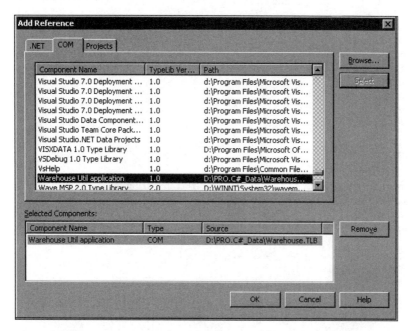

We will have to search for the COMTI component in order to select it and add it to our project. Previously, HIS and .NET incompatibility was mentioned, and the following message box may appear after we try to add the reference:

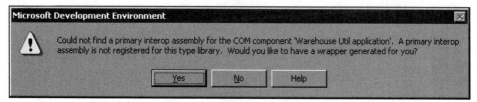

If this does occur, allow the wrapper to be generated (although in RC1 this may be done without the prompt).

Now we can add a Check button to call the COMTI object QTY() method:

```
private void btnCheck_Click(object sender, System.EventArgs e)
{
    if (lvOrders.SelectedItems.Count > 0)
    {
        // Create an instance of the COMTI object
        Warehouse.Util check = new Warehouse.Util();
```

If the user has selected an item in the list, the code creates an object from the COMTI COM+ component.

This code retrieves the product SKU from the selected ListView item and passes it to the QTY() method:

```
// Retrieve the selected ListView item
ListViewItem item = lvOrders.SelectedItems[0];
// Retrieve the product SKU and the quantity
string strSKU = item.SubItems[1].Text;
short sQTY = check.QTY(strSKU);
```

If the product quantity available in the warehouse is less than the required one, a new message will be sent to the tobltstore private queue to inform the store messaging system:

```
// If the quantity available in the warehouse is less
// than quantity required, then a out of stock message
// is sent to the tobltsore private queue.
if (sQTY < Convert.ToInt16(item.SubItems[3].Text))
{
```

The code above uses the ToInt16() method to convert the string into a small integer in order to be compared to the quantity.

In the final part of the code a reference to the queue is created and a new message is sent to the store:

```
// Send a confirming message to the store
if(MessageQueue.Exists(@".\Private$\tobltstore"))
{
    // Retrieve the queue
    MessageQueue q = new
    MessageQueue(@".\Private$\tobltstore");

    // Send the message
    q.Send("OUT OF ORDER", strSKU);

    // Close the queue
    q.Close();
}
    }
  }
}
```

Data Integration

As we said earlier, Microsoft HIS provides a series of OLE DB providers to interact with the most diverse data sources running on mainframe systems. These are:

❑ OLE DB provider for AS/400 and VSAM

❑ OLE DB provider for DB2

Moreover, HIS provides an ODBC driver for DB2, and other powerful services to implement file transfers between Windows and legacy systems.

Using an HIS OLE DB provider in a .NET application written in C# is similar to a standard C#
application retrieving data from a generic database with the OLE DB data provider. We only have to
change the connection string to the database using the usual OLE DB classes. For example:

```csharp
using System;
using System.Data;
using System.Data.OleDb;

namespace ConsoleApplication2
{
    /// <summary>
    /// Summary description for Class1.
    /// </summary>
    class Class1
    {
        static void Main(string[] args)
        {
            OleDbConnection dbConn = new OleDbConnection
                                ("Provider=DB2OLEDB;NetLib=SNA;
                                NetAddr=;NetPort=;RemoteLU=DRDAD
                                EMO;LocalLU=LOCAL;
                                ModeName=QPCSUPP;UID=SNA;
                                PWD=SNA;InitCat=WAREHOUSEDB;
                                TPName=0X07F9F9F9;
                                AccMode=ReadWrite;CCSID=37;
                                PCCodePage=1252;BinAsChar=NO;
                                DSN=WarehouseDSN;");
            dbConn.Open();

            OleDbCommand dbComm = new OleDbCommand("SELECT QTY FROM " +
                "tabProducts WHERE SKU='HIPZIPS001'", dbConn);

            int iQTY = (int) dbComm.ExecuteScalar();

            dbConn.Close();
        }
    }
}
```

Summary

In this final chapter we've looked at using Internet-oriented .NET applications to work with legacy systems.
We began by identifying some of the potential areas of conflict between applications designed for the Internet
and those systems designed using older network solutions, namely availability, performance, and scalability.

Then, using the simple scenario of a small store that goes on-line but needs to organize re-stocking from a
large warehouse, we identified two possible solutions. Firstly, we looked at using Message Queuing to
establish a link between the web site (that we constructed) and the warehouse. Secondly, we briefly looked at
some of the features of Host Integration Server that allow more direct integration with the legacy system.

.NET Evolution

Microsoft first released .NET to the public at PDC (Professional Developers Conference) 2000. This release was soon followed by the .NET SDK Beta 1 in October 2000. The Beta 1 release was given a warm welcome and lots of code started to show up on numerous web sites devoted to the .NET and C# cause. Seldom has any product in history been able to generate this much popularity at such an early stage. At Tech-Ed 2001, Microsoft released the Beta 2 version of the .NET SDK. In Beta 2, Microsoft has not only fixed the bugs that surfaced in Beta 1, but has also made a lot of changes to the namespace and class structures, so they would be more extensible in the future.

Because of this, Beta 1 code has to be manually converted to Beta 2. Fortunately, most of the conversion can easily be achieved by carrying out simple find and replace operations. This section will summarize some of the common changes that have occurred.

> At the time of writing, Microsoft has just released the .NET Release Candidate 1 at PDC 2001 however, according to Microsoft, this release is only recommended for users who have not installed Beta 2, hence this appendix will only look at the Beta 1 to Beta 2 transition.
>
> There are several changes between Beta 2 and RC1, which are detailed at appropriate points in the book. Further information on changes that affect material in the book will be posted on www.wrox.com.

One significant change that Microsoft has made in Beta 2 is that now the base class library follows a consistent naming convention of using **Pascal casing**, where the first letter of every word is capitalized and rest of the letters are in lower case.

Primitive Data Type Conversion

The String class from the System namespace no longer contains methods to convert strings into various primitive data types in Beta 2. Instead, each of the primitive data type classes now has separate methods to parse data from strings. Also, more methods have been added to the Convert class, which specifically look after converting data into different types:

Beta 1	Beta 2	Description
String.ToBoolean	Boolean.Parse	Convert from String to Boolean
String.ToByte	Byte.Parse	Convert from String to Byte
String.ToChar	Char.Parse	Convert from String to Char
String.ToDateTime	DateTime.Parse	Convert from String to DateTime
String.ToDecimal	Decimal.Parse	Convert from String to Decimal
String.ToDouble	Double.Parse	Convert from String to Double
String.ToInt16	Int16.Parse	Convert from String to Int16
String.ToInt32	Int32.Parse	Convert from String to Int32
String.ToInt64	Int64.Parse	Convert from String to Int64
String.ToSingle	Single.Parse	Convert from String to Single

Increased XML Capabilities of the DataSet Object

Beta 2 introduces the methods GetXml(), GetXmlSchema(), and InferXmlSchema() to the DataSet object (in the System.Data namespace). These methods facilitate easy conversion of the data and schema in XML format into a string object (in the case of the first two methods) or to a TextReader object (in the third case).

The ReadXmlData() and WriteXmlData() methods from Beta 1 have been dropped and the ReadXml() and WriteXml() methods have been overloaded with XmlReadMode() Enumeration and XmlWriteMode() Enumeration to have the same effect.

SQL Managed Provider

The MS SQL managed provider was placed under the System.Data.SQL namespace in Beta 1. In Beta 2, this namespace has been renamed to System.Data.SqlClient. Also, all the classes under the System.Data.SQL namespace that had a prefix of SQL in the class name in Beta 1 have a prefix of Sql before the class name in Beta 2 (case is important):

Beta 1	Beta 2
SQLCommand	SqlCommand
SQLConnection	SqlConnection
SQLDataReader	SqlDataReader
SQLDataSetCommand	SqlDataAdapter

Many new methods have been added to the SQLCommand class, which have been renamed to SqlCommand in Beta2.

Beta 1	Beta 2	Description
SQLCommand. Execute()	Removed in Beta 2	This method was used in Beta 1 to build a DataReader object
Not present	SqlCommand. ExecuteReader()	This method is used in Beta 2 to build a DataReader object
Not present	SqlCommand. ExecuteScalar()	This method executes the query and returns the first column and the first row from the result set
Not present	SqlCommand. ExecuteXmlReader()	This method is used to return an XmlReader object in cases where the FOR XML clause has been used in the SQL query to return an XML fragment from MS SQL 2000

The properties HasMoreResults and HasMoreRows from the SQLDataReader class, that were used to check for availability of more result sets and rows in Beta 1, have been dropped from the SqlDataReader class in Beta 2 for performance reasons.

A standard way to connect to a data source and read some rows using the DataReader is shown below:

Beta 1

```
string myQuery = "SELECT firstName FROM Author";
SQLConnection myConnection = new SQLConnection(myConnString);
SQLCommand myCommand = new SQLCommand(myQuery,myConnection);
myConnection.Open(); //Open the connection
SQLDataReader myDataReader;
myCommand.Execute(out myDataReader); //Get the DataReader

while (myDataReader.Read()) {

  Console.WriteLine(myDataReader.GetString(0));
  //Print out the values

}
myDataReader.Close(); //Close the DataReader
myConnection.Close(); //Close the Connection
```

Beta 2

```
string myQuery = "SELECT firstName FROM Author";
SqlConnection myConnection = new SqlConnection(myConnString);
SqlCommand myCommand = new SqlCommand(myQuery,myConnection);
myConnection.Open(); //Open the connection
SqlDataReader myDataReader;
myDataReader = myCommand.ExecuteReader(); //Get the DataReader

while (myDataReader.Read()) {

   Console.WriteLine(myDataReader.GetString(0));
   //Print out the values

}
myDataReader.Close(); //Close the DataReader
myConnection.Close(); //Close the Connection
```

The `FillDataSet()` method from the `SQLDataSetCommand` class used to populate a `DataSet` object in Beta 1 has been renamed to `Fill()` in the `SqlDataAdapter` class used in Beta2. Another helper class, `SqlCommandBuilder`, has been introduced in Beta 2 to help automatically generate SQL queries in `SqlDataAdapter` to facilitate reconciliation of a single tabled `DataSet` object with its data source.

OLE DB and ODBC Managed Providers

In Beta 1, classes under the `System.Data.ADO` namespace were used to connect to databases using an OLE DB provider or an ODBC DSN. In Beta 2, two managed providers, namely `OleDb.NET` and `Odbc.NET` have been created separately to provide the respective connectivity. Hence all the classes that were prefixed with `ADO` in Beta 1 are now prefixed with `OleDb` in the case of `OleDb.NET`, and `Odbc` in the case of `Odbc.NET`.

Beta 1	Beta 2 OleDb.NET	Beta 2 Odbc.NET
ADOCommand	OleDbCommand	OdbcCommand
ADOConnection	OleDbConnection	OdbcConnection
ADODataReader	OleDbDataReader	OdbcDataReader
ADODataSetCommand	OleDbDataAdapter	OleDbDataAdapter

Similar to the case of the `SqlCommand` class from the SQL managed provider, in OLE DB and ODBC command classes, the `Execute()` method from Beta 1 has been removed, and `ExecuteReader()` and `ExecuteScalar()` methods have been added.

The `HasMoreResults` and `HasMoreRows` properties from the `ADODataReader` class have also been removed in Beta 2.

The `ADODataSetCommand` from Beta 1 has been renamed to `OleDbDataAdapter`/ `OdbcDataAdapter` in Beta 2. Also, the `FillDataSet()` method from the `ADODataSetCommand` class has been replaced by the method `Fill()`. Also, in the OleDB / ODBC Managed Providers, the `CommandBuilder` class has been added in Beta 2 to help reconcile the `DataSet` object with the data source.

A standard way to fill a `DataSet` from the data source is shown opposite:

Beta 1

```
string myQuery = "SELECT firstName FROM Author";
ADOConnection myAccessConn = new ADOConnection(myConnectionStr);
ADODataSetCommand myAccessDataSetCmd =
  new ADODataSetCommand(myQuery,myAccessConn);
    DataSet myDataSet = new DataSet();
myAccessDataSetCmd.FillDataSet(myDataSet,"Author"); //Fill the DataSet
```

Beta 2

```
string myQuery = "SELECT firstName FROM Author";
OleDbDataAdapter myAdapter =
  new OleDbDataAdapter(myQuery,myConnectionStr);
    DataSet myDataSet = new DataSet();
myAdapter.Fill(myDataSet,"Author"); //Fill the DataSet
```

COM Components

In Beta 1, classes like `ServicedComponent` placed in the `Microsoft.ComServices` namespace were used to create COM components. In Beta 2 these classes have been shifted to the `System.EnterpriseServices` namespace.

File and Directory Manipulation

The `File` and `Directory` classes used for file and directory manipulation respectively in Beta 1 have been split into two classes each in Beta 2, `File` and `FileInfo` classes for dealing with file manipulation and `Directory` and `DirectoryInfo` classes for dealing with directory manipulation. The functionality of the classes remains the same, but the `File` and `Directory` classes have static methods while the `FileInfo` and the `DirectoryInfo` classes have instance methods to deal with file and directory manipulation.

Beta 1	Beta 2
File	File (static methods) and FileInfo
Directory	Directory (static methods) and DirectoryInfo

Sending E-Mails

The .NET Beta 1 SDK provided classes like `MailMessage`, `MailAttachment`, and `SmtpMail` under the `System.Web.Util` namespace to enable quick composition and sending of e-mails using the underlying IIS mailing components. In Beta 2, a separate namespace, `System.Web.Mail`, now hosts these classes.

Templates

In Beta 2 there have been a lot of changes in the template names of the templates under the `System.Web.UI.WebControls` namespace used in controls like `DataGrid`, `DataList`, and `Repeater`.

Style Templates

Beta 1	Beta 2
`<property name="HeaderStyle"></property>`	`<HeaderStyle></HeaderStyle>`
`<property name="ItemStyle"></property>`	`<ItemStyle></ItemStyle>`
`<property name="AlternatingItemstyle"></property>`	`<AlternatingItemstyle></AlternatingItemstyle>`

Item Templates

Beta 1	Beta 2
`<template name="HeaderTemplate"></template>`	`<HeaderTemplate></HeaderTemplate>`
`<template name="ItemTemplate"></template>`	`<ItemTemplate></ItemTemplate>`
`<template name="EditItemTemplate"></template>`	`<EditItemTemplate></EditItemTemplate>`
`<template name="FooterTemplate"></template>`	`<FooterTemplate></FooterTemplate>`

Windows Forms Applications

The `System.WinForms` namespace hosted all the classes to build rich Windows applications in Beta 1. All these classes have been shifted to the `System.Windows.Forms` namespace in Beta 2. Also, the `TrayIcon` class used to create applications that run from the system tray has been renamed to the `NotifyIcon` class in Beta 2.

Support for the Latest XML Standards

The `System.Xml` namespace comprises classes that deal with XML and its derivatives. In Beta 2, Microsoft has shown a firm support for XML and adopted the latest W3C XML specifications as given below:

❑   XML 1.0 – http://www.w3.org/TR/REC-xml

❑   XML Namespaces – http://www.w3.org/TR/REC-xml-names/

❑   XML Schemas – http://www.w3.org/TR/xmlschema-1/

❑   XPath expressions – http://www.w3.org/TR/xpath

❑   XSLT transformations – http://www.w3.org/TR/xslt

❑   DOM Level 2 Core – http://www.w3.org/TR/DOM-Level-2/

❑   SOAP 1.1 – http://msdn.Microsoft.com/xml/general/soapspec.asp

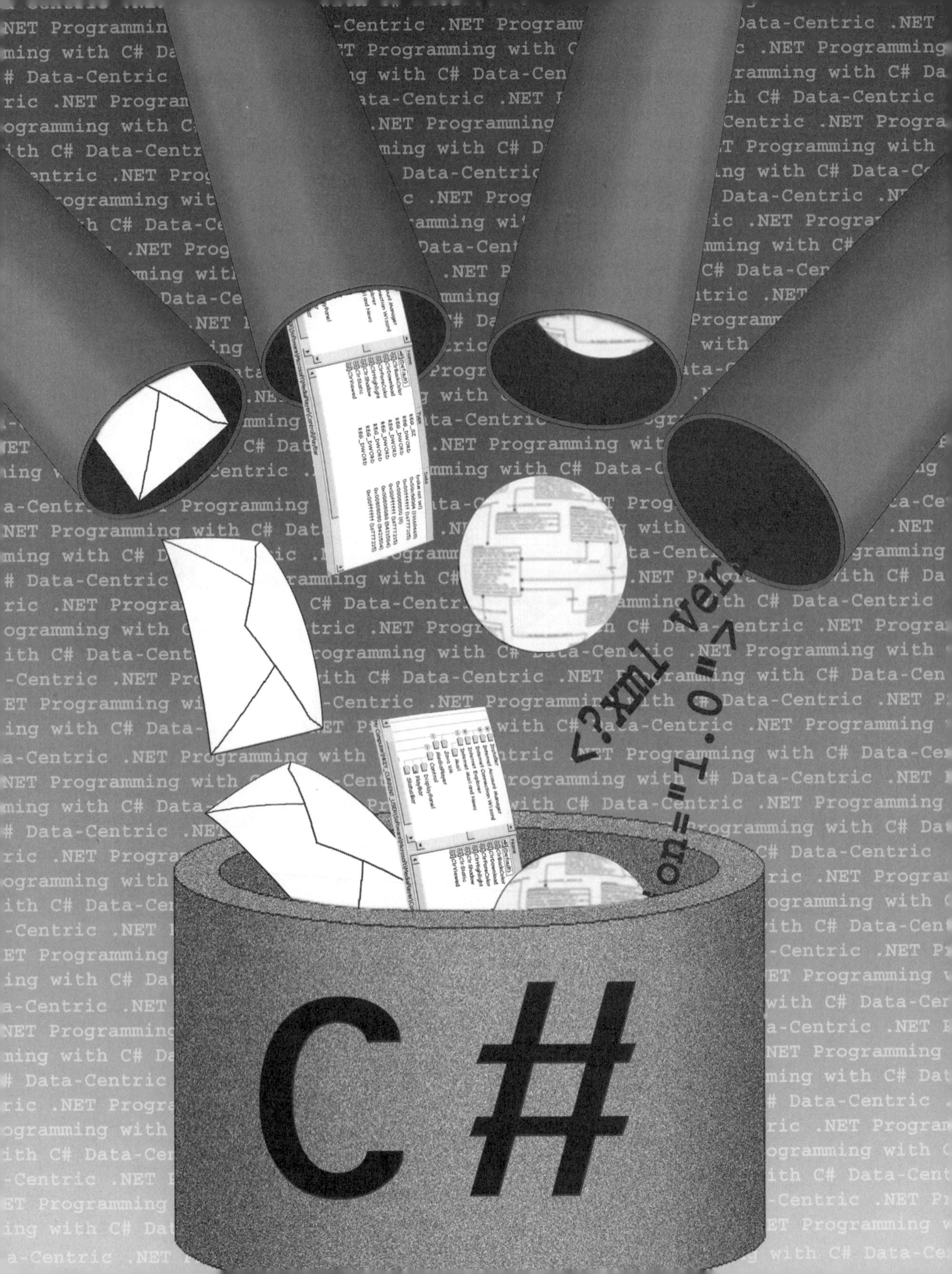
Data-Centric .NET Programming with C#
<?xml ver
on="1.0"?>
C#

ADO.NET Object Model

The .NET Class Library is massive, and the classes listed in this appendix are focused on data-related tasks. We will not be including all of the members for base classes. We will provide the hierarchy of the class and any overridden members within each class's model.

Command Classes

SqlCommand Hierarchy:	OleDbCommand Hierarchy:
Object	Object
MarshalByRefObject	MarshalByRefObject
Component	Component
SqlCommand	*OleDbCommand*

These classes represent a SQL statement or stored procedure to execute on or against a data source. There is one for Microsoft SQL Server, the `SqlCommand` class, and one for all other OleDb Providers, the `OleDbCommand` class.

Command Properties

Name	Type	Description
CommandText	string	Read/Write string that will be a SQL statement or stored procedure to execute against the data source.
CommandTimeout	int	Gets or Sets the timeout period for which an execution attempt of the current Command will wait before quitting and return an error. Default value: 30 (Seconds).
CommandType	CommandType Enum	Read-write property allowing us to specify the type of command that is passed to the data source in the CommandText property. Default value: Text.
Connection	Connection	Read-write property allowing you to specify which connection object this command will use.
Parameters	Collection	Returns the ParameterCollection object. Default value: empty collection.
Transaction	Transaction	Read/write property that allows the assignment or retrieval of the transaction that this command instance will execute within. Default value: null reference.
UpdatedRowSource	UpdateRowSource Enum	Read-write property to determine how results will be applied to the DataRow object when the DbDataAdapter.Update method is invoked.

Command Methods

Name	Returns	Description
Cancel		Cancels the executing command.
CreateParameter	Parameter	Returns a new instance of a SqlParameter or OleDbParameter object.
ExecuteNonQuery	int	Executes the command and returns the number of affected rows only.

Name	Returns	Description
ExecuteReader	DataReader	Executes the command and returns a new instance of the DataReader object.
ExecuteScalar	Object	Executes the command, and returns the value in the first column of the first row in the result set.
ExecuteXmlReader (SqlCommand Only)	XmlReader	Executes the command and returns a new instance of the XmlReader object.
Prepare		Creates a compiled version of the command to issue to the data source.
ResetCommand Timeout		Sets the CommandTimeout property back to its default value.

Connection Classes

SqlConnection Hierarchy:	OleDbConnection Hierarchy:
Object	Object
MarshalByRefObject	MarshalByRefObject
Component	Component
SqlConnection	*OleDbConnection*

There are two connection classes – the SqlConnection class used to connect to a Microsoft SQL Server, and the OleDbConnection class, which is used to connect to a data source with an OLE DB provider. Once opened these classes represent an open connection or session to the data source.

Connection Properties

Name	Type	Description
ConnectionString	String	Read/write property that contains the data-source specific information required to connect to the source.
ConnectionTimeout	Int	Read/write property that sets the amount of time, in seconds, to wait for a connection to open. The default is 15; a value of 0 will cause the connection to wait indefinitely.

Table continued on following page

Name	Type	Description
Database	String	Returns the name of the database that you are connected to.
DataSource	String	Returns the name of the server that you are connected to.
PacketSize (SqlConnection only)	Int	Returns the size, in bytes, of the network packets used to connect to a SQL Server. The default value is 8192.
Provider (OleDbConnection only)	String	Returns the name of the provider as defined in the ConnectionString property.
ServerVersion	String	Returns the version information for the server that you are connected to.
State	Connection State Enum	Returns the current status of the connection (Open or Closed).
WorkstationId (SqlConnection only)	String	Returns the host name of the workstation that is making the connection.

Connection Methods

Name	Returns	Description
BeginTransaction	Transaction object	Begins a database transaction.
ChangeDatabase		Changes the current database for the open connection to the one specified.
Close		Closes the connection to the database.
CreateCommand	Command object	Creates and returns a Command object.
Open		Opens a connection to the database with the information specified in the connection string.

Connection Events

Name	Description
InfoMessage	Occurs following the addition of an information message.
StateChange	Occurs following a change in connection state.

DataAdapter Classes

SqlDbDataAdapter Hierarchy:	OleDbDataAdapter Hierarchy:
Object	Object
MarshalByRefObject	MarshalByRefObject
Component	Component
DataAdapter	DataAdapter
DbDataAdapter	DbDataAdapter
SqlDbDataAdapter	*OleDbDataAdapter*

Used to populate a `DataSet`, these classes represent a connection and a set of data commands.

DataAdapter Properties

Name	Type	Description
AcceptChangesDuring Fill	bool	Read/write property that will determine whether or not the `DataRow.AcceptChanges` method is called after it has been added to the `DataTable`.
DeleteCommand	Command	Read/write property that that will return or assign a SQL statement to delete records from a `DataSet`.
InsertCommand	Command	Read/write property that that will return or assign a SQL statement to insert new records into the data source.
MissingMappingAction	MissingMappingAc tion Enumeration	Determines the action to take when incoming data does not have a matching table or column. Default is passthrough.
MissingSchemaAction	MissingSchemaAct ion Enumeration	Determines the action to take when existing `DataSet` schema does not match incoming data. Default is `Add`.
TableMappings	Collection	Gets a collection that provides the master mapping between a source table and a `DataTable`. Default is an empty collection.

Table continued on following page

Name	Type	Description
SelectCommand	Command	Read/write property that that will return or assign a SQL statement to select records from a DataSet.
UpdateCommand	Command	Read/write property that that will return or assign a SQL statement to update records from a DataSet.

DataAdapter Methods

Name	Returns	Description
CloneInternals	DataAdapter	Makes a copy of the current DataAdapter.
CreateTableMappings	DataTableMapping Collection	Creates a new DataTableMapping Collection.
Fill	int	Updates the rows in the DataSet to match those within the data source.
FillSchema	DataTable Array	Adds a DataTable with schema generated from the data source to an existing DataSet.
GetFillParameters	IDataParameters Array	Retrieves the parameters as set when executing a SQL select statement.
ShouldSerializeTableMappings	bool	Returns whether or not at least one DataTableMapping object exists and should be persisted.
Update	int	Executes the respective INSERT, UPDATE, or DELETE statements on the data source for each inserted, updated, or deleted row in the DataSet. Returns the number of rows successfully updated.

DataAdapter Events

Name	Description
RowUpdated	Occurs *after* an update command is executed on a data source.
RowUpdating	Occurs *prior* to an update command being executed on a data source.
OnRowUpdated	Raises the RowUpdated event.
OnRowUpdating	Raises the RowUpdating event.

DataColumn Class

DataColumn Hierarchy:
Object
MarshalByValueComponent
DataColumn

The DataColumn class represents the schema of a column within a DataTable.

DataColumn Properties

Name	Type	Description
AllowDBNull	bool	Read-write property that determines whether the current column will allow null values.
AutoIncrement	bool	Read-write property that will determine whether or not newly inserted rows will be auto-numbered.
AutoIncrementSeed	long	Read-write property, if the AutoIncrement propert is set to true, this property will determine the starting value of the auto-numbering.
AutoIncrementStep	long	Read-write property, if the AutoIncrement propert is set to true, this property will determine the increment between auto generated numbers.
Caption	string	Read/write property that will assign or return the caption of the current column.

Table continued on following page

Name	Type	Description
ColumnMapping	Mapping Type Enum	Read/write property that will assign or return the MappingType of the column.
ColumnName	string	Read/write property that determines the name of the column in the DataColumnCollection.
DataType	Type	Read/write property that determines the type of data stored in the column.
DefaultValue	Object	Read/write property that will set or return the default value for the current column when new rows are inserted.
Expression	string	Read/write property that sets or returns the expression used to filter rows, calculate the values in a column, or create an aggregate column.
ExtendedProperties	Property Collection	Returns the collection of custom information.
MaxLength	int	Read/write property used to set or read the maximum length of a text column.
Namespace	string	Assigns or returns the namespace of the current DataColumn.
Ordinal	int	Returns the location of the column in the DataColumnCollection collection.
Prefix	string	Assigns or returns the XML prefix that aliases the namespace of the DataTable.
ReadOnly	bool	Read/write property that determines whether the column allows changes once a row has been added to the table.
Table	DataTable	Returns the DataTable to which the current column belongs.
Unique	bool	Read/write property that determines whether the current column's value must be unique when compared to other rows within the same table.

DataColumn Methods

Name	Returns	Description
`OnPropertyChanging`		Causes the `OnPropertyChanging` Event to fire.
`RaisePropertyChanging`		Sends a notification that the supplied `DataColumn` property is about to change.
`ToString` (Overridden)	`string`	Returns the `Expression` of the column, if there is one.

DataColumnMapping Class

DataColumnMapping Hierarchy:
Object
MarshalByRefObject
DataColumnMapping

This class allows us to have columns whose names within a `DataSet` differ from the actual column names as defined within the data source. This class maps between the two names.

DataColumnMapping Properties

Name	Type	Description
`DataSetColumn`	`string`	Read/write property that assigns or returns the name of the column from the `DataSet` to map to.
`SourceColumn`	`string`	Read/Write property that assigns or returns the column name from a data source to map from. (This value is case-sensitive, even if the data source is not.)

DataColumnMapping Methods

Name	Returns	Description
GetDataColumnBySchema Action	DataColumn	Returns a `DataColumn` from the supplied `DataTable`.
ToString (Overridden)	String	Returns the current `SourceColumn` name.

DataReader Classes

SqlDataReader Hierarchy:	OleDbDataReader Hierarchy:
Object	Object
MarshalByRefObject	MarshalByRefObject
SqlDataReader	*OleDbDataReader*

The `DataReader` object allows us to read a forward-only stream of data from a data source. It is similar to an ADO `Recordset` with a `ForwardOnly` cursor.

DataReader Properties

Name	Returns	Description
Depth	int	Depth of nesting for the current row. (The SQL Server .NET provider will always return 0.)
FieldCount	int	Returns the number of columns (fields) in the current row.
IsClosed	bool	Returns whether or not the `DataReader` is closed.
Item	Object	Returns the value of a supplied column. Also acts as the indexer of the `DataReader` class.
RecordsAffected	int	Returns the number of rows that were updated, inserted, or deleted as a result of the SQL statement.

DataReader Methods

Name	Returns	Description
Close		Closes the `DataReader` object.
GetBoolean	bool	Returns the value of the supplied column as a Boolean.
GetByte	byte	Returns the value of the supplied column as a byte.
GetBytes	long	Returns the number of bytes read.
GetChar	char	Returns the value of the supplied column as a single character.
GetChars	long	Returns the actual number of characters read.
GetDataTypeName	string	Returns the name of the data type as defined on the data source.
GetDateTime	DateTime	Returns the value of the supplied column as a `DateTime` object.
GetDecimal	Decimal	Returns the value of the supplied column as a `Decimal` object.
GetDouble	double	Returns the value of the supplied column as a double-precision floating-point number.
GetFieldType	Type	Returns the `Type` that matches the data type of the field.
GetFloat	float	Returns the value of the supplied column as a single-precision floating-point number.
GetGuid	guid	Returns the value of the supplied column as a globally-unique identifier (GUID).
GetInt16	Short	Returns the value of the supplied column as a 16 bit signed integer.
GetInt32	int	Returns the value of the supplied column as a 32 bit signed integer.
GetInt64	long	Returns the value of the supplied column as a 32 bit signed integer.
GetName	string	Returns the name of the column supplied.
GetOrdinal	int	Returns the ordinal (position) of the column supplied.
GetSchemaTable	DataTable	Returns a `DataTable` object that describes the column metadata of the `DataReader`.

Table continued on following page

Name	Returns	Description
GetSqlBinary (SqlDataReader only)	SqlBinary	Returns the value of the supplied column as a SqlBinary.
GetSqlBoolean (SqlDataReader only)	SqlBoolean	Returns the value of the supplied column as a SqlBoolean.
GetSqlByte (SqlDataReader only)	SqlByte	Returns the value of the supplied column as a SqlByte.
GetSqlDateTime (SqlDataReader only)	SqlDateTime	Returns the value of the supplied column as a SqlDateTime.
GetSqlDouble (SqlDataReader only)	SqlDouble	Returns the value of the supplied column as a SqlDouble.
GetSqlGuid (SqlDataReader only)	SqlGuid	Returns the value of the supplied column as a SqlGuid.
GetSqlInt16 (SqlDataReader Only)	SqlInt16	Returns the value of the supplied column as a SqlInt16.
GetSqlInt32 (SqlDataReader Only)	SqlInt32	Returns the value of the supplied column as a SqlInt32.
GetSqlInt64 (SqlDataReader only)	SqlInt64	Returns the value of the supplied column as a SqlInt64.
GetSqlMoney (SqlDataReader only)	SqlMoney	Returns the value of the supplied column as a SqlMoney.
GetSqlSingle (SqlDataReader only)	SqlSingle	Returns the value of the supplied column as a SqlSingle.

Name	Returns	Description
GetSqlString (SqlDataReader only)	SqlString	Returns the value of the supplied column as a SqlString.
GetSqlValue (SqlDataReader only)	Object	Returns an Object that represents SQL Server's Variant data type.
GetSqlValues (SqlDataReader only)	int	Returns the attribute columns from the current row in the DataReader.
GetString	string	Returns the value of the supplied column as a String.
GetTimeSpan (OleDbDataReader only)	TimeSpan	Returns the value of the supplied column as an interval of time using the TimeSpan object.
GetValue	Object	Returns the value of the supplied column in its original format.
GetValues	int	Passes out all of the attribute columns within the current row as an array parameter.
IsDBNull	bool	Returns true if the supplied column is null, false otherwise.
NextResult	bool	Moves the DataReader to the next result when reading the results of a SQL batch.
Read	bool	Moves the DataReader to the next record.

DataRelation Class

DataRelation Hierarchy:
Object
DataRelation

The DataRelation class is used to maintain a parent-child relationship between two DataTable objects.

DataRelation Properties

Name	Type	Description
ChildColumns	DataColumn Array	Returns the child DataColumn of this relation.
ChildKey Constraint	ForeignKeyConstraint	Returns the ForeignKeyConstraint for this relation.
ChildTable	DataTable	Returns the child table of this relation.
DataSet	DataSet	Returns the DataSet to which the current DataRelation belongs.
Extended Properties	PropertyCollection	Returns the collection that stores the extended or custom properties.
Nested	bool	Read/write property that will determine whether the current DataRelation objects are nested.
ParentColumns	DataColumn Array	Returns an array of DataColumn objects that are the parent columns of the current DataRelation.
ParentKey Constraint	UniqueConstraint	Returns the UniqueConstraint object that guarantees the uniqueness of the parent column.
ParentTable	DataTable	Returns the parent DataTable for the current DataRelation instance.
RelationName	string	Read/write property that references the name used to get a DataRelation from the DataRelationCollection.

DataRelation Methods

Name	Returns	Description
CheckStateFor Property		Guarantees that the current DataRelation is a valid object.
ToString (Overridden)	String	Returns the RelationName as a string.

DataRow Class

DataRow Hierarchy:
Object
DataRow

This class is used to represent a row within a `DataTable`.

DataRow Properties

Name	Type	Description
HasErrors	bool	Returns a value indicating whether or not there are errors in the columns collection.
Item	Object	Gets or sets data stored in a supplied column. In C# Indexer for the `DataRow` class.
ItemArray	Object Array	Gets or sets all of the values for this row through an array.
RowError	string	Gets or sets the custom error description for a row.
RowState	DataRowState	Gets the current state of the row in regards to its relationship to the `DataRowCollection`.
Table	DataTable	Gets the `DataTable` for which this row has a schema.

DataRow Methods

Name	Return Type	Description
AcceptChanges		Commits all the changes made to this since the last time this method was invoked.
BeginEdit		Begins an edit operation on a `DataRow` object.
CancelEdit		Cancels the current edit on the row.
ClearErrors		Clears the errors for the row, including the `RowError` and errors set with `SetColumnError`.
Delete		Deletes the row.
EndEdit		Ends the edit currently in action on the row.
GetChildRows	DataRow Array	Gets the child rows of a `DataRow`.

Table continued on following page

Name	Return Type	Description
GetColumnError	string	Gets the error description for a column.
GetColumns InError	DataColumn Array	Gets an array of columns that have error.
GetParentRow	DataRow	Gets the parent row of a DataRow.
GetParentRows	DataRow Array	Gets the parent rows of a DataRow.
HasVersion	bool	Gets a value indicating whether a specified version exists.
IsNull	bool	Gets a value indicating whether the supplied column contains a null value.
RejectChanges		Rejects all changes made to the row since AcceptChanges was last invoked/
SetColumnError		Sets the error description for a column.
SetNull		Sets the value of the supplied DataColumn to a null value.
SetParentRow		Sets the parent row of a DataRow.
SetUnspecified		Sets the value of a DataColumn with the supplied name to unspecified.

DataRow Events

Name	Description
ColumnChanged	Fires after a value has been changed in a specified DataColumn within a DataRow.
ColumnChanging	Fires when a value is in the process of being changed for a supplied DataColumn within a DataRow.
RowChanged	Fires following a successful change to a DataRow.
RowChanging	Fires while a DataRow is in the process of changing.
RowDeleted	Fires following a successful deletion of a row.
RowDeleting	When deleting a row this event will fire prior to the actual removal of the row.

DataSet Class

DataSet Hierarchy:
Object
MarshalByValueComponent
DataSet

This class represents the cache of data retrieved from the data source and kept in memory. This is one of the major classes with the ADO.NET architecture and is made up of `DataTable` and `DataRelation` objects.

DataSet Properties

Name	Type	Description
CaseSensitive	bool	Read-write property determining whether or not string comparisons are case-sensitive within the `DataSet`. The default is `false`.
DataSetName	string	Read/write property either assigning or returning the name of the current `DataSet`.
DefaultViewManager	DataViewManager	Retrieves a custom view of the data within the `DataSet` that allows filtering, searching, and navigation using a custom `DataViewManager`.
EnforceConstraints	bool	Read/write property that determines whether or not constraints will be enforced when attempting update operations.
ExtendedProperties	PropertyCollection	Returns the collection of custom information.
HasErrors	bool	Retrieves whether or not there are errors in any of the rows within any of the tables in this `DataSet`.
Locale	string	Read/write property that returns or assigns the locale information used for string comparisons within the table. Defaults to a null reference.

Table continued on following page

Name	Type	Description
Namespace	string	Read/write property that returns or assigns the NameSpace of the DataSet.
Prefix	string	Read/write property that will return or assign an XML prefix aliasing the namespace of the DataSet. Used in conjunction with the ReadXml method.
Relations	DataRelationCollection	Returns the DataRelationCollection that defines the relationships from parent tables to child tables. If no DataRelation objects exist, it defaults to null.
Site	ISite	Assigns or returns a System.ComponentModel.ISite for the current DataSet object.
Tables	DataTableCollection	Returns the DataTablecollection object consisting of the tables within the DataSet.

DataSet Methods

Name	Returns	Description
AcceptChanges		Commits all changes made to the DataSet since it was loaded or since the last time this method was invoked.
BeginInit		Starts the initialization of the current DataSet instance that is used on a form or used by some other component.
Clear		Removes all rows in all tables within the DataSet. (Erases the data, keeps the schema.)
Clone	DataSet	Clones the structure of the current DataSet.
Copy	DataSet	Copies the structure as well as the data of the current DataSet.
EndInit		Completes the initialization of the current DataSet instance that is used on a form or used by some other component.

Name	Returns	Description
GetChanges	DataSet	Returns a new DataSet that is a copy of the current DataSet with all changes that were made to it since it was loaded or the AcceptChanges method was invoked.
GetSchema Serializeable	XmlTextReader	Retrieves an XmlTextReader object in order to implement IXmlSerializeable.
GetSerialization Data	SerializationInfo & StreamingContext	Retrieves SerializationInfo and StreamingContext information in order to implement IXmlSerializeable.
GetXml	string	Retrieves the data stored in the DataSet and renders it as XML.
GetXmlSchema	string	Retrieves the XSD schema for the data in the current DataSet when the data is rendered as XML.
HasChanges	bool	Retrieves a value determining whether or not there have been changes (Insert, Update, or Delete) to the DataSet.
HasSchemaChanged	bool	Returns whether or not the schema has been altered.
InferXmlSchema		Enacts schema on the DataSet as predefined within a file or TextReader object.
Merge		Merges the current DataSet with a supplied DataSet.
OnPropertyChanging		Causes the OnPropertyChanging event to fire.
OnRemoveRelation		Exists to be overridden in order to prohibit the removal of tables.
OnRemoveTable		Fires when a DataTable is removed from the current DataSet.
RaiseProperty Changing		Causes a notification to be sent that the supplied property is about to be changed.
ReadXml		Reads XML schema and data into the DataSet.

Table continued on following page

Name	Returns	Description
ReadXmlSchema		Reads an XML Schema into the current `DataSet` object from a specified source.
ReadXml Serializeable	XmlTextReader	Reads the XML serialization information to facilitate the implementation of `IXmlSerializeable`.
RejectChanges		Undoes changes that were made to the `DataSet` from the later of being created or having the `AcceptChanges` method invoked.
Reset		Puts the `DataSet` back into the state in which it was upon being created.
ShouldSerialize Relations	bool	Returns whether the `Relations` property should persist.
ShouleSerialize Tables	bool	Returns whether the `Tables` property should persist.
WriteXml		Sends the current `DataSet` object's XML Schema and data to the specified destination (such as a File, String, or `TextWriter`).
WriteXmlSchema		Sends just the XML Schema of the current `DataSet` to the specified destination.

DataSet Events

Name	Description
MergeFailed	If the `EnforceConstraints` property is set to `true`, this event will occur if two rows are being merged from separate `DataSet` objects and have the same value for a primary key column.

DataTable Class

DataTable Hierarchy:
Object
MarshalByValueComponent
DataTable

The `DataTable`, which represents a typical database table, exists in memory and belongs to a `DataSet`.

DataTable Properties

Name	Type	Description
CaseSensitive	bool	Whether or not string comparisons will be case-sensitive within this table.
ChildRelations	DataRelation Collection	Gets the collection of child relations for the current DataTable.
Columns	DataColumn Collection	Gets the collection of columns that belong to the current DataTable.
Constraints	Constraint Collection	Gets the collection of constraints maintained on this table.
DataSet	DataSet	Gets the DataSet that this DataTable belongs to.
DefaultView	DataView	Gets a customized view of the table, which could include a filtered view or a cursor position.
DisplayExpression	string	Gets or sets the expression that will return a value used to display this table in a user interface.
ExtendedProperties	Property Collection	Gets the collection of customized information.
HasErrors	bool	Whether or not there are errors in any of the rows in any of the tables of the DataSet for which this table is a member.
Locale	CultureInfo	Gets or sets the locale information used to compare strings within the table.
MinimumCapacity	int	Gets or sets the starting size for this table.
Namespace	string	Gets or sets the namespace for the XML representation of the data stored in the DataTable.
ParentRelations	DataRelation Collection	Gets the collection of parent relations for this DataTable.
Prefix	string	Gets or set the namespace for the XML representation of the data stored in the current DataTable.
PrimaryKey	DataColumn Array	Gets or sets an array of columns that will function as primary keys for the DataTable.

Table continued on following page

Name	Type	Description
Rows	DataRow Collection	Gets the collection of rows that belong to this table.
Site (Overridden)	Isite	Read/write property that returns or assigns a `System.DCOmponentModel.ISite` for the current `DataTable`.
TableName	string	Gets or sets the name of the `DataTable`.

DataTable Methods

Name	Return Type	Description
AcceptChanges		Commits all the changes made to this table since the last time this method was invoked.
BeginInit		
BeginLoadData		Turns off the notifications, index maintenance, and constraints while loading data.
Clear		Clears the `DataTable` of all data.
Clone	DataTable	Clones the structure of the `DataTable`.
Compute	Object	Computes the given expression on the current rows that pass the filter criteria.
Copy	DataTable	Copies both the structure and the data from this `DataTable`.
EndLoadData		Turns back on the notifications, index maintenance, and constraints after loading data.
GetChanges	DataTable	Gets a copy of the `DataTable` containing all changes made to it since it was last loaded, or since the last `AcceptChanges` method invocation.
GetErrors	DataRow Array	Gets an array of `DataRow` objects that contain errors.
GetRowType	Type	Returns the row type.
HasSchemaChanged	bool	Returns whether or not the amount of columns that exist in the current `DataTable` instance has changed.

Name	Return Type	Description
ImportRow		Copies a `DataRow`, including original and current values, `DataRowState` values, and errors, into a `DataTable`.
LoadDataRow	DataRow	Finds and updates a specific row. If a matching row isn't found, a new row will be created with the given values.
NewRow	DataRow	Creates a new `DataRow` with the same schema as the table.
OnColumnChanged		Raises the `ColumnChanged` event.
OnColumnChanging		Raises the `ColumnChanging` event.
OnProperty Changing		Raises the `OnPropertyChanging` event.
OnRemoveColumn		Alerts the `DataTable` that a `DataColumn` is being removed from the current `DataTable` instance.
OnRowChanged		Raises the `RowChanged` event.
OnRowChanging		Raises the `OnRowChanging` event.
OnRowDeleted		Raises the `OnRowDeleted` event.
OnRowDeleting		Raises the `OnRowDeleting` event.
RejectChanges		Rolls back all changes that have been made to the table since it was loaded, or since the last `AcceptChanges` method was invoked.
Select	DataRow Array	Gets an array of `DataRow` objects.
ToString (Overridden)	string	Returns a string that is made up of the name of the table and the `DisplayExpression` if there is one concatenated after the name of the table in the string.

DataTableMapping Class

DataTableMapping Hierarchy:
Object
MarshalByRefObject
DataTableMapping

Used by the `DataAdapter` class when populating a `DataSet`, this class maintains the relationship between column names in a `DataTable` within a `DataSet` and the corresponding column names in the data source.

DataTableMapping Properties

Name	Type	Description
ColumnMappings	DataTableMapping Collection	Returns the `DataColumnMappingCollection` for the `DataTable`.
DataSetTable	string	Read/write property that will return or assign the table name from a `DataSet`.
SourceTable	string	Read/write property that will return or assign the source table name from a data source (case-sensitive).

DataTableMapping Methods

Name	Returns	Description
GetColumnMappingBy SchemaAction	DataColumn	Returns a `DataColumn` from the supplied `DataTable` using the `MissingMappingAction` that was specified and the name of the `DataColumn`.
GetDataTableBy SchemaAction	DataTable	Returns the current `DataTable` for the supplied `DataSet` using the supplied `MissingSchemaAction` value.
ToString (Overridden)	string	Returns the name of the current `SourceTable` as a string.

DataView Class

DataView Hierarchy:
Object
MarshalByValueComponent
DataView

The `DataView` class represents a customized view of the data to which it is bound. This view can then be sorted, filtered, edited, searched, and navigated. This class is similar to a view in a database.

DataView Properties

Name	Type	Description
AllowDelete	bool	Read/write property that determines whether deletes are allowed.
AllowEdit	bool	Read/write property that determines whether edits are allowed.
AllowNew	bool	Read/write property that determines whether new rows can be inserted using the AddNew method.
ApplyDefaultSort	bool	Read/write property that determines whether to use the default sort.
Count	int	Returns the number of records in the DataView after both RowFilter and RowStateFilter have been applied.
DataViewManager	DataViewManager	Returns the DataViewManager associated with this view.
IsOpen	bool	Returns whether the data source is currently open and applying views of the data on the DataTable.
Item	DataRowView	This property acts as the indexer for the DataView class.
RowFilter	string	Read/write property that will act as the clause used to filter which rows are viewed through the DataView.
RowStateFilter	DataViewRowState	Read/write property that will assign or return the DataViewRowState filter used within the DataView.
Sort	string	Read/write property that will assign or return the sorted column(s) and sort order.
Table	DataTable	Read/write property that will assign or return the source DataTable.

DataView Methods

Name	Returns	Description
AddNew	DataRowView	Inserts a new row into the DataView.
BeginInit		Begins the initialization of a DataView that is used by another component.
Close		Closes the current DataView.
Delete		Deletes the row at the supplied index location.
EndInit		Ends the initialization started from the BeginInit method.
GetEnumerator	IEnumerator	Returns an enumerator for the current DataView.
IndexListChanged		Invoked following a successful change to the DataView.
OnListChanged		Causes the ListChanged event to fire.
Open		Opens the current DataView.

DataView Events

Name	Description
ListChanged	Fires when the list controlled by the DataView is altered.

DataViewManager Class

DataViewManager Hierarchy:
Object
MarshalByValueComponent
DataViewManager

This class maintains the default DataViewSetting collection for each DataTable that exists within a DataSet.

DataViewManager Properties

Name	Type	Description
DataSet	DataSet	Read/write property that will assign or return the DataSet to use with the current DataViewManager.
DataViewSettings	DataViewSetting Collection	Returns the DataViewSettingCollection for each DataTable within the DataSet.

DataViewManager Methods

Name	Returns	Description
CreateDataView	DataView	Creates a DataView for the specified DataTable.
OnListChanged		Causes the ListChanged event to fire.
RelationCollection Changed		Causes a CollectionChanged event to fire when a DataRelation object is inserted in or deleted from the DataRelationCollection.
TableCollection Changed		Causes the CollectionChanged event to fire when a DataTable is inserted in or deleted from the DataTableCollection.

DataViewManager Events

Name	Description
ListChanged	Fires when a row is added to or removed from a DataView.

DataViewSetting Class

DataViewSetting Hierarchy:
Object
DataViewSetting

This class represents the default settings ApplyDefaultSort, DataViewManager, RowFilter, RowStateFilter, Sort, and Table for DataView objects that were created by the DataViewManager.

DataViewSetting Properties

Name	Type	Description
ApplyDefaultSort	bool	Read/write property that determines whether or not to use the default sort.
DataViewManager	DataViewManager	Returns the DataViewManager that contains the current DataViewSetting.
RowFilter	string	Read/write property that returns or assigns the filter to use within the DataView.
RowStateFilter	DataViewRowState	Read/write property that determines which types of rows in the DataView.
Sort	string	Read/write property that determines the Sort to use for the DataView.
Table	DataTable	Returns the DataTable that the current DataViewSetting properties apply to.

OleDbError Class

OleDbError Hierarchy:
Object
OleDbError

When an OleDb data source returns an error or warning this is the object that collects the information.

OleDbError Properties

Name	Type	Description
Message	string	Returns a short description of the error.
NativeError	int	Returns the proprietary error message from the data source.
Source	string	Returns the name of the provider that generated the error.
SqlState	string	Returns the code following the ANSI standard for the database.

OleDbError Methods

Name	Return Type	Description
ToString (Overridden)	string	Returns the complete error message.

OleDbException Class

OleDbException Hierarchy:
Object
Exception
SystemException
ExternalException
OleDbException

When an OleDb data source returns an error or warning this is the exception that is thrown.

OleDbException Properties

Name	Type	Description
Errors	OleDbError Collection	Returns a collection of OleDbError objects.
Message (Overridden)	string	Returns the error message.
Source (Overridden)	string	Returns the name of the provider that generated the error.

OleDbException Methods

Name	Return Type	Description
ToString (Overridden)	string	Returns the fully qualified name of the current exception as a string.

Parameter Classes

SqlParameter Hierarchy:	OleDbParameter Hierarchy:
Object	Object
MarshalByRefObject	MarshalByRefObject
SqlParameter	*OleDbParameter*

The parameter classes represent the parameters passed into, or out from a command object.

Parameter Properties

Name	Type	Description
DbType	DbType Enum	Read/write property that will return or assign the DbType of the parameter.
Direction	Parameter Direction Enum	Read/write property that will determine the type of parameter: Input, Output, Input/Output (Bi-Directional), or stored procedure return value.
IsNullable	bool	Read/write property that will return or assign whether or not this parameter accepts null values.
Offset	int	Read/write property that will return or assign the offset to the Value property.
OleDbType (OleDbParameter only)	OleDbType Enum	Returns or assigns the OleDbType of the current parameter.
ParameterName	string	Returns or assigns the name of the parameter.
Precision	byte	Returns or assigns the numeric precision (number of digits) used for the value property.
Scale	byte	Returns or assigns the numeric scale (number of decimal places) that the value will be represented.
Size	int	Returns or assigns the number of bytes used to store the value within the column.

Name	Type	Description
SourceColumn	string	Returns or assigns the name of the column that was mapped to the DataSet.
SourceVersion	DataRowVersion Enum	Returns or assigns the DataRowVersion to use when loading a value.
SqlDbType (SqlParameter only)	SqlDbType Enum	Returns or assigns the SqlDbType of the parameter.
Value	Object	Returns or assigns the actual value of the parameter.

Parameter Methods

Name	Returns	Description
ToString (Overridden)	string	Returns the ParameterName as a string.

SqlError Class

SqlError Hierarchy:
Object
SqlError

When SQL Server returns an error or a warning, this class collects the information.

SqlError Properties

Name	Type	Description
Class	byte	Returns the severity level as defined from the SQL Server .NET Data Provider.
LineNumber	int	Returns the line number from the T-SQL command that caused the error.
Message	string	Returns the string describing the error.
Number	int	Returns the error number.

Table continued on following page

Name	Type	Description
Procedure	string	Returns the name of the stored procedure or remote procedure call (RPC).
Server	string	Returns the name of the SQL Server that generated the error.
Source	string	Returns the name of the provider that generated the error.
State	byte	Returns the number altering the error to provide additional information.

SqlError Methods

Name	Return Type	Description
ToString (Overridden)	String	Returns the complete error message.

SqlException Class

SqlException Hierarchy:
Object
Exception
SystemException
SqlException

The SqlException is the exception that is thrown when SQL Server raises a warning or error.

SqlException Properties

Name	Type	Description
Class	byte	Returns the severity level as defined from the SQL Server .NET Data Provider.
Errors	SqlError Collection	Returns a collection of SqlError objects.

Name	Type	Description
LineNumber	int	Returns the line number from the T-SQL command that caused the error.
Message (Overridden)	string	Returns the description of the error.
Number	int	Returns the error number.
Procedure	string	Returns the name of the stored procedure or remote procedure call (RPC)
Server	string	Returns the name of the SQL Server that generated the error.
Source (Overridden)	string	Returns the name of the provider that generated the error.
State	string	Returns the number altering the error to provide additional information.

SqlException Methods

Name	Return Type	Description
ToString (Overridden)	string	Returns the fully qualified name of the current exception.

Transaction Classes

SqlTransaction Hierarchy:	OleDbTransaction Hierarchy:
Object	Object
MarshalByRefObject	MarshalByRefObject
SqlTransaction	*OleDbTransaction*

The transaction class represents a SQL transaction in the data source.

Transaction Properties

Name	Type	Description
IsolationLevel	IsolationLevel Enum	Returns the selected IsolationLevel or assigns a value from the IsolationLevel enum.

Transaction Methods

Name	Returns	Description
Begin (OleDbTransaction only)		Starts a nested database transaction.
Commit		Commits the transaction
Rollback		Rolls back a transaction.
Save (SqlTransaction only)		Constructs a savepoint in the transaction. Note that OleDb provides nested transactions instead of savepoints.

C

Using Non-SQL Server RDBMS

In this appendix, we will demonstrate how to connect to the following relational databases:

❏   Microsoft Access

❏   Oracle 8i

❏   DB2

ADO.NET offers a rich set of classes for connecting to databases, executing SQL statements, and calling stored procedures. Connecting to SQL Server database version 7.0 or later is performed using the SqlConnection class, whereas connecting to SQL Server database version 6.0 or earlier, and other RDBMS such as Microsoft Access, or Oracle is achieved using the OleDbConnection class. The appropriate .NET data provider must be used. For SQL Server 6.x or earlier the provider is SQLOLEDB.

Connecting to Different Databases

In OleDbConnection the provider is a mandatory property, which needs to be set before making a database connection. Providers are essentially a core set of OLE DB interfaces that help make connections and gain access to databases.

In this section first we will revisit the connection to SQL Server database and later we will see how this is different from non-SQL Server connections. The following code illustrates a SqlConnection to a SQL Server 7.0 database. Here, ent01h02 is the server name of the data source, and northwind is the database name:

```
SqlConnection sqlConn = new SqlConnection("Data Source=ent01h02;"+
                  "Integrated Security=SSPI;Initial Catalog=northwind");
```

The following code illustrates how to connect to a SQL Server 6.x database using the `OleDbConnection` class. Here `SQLOLEDB` is the provider name for SQL Server 6.x and earlier versions:

```
OleDbConnection oleDbConn = new OleDbConnection("Provider=SQLOLEDB;" +
                  "Data Source=ent01h02;Integrated Security=SSPI;" +
                  "Initial Catalog=northwind");
```

Apart from the database connections, the `OleDbDataAdapter` and `OleDbCommand` classes are similar to their SQL Server 7.0 and above counterparts, which are `SqlDataAdapter`, and `SqlCommand` respectively.

OLE DB with a Microsoft Access Database

In this section, we will look at the use of various methods of the `OleDbConnection`, `OleDbDataAdapter`, and `DataSet` classes. We will connect to a Microsoft Access database using the `OleDbConnection` class, and retrieve data using the `OleDbDataAdapter` and `DataSet` classes. Later, we will develop an application called `Student Maintenance`, which illustrates in detail how to insert to and update an Access database using the `OleDbDataAdapter` and `DataSet` classes. Student Maintenance is a simple master maintenance kind of application, which selects data from Access database and displays it in a `DataGrid` control. The user is allowed to insert new rows or modify the existing rows in the `DataGrid` control, which can be saved back to the database.

Open up Microsoft Access and create a database. In our `Student` database, we will have a single table called `Student`, which holds student information. Alternatively, the `Student.mdb` access database file can be downloaded from Wrox site, http://www.wrox.com. Let's look the student table design, which we can see in the screenshot below:

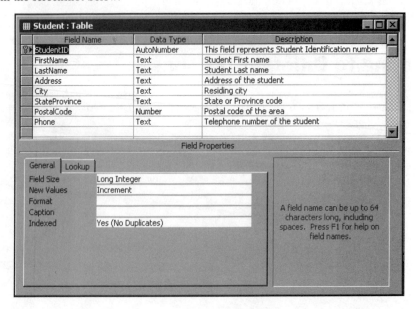

The `StudentID` column is defined as **AutoNumber** and it is the primary key. The other columns allow null values.

The following screenshot shows the data from the `Student` table:

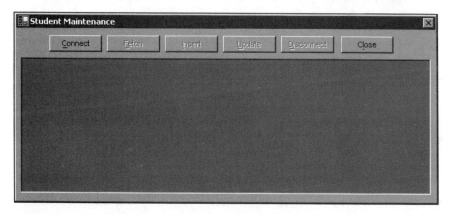

Now we will see how to use the `OleDbDataAdapter` and `DataSet` classes to retrieve data. Our `Student Maintenance` application will have a `DataGrid` control that will be bound to a `DataSet` object.

Start Visual Studio .NET and create a new **Windows Application C# Project**. Design a form as shown in the screenshot below. In the form, we will have six `Button` controls and a `DataGrid` control (the gray area) occupying the rest of the window. Add handlers for the click event of all the buttons. Set the `DataGrid` control's `Name` property to `m_dgStudentDetails` and its `CaptionVisible` property to `false`. Similarly we need to set `Name` and `Text` properties, and `Click` event handlers for all button controls. The form should look like this:

Declare the following members with `private` access in our Form class. These are the key members, which aid in database connection and manipulation of data:

```
private OleDbConnection m_dbConnection;
private OleDbDataAdapter m_dbDataAdapter;
private DataSet m_dsStudent;
private OleDbCommandBuilder m_dbCommBuilder;
```

The `m_dbConnection` object represents a database connection. `m_dbDataAdapter` is our `OleDbDataAdapter` object, which acts as a bridge between the `OleDbConnection` and `DataSet` objects. We will see the importance of the objects derived from the `OleDbCommandBuilder` class while inserting and updating data. For the moment, we will focus on connecting to databases and retrieving data.

On clicking the **Connect** button, we will connect to our Access database, `Student.mdb`. On a successful database connection, the buttons **Fetch**, **Insert**, **Update**, and **Disconnect** will be enabled.

The `OleDbConnection` class implements a database connection. An instance of this class is created by passing a database connection string to its overloaded constructor. The main difference between this and using the `SqlConnection` is the connection string. For OleDb connections, we need to set the `Provider` parameter, which specifies the software we will use to access the database. See the following code, which connects to an Access database with an `OleDbConnection` object:

```
/* Build connect string */
string l_strConnectString =@"Provider=Microsoft.Jet.OLEDB.4.0;" +
        "Password="""";User "+ "ID=Admin;" +
        "Data Source=D:\Niranjan\Sairam\MyProjects\"+
        "VisualStudio.NET Beta2\CSharp\RDBMSDatabases\StudentDB.mdb;";

/* Open database connection */
m_dbConnection.Open(l_strConnectString);
```

Here, the `Provider` parameter specifies the Jet database engine, which is used to access Microsoft Access databases. A `Provider` is a made up of one or more COM objects, which is responsible for transferring data from a data source to the consumer or client. The `User ID` and `Password` parameters provide user authentication. In our case, the user ID is `Admin` and password is `null`. The next important parameter is the `Data Source`, which is the Access database file name: `Student.mdb`.

The next step is to call the `Open()` method of the `OleDbConnection`, which opens the actual database connection. In the case of connection failure, an `OleDbException` will be raised. If the connection is already open, an `InvalidOperationException` will be thrown.

We will fill our `DataGrid` control using the `DataSet` class. The `OleDbDataAdapter` class is the one that acts as a bridge between our database connection, `OleDbConnection`, and our `DataSet`. In order to fetch data using our `DataSet` – `m_dsStudent` – the `OleDbDataAdapter` object must be created and passed a valid SQL `SELECT` statement. The overloaded constructor of this class allows you to create an instance by passing a SQL `SELECT` statement and an `OleDbConnection` object (in our case `m_dbConnection`) as parameters. The following code illustrates the creation of an `OleDbDataAdapter` object called `m_dbDataAdapter`, and associates this object with the connection object. Also, note that this `SELECT` statement returns all the rows and columns from the student table:

```
/* Create Data Adapter object */
m_dbDataAdapter = new OleDbDataAdapter("SELECT * FROM STUDENT",
                                               m_dbConnection);

/* Create Command Builder object for generating SQL statements */
m_dbCommBuilder = new OleDbCommandBuilder(m_dbDataAdapter);
```

To insert or update data from the `DataSet` to the `Database`, we need the `OleDbCommandBuilder` object. Therefore, we create this object using its overloaded constructor by passing in an `OleDbDataAdapter` instance. Later we will use the `OleDbCommandBuilder` class to insert and update data from `DataSet` to database.

Next, we will populate the `DataGrid` control using the `DataSet`. This takes the following steps:

❑ Create a `DataSet` object in the click event handler of the **Fetch** button.

❑ Load the `DataSet` with data from database using the `Fill()` method of the `OleDbDataAdapter` object and give a name to this table. In the code fragment shown below, the table name is `Student`.

❑ Design your grid control to customize the style, format, coloring, and other settings.

❑ Call the `SetDataBinding()` method of the `DataGrid`, which will display the data in the grid control.

The following code snippet is taken from the click event handler of the **Fetch** button:

```
/* Create a DataSet */
m_dsStudent = new DataSet();

/* Fill Data Set using Data Adapter */
m_dbDataAdapter.Fill(m_dsStudent,"Student");

/* Design your Grid control */
DesignDataGridControl();

/* Fill Grid control with the data from DataSet object */
m_dgStudentDetails.SetDataBinding(m_dsStudent,"Student");
```

In the above code, first the `DataSet` is created then the `Fill()` method of `OleDbDataAdapter` is called to populate data from the `Student` table into the `DataSet` object. While filling data, we also give a name to the data that resides in the `DataSet` object. Remember that the `DataSet` is an in-memory cache of the database, which works in a disconnected manner. It can hold data from one or more tables. Therefore, we need to give a table name (this can be anything and not necessarily the database table name) that we can use to refer to. The `SetDataBinding` method of the `DataGrid` will populate the data from the `Student` table of the `DataSet` object.

`DesignDataGridControl()` is our private method that customizes the grid columns. In our application, Student ID is an auto-generated number, so we will hide it. In addition, we will give custom headers for all the columns. The `DataGridTableStyle` class is used to customize the `DataGrid` control. First, we need to create this object and, for every column, we need to create an instance of the `DataGridColumnStyle` class and attach this to the `DataGridTableStyle` object. Finally, the `DataGrid` control is associated with the table style using `TableStyles` public instance property. The `MappingName` property of the `DataGridTableStyle` class should be same as the table name given to the result set of the `DataSet` object in the `Fill()` method of the `OleDbDataAdapter` class. See the following code:

```
private void DesignDataGridControl(){
    try {

        /* Create a new Table Style */
        DataGridTableStyle l_dgtsObj = new DataGridTableStyle();
        l_dgtsObj.MappingName = "Student";

        /* Student ID */
        DataGridColumnStyle l_gdcsStudentID = new DataGridTextBoxColumn();
        l_gdcsStudentID.MappingName = "StudentID";
        l_gdcsStudentID.HeaderText = "ID";
        l_gdcsStudentID.Width = 0;
        l_dgtsObj.GridColumnStyles.Add(l_gdcsStudentID);
```

```
        /* First Name */
        DataGridColumnStyle l_gdcsFirstName = new DataGridTextBoxColumn();
        l_gdcsFirstName.MappingName = "FirstName";
        l_gdcsFirstName.HeaderText = "First Name";
        l_gdcsFirstName.Width = 100;
        l_dgtsObj.GridColumnStyles.Add(l_gdcsFirstName);

        /* Last Name */
        DataGridColumnStyle l_gdcsLastName = new DataGridTextBoxColumn();
        l_gdcsLastName.MappingName = "LastName";
        l_gdcsLastName.HeaderText = "Last Name";
        l_gdcsLastName.Width = 100;
        l_dgtsObj.GridColumnStyles.Add(l_gdcsLastName);

        /* Address */
        DataGridColumnStyle l_gdcsAddress = new DataGridTextBoxColumn();
        l_gdcsAddress.MappingName = "Address";
        l_gdcsAddress.HeaderText = "Address";
        l_gdcsAddress.Width = 150;
        l_dgtsObj.GridColumnStyles.Add(l_gdcsAddress);

        /* City */
        DataGridColumnStyle l_gdcsCity = new DataGridTextBoxColumn();
        l_gdcsCity.MappingName = "City";
        l_gdcsCity.HeaderText = "City";
        l_gdcsCity.Width = 50;
        l_dgtsObj.GridColumnStyles.Add(l_gdcsCity);

        /* StateProvince */
        DataGridColumnStyle l_gdcsSP = new DataGridTextBoxColumn();
        l_gdcsSP.MappingName = "StateProvince";
        l_gdcsSP.HeaderText = "State/Province";
        l_gdcsSP.Width = 50;
        l_dgtsObj.GridColumnStyles.Add(l_gdcsSP);

        /* Postal Code */
        DataGridColumnStyle l_gdcsPostalCode = new DataGridTextBoxColumn();
        l_gdcsPostalCode.MappingName = "Postal Code";
        l_gdcsPostalCode.HeaderText = "Postal Code";
        l_gdcsPostalCode.Width = 50;
        l_dgtsObj.GridColumnStyles.Add(l_gdcsPostalCode);

        /* Phone */
        DataGridColumnStyle l_gdcsPhone = new DataGridTextBoxColumn();
        l_gdcsPhone.MappingName = "Phone";
        l_gdcsPhone.HeaderText = "Phone";
        l_gdcsPhone.Width = 100;
        l_dgtsObj.GridColumnStyles.Add(l_gdcsPhone);

        /* Add the collection to DataGrid Control */
        m_dgStudentDetails.TableStyles.Add(l_dgtsObj);
    }
    catch ( Exception e )
    {
        throw new Exception("Error while customizing DataGrid Control");
    }
}
```

The `DataGridColumnStyle` class is an abstract class that specifies the appearance and behavior of the grid column. A column can be represented as either a radio button or a text box in a `DataGrid` control. Therefore, the `DataGridColumnStyle` object can be created with either a `DataGridTextBoxColumn` object or a `DataGridBoolColumn` object. In our table we don't have any Boolean columns, so all columns are created with the textbox type. The `MappingName` property of the `DataGridColumnStyle` class represents the name of the database column. `HeaderText` is the text that appears on the header in the `DataGrid` of each column. The `GridColumnStyles.Add()` method of the `DataGridTableStyle` object allows us to add a `DataGridColumnStyle` object. The screenshot below shows our data in a `DataGrid` column with styles applied to it:

Now we have seen how to list data in a `DataGrid` control. Next, we will focus writing data from a `DataGrid` to a database, using the `DataSet` object. Inserting data using a `DataSet` is a two step process. First we will be inserting data into the `DataSet`, and then into the underlying database. This helps to minimize the load on the database. If there are any problems with the newly inserted rows, such as integrity or constraint violations, they can be validated at the `DataSet` level. Only when the `DataSet` is updated successfully will any load be placed on the underlying database. By default, the `DataGrid` control will display an empty row at the bottom. The user is allowed to enter values into this row. We need to write the following code for the Insert button's click event to insert the row into database:

```
/* If no new records found, then exit from the function */
if ( m_dsStudent.HasChanges(DataRowState.Added) == false )
{
    MessageBox.Show("No new records added to Grid control. " +
                        "Add records and click Insert button !!!",
                    "Student Maintenance", MessageBoxButtons.OK,
                            MessageBoxIcon.Information);
    return;
}
else
{
    try
    {
        this.Cursor = Cursors.WaitCursor;

        /* Get only New records data */
        DataSet l_dsAdded = m_dsStudent.GetChanges(DataRowState.Added);

        /* Accept the changes */
        m_dsStudent.AcceptChanges();
```

```
        DataTable l_dtAdded = l_dsAdded.Tables[0];
        m_dbCommBuilder = new OleDbCommandBuilder(m_dbDataAdapter);

        /* Insert to database */
        int l_iRowsAffected = m_dbDataAdapter.Update(l_dtAdded);
        string l_strMessage = "Successfully inserted " +
                      l_iRowsAffected.ToString() + " student record(s)";

        this.Cursor = Cursors.Arrow;
        MessageBox.Show(l_strMessage,"Student Maintenance",
                    MessageBoxButtons.OK ,MessageBoxIcon.Exclamation);
    }
    catch ( Exception e1 )
    {
        string l_strError = "Error while Inserting data :" + e1.Message;
        this.Cursor = Cursors.Arrow;
        MessageBox.Show(l_strError,"Student Maintenance - Error",
                      MessageBoxButtons.OK,MessageBoxIcon.Error);
    }
}
```

Inserting a new row into a DataGrid will automatically notify the DataSet object associated with it. First, we determine whether there are any new rows added to the DataSet object using HasChanges(). This function takes a DataRowState enumerated parameter and returns a Boolean value. The DataRowState.Added value represents new rows added to DataSet. If HasChanges() returns false, it means that there are no new rows added to the DataGrid, so we will display a message and exit the function. If it returns true, we need to get the new rows and insert them into the database. This is done by calling the GetChanges() method of the DataSet class. GetChanges() takes DataRowState.Added as a parameter and returns a new DataSet with rows added to original DataSet:

```
/* Get only New records data */
DataSet l_dsAdded = m_dsStudent.GetChanges(DataRowState.Added);
```

Here l_dsAdded will contain only the new rows added to the DataSet. Next, we get the table (which contains new rows) from the DataSet using the Tables property. The Update() method of the OleDbDataAdapter object will insert new rows from the DataTable into the database, and it returns the number of affected rows.

The Update() method of the OleDbDataAdapter needs a SQL insert statement in order to do this insertion. This is where the OleDbCommandBuilder object will be helpful. The Update() method internally refers to its attached OleDbCommandBuilder object (m_dbCommBuilder) to issue SQL statements to the database. The OleDbCommandBuilder class automatically generates appropriate SQL statements. Remember in our database connection function, this object is created using its overloaded constructor and passing an OleDbDataAdapter object. This is where the OleDbCommandBuilder object is useful. Its helps in generating SQL statements for when we call Update().

Calling AcceptChanges() on the DataSet will commit all the changes since it was loaded, or the previous AcceptChanges() call. See the following code fragment, which can be found after creating a new DataSet and before calling Update(). If AcceptChanges() is not called, then calling GetChanges() next time will return this new row, and in this case if Update() is called, it will try to insert the same row again which will cause duplication of the data in the database:

```
/* Accept the changes */
m_dsStudent.AcceptChanges();
```

Now we have finished inserting data from the `DataSet` to the database. The next step will be to update the data.

Updating of data is very similar to the insertion function, except for two differences. The first difference is in determining the changes made to `DataGrid` using the `HasChanges()` method. In the case of updating, we pass the `DataRowState.Modified` value to check for any modifications done in `DataGrid` control. See the following code fragment:

```
if ( m_dsStudent.HasChanges(DataRowState.Modified) == false )
{
```

The next difference is the parameter being passed to the `GetChanges()` method. Here we pass the `DataRowState.Modified` value to determine the changed rows:

```
/* Get only Modified data */
DataSet l_dsModified = m_dsStudent.GetChanges(DataRowState.Modified);
```

We've now completed our application to the level needed to demonstrate the basic principles we're interested in – deleting a row from the `DataGrid`, and updating the changes to its `DataSet`, is left as an area for the reader's exploration.

OLE DB with an Oracle 8i Database

In this section we will discuss connecting to and manipulating data in an Oracle 8i database from C# using .NET OLE DB classes. We will also see how to call Oracle stored procedures from C#. Connecting to Oracle databases is very similar to connecting to Access databases, except that we use a different provider. The provider that we use is the **Microsoft OLE DB Provider for Oracle**. In this application, I have illustrated connectivity to Oracle 8i installed on Sun Solaris. Apart from connecting to an Oracle database, this section also explains how to call stored procedures using `OleDb` classes.

Before getting into the connectivity to Oracle, let's first see how to configure our client machine to access Oracle server. To connect to Oracle 8i server, Oracle Client needs to be installed in our machine. When installing the Oracle client, necessary network configuration applications will be installed by default. Open the "Net8 Easy Config" application from the programs menu as shown in the figure overleaf:

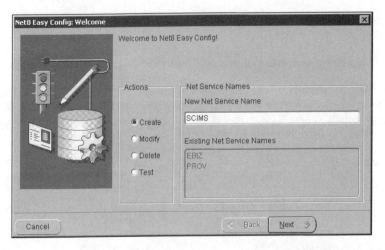

Select the **Create** option, enter your service name, and click **Next**. I have given SCIMS here. In the second window select the appropriate protocol. Here I have selected TCP/IP:

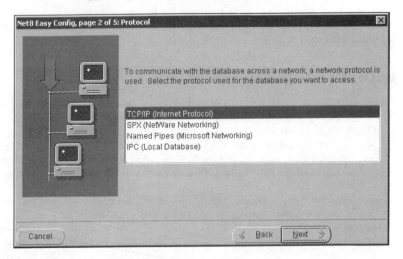

In the next window enter the name or IP address of your server where the Oracle database resides. By default the Oracle Listener will be listening at port 1521. So leave it as it is and click **Next**:

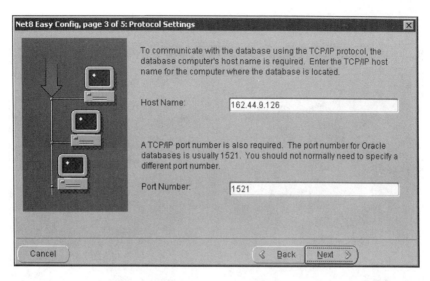

In the next window, we need to give the Oracle service name. Depending upon the Oracle release SID (Service ID) or Service Name should be given. I have entered TEST1 as my SID:

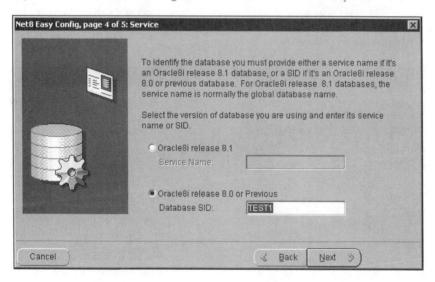

The next window, test your connection parameters by clicking the Test button:

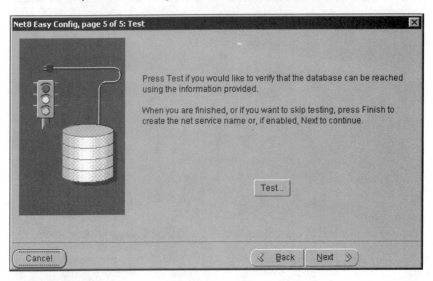

When the Test button is clicked, this tool attempts to connect to the database using the user ID 'scott' and password 'tiger'. Change the user ID and password and click the Test button. I have given 'cg1104' as user ID and 'cg1104' as the password:

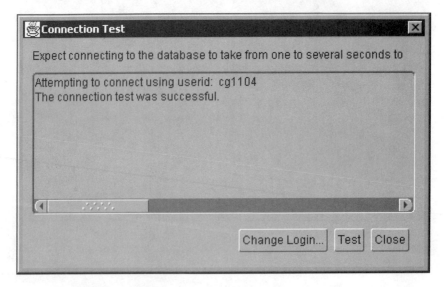

Close this window and click the Finish button in the next window to save the settings.

Now we are configured to connect to our Oracle database. This will add an entry into the tnsnames.ora file, which holds the connection information for Oracle databases.

The next step is adding a DSN that points to this SCIMS service name. To do this, go to Control Panel, open **ODBC data sources**, select the **System DSN** tab, and click the **Add** button. This will show the list of drivers installed on your machine. From the list select **Microsoft ODBC Driver for Oracle**, enter your DSN name in the **Data Source Name** textbox. I have given "SCIMS" as my DSN. The next two boxes can be left blank. In the last box, enter the Service name given in the Oracle Net8 configuration box. In our case this is "SCIMS". So enter the same and click **OK**. That's all – we have finished configuring Oracle:

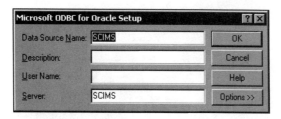

Here we will develop a different application, Student Modification, which populates a combobox with the Student ID and allows us to modify student details. The database is updated with the modified details using an Oracle stored procedure. The `Student` table is the same as in the Access sample application. The table scripts are given below:

```
/* Table creation script */
Create table Student (
      StudentID number(5) Primary Key,
      FirstName Varchar2(25),
      LastName Varchar2(25),
      Address Varchar2(30),
      City Varchar2(15),
      StateProvince Varchar2(2),
      PostalCode Varchar2(10),
      Phone Varchar2(15)
);
```

```
/* Insert scripts */
Insert into Student Values ( 1,'Niranjan','Kumar','507 - 20th Ave. E.Apt.
                          2A','Seattle','WA','98122','(514) 555-8978');
Insert into Student Values ( 2,'Roopa','Sairam','908 W. Capital
                          Way','Tacoma','WA','98401','(514) 555-9482');
Insert into Student Values ( 3,'Brandon','Coake','722 Moss Bay
                       Blvd.','Kirkland','WA','98033','(514) 555-3412');
Insert into Student Values ( 4,'Margaret','Peacock','4110 Old Redmond
                       Rd.','Redmond','WA','98052','(514) 555-8122');
Insert into Student Values ( 5,'Matthew','Dunn','14 Garrett Hill',
                          'Seattle','WA','98105','(514) 555-1189');
Insert into Student Values ( 6,'Helvetius','Nagy','722 DaVinci Blvd.',
                          'Kirkland','WA','98034','(514) 555-8257');
Insert into Student Values ( 7,'Deborah','Peterson','305 - 14th Ave.
                       S.Suite 3B','Seattle','WA','98128','(514) 555-4112');
Insert into Student Values ( 13,'Aparna','Sairam','908 W. Capital Way',
                          'Tacoma','WA','98401','(514) 555-9482');
commit;
```

The main application window looks like this:

The following table shows the structure of the Student table in the Oracle database:

Column	Data Type
STUDENTID	NUMBER(5) NOT NULL - PRIMARY KEY
FIRSTNAME	VARCHAR2(25)
LASTNAME	VARCHAR2(25)
ADDRESS	VARCHAR2(30)
CITY	VARCHAR2(15)
STATEPROVINCE	VARCHAR2(2)
POSTALCODE	VARCHAR2(10)
PHONE	VARCHAR2(15)

Let's see how to connect to Oracle database. Start VS .NET, and create a new C# Windows Application. Design the form as shown in the previous screenshot. Our form has one ComboBox control, seven TextBox controls, and two Button controls. Drag and drop one OleDbConnection control from the toolbox and open its **Properties** window.

Here we will see how to connect to Oracle database at design time, and how to set the OleDbConnection parameters accordingly. Select the ConnectionString property combobox and click the **New Connection** option, as shown in the screenshot opposite:

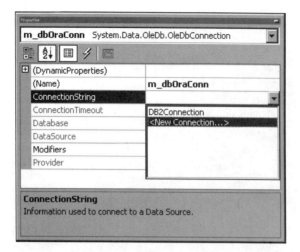

When you select this option, you will get a Data Link Properties window as shown below:

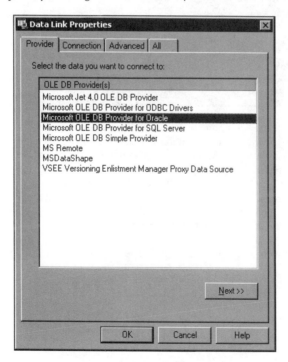

From this dialog, we will specify our Oracle database and connection parameters. Here, select the Microsoft OLE DB Provider for Oracle option and click the Next button, which will take you to the Connection as shown overleaf:

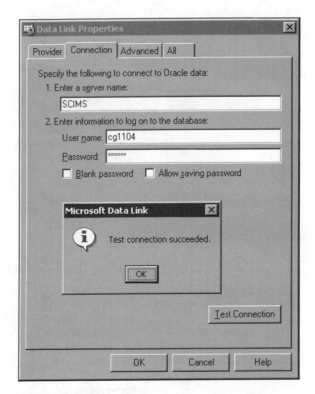

In this window, enter the service name in the Server name text box, and the user name and password in their respective fields. For my Oracle database, SCIMS is the server name (remember the service name that is given in the Net8 Easy Config application), CG1104 is the User name, and CG1104 is the Password (for security reasons the password is shown as * characters). After entering the database connection details, clicking the Test Connection button will attempt to connect to the database with the details given. If successfully connected, a Test connection succeeded message will be displayed; otherwise an error message will be displayed. When successfully connected, click the OK button to save the connection details and close this Data Link Properties window.

When you click the OK button in the Data Link Properties window, a connection window will appear:

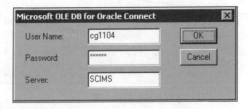

Entering the correct password and clicking the OK button will set the ConnectionString property of the OleDbConnection object with proper values as shown in the following screenshot. This screenshot shows the entire ConnectionString value in the ToolTip:

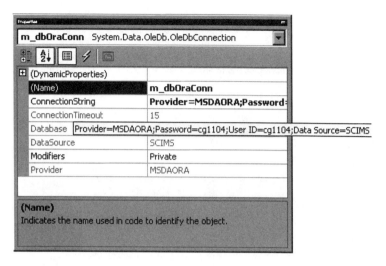

The `ConnectionString` for `m_dbOraConn` will be set as shown below.

```
//
// m_dbOraConn
//
this.m_dbOraConn.ConnectionString = "Provider=MSDAORA;Password=cg1104;User
ID=cg1104;Data Source=SCIMS";
```

We have completed our design time Oracle connection. This database connection will be added to the VS Server Explorer as shown in the screenshot below:

Our next step is to write code to connect to the database at run time, populate the Student ID `ComboBox`, modify details of the `Student` table, and store it in database. We will connect to the database and populate the `ComboBox` with the Student ID during the loading of the form. Add an event handler to the `Load` event of the form and write the following code as shown below:

```
private void OnLoadStudentDlg(object sender, System.EventArgs e)
{
    OleDbCommand l_dbComm = null;
    try
```

```
{
   /* Connect to database */
   m_dbOraConn.Open();

   l_dbComm = new OleDbCommand("SELECT StudentID From Student",
                                                m_dbOraConn);
   OleDbDataReader l_drStudent = l_dbComm.ExecuteReader();

   /* Add Student ID to Combo Box */
   decimal l_dStudentID = 0;
   for ( ; l_drStudent.Read() ; )
   {
      l_dStudentID = l_drStudent.GetDecimal(0);
      m_cbStudentID.Items.Add((object)l_dStudentID);
   }
   m_cbStudentID.Focus();

   /* If there are no items in Combo box then disable
      Save button and return */
   if ( m_cbStudentID.Items.Count == 0 )
   {
      m_bnSave.Enabled = false;
      return;
   }
}
catch ( Exception e1)
{
   MessageBox.Show(e1.Message,"Student Maintenance",
                   MessageBoxButtons.OK, MessageBoxIcon.Error);
   Close();
}
finally
{
   if ( l_dbComm != null ){
      l_dbComm.Dispose();
   }
}

/* Select First Record by default */
m_cbStudentID.SelectedIndex = 0;
}
```

The Open() method of the OleDbConnection class connects to the database with the specified ConnectionString. If there are any run time errors, then an exception will be thrown which is caught in the catch block. Remember that we have set our ConnectionString property during design time.

Here are the steps to retrieve data using the OleDbCommand and OleDbDataReader classes:

❑   Create an OleDbCommand object by passing a SQL SELECT statement and an OleDbConnection object as parameters to its overloaded constructor

❑   Call the ExecuteReader() method of the OleDbCommand object and store the returned OleDbDataReader object

❑   Call the Read() method of the OleDbDataReader until it returns false

❑   Retrieve data using the Get() methods of the OleDbDataReader object

To populate our ComboBox with the Student ID from the Student table we will use the OleDbCommand class, which is responsible for executing SQL statements and returning results. Here we create an OleDbCommand object with a SQL statement, which retrieves the StudentID from the Student table. The ExecuteReader() method of the OleDbCommand class executes the SQL statement and returns an OleDbDataReader object. The OleDbDataReader class's Read() method will retrieve one row at a time, and return false if it reaches the end-of-record marker. This class implements a forward-only, read-only cursor. Inside the for loop, the StudentID value is retrieved using the OleDbDataReader object's GetDecimal() method, which returns the data in decimal format. For more details about the OleDbDataReader object, visit the MSDN web site, or the Visual Studio .NET Combined Help Collection. After retrieving the StudentID, the value is added to the ComboBox using the ComboBox class's Add() method.

When the form is shown in the beginning, the first record should be displayed by default. Therefore, set the SelectedIndex property to 0 (zero). This statement will fire the SelectedIndexChanged event of the ComboBox. When the user selects a Student ID from the ComboBox we will display the student details in this event handler. The following code takes the selected student ID from the ComboBox and displays the corresponding student details from the Student table using the OleDbCommand and OleDbDataReader classes:

```
private void OnSelIndChangedStudentID(object sender, System.EventArgs e)
{
    object l_obj = m_cbStudentID.SelectedItem;
    string l_strStudentID = l_obj.ToString();

    OleDbCommand l_dbComm = null;

    try {
        string l_strSQL = "SELECT FirstName,LastName,Address,City, " +
                          "StateProvince, PostalCode,Phone " +
                          "FROM Student WHERE StudentID = " +
                          "'" + l_strStudentID + "'";
        l_dbComm = new OleDbCommand(l_strSQL,m_dbOraConn);
        OleDbDataReader l_drStudent = l_dbComm.ExecuteReader();

        string l_strData = "";
        for ( ; l_drStudent.Read() ; )
        {

            l_strData = l_drStudent.GetString(0);
            m_ebFirstName.Text = l_strData;

            l_strData = l_drStudent.GetString(1);
            m_ebLastName.Text = l_strData;

            l_strData = l_drStudent.GetString(2);
            m_ebAddress.Text = l_strData;

            l_strData = l_drStudent.GetString(3);
            m_ebCity.Text = l_strData;

            l_strData = l_drStudent.GetString(4);
            m_ebSP.Text = l_strData;

            l_strData = l_drStudent.GetString(5);
            m_ebPostalCode.Text = l_strData;
```

```
l_strData = l_drStudent.GetString(6);
        m_ebPhone.Text = l_strData;
    }
    m_ebAddress.Focus();
}
catch ( Exception e1)
{
    MessageBox.Show(e1.Message,"Student Maintenance - Error",
                    MessageBoxButtons.OK,MessageBoxIcon.Error);
    Close();
}
finally
{
    if ( l_dbComm != null )
    {
        l_dbComm.Dispose();
    }
}
}
```

Note that the GetString() method of the OleDbDataReader class is being used here, because all of our database columns (except for StudentID) in the Student table are of type Varchar2.

The next step in our application is to allow the user to edit the student details, such as the Address, City, StateProvince, PostalCode, and Phone, and store the changed details in the database using a stored procedure. We will not allow the FirstName and LastName columns to be modified, so set the ReadOnly property to true and the TabStop property to false. The ReadOnly property will determine whether the value of the TextBox can be changed or not, while the TabStop property will determine whether the control can be navigated using the *Tab* key.

First let's look at the Oracle stored procedure code, which is as shown below. Oracle procedures can be written in any text editor and can be compiled using the Oracle SQL Plus tool. This tool will be installed along with your Oracle 8i client. Remember Oracle procedures cannot be created using VS .NET Server Explorer. This procedure accepts the following input parameters: StudentID, Address, City, StateProvince, PostalCode, and Phone. It also returns the result in the form of the out parameters Status and Message. Status will be 1 if the procedure is executed successfully, otherwise it will be 0. The Message out parameter gives the success or failure message from the procedure. Note that all input parameters are prefixed with the I character, and output parameters with an O. This is just a coding convention that I follow for stored procedures. Here's the code:

```
Create Or Replace Procedure Update_Student (
    IStudentID in Number, IAddress in Varchar2,
    ICity in Varchar2, IStateProvince in Varchar2,
    IPostalCode in Varchar2, IPhone in Varchar2,
    OStatus out Integer, OMessage out Varchar2)
As
Begin

    /* Update student detail */
    Update Student Set Address = IAddress, City = ICity,
        StateProvince = IStateProvince, PostalCode = IPostalCode,
        Phone = IPhone
    Where StudentID = IStudentID;
```

```
      /* Commit the transaction and exit with success code */
      Commit;
      OStatus := 1;
      OMessage := 'Successfully updated student detail';
      Exception
      /* Exit with error code and error message */
      When Others Then
          OStatus := 0;
          OMessage := 'Error :' || SQLErrm(SQLCode);
  End Update_Student;
```

If you note the procedure parameters, you can see the keywords in and out before the parameter name. When the keyword in is found before a parameter, it means that the parameter is an input parameter. Inside the procedure you cannot change the value of this parameter. On the other hand, parameters with the out keyword are output parameters and are used to return values from the procedure. By default the parameter is considered to be input parameter when no keyword is given before it. When you want a parameter to be used as input and output as well, both these keywords can be used. For example in the following declaration param in out varchar2 will allow the variable to be used as input and output.

Having seen the parameter types, let's concentrate on the procedure body. Inside the procedure the SQL update statement is used to update the student details. When the update statement is executed successfully, the change is committed to the database. If there are any errors inside the procedure, the exception block will be executed, which is handled using the Others exception handler. The Others exception handler can be compared with the Exception class in C#. It handles all exceptions inside a PL/SQL block. The error message is retrieved using the SQLERRM() function by passing the SQLCODE which contains the Oracle error number.

Now let's see how to call this Oracle procedure from our C# program. The user is expected to change the details of a student and click the **Save** button. In the Click event of the **Save** button we will call our Oracle procedure and update the changes to the database.

Steps to call a Stored Procedure are:

❑ Create an OleDbCommand object using the overloaded constructor with the procedure name and the OleDbConnection object as parameters.

❑ Set the CommandType property to CommandType.StoredProcedure.

❑ Create parameters with OleDbParameter using its overloaded constructor, by passing the parameter name and data type. Note that the parameter name should match the database parameter name, or else an exception will be thrown.

❑ Assign values to input parameters using the Value property. Set the Direction property to output parameters.

❑ Add all parameters to the OleDbCommand object.

❑ Call the procedure using ExecuteNonQuery().

❑ Retrieve values from the output parameters (if any).

Look at the following code. Before calling the procedure, the Size property needs to be set for output parameters of type Varchar, or else an exception will be thrown while executing the procedure. The values from the output parameters are obtained using the Value parameter. Note that the Value parameter returns object so it needs to be typecast accordingly:

```
private void OnClickSave(object sender, System.EventArgs e)
{
    OleDbCommand l_dbComm = null;

    try
    {
        this.Cursor = Cursors.WaitCursor;

        /* Create command object */
        l_dbComm = new OleDbCommand("Update_Student",m_dbOraConn);

        /* Set command type to StoredProcedure */
        l_dbComm.CommandType = CommandType.StoredProcedure;

        /* Create parameters */
        OleDbParameter l_paramStudentID = new
                            OleDbParameter("IStudentID",OleDbType.Numeric);
        OleDbParameter l_paramAddress = new
                             OleDbParameter("IAddress",OleDbType.VarChar);
        OleDbParameter l_paramCity = new
                                OleDbParameter("ICity",OleDbType.VarChar);
        OleDbParameter l_paramSP = new
                          OleDbParameter("IStateProvince",OleDbType.VarChar);
        OleDbParameter l_paramPostalCode = new
                            OleDbParameter("IPostalCode",OleDbType.VarChar);
        OleDbParameter l_paramPhone = new
                               OleDbParameter("IPhone",OleDbType.VarChar);
        OleDbParameter l_paramStatus = new
                                OleDbParameter("OStatus",OleDbType.Integer);
        OleDbParameter l_paramMessage = new
                               OleDbParameter("OMessage",OleDbType.VarChar);

        /* Set value to input parameters */
        l_paramStudentID.Value = int.Parse(m_cbStudentID.Text);
        l_paramAddress.Value = m_ebAddress.Text;
        l_paramCity.Value = m_ebCity.Text;
        l_paramSP.Value = m_ebSP.Text;
        l_paramPostalCode.Value = m_ebPostalCode.Text;
        l_paramPhone.Value = m_ebPhone.Text;

        /* Output parameters */
        l_paramStatus.Direction = ParameterDirection.Output;
        l_paramMessage.Direction = ParameterDirection.Output;
        l_paramMessage.Size = 4000;

        /* Add parameters to Command object */
        l_dbComm.Parameters.Add(l_paramStudentID);
        l_dbComm.Parameters.Add(l_paramAddress);
        l_dbComm.Parameters.Add(l_paramCity);
        l_dbComm.Parameters.Add(l_paramSP);
        l_dbComm.Parameters.Add(l_paramPostalCode);
        l_dbComm.Parameters.Add(l_paramPhone);
        l_dbComm.Parameters.Add(l_paramStatus);
        l_dbComm.Parameters.Add(l_paramMessage);

        /* Execute the procedure */
        int l_iRetval = l_dbComm.ExecuteNonQuery();
        l_iRetval = (int) l_paramStatus.Value;
```

```
        string l_strMessage = (string) l_paramMessage.Value;
        this.Cursor = Cursors.Arrow;
        if ( l_iRetval == 1 ){
           MessageBox.Show(l_strMessage,"Student Maintenance",
                          MessageBoxButtons.OK,MessageBoxIcon.Exclamation);
        }
        else
        {
           MessageBox.Show(l_strMessage,"Student Maintenance - Error",
                          MessageBoxButtons.OK,MessageBoxIcon.Error);
        }
    }
    catch ( Exception e1)#
    {
        this.Cursor = Cursors.Arrow;
        MessageBox.Show(e1.Message,"Student Maintenance - Error",
                       MessageBoxButtons.OK,MessageBoxIcon.Error);
    }
    finally
    {
        if ( l_dbComm != null )
        {
            l_dbComm.Dispose();
            l_dbComm = null;
        }
    }
}
```

Finally, we display messages in the MessageBox with different styles, based on the Status output value. With this, we have completed our "Student Modification" application.

OLE DB with a DB2 Database

This section will explain in detail about connecting to a DB2 database in C# using the .NET classes. Apart from connecting to a DB2 database, this section will give you an overview of how to delete rows from a table using the OleDbCommand class. We will extend the same Student database, and will see how to connect to a DB2 database using the OleDbConnection object, and how to call SQL statements using the OleDbCommand object. Connecting to DB2 is similar to connecting to an Oracle database. The only difference is the use of a different provider and a slight change in the ConnectionString. The platform is DB2 installed on IBM-AIX version 4.5.

We will develop a dialog based "Student Removal" application, which allows the removal of student records from the database. Start VS .NET and create a new C# Windows Application project. Design our main window as shown in the screenshot overleaf:

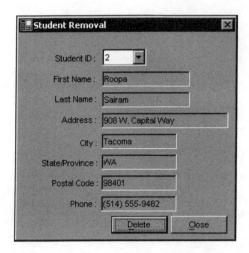

Drag and drop a `ComboBox` and set its `DropDownStyle` property to `DropDownList`. Drag and drop `TextBox` controls for the other columns and set their `ReadOnly` properties to `true`, and their `TabStop` properties to `false`. Drag and drop two buttons, **Delete** and **Close**. Add a click event handler to these buttons. The next step is setting the connection to the DB2 database. The table below shows the structure of `Student` table in the DB2 database:

Column	Data Type
STUDENTID	INTEGER NOT NULL PRIMARY KEY
FIRSTNAME	VARCHAR(25)
LASTNAME	VARCHAR(25)
ADDRESS	VARCHAR(30)
CITY	VARCHAR(15)
STATEPROVINCE	CHARACTER(2)
PHONE	VARCHAR(15)
POSTALCODE	INTEGER

The table creation script is:

```
/* Create the table */
CREATE TABLE DB2INST1.STUDENT
(STUDENTID INTEGER  NOT NULL  DEFAULT 0,
FIRSTNAME VARCHAR (25) ,
LASTNAME VARCHAR (25) ,
ADDRESS VARCHAR (30) ,
CITY VARCHAR (15) ,
STATEPROVINCE CHARACTER (2) ,
PHONE VARCHAR (15) ,
POSTALCODE INTEGER ,
PRIMARY KEY (STUDENTID)  )  DATA CAPTURE NONE;
```

The insert scripts for the `Student` table are:

```
/* Insert scripts for the table */
INSERT INTO STUDENT VALUES (1,"Niranjan","Kumar","Lloyds Road",
                            "Chennai","IL","(514) 555-8978",98122);
INSERT INTO STUDENT VALUES (2,"Roopa","Sairam","908 W. Capital Way",
                            "Tacoma","WA","(514) 555-9482",98401);
INSERT INTO STUDENT VALUES (3,"Brandon","Coake","722 Moss Bay Blvd.",
                            "Kirkland","WA","(514) 555-3412",98033);
INSERT INTO STUDENT VALUES (4,"Margaret","Peacock","4110 Old Redmond Rd.",
                            "Redmond","WA","(514) 555-8122",98052);
INSERT INTO STUDENT VALUES (5,"Matthew","Dunn","14 Garrett Hill",
                            "Seattle","WA","(514) 555-1189",98105);
INSERT INTO STUDENT VALUES (6,"Helvetius","Nagy","722 DaVinci Blvd.",
                            "Kirkland","WA","(514) 555-8257",98034);
INSERT INTO STUDENT VALUES (7,"Deborah","Peterson",
        "305 - 14th Ave. S.Suite 3B","Seattle","WA","(514) 555-4112",98128);
INSERT INTO STUDENT VALUES (13,"Aparna","Sairam","908 W. Capital Way",
                            "Tacoma","WA","(514) 555-9482",98401);
```

Drag and drop an `OleDbConnection` control and open its property window, and select the New Connection option from the `ConnectionString` combo as shown in the screenshot below:

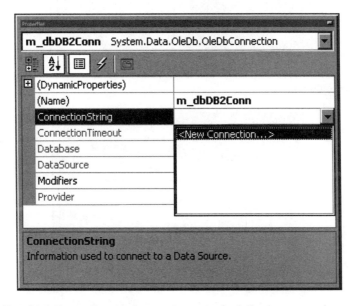

You will get a **Data Link Properties** window as shown in the following screenshot:

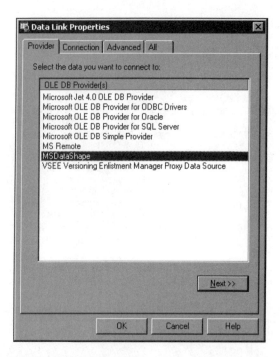

In the **Data Link Properties** dialog, select the `MSDataShape` option from the **OLE DB Provider(s)** list and click the **Next** button:

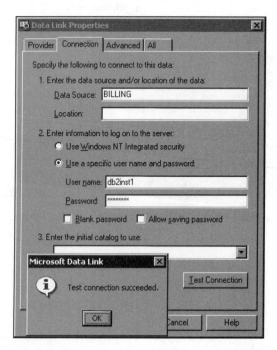

Enter your data source name into the **Data Source** textbox, click the **Use a specific user name and password** radio button, and enter the database user ID and password. Leave the other options empty. For my database, the data source name is `BILLING`, the user id is `db2inst1`, and the password is `db2inst1` (the password will be shown as * for security reasons). On clicking on the **Test Connection** button, you should get a **Test connection succeeded** message as shown in the screenshot above. If the connection isn't successful, then an appropriate error message will be displayed.

After successfully testing, click the **Data Link Properties** window's **OK** button. The DB2 database connection window will appear as shown below:

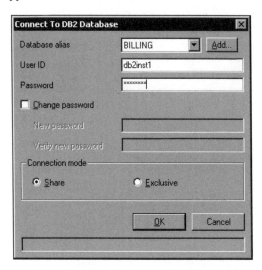

In this window, enter the database user ID and password and click **OK** to save the information. After successfully connecting to the database, this connection is added to the VS .NET Server Explorer as we can see in the following screenshot:

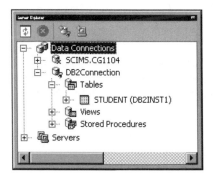

Now we have completed the design stage of the Student Removal application. We will connect to the database in the Form Load event. Therefore, add a handler to the Form Load event and insert the following code fragment:

```
OleDbCommand l_dbComm = null;
try {

    m_dbDB2Conn.Open();

    l_dbComm = new OleDbCommand("SELECT StudentID From Student",m_dbDB2Conn);
    OleDbDataReader l_drStudent = l_dbComm.ExecuteReader();

    /* Add Student ID to Combo Box */
    int l_iStudentID = 0;
    for ( ; l_drStudent.Read() ; )
    {
        l_iStudentID = l_drStudent.GetInt32(0);
        m_cbStudentID.Items.Add((object)l_iStudentID);
    }
    m_cbStudentID.Focus();

    /* If there are no items in the ComboBox then disable
       Delete button and return */
    if ( m_cbStudentID.Items.Count == 0 )
    {
        m_bnDelete.Enabled = false;
        return;
    }
}
catch ( Exception e1 )
{
    MessageBox.Show(e1.Message,"Student Removal - Error",
                    MessageBoxButtons.OK,MessageBoxIcon.Error);
    Close();
}
finally
{
    if ( l_dbComm != null )
    {
        l_dbComm.Dispose();
    }
}

/* Select First record by default */
m_cbStudentID.SelectedIndex = 0;
```

There is not much difference between this code and the code that we wrote to connect to the Oracle database. When using the DB2 database, the ConnectionString property has a different value for the Provider parameter, and there is an additional parameter: Data Provider. The ConnectionString for a DB2 database is shown below. Here m_dbDB2Conn is an instance of the OleDbConnection class:

```
//
// m_dbDB2Conn
//
this.m_dbDB2Conn.ConnectionString = "Provider=MSDataShape.1;Persist Security
Info=False;Data Source=BILLING;User ID=db" +
"2inst1;Password=db2inst1;Data Provider=MSDASQL";
```

We call the Open() method, create an OleDbCommand object, passing a SQL SELECT statement into its constructor, fill our OleDbDataReader object using the ExecuteReader() method, retrieve the row using the Read() method, and retrieve the data using the GetInt32() method. Since the StudentID column is defined as an INTEGER data type in the database, we use the GetInt32() method here.

When a Student ID is selected from the ComboBox, we will fetch the student details from the database and display them in the TextBox controls. The code is the same as we had in our Oracle sample. Therefore, let's concentrate on how to delete a record when the user clicks the Delete button. Add the event handler for the Click event of the Delete button, and write the following code to delete a selected Student ID:

```
try {
    int l_iIndex = m_cbStudentID.SelectedIndex;
    int l_iStudentID = (int) m_cbStudentID.Items[l_iIndex];

    string l_strSQL = "DELETE FROM STUDENT WHERE STUDENTID = " +
                        l_iStudentID.ToString();
    OleDbCommand l_dbComm = new OleDbCommand(l_strSQL,m_dbDB2Conn);
    int l_iRetval = l_dbComm.ExecuteNonQuery();
    if (l_iRetval == 1 )
    {
        m_cbStudentID.Items.RemoveAt(l_iIndex);
        m_ebFirstName.Text = "";
        m_ebLastName.Text = "";
        m_ebAddress.Text = "";
        m_ebCity.Text = "";
        m_ebSP.Text = "";
        m_ebPostalCode.Text = "";
        m_ebPhone.Text = "";
    }
    if ( m_cbStudentID.Items.Count == 0 )
    {
        m_bnDelete.Enabled = false;
    }
    m_cbStudentID.Focus();
}
catch ( Exception e1)
{
    string l_strError = "Error : " + e1.Message;
    MessageBox.Show(l_strError,"Student Removal - Error",
                MessageBoxButtons.OK, MessageBoxIcon.Error);
}
```

First, we get the selected Student ID from the ComboBox. The next step is to build the delete SQL statement and pass it to the OleDbCommand object. Then call the ExecuteNonQuery() method to execute the statement. This method will return the number of affected rows if it was successfully executed, but it returns 0 if execution fails. The return value of this method is checked, and according to the value, the ComboBox item is removed and other fields are cleared.

In this appendix, we have discussed OLE DB database connections and manipulating data with the OLE DB .NET classes. We have seen how to connect to various RDBMS databases such as Microsoft Access, Oracle, and DB2. We also had hands on experience in writing sample applications, and learnt about various .NET classes and how they make it easy to programmatically manipulate the data.

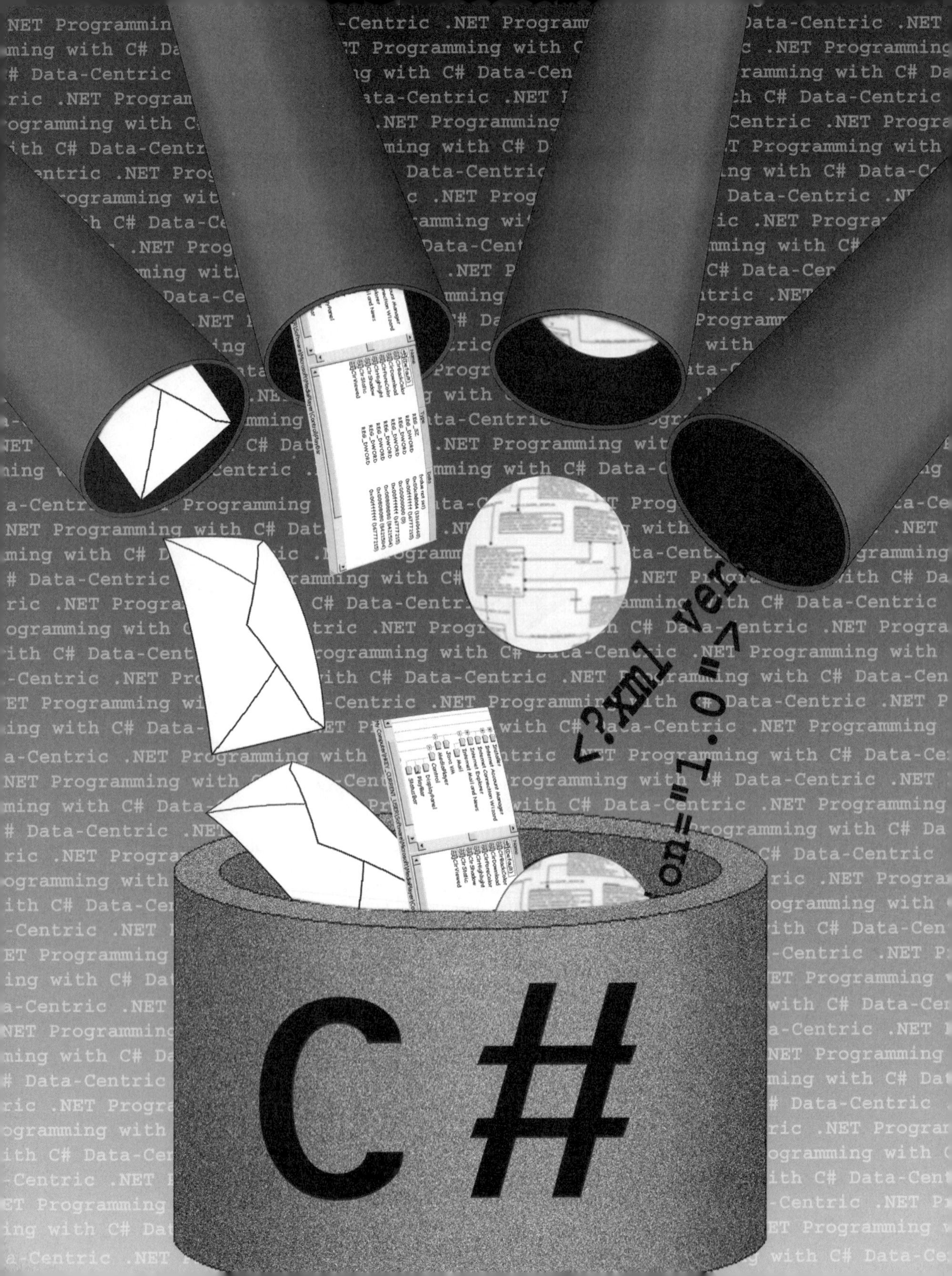
Data-Centric .NET Programming with C#
<?xml ver
on="1.0"?>
C#

Index

A Guide to the Index

The index is arranged hierarchically, in alphabetical order, with symbols preceding the letter A. Most second-level entries and many third-level entries also occur as first-level entries. This is to ensure that users will find the information they require however they choose to search for it.

The ~ character is used to reduce the need to duplicate almost identical entries (e.g. GetX/~Y means GetX/GetY)

Symbols

$ character
 XsltArgumentList class, 323
@ character
 ignoring the backslash, 61
\ character
 ignoring with ampersand, 61

A

abstract classes, System.IO namespace, 433
AcceptChanges method, DataRow class, 96, 709
AcceptChanges method, DataSet class, 94, 712
AcceptChanges method, DataTable class, 95, 716
AcceptChangesDuringFill property, DataAdapter classes, 699
access control lists
 securing a message queue, 380
 setting, 416
Acknowledgement Queues, 411
AcknowledgeType property
 table of enumerated values, 411
Activate method, ServicedComponent class, 223
Active Directory
 accessing, 352
 Directory Services information store, 333
 global catalog, 365
 sample applications, 365
 Searcher, sample application, 360
 searching for service, 370
 service registration, 366
Active DS Type Library (activeds.tlb)
 ADSI availability, 357
 .NET wrapper class, 358
ActiveXMessageFormatter class, System.Messaging namespace, 394
adAsyncConnect constant
 .NET work arounds, 25
adConnectUnspecified constant

 .NET work arounds, 25
AddChildren method
 adding DirectoryEntry objects, 346
AddingRecord method
 creating command object, 71
AddNew method, DataView class, 720
administration queues
 message queue type, 381
AdministrationQueue property, System.Messaging namespace
 Acknowledgement Queues, 411
ADO (ActiveX Data Objects)
 ADO.NET
  comparison between, 35
  future with ADO.NET, 43
  object model and differences to, 39
 avoiding in new .NET solutions, 35
 C# and ADO, 19
 C# programming, 22
  lessons learned, 34
 classes
  Command classes, 21
   ADO.NET object model, 39
  Connection classes, 21
   ADO.NET object model, 40
  Record class, 21
  Recordset class, 21
  Stream class, 21
 connection string syntax, 40
 errors, data source to application, 40
 historical background, 20
 IPP, gateway to accessing web space, 29
 programming steps, 22
 referencing ADO, 23
 relational databases
  key points, 27
  using with, 24
 semi-structured data sources, 28
 shortcomings in .NET environment, 46
ADO MD, 21
ADO.NET
 ADO comparison, 35
  illustrated, 39
 building applications, Web/Windows Forms, 145

F

facets
user-defined data type restrictions, 282
Failover Clustering
SQL Server, 521
FieldCount property, DataReader classes, 704
Fields collection
Recordset class, ADO, 21
File class, System.IO namespace, 433
access compared to FileInfo class, 434
static methods, 434
FileAccess property/enumeration, FileStream class
members, 437
FileInfo class, System.IO namespace, 433, 434
access compared to File class, 434
Beta 2 changes, 691
methods similar to File class, 435
properties and descriptions, 435
FileMode property/enumeration, FileStream class
members, 437
FileShare property/enumeration, FileStream class
members, 437
FileStream class, System.IO namespace, 433, 436
asynchronous data access, 441
constructor exceptions, 438
constructor specifying properties, 447
data reading methods, 438
data writing methods, 440
default enumeration values, 438
FileAccess property/enumeration, 437
FileMode property/enumeration, 437
FileShare property/enumeration, 437
Fill method, DataAdapter classes, 700
DataSet, filling, 64
OleDbDataAdapter class
example, 735
FillSchema method, DataAdapter classes, 700
FillSchemaGridOdbc method
Buoy database case study, 563
FillSchemaGridOleDb method
Buoy database case study, 563, 568
FillTreeView method, XmlTreeNode class
using MSXML, 239
Filter property, DirectorySearcher class
search string, 359
filters
LDAP filter, 359
FindAll method, DirectorySearcher class
paged search, 364
firewalls
DataSet class, 93
FlatMode property, DataGrid class, 147
Font property, DataGrid class, 147
ForeColor property, DataGrid class, 147
Foreign Key constraint
Primary Key constraint relationship, 100, 104
ForeignKeyConstraint constructors, Constraint class, 99
FormatName value, MessageQueue class
hostname independent, 391
formatter objects
example, 472
serialization, 472
Serialize methods caled, 474

Formatter property, MessageQueue class, 394
formatters
ActiveXMessageFormatter class, 394
BinaryMessageFormatter class, 394
System.Messaging namespace, 394
XmlMessageFormatter class, 394
frmMain class, 130
Buoy data viewer, 569
Buoy database case study, 563

G

garbage collection
CLR , 9
MSDN article, web site, 201
Gatekeeper
Commerce Server implementation, 530
GetAllMessages, MessageQueue class
BLTStore case study, 667
GetAttribute method, XmlTextReader class
processing attributes, 256
GetBoolean method, DataReader classes, 705
GetByte(s) methods, DataReader classes, 705
GetChanges method, DataSet class, 94, 713
GetChanges method, DataTable class, 95, 716
GetChar(s) methods, DataReader classes, 705
GetChildRows method, DataRow class, 96, 709
GetColumnError method, DataRow class, 96, 710
GetColumnMappingBySchemaAction method, DataTableMapping class, 718
GetColumnsInError method, DataRow class, 96, 710
GetDataColumnBySchemaAction method, DataColumnMapping class, 704
GetDataTableBySchemaAction method, DataTableMapping class, 718
GetDataTypeName method, DataReader classes, 705
GetDateTime method, DataReader classes, 705
GetDecimal method, DataReader classes, 705
GetDirectories method, Directory class, 434
GetDirectoryEntry method
Active Directory Searcher, sample application, 363
GetDirectoryNames method, IsolatedStorageFile class, 463
GetDouble method, DataReader classes, 705
GetEnumerator method, DataView class, 720
GetErrors method, DataTable class, 95, 716
GetFieldType method, DataReader classes, 705
GetFileNames method, IsolatedStorageFile class, 463
GetFiles method, Directory class, 434
GetFillParameters method, DataAdapter classes, 700
GetFloat methods, DataReader classes, 705
GetGuid method, DataReader classes, 705
GetInt16/32/64 methods, DataReader classes, 705
GetMessageEnumerator method, Message Queue class
BLTStore case study, 671
GetMessageQueueEnumerator method, MessageQueue class
finding queue, 390

M

Notes

Notes

Notes

Notes

wrox

Programmer to Programmer™

Wrox writes books for you. Any suggestions, or ideas about how you want
information given in your ideal book will be studied by our team.
Your comments are always valued at Wrox.

Free phone in USA 800-USE-WROX
Fax (312) 893 8001

UK Tel.: (0121) 687 4100   Fax: (0121) 687 4101

Data-Centric .NET Programming with C# – Registration Card

Name _____

Address _____

_____

_____

_____

City _____ State/Region _____

Country _____ Postcode/Zip _____

E-Mail _____

Occupation _____

How did you hear about this book?

☐ Book review (name) _____

☐ Advertisement (name) _____

☐ Recommendation _____

☐ Catalog _____

☐ Other _____

Where did you buy this book?

☐ Bookstore (name) _____ City _____

☐ Computer store (name) _____

☐ Mail order _____

☐ Other _____

What influenced you in the purchase of this book?

☐ Cover Design   ☐ Contents   ☐ Other (please specify):

How did you rate the overall content of this book?

☐ Excellent   ☐ Good   ☐ Average   ☐ Poor

What did you find most useful about this book? _____

_____

What did you find least useful about this book? _____

_____

Please add any additional comments. _____

_____

What other subjects will you buy a computer book on soon?

_____

What is the best computer book you have used this year?

_____

Note: This information will only be used to keep you updated
about new Wrox Press titles and will not be used for
any other purpose or passed to any other third party.

wrox

Programmer to Programmer™

Note: If you post the bounce back card below in the UK, please send it to:

Wrox Press Limited, Arden House, 1102 Warwick Road,
Acocks Green, Birmingham B27 6HB. UK.

Computer Book Publishers